ENGLAND

ACADEMY BOOKS

Uniform
with this volume

ENGLAND

BY

WILHELM DIBELIUS

JONATHAN CAPE
THIRTY BEDFORD SQUARE
LONDON

FIRST PUBLISHED SEPTEMBER 1929
SECOND IMPRESSION MARCH 1930
THIRD IMPRESSION JULY 1930
FOURTH IMPRESSION APRIL 1931
RE-ISSUED IN ACADEMY BOOKS 1934

The original German edition was published in 1922;
the revised fifth German edition is the
basis of the English translation

JONATHAN CAPE LTD. 30 BEDFORD SQUARE LONDON
AND 91 WELLINGTON STREET WEST, TORONTO

PRINTED IN GREAT BRITAIN
BY BUTLER AND TANNER LTD. FROME AND LONDON
BOUND BY A. W. BAIN AND CO. LTD.
PAPER MADE BY JOHN DICKINSON AND CO. LTD.

CONTENTS
BOOK I
THE COUNTRY AND ITS PEOPLE

I

CONTENTS

CONTENTS

CONTENTS

CONTENTS

5

INTRODUCTION

I READ Herr Dibelius' book for the first time in 1923. The German edition had a preface which is for understandable reasons omitted in this translation. I shall nevertheless quote the first two sentences of that preface, for they help to an understanding of the book.

'The idea of writing this book came to me,' Herr Dibelius begins, 'in the war. It forced itself on me from my overwhelming sense of a people giving its best in fighting an enemy which it did not know.'

This book is therefore in a sense a war book, but of a remarkable and, I think, a noble kind. It is addressed to a German and not to an English public, designed as it is to help the German people to understand the people with whom they have been fighting. The author has a proper pride in his own people, is convinced that they have made their own unique contribution to the civilization of the world: but he is trying with all his might to understand – as sympathetically and objectively as he can – the contribution made by England.

But though this book was meant originally to be read not by Englishmen but by Germans, it seems to me that it must be of interest and value to us; and though it was written in a sense as a war book, it is more adapted to serve the purposes of peace. For if we are going to direct the civilization of the world by co-operation instead of by war, men of different nations will have to learn to understand one another, and one of the most enlightening things about other people is the peculiar way we strike them. 'To see ourselves as others see us' helps us, no doubt, to understand ourselves. For the things about us that strike other people – and this is perhaps even truer of nations than of individuals – are mostly the things we ourselves so much take for granted that we are ourselves hardly conscious of them. All nations – but perhaps above all the English – are apt to take for granted that their own ways of doing things and of looking at the world are the natural and inevitable ways, and that foreigners are just funny. We have got to learn to go on being proud of our own national culture and yet to appreciate the distinctive culture of others. This is what Herr Dibelius is doing in this book, and to follow him trying to understand us will make us understand both ourselves and Germans better.

7

INTRODUCTION

The form of this book is of course determined by the fact that it is written for a German public. There is much in it which is for us unnecessary information. There are, no doubt, books written by men of other countries about English institutions which are the classical accounts of such institutions. It is a curious thing that the best book on the United States is Bryce's *American Commonwealth*, and the best book on English government Lowell's *Government of England*. So Dr. Redlich's books on English Local Government and English Parliamentary Procedure, and Professor Halévy's great history of England in the Nineteenth Century, are authorities in this country. This is not a book of that kind. English institutions are described not for their own sake but for the light they throw on English character. The interest for us of those parts of the book which describe our system of government or of education is not their information, but that they make us see how our institutions look to the eyes of a German. 'Critics will easily find details to criticize,' says the author in his German preface. I have myself noticed, as was natural, that he confuses the founder of my College with his son; and there are no doubt other mistakes of detail. But the author declares that his book 'is not meant to be a compendium of facts, but to help to make understood the soul of a people.'

We are apt in this country to be a little shy of attempts to depict national 'souls.' We feel, as Charlie Lomax said about the Salvation Army, that 'there is a certain amount of tosh' about national psychology. So there is. It has to be done with too broad a brush. It is as possible not to see the trees for the wood as not to see the wood for the trees: and when we are the trees of this wood which is being described we feel that our individual differences (which the broad brush of the national psychologist omits) are much more important than the samenesses which it reproduces. A Scotsman squirms when in America remarks are made on his English accent. An Englishman, indeed, does not like it either, but that is because he thinks that Scotsmen and Welsh and Irish speak English with an accent, while he just speaks English. The Scotsman recognizes the truth of Mark Twain's remark that even the angels in heaven speak English with an accent, but he finds it hard to understand how Americans can possibly suppose that the noises he makes sound like those made by the English. But to the foreigner, as to the outsider seeing a family for the first time, the common resemblances peculiar to a nation are more striking than the differences within the nation.

8

INTRODUCTION

Only a foreigner can see the resemblances, and so only a foreigner can describe a nation's 'soul.' And for all our prejudice against such generalizations we are beginning to recognize that there is something in these broad national characters. As we sit in international conference, we can notice that the Frenchmen and the Germans and the Italians are behaving each in their characteristically national way; and if we are honest with ourselves, we must recognize that we are probably doing the same. When we come to understand these broad national differences, then and then only are we likely to be able to see the individuality as well.

We are to read this book, then, not for its details but to see what we look like to an intelligent observer of another nation, and if we will do that we shall find much illumination in it.

It would be tempting to quote in the foreword what seem to me the most penetrating of the author's remarks, but that process of 'picking out the plums' is as unfair as to give away the end of a detective novel. But I should like to call attention to the way in which the author deals (on page 106) with what is so often regarded on the continent as our hypocrisy.

'The whole of this international spiritual propaganda is apt to be completely misunderstood on the continent. Non-English nations are apt to see in it nothing but Machiavellian cunning harnessing the world's idealism to England's triumphal car. Such a judgment overlooks the fact that purely idealistic movements, rare in the world we live in, are only too constantly forced to make terms, and very unexhilarating terms at that, with the world's political, economic, and egotistic forces. . . . English policy has never been infected by that myth of a materialistic age which sees political events as mere struggles for food and shelter. On the contrary, it has shown quite incomparable intelligence in appreciating the mighty force of the movements of ideas and using them for political purposes.'

Or again, the author's analysis of the part played in English life by what he calls in Chapter VI the ideal of a gentleman, its advantages and its shortcomings, seems to me full of insight.

But I am beginning to do what I have just said is unfair, and I shall end by quoting a sentence at the end of the book which summarizes a great deal of what Herr Dibelius has to say. 'The English

9

state rests on two specifically English assumptions – common sense, and the transformation of the antagonist into a privileged colleague.' That is surely an interesting thesis. The book is largely an explication of it.

A. D. LINDSAY

BOOK I
THE COUNTRY AND
ITS PEOPLE

CHAPTER I
THE BACKGROUND OF HISTORY

§ I

THE island of Britain, in the far north-west, was known to the earliest geographers. The Phœnicians dug tin in the mines of Cornwall; the geographer Pytheas of Marseilles is said to have visited Britain; Julius Cæsar occupied the southern coast for a brief period; Agricola, general of the Emperor Claudius, made the island, as far north as the Firth of Forth, a Roman colony.

Of the original inhabitants we know little. Some think that they are represented in the dark, round-skulled type, comparatively common in Wales and Ireland, and belong to the primitive Mediterranean stock. Others see the original inhabitants as surviving in the singular race of Picts, who occupied the north-east of Scotland at the Roman invasion, painting and tattooing their bodies and living under a form of matriarchy. Anyhow, by the beginning of the historical period, Celts were living in the country, known as the Cymri in Wales and Gaels elsewhere in Britain and in Ireland. They probably were invaders who conquered the original race and in the long run largely mixed with it. They were a gifted race, artistically sensitive, and of quick intelligence, but never outgrew the clan form of government or developed any economic life beyond a semi-village communism. They were later subdued by the Romans. The conquerors made a military colony of the country, with a network of military roads which laid the main lines followed by highways and railway tracks to-day; with camps, and a certain number of self-governing cities – the old *castra* and *colonia* survive in place-names like Chester, Lancaster and Lincoln; but although there was a thin layer of upper-class people, who built after the Roman fashion, spoke in Latin, lived with a certain degree of Roman provincial luxury, and worshipped the Mediterranean gods, there was no such far-reaching Romanization as took place in France or Spain; there are no traces of the development of a Romanic language on British soil. Late Roman coinage terms, like *L(ibra)*, *s(olidus)* and *d(enarius)*, which later were adopted by the Anglo-Saxons, have survived to the present day.

When the Western Roman Empire needed its legions in Italy, Britain was invaded by Germanic tribes. First Saxons from the mouths of the Elbe and the Weser crossed the Channel, probably leaving newly acquired possessions in Normandy behind them, and, constantly reinforced, occupied the country as far as the Thames (about 450). Two generations later they were followed by the Angles from Schleswig-Holstein and the Lower Elbe, who, after heavy fighting with the Celts, settled down in the eastern two-thirds of the country, between the Thames and the Firth of Forth. They established kingdoms whose names and boundaries still survive in the names of counties and dioceses. The Saxons had Wessex, Sussex and Essex; the counties of Kent and Hampshire formed the kingdom of the Jutes; East Anglia (Norfolk and Suffolk) that of the Angles, who also consolidated themselves against the Celts in Mercia and in Northumbria, the kingdom between the mouth of the Humber and the Firth of Forth, including the whole of the Scottish Lowlands. In 829 Ecgberht of Wessex united the whole of Germanic Britain under his sway.

Bitter as are the complaints of historians, from the very earliest times, of the ferocity of the invaders, it is hard to believe that the Celts were completely exterminated. Celtic lingered down to quite recent times both in the north-west (in Cumberland) and in the south-west (in Cornwall); a large number of place-names (Pen-zance, Lei(r)cester, Carlisle, London, Dunbar) and names of rivers (Avon, Severn, Thames, Trent, Dee) are certainly of Celtic origin. The facial Celtic type is too common in England to this day to be completely accounted for by immigration from Ireland. The intensity of the imaginative element in English literature as it appears, for example, in Shakespeare and Spenser, Shelley and Keats, is certainly not typically Germanic. Notable, too, is the high degree of suggestibility of the English lower orders. True, they may be hard to move so long as they are comfortable; yet, let any scare be raised – in the seventeenth or eighteenth century, generally 'No Popery!'; in the nineteenth, French; in the twentieth, German, invasion – and the whole mass is automatically in a seething state. Treacherous as is any attempt to make ethnographic national charts with indefinite indices, the existence of a strong Celtic infusion in the Germanic blood must be recognized as highly probable in England. In Wales, Scotland and Ireland, Celtic is still a spoken language. In Wales it is indigenous; 30·8 per cent of the total population of the Principality and the adjacent English county of Monmouth were Welsh-speaking in 1921, while in two counties more than half the population had no other language. In Scotland, in the northern counties (Argyle, Inverness, Ross and Cromarty, and Sutherland) 4 per cent spoke nothing but Gaelic, and

32–50 per cent both Gaelic and English (1921). In Ireland, English repression reduced the proportion of people who could speak only Irish to rather more than a third per cent; the only considerable proportions of non-English speaking people exist in Donegal (2·8 per cent) and Galway (4·2 per cent). The active nationalist agitation of the last generation, which insists on the teaching of the Irish language, and since the establishment of the Free State is backed up by all the forces of the State, has at least had the result of increasing the number of bi-linguals; it hardly will succeed in making Irish the mother-tongue of Ireland once more.[1]

Christianity came early to the land. In the first instance from Ireland, where the new teachings had never been lost since the days of St. Patrick. This type of Christianity was comparatively free of Roman influences, with a certain Celtic strain in many details, averse from the world and based almost exclusively on the cloister. Its earliest British home was in the remote Hebridean island of Iona. A little later, in 597, missionaries from Rome brought the Papal form of Christianity to the south of Britain. After bitter struggles the Roman form prevailed, and, with it, the universal Church ousted the narrowness of Nationalism (though English Christianity has never lost a certain national complexion); the practical culture that accepts this world triumphed over the mysticism of the cloister.

The youthful Germano-Christian Church had soon to meet a grave danger in the invasion of pagan Scandinavians, whom the Anglo-Saxons generally called Danes. They actually ruled, for a considerable time, over the Scottish islands and the Isle of Man; in Ireland too, they founded hereditary dynasties: the towns of Dublin (840) and Cork (860) are of Scandinavian foundation. The raiders went on ravaging and laying waste in England, decade after decade. King Alfred (871–901) freed his country from the worst danger; the Danes accepted Christianity and became vassals of the Anglo-Saxon king, but, at the same time, they were given the whole of the eastern portion of Anglia to settle in; towns like Der-by, Whit-by still retain the Danish word for town in their names, and in the English vocabulary of to-day there are a considerable number of words of Scandinavian origin, including such old Norse everyday words as 'they' and 'their.' On Alfred's death there was a renewal of war: Canute the Great (d. 1035) ruled over England as well as Scandinavia. On his death, the national dynasty returned to the helm with Edward the Confessor, but the signs of coming disaster were plain to see. The King was half a Norman in character, and the Anglo-Saxon national opposition threatened to divide the country once more into the old separate Anglian and Saxon kingdoms which had been fused into one realm by Ecgberht and Alfred. Under Harold, in 1066, the Anglo-Saxon kingdom fell under the sway of the Norman, William the Conqueror.

§ 2

The new dynasty brought a flood of French culture over the land which, at first, threatened to submerge everything Anglo-Saxon. The danger was the greater that, from the earliest times, relations between Britain and what is present-day France had been extremely close, as even Cæsar noted; further, during the whole Anglo-Saxon period, Frankish culture came across to England; indeed, from the very beginning England's access to Continental culture lay through France. In 597 the acceptance of Christianity by the Anglo-Saxons was promoted by a Queen of Kent of Frankish descent; King Ecgberht, the unifier of the Anglo-Saxons, spent a considerable time in the Frankish realm; Alfred the Great himself had a daughter of Charles le Chauve as his stepmother. Both in architecture and in painting, Frankish influence on Anglo-Saxon culture is evident, and to some extent mutual. In the later Anglo-Saxon period, French feudal and military terms make their appearance in the English language; the court of King Edward the Confessor was almost purely Norman. The new dynasty brought with it the danger of a complete suppression of the Germanic elements.

This new dynasty dominated the resistance of the Anglo-Saxons by a rigidly centralized feudal system, admitting no territorial magnates of the German type, supported by Norman nobility, Norman bishops, and French culture. Richard Cœur-de-Lion, the most famous if by far from the greatest of the Plantagenet kings, was a French troubadour; not till the fourteenth century was the King English, and English the language of the law courts and the parliament. When in the twentieth century the King marks his acceptance of a new law with the formula 'le roi le veult,' and the entry of a high dignitary or judge is heralded with 'oyez,' the last traces of the old French state language appear. The Plantagenets defended the French possessions of the Norman crown with great tenacity; under Edward III (1327–1377) and Henry V (1413–1422) they even sought to conquer the whole of France. Their attempt, however, was vain: even Calais had to be surrendered in 1559. The separation from the Continent was thereby completed; though, in the seventeenth century (1658), Dunkirk fell into English hands, this bridge-head was handed back again four years later.

Actually, Anglo-Saxondom defended its culture with mighty energy against the foreign elements that seemed to overwhelm it, and in the end absorbed the invaders into itself. French words overflowed into the language, but its structural form has remained purely Germanic. Constitution and administration were, at first, entirely Norman: ultimately, however, Anglo-Saxon elements forced their way through. Architecture, at first, was French; but by the close of the Middle Ages England had developed a style of building of its own, which has no analogue on the Continent. In the same way, the Norman nobility died out, and, though pedigrees may often conceal the fact, was replaced, by the end of the Middle Ages, by newly risen Anglo-Saxons. Towards the great mediæval cultural movements, England presented a truly Low-German-Anglo-Saxon aloofness; the idea of the Minnesaenger waked but a feeble echo in England, that of the Crusades even less. Understanding of the ethical side of the Holy Roman Empire was completely lacking. Again and again did the strife between Emperor and Pope, notably under Henry II, lead to conflict: Archbishop Thomas à Becket was a martyr for the Church.

The conflict left the nation quite cold. At the time of a grave political crisis, under John (1199–1216), Innocent III succeeded in making the country a vassal of the Papacy; a hundred years passed, the English monarchy recovered its strength, and when a later Pope endeavoured to renew these claims, all England, under Wycliffe's leadership, rose in resistance to Rome. By this time, Anglo-Saxons and Normans, together with what remained of the Celtic elements, had been fused into a national unity. Its basis was the Low German peasant stock: materialistic, formless, crude, liberty-loving, hard and tough, with a strong strain of Germanic inwardness; shot through with a curious imaginative gleam, and capable of periodic outbursts reminiscent of the sleeping Celt within. Superimposed on this is a stout layer of superficial culture, in the main of Norman origin. Norman, too, is that diplomatic skill in handling men which is as native to the upper-class Englishman as it is foreign to the average; Norman, too, the sense of form which wars so incessantly with the somewhat crude inwardness of the Germanic type: that sense of form which comes out in religion, in the Oxford Movement and the High Church, and in poetry, in the Cavalier poets, in Dryden and in Pope. From the close of the Middle Ages England as a whole, feels itself a nation – a unified and proud nation, rejecting everything foreign with a sort of lofty scorn, which those same foreigners were quick enough to observe.

The Norman rule was, at first, a feudal absolutism. As such it was strong enough to prevent the rise of those particularist powers which in Germany gradually pushed the Crown into the background. Royal courts of justice and royal taxes were successfully introduced; in the feudal hierarchy the ultimate power remained in the hands of the King, not in those of the barons of the realm dependent upon him. Also, in relation to the Church, it was the King who represented the interests of the realm as a whole. The right of private war never developed. Among the nobles on the Borders, in the Marches of Wales and Scotland, certain noblemen (the rulers of Northumberland, Lancaster, Chester, Shrewsbury, Hereford, and the Bishop of Durham) repeatedly established, though they never maintained, a certain independence as against the royal power; a state of things still reflected in the existence of a Chancellor of the Duchy of Lancaster, who sits in the English Cabinet as a Minister without portfolio. Wales alone, first conquered by Edward I (1282), had a really independent administration down to the time of Henry VIII. The results of this strong centralization are patent. No particularist movement or feeling has ever arisen within the people itself. The obverse of the medal is the uniformity of human type imposed on an entire nation – a uniformity that, in comparison with the rich variety of German or French stocks, seems a defect. The speech of the educated Englishman, in contradistinction to that of the Scot or the American, lacks the dialectical colour that often marks the educated German. True, there are local variations in national type, as in manners and customs, which separate the folk from one part of the country from that of another, but they are much less marked than in Germany and France. Apart from Scotland, English national life, contrasted with the rich variations of the Continent, presents a picture of drab uniformity, fatally congenial to the creation of a featureless and spineless urban population.

Royal absolutism notwithstanding, the germs of Anglo-Saxon self-government persisted throughout Norman times, when the constant conflicts between the King, the great territorial lords, and the Church, soon gave a certain importance to the lesser barons and the cities. Although the significance of Magna Charta was for long greatly overrated, it did at least provide the Barons and the capital with a certain protection from royal absolutism. In 1265, the Barons attempted to strengthen this opposition by enlisting representatives of the towns; and in the fourteenth century parliament – the assembly of the three estates of the realm, the feudal lords, the clergy, and the common vassals (i.e. property-holders and representatives of the towns) – gradually developed. By degrees this assembly established its right to vote taxes, to insist on the King's repressing the malpractices of, and even dismissing, counsellors whom it disliked, and became more and more the decisive voice in State life; twice, indeed, a king was deposed – Edward II in 1327, and Richard II in 1399. Under the Tudors (from Henry VII, 1485–1509), the power of parliament was gradually reduced, but in the contest with Charles I, it rose again to supremacy, and, after a second revolution in 1688, the Crown dwindled down almost to impotence.

§ 3

In the Reformation, England took a very active part. Both its political aspect, the rising of nations against the political claims of the Pope, and its dogmatic aspect, doubt as to Transubstantiation and implicitly the very basis of priesthood and Church, first came to the front in England, with John Wycliffe (d. 1384). Even in this first onset of the new movement, the characteristic marks of English religious life appear. While a considerable minority – Lollards in the fifteenth, and Puritans in the sixteenth and seventeenth centuries – felt vital spiritual issues involved, the great majority was interested only in the idea of liberty. And even for the Lollards and the Puritans this was the decisive element in the Reform movement. Under Wycliffe, Papal influence in England was definitely reduced; under Henry VIII a decisive break with Rome followed. The more radical Protestants endeavoured, through the formation of various sects (Presbyterians, Independents, etc.), to lessen or entirely abolish the influence of the priest in the Church. In so far as the conflict raged round the issue of the independence of the individual from ecclesiastical dominance, the fight was carried on with bitterness, tenacity, and an heroic spirit of sacrifice. But while individuals might be interested in the intellectual form of religious life, the mass cared nothing for doctrinal questions. Henry VIII, a great despot, utilized the new tendencies in religion to provide religious sanction for his Cæsarian instincts and polygamous desires. He broke with Rome when the Pope refused him a divorce from his first wife, and imposed upon his people a religion of his own creation, in which Catholicism and Protestantism were blended. His successor, Edward VI (1547–1553), introduced a definitely Calvinist form; after a brief Catholic episode under Mary (1553–1558), Elizabeth founded a religion which, while mainly Protestant in doctrine, retained the Catholic hierarchy and the Catholic form of worship. The majority of the people took all this quite calmly; the Puritan minority, in loud opposition, fought rather against the hierarchy than against the Roman dogma of Communion or any other of the hotly disputed dogmas of the day.

In England the Reformation did not produce a unified result. This fact had momentous consequences. Catholicism, it is true, at least so far as England itself and Scotland were concerned, was expelled; but the new Anglican national Church was never more than the Church of the politically and socially dominant classes and some of their adherents in the lower strata. The middle and lower classes as a whole did not and do not belong to it: they are Dissenters or Nonconformists (called Puritans in the seventeenth century) – in other words, adherents of a number of denominations of definitely democratic organization, much more hostile to Catholicism than is the Anglican Church. The separation between Anglicans and Dissenters is quite as marked as that in other countries between Catholics and Evangelicals. The difference, however, is not one of doctrine but of social class: a distinction between lower and higher, between the privileged and the merely tolerated, that is saved from being felt in all its harshness only by the tendency of Dissenters to pass over into the Church as they rise in the social scale. For long, and to some extent even to-day, there was an analogous cultural gap. Anglicanism has the large religious latitude of most State Churches. There is room in it for all forms, from the religious fervour and intensity of a Crashaw and a Christina Rossetti to the formal conventionalism of such a realist and man of the world as the eighteenth-century Bolingbroke. Therefore it is mainly within the Anglican fold that those leaders of English scientific and literary culture are to be found who know other ideals than the religious. The Nonconformist, on the other hand, is apt to be exclusively religious. The forms of his religion vary, from the zealotry and literalism of Old Testament piety to the finest mysticism of seeing and feeling; but he is religious, first, last and all the time: prosaically good and dull, unæsthetic, banausic and middle class. About 1630, this contrast became sharply

merely mechanical

20

visible. On the Anglican side, the Cavaliers, full of the joy of life, artistic, light-minded, coquetting with the Renaissance ideas of a superman which in Charles I passed over into arrogant cruelty and falseness. On the other, the Puritans, honest, pious, full of banausic hatred of the arts: their great Renaissance poet, Milton, an almost solitary exception. Their short period of rule (1640 or 1649 to 1660) killed the English theatre and English music. Down to this day, there has been no full recovery in these two forms of art, dependent as they are upon the public, since, unlike the lyric or the novel, they cannot unfold in solitude, independent of the favour and disfavour of authority. And the Puritan closure of the theatres was but one epoch in the persecution of the stage; a second, whose real conclusion is not yet, began when, though the Anglicans had triumphed (1660), the Puritan spirit of the lower orders had begun to infiltrate Anglicanism itself, in the eighteenth century. As the Puritans passed up, they gradually dropped their dogmatic tendencies and ecclesiastical-political ideals; but the majority of them retain to this day the religious one-sidedness of their notion of culture.

The absolutist tendencies of the English Crown, which, from the beginning of the Middle Ages on, came, again and again, into sharp collision with the powers and freedom of the individual, ended with the deposition of the last of the Stuart kings, James II (1688). Absolutism was replaced by oligarchy. Especially after the advent of a foreign dynasty, the House of Hanover, to the throne in 1714, the Crown was pushed more and more into the background. A final effort on the part of George III (1760–1820) to free himself and the country from oligarchy, ended in complete failure. Down to 1832 the nobles ruled the State through alternating Whig and Tory Governments. The rule of the gentry is the basic fact in modern English life, and one which has exerted and exerts a profound influence not only on the Constitution but on national character and life.

In every department of political life, power was in the hands of the nobles. A series of apparently insignificant measures had effectively excluded the masses from any share in it. Local government was in the hands of the Justices of the Peace, drawn to a man from the ranks of entrenched property. In the towns, the restrictions on the franchise, introduced by the Stuarts in every direction, were left intact, because they favoured the oligarchy. The administration of the towns had fallen entirely into the hands of small interested groups, practically exempt from outside supervision, which filled vacancies from among their own number, and were easily persuaded or bribed to act as agents for the great landowners; in the towns, before the Industrial Revolution, economic life was absolutely dependent on the big families in the neighbourhood. Parliamentary elections were in the main in the hands of local corporations, with a very small number of highly amenable electors. The rapidly rising industrial centres, which might easily constitute independent factors dangerous to the oligarchy, like Leeds, Manchester, Birmingham, Bradford, Sheffield, returned no members to Parliament, whereas miserable hamlets in the rural districts, and even groups consisting merely of the inhabitants of a park, acted as convenient bulwarks of the territorial interest, and as such retained their franchise. Moreover, any possible defence of their own interests on the part of the poorer classes was cut off by the gentlemanly provision that any and every form of participation in government, from the sessions of the J.P.s to the meeting of parliaments, was unpaid: even travelling expenses were not reimbursed. This meant that no one could be a J.P. or a M.P. who did not possess considerable private means. Politics in any and every form was thereby made the monopoly of the possessing classes.

Equally impossible was the creation of an opposition from the ranks of the intellectuals, since all the intellectual professions were likewise the monopoly of those in possession and their friends. The Universities in their entirety, and more than nine-tenths of the schools, were in the hands of the State Church, which excluded from study all but its well-wishers and thereby made the clergy, medicine and the law nearly exclusively Anglican; that means all these professions were manned and recruited from the good old families. No one, not even the staunchest opponent, could escape the influence of the Anglican Church, for no baptism, no marriage was legal, unless celebrated with Anglican rites: no one could officiate at a burial service except the parish priest or his deputy. The power of the oligarchy did not stop here. It even reached to the writer. Most of the leading minds of the eighteenth century belonged to the ruling class like Steele, Bolingbroke, Shaftesbury, Chesterfield, Fielding, Shenstone, Horace Walpole, or were their protégés, like Addison, Pope, Swift, or Young. Literature could not yet support its offspring: the way to success was through the great man's ante-chamber. Thither went great men like Pope and Swift, as Spenser had done in the sixteenth century; Defoe, who attempted, at first, to work through the opposition, ended by being a government agent. Only Samuel Johnson succeeded

22

in dispensing with outside help. And even he made no political opposition. Any pungency in political opposition, such as the *Letters of Junius* (1768–1773) displayed, caused a sensation which is difficult to understand to this day and had to remain anonymous; when a literary freebooter like John Wilkes ventured to organize a political opposition, he met with a persecution that stopped at nothing.

By such simple and apparently innocent means a class domination was set up of an absolutely unprecedented completeness and cleverness. Home policy was ruthlessly dictated by the agricultural interest: the object of economic policy being a high price of corn. The landlords did their best to lessen their share in taxation, notably in the Poor-rates, which had gone up alarmingly with the onset of industrialization. The oppressive Game Laws were solely motived by their sporting interests. Dissent, which comprised the organization of the lower classes, was ruthlessly repressed. Dissenters were not allowed a place in civil administration till 1828. In 1812 the last of the Stuart restrictions on their worship were removed, but they were not relieved of Church rates till 1868. Until the Register of Births, etc., Act of 1836 and the Burials Act of 1880, marriages and funerals could only be conducted by the State Church. Down to the middle of the nineteenth century, the Dissenters continued to be an unwillingly tolerated half, if not actual majority, of the population. But heavy as the domination of the few on the country, its form was mild; and while its monopoly position was resolutely maintained, an effort was made to soften the application of the law through a friendly insistence on the human standpoint. What, however, mainly distinguishes this from all other oligarchies is the skill it invariably showed in continuously infusing itself with fresh blood. This long vision, proper to the really powerful, as distinguished from the merely would-be powerful – this sense of the limits of power – seems to be in the English blood. Even in the Middle Ages, the lesser nobility, or gentry, never aimed at being the hangers-on of the great aristocrats. When the division into Upper and Lower Houses took place in Parliament, the gentry joined the town representatives in the Lower House. For centuries the towns held the balance there, but the nobles, in the long run, acquired ascendancy for themselves. The working of the law of Primogeniture prevented the creation of a poor and proud, but politically inefficient, nobility, and fused the nobles and the middle class. As early as the fourteenth century, great families like the de la Poles appear as great merchants, returning later to the ranks of the aristocracy with fresh patents. Or a thoroughly middle-class man like the poet Chaucer, again in the fourteenth century, fills purely noble positions, as page, diplomat and court troubadour.

In the eighteenth century, too, the ruling nobility showed skill in broadening its base, with the result that it maintained its oligarchy for a century. The gifted son of the artisan was not excluded from the high school, might, often enough, make his way, through the University, to the highest station in the land – provided only he adhered to the Anglicanism of the ruling caste. Since, theoretically, the State Church was the one and only, no conversion, no solemn abjuration, was necessary in joining it; all that the student had to do, on entering college, was to state his acceptance of the Thirty-nine Articles, and no external obstacles, no inquisitorial inquiry, no compulsion to the profession of conformity then barred his upward path to power. If a wealthy merchant or leading industrialist sought recognition by ruling circles, he had only to join the State Church, which, again, asked for no conversion, and whose doctrine comprised in its ample scope almost all the teachings of the separate denominations. If his means made him a real force, he had every prospect of finding a titled son-in-law or even crowning his career with a peerage, and serving, with his wealth, as one more firm support of the ruling caste. In this way the vast wealth that poured into England from India in the course of the eighteenth century was largely absorbed into the nobility, either through marriage or ennoblement. This process of absorption is still going on; indeed, it has accelerated during the last generation with a speed which may ultimately prove a danger to the old aristocratic type. At the end of any more than ordinarily successful business career, the English capitalist sees shining before him either the knighthood or baronetcy that admit him to the ranks of the gentry, or the peerage that elevates him to the aristocracy and the Upper House.

§ 4

The Industrial Revolution of the turn of the eighteenth century, bringing an accession of new wealth, mainly in the hands of Dissenters, more rapid than could be their absorption into the oligarchy, gave birth to an opposition to the ruling caste which, by 1832, culminated in the complete victory of the middle class. This laid the foundations of modern England. 1832 swept away the rotten boroughs and gave votes to the new industrial centres; 1835 substituted a new system of municipal government for the network of private interests in the hands of the gentry. The civil marriage law of 1836 freed Dissenters from subjection to the hated Establishment in the most important contingencies of private life. By 1829, the vote had been granted to Catholics and a breach made in the Anglican monopoly of State control: the establishment of University College, London, on an undenominational basis (1828), broke the monopoly of higher education. The domination of the gentry was gone, but England was still far from being a democracy. The Reform Act admitted only the upper ranks among the merchants and business men to the franchise; up to 1867 a series of complicated rules combined to exclude the whole of the fourth estate from the vote. The newly ascendant class consolidated its economic position unassailably by the introduction of Free Trade (1846), which dealt a deadly blow at the agricultural interest of the great landed proprietors, and made trade and industry the permanent basis of English economics. Just as in 1688 the landed aristocracy cheated their allies, the Dissenters, of their share of the fruits of victory, so now the new capitalists endeavoured to deprive the lower classes, who had fought in the first line for the 1832 Reform Bill, of their part in its benefits. The period from 1832–1848 is filled with revolutionary efforts on the part of the masses and attempts to achieve a democratic franchise and a liberal Trade Union law. Earnest thinkers like Carlyle, Kingsley and Dickens made it their life-work to fight the more and more obvious Mammonism of the ruling caste, and preach social reconciliation as a new social ideal. But the first step towards strengthening democracy was taken in 1866, when defeated Conservatives decided to exploit democratic tendencies for their own ends. In 1867 a Conservative Government broadened the franchise, and in 1884 the Liberals, afraid for their own power, carried the work a stage further, though not so far as universal suffrage. From this time on, the tendency of legislation becomes more and more definitely democratic; in 1870 and 1876 Shakespeare's country at last followed the example long before set it by half the continent of Europe and introduced compulsory education. In 1871 the religious tests that still hampered Nonconformist access to the Universities were abolished; the opening years of the twentieth century saw new modern Universities like Manchester, Liverpool, Leeds, springing up throughout industrial England, and opening the way for the son of the artisan and craftsman to pass into the upper social grades.

In 1880 the permission to conduct funerals outside the rites of the Church swept away the last remnant of Anglican compulsion over other denominations. Every decade showed an increase in the influence of the working class in public life. In 1871 and 1876 legal recognition was given to Trade Unions: in 1906 a Bill, originating in a legal decision in a case on the Taff Vale Railway, made it practically impossible to attach Trade Unions funds for strike damages, and legalized the strike as an industrial weapon. In the eighties England in its turn witnessed the rise of a Labour movement. In 1905 John Burns was the first working man to be member of an English Cabinet. In 1909–11, Lloyd George introduced his Unemployment and Health Insurance Bills, and in 1909 his famous Budget, with taxes on land and capital at what were then thought to be revolutionary rates; in 1911 the resistance of the Upper House to all these reforms was broken by the abolition of its unqualified right of veto; and, in 1918, the process culminated in a Franchise Bill which, though still leaving a modified form of plural voting in the hands of property-owners, was in general thoroughly democratic. The Act of 1918 (with an amendment passed in 1928) even extended the principles of democracy into the world of women.

§ 5

The political struggles of the nineteenth century produced many alterations in the spirit of the English State. Before 1832, England was aristocratic; then followed the period of middle-class capitalist ascendancy; with the Franchise Act of 1918, the structure of democracy is complete. Always, however, the new, instead of driving out the old, comes in and fuses the old into itself. Revolution does not occur in this deeply conservative country, only development. Up to 1832 the tone was set exclusively by the aristocracy; after 1832, and even after 1918, its power is not so much abolished as painfully reduced by the middle and working classes. Capitalism, which begins in 1832 to be the most powerful factor in English life, was by no means superseded in 1918. The masses have acquired an influence they never had before, but they are a long way from ruling alone. The old forces in the life of the State have accommodated themselves to present-day democratic forms; by admitting the masses to a share of power they have skilfully secured for themselves a good measure of their old ascendancy.

A more detailed study will be made of the three forces in English politics – aristocracy, middle-class Capitalism, and Labour. For the moment, a brief indication of their influence on the last century of English history must suffice.

Down to 1832, the hereditary aristocracy ruled the State along paternal, feudal lines. They felt themselves a privileged class, the real England, strong, ruthlessly severe towards Dissenters, Irish and Nonconformists, but intelligent and always alert to receive capitalist competitors into their ranks. The lower orders they dominated with patronizing superiority, doing little for them, yet not repressing them too harshly. Their foreign policy was strong and far sighted; they took up Louis XIV's challenging bid for world supremacy, and that of Napoleon, and beat them both.

When, in 1832, the middle-class capitalists came to the helm, they at first played the part of the saturated parvenu. They consolidated their power, at the expense of the aristocracy, in every possible direction: economically through Free Trade, politically through electoral reform, both national and local, spiritually by overthrowing the aristocratic monopoly of University education.

At the same time they did everything in their power to block any further reform. Every political or social aspiration of the fourth estate met with an absolute no. The appalling condition of the factory-worker, the hideous slums of the great cities, the spiritual destitution of a nation growing up without any system of general education – none of this touched the moral deadness of these hard-faced men. On the contrary, whereas the roots of these evils may have struck under the regime of aristocracy, it was only under Capitalism that they grew up to the proportion of evils crying aloud to Heaven. The new plutocrats regarded the town and the factory as their domain, in which it was theirs alone to command, as the noble did on his estate; to attack this sacred right of theirs was to preach revolution and Jacobinism. And in the town, in the factory, and throughout the life of the State, the individual had got, so ran the ruling philosophy, to be self-supporting. Never did even the particularism of the Lower Saxon peasant lead to such sinister conclusions as were promulgated by his descendants of the English towns. To this Radical Manchesterism, as preached by Adam Smith and Jeremy Bentham at the turn of the eighteenth and nineteenth centuries, we shall have to return. In it the crudest greed of gain clothed its nakedness in the threadbare garment of the idealistic catchwords of philosophic rationalism. According to it, sanitary conditions in the factory

27

or in the dwelling of the worker, nay even the ultimate bases of every community, the increase and education of its population, ought to be exclusively governed by the laws of supply and demand, which were sacrosanct. The same applied to questions of foreign policy.

In principle, the development of State power was objectionable, since it might disturb the course of trade: in principle, war was opposed and the Colonies regarded as relics of outworn Mercantilism. In practice, however, a friendly eye was turned on war, even on so shameful a piece of exploitation as the Opium War on China, if it seemed likely to yield large profits at a small expense. Since these middle-class people shrank from responsibility, their policy in relation to big States like France, Russia or America was one of clever concession; smaller ones were treated to wordy threats upon which they generally would turn back cautiously when threats did not sufficiently awe the culprits. Fortunately for England, sheer Capitalism has never dominated its foreign policy. In this sphere the 1832 Reform Act only temporarily displaced without dispossessing the old nobility: throughout the nineteenth century the direction of foreign policy remained in aristocratic hands. At the same time, the lower middle-class note, characteristic of this era, sounds in the lack of interest shown by England in its Colonies, in the weakness of its action at the time of the Crimean War, in the mixture of arrogant brutality and irresolution in the policy of an aristocratic foreign minister like Palmerston, it is even visible.

The real difference between the political life of the century of middle-class predominance and that of its aristocratic precursor lies in its characteristic idea. The old aristocrat of the eighteenth century might toy with certain catchwords, such as liberty, Protestantism, order, but, in the main, his policy, both at home and abroad, was a policy of power and interests, and he was not ashamed of calling it so. The new middle class, while looking with even greater egotism after its own interests, had charity, progress, humanity, the brotherhood of nations, eternal peace, for ever on its lips. The men of 1832 are the lineal descendants of the old Puritans; the old Calvinistic enthusiasm for making the earth into the Kingdom of God persists through all the critical realism professed by the posterity of Cromwell and Hampden in matters of religion.

The transformation of this capitalistic into the modern democratic State began with the establishment of the capitalist State itself. The excluded masses organized in their Trade Unions, after the abolition of the Combination Laws in 1824 and 1825. With the aid of this weapon, they have gradually conquered the purely capitalist State. Unconditional individualism, the ideal of middle-class capitalism, is now dead. For centuries, even before it arrived at mastery, it was fought by every workman who suffered under it, and every conservatively-minded man who saw in it a destructive force. For Coleridge and for certain groups round Cardinal Newman and Lord Shaftesbury, it was the fig-leaf of naked materialism. Social reformers like Kingsley and Carlyle, novelists like Dickens, fought it as the poison that disintegrates and rots every form of human association. Nor was the old individualism unchallenged in England's relations with the outer world. A foreign policy of ideas centring round imperialistic tenets has, ever since the middle of the nineteenth century, been the cry of a body of opinion that, growing from decade to decade, has, since the Boer War, actually dominated English thought. For them the Colonies represent not so much economic as ideal values, since in them lie possibilities of a British world-power that might rule the world and at the same time serve to spread Christian and ideal ends over the Universe.

But the new English State of 1918 is in no sense a break-away from the old. Politically, economically, and mentally, Aristocracy and Capitalism are still immensely strong in it. The great weapons of control – Parliament and the Press – are completely in their hands. The powers of the old State are indeed so strong that they can dominate through the new democratic forms and over the new community. Labour strives to organize the entire State in accordance with the forms of Trade Unionism. Derived, essentially, from mediæval ideas of organization, these forms cut right across the dominant individualistic outlook. But Individualism could not have ruled as it has for a century if it were not rooted in certain primary needs of the English soul, which are not easily to be uprooted. Labour demands the interposition of the State to protect the individual by Factory codes, housing regulations, compulsory education, and so forth, all under statutory supervision. Labour now demands a guaranteed high minimum wage for all, to be provided out of the maximum wealth of the few. So far, the middle-class Radicals have kept march with the Labourites. But English Individualism passionately opposes any revival of mediæval ideas which would make workmen and masters partners in a co-operative enterprise and set above them the directing, controlling, profit-limiting, force of the State. The struggles round this issue that started about 1900 are far yet from their conclusion. We shall have to examine some of their most important phases later on.

In the sphere of foreign policy, too, everything is in flux. The two great forces which made for the world war in England were the old English aristocratic struggle for unlimited political power and the newer desire of Capitalism for unlimited economic expansion. During the war the Little England ideal of the Victorian era collapsed completely. That little British State which could make nothing of its Colonies, has become a world commonwealth in which the Motherland and the Colonies are partners with equal rights; while the hope of a permanent good understanding with the United States holds out the prospect of a dawning era of Anglo-Saxon dominance over the world. This sense of the mission of their race now inspires practically the whole people, including most of the workers. Differences turn not on fact but on ethical interpretation. For some, Anglo-Saxon Imperialism connotes only power, exploitation, profits. Before others there sways a dim but dazzling vision of a millennium to be brought to the world by the Anglo-Saxons. For the moment, these last constitute a leaderless minority, with no definite aim, no plan of action, without influence on practical politics, blind tools in the hands of the politicians and capitalists. But the existence of such a man as Lord Robert Cecil, and the efforts towards founding a world community of Christian churches, show a genuine enthusiasm behind this aspiration which can hardly be wholly ineffective.

CHAPTER II
ENGLAND AND THE BRITISH ISLES

§ 1

By the close of the Middle Ages, England had started on a steady and almost uninterrupted rise to world power. The motives for expansion were, in the first instance, exclusively economic and political. A tinge, but hardly more, of romantic idealism may be found in the French wars of the Plantagenets and Lancastrian kings, coming out in such masterful characters as Henry II, Edward I, and his two great-grandsons, the Black Prince and John of Gaunt. But the essential factor in these French wars was economic – the need of a purely agricultural state, at a low cultural level, for the territories of a country at a higher one; together with the sheer drive of the Anglo-Saxon race towards rule and conquest.

In mediæval times this drive had two objects. The dynasty endeavoured to pursue its family interests in France. The national interest demanded the fusion of the two British islands into a single realm. By 1450 the anti-French, Continental policy of the Plantagenets and Lancastrians collapsed; fortunately for England, since the only result of a lasting connexion with France and its higher level of culture would have been that England must have fallen to the position of a dependency. All its great future was bound up with an insular policy, and for such a policy the foundations were laid during the Middle Ages.

Edward I conquered Wales between 1277 and 1284. At first, the country was placed under military rule, but local traditions were respected so far as they were consistent with the final aim of the conqueror. Wales continued to be an independent Principality, with the heir to the throne as Prince over it, guarded by fortresses like Carnarvon at every vital point. There was a crisis when Henry VIII abrogated the independent constitution and introduced the Reformation, with English as the language of the Church. Wales had to submit. But the reaction came in the eighteenth century, when Methodism arrived and Wesley's followers started preaching in Cymric; the whole of Wales, with the exception of the English gentry, the progeny of the conquering families, fell away from Anglicanism, and created a Cymric church service, which led, gradually, to the revival of a secular literature in Cymric also. Since its power was in no way affected, England let this be, and to-day Wales is to all intents and purposes a

31

Celtic country again. In 1918, after protracted struggles, the Anglican Church in Wales – to the Welsh the symbol of the foreign rule – was disestablished. To-day it is but one among the other denominations, and far less important than Methodism, Congregationalism or Baptist faith in Wales. Welsh is taught in all schools, and is the medium of instruction in many: England offers no opposition. There is an active Home Rule movement, aiming at making Wales a quasi-independent State with an independent administration; England lets it be. It has unchallenged power in the country; Wales has given England a Prime Minister. Always, England is liberal, where its power is safe. *Minima non curat praetor* is part of the creed of the English gentleman.

§ 2

Scotland presented far greater difficulties to the conqueror. As far back as 1018, the Scots had seized land that was originally Anglo-Saxon, together with Edinburgh, founded by Eadwine of Northumbria (617–633). England had had to look on while the Celts of the Scottish north and the Anglo-Saxons of the Scottish south set up an independent kingdom there. Attempts to give reality to the shadowy over-lordship of England over the northern half of the island never came to anything. There was a constant state of tension between the two. The Border was given over to a chronic state of feud. Scotland made itself as unpleasant to its neighbour as it knew how, by assiduously cultivating political and social ties with England's rival, France. For long, indeed, Scotland presented a very curious mixture of natural boorishness and French polish. After the death of Elizabeth in 1603, James VI of Scotland became James I of England; but religious differences – like those which, in a different form, developed in Ireland – split the country afresh, and created a contrast between the English and the Scots that persists to this day, and is, in fact, the single essential local differentiation that does exist within Anglo-Saxondom. Under Charles I, England was Anglican, if with a strong Puritan opposition; Scotland definitely Puritan. Attempts to impose Anglicanism met with resolute resistance. The National Covenant of 1638 eventually cost Charles his throne, and showed, once and for all, the futility of any idea of forcing the Scots out of their Presbyterianism. True, the Stuarts came back. When Charles II (1660–85) and James II (1685–8) renewed the attempt to introduce absolutism and Catholicism into England, they were finally driven out by the Revolution of 1688. Scotland, however, had never

32

forgotten that the Stuarts were its national dynasty; this, conjoined with a dislike of England, led to a series of Stuart risings, first in 1689, and, later and more effectively, in 1715 and 1745. All these risings were put down with appalling ferocity. English special tribunals rushed the rebels to the scaffold, without too careful inquiry into evidence. On one occasion a whole Catholic clan – the Macdonalds with their women and children – were butchered (Glencoe, 13 February 1692) when peace had already been concluded. A Protestant Scot, who held the local command, issued the order thinking himself to be authorized by a somewhat vague order of the London Government. This terrible massacre never has been atoned for. Free play was given to all the freebooting instincts of the English soldiery, and no one raised a finger in England for the protection of the Scots. Here, too, as in Wales, England went no further than its need of power demanded. True, the constitutional Union of 1707 was forced upon the country by some questionable intriguing behind the scenes, but the conditions were generous; nor was there any attempt, after the fall of the Stuarts, to force Anglicanism upon Scotland. The use of Gaelic and the wearing of Gaelic dress was heavily penalized, so long as it was a living symbol of hostility to England; not a second after it ceased to be so. In the Hebrides, in Argyle and Inverness, and other counties, Gaelic is the speech of the people to-day: Church services are conducted in Gaelic. It is tolerated, even encouraged. Old traditions are fostered: Scottish garb, which was once enough to send a man to prison, is now used for regiments of the line, and worn on dress occasions by Scottish nobles related by marriage to the Royal Family. Now that nationalism is no longer dangerous to England, it is petted: the effort is to use the ideal elements in this nationalist feeling in the service of England. By the seventeenth century, it was said, by way of flattery of the Scottish nobles, that Scotland had given England a dynasty, and so rather ruled England than was ruled by her. At the same time, the idea of economic advantages was held out to the mass of the people.

Scotland had enjoyed a certain trading importance thanks to its connexion with France and its own weaving industry, but the Union with its stronger and more advanced neighbour opened up the English market to Scottish industry and gave it a share in the markets of the world. The hungry, thrifty, barbarous Scot was a favourite butt of the eighteenth-century English satirists. Now this same Scot made his way not only to court but into the city: and, very soon, efficiency brought him to the top in almost every sphere. One need only mention, to cite relatively modern instances, statesmen like Lord Balfour, Lord Rosebery, Lord Haldane, and Sir Henry Campbell-Bannerman; business men like Lord Strathcona and Andrew Carnegie; writers like Adam Smith, Smollett, Macpherson, Burns, Scott, Carlyle, Ruskin, R. L. Stevenson or Andrew Lang. Immigrant Scots compose the Ulster garrison in Ireland which will serve the interests of England with its latest breath. In America, too, Ulster Scots, like McKinley, have played a prominent part; while in Australia and in Canada, Scots are an important and generally strongly Imperialistic element in the population. In view of this close interweaving of Scottish and English interests, what does it matter if there is in Scotland, too, a Home Rule movement, demanding greater freedom from the central Government in London? Already, Scotland has its own local government system and its own educational system, centred in Edinburgh; it retains its own Courts of Justice and its own system of law. Further decentralization is a purely practical question, entirely irrelevant to the policy of the realm as a whole: as irrelevant as the question whether or no more scope shall be given to the teaching of Gaelic in the schools in the north-west of Scotland.

§ 3

Scotland accommodated itself; Ireland did not. For that reason, Ireland had to feel the whole weight of English power. Motives of power alone operated in the conquest of Ireland. The religious dedication of Henry II's campaign in 1171, as of his ancestor, William I's expedition against Harold, was merely the conventional mediæval form, and one which England has employed, with real virtuosity, down to modern times. (Both the war against Napoleon and that against Wilhelm II were invested with the religious sanctions of a Crusade.) The conquest of Ireland was only partially successful. During the Middle Ages, England never had enough men to occupy more than half the island. In the Pale, the English fringe on the eastern and southern coast, English towns were built whence settlers went out into the interior, the rest remained a Celtic country, in ill-defined dependence on the English Crown. Even in the Pale, English dominion was not unchallenged. The handful of English colonists tended to become Celts as time went by; the second generation often figuring as leaders in Irish resistance. After the complete failure of the Reformation in Ireland, differences of religion aggravated national hatreds, and an impassable gulf yawned between the two countries. Failing to pacify the land, and finding that the Irish took every opportunity of attempting to shake off the yoke, England settled down to the task of reducing it with unscrupulous brutality. The use of the Irish speech was forbidden, under inhuman penalties. Since the English settlers tended to marry Irish girls and bring up their children as Irish, this, and the use of the language, the wearing of Irish garb or an Irish beard, were made punishable offences by the Kilkenny Parliament (1367). For any kind of firm hold on the country, it was necessary to carry through some sort of mass-settlement; this was actually effected through an unprecedented act of constitutional violence. After a fruitless rebellion against the English throne, led by Tyrconnel, Tyrone and others, at the time of Elizabeth, James I proclaimed the whole of their lands, i.e. the province of Ulster, as forfeit. By a piece of juristic sharp practice, English feudal law was, in fact, carried over to a country where a different system of tenure prevailed, half communist, with a very limited right inhering in the clan lords over the estates of their tenants. The expulsion of the Irish from the greater part of Ulster, and the settlement of Scotsmen and Englishmen there in 1609, created a bulwark for England that exists down to this day. In 1653–5 Cromwell repeated the experiment, with small success, in the southern provinces, driving the Irish out of Leinster and Munster and endeavouring to confine them in the stony and marshy region of Connaught and to settle English soldiers in the regions they had vacated. A brutal solution was found for the Church and Education Questions, by making all schools and churches English and Anglican. Down to 1869, tithes for the support of the Church of the oppressor were wrung from the desperate poverty of the Irish peasant, even in parishes without a single Protestant, whose wretched potato fields had, in addition, to maintain an Irish Catholic priest – and this although, when the last Irish garrison left the country under the Treaty of Limerick (1691), the Irish were guaranteed the possession of their old religious freedom. Economically, too, English policy systematically aimed at reducing the Irish to a nation of pariahs through a long chain of penal laws. Consequential legislation for Ireland, following on Cromwell's Navigation Act (1651), forbade direct trade between Ireland and France and other countries. Ireland remained shut off from world trade. Although rich in splendid natural harbours, with a west coast constituting the natural point of departure from Europe to America, no world-shipping line so much as touched there before the war. Protective taxes, imposed in the interest of the English woollen trade and English cattle, destroyed the Irish woollen industry about 1700; while, for a century, the export to England of Irish cattle was prohibited. The object here was plainly not religious but merely confiscatory; the injury fell, in the first instance, on the Irish cloth manufacturers of Ulster, Protestant settlers, forgotten by the predatory policy of the eighteenth century. A cunning property law contrived that, in the case of Catholic (Irish) succession, property was divided at death among the children – i.e. cut up into small parcels – while in that of Protestant (English) it remained undivided. Further, Irishmen could not own their land; they could only obtain it on lease, subject to conditions that made economic progress impossible. In the towns, the English artisan could have as many apprentices as he liked, but the Irish only two; the development and yield of any undertaking, of course, depended upon the number of apprentices. In many areas, notably in the neighbourhood of towns designed to be kept, or made, entirely English, Irishmen could hold no land. Catholics (i.e. Irishmen) had no votes either for national or local government, although, as a result, in Londonderry only thirty-eight, and in Belfast only twenty-one, persons were entitled to vote. As a Catholic, again, the Irishman was excluded from every kind of school, and, of course, from the solitary University, Trinity College, Dublin; he could become neither a lawyer nor a doctor; there was not a single institution for the education of Catholic priests. He could be a proletarian, a hodman in the towns, a little artisan or pot-house keeper, or a tenant in the country of a miserable little plot which, in good years, brought in just enough to pay rent to the English landlord. That was all. He was to be proletarianized; and he has been. The best of the people emigrated to America, above all the Irish Protestants from Ulster. From the end of the eighteenth century on, there was a steady stream of emigrants to the United States and to some extent also to the Colonies. Ireland is the single country in Europe to show a decline in population in the course of the nineteenth century. In 1821 it had 6·8 million inhabitants; in 1841, 8·2; since then the number fell steadily to 4·2 millions in 1926. The vast sums of money that poured back to Ireland from America saved it from complete proletarianization; they also stimulated such resistance to England that England itself entered upon a completely new policy in relation to Ireland. But English oppression made Ireland economically wholly dependent upon England. The entire soil of the country passed into English hands; about 1830, the entire upper class was exclusively English and Protestant. Further, Ireland lost its language. All that it retained, throughout this terrible period of oppression, was its religion. When, in 1831, England gave the country some sort of educational system, the Irish language represented the cultural life of a primitive shepherd people. At the time when it might have been used, no Irishman thought of learning as much as the A B C in this language.

When England perceived that Ireland could be repressed but not broken, it modified its policy. From 1840 on, the main course of English statesmen in Ireland is towards conciliation. There have been long breaks in this policy, but its main trend is unmistakable. Every measure of conciliation, while it might attract an infinitesimal section of Irish opinion to the English camp, invariably acted, with the great mass of the people, as simply to stimulate the hunger of the freed slave for more, and always more. Every concession on the part of the English Government was the signal for conspiracies, acts of violence, and movements of protest, which England had then to repress by violence, which violence again produced a fresh crop of conspiracies, boycotts and risings. About 1840, Daniel O'Connell raised the standard of the Repeal of the Union forced on the country by England, after the rebellion of 1798, by force, bribery and corruption (1800). Isaac Butt (1871) and, after him, Charles Stewart Parnell (d. 1891) revived the campaign in the much more modest form of a Home Rule movement; from 1906 on, the Sinn Feiners openly raised the demand for complete political independence. In view of the economic destitution of the country, O'Connell advocated a refusal of rent; Parnell's Land League in 1879 renewed the struggle; the aim of Sinn Fein was to promote native Irish industry by boycotting English and to drive England gradually out of the country, through the institution of an Irish Parliament and Irish Courts of Justice. Throughout Irish politics there is an accompaniment of terrible outbreaks of fanaticism, like the Fenian outrages of the sixties and the Phœnix Park murders in 1882.

The strongest methods were employed by England for the establishment of order in Ireland – courts-martial, military occupation, substitution of military for civil law and the establishment of special commissions operating with the savagery of the conqueror. But this is only one side of the matter, if the more obvious one. What is more important is that England, through its nineteenth-century fiasco in

Ireland, learned a larger conception of policy, one which discerns the friend of to-morrow behind the cruelly defeated enemy of to-day, and has the courage to hold its hand once victory has been attained. So, in the nineteenth century, Ireland was hardly subdued before England called off its bloodhounds and sent for its statesmen. True, England has never of its own free will made concessions to Ireland; always under the compulsion exercised by 3 million heroic Catholic Irishmen, who have been able to hold a great Empire in check. Nevertheless there is greatness in the courage with which England held true from 1840 on to a line of policy directed towards conciliation, in the face of the perpetual accusations of cowardice and treachery levelled at it by its own Die-hards. For the sake of this idea, England made sacrifices such as have never been made by an externally victorious nation. A radical break was made with the seventeenth- and eighteenth-century policy of ruling the Celtic masses through an English Protestant upper class, which owned the whole of the land of the country. In 1831 Ireland was given an educational system of its own. When the undenominational education, a product of the green table of English Liberalism, failed in practice, the country was allowed quietly and by degrees to Catholicize the schools, and, in Ulster, to Protestantize them. The monopoly position of the Protestant University, Trinity College, Dublin, was broken by the establishment of the undenominational Queen's Colleges, in Belfast, Cork and Galway (1845). This, however, proved no lasting solution, and in 1909 a Catholic University was founded in Dublin, with branches in Cork and Galway. To the horror of Anglicanism, Gladstone in 1869 disestablished the Anglican Church in Ireland, restored most of the old mediæval Church property to Ireland, and even went so far as to endow the new Catholic seminary at Maynooth.

In the nineties, when a movement arose in Ireland for the encouragement, in schools, of the Irish language, still struggling for existence in outlying districts, concessions were made to meet it. It was used in many schools as the language of instruction, and in more taught as a school subject; before 1914 it became compulsory for admission to the National University; one saw everywhere names of shops and streets written in mediæval Irish script (which no Englishman can read) – the English Government made no objection. Above all, England gave the land back to the Irish. From 1881 on, English Land Commissions systematically reduced the exorbitant rents, and that without a penny of compensation for the English landlord; it was a Liberal Minister, Mr. Gladstone, who carried through this unheard-of attack on the sacred rights of private property. Before this, in 1870, the tenant acquired rights in his land and the landlord's power of eviction was severely restricted.

Finally, with the help of the State, the landlords were bought out, and the tenant became a free man. By the revolutionary Land Act introduced by the Conservative George Wyndham (1903), representative of a party which had once been the spokesman of the Irish landlords, four-fifths of the land was handed over to Irish peasant proprietors. Politically, too, England retreated; in 1829 the Irish were given the Parliamentary vote; in 1898 the English system of local government, which handed control over practically all their local bodies to them, was introduced; in 1886, and again in 1893, Gladstone, and in 1912 Asquith, following in his footsteps, attempted to give Ireland a parliament of its own, with wide powers.

England has learnt an immense amount from its Irish policy. Its outlook was powerfully widened. A country of rigid individualism, and deep distrust of any kind of State action, learned to work through a bureaucracy and to carry out a State educational system and a State policy of land settlement. Great Britain, whose officials at home are little more than peripatetic controllers, envoys from the centre who supervised the execution of the laws, maintained, in Ireland, a resident bureaucracy, mainly in Dublin, but also to some extent in the smaller places, which learned how to act on its own initiative, working out draft bills and carrying on the practical business of administration. The Irish experiment forced even the Manchester man to learn that a bureaucracy can do things, as well as prevent them from being done – although he may still resist the proof thus forcibly put under his eye. The strongly Protestant State has learned to come to terms with Catholicism. Ireland burst the framework of the purely Protestant State when, in 1829, it secured the political emancipation of the Catholics. (The subsequent disestablishment of the Church both in Ireland and in Wales, the almost complete equality secured in England by the Nonconformists, and the removal of the schools from Church control, were the inevitable results of this first step.) The country, which oppressed and persecuted Catholicism more than any other in the world, succeeded in making Catholicism one of the pillars of its power, in a manner to be described later on (cf. page 359). But the outstanding thing is that England came to see that it could never win by sheer force. In England itself, from 1840 on, hostility to official Irish policy grew in working class and Radical circles, came to the fore in social movements, like Chartism and others, and spread thence to the Continent, where the contrast between England's humanitarian preachings and its practice began to be very unkindly pointed out. In the United States, and even in the Colonies, the Irish began to be a danger. From America the Fenians (mainly 1865–8) launched their propaganda of the deed – assaults on persons and property, revived in 1916 – and there, too, hatred against England was brewed, down to the days of the World War. The Irish element in the Colonies was passionately opposed to every Imperialistic tendency of the close of the century. It was the Irish, in the main, who blocked Conscription in Australia at the time of the war, and the anti-English agitation of the Irish-Americans constantly led to painful incidents and even compelled American Presidential candidates to take a line on the Irish Question by no means agreeable to England.

The World War made a solution of the Irish Question a matter of urgency. In 1914 the prospects were not bad. The Catholic Primate, Cardinal Logue, Archbishop of Armagh, and John Redmond, the political leader of the country, came out unconditionally on the English side. True, the introduction of the Home Rule Act had to be postponed. Under Sir Edward Carson, the descendants of James I's Protestant settlers rose in opposition to separation from England, and, in time of peace, organized an army and a provisional government. Home Rule could not be put into operation without armed conflict between Ireland and Ulster. Its suspension fed the bitterness of the Sinn Feiners, who were not satisfied with Home Rule, and now felt that they were completely betrayed by England. Lack of confidence, on England's part, even in Redmond, was shown by a whole series of trifling military regulations at the expense of Irish recruits and Irish officers, as well as by the influential part played in England by Sir Edward Carson, the leader of the Ulster rebels. Thus, the Irish Volunteers, originally raised against Ulster, gradually under Sinn Fein influence became an anti-English force, and Easter Monday, 1916, saw the outbreak of rebellion in Dublin. From the start, the military chances were hopeless: the 'rebellion' was a *Putsch* on the part of a few inexperienced, heroically-minded young literary men and a handful of Socialistic workmen, with little or nothing behind them. The new peasant proprietors – the decisive element in the country – stood aloof: a sign of the success of the policy of conciliation. Nevertheless, the liberation of Ireland dates from the Easter coup of the Dublin martyrs. The military reign of terror after the shooting of the rebels soon fanned the hidden fires almost everywhere to open flame. After demobilization in 1919, an irregular gendarmerie, the Black and Tans, so called after the colour of their uniforms, was cast into the unhappy island, and a guerrilla warfare started, conducted with ruthless bitterness and incredible self-sacrifice, that seemed to have conjured up anew the anarchy of Cromwellian times. Up and down the country, revolutionary Irish authorities were established, a local tax system began to function, along more or less confiscatory lines, the voluntary tribunals that exist everywhere on British soil transformed themselves into an Irish national judicial system, the English organization was simply boycotted, in accordance with Sinn Fein tactics, and the Irish members, elected to the Parliament at Westminster, met in Dublin and constituted an Irish National Assembly, the Dail Eireann. Even so, the armed hand of a victorious world-power lay heavy on the unhappy land. For long it seemed as though Ireland, this time, was to receive the knock-out blow. Gradually, however, another aspect asserted itself. Ireland had become a question of world-policy: as such it stood in the way of England's Imperialist design. Warning voices sounded from South Africa and Australia, which had begun to influence England's foreign policy to a notable extent: they sounded, too, from America. The Washington Conference was imminent, and England's Anglo-Saxon partners were of uncommon importance for her. In this situation England made one of those clever turns that have always characterized her world-policy; peace was made with Ireland. The world power capitulated to 3 million rebels, most of whom had to be brought out of their prisons for the purpose of concluding peace. The Treaty of London of December 6, 1921, makes far greater concessions to Ireland than had ever been dreamed of by the most radical of Home Rulers. The obvious demands of security are limited to an irreducible minimum. Ireland receives an English Governor-General; its members of Parliament have to take an oath of fealty[1] to the English king, of a very restricted character, coast defences are, for the present time, entrusted to the English Fleet, four harbours are subject to the English Admiralty, and certain conditions provide for the protection of the Protestant minority. But Ireland has become a Dominion – the Irish Free State, no English troops are maintained there; its status is the same as that of Canada. Administratively, it is entirely autonomous; Irish officials take the place of English; Ireland levies its own taxes and even forms its own tariff, against the outer world as well as against England; it sends Irish Ambassadors abroad. The consent of the Irish Parliament to the nomination of the Governor-General may follow. For the future, the provision by Ireland of some part of its own coast defence, i.e. of an Irish naval contingent, is envisaged. The Irish Constitution, as based on the London Treaty, assumes that – invasion apart – the Irish Parliament has a voice in peace and war; in other words, Ireland has self-determination in this most vital issue of foreign politics. Such are the concessions that the death of the Easter martyrs wrung from the victors in World War.

Not that the Irish Question was thereby settled. The 1921 Treaty's first result was to break the unity into which the people had been welded by the national fight. In a country which had never known peace, there had never been any opportunity for solving the conflicting problems of modern life. They now all burst forth at once, demanding an instant solution. Up to 1900, the dominant factors in the country have been the Catholic priests on the one hand and, on the other, the peasants and shopkeepers, led by lawyers and petty tradesmen. Feeling had never been too good between them, since the political leaders of the second group were apt to be Protestants; but against a common foe they had managed to work together. The new century brought new groups forward, clamorous to be heard. A strike of unusual magnitude in Dublin in 1913 revealed the existence of grim industrial poverty and advanced Labour ideas in the Irish capital. Moreover, about the turn of the century, Irish Nationalism raised its head afresh. True, the policy of the parliamentary party, under O'Connell, Parnell and Redmond, had been Nationalist, but it was predominantly Catholic and economic. It was always against the Irish Protestants, took little interest in the maintenance of Irish speech and Irish customs, and had almost always been ready to buy peace with England at the price of religious or economic concessions. That genuine Irish Nationalism which preached 'Free from England, at any price,' and even greeted the Ulster Protestant as a brother, had never been more than an impotent undercurrent. From 1900 on, however, it gained greatly in strength. In 1893 John MacNeill and Douglas Hyde founded the Gaelic League, which sought to re-create a living, literary language out of the dying Irish dialects, and employ every instrument of agitation for its restoration as a national tongue. It was a purely cultural movement, non-political in aim. From 1905 on, Sinn Fein[2] carried cultural Nationalism to its logical, political results – the expulsion of the hated alien by boycott and, if boycott failed, by rebellion. The war and the Easter rising made Sinn Fein master of the country. Victory once secured, the opposition elements reasserted themselves; the clergy, the peasants, and the middle classes revolted against the extreme Nationalism of the Republicans (*Fianna Fail*) who, led by dreamy (and to a large extent anti-Clerical), town-bred, literary men, threatened to isolate little Ireland, culturally and economically, from the rest of the world, through their policy of national speech, schools, university, and their impregnable tariff wall against England.

The first years of Irish freedom were full of a bitter feud between the Moderates and the radical Republicans. For the Moderates the Free State, which Ireland had at last won, was an enormous step forward, not the ultimate goal perhaps, but a reality upon which it was necessary to build Ireland's future. For the radical Republican, on the other hand, under Edmund de Valera, the Free State was a fake, a dodge of England to throw dust into Ireland's eyes. Their goal was complete independence, a republic without any official connexions with England, if possible with Irish as the official language, with an Irish coinage, and economic independence as well.

Until 1923 Ireland was in the throes of a civil war. Even after their defeat the Republicans are still a certain danger for the new Free State, which has not yet passed the danger-zone completely.

Danger at least as serious threatened the new State from the north, from Ulster. The passionate hostility of the North to the South persists. The pride of the Scottish peasant, the bigotry of the Puritan, and sheer economic interest had created an almost impassable wall of hate. The great Ulster manufacturers and the peasants were afraid of being plundered economically by the small men who would set the tune in the Dublin Parliament. They mobilized Ulster against the South by an appeal to religious prejudices. Seventeenth-century Puritanism lives on, rigid and unyielding, in the mass of the Ulster peasantry; they hate the Catholic of the South and believe that were Dublin to rule over the North, they would be put to the sword. This mingle of economic and religious impulses, surprising to no one familiar with Anglo-Saxon life, led to the signing of the Covenant of September 28, 1912, a revived form of the religious bond once used by the Scots against England. After the war, the London Imperialist press, which had once extolled the Ulster rebels to the skies, suddenly swung over into the opposite camp, because for the Imperialist, America counts more than little Ulster. But the religious passions of the North, for ten years blown to fever-heat, were not to be so easily assuaged. Ulster organized itself as an independent state under the English Crown. Since May, 1921, it has been governed by a Parliament in Belfast. Ireland is divided into a northern part with 1·25 and a southern part with 2·97 millions of inhabitants, who economically ought to form one body. Northern Ireland sends its members of Parliament to Westminster. Diplomatically and economically it is a part of Great Britain. It pays its quota to the general expenses of the Motherland, but has its own Parliament and Cabinet, its own judicature; it is part of Great Britain but autonomous. Its territory comprises the Protestant counties of Ulster (Antrim, Armagh, Down, Fermanagh, Londonderry, Tyrone) which have been cut off from the Free State politically, and economically as well, whereas the more or less Catholic counties of Ulster (Donegal, Cavan, Monaghan) have remained part of the Free State. This separation is hardly final. So long as the linen and shipping industries of the North remain outside, Southern Ireland is financially and economically hampered. The Treaty between England and the Free State envisages immediate negotiations with Ulster; the completion of the constitutional form there set out depends upon this; so far, however, the union of North and South, subject to a certain measure of autonomy for the North, seems absolutely impossible. The Catholic Free State loudly complains that the Catholic minority which had to be left in Ulster, is systematically being deprived of all higher offices there. The negotiations about the final boundary, by which the Free State hoped to recover part of the territories inhabited by Catholic minorities, have broken down completely. Until an accommodation is reached, there must remain a wound in the body of the English State, dangerous because so near its centre.

There was bitter opposition in England to the Irish Treaty: talk of disgrace and treachery to Ulster. But Lloyd George went ahead. Irish peace was necessary. Ulster itself is most useful to England as a support to the English spirit in Ireland. Reinforced by a round million of Ulster Protestants, absolutely pro-English, the scattered quarter of a million Protestants in the south and centre of Ireland have some weight and importance: without Ulster, they are helpless. It may be hoped that the existence of this million of pro-English Irish Protestants may prevent the three and a third million of Irish Catholics from carrying on an anti-English policy. Economic forces are certainly on their side. The Free State has been up to the present an agricultural country; beer and whisky are brewed in the Free State, but the main Irish industries – shipbuilding and linen-spinning – are centred in Belfast. Practically all the industrial goods which the Free State wants come from England in spite of a protective tariff behind which Irish industries of the future, it is ardently hoped, will develop. Ireland's railways are still in the hands of English capital; its money comes in the main from the London market.

The Ireland of the future will probably be a rich agrarian country, when a new independent peasantry, which is gradually developing in consequence of the English agricultural reforms, will be the main factor of her economic life. The great Shannon power plans which are at present being constructed by German engineers, will distribute cheap electrical power all over the country. Agricultural co-operative unions are spreading in the country, and will largely contribute to make Irish agriculture efficient again; but all these new enterprises, together with the enterprises of the future, like new harbours, new coal-mines and afforestation, are extremely costly. According to the old Sinn Fein programme an enormous stream of American money would fertilize the country as soon as Ireland would have recovered her liberty. The American financiers, however, have on the whole been very reluctant. At the present moment practically all Irish money comes from Great Britain. Irish banks are practically branches of the great London banks. Of the Irish exports of 1927 (£44·9 millions) £37·8 millions went to England; of the Irish imports (£60·8 millions) no less than £40·6 millions came from England. Ireland has been and will be for a very long period to come in all economic aspects a branch of the English head office. She may be independent, but is riveted to England by economic bonds of the greatest strength. To change this may be the legitimate aim of Irish politics, but it cannot be changed by Radical declamations, only by the sturdy, silent, economic work of many generations.

CHAPTER III
THE RISE OF COLONIAL EMPIRE

§ 1

ENGLAND's instinctive isolation notwithstanding, its relations with the Continent have always been extraordinarily close. Back in prehistoric times, the religious contact existed between the Celts of France and those of the island: even then, the Channel was a superb strategic line of defence rather than any kind of cultural barrier. Economically, England was long dependent on the foreigner. Up to Reformation times, it was predominantly an agricultural country, growing corn and wool, but manufacturing only a small portion of its produce. Luxuries came exclusively from abroad; England imported cloth from Flanders, woven from the wool of its own sheep: wines from the south of France and from Germany: such commodities as silks, carpets, weapons, watches, organs, hats of fine quality, and leather wares came from the Continent, carried, for the most part in German, Hanseatic, bottoms. Its intellectual life was profoundly influenced by foreigners. In literature, French influence, after the thirteenth century, and Italian, too, after the fourteenth, is everywhere perceptible: after the Renaissance, first Italian artists, then German, like Holbein, Lely and Kneller, or a Fleming, like Van Dyck, were the painters of the English Court and society: music shows strong Italian, and also German, influences; architecture reveals French, and, above all, Italian, models everywhere. And yet, from the earliest times, the effort towards national independence is strongly marked. A wave of anti-foreign feeling passes over the country at least every second century. Whether the massacre of St. Brice in 1000, when the Anglo-Saxon King Æthelred II put the Danes in England to the sword, should count among them, may be doubtful. But Earl Godwine successfully led a national reaction against the Normans whom Edward the Confessor had brought to court with him: two hundred years later, English nationalism turned against the Italians and the Frenchmen at the court of Henry III (1216–72): in Elizabeth's time, it rose against Flemings and Hansa men, and had them deprived of their privileges. The national attitude to foreign intellectual influences is cold and critical.

Supremacy is permitted to foreigners in spheres where competition seems impossible, for example, in painting and music. But where a native product exists, as in literature, only the smaller men

46

turn joyously to foreign inspiration; the stronger are definitely critical of everything foreign. Modern movements of predominantly Continental origin, like the Reformation, the Renaissance, Nationalism or Socialism, have to pass through a considerable period of proud rejection before they take hold in England, and even then do so, without exception, only after they have been definitely adjusted to the insular tradition. English men of letters were in touch with Italy from about 1370 on, but it was not till about 1500 that anything like a Renaissance movement comes into being, nor is its full growth realized till after 1570, by which time it was nearly over in other countries. All the essential elements of the Renaissance stream over to England, are greeted there with enthusiasm and accepted by every one who cares for æsthetic life; but the really creative minds in the country either submit them to a national transmutation or reject them out of hand. Thus the typical Renaissance lyric form, the sonnet, only appears, in England, in a vulgarized form, in which the rhyme sequence and composition of the original are changed out of recognition, and nothing survives but the purely external element – the number of lines. In the same way, Renaissance drama, based on Aristotelian or pseudo-Aristotelian laws, rejecting all crude theatrical effects, adhering strictly to a measured and formal verse, and sharply divided between purely pathetic tragedy and purely comic comedy, is accepted in England, but only to yield pride of place to Shakespearean drama. Shakespearean drama fuses comedy and tragedy; permits its blank verse to range over the whole gamut of expression, from declamatory narrative to conversational prose and the stammering staccato of passion; it puts the most violent action on the stage and rejoices in the movement of loud and excited masses in every form of violent contrast. Renaissance imitation of the antique, quantitatively stressed hexameter and the Horatian mode, was cut off, as early as 1602, by Samuel Daniel's conscious reversion to national rhyming verse. Continental Humanists proudly rejected the Middle Ages: but England's most distinguished Renaissance poet, Edmund Spenser, resurrected them, and, right down to the eighteenth century, they were not forgotten. The Italian tour, which every sixteenth-century mind regarded as the ideal gate to culture, was decried by the Humanist, Roger Ascham (d. 1568), as superfluous and dangerous. The fostering of their native tongue by the side of and in preference to Latin, the English book as against the Latin, was universally demanded in England at a time when few Germans showed any sort of national interest. At the beginning of the nine-teenth century, Coleridge, Carlyle and George Eliot enthusiastically commended the study of German philosophy and literature, and certainly had considerable influence on intellectual leaders; but the majority rejected the whole thing as 'German mysticism.' German Socialism was actually born in London about 1840, but it is not till 1880–90 that it begins to have any effect in England, and then the individualist and visionary German elements in it are forcibly ex-truded. From time immemorial 'foreign' has connoted, in England, 'disagreeable,' 'inferior,' and, in part 'morally suspect.' The proud sense of superiority to the alien, which struck foreign travellers even in the fifteenth century as typically English, has always been the Englishman's strongest weapon against any kind of foreign intellec-tual influence.

§ 2

French influence has always been patent in England, but it has never sunk very deep. Before the middle of the eleventh century Norman knights are to be met with at the court of the penultimate Anglo-Saxon king. In the Middle Ages, French troubadours, French lyric forms and the French epic, find their way to England; in modern times, French dramatic technique. The English bill of fare even of the private household is French; the ox, the sheep, the calf come on the English dinner-table with their French names, as beef, mutton, veal; the old Christian names have either disappeared or have been romanized early in the Middle Ages. Names like Matthew, Andrew and even William plainly reveal to the philologist traces of an earlier romanized form. The wife of Charles I was the last of several French princesses to sit upon the English throne. From about 1630 right on to the second half of the eighteenth cen-tury, French taste in architecture, literature, clothes, cooking and the form of life generally, was regarded as 'the thing': by many educated persons as the only thing. England, as a whole, however, always rejected it: native developments overwhelmed foreign.

Even to-day France – certainly not Germany – is the one Con-tinental country that is more or less well known, and the one whose culture ranks, with the native, as worth knowing. Trifles indicate the general trend. Thus, the Continental window, opening, unlike the English, not from above downwards, but sidewards, is called simply, 'French window.' A German invention like the taxi-cab (*Taxameter*

48

droschke in German ; in the French, taxi, from *taximètre*) found its way in its French form into England after it had been adopted in Paris. German and Italian names pass into English in their French form: one talks of Cologne, Aix-la-Chapelle, Mayence, Ratisbon, Vienna; of Naples, Florence, Milan and Venice. French is the one modern foreign language the educated Englishman is apt to learn at school: French books the only ones the ordinary English paper is apt to take count of. France, not Germany, has always been the bridge between England and the Continent.

In mediæval times, English foreign policy was essentially based upon England's relations with France. Relations to other powers, Spain, the German Empire, the Flemish magnates, were, as a rule, fostered only in so far as they might serve as allies against France. If, throughout the Middle Ages, good feeling with Flanders was assiduously fostered; if an English prince, Richard, Earl of Cornwall, strove for the Imperial German crown; if the German king, Adolf of Nassau, received English moneys; if Edward III made, in 1338, an alliance with Louis of Bavaria – the invariable reason has always been the effort to encircle France. Only with the final shattering of the dynastic ambitions of English kings to the throne of France, in the fifteenth century, did the aim of English policy become widened and diversified.

Opposition to France gave way to the new antagonism to Spain. In this, both idealistic and economic forces played their part. Ever since Elizabeth's day, England felt itself the guardian of Protestantism; it also sought to acquire a share in the new Colonial world. From either point of view, Spain was the real enemy. Every kind of flattery and pressure was used upon France, to induce it to act as an ally against Spain, but without success. Spain's other neighbour, Portugal, became, on the other hand, from the seventeenth century on, more and more dependent upon England. England guaranteed its political independence to Spain, at the price of one of its Indian colonies, Bombay (1662), while the Methuen Treaty of 1703 made it economically England's vassal. That this carried with it complete political dependence was proved when Portugal, with absolutely no quarrel with Germany, was compelled to declare war against it in 1916.

Of the two motives governing English Continental policy in the sixteenth and seventeenth centuries, the idealistic and the economic, the first is by far the weaker. England was the champion of Protestantism, so long as it risked little and ran no essential danger in being so. Henry VIII and Elizabeth were most careful to avoid any close alliance with the German Protestants. Elizabeth did support the rebellious Netherlands against Catholic Spain, but grudgingly, and with the utmost stinginess. England undertook no regular war against Spain, contenting itself with encouraging freebooters like Drake and Hawkins to burn Spanish harbours and raid the Spanish specie fleet. When Spain roused itself to revenge and sent out the Armada, England repulsed it with the utmost skill and energy, and actually did save Protestantism, at a minimum of cost to itself.

But the real driving force in English policy of that time was economic advantage. It was this that sent it out, in search of colonies, to India, which the world at that time located in the West Indies.

In Henry VII's service, John Cabot, a Genoese, discovered Newfoundland; under Mary and Elizabeth, English travellers went out in search of distant India through Russia and Siberia, and came to China, Bokhara, and Nova Zembla. Refusing to recognize the Pope's division of the New World between Spain and Portugal, English merchant adventurers, under Hawkins and Drake, broke their way into the Spanish sphere of influence, to carry on peaceful trading or armed piracy, as luck might hap. In 1584, Walter Raleigh founded the first colony in Virginia; in 1591-4, the first expedition to India sailed; in 1600, the East India Company was formed. During the seventeenth century, Colonial guerrilla war was the rule. England was mostly officially at peace with all the Powers. None the less, English freebooters and colonists fought the French at the mouth of the St. Lawrence in Canada; the Spaniards in the West Indies, the Dutch and the Portuguese in India and the Malay Archipelago. In this warfare the motive was merely material profit. The fact that the French or Spanish opponent also happened to be an accursed Papist was useful enough in justifying anything dubious in the procedure in the eyes of the world, but hardly imported any loftier motive into economic guerrilla warfare. Every competitor strove to drive his rival out of the market, and regarded himself as having a monopoly over the disputed area. No one thought of liberty of trade. No one was in any position to throw moral stones at anyone else. The whole thing was carried on by bold adventurers, not taken too seriously by the statesmen at home. Their services were accepted, sometimes rewarded; they could always be disowned if any other Power complained.

Spain, England's most dangerous rival, more or less faded out after the death of Philip II. In the case of Holland, however, which had succeeded the Hanseatic League as indispensable purveyor of the carrying trade, guerrilla Colonial war developed into an affair of bitter seriousness. Cromwell's Navigation Act (1651) made an end of Holland's carrying trade between English ports and the manufacturing nations, and, after repeated wars (1652–4, 1665–7, 1672–4) Dutch resistance was broken.

Here again, we meet, for a time, a combination of idealistic and economic motives. Cromwell felt himself the protagonist of Protestantism, and played with the idea of a combination of all the Protestant powers, including Holland, under England's leadership – an idea which did not in the least prevent his doing all the harm he could to Dutch trade.

After this, England's real rival was, as in the Middle Ages, France – enemy this time not merely of the dynasty, but of the entire nation. Louis XIV strove to make his country supreme in Europe. England felt this as a threat to its security,. and therefore attempted to play off the smaller powers against France – Prussia, Austria, even its defeated enemies, Spain and Holland. Just as in the Middle Ages, its resistance toughened when France again began to extend its sway in the direction of Belgium, and so enlarge the coast area confronting Englands'.

War with France really begins with the accession of William of Orange (1688), and ends with the downfall of Napoleon in 1815. Throughout, England is the 'protector of small nations' threatened by France. Again and again, England sets them at war; they carry it on with English money; but in every peace treaty, their interests are ruthlessly sacrificed to England's. England, as a rule, only takes part in naval warfare; the English armies that took the field, for example, under Marlborough in the war of the Spanish Succession, or under Wellington in Spain and Flanders, are composed for the most part of mercenaries, drawn from the Continent, from Ireland, and to some extent from Scotland, though their officers are English. The result of a period of a hundred and thirty years of war was the complete destruction of French plans of world supremacy. Belgium, cockpit of Europe, was made into a buffer State under English influence; the overseas possessions in dispute, India and Canada, were ceded to England by France (in 1763).

In these wars, the driving force was indubitably the struggle for political power and economic influence. At the same time, a certain idealistic point of view was present, too, to lend a sort of consecration to the strife for power. For the nation, the hundred years' fight against France wore the aspect of a mighty duel between two principles, with England as the champion of freedom against Continental despotism. Contemporary history can admit this unmeasured claim only within narrow limits; we know, to-day, that freedom, in eighteenth-century England, was the privilege only of the landed gentry, that they alone were, in the full sense, citizens. We know, further, that, in comparison with the complacent selfishness and corruption of English administration, autocracy, in Prussia if not in France, certainly represented a higher type of government. Nevertheless, England had discovered a slogan in which every Englishman honestly believed. Like any other Gospel, it worked, not only with humanity as a whole, but even with its believers, to remove the dross that still hindered its efficacy. The question whether the idea of English liberty in the eighteenth century was truth or a legend is not essential to its history in the world. What is essential is, England had a watchword for humanity at a time when the rest of the Powers of the world only played the game of huckstering villages, souls and alliances. England knew how to play that game with consummate mastery; but besides it, England alone knew how to rouse something like an ethical feeling all over the world. Its new watchword worked at home and abroad. The English aristocrat had dangled the notion that they were the only free people in the world so often before the English masses, that, in the course of the nineteenth century, these presumedly free persons did actually demand and acquire from the gentlemen a great share of that same freedom. And for the peoples of Europe who saw, about 1800, that English freedom, unlike the freedom of the French Revolution, kept order at home and allowed other nations – Ireland always excepted – to live their own lives in all essentials: for them, the slogan seemed a veritable Gospel. The end of the eighteenth century saw England a world-power. It rules over a good part of the world's surface and – which is part of the story – gives the world over which it rules a principle of life such as it needed, at the time, and one whose force is not yet worked out. Whether it is, in fact, the true, ultimate principle of life in the world, is a fundamental question irrelevant to the history of the period from 1750 to 1918, since no Power throughout that epoch has had anything better to offer the world.

§ 3

England's rise to world dominion, viewed externally, proceeded along two different lines. The one, foreshadowed by Henry VIII and Elizabeth, set as its object the Balance of Power. This assumes such a grouping among the Powers of Europe that England, remaining outside both groups, is always in a position to give a casting vote. The main assets of English policy in this game are, first, the existence of a certain sympathy for England at least in some circles in every European capital; second, England's wealth, through which it can invariably purchase and subsidize allies; third, its fleet, based on a practically unassailable geographical position. The English fleet enters European politics in the fourteenth century: during Edward III's wars with France it fought the first notable naval action in European history, at Sluys in 1340. At that time, the fleet was merely a means of securing English control over the Channel. In Elizabeth's time, it kept the Armada from attacking the British Isles by a skilful defensive action; it 'singed the King of Spain's beard' in all sorts of pirate expeditions; but it was not capable of anything on a large scale. It is under Cromwell that it first appears as an instrument of world power. Then, it destroyed the Dutch shipping trade; later it played a great part in the overthrow of Napoleon, by cutting France off from the sea. Finally, in the World War – again, as at the time of the Armada, at the most modest cost – it decided everything.

There is nothing specially English in the methods of the Balance of Power policy. Essentially, it is the time-honoured cabinet policy of wearing down an adversary by a combination of allies. England, however, thanks to its geographical situation, is able to undertake it at an exceptionally small risk to itself.

We shall see later on that the Balance of Power is not the only instrument of English world politics, but that an extremely clever manipulation of idealistic feelings proved nearly as successful as the use of force (*comp*. p. 101 *seq*.). But before this second factor in English world politics was fully developed, England had already become a great Colonial Empire.

§ 4

The building of the English world empire was begun in America. Virginia was settled in 1584. The loss of the American colonies, however, interrupted this line of development. The area retained by

England, Canada (taken from the French in 1763) became after many disappointments the scene of the most momentous development in English Colonial history. When it became British, the principal area, Quebec, was French speaking, inhabited by Catholic peasants, and ruled over by Catholic priests. The English Government, after a considerable time of vacillation took the bold course of allowing this state of things to continue. At a time when Catholics were not allowed the most elementary civic rights in England itself, England allowed in its chief colony the growth of a kind of Church State, where Catholicism is everything; the Catholic priest is master over the church, the school, and the press, and church tithe is a legal obligation on all Catholics. The fruits of this bold policy appeared as early as the American War of Independence. Canada, faced with the choice between joining the rebellious colonies and adhering to England, preferred England. The Colonies might promise religious liberty to Catholicism – but England had actually given it: nor did the bigoted Puritan of Massachusetts appear the safest guardian of toleration. England weathered the storm; Canada remained within the Empire. After the peace England quietly but very effectively insured itself against any possible recrudescence of anti-English feelings among the Canadian French by swamping the country with English colonists. The stream of English Loyalists, driven out of the United States at the conclusion of peace, was directed to Canada, and Ontario, a new State, to all intents and purposes entirely English, was created where the St. Lawrence emerges from the Great Lakes. After the Napoleonic wars, emigration was systematically diverted to Canada. As a result, the French were soon in the minority everywhere outside of Quebec. But even then, the game was not quite won. There was no end of troubles in Canada. It was the hey-day of the hole and corner type of Colonial policy. Petty little bureaucrats, with a staff of time-servers hungry for emoluments, ruled over an equally petty little settlement, which expected nothing but profit from the homeland while refusing to do anything for the Mother Country. The rising under Louis Papineau in 1837 showed how critical the situation really was. Lord Durham's historic Report recommended Anglicization of the French, by extinguishing the identity of Quebec in a united Canadian State (1838 *seq.*). This failed completely, and a final solution was not found till a quarter of a century later, when settlement of the country had developed more fully. All the Canadian colonies – with the exception of Newfoundland, independent to this day – were combined in a single Dominion, by the British North America Act of 1867. The Dominion is more strongly centralized than the United States; the Union has at least a nominal right of veto as against the individual provinces. There is no longer a serious national problem between the English and the French element. In Quebec, the French element predominates; in Ontario and the whole west, the English. But in Ontario and the Prairie the considerable French speaking minorities have been granted certain important rights in the schools. All these questions have been delegated to the provincial authorities. England does not care how much French is taught, how much Catholicism grows in Saskatchewan. England is only interested in the great issues of politics. How far Canada will follow the English lead in great imperial questions and in all these questions is not decided in the provinces, but in the Dominion Parliament, where English members have a safe majority. In the Dominion Parliament forward-looking English and Scotsmen settle all those economic questions which, in a young colony, are the great questions of the day: the French, taking small part in industry, often old-fashioned and conservative in their ideas, are strong mainly in the rural areas. Race distinction is so little of a factor in politics that there are English and Frenchmen in both the political parties.

But although the nationalist question is no longer a difficulty, England's relations to Canada still cause it some concern. So far, it has not succeeded in forging economic ties between the Dominion and the Mother Country strong enough to resist the economic magnetism of the United States. There is in itself no inclination in Canada to join the United States. The French element is against it, because in Canada it is a very powerful ethnical and political factor (1921: 2·5 French to 4·9 million English), whereas in the United States the French would be but a tiny island in the Anglo-Saxon sea. Canadian industry is, in the main, against it. Though it can and does protect itself against the Mother Country by tariffs (a Canadian protective tariff has existed since 1859 and 1879), it would be powerless against the mighty Trusts of the Union. The interests of the various industrial groups are, however, very diverse, and agriculture certainly seems to hope more from the American market than it fears from American competition. American immigration into the newly settled Western provinces is growing steadily, as does the financing of Canadian undertakings by American capital and the placing of

Canadian State and provincial loans on the New York market. It is not easy for the Mother Country to oppose the pull of the United States. Its own Free Trade system prevents it from giving Canadian wheat any preference on the home market. Joseph Chamberlain's attempt to reintroduce a tariff with preferential duties on Colonial imports was a complete failure. All that remains is Canada's dependence on the London capital market, and the political protection afforded to 9 million colonials by the prestige of the Mother Country. Here are considerations of immense weight against any idea of independence, but hardly against the United States, which could offer the same advantages.

England relies on the powerful political and economic interests which are still speaking for the Mother Country in Canada, and the faculty of standing pat, so strong in every Anglo-Saxon. It deals tenderly with the unbridled egotism of the Canadians (as of all other colonials), and goes to meet it with concessions often hardly compatible with the unity of the Empire. No protest was made when, in 1879, Canada introduced a protective tariff on all foreign goods, including English, the force of which is by no means neutralized by a system of preferential treatment in favour of England (since 1897). Politically, the Dominion is to all intents and purposes independent. The ties that unite it to the Motherland are very slender. True, England sends out a Governor-General, generally a personage of high rank, who theoretically has a veto on Dominion legislation. This right is now lost. The last time when a Governor-General (Lord Byng) tried to interfere in Canadian politics (in 1926 he refused to the Prime Minister the right to dissolve Parliament) the first consequence was a complete victory of the party which he had injured, the second his own downfall, and the third the Imperial Conference of 1926 which took all political power from the Governor-General. Juridically, the Privy Council in London is the court of last instance for Canada – a fact which often rouses sharp opposition in the Colony. Canada has always refused to have to participate in the costs of British military expenditure. The only contribution to Imperial defence Canada was willing to make, was the building of a small fleet and a militia of its own (1911). The last English garrisons had to be removed from Canada in 1904. Long before 1914 it had become plain that only on condition that Canada had itself approved of war would it place its troops under the orders of the English Commander-in-Chief. No obligation ever was admitted to send

Canadian troops to fight the battles of the Mother Country. Both in the Boer War and in the World War, important volunteer contingents were dispatched to the aid of the Mother Country: in the World War even conscription was introduced, when voluntary enlistment began to dry up. But the greatest emphasis was laid upon the fact that this was a voluntary assistance. In Quebec, when French Canadians protested passionately against conscription, it was allowed to remain a dead letter. Canada has even gradually achieved a very large freedom in diplomatic questions. It never had any love for the British Foreign Office. Canadian interests have so often been sacrificed to peace with the United States – as, for instance, in the question of fishing rights off the coasts of Nova Scotia, and the boundaries of the Klondyke gold-fields – that the Dominion now demands independent representation. A Department of External Affairs already exists, as a liaison both with the Government in London and the English Ambassador in Washington, with the Colonies and the foreign consuls in Canada. When in 1923 a treaty was concluded with the United States concerning the Halibut Fisheries on the Canadian coast, it was a Canadian minister, not the British Ambassador at Washington, who signed it. A Canadian ambassador has been in residence at Washington since 1926, and when England concluded the peace treaty with Turkey at Lausanne (1923), it had to be ratified not only in London, but at Ottawa as well. There are even hopes in certain Canadian quarters that it will be possible to create a tropical Colonial Empire for itself, by some sort of connexion with the West Indian islands. The Imperial Conference of 1926 has made Canada practically an independent country.

§ 5

India became a British colony at the same time as Canada. When Frederick the Great was keeping the French busy in Europe, thanks to English subsidies, in the Seven Years' War, Quebec fell into English hands in 1759, and Clive defeated the French at Plassey in 1757. Ever since the Treaty of Paris (1763), India has been the brightest jewel in the Imperial Crown.

India, at first, was an economic colony. Wealth rather than power was sought there. India made England rich. All the agents of the East India Company (founded 1600), who looked after trading stations in India, or, later, administered whole districts for the Company, came home millionaires. Indian gold flowed in streams to

London; the Indian merchant princes married into the peerage and were themselves ennobled: it was in the main Indian gold that lifted the middle class up into the aristocracy. Now the treasuries of Indian nabobs are no longer pillaged or defrauded, but Indian trade is still absolutely vital to English economy. The Englishman cannot get on without his Indian tea, Indian cotton and oil seeds, wheat from the Punjaub, jute and rice from Bengal: India is the largest customer of his cotton and metal industries. India's recent development of a local cotton industry, protected by duties against Lancashire competition, is felt in England as a disagreeable threat to the home industry.

Even to-day India is the country in which Englishmen grow rich. The administration is in the hands of English officials. Up to quite recent times, every economic and cultural improvement has been due to the work of some thousands of young Englishmen. In sharp contrast to English practice elsewhere, India – like Ireland, up to quite recent date – has been administrated by a bureaucratic hierarchy. The Indian Civil Service attracts young men of talent from good families without considerable worldly goods, and assures to every one who shows any merit a very handsome salary while he is still young and a more than adequate pension at the end of his service. The wealth of India goes far to account for the fact that the standard of life in England is markedly higher than in other countries.

To-day, however, India is more important politically even than it is economically. India is the great central barracks of Empire. The army in India is there not merely to keep order within the country, but to serve as a mobile reserve, behind foreign policy, available for use in Asia, Africa, and even, possibly, Australia. In 1899, in the Boer War, it was Indian troops that saved Cape Colony; in 1900, at the time of the Boxer rising, Indian troops relieved the Peking Embassies; in the World War they fought in German East Africa, in Palestine, and in Mesopotamia; were Australia ever to be threatened by Japan, they are there to defend it. Eternal petty feuds on the North-West Frontier keep a body of men and officers in existence who know what war is from direct experience. By ruling India, with its 60 millions of Moslems, England is the greatest Mohammedan power of the world. In India it rules over a population nearly as numerous as that of Europe (1921, 319 millions) divided into countless races, religious sects and social castes. India is the training ground, on which England has learned how to deal with jealousies between nations, states and social classes, with religious prejudices and religious fanaticism. The necessity of protecting India from without has widened the area of English policy from decade to decade. To safeguard the sea route to India the Cape was occupied and Egypt taken over: and, in the World War, bridges created between it and the Mediterranean in Persia, Palestine and Mesopotamia.

India came gradually under English sway. The trading company that exercised the authority of the State until 1859 had only one interest there – that of making dividends. This was accomplished more surely and cheaply by erecting trading stations than by hoisting the flag. Administration was left in the hands of the native princes: the Company had Residents at their courts entrusted with the duty of keeping their policy along satisfactory lines. Their instruments for this task were personal force and dignity, and the use of every kind of intrigue and bribery. In the name of order, the Resident would support the power of the Great Mogul against the lesser feudal chiefs; in the name of liberty, the power of the lesser magnate against the greater. He would discover a bloody tyranny here, that must be overthrown: a little group of people there being oppressed by some one or other: women and children, who had got to be helped. Circumstances varied, but the person to be trusted and protected always happened also to be a friend to England. All these lesser potentates gradually had to hand over the direction of their foreign policy to England. So, France was cut out. For the rest, they retained their sovereignties. Indirect rule over men, avoiding any appearance of command: influence, without flag-wagging, such was the *modus operandi* in India. True, it could not be pursued invariably. If trade were to flourish, India must be at peace. But peace could only be secured at the price of interfering in every disputed succession and every court intrigue, everywhere protecting the pro-English candidate, and casting an appreciable weight into the scales against France. This could not be done without some sort of an army. Economic security was indispensable to trade. Since the Indian officials of the smaller potentates were not to be trusted, English tax-collectors had to be instituted. So, under the two first great English rulers in India, Robert Clive (Governor 1757–60) and Warren Hastings (1772–85), an extensive system of government and administration developed – regarded merely as an emergency system, less government being preferred to more, and direct administration restricted as far as possible to the Coromandel coast and the Ganges Valley, the rest of the country being left to the native princes. Subject even to these limitations, the policy could not be carried out without a large body of men dependent on the general representative of a trading company : the commercial rulers of India even became a figure in world politics. The question of peace or war between England and France was not in the last analysis, settled by the Cabinets of Europe, but by the officer of a merchant company in Calcutta, with a considerable army at his disposal.

This impossible state of things was opposed, at home, by everybody who, not being a member of the dividend-earning Company, was therefore ruthlessly shut out from any share in Indian trade. Further it was by no means satisfactory to the State which, having given the Company dictatorial powers, now felt itself pushed into a back seat. At each renewal of the Charter, therefore, the State extended its powers. First, in 1773, it claimed the right to approve nominations for Governor, and limited his autocracy by establishing a Council of officials at his side. In 1784, the whole of Indian administration was put under a Board of Control in London, which finally developed into the present India Office. In the course of the nineteenth century the area of direct administration was constantly extended until it covered two-thirds of the country.

The growing anarchy of the native States called for firm handling: English administration was far more productive economically than the Oriental government of the Maharajahs. On top of this, philanthropists at home began to talk of England's civilizing mission in India, and say that it could only be carried out if the country was under direct government control. A violent break came with the mighty uprising of the Indian East against the European West, which, in 1857–59, shook English rule to its foundations. It was a revolt on the part of every group in India that saw itself as threatened with being swept out of honours (often questionable enough) and offices by the English administration, in combination with religious zealots who saw the approach of Christendom. It was an immense danger to English rule, and it led to a complete change of policy. The East India Company was abolished and the country made directly subject to the English Crown, which in 1877 took the title of Emperor of India. But there was no extension of direct administration. Even to-day, 38 per cent of the area and 22 per cent of the population remain under the rule of native princes, whose rule England does everything to strengthen. It has, moreover, made energetic efforts to foster the co-operation of Indians in the administration of their country.

The creation of a native element civilized in the European sense and at the same time attached to England, is the central problem of the English rule. It is obviously impossible to rule a country of 319 millions merely by importing English officials. In the long run, India can only be held if its natives take part in the administration and willingly direct it into an English channel: if in other words they can see a broad correspondence between England's advantage and their own.

There are two possible solutions to the relation between ruler and ruled. One is the assimilation of the ruled to their conquerors. Or, on the other hand, the progress and material welfare of the dependent people may be encouraged in every way, subject to the maintenance of a sharp line of distinction between two social classes, never to be obliterated. The first method approximates more nearly to the political principles of English statesmanship, the second represents the feeling of the average Englishman. Assimilation was the goal of English policy in Ireland, after it had come of age: assimilation is what it has striven for in Canada and South Africa; in the United States and Canada, it is the Anglo-Saxon policy *vis-à-vis* all the other nationalities in the Union. It has been attempted in India. Here, however, it meets a very significant limitation, set by the white man's sense of superiority to the coloured. In 1835, the historian Macaulay introduced a system of education, on the English model, into India. The young Indian reads Milton and Shakespeare, Wordsworth and Tennyson, and is nurtured on Western ideas of freedom and self-determination. Since 1857 there has been a network of Universities in existence, organized entirely on the English model. The supreme aim of education is to convey the youthful Indian to Oxford or Cambridge and return him to his native land an Europeanized Indian. This does happen, if to a much smaller extent than Macaulay dreamed of, but its result in nine cases out of ten is an Indian who loathes England from the depths of his soul. He returns to India, with the title of M.A. and the consciousness, that, in knowledge and experience of life, he is the equal of his rulers. He finds that he remains the ruled. Every honourable and distinguished career is open to him. But in the army he can only become a junior officer, and no Englishman is ever put under his command. A proportion of the higher administrative posts are filled by Indians, but the prospect, for any given individual, of reaching one of them is infinitesimal. European education, painfully acquired, admits him only to the outer courts of the Temple. And most painful of all – let the Indian come from the most distinguished caste, let him be blessed in abundance with this world's goods, let him hold a high administrative post, and be honoured by the Viceroy: he still finds the doors of the clubs, thrown wide to every English subaltern, closed in his face. Socially, he remains the 'dirty nigger.' Nor is dissatisfaction confined to the successful. It was estimated in Lord Curzon's administration that not more than 8 per cent of entrants for matriculation – a point often reached only after years of strenuous diligence and incredible sacrifice on the part of the candidate's family – pass the examination of B.A. For the rest, immense efforts end in nothing but failure. Thus those who appear outwardly successful, but with the inward grudge of the humiliated, are perpetually being reinforced by an army of disappointed men, whose dream of the higher administration ends up in the enforced modesty of a pleader or clerk.

Any attempt to Anglicize the Indian is an attempt to square the circle. English education demands a pedantic respect for truth from born poets and dreamers, strong action from ascetics who say Nay to life. What it accomplishes is the production of a race that corresponds to no English ideal, but has contemptuously sloughed off all the good qualities of its own. What England gives to the Europeanized Indian neither is nor can be enough to satisfy his wants, but it is more than enough to irritate conservative India. Those who adhere to the ancient ways see with disgust that they are ruled over by renegades, by men who, though they may not have become Christian, nevertheless eschew native rites and abandon the sacred moral codes of their home.

A national movement against England, the defiler of Oriental morality, began to grow up, about the turn of the century, and has developed in imposing force since. Its leaders, first Bal Gangadhar Tilak (d. 1920), and now, Gandhi, demand the expulsion of the English, in the name of morality, purity, and national self-determination. Opposition to England unites those whom England has Europeanized too much and those whom it has Europeanized too little. Indian fanaticism omits to inquire who is to maintain order after the English have been driven out, in a country atomized by differences of religion, nationality and social custom, where, ever since the tenth century, order has only been maintained by foreign conquerors. It is blind to the immense rise in civilization India owes to the Englishman. It sees only the undeniable evil of the obverse of the medal – Indian soldiers fighting England's battles, Indian finances largely mobilized for the maintenance of English power: huge sums drawn to England as official pensions, miserably small ones devoted to the education of the Indian.

The movement has become extraordinarily dangerous. The storms on the political horizon to-day are more threatening than those of sixty years ago. The great uprising of 1857 was at bottom a mere military revolt: the country as a whole looked on, passively. To this day, of course, the millions of Indian peasants are really only objects of rule, with a political outlook bounded by the interest in the tax-gatherer. But they follow their leaders like sheep. Almost every village now has its half-educated agitator, with just enough European culture to make him discontented; and, again in every village, his counterpart, the fanatical Asiatic, is busy preaching revolution. Against European culture and its English exponent in Oxford and London, Indian students read exciting European literature, and learn the technique of revolution from Russians and Irishmen. They bring home with them the art of the boycott, the forceful levy of money, and the bomb. In India, as elsewhere, the demobilized soldiers of the World War are a focus of political discontent; they have seen England in defeat, and have been cured of their respect for the white race by an acquaintance with the white brothel. Moreover, in trying to educate Indians for self-government England has taught them how to carry on political agitation. Since 1877, the Legislative Councils – parliamentary bodies, which slightly limit the omnipotence of the Governors of the Provinces and the Viceroy – have included elected representatives of urban communes and Chambers of Commerce, most of them Indian natives. A vernacular press disseminates political reports and leading articles, all over the country, for the most part of a highly seditious character. In 1884, dissatisfied Europeanized Indian groups associated together to form the Indian National Congress, and this organization has ever since carried on a more or less openly anti-English propaganda throughout India. Until recently, the immemorial antagonism between the Hindu majority and the Moslem minority was one of the pillars of the English rule, but England's anti-Turkish policy has, since 1900, driven the Mohammedan more and more into a greater opposition to England than could be counterbalanced by his aversion to the Hindu; and in 1916, the two great nationalist organizations, the Indian National Congress and the Moslem League, accepted a programme of common action, and united on a demand for Dominion status for India within the British Commonwealth. This implies complete independence of the India Office, the filling of at least half the higher posts of the country with Indians and the establishment of a national Indian army, with Indian officers. This alliance of the old antagonists was a landmark in Indian history. England gave way at once. In 1919 a new Constitution was promulgated by Edwin Montagu, then Indian Secretary, establishing parliamentary government, to be reached by cautious stages. A form of dual administration is introduced in the provinces (with a few concessions also in the central administration at Delhi). The old bureaucratic autocracy remains responsible in all the more important departments. But part of the administration of the provinces is handed over to a parliamentary government, composed, on the English model, of ministers drawn from a parliamentary assembly, who have to resign office, when they should lose their seat in parliament. Along these lines, Indians are to learn to apply intelligent criticism and even gradually to accept responsibility.

So far, the result of these concessions has been small. Europeanized Indian Radicals spurned a constitution which gave them for the moment only the forms of parliamentarism, while leaving the decisive voice on all major issues to Governors and Viceroy. Under Gandhi a popular movement of immense volume mobilized all the Indian conservative, anti-European and anti-English elements against the new constitution. Through his slogan, non-cooperation, Gandhi succeeded in inducing the vast hordes of his adherents to abstain from any part in the elections of 1920. Others less radical did cooperate, only, when themselves elected to Parliament, to pursue determined obstruction there. For this reason, the constitution can hardly be said to have functioned freely so far; the veto or fiat of the British administration, which ought only to be employed in exceptional cases, has had to be used constantly, in a way by no means intended or desired. At the same time, the danger of this popular movement's developing into a new Indian rising appears to have passed. The alliance between Western reformers and the opposition under Gandhi was too unnatural to last: the fighting bond between Hindus and Mohammedans has likewise broken down and skulls are freely broken again on both sides. Very quietly, Britain is making one breach after another in the ranks of the allies. The more vociferous Radicals are promoted to ministerial posts and become interested in maintaining the existing order. The Nationalist opposition finds adversaries springing up, too, within its own ranks. It is in the hands, in the main, of the old Brahmin castes: suddenly, an anti-Brahmin movement rises in the South, to fight privileged Indian aristocracy in the name of Western democracy. Indian industrialists and capitalists, who have been exploiting their workpeople with all the soullessness of the Europeanized Oriental, are surprised to find themselves faced with stirrings of revolt among the down-trodden proletariat. The British Government, after turning a blind eye to all this, decade after decade, displays a sudden interest in every form of social evil, allows it to be seen that it is in its power to demand, in the name of humanity, very inconvenient and costly reforms, and that Lancashire has long been unable to comprehend why Indian industry alone should possess an unrestricted right to extract the last ounce of effort out of its workers. This social problem is proving a decisive danger point on the Nationalist front. In Bengal, the Indian landlords who, under the workings of an antiquated tax system, have enjoyed what seem to Europeans to be quite extraordinary privileges, at the expense of their tenants, are so far apt to be instinctively on the side of government, since it alone can guarantee them order and security; but occasionally the British Government throws out a warning that should the landlords become unreliable, there is nothing to prevent its altering the land taxation system in the interest of the hard-pressed tenants. Quickly and carefully the Government tries to make the native princes of India – who in their old Oriental dignity see with disgust native lawyers and journalists gaining political power in the country – an active support of English power. Gradually the Government try to give them political influence. The policy of Lord Dalhousie, which tried gradually to discard these remnants of non-English power in the country, has been totally abandoned. Moreover, concurrently with the Europeanized system of education, created, in broad outline, by Macaulay, assistance has recently been given to schools based, essentially, on the Oriental standpoint, and designed to bring up a Conservative upper class, familiar with European thought, but imbued *au fond* with ancient indigenous culture. The Mohammedan College at Aligarh (1883) and the Central Hindu College at Benares (1898) are instances of this changed course.

That the danger in India is real, is sufficiently indicated by the apparent readiness of the home government to subordinate home to Indian interests in matters of real importance, and by the tendency of high Indian officials to regard themselves not so much as representatives of English purposes in India as advocates of Indian interests in London. Here is an evident sign that England feels itself up against a resistance that it cannot overcome. The English Government of India has long, though vainly, endeavoured to achieve complete freedom of access for Indians, throughout the British Empire, as against the troublesome restrictions imposed for example by South Africa, on Indian immigration. During the war India put on protective duties for its cotton industry and maintained them, in the face of a storm of protest from Lancashire.[1] With extreme definiteness, the increased demands of the War Office for military and financial assistance from India were rejected by the English administration in India. That England will have to make large concessions in India is not open to doubt. Gone, irretrievably, is the day when India's waging England's wars at its own expense was taken as a matter of course. No longer does India provide the obvious career for the able son of the English middle class: among the most momentous of post-war decisions is that of 1924, which undertakes that, within the next fifteen years, 50 per cent of places in the higher ranks of the civil service and, within twenty-five years, in the police, are to be filled by Indians – a very serious blow to England's political monopoly in the country. Further, inasmuch as India is free to carry on a protective policy against England, its economic monopoly there is severely shaken, since India, in addition to weaving its own cotton, is beginning to produce its own coal and steel. In these circumstances, India can no longer be counted on to be, in the future as in the past, the greatest customer for English exports: almost as important as Germany and France together.

But, withdrawal, even on a large scale, does not necessarily spell catastrophe. If the Europeanization of India proceeds – and, despite Gandhi's efforts, all the evidence is that it will – the decline in imports of raw materials such as coal and low-grade textiles may well be compensated by an increase in those of high-grade articles, since generations will have to pass before India can supply these needs from its home production. So, while the number of English administrative officials goes down, that of engineers, forestry and technical experts will rise. It may be that, here and there, non-English Europeans and non-English commodities will appear, but a country whose culture is based on the English school and on the English press must always tend to turn to England; after all, English is the sole European language which is understood in India. So deep, too, are the internal divisions, of religion, of race, of caste, or interest, that let one group take up an anti-English line and its opponent is, *ipso facto*, driven into the arms of England. Thus, while a decline in British power in India is taking place, there is as yet no sign of its being driven out. Not for nothing has English policy applied to India for three hundred years the science of *divide et impera*.

§ 6

As far back as the eighteenth century, England regarded India's economic treasures as its most precious possession; and, ever since, political efforts have been directed to securing a firmer grasp on this jewel in its crown. The 'road to India' must be defended. To this end, Aden (1839) and Socotra (1835) were occupied, the Cape of Good Hope taken from the Dutch (1815), and Zanzibar on the east (1890) and St. Helena on the west (1815) coast of Africa acquired, with the result that all the more important harbours on the old route to India are now in British hands. The motive in the acquisition of two great colonies, South Africa and Egypt, was, again, the safety of India. Finally, when there seemed a danger that the two States between India and Egypt might fall under alien political influences, both Turkey was overrun and Persia at least isolated during the World War: the land bridge from Egypt to India in British hands is now nearing completion. There is also a combined land and sea route to India through the Mediterranean and Turkey. In Cromwell's day, with mixed idealistic, Christian and economic motives, ships were sent to defend English trade against the North African pirates; for similar reasons, Charles II acquired Tangier (1661), although he gave it up again, when it proved more expensive than it seemed worth at that time. In the eighteenth-century wars with France, the Mediterranean recovered some of the importance it had possessed in Roman times. To-day, it has become nearly an English sea. Gibraltar, at the entrance, has been an English fortress since 1704. In 1708, Minorca was added as an operations base to face Toulon, but abandoned later on. Malta, in the centre, fell into English hands in 1800, and serves to hold Italy, France, Greece, and Egypt simultaneously in check. Cyprus, to the east, was acquired in 1879, and for a time (1815–63), the Ionian Islands also. Above all, England established a firm hold on Turkey – and Turkey was suzerain over Mesopotamia and Persia, the old trading route to India. For a whole century England defended Turkey against Russia's forcible attempts to break it up; it was in

Turkey's defence that it entered on the Crimean War, in 1854–56. There was disquiet in England over such a close relationship to Islam, but, as in Cromwell's day, power proved a stronger motive than religion. But at the same time, English policy was always directed to securing a proper share of the Turk's inheritance, if the Ottoman Empire should prove impossible at last. The Battle of Navarino, which gave Greece its independence, was officially characterized as an 'untoward event,' but no objection was made to Lord Byron's dying melodramatically for Greece; on the contrary, the newly-formed State was promptly taken under sympathetic protection. In Egypt, whose separation from Turkey was plainly only a matter of time, from 1800 on, France was defeated, after long and obstinate struggles. When Disraeli, in 1875, bought the Suez Canal shares from the Khedive – the first instance in history of a political coup accomplished in a single financial transaction – one of the main arteries of modern Egypt, the road to the East, was in English hands. When, in 1882, a native rising caused England to occupy the country, and above all, after Kitchener had driven the Mahdi out of the Nile basin, out of Khartoum and Fashoda (1898), the second and even more important artery, the Nile, had become English too. The withdrawal of France from Egypt (1904), and the proclamation of the English Protectorate (1914) were then only questions of time.

§ 7

In 1882 England laid its hands on Egypt, and, despite all its promises, has never evacuated it. In 1914 a Protectorate was formally proclaimed. By 1904 France, which had so long disputed possession of the country, withdrew: the World War swept away all that was left of consideration for the ancient suzerainty of Turkey over the regions of the Nile. By 1918, British control was complete. Here, as in India and in Ireland, retreat followed hard on success. In December, 1921, Britain capitulated to Ireland; in March, 1922, an independent kingdom was offered to the rebellious Egyptians. How is this inconsistency to be explained?

England's promises of evacuating Egypt have always been regarded by foreigners as the supreme instance of English hypocrisy. And yet they were quite sincere – subject only to a highly characteristic subconscious mental reservation. And the final evacuation of Egypt after victory in the World War is in perfect harmony with the ultimate implications of that policy.

When England occupied Egypt in 1882, Gladstone was at the helm. He knew little of foreign policy and had grown up in the traditions of Little Englandism. His ideal in foreign policy was the utmost freedom of trade and the absence of responsibilities that might lead to war. He was the man to make a very disadvantageous peace with the Boers when an exiguous body of English troops were defeated at Majuba in 1881. His views of Egyptian policy comprised the restoration of order in the anarchic, bankrupt country, the establishment of the closest possible trade relations, the deflection of the strong current of sympathy with France, and, finally, the withdrawal of military garrisons. The soldier, for Gladstone, was an unsympathetic figure, the sooner dispensed with the better. This type of mind would take it for granted that Egypt, once independent both of Turkish and of French influence, would automatically and peacefully run in English leading strings. Egypt was to be evacuated, not, as simple folk imagined, to make it independent, but to make it easier and cheaper to rule.

But the time, when this was to be possible, refused to come. French influence in the country was so strong that an early withdrawal would have meant French predominance, a possibility that even a Little Englander like Gladstone could not contemplate. There were grave difficulties in the path of economic reconstruction in a country without any available native officials. Further there were the usual results of occupying a land which had no frontier. At the gates of Egypt, a new colony, the Sudan, had to be conquered to make Egypt safe. And the new conquest was hard to hold, unless the single means of access, the Nile, was also completely controlled. The Sudan was conquered to make Egypt safe, and Egypt had to remain occupied in order to hold the Sudan. So the date at which the country was to be evacuated seemed remitted indefinitely, and when Turkish suzerainty was abrogated in 1914, people in England had practically given up the idea that the *status quo* was ever to be changed, and the proclamation of the Protectorate was hailed by all as the only practicable way out of an impossible situation.

England ruled Egypt with extraordinary skill – on Indian lines. The country was in all appearance governed by an Egyptian monarch and an Egyptian ministry. All laws were issued in their names. But there were English 'advisers' in every ministry. How could it be otherwise, when the task before them was to exploit every resource of a naturally not very rich country so as to save it from falling into the abyss of bankruptcy, on whose very edge it stood? Orientals never could have coped with such a task. They had, however, to meet the extremely unpopular one of enacting and collecting the necessary taxes. The same game was repeated in local administration The provincial chief, the Egyptian *mudir*, was responsible; but he was guided by some English overlord or expert who, as a rule, had learned in India how to make the vast elephant move at the touch of the pin. Behind the whole political façade, which included the forms of parliamentarism, in the shape of a General Assembly with elected representatives but no power, was a modest English consul-general. Hardly visible from without, he was in fact – Lord Cromer filled this post from 1883 to 1907 – the ruler of Egypt, since in his more or less unseen hands were the strings which compelled Khedive, Ministers, *mudirs* to dance to England's tune. Economically, the country was entirely dependent on England. It could not even feed itself, since every square foot was sown with cotton seed; since Lancashire wished to have it so and cotton brought better returns to the bondholders than wheat. And England's invisible grip grew closer and closer. The Suez Canal was regulated, nominally by an international company, really by England. In the Sudan, the British and Egyptian flags waved side by side. Egypt taking the major share of the cost, and no share at all of the power, the constitutional position of the Sudan remained undefined. The Sudan, a predominantly negro country, was, for the moment, autocratically governed, under military rule. Any intrusion by Egyptian officials was therefore excluded. The actual ruler of the country was the Governor, an Englishman, appointed by England and the Khedive to rule the Sudan in England's interest. The same general was at the same time, Sirdar, commander-in-chief of the Egyptian army, appointed by the Khedive, and commander of the English contingent, appointed by England. He was in reality, together with the consul-general, the effective director of the destiny of the entire region of the Nile. For greater security, a railway was laid in 1905 between Khartoum and Port Sudan at the Red Sea, which made the Sudan accessible from the east. The result was to make the Sudan more independent of Egypt and the political pressure of the Upper Nile region stronger on the lower. Above all, the Sudan and Egypt share a common life-nerve – the Nile. Mighty dams and irrigation plants distribute the Nile water over great areas both in the Sudan and in Egypt. Any failure of Sudan irrigation control might mean catastrophe for Egypt. So, the ruler over the Upper Nile has a power over the Lower that may be of crucial importance, politically.

In Egypt, as in India, England is faced with the problem of the Europeanized Oriental. In Egypt this problem is older than in India, since Egypt, from time immemorial, has been one of the meeting-points of East and West. For that reason there has been no need to create an Anglicized Oriental class, as in India. The country's revenues barely cover the costs of Nile control, irrigation, cotton growing, and State debt. There was practically no money available for education. It was not till 1907 that an Egyptian university with carefully moderated European curricula was added to the old Mohammedan high school of El Azhar which till then had the monopoly of education. But the hesitant education policy pursued in Egypt has had the same results as the more energetic one followed in India. The Europeanized Egyptian of the higher class thinks that he is able to rule the country, and desires to drive the hated usurpers out of it. This strain of feeling was aggravated by the World War, during which the Australian garrison gave full vent to its idea of superiority, with all the arrogance of the half-educated white man. Further, anti-Turkish policy roused Mohammedan passions to fever-heat. Soon after the close of the war, Saad Zaghlul (1921) revived the Nationalist movement which began with the short-lived rising of Achmet Arabi in 1881, and had never subsequently died out completely. The movement developed with such tremendous force that England had to decide to treat with it. The result was the recognition of Egyptian independence in March, 1922.

Not that England has any intention of giving Egypt up. It is rather reverting to the Gladstone policy. Up to 1914, it ruled Egypt indirectly: in the future, its rule will be even less direct. It still holds the country in its grip, by enclosing it between the Sudan in the south and the Suez Canal in the east. In all its negotiations with the Egyptian Nationalists it has never budged from the point that there can be no question of loosening the grip on either side. The British army will, under certain conditions, evacuate Egypt proper, but remain in Khartoum and the Suez Canal. The World War actually added a third and fourth trench round Egypt, Palestine and Arabia. In both countries, 'Free' states have been set up, the Zionist realm and the Hedjaz 'kingdom,' but both are indirect objects of British world power. The old competitors for control over Egypt have gone. France renounced its claim in 1904, Turkey has been pushed back into Asia Minor by the war, and no longer has the German Empire behind it. A Monroe doctrine for Egypt is to keep all foreign powers out. Such foreign officials as Egypt will need – and it is quite impossible for it to get on without them, in the long run – will be English. The Egyptian Finance Minister will realize that money is easier to raise on the London market if the country submits willingly to English direction. And the Egyptian will be proud of his independence – just like the Indian.

§ 8

The South African Union is another offshoot of British colonization of India. In 1652, the Dutch established a supply station for ships sailing from Europe to India at the Cape of Good Hope. The English had similar arrangements at St. Helena. In 1795, during the French Revolution wars, the English fortified the Cape, to defend it for its legal owners, the Dutch, against Napoleon. In 1803 they handed it back: in 1806 they occupied it again, and in 1814 finally acquired possession of it, together with St. Helena. It was a small colony then, confined to the southern coast, inhabited by some 26,000 Dutchmen and twice that number of natives, in continual danger of destruction by attack from the mighty Zulu kingdom to the north. The Colony produced cattle, corn and wine for its own use. It seemed to have no particular value beyond the purpose for which it served, that of a victualling station for ships sailing to Asia. The British Government therefore rejected the idea of any extension of the Colony that might bring it into conflict with the war-like Zulus. It refused to recognize Natal, on the east coast, as a colony, even after English naval officers had occupied land there in 1824. When the Cape colonists pushed over the old frontier of the Dutch settlement, across the Fish River, into Zululand, the London Government protested and recalled Governor D'Urban (1835). Equally firmly did the homeland refuse the appeals of the Cape Government for an extension of the British sphere of influence to the south-west coast of Angra Pequena (1867, 1877). It contented itself with raising the flag in Walfish Bay (1878). No foreign power threatened to establish itself in South Africa at the time; to occupy more land would therefore have been useless expenditure. From 1836 on, however, the restless Dutch element, constantly fighting with the Zulus, left the Colony and established new settlements outside the English area (Natal, the Orange State, the Transvaal). Even so, the British

Government was content to promulgate a decree to the effect that British subjects, leaving British territory, still remained subjects of the Crown. It thus proclaimed a sort of suzerainty over all the States founded from South Africa, but formal annexation took place only in the case of Natal (1843). At the same time, the negative policy of the Government was constantly crossed by the active proceedings of governors and private individuals, now here now there, who busied themselves with acquiring influence inside the Boer States, and thereby perpetually caused fresh conflicts. Things were in this state of flux when the discovery of diamonds in South Africa took place in 1870, and, ten years later, the Transvaal proved to be one of the richest goldfields in the world. This at once led to a more forward policy. In 1871 an important section of the diamond fields, the Kimberley area, was taken from the Orange Free State, on very dubious legal grounds. Gladstone, on the other hand, showed incomprehensible weakness in the case of the Transvaal Boers, after they took up arms against the English, and inflicted a trifling defeat on them at Majuba (1881). Although he demanded their recognition of British supremacy, which made a foreign policy of their own impossible for them, he actually sacrificed the High Commissioner Sir Bartle Frere, the leader of a forward British policy in South Africa at the time.

The scene was changed with the appearance of two new factors: Bismarck and Cecil Rhodes. In 1884, Germany annexed South-West Africa, and Bismarck entered into relations with the Boers. This led to a complete *volte-face* in British policy. Unexpectedly, the economic value of the colony had gone up: the appearance of a competitor on the horizon made it necessary to have the constitutional question cleared. And Cecil Rhodes (1853–1902) began to direct British policy along wholly new lines. He was one of the most singular figures in the world of modern England: hard and tenacious, energetic and unscrupulous, a true Conquistador, full of contempt for the human race, since he had found out that every man had his price, self-contained, and lonely, but with the imagination that always marks the genuinely great man, a dreamer of worlds lit by 'the gleam that never was on sea or land.' His dreams took nothing from his extraordinary concentration: on the contrary, they gave to his thought a lift which was the secret of his power over men. Although money-making was his element, his ambition was power for himself and greatness for England; in personal matters his tastes were Spartan. As a young man of four and twenty he made over his entire fortune to a secret society of his imagination, which was to spread British dominion over the entire globe.[2] The whole of Africa was to be English, Palestine, Mesopotamia, the whole of Southern America; the United States were to be rejoined to the British Empire, and an Anglo-Saxon power thus come into being which should rule the world and make war impossible. Not mere conquest, but world dominion for an ethical end. This man, who lorded it over the world of company promoters and mining speculators of Johannesburg, nevertheless believed in ethical values. When, in the prime of life, he died, he left the greater part of his fortune to be devoted to training typical English gentlemen; the Rhodes Trust sends the best of the young Colonials to study at Oxford, thence to plant the stock afresh in the Colonies. Rhodes reconquered South Africa for England. Under his influence, the method of encirclement, as exemplified in Canada and Egypt (cf. pp. 54, 69), was applied to South Africa. The Boers had steadily pressed back from the coast to the interior, now their further extension there was blocked by the establishment of a new British colony, Rhodesia to the north of the Transvaal. This was the territory of the new Chartered Company of South Africa, a trading company clothed with rights of supremacy and constructed on the East India Company model. Set up in 1889, the Chartered Company blocked any union between the Transvaal and German East Africa. From the west, too, the Boers were cut off by the conclusion of a treaty with Germany in 1890, and the occupation of the new Boer republics that had sprung up in Bechuanaland. But while Rhodes' policy was directed against the Boers, his intention was to keep them within the Empire, not to subdue them. Both in Rhodesia and in Bechuanaland he insisted on having Boers among his settlers. In a territory belonging to a trading company it was possible to avoid having any large self-contained foreign settlements such as might have jeopardized the British character of the whole. Once the ring was complete, pressure was brought to bear on the Transvaal, the land of gold, and, later, of diamonds too. An industry had developed in Johannesburg that was bringing almost fabulous riches to the hitherto well-nigh bankrupt State, run by old-fashioned farmers. That wealth was not the work of the Boers themselves. It was the product of an inrush of gold-diggers and stock exchange speculators, who made up a new society there, international with many sinister forces and mainly English speaking. These people financed the entire State, but, as aliens, were excluded from all participation in political life. They demanded the vote. The Boers had to refuse it; they would otherwise have very soon been left in a decided minority. In this struggle between a patriarchal, rural, family economy which was slowly breaking up, and the inrush of the worst type of modern capitalism, reconciliation was impossible. The capitalist party attempted to seize government, by a coup under Starr Jameson in 1895. The mind behind this conspiracy, Cecil Rhodes, kept well in the background. But he was the soul of the diplomatic offensive against the Boers conducted in the course of the next few years by the leader of England's new Colonial policy, Joseph Chamberlain, Colonial Secretary at the time. England's demand that those who created the wealth of the Transvaal should have a voice in the spending of it was at once so popular in England and so impossible to the Boers, who could not be expected to sign their own death warrant, that a decision had to be reached by force of arms. In three years of heroic struggle, between 1899–1902, the Boers tried to hold back the chariot of history. They were defeated less as the result of military operations, which could hardly bring a decision in a country so vast and so thinly populated, than by the systematic devastation of their country and the horrors of the concentration camps behind the lines. Their farms were burned and the bases for guerrilla warfare destroyed; their women and children were driven into concentration camps. There they were well looked after – as far as was possible in a country practically without any industry and with few railways – where the most elementary articles of hygiene had all to be fetched from the coast and from England. The awful mortality of women and children that was unavoidable had much to do with breaking down the resistance of the men in the field.

The land had been subdued by Irish methods, but the Irish method, the policy of conciliation, was then introduced on a grand scale. Immediately on the conclusion of peace, the ravaged land was rebuilt with English money. The leaders of the new policy, Joseph Chamberlain and Alfred Milner, applied the methods that had succeeded in Canada in effecting reconciliation. The Transvaal, the Orange Free State, Natal and the Cape were made autonomous provinces, with complete self-government. In the Free State, almost wholly Dutch, the Boers were left entirely free and there, as in the Transvaal they can, so long as they are in a majority, regulate the franchise as they choose, i.e., exclude the blacks from it; and institute Dutch schools. The Transvaal and the Orange Free State are however, united with Cape Colony and Natal to form the Union of South Africa. It is in the Union Parliament at Capetown that the questions that concern England are decided, and in it England hopes always to have a majority. True, the Dutch population is actually in a majority in the country, and the rate of increase has, down to very late years, been so rapid among the Boers that British immigration must be maintained at a very high figure if it is to keep pace with it. Even if there should fail to be an English majority in the Union Parliament, however, the racial question can always be used as an excuse for unfurling the flag of humanitarianism. Only a very small proportion of natives have the franchise. Since however there were, in 1921, $1\frac{1}{2}$ million whites [3] to 4·6 million blacks, and the Boers repress the blacks and coloured people rigorously, a certain reserve of friends for England can be gathered, at the worst, from among their number. So far, it has not been necessary to have resort to this extreme measure. From the first, it proved possible to form a government under Boer leadership (first Botha, then Smuts) with a majority composed of Boers and Englishmen behind it.

The opposition was originally composed of the old-type Boers in the Backveld, who cannot forget the concentration camps, and hate England as the exponent of European capitalism. Nowadays it has been reinforced by the Dutch youth in the university, who hope to make South Africa one day an independent Dutch republic with Afrikaans as national tongue. These circles have a categorical No for all imperialistic wishes of England, and as their leader, General Hertzog, has been Premier since 1926 they are the strongest group in the country.

It does not actually constitute a danger to the unity of South Africa. But it is strong enough to compel all South African leaders to move very cautiously in any questions touching the Empire. The utmost to be expected of the Union, during the World War, was the 'conquest' of German South-West (and East), a territory hardly capable of defence, and the enlistment of a volunteer corps from South Africa. Even this was got through Parliament with the greatest difficulty, at the cost of constant deception of the public. Thus, it was reported in September, 1914, that the German army had been completely destroyed on the Marne, and that the only question was whether the booty should be collected by England or South Africa.

After the war, South Africa has slipped almost entirely out of England's hands. The 'German peril,' which used to serve as a bogey, had gone, and there was no other to take its place. England now is not much more than the protector of the Indians – in 1921 there were 142,000 Asiatics in Natal, almost all of them Indian, against 137,000 whites – and, by encouraging their claims to equal treatment with the whites, serves indirectly to encourage ever fresh demands on the part of the blacks. South Africa's contribution to Imperial defence is negligible: no colony is less accommodating in its attitude to British industry. Hertzog, the present Premier, may not seek to sever the British connexion – why should he? since it gives South Africa privileges without duties – but it is absolutely plain that in any world crisis that may arise, England can count on no help from South Africa.

§ 9

Contemporaneously with South Africa, a new British colony grew up in Australia. There too development coincided with a period of lassitude in Colonial matters on the part of the home Government; the Colony grew up as the result of the energy of the race, more or less against the will of the London Government. In Port Jackson, the present-day Sydney, a penal settlement had been established in 1788. Other convict settlements grew up in 1804 in the neighbourhood of Victoria, in 1826 at Brisbane in Queensland, and in 1825 in Western Australia. The Government's ideas about the Colony did not extend beyond that. Captain James Cook had hoisted the flag in New Zealand, but London refused to recognize his action. In 1835 the Government determined on giving up Brisbane. The flag was not raised over Western Australia (1825) or New Zealand (1840) until French ships were actually on the way for a similar purpose. The English Government saw in Australia a country for the deportation of criminals, since America which to some extent had served as a dumping-ground for undesirables (Puritans and criminals alike) was no longer English. But it had no desire to make a European colony out of a wild desert where every ounce of flour, every nail, and every button was an article of importation. And a country like England without a trained bureaucracy seemed hardly able to develop a country where the population consisted of criminals whose only desire was to shirk every work which the iron rod of the gang-master could not force them to do.

The conditions of the Colony in the first generation were terrible indeed.

In Sydney a settlement grew up in which drunkenness among the highest officials was too common to be noticed, where a legitimate child was an exception, where most of the women were convicted prostitutes, where wages were measured in rum, and the officers sold Government supplies to the prisoners at extortionate prices. A mutiny of police in 1809, who held Governor Bligh prisoner for a year until he promised to go back to England, showed plainly that things had become unbearable. Some sort of order was at last brought out of chaos by Governor Macquarie (1809–21). Among the convicts, there were a certain number of Irish and other political prisoners, out of whom something could be made. Bit by bit it became possible to draw free settlers into the Colony: deportations ceased at last; but even to-day it is by no means an honour in Australia to count back more than three generations in the country.

Serious problems were at once presented by the association of released convicts and free settlers. Transportation implied that the former, on the expiration of their sentences, should enjoy full equality and be admitted without distinction to offices, positions of trust, and social intercourse. This, however, was energetically opposed by the free settlers. There was therefore nothing for it but to abandon transportation which had also strong opponents on humanitarian grounds, and send out free emigrants. A fresh problem then arose. How were the officers, officials, and soldiers of the garrison to work the lands granted to them, if cheap convict labour was no longer available? All sorts of Colonizing Societies stepped into the breach: in 1830 Edward Gibbon Wakefield founded a society for establishing *free settlers*, first in South Australia (1836), and then in New Zealand (1840). Wakefield's idea was to keep up the price of plots, so that the immigrants had to work as day labourers to earn the price of a holding. By this means, he hoped at once to solve the labour problem and prevent either wastage of or speculation in land. In this, his success was only very partial; what was achieved, however, was that settlement based on free labour became possible at last.

As soon as the settlers crossed the mountains near the coast and reached the wide plains of the interior, admirably suited for cattle raising, the native grit of the race began to develop the Colony with such success that even the home Government was converted. To-day, despite the periodic droughts, a sixth of the world's wool production comes from the inland plateaux of Australia. Further, from 1851 on, Australia became one of the world's great goldfields: accounting for a quarter of the world's production. Nevertheless, development has been exceedingly slow, and the country become the scene of some of the sternest fights between capital and labour.

The history of settlement in Australia is quite different from that in America. In the seventeenth century there streamed across to America a population, in the main, of uniform character, which settled on a soil of more or less uniform quality, from an economic point of view. In Australia, the soil varied in quality, widely. In one place large-scale production was possible, in another small. Periodic droughts involved an element of uncertainty such as only the capitalist could face. Great stretches of territory, large as English counties, soon fell into the hands of single individuals. There were orgies of land speculation. But the other side of the account was presented by the workman, for here there were no negro slaves, as in the Southern States of the American Union. The capitalist needed the free workman, and his worth consequently rose enormously. Moreover, he knew his price: often, he came from industrial areas in England where Trade Union organization was familiar. The whole of the second half-century of Australian history is dominated by a stubborn struggle between capital and labour, of a bitterness and extent unparalleled in the world. The capitalist, there, is rather a real estate-owner, great sheep-raiser and land speculator than a manufacturer. The workman strives to break his land monopoly by laws of settlement, by turning the screw of taxation, and by raising wages and industrial conditions, at the expense of the capitalist. His progress has been uninterrupted, since the great Australian Trade Union Congress of 1884 in Melbourne. Almost everywhere he has won equal and universal suffrage. Moreover, ever since the Sydney Trade Union Congress of 1902, State socialistic ideas are everywhere – workman's insurance, compulsory arbitration in labour disputes, designed to make strikes impossible (but actually only making them less frequent but more cruel and bitter), fixation of prices by the State in all directions, all sorts of State banking, building, and insurance institutions, as well as State land settlement schemes. A workman's paradise has arisen, without analogue elsewhere, whose darker side is a universal drab uniformity that presents real obstacles to progress. There is a dead level of average comfort – no proletariat, no great wealth: a democratic population, hostile to any deviation from the mean, whose interests are bounded by the universal Anglo-Saxon passion for sport, without a literature or any other form of higher intellectual life; a dull stagnation in the comfortable average. True, there is opposition from employers. From time to time, they try to break the white workman's monopoly by introducing Chinese, Japanese, and Kanaka boys. As a rule, however, all such efforts are nipped in the bud by the resolute opposition of the Labour parties. 'White Australia' is the Magna Charta of all Australian liberties. The increase of the population is small: the Australian looks askance even on white immigration since it might produce an undesirable increase in the supply of labour. In the upshot, a continent nearly as large as Europe had only 5,435,734 inhabitants in 1921; New Zealand, 1,320,275.

Vast distances divide the different settlements, and politically they were therefore, at first, completely isolated. In 1900, however, a Commonwealth of Australia was established, with a constitution in the main on the American model. New Zealand continues to be independent. Relations to England are of the loose nature already observed in Canada and South Africa, expressed through the Governor-General, Privy Council, Imperial Conference. There is a sense almost of complete independence of the Mother Country. Australia, like most of the other Colonies, has proved not very tractable at Colonial Conferences. Only New Zealand, too small to provide a fleet or carry on a foreign policy of its own, has always been in favour of contributions to the Imperial navy; but in the case of Australia the rudest threats of German peril were required to bring it to the point of making any contribution, and when it did reach that point, it did not provide money for the British navy but constructed a fleet of its own, and even New Zealand followed suit in building a separate cruiser. Like Canada, it aspires to found a Colonial Empire of its own, which might ultimately unite all the islands of the Australian Archipelago to the continent. During the war, it sent a notable volunteer contingent, which fought gallantly at Gallipoli; and displayed unparalleled ruthlessness towards German property, notably in the case of the Zinc monopoly belonging to the German Merton Company. But as the war dragged on, Irish Nationalist and extreme Socialist ideas came to the front, and when Premier W. M. Hughes attempted to introduce conscription, it was twice rejected, after a referendum.

England's alliance with Japan was extremely unpopular in Australia. Every Australian knows that the overcrowded island Empire has long cast envious eyes on this sparsely populated continent, which could hardly be defended against Japanese cannon. Population is concentrated on the coast, in a couple of big cities. Of the 4·24 million inhabitants of New South Wales, Victoria and South Australia (in 1921), nearly half (2·10) are in the three great cities of Sydney, Melbourne and Adelaide. There is no system of inland transport available for military purposes. Against an enemy coup, there is no protection save the British fleet and, possibly, the Indian army; but, to Australia, protection offered in the form of an alliance with the enemy came in but a questionable shape. In a fashion very disagreeable to London, Australia began to look over to the United States in its search for protection. The decision, in 1921, not to renew the Anglo-Japanese Alliance is largely attributable to a recognition of the difficulties created by that Alliance in England's relations to Australia. Similarly, the new Imperial docks at Singapore are to a very large extent meant for the protection of Australia against Japan.

§ 10

Both South Africa and Australia developed into colonies of the first rank against the wishes of the Colonial Office. Only in the case of India was there an early recognition of its significance, and a prompt direction of foreign policy to that end. The other colonies, acquired in war, were held if they did not cost too much, and viewed mainly as bargaining counters when it came to peace negotiations. Louisburg, the French fort commanding the estuary of the St. Lawrence, fell into English hands in 1745, to be given up in 1748, and not reconquered till 1758. Tangier, English from 1662 to 1683, was given up, as too expensive. Minorca, conquered in 1708, was lost again in 1756. The West Indian Islands and West African Colonies perpetually changed hands between England and France in the eighteenth century. In 1762, Havana and Manila were English, only to be given up in the following year; Java and Sumatra were taken in 1810, and given back to Holland in 1815. Among the English of the period only Chatham and Pitt knew that the Colonies had an intrinsic value of their own. Public opinion in general regarded colonies with complete indifference. The American rebellion seemed to show that they were an unproductive experiment. At endless expense, a fruit was matured only to break off from the parent stem as soon as it was ripe. On apparently incontrovertible grounds, the Free Trade theory demonstrated that trade with independent nations was more profitable than the ownership of colonies. It was more or less taken for granted that Canada's separation from the Mother Country was only a matter of time.

This was the natural standpoint of a trading middle class which valued everything according to its money worth alone. The great moral reaction against Manchesterism, as it gathered force in the course of the nineteenth century, was bound to raise the appreciation of Colonial Empire. In almost all his social writings, from *Chartism* (1839) on, Carlyle refers continually to the Colonies. For him, British colonization was a moral act, the possession of colonies had ethical value: colonies are at once the proud inheritance of a great past and an opportunity designed to take up the stream of emigration and carry the ideas of Anglo-Saxon culture to all the corners of the earth. So, in his novel *Westward Ho!* (1855), Charles Kingsley preached to his own generation the greatness of the Elizabethan colonizing ad enturers. A similar spirit breathes through such an heroic representation of that epoch in history as is contained in the works of James Anthony Froude (1856-70).

In 1868 appeared Charles Dilke's *Greater Britain*, which may be said to have given a programme to the young men of its day. It describes the Colonies, their scenery, their economic and political problems, and sets out a great plan of future Anglo-Saxon dominion over the world. England is to acquire Asia and Africa, and parts of South America, and seize the land bridges between itself and India. If the Colonies should become independent, the Triple Alliance of Britain, the Colonies, and the United States, a union of the Anglo-Saxon race, will dominate the world and bring about its salvation. In this book, English Imperialism, militant and aggressive, but with a great programme of universal civilization, presents itself to the world of the non-elect. The same line of thought, deepened and more enlightened, appears in the two books, *The Expansion of England* (1883) and *The Growth of British Policy* (1895), in which a Cambridge historian, John Robert Seeley (d. 1895) set the rise of the British Empire before his contemporaries as the embodiment of British efficiency.

After the jubilee of Queen Victoria in 1887, which set the unity of the Empire for the first time before the world in a guise to strike its imagination, English Imperialism becomes a political force. A sense that the Colonies were threatened began to rise, with the perilous advance of Russia on India and the Persian Gulf, and the development of the Colonial instinct in Germany. As French policy caused the English flag to be raised over Australia, so the awakening of a Colonial interest in Germany helped English Imperialism to wake to life. In connexion with the Queen's Jubilee, the first Colonial Conference took place in London. In 1895 Joseph Chamberlain, the reorganizer of the Colonial Empire, and Colonial Secretary from 1895 to 1903, launched his campaign for the creation of a British Tariff Union. He sees Free Trade England threatened, at home, by foreign, and, above all, by German competition, and powerless against the danger because it can set up no tariff walls to protect itself against a world shut off against it behind them. He sees Canada being more and more drawn out of the British into the American sphere of influence, because the Mother Country has nothing to offer it, and fears that the other Colonies will go the same way. He seeks to prevent this, by renewing the system of Imperial preferences between Britain and the Colonies which Free Trade had superseded. He will leave the Colonies free to set up tariffs of their own, but complete the structure by a British tariff system. British preferences to the Colonies are to give Canada and Australia, in Britain, a safe market for their corn and meat, and Australia and South Africa for their wool. Colonial preferences for Britain are to secure the Colonial market for British industry, against their German and American competitors. Economic bonds are to unite the Empire at a time when political ties are beginning to fray. Chamberlain's programme was not realized. True, Canada gave Britain a preference in 1897, and Australia followed in 1908. But the effort to introduce protective taxes on food, the indispensable premise of a Colonial preferential tariff in England, failed. The workers feared a rise in their cost of living: cotton-spinners and financiers regarded Free Trade as the foundation of England's export strength and the world position of the London pound.

Imperialism, however, had a mighty effect on the English mind. Chamberlain exploited the Boer War to whip up Imperialist feelings throughout the British world. The Colonial volunteer troops, from all the quarters of the globe, contributed little to the military decision; but as proof of the unity of Anglo-Saxon feeling they were invaluable. Fortified by this demonstration and its effect, Chamberlain went on to create a great common armament. By 1904 it had been settled that England's future foreign policy must run with that of France, not of Germany. From that time on, Germany became more and more the bugbear for the terrified imaginations across the oceans. Its reply to Canada's preferences to Britain with a tariff war: the Kruger telegram of the German Emperor and the anti-English attitude of German public opinion at the time of the Boer War, were the starting-points of the anti-German agitation. Everything, from Germany's naval programme, down to the short-sighted rejection of peace ideas by the German spokesmen at The Hague Conference of 1907, was used to fan Colonial apprehensions of Germany's world ambitions to an intolerable point. During the war the propaganda of lies was developed to a positively diabolical system. For Canada, there was the story of the Canadian soldier crucified on the barn-door; for India, that of the German cannibals, who boiled corpses down to fat; and so on: and they worked. In the same way the military pinpricks that German Zeppelins made at the Empire through London were taken in Canada and Australia as prophetic of the doom Germany had got ready for Montreal and Melbourne. Fear of Germany was grist to the Empire's mill.

During the war, too, the Colonies were induced to send great bodies of recruits. But the idea of organizing the Empire on a unified military plan collapsed completely. All the Colonies sent their army corps as voluntary contingents. There was no persuading them to make regular financial contribution to the upkeep of the British navy. Canada and Australia, instead, have set up naval units of their own, very loosely connected with the British navy and available only for service under the English Admiral in the event of war. Whether or no the declaration of the London Government constitutes the event of war is nowhere stated.

The London Imperial Conference of 1921, which was to provide a new organization for the Empire, really came to nothing, despite the patriotic salvos which accompanied it throughout its course. At the Versailles Conference, Anglo-Saxon world dominion appeared in the shape of a loose confederation of Anglo-Saxon States. They acted together in negotiation, but each signed separately, and each entered the League of Nations as an independent member.

The Imperial Conference in London, in December, 1926, gave to the Empire a kind of new constitution in which all the new centrifugal tendencies of modern times culminate, though their wording is a triumph of official sugar-coating. From now on the Governor-General, appointed from London, is merely the King's represent-ative, and may take no part in Colonial politics. In Colonial affairs, the King will consult the Colonial Premier. Practically, this implies that both the King himself and the Governor-General have become decorative appanages: any power of veto by the King and the London Government is practically gone. The Dominions may restrict the appeal from their courts to the highest tribunal of the Empire, the Privy Council, though they will not do it now without consultation with England. This means that, except in so far as a colony itself desires to maintain it, the last remains of any power of effective intervention on the part of London has disappeared. Ominous, from this point of view, is the recognition of the right of all the Dominions to make treaties with other states – a right only limited by the provision that other parts of the Empire (i.e. Britain itself) must be asked whether any such treaty might affect them. Since there is no provision for the event of an opposition of interests, should such arise, this obligation is not of great value. True, a common Imperial foreign policy is envisaged, and the main responsibility for it, as for the military defence of the Empire, remains with Great Britain, but this amounts to no more than a polite circumlocution of the fact that the Colonies recognize no obligation to make sacrifices for or actively participate in any such common foreign policy. On the contrary, what they emphasize is that the Dominions have equal rights but no responsibilities beyond those they voluntarily undertake. The word 'independence' is avoided: through the King, the Colonies continue to be united to the Mother Country: if war is declared, the fact that the declaration proceeds from a common Sovereign deprives them of the possibility of remaining neutral, but does not impose upon them of necessity any independent contributions towards the carrying on of the war. That the relations of the Dominions with London will be in future, like those of other states, conducted through diplomatic representatives, is the visible and external signal of the fact that the Empire is in act of transformation into a Union of British States or British Commonwealth of Nations under the nominal headship of a common monarch. The inspired enthusiasm of the British press, which hailed this new constitution as a sign of undestructible unity, can deceive no one who recalls that for thirty or forty years the British Government's efforts have all been directed to the exactly opposite result. What they sought to secure was the establishment of a vigorous foreign policy based, as far as possible, on the existence of a common Imperial navy, to which the Colonies would make pecuniary contributions, and a standing Colonial reserve army for Imperial purposes (Colonial Conference, 1902), and a common foreign policy, whose organ, certainly, was never precisely defined. Even at the time of the Versailles Conference, even under the MacDonald Government (in 1924) this aim was pursued: extreme pressure had to be used by Canada to achieve its independent representation at the Peace Conference and the right to independent signature of the Halibut Treaty (p. 57). No one who knows the facts can deny that the new Constitution of the British Commonwealth represents a real weakening of the Empire. At the same time, however, it provides Britain with a new incentive to securing, by spiritual and economic ties, what it can no longer hold to it by political bonds.

Indubitably, the effort will be to draw the Colonies more closely to Britain. All the Dominions could maintain greatly increased populations, but only on condition of immense extension of irrigation, railway development and the establishment of canal and electric power stations to reclaim the waste parts of their territories. Politically they will incline to the sources of easy monetary supply. To-day this is London: to-morrow it may well be New York. The huge sacrifices made, very soon after the war, for the sake of restoring the pound to gold parity afford clear proof of London's desire to remain the source to which its Colonies go for loans.

Further, there are large numbers of people in England, notably in the Conservative Party, who clamour for the execution of the repeated resolutions passed at Colonial Conferences in favour of Preference duties for Colonial raw products – in other words the revival of Joseph Chamberlain's ideas (cf. p. 83). Since 1900, trade with the Colonies has greatly gained in value, and amounts to-day to more than that with Europe. It would doubtless help to consolidate Imperial ties to have Canadian wheat and Australian meat secured in the possession of a steadily expanding market in England; and Conservative policy seems to be tending in this direction. Is it to be expected, however, that the British workman will give up his objection to taxes on food? Will the Colonies, in return, open their ports to British industrial products with a completeness that would compensate England for the abandonment of all the benefits of Free Trade? So far there is no sign of this happening. The preferences granted by the Colonies to Britain are far too small to exercise any noticeable influence upon trade; they neither prevent the Colonies themselves from taking a larger and larger part in world trade and the British proportion of their imports from sinking in comparison with the American: nor do they restrain the Colonies from an energetic effort to build up industries of their own – which is almost invariably at the expense of Britain's export trade.

Active efforts are also going on to draw the spiritual bonds of Empire closer and lessen the distances that separate the Colonies from the Mother Country. England tries to develop commercial aviation as quickly as possible – not military, as does France – and tries to establish a great chain of wireless stations throughout the world; the chief motive of all this Imperialist. It might mean a great advantage, if it were possible to operate great aerial routes between Canada, Australia and Britain a generation sooner than they will be established with the United States. It would strengthen the Imperial tie if it were possible for a Colonial Premier, who comes to London to negotiate a loan, to have his electoral speeches wirelessed home thence. Wireless, the aeroplane and the airship, may all serve to enable history to correct geography. Chamberlain was thinking Imperially when he in 1900, by the Colonial Stocks Act, made the loans of the Colonies first-class securities in England and enabled letters and papers from England to reach the Colonies (at that time) more cheaply than did postal matter from the United States; and wireless and airship may draw the bonds tighter still. Every colony contains wide circles of people whose thinking and feeling is still Imperialist and for whom any threat to British interests seems a threat to their own existence; and this tendency England seems to strengthen. Every possible means is employed for consolidating all-British sentiment. The Church organizes Pan-Anglican conferences; the Universities, through the Rhodes scholarships, attract Colonial students; the Board of Education experiments in an interchange of teachers; the Boy Scouts carry on Imperial propaganda among the young; and Overseas Clubs are founded everywhere to promote friendship between Britishers and Colonials. Above all, there has, since the war, been a systematic effort to direct British emigrants to the Colonies. The Wembley Exhibition (1924) was intended as a mighty display of what the Colonies have to offer the world, and above all the Mother Country, economically. If it proves possible to direct a great flow of patriotically-minded British land workers – the only kind of workers still welcome there – to the Colonies, the Empire is far from being lost. The only question is whether Britain, deeply concerned at the moment with the effort to create a new peasantry at home, now possesses a sufficient supply of human material of this type to enable it to fill up Canada, Australia and South Africa with Englishmen?

There is further a certain hope that outstanding British statesmen may yet achieve unforeseen political results, through the very freedom and looseness of the new form of the British Commonwealth, such as it is impossible even to estimate at the present hour. The Dominions are to be independent in foreign policy, but all of them, thanks to their education and their speech, are bound to look upon what happens in the world with English eyes, while every Colony contains influential groups whose minds are consciously set to carrying on their policy along English lines. Is the picture really so different when we turn to the United States? Is it not possible to hope that, on the basis of complete independence in detail but the pursuance of common aims in most larger questions, America too may be brought into a kind of All-British Confederation in spite of all tendencies that are pointing in the opposite direction? And may not patriotic optimism even look farther still? Under the British flag, Dutchmen and Frenchmen enjoy complete autonomy. Hindus and Mohammedans will in all probability soon achieve the same: Jews and Arabs possibly likewise. Is it not possible that an Empire of this character, which while compelling none influences all, and gives to those within it the guarantee of complete peace, may exert a certain attractive force over other nations? Is the hope quite excluded that, one day, a British League of Nations may stand over against the League of Nations in Geneva?

This is not a question to which anyone is as yet in a position to give the answer. Its future depends on the British Empire, during the next few decades, having men of the highest calibre to conduct its destinies: men capable of transforming the defeat of to-day into the victory of to-morrow. What is, however, certain is that consideration for the Colonies, who must be kept unconditionally attached to the Empire, will force England to avoid all military adventure in the immediate future. A warlike policy in Eastern Asia might find Canada and Australia on Britain's side, but not a warlike policy in Europe; South Africa and Ireland would probably stand aloof in any case. A war with America would certainly mean the loss of Canada. For the moment, this fact that all its opponents are perfectly well aware that Britain can afford to run no great risks, certainly hampers British foreign policy against some of its rivals. Yet, in a war-weary world like that of to-day this disadvantage is not so serious. Against it may be set the fact that, in every country, the friends of peace look to England. This, of course, does not mean that British foreign policy will

88

everywhere go slow: it means, rather, that it will work more strongly than before along the lines of moral and economic pressure; the use of diplomacy, understandings, temporary or permanent; the effort to encircle its rivals from without or divide them from within, supported by press propaganda of every kind, in all the keys, from enthusiastic flattery to ruthless terrorism. For Britain, therefore, the platform of the League of Nations at Geneva, where the new forms of bloodless warfare are being developed, is more important than for any other nation.

England has signed the Kellogg Pact (1928) which is to make offensive war impossible, subject, however, to a declaration by its Foreign Secretary of reservation of liberty of action with regard to certain areas (Egypt, Suez Canal). Diplomatically, therefore, the Pact means little. Openly offensive wars are things of the past; all modern wars have arisen out of a situation in which a nation felt itself attacked – or threatened with attack. Even the invasion of a neutral State, resulting from a state of war between two powers on its borders, would be a defensive action, inasmuch as each belligerent would fear the invasion, by the other, of the said neutral State, with consequent access to its own territory. But the psychological effect of the Pact remains, and can hardly be exaggerated. There are now in every country large sections of pacifist opinion; no Government will find it easy to convince confirmed pacifists that they are being attacked and therefore must vote war-credits and endorse a declaration of war. Thus any nation which, like the British, is, for other reasons, bound to be averse to war, must see an advantage in the Pact, which, while not absolutely restraining its liberty of action, nevertheless does set obstacles in the way of a declaration of war by others. Considerations like these may seem of doubtful value to the pacifist mind. But they have their value. In the present state of the world, where there are pacifists everywhere, but few pacifists willing to make sacrifices, the main necessity, from the pacifist's point of view, must be that no new war should arise now, and the motives leading to this must be a matter of secondary importance.

CHAPTER IV

WORLD DOMINION – BRITAIN, GERMANY AND THE UNITED STATES

§ 1

THE English nation as a whole has never entertained cordial feelings with any other, least of all with Germany. Yet the ties of common race and common feeling are unmistakable and occasionally show themselves with surprising strength. Minds as profound and genuinely English as Coleridge, Carlyle, Kingsley, and George Eliot, showed a deeper comprehension of what is essential in Germany than any Latin civilization has ever received at English hands. Real understanding, however, whether of the Reformation in the sixteenth, or of German literature and philosophy in the nineteenth century, has always been confined to a very small though distinguished minority. The mass mind, ever since the sixteenth century, has been dominated by two rough and ready ideas about Germany. First, it is a country at a low and crude level of civilization. After the decline of the German cities, in the course of the sixteenth century, this view spread more and more. A pleasing sense of personal superiority was bred by the contemplation of German boorishness, the rudimentary standard of comfort, the drunken habits of the people, and the ridiculous pretentiousness of the twopenny-halfpenny little German courts. Germany, further, is the *terra incognita*, the land of strange, adventurous occurrences, and mysterious forests, mentioned even by Tacitus, which gave birth to such singular and unfathomable creatures as Dr. Faustus and Paracelsus. The German quack, phrenologist, adept and professor are objects of mirth, despite a certain undertone of unwilling respect in the laughter they arouse. A change came when the Romantic movement suddenly brought everything simple, genuine, popular and mystic into fashion. There now begins the long line of German appreciators, men like Coleridge, Carlyle, De Quincey, George Eliot, and Matthew Arnold, for whom German philosophy and theology, literature and art, were a veritable fount of youth, a healing well, for the hypertrophy from which England seemed to them to be suffering for its Mammon-worship. From this time on, philosophy, theology, natural science and medicine are profoundly influenced by Germany, and the first generation of English philology was practically a German science. Praise of German education, from the national school up to the University, is universal: practical imitation remains exiguous.

Certain distinguished groups respond to German influences, but the mass either has no reaction at all, or one of scorn or ill-concealed distaste. Germany is practically unknown. While the average Englishman can make some sort of show of reading a French newspaper, a German book presents well-nigh insuperable difficulties even to the English scholar.

The educated Englishman knows Paris and the resorts of Normandy and Brittany, but a visit to the Rhine was the habit – even then a habit confined to intellectual circles – only between the time of Byron and Thackeray and the youth of Meredith. Any personal contact of English Society with Germany was buried with Queen Victoria. Instinctively, the average Englishman regards the best thing Germany has to offer him – the habit of thinking problems out to their ultimate conclusion – as superfluous and harmful, just as he looks upon German philosophy and German liberal theology as godless errors. The discipline of the German military state, so enthusiastically praised by Carlyle, strikes the islander, accustomed to liberty, as abominable barbarism, and this though the whole course of Army reform from 1870 on is clearly stamped by German – as well as by French – influences. The development of German trade, industry and technical efficiency is, for him, something sinister and detestable. His ideas of everything German follow the old lines, and make little or no allowance for modern developments. As in the sixteenth century, so now, he sees the German as a rudimentary, uncivilized creature, with the further peculiarity of working, with sinister efficiency, for such long hours and low wages, whether as clerk or waiter, as force a higher rate of production and more modern methods on his English competitor. With equal disgust does the Englishman regard the occasional habit of German industry (like all other industries) of depressing prices by 'dumping' and so capturing foreign markets. Here, the inferior German of the Renaissance reappears in modern garb. In the same way, traits of the suspect German magician of the Faustus epoch, or the unfathomable German mystic of the Romantic era, present themselves anew in the German industrialist, whose uncanny powers of combination put the world's supply of zinc and munitions metals in his power, so that he now dominates entire regions and will soon bring fresh ones under his yoke. By a convenient distortion tendencies general to capitalism are interpreted as specific machinations of German craft. The same type of misconception appears in the picture of the German Headquarters staff encompassing the inmost secrets of an English officers' mess with their sinister network of spies, and drilling millions of men to move in perfect time to a single purpose. It reaches its zenith in the vision of a German Kaiser, in whose service officers and technicians of matchless skill fill earth, air and sea with awful masterpieces of engineering genius; at whose nod merchants and exporters direct the concentrated force of the German brain to the immediate object of a conquering Cæsarian; at whose beck and call every German professor and minister of the Gospel falls to the work of perverting the minds of the young in blind adoration of this Imperial mania; at whose command the whole gigantic engine of hideously mechanized humanity casts itself, in a blind fury of destruction and extermination, on a single little nation. Even to-day, after the collapse, the myth of immeasurable German potency lives on. Loss of men, loss of territory, loss of materials, reparations running into incalculable figures—these things are, apparently, powerless to prevent the land of Dr. Faustus from resuming its plan of world conquest within a few years! Every superficial traveller's impression of German cities, seething with war profiteers, revivifies the phantom of 1914, and the invulnerability of the non-existent routs every normal and logical calculation.

Up to about 1800, political relations between England and Germany were unimportant. From the days of Richard of Cornwall to those of Frederick the Great, who was dropped in 1762, when he had served his purpose, Germany was made use of as an ally in the attempted encirclement of France. German unification was regarded with very mixed feelings. In itself, the reunion of scattered national elements was altogether in the line of the Liberal programme, which, for example, supported the unification of Italy with all its might. Once again, however, the instinct of domination was to prove stronger than idealism, just as the spectre of Dutch economic supremacy proved stronger than the sense of Protestant solidarity. The Zollverein threatened British economic supremacy in Central Europe; moreover, a united Germany was bound to be a North Sea power. This tilted the balance of favour against Germany. Palmerston was decidedly anti-German, but the influence of the pro-German court and other exigencies of the situation helped to maintain neutrality. The battle of Sedan (1870) was received with rather mixed feelings in which uneasiness at the rise of a new Continental power tended to prevail over satisfaction at the downfall of France. Relations with the new Germany were satisfactory; there were men of the first weight in politics who felt that a policy based on an alliance with Germany and directed against Russia and France promised as much success and possibly would cost less sacrifice than one directed against Central Europe. It seems that, about 1900, Germany was approached by England, but did not encourage any overtures. Anyhow, from 1901 on, the opposite tendency dominates British policy; in 1902 an alliance with Japan, from which Germany was excluded, cleared up the Far Eastern Question; in 1904 France was won over and Germany shut out of Morocco ; in 1907 Russia was drawn into the common front against Germany's Eastern policy. Sir Edward Grey, however, carefully avoided any binding and absolute engagements. From 1906 on, there was consultation between the English and French military staffs about common military action against Germany, and plans were laid down that involved Belgium; almost the whole British fleet was concentrated in the North Sea against Germany, and in 1914 a naval agreement for action in eventualities was concluded with Russia. But the Entente between the three Powers did not become an alliance – rather, to the great disquietude of its other members, feelers continued to be extended towards Germany with a view to securing a relaxation of tension. This can hardly have been mere conscious duplicity, hardly a mere opportunist regard to the opinion of the British electorate, which was opposed to any alliance policy, and, in the main, to war of any sort. There was – or so it seemed – always the possibility that, peaceably, by the use of threats of war, Britain might compel Germany to go back on its naval policy and so itself become the all-powerful arbiter between the two groups of Continental powers. Haldane's Berlin mission in 1912 seemed to indicate something of this kind. A favourable arrangement about Colonial possessions might have been the price offered to Germany in return for a renunciation on its part of naval ambitions.

But when the Serajevo crime brought the risk of war, Grey was no longer sole master, able to decide between war and peace. He was not in a position to put the decisive question straight and clear to the Central Powers, since any open threat of war would have split his Cabinet. Nor could he even try to reach an honourable compromise that would have been just to all parties, since his allies, France and Russia, would accept no peaceful solution save one that brought them measureably nearer to their aims, the recovery of Alsace-Lorraine and the break-up of Austria; any other would have broken up the Entente and left Britain isolated, for the secret military pact had raised hopes which, if disappointed, would have precipitated a breach. Peace, therefore, could only be maintained if Germany abandoned its ally, and withdrew from conflict with a complete loss of moral prestige such as it had experienced at Olmütz in 1850. This seems to have been the aim of British policy; on such terms (which of course imply a limitation that almost destroys the thesis) it sought peace; such a solution would have been enthusiastically acclaimed at home, both by the conscious friends of peace there, and by the conscious anti-Germans. Grey was no longer in a position to pursue a policy that would have honestly aimed at a peace which maintained the moral *status quo*, since, except at the price of risking British isolation, he had no means of exercising pressure on his allies; and when, on August 1, 1914, he told the German Ambassador that he could not guarantee British neutrality, even if Belgian neutrality were not violated and Germany had no designs on French Colonial possessions, he knew that this reply signified war and that it could only be a question of days before the violation of the Belgian frontier would provide a popular excuse for it.

In taking farewell of the German Ambassador in August, 1914, Grey implied that it was his intention to spare a defeated Germany. He most probably meant what he said. Had Germany speedily collapsed under the incredible pressure from all sides, it would certainly have lost its fleet but would probably have been allowed to maintain a more or less tolerable position, within a balance of power system dominated by Britain, as a useful counterpoise to France and Russia. But to win the war required the stimulation of national hatred of Germany to the last pitch, while every covetous instinct in the masses was fanned to fever heat by the confiscation and expropriation of German private property throughout the whole area over which the Entente had control. Then the utter helplessness of Germany at the end of the fighting roused all the victors to a frenzy of senseless violence. No government in the world would have had the strength to curb these orgies of hatred. Hence the Treaty of Versailles. It forced the British Government, contrary to its own intentions, to continue the policy of repression against Germany. To the Englishman it was perfectly inconceivable that any German government whatsoever would honourably maintain such a peace, no matter how many German pacifists were ready to accept any and every humiliation. Since at Versailles British policy was unable to prevent the complete disarmament of Germany, and since a Germany with neither aircraft nor heavy artillery could never serve as counterpoise to France, there was nothing for it but to continue the policy of the Entente, perhaps raising some objection, in detail, to the policy of military and political oppression of Germany, but never offering effective opposition to any really serious demand on the part of France, since to do so might have broken up the Entente. This applied to economic as well as to military measures. Germany had shown such astonishing power, resistance of the Blockade had revealed such mighty reserves of strength, both material and moral, in the country, that even after a victory externally so tremendous, the feeling persisted that Germany had not been wholly overthrown. A nation endowed with such vitality must, once the united pressure of a whole victorious world was lifted, be able to develop new and portentous economic strength and seemed, in the economic sphere, more dangerous than France. When France in 1923 occupied the Ruhr and bled Germany's greatest industry white, this event offered the hope of ridding England for a long period of the most dangerous economic competitor in Central Europe; and if the price was that France, for a while, was thereby strengthened, this might seem the lesser evil of the two. Yet to crush Germany absolutely, as France desired, could not be permitted; it had got to rehabilitate its currency if only because the constant fall of the mark acted as an export premium for German goods; the interests of British industry required to have Germany at least so far restored as to make it once more an importer of British products. At the same time it was altogether desirable, from the British standpoint, to have the Dawes Settlement (1924) burden it for an unlimited period with such a weight of Reparations payments as would prevent it from becoming a dangerous competitor on foreign markets for a generation or two. So, political and economic arguments led to one and the same result – England could tolerate no destruction of Germany, it could not help to make France the unchallenged political and economic master of the Continent; but in all this the major consideration still was the maintenance of the Entente and the exercise of steady but moderate pressure on Germany. A policy like this, which implied a restraining hand on French action in all minor matters, might further make England, up to a point, appear as the generous protector of Germany in German eyes and prevent too speedy a reconciliation between Germany and France. It was this policy that led to Locarno and Germany's admission to the League. From the British point of view, the two latter events imply the admission of Germany to the Western power combination and the voluntary recognition of the new Rhine frontier subject to the maintenance of concentrated pressure upon Germany from the west and the east – since France's connexion with Poland continues – in return for the single concession of the evacuation of the Cologne area, with the possible opening of discussion of further evacuation; but England, in the event, strictly refuse to exert any pressure on France to bring this about (Geneva, 1928).

The policy here described is that pursued by the English Foreign Office under successive administrations, no matter whether the Notes bore the signature of a Conservative or of a Labour Foreign Minister, and no matter what the personal angle of the Foreign Secretary himself might be to the problems concerned. This foreign policy has the support of Conservative public opinion, of the captains of industry, and, to a large extent, of the great exporters. But there are large sections of public opinion in England to-day which take a different view. In Labour and Liberal circles, among scholars, Churchmen, and above all among the young, a genuine policy of reconciliation with the defeated foe is sincerely and earnestly desired. There, people remember war lies with shame, regard the directors of national wartime policy with deep suspicion, and seek, in human friendliness, to draw near to the enemy of yesterday. They have learned to respect him and feel an honest indignation at any form of exploitation of the helpless. It is hard to say if and when this mood will be reflected, politically. It is at the moment of great human value and no one can meet it without a desire, gratefully, to foster the human possibilities it promises; but at the moment it does not yet count politically. Even in this camp there is but a tiny handful of men of broader political outlook who perceive that an understanding between Britain and Germany can only be reached through a revision of the Treaty. There is no other way. The pacifists who accept this fact are the only ones who can be taken seriously. The others may be kind and distinguished gentlemen, but in politics they do more harm than good. They care only for peace and reconciliation at any price, and if, unfortunately, the victor proves determined to let go none of the spoils, they regretfully feel that the vanquished must give up his claims for the sake of peace. Pacifists of this school will never count in politics: they may deprecate and complain but will never influence or prevent any policy which they call wrong.

§ 2

Across the Atlantic, in America, a new England arose in the course of the seventeenth and eighteenth centuries, which in 1776 severed itself by force from the Mother Country. To its growth multitudes from every country have contributed, yet the nation created from this mixture of strains has unmistakable English traits, and only English. The spirit of a solitary Frenchman, Montesquieu, sponsored the Constitution. Here and there – far more rarely than is generally assumed – Germany influenced the schools and universities. But the nation is English. There is no understanding America except through England. It is England transplanted to a region of vast aggregations of people and vast stretches of land; an England without the strong influence of a deep-rooted aristocratic tradition. A far-reaching limitation, this last. It means that, across the ocean, a superficial English stamp has been pressed upon millions of immigrants, to a large extent from non-Anglo-Saxon countries, who knew nothing of the limitations which a powerful old tradition imposes upon the working of a masterly will. This means that free play was given to all the hardness, all the materialism, all the warring instincts of the race. Nor were its virtues absent: an enthusiastic love for the self-elected leader, a high veneration for woman, respect for the home. But all this is formless, undisciplined, often futile (the genuine old English homes in Boston, Virginia and elsewhere on the eastern coast are, of course, excepted). Public life is mainly fight, as in England, but very often untrammelled by the chivalrous tradition of the Mother Country; the idea that the spoils are for the victor survived in its crudest form for half a century after it had died out in England.

Religious movements, unrestrained by any settled Church usages, occasionally touch mania in their exaltation and vulgarization. The tendency to create a uniform human type, limited, in England, by a certain recognition of the worth of individuality, here triumphs in a pitiless equalitarian democracy. A uniform level of material prosperity in all classes, accompanied by a dull intellectual sameness, is reflected in school, university and press. To do, to will and to believe in accordance with 'public opinion' is the effective ethical code, the lowest that has ever been formed in history. All this is England, multiplied, magnified, raised to the nth degree. English capitalism reappears in the worship of the Almighty Dollar, English pride of race in the lynching of negroes, English reverence for woman

97

in the domination of the female, the self-possession of the English child in the indiscipline of the young, English cant in a naïve, immovable belief that America can do no wrong, English humanitarianism in philanthropy on an unthinkably large scale, English optimism in a cocksureness that overleaps all obstacles, and even has a sort of childish charm. Throughout the great spaces of a vast continent, one finds English traits everywhere exaggerated to gigantic proportions. Wherever the formless aggregation of people is raised to a society, and literature and culture are recognized as living forces, it is patent that the nation lives on English ideas: nay, more, that English Liberalism has supplied the American with his spiritual diet for good and evil. When one rises in the social scale to the altitudes where, instead of living only in the daily hunt for dollars and power, men have time for reflection and seek to understand historic development, the English traits come out more prominently still. There is the reserve in outward behaviour, there is the gentleman with all his virtues after the English model. There, non-Anglo-Saxon descent is felt as a slur; there, the manners of the English drawing-room are the pattern to which everybody conforms; there, the millionaire seeks to marry his daughters to an English duke, and covers the nakedness of his own pedigree by the portrait of some forebear who came over in the *Mayflower*. Whether this state of things is to last indefinitely nobody can say as yet. There are considerable counter-movements against the English influence in politics, economics, literature, even against English standards of speech; they will become stronger in the same measure as American universities develop and American authors arise who have something entirely American to say. For the moment, and taking the American millions as a whole, the English type is still predominant.

German optimism is perhaps hardly to be blamed for having irrationally overstressed the differences between England and America, in the effort to unearth German influences in American civilization. Up to 1870 most Englishmen did the same; they saw nothing but differences. English Radicals sang pæans to the Land of Liberty, which they saw as better than their brightest dreams. English Conservatives derided the land of shirt-sleeves, spittoons and indistinction. In the long run theirs was the predominant voice, during the first generation after separation; many went over, like Charles Dickens, as enthusiasts for freedom, to return, as he did, having discovered nothing but inflated egotism. On the other side of the Atlantic, school books teem with infantile legends of the base tyrant George III and the noble citizen, Franklin, who rose against him. Politically, England and America were almost always on opposite sides. English and American diplomacy were at daggers drawn in Mexico (including Californiaand theSalt Lake region), in Central America and in China. In the American War of Secession, England was the barely concealed partisan of the South, because it thought it could cope more easily with two Americas than with one. England's claim to a right of search on the high seas was always passionately opposed by America. The frontiers of Maine (1842) and of Oregon (1845) were only settled after threats of war on both sides. In neutral territory, for example in Venezuela, in Panama, and in China, the two powers were generally to be found on opposing sides.

Nevertheless national similarity between the two has grown stronger, and is gradually becoming conscious. The more keenly England feels about her own colonization, the more must she admire the vast Colonial achievement of her sister nation. England's emancipation of the slaves, under Wilberforce, is beginning to be compared with Lincoln's emancipation of the slaves in the Southern States.

The reaction against the mere profit and loss economy of Manchesterism in foreign policy led to the search for a more civilized substitute, and the Boer War, in 1899, was joyously hailed as its achievement. About the same time, an Imperialist movement developed in America, at the period of the war in Cuba (1898). Here, as in the Boer War, a flame-like enthusiasm on the part of the young was exploited by capitalist greed. The methods applied by America to the indirect rule of the 'free' peoples of Cuba and the Philippines, as to the relief of the 'oppressed' peoples of Panama of the burden of carrying on their own foreign policy, are identical with the methods most perfectly developed by England in India. Dilke's book, already referred to (p. 82), is so completely under the influence of the new current of ideas that the points of separation hardly seem to count, in comparison with the points of contact. England and the United States are, here, two daughters of one house; which of them wears the crown is a matter of indifference. In 1902, the Pacifist, William Stead, wrote *The Americanization of the World*, a book with a wide circulation, whose main idea was that the union of England and America was the great task of the twentieth century.

Contemporaneously, diplomats on either side came together. At the time when England chose the side of France it reached an understanding, informal – probably, after the fashion of Anglo-Saxon gentlemen, unwritten – with America. By a sudden *volte-face* England signed the Hay-Pauncefote Treaties (1900–1) and so gave up its indisputable, and long and jealously maintained rights in the Panama Zone. The Panama Canal was constructed as an American undertaking, and became an instrument of American political and military dominion. Thanks to this, America was England's ally in the World War. When the hour struck, it made the decisive cast. By Wilson's own admission, it would have done so without the submarine. Large bodies of opinion on both sides of the Atlantic were favourable to the continuation of the war-time alliance, after the war, in the form of a great Anglo-Saxon Entente aiming at Anglo-American world supremacy, despite the widespread dislike in the United States to any European entanglements. To this end, Britain made very great sacrifices. At Washington, in 1922, it not only abandoned its alliance with Japan, but gave up the goal pursued by its naval policy for many centuries; it no longer claims absolute naval supremacy, but accepts parity in men-of-war with the United States, under the formula allowing Great Britain, America and Japan to build battleships in the ratio 5–5–3. But this was not sufficient to establish harmony. There were misunderstandings about the war-debt, and grave economical disagreements. The Oil question still yawns unsettled between the two countries. Petroleum seems, in the period of the Diesel engine, aerial transport, and the submarine, designed to take the place of coal and steam as a motor force. The oil-bearing areas of the world seem to have prospects for the future analogous to those which steam once opened up to the great industrial regions of Britain. Throughout the world, the great Oil Groups – Rockefeller in America, Shell-Royal Dutch in Britain – are at grips. There are other economic factors making against a lasting settlement. When Britain, which owns, in the Malay States, the greatest rubber plantations in the world, restricted the export of rubber in the years after the war, the action was resented as a blow not only to the powerful American motor-car industry but to the United States as a whole. On the other hand, the United States, having become the greatest creditor nation in the world, is exerting powerful pressure upon Britain. Inter-allied war-debts are not cancelled, less for financial reasons than because the United States wants to keep its position as the great creditor nation with all the possibilities of diplomatic pressure it implies. Further, the money sent across the Atlantic in payment of war-debts is safe from being used to build battleships which might reduce America's political influence in the world. Very strong ill-will between the two countries was engendered by the failure of the effort, made at the Geneva Naval Conference in 1927, to apply Washington standards to cruisers and smaller craft. MacDonald, the new Prime Minister, made it his first duty to reopen the question. His journey to America has already resulted in a solemn declaration (October 1929) which may lead up to a complete entente between the two countries, if very important questions as to armaments and naval rights can be solved satisfactorily.

§ 3

England's rise to world-dominion cost her relatively few wars. She certainly used her elbows without much scruple, but not, for the most part, in war. From 1700 on, there are few wars in which England did not play a determinant part, yet it never risked any great expenditure of strength of its own. After 1066, no foreign conqueror set foot on its soil. The last battle – and that a purely dynastic one – on British ground was that of Culloden in 1746, between the troops of George II and of the Pretender, Charles Edward Stuart. Its legendary pacific character is based solely upon the fact that it never went in for arming to the teeth like Prussia or Russia, but always contrived to keep almost the whole of its own population peacefully at work. This made the world forget that practically every war between 1700 and 1918 ended with a victory for Britain, which in most cases was not the power which had done most of the fighting.

This policy of setting others to work is one of the old secrets of cabinet policy. It is a method recommended by so rare a Humanist as Sir Thomas More in his *Utopia*. The arts of dexterously making use of others were developed to the point of virtuosity by practice in yet another school – India. France and Spain, full of knightly, crusading notions, dreamed of founding a new Europe across the seas, Catholic, Christian, feudalistic, a true mirror of the homeland, with the bishop at least as powerful in it as the Governor and the tax-collector. England, on the other hand, drily realist, exclusively concerned with profit and loss, founded a trading colony in India. Missionaries were carefully excluded; they might have disturbed trade and brought trouble, perhaps even war. (Thus, in America, the Puritans found a convenient excuse for not busying themselves with distasteful missionary efforts in the handy Calvinist formula which stigmatized the Indians as the progeny of Ham, designed for damnation by God, whose purposes must not be crossed by any attempt to convert them.) Nor did they like flag-hoisting. This, again, was apt to create unrest and lead to punitive expeditions and other costly debit items. It was cheaper and more convenient to make a party at the court of this or that native prince and so rule, indirectly, over the largest possible territory. From the beginning, England governed the greater number of Indian States in the benevolent twilight of a semi-suzerainty. This permitted English influence to be more or less prominent, as need dictated; permitted troops to be brought in to defend the 'independence' of the country, English 'advisers' to be inserted into every department of government, and the economic resources of the area to be developed to the full. The same method is employed to-day in 'independent' Egypt, and is being applied to control Mesopotamia, Arabia, and the Zionist State of Palestine. Undoubtedly it is, for England, the ideal form of government. The moving complaints of the Englishman about 'the white man's burden,' and the declarations solemnly made by the Press, before every new extension of Colonial boundaries, that England has no 'desire to increase its responsibilities' are perfectly honest. They are but regrets over the passing of that ideal state of things, when England could control, more or less gratis, vast areas of the world's surface.

But there is another side to all this, to which hostile criticism obstinately closes its eyes. Far from disinterested as is English policy, it must appear disinterested to the world. While France, since Richelieu's day, has kept the world busy and excited by plans of expansion and perpetual flag-hoisting, England quietly grows, waving its flag as seldom as possible. In the seventeenth century, France was perpetually nibbling off pieces of Belgium. England defended Holland and Belgium, and then withdrew without retaining either Nieuport or Flushing. There are important strategic points, like Dunkirk, Minorca, and the Ionian Islands, which it conquered and then gave back. Its ambassador rules in Lisbon and Athens, but the national government is not interfered with in any way. Denmark was protected, but no hold on Danish waters sought. Where it does hoist its flag, the place generally happens to be some sterile promontory or cape which represents no great loss to the Power that yields it up, but gives a most powerful position into the hands of a naval nation. Malta, St. Helena, Cape Town, Aden, Singapore, and Hong Kong are cases in point; Gibraltar is not much different. Obviously, it never was to the interest of a purely naval power to create an Alsace-Lorraine or indulge in Polish partitions. The example of Ireland is there to show how little humanitarianism would have availed to stay Britain's hand. But the fact remains that Britain is the solitary great Power which has never injured the vital interest of another European people by annexation: and it is a fact of immeasurable moral effect in a period dominated by the principle of nationality.

There is another point to notice. Britain's wars have been fought, in general, by sea and not by land. The logical difference is non-existent: the psychological, immense. A modern territorial army involves the slaughter of millions, the devastation of large areas, the laming of trade and industry throughout provinces. It sets before the eyes of millions a spectacle, repeated day after day, of trains of wounded being brought in, endless ranks of war graves, processions of lethal engines of every sort, air raids, and militarism dominant, far behind the front. Men see the khaki worm devouring their country. But a fleet fights its battles in the invisible spaces of the ocean. Men hear nothing but stories of heroic deeds; the horrors of a naval fight are known only to the sharks. An army is like an uncontrolled Briareus. Even in peace time its foot is on the country; it seizes hold of civil life with its thousand arms, is everywhere felt as destructive and restrictive; for the man of to-day it is an evil inheritance from an outworn past. A fleet, on the other hand, works noiselessly; except for the folk in the harbour towns, no one is aware of it. Of all implements of mass murder, it is the most sophisticated. The striking force, the drive of will and the destructive skill of entire nations are concentrated in a couple of gigantic hulls. Millions of warriors can annihilate provinces, but hardly destroy a whole nation: a dozen grey dreadnoughts, besieging a country, invisible in the far distance, can spread hunger and misery over an entire continent. The nation which wields supreme power over this instrument is, for war, the most potent in the world. Earlier nations knew this. But the superficial judgment of a democratic epoch is easily persuaded to believe that this nation is the most pacific of all.

§ 4

Whence does England derive the influence that enables it to maintain an English party in practically every country? Of course there is the Almighty Pound Sterling, and the more Oriental the country, the more effective is its influence. But it is least of all the powers which make influence. England has always possessed a skill superior to that of any other country to direct economic and intellectual forces. Where it can, it overruns the country with men and women of English birth. Ulster, Ontario, Rhodesia are examples of this. Otherwise, a handful of Englishmen in prominent positions will influence the policy of a country in a pro-English sense. Sometimes English princesses have occupied (though not always utilized) key positions in Europe – the Empress Frederick in Berlin, Queen Maud in Oslo, Queen Ena in Madrid. Or a British press correspondent, or some British missionary, will acquire an influence extending far beyond the bounds of his office. That every bank, every railway, every electric line, and every factory in Ireland is financed from England is the basic fact that prevents Ireland's separation from England, all revolutions notwithstanding. The rise and fall in English Bank rate is still the index of economic life in Canada; England is still the most extensive purchaser of Canadian wheat; England's economic influence is paramount in Australia and South Africa, in most of the South American States, in China and Japan, in Norway, Portugal and Greece, although, outside Europe, the United States is more and more busy attempting to break down the age-long economic and financial monopoly of Great Britain. A vast amount of basic raw materials is contained within the British Empire. In South Africa, Australia and Canada, Britain accounts for 56 per cent of the world's gold production; in the Malay Peninsula and West Africa, for the greater proportion of its rubber; in Wales for the outstanding supply of anthracite; in Australia, South Africa, and at home for nearly half (43 per cent) of the world's production of wool; in Australia and, above all, the Malay Peninsula, for four-fifths of the world's production of tin; and in Canada and Australia for a good proportion (a fifth) of the world's production of wheat. Its acquisition of the Persian and Mesopotamian oil-fields means that it is independent of the outer world in respect of the new economic raw material, oil and petrol, although in respect of cotton it is still dependent on America. All this means influence, and it may mean decisive power in great historical moments. During the World War a ruthless use of economic power, the refusal of bunker coal here, of wheat there, enabled England to force almost the whole of the world's shipping into its service and throttle Germany's trade, by its black lists, almost all over the world.

But even more important than all economic influence has been

England's rôle as champion of spiritual movements in the world. Under the purely humane inspiration of Wilberforce and Clarkson, it eradicated slavery everywhere. True, this was accomplished at an epoch when the economic consequences were no longer likely to be catastrophic. Moreover, the greatest skill was displayed in turning this moral achievement to political advantage. Weaker competitors, threatened with economic ruin by abolition, were made politically pliable by the constant pressure of humane demands. And England, liberator of millions of slaves, felt quite free to take the side of the slave-owning South in the American Civil War, since the South might perhaps succeed in eliminating the political peril of America as a great Power.

Throughout the world, England is the political ally of every great religious force. After conquering French Catholic Canada in 1763, it made peace with Catholicism, and set up a little Church State in Quebec. When the hour of conciliation sounded in Ireland, the Canadian experiment was repeated, on a smaller scale. The Catholic hierarchy sided with England against Parnell and Sinn Fein (p. 359). In India, it is the protector of Hindu and Mohammedan alike, and strong pressure from home was required before the missionary was gradually granted admission to the country. During the war, the Zionist movement was placed in English leading-strings, and the Jewish National State – so often decried and derided – was set up under British protection. The world's Holy Places are almost all under British protection: Jerusalem, Constantinople, the Ganges, Mecca, and Medina, Kerbela and Nedschef. Britain is not only one of the greatest of Protestant Powers, it is at the same time the greatest of Islamic Powers

When the movement for International peace was launched by the Czar's invitation to the first Hague Conference, in 1899, Britain, alone among the European Powers, recognized the realist significance of a movement that, Utopian as it might appear at the moment, nevertheless corresponded to the actual necessities of the time, and speedily took the lead into its own hands. At the second Hague Conference in 1907, in the months when the Anglo-Russian Treaty was being riveted round Germany, it very cleverly took a line that did more than any other circumstance to present Germany as the wilful enemy of peace and create the universal anti-German public opinion of 1914. Wherever any international question arises, whether inside the Protestant Churches (the Evangelical Alliance was founded in England in 1846), the Labour movement, the Women's Question, the War on Alcohol, the Youth movement or the Mission field – England will be behind it, sympathetic, disinterested, but, all the time, carefully and skilfully gathering up any political by-products that it may yield.

The whole of this international spiritual propaganda is apt to be completely misunderstood on the Continent. Non-English nations are apt to see in it nothing but Machiavellian cunning harnessing the world's idealism to England's triumphal car. Such a judgment overlooks the fact that purely idealistic movements, rare in the world we live in, are only too constantly forced to make terms, and very unexhilarating terms at that, with the world's political, economic and egotistic forces. No great idealistic, ethical, national or religious movement can remain long in complete isolation from the economic and political struggle of humanity.

The distribution of egotistic and altruistic motives varies with the individual: the altruistic will dominate in the great ethical leader, the egotistic in the responsible statesman, without either excluding the other. Great idealists who had no cunning side motives up their sleeve generally initiated England's humanitarian campaigns, whether for the emancipation of the slave or the assistance of this or that persecuted race or people. But the forces they released were very often employed by British statesmen to serve British political ends. English policy has never been infected by that myth of a materialistic age which sees political events as mere struggles for food and shelter. On the contrary, it has shown quite incomparable intelligence in appreciating the mighty force of the movements of ideas and using them for political purposes. A typical illustration will serve. The discovery of the atrocities being perpetrated in the Belgian Congo was the work of a very young and entirely uninfluential employee in a Liverpool shipping company, E. D. Morel, who from 1900 onward risked his income, his life and his position for the sake of making an end of this outrage to humanity. Missionaries and clergymen ranged themselves on his side. Gradually, they were joined by a handful of partisans of a less idealistic character, drawn from those industrial circles in Britain that, contrary to treaty provisions, had been excluded from trading in the Congo, and now found a highly effective weapon in their grasp for rousing the world against Leopold II. Even the Government was ready to lend an ear; it wanted to attach Belgium to the anti-German Entente; here was a means of exerting pressure upon it. Once that end was attained, official England found, all at once, that the reports from Africa were grossly exaggerated. Morel continued his agitation unweariedly, but the response from public opinion and the Government obviously grew fainter, and the fearless idealist began to speak with unconcealed bitterness of the duplicity of his own Government.

The British Government creates no movements of ideas, but it has always known how to give or withhold from them the gigantic weight of its support, according as they were or were not in the line of its political purposes. Agitations that did not suit it soon collapsed, like the Armenian propaganda of 1896; then the humanitarians were left to themselves. Wherever possible, however, English statesmanship would take a hand, finding in the humanitarian excitement created throughout the world a striking force that could never have been achieved through purely diplomatic pressure. The notorious 'profit and loss' business of this 'nation of shopkeepers' has always had the keenest sense of the potency of spiritual values. So, the declaration of war in 1914 was followed up by a 'war of ideas,' carried on with an unscrupulous virtuosity impossible to a people that did not rate spiritual values at least as high as dreadnoughts and black lists.

When British propaganda succeeds in using spiritual and material forces, the idealists and the egotists, concurrently, it is almost irresistible. Here is the secret of its Free Trade propaganda in the nineteenth century. It was no cunning effort to promote the unrestricted importation of British goods under the banner of the ideal. That has been its effect, no doubt; but the motives of the propaganda were pure. The parents of Free Trade were not politicians, but scholars like Adam Smith and Jeremy Bentham. With honest conviction they saw it as the whole world's salvation. They believed, sincerely, that every nation must be capable of producing some commodity or other so cheaply and effectively as to secure for it the same monopoly as England possessed of the manufacture of cotton goods. How could a temporary advantage of this nation or that weigh in the balance against a principle designed to make war impossible and bring the millennium to the world! Something here, for every element in the nation, for every constructive, imaginative, efficient and progressive spirit. Free Trade held out the prospect, to the egotist, of prosperity for his own industry, thanks to an unlimited supply of raw material from abroad; to the patriot, the prosperity of his native land, once free of the red tape tied round its limbs by the bureaucratic limitations of the old state; to the idealist and the philanthropist, an end of poverty, of destitution and of war, throughout the world. No one saw anything suspicious in the fact that England stood to profit, first and foremost, by all this; that fact merely afforded further confirmation of the theory that, at bottom, the interests of the whole of mankind are identical.

Similarly with England's championship of small nations. Again, the policy was thoroughly in line with its own interests. It was vital, for England, to support Portugal as a permanently faithful vassal against Spain; vital, to support Holland, Belgium, and in the eighteenth century, Prussia, against France, and, later, Denmark against the threat of Prusso-German domination over the coasts of the North Sea and the Baltic. In its colonial policy, a large part was played by the erection or protection of buffer States, to ward off a powerful neighbour – Afghanistan and Persia against Russia; Siam; and recently, Transjordania against France. Not that this in the least prevented an abandonment or blank seizure of the little protégé if and when necessity arose. Prussia was left in the lurch in 1762; Denmark in 1864; Portugal, in 1890, was compelled to yield the whole of its Colonial hinterland in Africa in the interest of Rhodesia. But such divagations of policy from its normal course are few and far between – and other States show the same. They made the less lasting impression that, on other occasions, when the normal course of policy did not seem convenient, England would appear as the energetic defender of the case of some small nation. Thus it broke off its Turkophil policy to come forward as the protector of Greece and the advocate of the persecuted Armenians; it set Crete free of the Turkish yoke; it pressed the unification of Italy against Austria with obstinate energy.

England is the single country in the world that, in looking after its own interest with meticulous care, has at the same time something to give to others; the single country where patriotism does not represent a threat or challenge to the rest of the world; the single country that invariably summons the most progressive, idealistic, and efficient forces in other nations to co-operate with it. Free Trade and the protection of small nations may not have any great part to play in the future. Their place may perhaps be taken by the League of Nations and the 'protection of order against Bolshevism.' But this does not alter the essential fact, which is that, so far, Britain is the solitary Great Power with a national programme which, while egotistic through and through, at the same time promises to the world as a whole something which the world passionately desires – order, progress, and eternal peace. All other nations, in so far as they have not been tied blindly to England's chariot-wheels, have, hitherto, merely resisted it, because they felt in England's growing power an encirclement that threatened to deprive them of freedom and the breath of life. But none of them has as yet succeeded in setting up, against the British ideal, an ideal of their own, national and international at the same time as the British. Only the Russians, recently, have found out this secret, and the result has shown how immense is the driving force which a national aspiration can acquire, once it has an international ideal behind it.

CHAPTER V
INDUSTRY AND POPULATION
§ 1

Down to about the close of the eighteenth century, England was a predominantly agricultural country. It fed itself, in the main, from the wheat grown more or less all over the land, with a yield well above the average. Pasturage, likewise at a high level of development, had, from of old, competed with tillage. Ever since the time of the Black Death (1349), whose ravages caused an unprecedented shortage of population, sheep-farming, and, later, cattle-raising, had been the favourite form of economics of the English landed proprietor, thanks to its relatively lower demand both for workpeople and for work, and the special advantages afforded by the dampness of the climate for the development of extensive meadow lands. But, about 1800, the production of wheat began to be insufficient to meet the needs of a rapidly rising population. In 1846 the sustained protests of consumers compelled the abolition of the Corn Laws. Nevertheless, attempts were then initiated to maintain corn production by intensive cultivation and the increased use of agricultural machinery. By the end of the century, foreign wheat (Russian, American, and Canadian) was coming on to the British market in such quantities that tillage was progressively replaced by pasturage. At the beginning of the twentieth century (1905), there were, in Great Britain and Ireland, 7·8 million acres under corn against 34·6 of pasture. At present (in 1927) 13·8 million acres of the soil of Great Britain (without Ireland) are stated as arable, 76·6 as pasture, 14·8 as rough grazing. Arable land predominates only in the south-east, east and south of a line drawn between Southampton and Birmingham and Nottingham, and thence towards Doncaster and Hull. Kent is devoted to hops, while fruit-growing covers large parts of the south, notably Devonshire and Somerset, largely for the purpose of cider manufacture. The agricultural yield is therefore not great. It consisted (Great Britain and Ireland) in 1926 of 1,397,000 tons of wheat, 1,170,000 barley, 3,171,000 oats, 6,663,000 potatoes. The characteristic feature of the country is the great, green meadow-lands, over which cattle are wont to roam the summer through. Here the level of production is high and the quality notable. Numerically, sheep are easily first, with 27,595,000 (figures for Great Britain and Ireland); there are 12,066,000 cattle, 3,388,000 pigs, 1,782,000 horses. During the war, there was a notable (but not lasting) increase in the cultivation of wheat, but Great Britain is still very far from being able to feed itself. Great Britain and Northern Ireland produced in 1924 24 per cent of its own consumption of wheat and flour, 46 per cent of its beef, 41 per cent of its mutton, 35 per cent of its pork, 18 per cent of its butter, and 32 per cent of its cheese.

To the extreme north of Scotland great stretches of land are un-cultivated. They may have grown barley in early times, but gradually the sheep took possession of them, and to-day the moorhen and the grouse have dispossessed the sheep, with a further contraction of the employment of men. Since it is the fashion for the Birmingham manufacturer and member of the London Stock Exchange to have a shooting in Scotland, it has become at once easier and more profitable to let these mountainous moors for sport than to put them under sheep. Economists may feel a certain bitterness in the spectacle of the gradual depopulation of regions where the grouse has driven the human inhabitants into the towns or across the ocean to the United States, but the State has proved powerless to curb the selfish egotism of the landlord. The forests, too, have been sacrificed to the greed of their owners. The mighty woodlands of Scotland, Wales and many parts of England are things of the past. Timber-felling was the handi-est financial resource of the proprietor during the eighteenth century, when the upper class could purchase a boundless extension of power by bribing complacent electors. In Britain to-day, a wood is a pictur-esque object. It is apt to have a special name, for example, Epping Forest outside London, the Forest of Dean near Gloucester, the New Forest near Southampton, or the Trossachs in Scotland. The great mountains of Scotland and Wales are, to-day, relatively bare; such woods as have escaped the axe of the owner are apt to be enclosed in parks, to which the public is not admitted. Almost the whole of the timber supply used in building and mining comes from Russia, Scandinavia, and Canada; during the war, the shortage of pit-props caused by the submarine campaign was almost more perilous to the mining industry than was the threat to the food supply. Since 1910, the Development Commissioners have been set up to assist, from State resources, in the reafforestation of the country. In 1921 in Eng-land and Wales 5·1 per cent of the surface were woodland, 6·1 per cen-in Scotland, 1·4 per cent in Ireland; as against 23·8 per cent in Gert many (1923). Further to accelerate reafforestation, the Forestry Commissioners were set up in 1919, with the specific object of bringing 150,000 acres of land under State ownership within ten years, and converting them into woods, and, further, of making grants to localities and private individuals for afforestation, by which it is hoped to add another 110,000 acres of woodland within the same period.

English agriculture works under a mixture of large landownership and tenancy, under which the owner supplies the capital, the tenant the labour. Originally (at the beginning of the Norman period, and even before that) the whole of the country was divided into manors, centring round the fief of some noble, with all sorts of tenures dependent upon it. The lord of the manor could demand plough and horse service on the demesne as well as other services from his tenants in socage; for the rest, the peasants carried on the economy of their part of the manor more or less independently. Theoretically the King is the only landowner; English law knows no absolutely free property of land. The outward form of feudal tenure disappeared in England earlier than on the Continent, but not its substance. No really free peasantry has arisen in England; the landlord has merely transformed himself from an owner who himself carried on the economy of the estate into a mere rent-receiver on a large scale. In the fourteenth century socage tenure gradually broke down, a process accelerated by the appalling depopulation of the country through the ravages of the Black Death in 1348-9; and the landlord let out his demesne to various tenants-in-chief, to whom he leased land, cattle, corn and buildings, and, later, capital, too, in return for a fixed rental. Where the soil was suitable, he converted arable land into sheep pasture, since it requires less labour and promises a higher rent. Further, the land was enclosed by hedges – and not the demesne only, but the commons, originally the common property of all the dwellers in the manor. This caused the gravest injury to the small men. For them the commons were vital as grazing land for a cow or a few pigs, and the meagre compensation they were given did not in the least furnish an equivalent. Deprived of subsistence, they either went into the towns or entered the service of the landlord or his tenant as hired labourers. So, the peasant became the labourer, the chattel of the estate. Even in the earlier period of enclosure, about 1500, it was plain that the State took no sufficient care of the small man. By the eighteenth century, when the King and the State had parted with all real influence in the land, and power was exclusively in the hands of the great landed proprietors, the labourers were utterly unprotected, and impotent to resist the new enclosures the owners now carried through, in their own economic interest. Economically this change meant progress, better farming, more intensive culture of the soil and better cattle. But it had also the sinister result of eliminating the free peasant. Driven away from the land, he either helped to swell the tragic army of the town proletariate or became the dependent tenant or almost disfranchised labourer.

The whole of the soil belongs to the landlords. Through purchase and marriage a vast area is united in a relatively small number of hands. Something like a sixth of the entire land of England and Wales was, in 1873, in the hands of some 400 persons,[1] two-fifths of the soil in the hands of less than 1,700. It is by no means rare to find areas equalling the size of a whole county in a single hand. Not only the agricultural produce yields an income to them, but also practically all the minerals below the surface, and nearly all the town land. From agriculture, mining, industry, commerce, and from the residential quarters of the towns, an immense stream of gold goes into the coffers of the landlord. The big landlord hardly contributes anything to the management of his estate. Generally he is simply the owner. He provides buildings, hedges and fences, undertakes drainage works on a larger scale, and keeps all these in order. He generally leases out his estate in parcels of middling size. The tenant, or farmer, does all the work, and bears the real risk. He takes on and dismisses the workers he needs, provides the agricultural machinery, buys the seed and harvests the yield. Below him stand the labourers. They are partly taken on singly or in groups, by some agent, and are engaged casually, for the harvest. Of these casual workers a large number are Irish. But the backbone of English country life is composed of resident labourers, dwelling in houses that belong to the landlord. Since all the cottages on the estate are his, the workers are completely in his power. He can nip any strike or disaffection in the bud by giving notice to quit to his cottagers. If the supply of labour is adequate, he often pulls down any superfluous dwellings, so that he may be incommoded by no excess of population, with a consequent rise in his Poor-rates. There can never be a sound village life in England so long as this condition of things persists. The so-called English village is a mere collection of workmen's cottages, which belong to the landlord and house poverty-stricken landworkers; an artisan or two, a few shopkeepers, and a handful of retired persons of the upper classes complete the picture.

The farmer, who employs the labourers, will live a little out of the village, on his own farm; still further off is the princely mansion where the landlord sits in state. Every effort on the part of Government to create anything like a strong communal life out of elements so various and hardly possessing anything in the nature of a common interest has, so far, been unavailing, because of the unnatural structure of rural society itself.

Yet the whole structure of English social life rests on the foundation of this agricultural system. The land is possessed by an aristocratic caste that, without doing any work or taking any real risks of its own, lives in the country on magnificent estates, in the enjoyment of princely revenues, occupying itself in the main, in a careless, unsystematic way, with hunting, sport and politics. This class has given England a series of notable men of letters – Surrey, Sidney, Lord Shaftesbury (the philosopher), Horace Walpole, Byron, Shelley, Bulwer Lytton; a fine array of statesmen – Lord Bolingbroke, Lord Shaftesbury (the social reformer), Lord Grey, Lord Palmerston, Lord Salisbury, Lord Lansdowne. More than that, it really ruled England between 1689 and 1832, and to this day exercises a strong influence over foreign and domestic policy, subject to a meticulous regard for the forms of democracy. In it, a formidable vitality is masked beneath the strictly regulated code of manners and affable address of the well-bred man of the world. It has no tinge of the Puritanic dryness of the middle class; it can hardly be accidental that all the poets who have come out of it belong to the Romantic and not the Classical type, or that it is here that we find mad rush for pleasure and a tendency to break over the narrow traces set by the Puritan code, notably in the relations of the sexes. A strong bent for action and an outspokenly militarist point of view further distinguish this class. It has no use for Pacifism, and, in foreign policy, inclines to the strong hand. Here, as elsewhere, tone and manner, cool, serene, and polished, bespeak the self-assurance of the born ruler, and conceal the passionate heart that beats beneath. Above all, this class has a matchless power of assimilation. All who belong to it have the dignity and breeding of little kings, the *noblesse oblige* of the old aristocrat is the guiding principle of them all, and this although we are not, here dealing, except to a very small extent, with a really old noble caste. More than half of the members of the British House of Lords have titles dating from after 1832.[2] Nothing shows the genius for leadership of this class more strikingly than its capacity to take up into itself the dominant men in the class below it, and so nip any really dangerous opposition in the bud.

The strongly centralized power of the Plantagenets not only prevented the rise of territorial powers, but of hereditary magnates, and while the individual holder of the feudal title was noble, his brothers and sons belonged to the middle class. There has never been a '*von*' to erect a barrier between noble and non-noble. Literally, the younger sons of the nobility belong to the bourgeoisie, although in fact to an intermediate group between the middle and upper classes. The other side of the picture is that, in England, any extraordinarily successful career will carry a man into the peerage. The really big industrialist or merchant, or even a distinguished poet like Tennyson, is taken into the circles which have governed the country for a century and a half. Rank, therefore, hangs as a tempting possibility before every one. No one, outside of a tiny handful of Radicals, sees it as exercising any pressure on the community – and this although the pressure is real enough. By owning practically all the land of the country, the nobility takes its toll not only from the peasant and the labourer on the land, but from every one who has to build a house or a factory, every one who extracts coal from a mine, every one who uses a canal or a railway. In a word, the ground rents of England pass, in the main, into the pockets of a nobility that is boundlessly rich, and does not work, but only governs. If the average Englishman is not conscious of all this, it is because the English nobleman has learned how to govern pleasantly. Not in law, but in fact, estates are strictly entailed. The son is made heir by his father only on condition that he hands his inheritance on, undiminished, to his own son, in turn.[3] Provision for younger sons is made out of capital, or else they have places found for them in the diplomatic service, in the army (to a far less degree than in Germany), in the Indian civil service, in the Church, or, more rarely, in trade and industry. Hitherto, nothing has shaken the position of the upper class. The leasehold system gives the tenant his chance of profit, and, in bad years, the landlord takes a reasonable view of arrears and abatements. The whole burden of the system rests on the labourer's back. Wretchedly paid, equally wretchedly housed, he is utterly dependent on the employer on whose good pleasure his sole chance of getting some sort of roof over his head depends. The patriarchal benevolence of his master may protect him from utter destitution, but it at the same time deprives him of any chance of bettering himself, so long as he remains upon the land. Therefore, all that is alert and energetic in the countryside leaves it; goes to the town, goes to America, goes to the Colonies, with the result that, despite the progressive introduction of machinery, the Labour Question is becoming more and more difficult there. In the sixties, the discontent of the labourers with the misery of their lot led to the foundation of Agricultural Unions, and a notable series of strikes of which the labourer, Joseph Arch, was the life and soul, between 1872 and 1874. But the landlords, who were also the local J.P.s, soon stamped the movement out by giving notices to quit to their labourers – i.e. evicting the 'unruly' *en bloc* – and a ruthless application of the laws. The very basis of their existence was threatened; they organized for its defence with the grim energy with which the Anglo-Saxon fights for his privileges.

The rural districts have been always the strongholds of the Conservative Party. The Liberals attempted to undermine their hold; for instance, in 1884, Gladstone gave votes to the previously disfranchised agricultural labourer. The result was meagre. And in 1888 the Conservatives put through a reorganization of the franchise for county councils – infinitely more important in the regulation of real issues in the daily life of the countryside – that kept the direction of local administration safely in their grip. No real change can come about until the agricultural labourer is made a free peasant again – in other words, until the whole course of development, beginning in the sixteenth century, which led to the degradation of the peasantry, is reversed.

In Ireland, under the threat of revolution, enough courage was mustered up to do this. Since 1881, and more particularly since 1903, four-fifths of the land has been given back to the peasants. In the Highlands of Scotland, too, a beginning has been made. Here, owing to the poverty of the soil, no such strong intermediate tenantry has developed as exists in England. The normal case is that of a boundlessly wealthy landlord on one side, and, on the other, a mass of wretched tiny crofters, who can just manage in good years, but succumb in bad. The life of Robert Burns gives a glimpse into the misery of their condition (though his tragedy was enacted in the Lowlands) – a misery that is the logical outcome of the ruthless oppression of the small man by the land-owning nobility. After the Union in 1707, English Courts did not recognize the semi-communistic constitution of the Celtic Highlands, but treated the land, originally the property of an entire clan, as the personal property of its Chief.

Hence the immense *latifundia* of the Dukes of Sutherland, Montrose, and Richmond, and the Marquis of Breadalbane. The landowner's clansmen were established, under miserable condition, as small crofters, and, even so, were driven out of their wretched crofts during the eighteenth century, when their land was put under sheep. Scottish immigration into Canada and the United States dates, in the main, from these evictions. In certain counties (Argyle, Sutherland, and Perthshire) the population in 1911 was actually below the figures for 1801. The worst of these conditions were ended by the legislation of 1886–1888. As in Ireland in 1881, there was a re-fixing of rents through the Crofters' Commission, which also freed the crofter from his utter dependence on the landlord, inasmuch as he was given security of tenure, and subject to fulfilment of contractual conditions, he, but not the landlord, can determine the tenancy. In 1911 crofters' rights were extended to all small holders of less than fifty acres. Finally, these improvements in the position of the tenant were extended to England. The Agricultural Holdings Act of 1908 gave the farmer compensation for his own improvements and also the right to a claim against unjust eviction, tantamount almost to an unlimited tenancy. Earlier than this, in the Allotments Act of 1887, an effort was initiated by the Government to arrest rural depopulation by giving local authorities power to create small allotments, chiefly for market-gardening, alienating land, if necessary, for that purpose. The results, however, were small. The District and County Councils, the preserves of land-ownership, simply did not work the Act, and it was not till the Small Holdings Act of 1907 gave the initiative to the Ministry of Agriculture that anything was really done. Along this line a new agricultural population is arising, independent of the great landlords, which though it does not produce much wheat does supply the big towns with fruit, vegetables, and eggs. The movement has been actively promoted by the Liberals, who would fain thus break the social monopoly of the land-owning class. But their aim is not the creation of a new class of free peasant proprietors – a solution the landlords are themselves beginning to accept. At best, the Liberals hope to break the power of the landlords by creating a new type of tenant. The new agrarian legislation guarantees the tenant independence *vis-à-vis* his landlord, and further permits the Ministry of Agriculture to intervene, as a sort of court of first instance, between landlord and tenant, notably in the direction of fixing a fair rent, on the Irish model. This – the creation, in the mind of the land-

THE COUNTRY AND ITS PEOPLE

lord, of the sense that he is subject to law in relation to the land – is the real object of the Liberals, and one which, naturally, meets with the stoutest opposition from the whole of the old land-owning interest. They may be brought to the point of reducing their own possessions by giving up the economically less profitable parts of the land, but only with the idea of there training up a peasant proprietorship at their door, likely to be brought, through the development of the instinctive hostility between town and country, into a conservative agrarian alliance with themselves, on the lines of France and Germany. And this is precisely what the Liberals seek to prevent. To them, tenancy is an instrument for keeping the small-holder in permanent opposition to the landlord, and the constant interference of bureaucracy to protect the tenant a means of preventing any such alliance.[4]

The old monopoly position of the landlord is threatened from another side. Gladstone's budget of 1853 made land liable to inheritance duty, and Lloyd George's revolutionary budget of 1909 imposed taxation more difficult for land to evade than for mobile capital. In the far from rare case of an estate of £50,000 value passing to an heir of the third degree, Estate duties of 10 per cent, and, on top of that, Legacy and Succession duties of a further 10 per cent are levied, which may rise in some cases to not less than 50 per cent of the total value of the inheritance. Nor can these burdens be readily shifted on to the tenant, who can give notice if his rent is greatly raised, and then claim compensation for disturbance and for improvements. Since 1909, to the deep disquiet of all Conservatives, something like a break-up of the old estates has been going on, accelerated by post-war developments which have brought the war profiteer into the market. A class that contains many rich and cultured individuals, who have deserved, as individuals, well of the State, is being deprived of the financial basis of their accustomed way of life. Looked at, however, from the standpoint of the community as a whole, the step is inevitable: no State in the world can to-day afford to maintain a non-working upper class in luxury and brilliance at the expense of the rest.

The rule of the landlords now depends on the continuance of Conservative government. Lloyd George's Liberal Land Policy seeks to assimilate all the landlord's rights in a State rent (normally 65 per cent of the present). The cultivating tenants are to retain and work their present holdings, but under the future supervision not of the landlord but of the State. They continue to bear the full risk, and enjoy property rights (passed on by inheritance), but a State department has the right to dispossess tenants of land which they fail to cultivate properly, and to exercise a right of purchase whenever a holding changes hands. Out of the land funds thus assembled they are to settle fresh tenants on the soil. Rural workers receive a legal minimum wage and the right to small holdings of half an acre. Even now the Liberals expressly reject the idea of transforming tenants into free peasants; they only want to see the old nobles disappear as owners of the land, and all future increases in ground rents (arising out of the value of land for mining, sport, housebuilding, etc.) accruing to the community.

English life is hardly conceivable without itsaristocratic influence – an influence, that, despite all its faults, drawbacks and prejudices has, in the long run, been beneficial. The aristocracy has lost all its external privileges. But it sits in the Upper House, which means that the head of any noble family may become a Minister without going through the political mill, while he is still young. At the moment, the great families are still, broadly speaking, in possession of a princely wealth that makes them completely independent. Above all, equalitarian democracy has not availed to shake the popular conviction of their natural leadership. The first claim to Ministerial posts, as to every honourable office in the State, national or local, belongs to the candidate who comes from one of these families. A hospital cannot be founded, or any political, social, scientific or humanitarian effort launched, without having some member of the nobility as its sponsor. Only literature and the arts have to get on as best they may without.

In Society, that perplexing but potent organ of English public life, rank enjoys an unchallenged supremacy. In Germany, certain definite objective qualities settle a man's personal status: noble birth, officer's rank, academic distinctions, an official position, membership of some student corps, or even the possession of an empty order or title. In England, rank takes precedence of everything else. A long way after it comes membership of some association closely connected with the nobility, such as the ancient colleges of the two historic Universities, or the old Inns of Court, as well as certain dignities of the Church. Social consideration, however, does not attach to the clergyman, as such, to the M.A., the Professor, the Civil servant, or even the Minister of the Crown. But it does attach to the man who is to be met with in the houses of the aristocracy, and, above all, to the man who has the honour of being invited to their country houses for hunting or shooting in spring or autumn.[5] *Entrée* there is what counts. This social calculus, wholly independent of the State organization, is one of the most characteristic traits of English life. In comparison with the caste system of Germany, there is something about it refreshingly individual, free and spontaneous: the way up is open to every one, without too many formalities to hedge it round. But this purely social standard of values may assign a far higher worth to a vacuous individual who happens to have social claims than to a man of real merit, and, as a matter of fact, the old, pre-1832 aristocratic character of the State has been largely bolstered up, to this day, as a result. If a man wants to get on in politics, if he is concerned with some great economic project, if he seeks fame as inventor, producer or writer, the road is clear before him, as it was in the eighteenth century, on condition that he has a foothold in Society. The only change is that this is no longer the only door to success.

In politics, the influence of Society is still extremely powerful. Again and again, the weaving of the webs that lead to a party's taking up a new political cry, cause the fall of a Minister, put a new man into a Cabinet, or change the course of foreign policy, takes place over the dinner-table in some great country house, or at Cowes, Henley or Ascot. The monarchs dethroned in 1832 still rule to a large extent under new forms, and Society, which takes its tone from the aristocracy, and in the last resort from the King, is the modern sphere of their dominance. Up to 1832 they ruled by force and corruption, and relied upon fear and greed; to-day they rule through human vanity. And, all that is petty and contemptible apart, there remains, in this, something fine; it can hardly be said that America, the Anglo-Saxon country without an aristocratic Society, is superior to England. If, despite the scramble for profits that characterizes the mass mind, and despite all the democratic tendencies of the last generation. England is still the land of a tradition of decency and *noblesse oblige*, it has to thank an aristocracy, a land-owning class, whose influence has gone on though its political privileges have been taken from it. It has impressed on the whole nation the sound ideal of a certain comfortable ease which is undoubtedly a useful corrective to the nerve-destroying contemporary scramble for gold. It has given it the moral ideal of the gentleman which, though not perhaps the highest from an ethical point of view, does secure a high average level of moral conduct and provide certain useful safeguards for a people whose temperament contains a strong infusion of animalism of the Viking strain.

§ 2

Great Britain has long ceased to be an agricultural country. Of the employed population in 1921, only 7·8 per cent were occupied in agriculture, against 30·5 per cent in Germany: a percentage hardly greater than that of domestic servants, 7·5 per cent against 3·2 per cent in Germany. The main occupation is industry, which took 51·5 per cent against 41·4 in Germany, and trade, with 22·2 per cent against 16·5 per cent in Germany.

Sheep-farming has made Britain a textile country. The process was very gradual. Throughout the Middle Ages, English wool was taken in Hanseatic bottoms to Flanders, to return thence as Flemish cloth to England, merchanted as a rule by Hanseatic dealers. One of the periodic outbursts against the hitherto indispensable foreigner made England independent in this connexion in the time of Queen Elizabeth. Woollen-weaving – at first as a domestic industry, after the close of the eighteenth century in factories – became the characteristic English industry, especially after Irish competition had been killed about 1700 by protective duties and prohibitions. With the introduction of cotton-spinning and weaving about the end of the eighteenth century, cotton took its place by the side of wool, and from the beginning of the nineteenth was the staple industry. To-day, wool and worsted are centred in Bradford, cotton in Manchester, linen in Belfast, jute in Dundee.

So far as its wool goes, a practical independence of foreign supplies has been reached. South Africa and Australia are the greatest producers of raw wool in the world. Out of 3060·7 million pounds produced in the world in 1926, 1,355 millions were grown within the Empire. For raw cotton, on the other hand, dependence on the United States has grown more and more uncomfortable, decade by decade. The cutting off of cotton supplies during the American Civil War (1861–64) threatened to produce a national disaster. Energetic efforts have therefore been made to reduce this dependence. Almost the entire soil of Egypt has been sown with cotton, although the consequence is that the country has to import almost all its food supplies in British ships. In the Sudan, too, in Nigeria, Uganda and in India, the greatest efforts are made to create cotton-growing lands; Mesopotamia's possibilities in this connexion rank only second to its importance for the route to India as a motive in British foreign policy. Still, 955 out of the total importation of 1,584 million pounds in 1924, came from the United States. Although the cotton industry is far from being a monopoly, as it was a hundred years ago, it has no effective competitor in Europe. In the moist climate of England a thread of unsurpassable fineness can be produced, which is therefore England's monopoly. Coarser yarns are often introduced from abroad. The (1926) consumption of raw cotton, 3·02 million (1913: 4·27) bales, is surpassed only by that of the United States (6·395 million); it was nearly thrice that of Germany (1·148). The number of spindles (1926) 57·3 millions, was far ahead of any other country's; after a considerable gap, come the United States, with 37·6 million; Germany with 10·48, etc. The large number of spindles is not a very happy feature: it goes to show that the U.S.A. with a very much smaller number of spindles, can deal with a much larger amount of cotton, that therefore methods and organization must be far from satisfactory in England.

§ 3

Coal has made Britain economically a great power. Mining is one of the oldest industries; even in Celtic times, there were tin, silver and copper mines in Cornwall. The value of the native iron was early recognized; Sheffield and Birmingham steel goods were known in the Middle Ages, although, right down to the seventeenth century, fine work came from Germany, France, and Italy. But it was the coal of Lancashire, Yorkshire, Northumberland and South Wales that really revolutionized national economy. It was the discovery of steam power based on coal that enabled looms to be set up and driven in hitherto unimagined numbers all over the country. And with that, Britain's great hour was come. For now looms could be set up in the vicinity of the coal-fields, and since in Britain, – unlike other countries, notably Germany and America – the mines were near to the ports, the whole process of production, from the obtaining of the raw material to its transport as finished goods, could be concentrated in the smallest possible space and carried through at the lowest possible cost. Further, the capital required for the new industrial processes was available in abundance to the country of Indian trade. All factors combined to promote the development, between Liverpool and Newcastle, of an industrial region of maximum density of population and efficiency of output.

The sources of Britain's wealth lie in three major coal-fields: the first stretching from the Firth of Forth to the Firth of Clyde, taking in Fife, Lanark and Ayrshire; the second extending from the eastern spurs of the Pennines in Durham and Northumberland, across West Yorkshire and down to Staffordshire; thence continuing on to the third, which runs right down to the coasts of South Wales and seems to be in connexion with unexploited layers in Kent. Whether there is any effective extension of the Scottish coal-field into Ireland remains to be discovered. In many districts, notably in Ayr and Lanark, and at Cleveland in Yorkshire, iron deposits are in proximity to the coal. Nearly everywhere coal is easy to get at, so that coal-mining, which practically everywhere in the world is the monopoly of great concerns, has in England been largely carried on by diminutive firms, who under modern conditions are certainly doomed to failure.

The British coal-fields are probably inferior in extent to the German and certainly to the inexhaustible supplies in the North American continent. But they are worked to give a yield whose huge dimensions has often caused anxiety in the minds of geologists. The output in millions of metric tons, in 1925, was – Britain 247·1, and Germany 272·3; moreover the British output contains only the best hard coals (including the valuable ships' coal of the Cardiff basin), whereas, in Germany, rather more than half the output was the less valuable brown coal. In steel, the superiority of Britain is immense; measured in million metric tons, in 1925, British production was 10·3 against German 5·9 – before the war, the ratio was reversed – and even so, Britain could not meet its huge needs from its own production. Pig-iron production 6·4 million tons in 1925 – was below the German (10·1).

Thanks to the power of British coal, other British industries also have attained a world position. Thus in shipbuilding Britain long enjoyed a monopoly and still leads the world. Of the tonnage built in 1924 nearly two-thirds were launched there. Its greatest docks are situated at the mouth of the rivers Clyde and Tyne, while Belfast has the largest docks in the world (Harland and Wolff). Pottery is another very important industry: since Josiah Wedgwood founded his factories at Etruria, North Staffordshire has led in this. Sheffield is the centre of the cutlery trade: Birmingham of munition factories and all sorts of metal work; since the war there has been a rapid development in the fine chemicals and dyemaking industries.

§ 4

The mercantile marine developed, at first, relatively slowly. In the Middle Ages English ships hardly ventured beyond the Channel coasts and the wine lands of Bordeaux. They were vastly inferior to Genoese and Hanseatic enterprise. Its rise dates from the end of the sixteenth century, when England began to share in the Indian trade. Wealth came with supremacy over India, in the eighteenth century. Rise to economic supremacy followed the rise of industry under amazingly favourable conditions, including the absence of any Continental competitor. It was then that Liverpool became one of the first ports of the world. Commanding the swiftest access both to coal and goods, it displaced both Bristol and London, and became the real exporting centre of the country. The development of nine-teenth-century capitalism, however, raised London again, as against Liverpool. As trade took on specifically capitalist forms, and the tendency grew to sell goods before arrival in England either on ship-board, or even in the harbour of origin, and the time factor became more and more important in the sale of goods, and the raising of credits upon them, the centre shifted back to London, the time-honoured seat of British capital and the greatest market for every type of commodity. The British mercantile marine is one of the great mainstays of British economical power. In 1914, before the war, it comprised two-fifths of the world's tonnage, and even to-day, when the United States, under the pressure of the German submarine cam-paign, has developed the second trading fleet of the world, Britain still stands first with 19·4 million tons (1926): next, United States with 14·9: then Germany, 3·1. Britain also controls 51 per cent of the world's fishing fleet.

The principal British exports are cotton goods; then coal, iron and steel; then machinery and woollen goods. Coal is exceptionally important; not only on account of its value, but because of the indirect results of its exportation. It is shipped in the main not in great vessels but in tramps to every port in Europe and a great many out-side it. The tramp always gives cheap freightage home and so reduces the price of many goods that Britain needs. Many European countries (Italy, Holland, Norway, Denmark) depend wholly or mainly on British coal. During the war, Britain met the German submarine campaign by supplying coal only to the countries which in return would help it with imports, with the result that almost the whole neutral tonnage of the world was forced into its service. Very serious is it therefore for Britain that to-day the world is beginning to use less British coal. (Export of coal, 1913, 73 million tons: 1925, only 50 millions.) Since the raw fuel is everywhere to-day being economically used, it lasts longer; further, the competition of oil is beginning to be severely felt. In addition, the price of British coal is rising, as a consequence of uneconomic management of the mines. The result of all these factors is that the greatest British industry has begun to work at a loss. The grave mining lock-out of 1926 was a result of this critical position.

Besides these visible exports, the invisible export of gold and credit has become, more and more, the dominating factor in the economic activities of Britain. Thanks to the fact that the interest on British capital lent to foreign countries runs into enormous figures, Britain can afford to pay for its enormous import of raw materials, and also of finished goods. British finance, the reputation enjoyed by London of being the place where the reliable merchant can count on easy and cheap credit facilities, the home of non-speculative and therefore absolutely safe banking, has made London the financial centre of the world ever since the eighteenth century. It has behind it the most efficient firms in the world and the strongest trade connexions. Nowhere in the world is it so easy to exchange goods for money. Since, moreover, London has connexions with traders everywhere, in every department, a good bill on London is equal to cash all over the world. The war has broken London's monopoly with regard to places on the American Continent, where New York has displaced it. But its position in Europe is practically unchanged. So long as London is in a Free Trade country and New York lies behind one of the highest tariff walls of the world, all goods will be much more easily marketable in England than in America.

§ 5

With the advent of trade and industry, a new type of man came to the front. The agents of economic progress were Puritans, men who fought with grim earnestness for the Kingdom of God upon earth, and, likewise, for their millions. They were men for whom property was something sacred, since a blessing upon His servants' earthly strivings was the sure sign of God's grace. Too much luxury and comfort was a danger to the soul. Religion permitted, nay, encouraged, the amassing of money, but enjoined caution in spending it. But the Christian altar was in perilous proximity to the Golden Calf. Every higher branch of culture, literature and the arts was stigmatized as profane. There was the Church, and there was property – that was all. Hardly surprising, therefore, to find the Puritan of the seventeenth and eighteenth centuries reappearing as the exponent of a soulless capitalism in the thinnest of Christian masks.[6]

In the seventeenth century this middle class had fought for its religion, and sent King Charles I to the block. Sufficient proof, here, of the formidable religious excitement of the time, and of the tremendous energy with which Cromwell was able to infuse his countrymen: for, naturally, the middle class is far from warlike. Fighting is the recreation of the aristocracy: from the Middle Ages down to the World War, the middle class avoided military service as far as possible. Whenever it could, it hired foreign mercenaries to fight its battles. Irishmen were willing recruits, but force and fraud were required to press the lower and middle-class Englishman into the army, throughout the eighteenth century. Nor does the spell of the sea extend much farther than the population of the seaboard. The average Englishman dwelt in his towns, enjoying a degree of comfort and even luxury that astonished the world outside, even in the sixteenth century, to all appearance clear of higher interests, until he was seized by Puritanism. His first ventures on the sea came after 1570, when he saw that there was something to be made there, and could cast a Christian cloak over his piratical raids on the Spanish silver argosies. Always, the English middle class has inclined to a base and soulless Utilitarianism. While an aristocrat, like Lord Shaftesbury, revived the study of Plato, and regarded æsthetic contemplation as the highest activity of the mind, the English bourgeoisie, the middle classes, – still conscious in the eighteenth century of Puritan descent, – worked out a dry, rationalist philosophy, in so far as it professed anything of the sort, for the genuine Puritan abjured philosophy altogether, as potentially dangerous to the soul, and of no value on the Stock Exchange. The English bourgeois found, in his chapel, a service of inconceivable bareness, and a sort of consecration of his energetic will and robust self-esteem. For the rest, he made money and eschewed all 'vague generalities' like literature, art, philosophy and music. His typical representative is the Utilitarian, Jeremy Bentham (1748–1832) – a man of penetrating intelligence, a brilliant jurist and fearless reformer, whose arid soul measured every action of the individual or the State merely according to whether it was or was not useful and how great the number of individuals to whom its utility could extend. For the utilitarian philosopher himself, utility might possess an ethical content; but it was natural enough that the great mass of the middle class, with absolutely no interest in philosophy, should translate utility into low, tangible and purely materialistic terms at a time when the increase of his banking account was the supreme ideal of human effort conceivable by the English arrivist.[7]

The discovery of steam power, at the turn of the century, opened up to such men the possibility of an immeasurable increase in wealth; the political transformation of the Revolutionary epoch enabled them, in 1832, to achieve political power. And Free Trade, as preached about this time by the Glasgow professor Adam Smith (1723–90), gave them an ideal which put an ethical gloss on their naked urge for money-making. The golden age seemed to be ushered in, when each individual was free to exercise his native energy in the economic sphere, unhampered by any restriction, State or other, and Free Trade with the whole world allowed him to cast the product of his efficiency on all markets. For the unrestricted expenditure of human energies must of necessity call out every latent power in each individual and, at the same time, draw the bonds between nations so close that economic conflicts and murderous war must be unthinkable, in the future. Away, therefore, with all domestic restrictions, all official price fixings, all supervision over the individual, all class privileges and distinctions: away, in foreign policy, with all tariffs, wars, and militarisms. For half a century the English middle class held high the banner of this ideal. It supplied dynamic energy for the mighty transformation of the whole life of the State that occupied the first half of the nineteenth century, and for the gigantic Free Trade propaganda that made Britain the protagonist of modern Liberalism all over the world. But the first effects of the removal of all restrictions at home was to unleash a frightful selfishness. The first-fruits of the new Gospel of the unlimited freedom of the employer were the horrors of child employment in factories about 1820, with children of seven years of age working fourteen or even sixteen hours, and men too old at forty-five: and the slums of the new industrial towns, where, down to this day, a wretched pariah race hides its rags in horrible holes and corners. The new capitalist had the power to force the poorest of the poor into barracks without air or light: there were no by-laws, then, to stop him.

This belief in the universal blessedness of economic freedom was severely shaken by the revealing work of men like Carlyle, Dickens, Kingsley and Ruskin. To-day no party stands for absolute freedom, in this sense. But, in his heart of hearts, the British trader and industrialist is still an individualist, and very much dislikes having to accommodate himself to a world which limits his freedom through officials and inspectors, factory codes and health regulations. The characteristic forms of modern capitalist economy, above all the impersonal business, in the shape of the Joint Stock Company, with limited liability, were first worked out in England. Nevertheless, no country has struggled so hard against the absolutism of this principle. The individual employer, operating on a considerable scale with his own capital or that of his family and friends, is still extremely general: the man who obstinately refuses to part with personal control over his business for the sake of securing greater gain thereby. In the same way, the great banking amalgamations have not crowded out the small and moderate-sized bank with personal relations to customers who are individually known to the banker; it still survives in England, though it has been pushed very much into the background on the Continent. Coal production, the most capitalistic branch of industry all over the world, is thinkable in England alone in the hands of small firms with very little capital and consequently very little success. Trusts and combines were fought against, as long as possible. Up to 1910 there was no English shipping line comparable in size with the two great German groups. The pressure of war, with its elimination of superfluous competition and transformation of nearly every department of industry into a gigantic trust under State control, was required to bring about a change over from individual to collective management in industry, banking and shipping.

The Puritan individualist, at once avaricious and pious, appears in other departments of English business life. The merchant and industrialist are still pious and honourable, and severely conscientious in all their dealings. Men of action, occupied, strictly, with making money; realists, they are almost totally devoid of understanding of intellectual life and almost as blank in the domain of the arts as were their Puritan forebears of the sixteenth and seventeenth centuries. But – and here we come upon a vital point, often overlooked by the Continental observer – there has been no such complete development of the pious business man as in the United States, where the only effective counterpoise to the immediacy of the hunt for the dollar is a smattering of Puritan religious ideas. In Britain, the trader, for all his materialism, shows a certain approach to the heroic ideal placed before him by the land-owning magnate. His final object is that of the landed proprietor-power. For the bigger men in trade and industry, the making of money is but the method, most readily available to their caste, of becoming in their own sphere such a kinglet as the landlord is in his. Often the manufacturer will crown a successful industrial career by becoming a peer, and end his days as a landed proprietor. Failing to reach these heights, he will lord it over his own people, in superior luxury and display, working hard, but not so hard as to wear himself out.[8] Always the Englishman has set his face against any vulgar notion of earning for earning's sake, any banausic work for work's sake. Manufacturer or merchant must have time for sport, within limits; plays his game of golf, requires a good dinner, and spends his evenings with his family or in social gatherings. Just as the squire regards it as obvious that he should take his part in local government and, if possible, get into Parliament, so the well-to-do manufacturer becomes, as a matter of course, an alderman or member of one or other of the countless urban councils, and often enough goes into the House. The sense of mastery and the consideration given by such positions are worth more, for him, than the loss of time and money which they cost; he is, indeed, pleased to meet the very heavy financial contributions which any sort of entry into public life exacts; he, too, accepts the *noblesse oblige* of the aristocrat. His aim in life is a position of dignity, distinction and consideration. True, wealth is desired; the average man may regard it not as means to an end, but, to a large extent, as an end in itself; but where there is a choice between wealth and position, position wins every time. Hence the British business man is not too keen to risk his position by entering on chancy enterprises. The average man, here, is altogether without the megalomaniac audacity of the American, and, to a large extent, of the German, trader. Whether or no he has inherited his position from his father, he likes safety in business. He has grown up to the view that trade with more or less undeveloped countries outside will bring him a sound profit without any very great risks. He objects, quite generally, to any methods of doing business that are not perfectly straight: dislikes excessive advertisement, or the capture of a market by means of price-cutting campaigns or dumping. And his objection to such competitive methods is not the fact that they contract his own profits, but that they offend his feelings as a gentleman. The London Exchange is a kind of aristocratic club, open only to a few select, and the doubtful industrial adventurer never enters its door. The British merchant has imposed capitalism upon the world. At the same time, he has raised himself from a tradesman to a gentleman, and averts his eyes from the results of the system he has himself developed. He sees, everywhere, unfair competition, reducing his own profits. He does not see that the day is past when half Europe, the whole of Asia and America, were demanding goods from Europe, and Britain alone was in a position to supply their needs: the day when immense returns could be earned by prudent business, carried on on decent, traditional lines, and making only moderate demands on time and energy. For him, the German competitor was not only a rival but an unfair rival. Thanks to his complete ignorance of economic developments, he saw the German, working longer hours and harder, studying his markets and meeting the wishes of his customers, giving longer credits and satisfying himself with a more modest rate of profit, as suddenly popping up as a competitor whose dirty methods justified the employment of any and every expedient against him.

The character of the middle-class merchant and industrialist stamped itself on the World War as on British warfare in general. From the eighteenth century on, Continental jurisprudence recognized war as a form of military and political struggle. The destruction of the enemy army, and of the enemy's political power was the end in view, and all economic measures against the enemy population justifiable in so far as they subserved this end; they were never ends in themselves, but merely means to the attainment of military ends. After the ruthless plunderings and massacres of the Thirty Years' War, an effort was made to develop on the Continent a new conception of warfare, distinguishing as sharply as possible between combatants and non-combatants. English theory – as well as practice – always opposed this conception, and took the economic destruction of the enemy to be as much part of the end of war as the political. The development of a code of naval warfare was opposed, and the attempt to establish the immunity of private property at sea always rejected. During the war, the economic possessions of the enemy were ruthlessly destroyed – it was openly avowed that one of the ends of war consisted in this. German businesses were not merely suspended for the duration, but for ever annihilated, and the object aimed at, in bringing other small and remote states into the war, was to extend this destruction throughout the world.

§ 6

The two bases of English economy hitherto, *private enterprise* without State interference, and *Free Trade*, have been seriously shaken by the aftermath of war. Inevitably, in England as elsewhere, the State was bound to take over the functions of the individual concern in war time. Since there was a shortage of shipping, only absolutely essential raw materials might be imported. Since there was a shortage of labour, only absolutely necessary works might be undertaken, and the State decided what work was necessary and what not. Industrial peace was essential, therefore the State fixed wages, hours, profits, prices and rents. Business individualism accepted war conditions very unwillingly, and could hardly wait for the day when the fetters were removed. Not so the workers: war-time conditions had given them a sort of State Socialism which they would gladly have retained. Moreover, when individual enterprise was restored after the war, business found it could not make things pay: trade did not revive. The whole world was impoverished. Great regions like Germany, Russia and Austria, which had been Britain's best customers, either passed out of the picture altogether or, thanks to depreciated currencies, began to offer unprecedentedly severe competition. During the war, new industries had been set up in Canada, Australia, South Africa, Spain, France and India in lines which had been British specialities (cotton-spinning, coal-mining and engineering). British exports showed the strain; under the pressure of post-war prices, home consumption proved much less elastic than had been hoped. A vast burden of unemployment (1921, 2·6: end of 1928, 1·3 million persons) weighed upon the country. The remedy for these economic distresses seemed to lie along the lines of drastic industrial Rationalization – which spelt, in practice, in the first instance reduction of wages and then a combination or grouping of individual businesses which probably would eliminate many workmen as superfluous. The workers – who did well during the war – naturally sprang to arms in resistance of any reduction of their standard of life, and went so far as to declare a General Strike (May, 1926) which however was a complete failure, since the miners, whom it was called to support, were defeated as the outcome of the protracted lock-out of the same year (May–December, 1926), and had to accept longer hours and lower wages. Combination and amalgamation of industrial units is now going on at an accelerating rate. This tendency was already noticeable before the war. With new industries, like the dyeing industry, founded during its course, this happened from the start; the same sort of organization has recently been adopted (1926) in the anthracite industry. There is even also a loose association of all the main industrial interests in the shape of the Federation of British Industries.

Even in a country as highly individualist as England, the formation of these huge Trusts, with their immense powers, is forcing the problem of State control to the front. The time has gone by when the State left all economic matters, on principle, to the individual to settle. During the war, the State had begun to participate in all sorts of undertakings planned with a view to future eventualities, based on war conditions, and designed to promote new industries after war was over – for instance, it took a hand in the new British Dye Stuffs Corporation which was to prevent the Germans from re-establishing their monopoly of dyes; in the Anglo-Persian Oil Company (existing since 1909); and in the Imperial Airways Company (1924); it gave British firms export credit insurance under the Exports Credit scheme of 1920 and the Trade Facilities Act of 1921; in 1915 a Committee (of the Privy Council) for Scientific and Industrial Research was set up to establish State research institutions or assist what was being done in this direction by industry itself; subsidies were given to local authorities for the building of dwelling-houses; a temporary sub-vention was granted to the coal-mining industry (1925–26), while the 1926 Royal Commission on the Coal-Mines recommended measures for the unification of the industry and the establishment of selling agencies, and that presided over by Mr. Justice Sankey (1919) even went so far as to recommend Nationalization of the mines. Under the new Electricity Act (1926) all electricity undertakings are to be grouped into large units on a geographical basis; the supply of current confined to a certain number of power stations, and the entire organization subject to the control of a single supervising authority which is to eliminate un-economic competition. In 1921 the railways were grouped into four great systems, non-competitive with one another, under State control of rates and wages. These things represent no inconsiderable progress in the direction of a unified national economic system, of a character that would have been thought inconceivable not so very long ago. They point to a new type of State, which, instead of standing apart and on high above millions of individual units in the old Manchester sense, organizes, controls and supervises economic life, composes its struggles and, possibly, indicates its goal.

Will this new national economic system of the future also seek to build itself in behind tariff walls? It looks as though the idea of Free Trade was fast losing ground. When England adopted Free Trade, it was the only country in the world with a strong and developed industry; if it could impose the new idea universally, the result would spell universal victory for itself. This hope was not realized; on the contrary, tariff walls rose higher and higher, and behind them, powerful industries grew up in Germany, France and the United States, which limited England's industrial expansion. Then came the war; and the new States of its creation are all bent on building up their own industries behind tariff walls. Has the time not come for saving what may still be saved, and endeavouring at least to hold the Empire together behind a tariff wall of its own? (see p. 86). England is still far from accepting Protection in principle; its old adversaries, the raw material interests are against it, as are great trading groups, shipping, insurance and banking circles, and the great mass of the working class. But there are Protectionist minorities already within all these groups. Protectionist ideas have largely captured the new free peasant class; an increased customs revenue presents itself as a possible means of reducing taxes; both employers and employed are beginning to have second thoughts. If workers, at a time of falling trade, are to maintain the higher standard of life won during the war, if the dangerous unemployment percentage is to sink, then England must make sure of the share of the world market that is still left to it. Australian and American example seems to prove that high wages and high profits can only be combined behind a tariff wall. This argument in many circles begins to outweigh everything that can be said upon the other side. The disquietude caused by the renewal of German competition goes hand in hand with patriotic concern about the Colonies to commend protective duties. Duties openly directed against German trade were prepared in 1915 by Reginald McKenna when Chancellor of the Exchequer, and introduced after the war ($33\frac{1}{3}$ per cent *ad valorem* on films, clocks, automobiles, tyres and musical instruments); removed in 1924 by Philip Snowden as part of the policy of the MacDonald Government, they were reimposed by Baldwin's Chancellor, Winston Churchill, and extended by a duty on silk. The Safeguarding of Industries Act (1921) further imposes a $33\frac{1}{3}$ per cent *ad valorem* duty on a number of individual commodities belonging to the most important of the so-called (wartime) Key Industries – optical and other scientific instruments, electrical and chemical articles, compass needles, etc., as well as on 'dumped' goods. Since 1925 it has been open to industries which on their own showing are exposed to 'exceptional' or 'unfair' competition, to ask for a duty and after examination of their claim by a tribunal to have it presented to Parliament for acceptance. A series of exceptions to the Protectionist system thus gradually built up has been introduced for the benefit of the Colonies, with the view of creating something like an Imperial tariff union. The results, under this head, are however paltry. True, since 1919, the duties on tea, cocoa, coffee, dried fruits, sugar goods, tobacco, wine and spirits have been materially reduced in favour of the Colonies, but this is all. Another measure, the partial lifting of the burdens imposed by the McKenna duties and the Safeguarding duties in favour of the Colonies, has a merely theoretic significance, since none of the Colonies is an exporter of industrial products. Every effort on the part of the Colonies, and notably of Australia, to secure a preferential duty on the articles of importance to it, like wheat and meat has failed so far, though many Conservatives, and particularly Baldwin would be glad to grant this in principle, because the preliminary condition is the introduction by England of a protective duty on articles of universal consumption for food. Snowden, Chancellor of the Exchequer in the Labour Government of 1924, actually reduced various Customs duties on which the Colonies were receiving preferential treatment, and no success has so far crowned any of Baldwin's efforts to do more to meet the wishes of the Colonies.

§ 7

The awful misery which Manchesterism brought to the factory worker led to the creation of a labour movement in England, which has set a third human type, the industrial worker, over against the landlord and the entrepreneur, and risen to be a dangerous and even a victorious adversary of the old individualistic state. After the workers had won the right of combination in 1824 and 1825 by a series of wholly and semi-revolutionary movements, they proceeded to build their Trade Unions into a state within the State, and one with an increasing power of bending society to its will. Individually weak and timid, the proletarians bound themselves into associations that grew steadily both in size and in importance. The Trade Union gave

the individual substantial support in time of sickness or any other
difficulty, and served, at the same time, as a weapon for exacting
steadily improving conditions from the employers, through strikes
or threats of strikes. The system rested upon a combination of
benefits and the strike. The prospect of immediate advantages
enabled the Union to induce even the least responsive spirits among
the workers to pay contributions by no means small, and these massed
contributions enabled them to hold out in the event of a strike. At
the same time, any strike might exhaust the benefit funds, within a
few weeks, and so leave no resources to meet the specific object for
which they had been collected. There were, thus, grave risks attached
to any strike, and, as time went on, the tendency grew to secure,
through negotiations with the employer and the mere threat of
coming out, all that might have been accomplished by a strike itself.
So serious a matter obviously could not be left to the blind passion
of the workers in any given local factory. The Unions, therefore,
began to organize in district and national associations, and the tendency was more and more to put the control over finance and the
employment of the perilous strike weapon into the hands of the
national executives. A bureaucracy was thus built up, consisting of
efficient, far-sighted workmen, elected by their comrades, and, in
their turn, exercising a practically dictatorial power over their constituents. In this machinery, the individual is nothing. He is compelled to join the Union and to pay contributions at a high rate or fall
out of employment: he has his vote in the election of the Trade Union
machine, and in the declaration and calling off of a strike. But he
must obey the order of the Union calling him to down tools; if he
disobeys, and is turned out of his Union, he forfeits all his hardly-
won claims to benefit. The scale of wages agreed on with the
employer is not fixed between the latter and the individual workman,
but between him and the Trade Union General Secretary. This same
secretary has to settle the thousand and one minor conflicts within the
factory, arising out of the fixation of piece-work price lists, the introduction of fresh machinery, and the dismissal of inefficient or
recalcitrant workers. To-day the Unions have a membership of
5·2 millions (1926): just after the war actually 8·1 millions. They are
organized in great national industrial groups, further united by
mutual arrangements; thus, for a time, there was a Triple Alliance
between the miners, railwaymen and transport workers, the three
strongest Unions in the country. In addition, every industrialized

area has the various local Trade Union branches organized into a Trades Council (since 1860). So, the time would not seem far distant when these labour associations can impose their will on the entire community. They are almost unassailable, thanks to the fact that the élite of the workers belong to them, and their effective power is safeguarded from any legal attachment through the provision (1906) by which strike funds, inasmuch as they are, at the same time, sick and unemployment benefit funds, cannot be made liable in costs for any damages inflicted on an employer by a strike. This enormous power has been somewhat reduced but not seriously weakened by recent legislation. After the collapse of the great strike of 1926, the Trade Disputes and Trade Unions Act of 1927 made the General Strike illegal, made picketing more difficult, and the enlistment of State employees into the General Unions impossible; but it left their main power unaltered.

The employers resisted the growth of this state within the State with the utmost energy and the most ruthless violence. They often succeeded in breaking individual strikes, but the movement, as a whole, has gone on over their heads. To understand the bitterness of this conflict, it must be recognized as one between fundamentally opposed views of social organization. The employers represent the modern, individualistic State, democratic in outward form, and the belief that the Reform Act of 1832, and its subsequent legislation, had swept the privileged classes and corporations out of the saddle. But the contemporaneous rise of freedom of association (1824-25) represented the development, within this free State, of a thoroughly reactionary form, a revival of the mediæval feudalistic and corporate State, with all its drawbacks. True, the external form of the workman's organization is modern, in so far as power is rooted in the masses. But it is altogether mediæval, if the workmen seek to establish a just, standard wage, which is to be paid, by every factory, regardless of differences in its profits (the Miners' abortive strike of 1921, for instance, was an effort to establish a National pool and so a National standard wage for all British miners). Mediæval, too, is their desire to secure to the craftsman in any trade a practical monopoly. They compel the unfortunate employer who seeks to have some simple machine defect put right by a couple of casual workers, to hold up the whole works for twenty-four hours until the engineer can be fetched to whom the job 'belongs'; since it is the unpardonable sin against Labour to 'take a man's job from him.' Mediæval, again, is the refusal to permit non-Unionists to work in a factory or shop, while, at the same time, regarding the Union as an instrument for extracting the best possible conditions for a more or less strongly placed minority of workers. Demarcation disputes of various kinds frequently hamper the introduction of a new industry: either there are not enough workers of the 'proper' category, or they have to be taken out of various categories, and each disputes the right of the others to employment. Wholly mediæval too, is the effort to secure a given fixed minimum wage, not merely for women and children, who may require a certain degree of legislative protection, but for adult males. This effort has been entirely successful: in 1909 the workers of some sweated industries accomplished the minimum wage; in 1912, the miners; 1917 and 1925, a large number of agricultural workers; 1921, the railwaymen. About half of the British workmen are at present in receipt of minimum wages. Analogous to this is the attempt, successfully made by the Unions since 1884, to compel Government Departments and local authorities to accept a fair wages clause; in other words, to bind themselves to give contracts only to firms who pay the rates recognized by the Unions. The Trade Union Secretary intervenes in every relation between capital and labour, with prescriptions and often with threats. Even genuinely humanitarian efforts to improve the workers' lot, like profit sharing, meet with energetic Trade Union opposition, since special local arrangements between capital and labour, which may detach those who are advantaged by them from the sphere of Trade Union control, may be dangerous to their efficiency. This is a spirit absolutely antagonistic to the time-honoured individualism of the British industrialist. So far, the honours of the fight have been with the workers. Here and there, Trades Unionism has met with heavy defeats. Their General Strike of 1926 ended in complete disaster. But, by and large, the spirit of industrial organization has gained steadily. A new State is arising, which puts all industrial undertakings under the supervision of the State, regulates the wages as well as the conditions of labour, replaces strikes by arbitration and draws a very large part of the employers' profits into the coffers of the State.

Very slowly, thanks to his Trade Union organization, the worker has become an effective member of the State. His upward march, here, was very gradual. Before the Trade Unions were formed, the great body of industrial workers were merely the masses. To a large extent they have remained the masses, dominated by dimly apprehended instincts of love and hate, capable of formidable, momentary achievements, and heroic self-sacrifice; but incapable, so far, of long views, incapable of action directed to a settled purpose, incapable of seeing themselves as responsible members of society. In the Trade Unions, however, a certain number of effective leaders have arisen, above the mass: men who possess the qualities lacking, as yet, to the many: men of longer vision, able to plan, to organize, and to rule, men who may grow to the point of seeing themselves and their class as part of the great State organism. The worker owes it to his Trade Unions that men of his class have formed a government (in 1924). They have broadened the basis on which the social pyramid rests. The old State, before 1832, was an aristocratic class State. The opposition that developed in the eighteenth century, thanks to Indian trade, shifted it, by incorporating the trade magnates and their posterity within its ranks. After 1832, it was a dualistic class State, in which control was shared between the nobles and the capitalist bourgeoisie. The Trade Union movement has now brought the upper section of the labouring mass in, as a living member of the whole organism. Not that there has been anything of conscious planning in this development, nor has it proceeded peaceably. Just as the bourgeoisie, in its day, wrested a share of political power in the teeth of violent opposition, so the Trade Unions reached their aim only after constant embittered struggles. Again, like that of the bourgeoisie, they, too, pushed their upper section up into the ruling circle at the price of sacrificing the demands of the mass. In 1830, the Radical bourgeoisie claimed to voice the opposition of the nation as a whole. In 1832, when its upper section had been admitted to a share of power, it was satisfied, felt that it was a pillar of the State, and drew a sharp line of demarcation between itself and the masses, still excluded from the franchise. The workers, in their turn, demanded political power and sanitary conditions for the whole of their class. In practice, however, all that happened was that, between 1820 and 1890, these goals were achieved by the upper sections of the working class, which, then, were on the whole satisfied. The Trade Unions did not take in the totality of workers, but only the upper ranks among them, relatively well paid, and gradually passing into a higher social status: their leaders had, indeed, been workers, but grew to belong, mentally and spiritually, wholly to the lower middle class. This upper section, standing between the bourgeoisie and the proletariate, gradually became conservative. It disliked strikes, since they might jeopardize all that had been won. So, despite all the fine talk about the solidarity of labour, the gulf between them and the real proletariate, the unskilled workers, became more and more evident. In the great London Docks strike of 1889, the voice of the hitherto unorganized masses made itself heard, uttering demands not only of society, but of the Trade Union leadership of the day, which seemed to the dispossessed to be slack and tainted with bourgeois mentality. Such a revolt on the part of the fifth estate is, obviously, just as dangerous as Chartism was, and as every mass movement has been, at every time. It can only be overcome by repression through sheer force, or by taking its own upper section up into the ruling circles. Since the expulsion of the Stuarts, there has been a constant broadening of the social basis of England. The question to-day is whether, once more, the heads of the mass of the fifth estate can be cut off by enlisting its hitherto absolutely Radical leaders in positive co-operation.

Since 1889 the masses have been in ferment, but the Trade Union leaders were always able to keep their hold over them, until the World War came, with the necessity of increased production. Co-operation had got to be secured on the part of workers by no means enthusiastic about the war and thoroughly indisposed to give a bigger output, if the result was to fill the employers' pockets. Lloyd George met them so far as to impose taxation high enough to divert the greater part of superfluous profits into the coffers of the State. At the same time he insisted on a suspension of all strikes and of Trade Union restrictions. Every man and every woman was to be put to work, whether or no members of Trade Unions. Munitions supply – in the widest sense of the word – was no longer to be the privileged job of certain Unions, with meticulous regulations on the number of apprentices, unskilled workers and women, and strict maintenance of the historic rights of each craft to its particular process: a vast supply had got to be produced by all means and at all speed. All at once, the privileged, skilled worker, who had hitherto been in unchallenged supremacy, became the exception; under dilution, the factories were flooded by a tide of unskilled workers, mostly women. At a stroke, the whole body of Trade Union regulations, the fruit of three generations of struggle and sacrifice, regarded by the skilled man as his Magna Charta, was swept aside – in the interest of winning the war. The process cost severe dislocations. Strikes could be penalized and forbidden, but not prevented. Grave disturbances on the Clyde and in South Wales, in 1916 and 1917, showed the seething bitterness bred in the workers by the fact that capitalist profiteering was going on gaily, despite the Excess Profits Tax, while their own cherished privileges had been swept away. Real patriotism was shown by the Trade Union leaders who sacrificed their rights on the altar of the country, in this crisis of its fate. But in doing so, they have brought on a new crisis. To a large extent they lost their dominant position within the working class, and made it easy for the vast unruly masses that now filled the factories to sweep the quieter spirits with them in wild wages demands, unauthorized by the leaders. Even the more level-headed sections among the workers began to be influenced by French Syndicalist and German Socialist ideas, of the most revolutionary character.

Genuine statesmanship was shown in the fact that, while the war was still on, the Prime Minister and certain influential industrial leaders addressed themselves to the task of utilizing the principles of this new movement to build up a new system governing the relations of employers and employed. To the industrialists, it seemed to be a favourable opportunity for breaking the power of the Trade Unions – minds in both camps clearly saw that after the war it would be impossible to revert to pre-war conditions entirely – and try to build the new society on a new basis. The new principle was suggested by the working, inside the same factory, of organized and unorganized workers. Further, the great systems of State Insurance, Old Age Pensions in 1909, and Unemployment and Health Insurance in 1911, in so far as they had diverted large parts of the previous activities of Trade Unions to the charge of the State, held out the possibility of making Trade Union organization less indispensable to the workmen in the future. At the same time, anyone who knew anything of politics was perfectly aware that there was no possibility of restoring the old patriarchal relations of obedient employee and dictatorial employer. Such were the premises out of which grew the Report of the Committee presided over by Mr. J. H. Whitley in the beginning of 1917. Its main idea was to give to Works Councils (composed of the non-organized workers and organized Trade Unionists belonging to all Unions represented in the establishment) the opportunity of adjusting wages and all disputes arising out of them, in conjunction with the employers – i.e. in place of the Trade Unions. These Works Councils, in their turn, were to create the feeling, in the workers, that instead of working for their employers, they are working with them. In the first instance, they may well prove a nuisance, and create new friction, since they are, in the first instance, representative of the unintelligent mass. As time goes on, however, it is assumed that leaders will develop from among Unionists and non-Unionists, i.e. the fourth and fifth estates, capable of co-operating in industrial leadership. The Works Councils are designed as the basis of a structure of collateral organizations of employers and employed.

The war had put the State, for the time being, in control over the whole supply of raw materials, and over the entire labour supply, and at the same time converted individualistically controlled private firms into great Trusts, under governmental supervision. It might be possible to continue them, in a modified form, and develop new organizations of a whole industry: Joint Industrial Councils, composed of representatives of Employers' Associations on the one side and of the employed on the other, to regulate working conditions and serve as official advisers to the State in all industrial questions. The right to strike is not abolished, but a law of 1919 (Industrial Courts Act) gives the Minister of Labour the power to intervene to bring a great proportion of industrial disputes before a court composed of representatives of employers and employed.

It is too soon to say how far the Whitley Councils prefigure the new social organization of the future. So far, owing to opposition from many employers and also from Trade Unions, which see them as threatening their own power, they have only been partially established, for the most part in minor industries, and, in the main, only function locally. At the same time, the main line of development is clear enough. Although for the moment the failure of the General Strike and of the coal-mining dispute of 1926 seemed to have left the old-fashioned individualist employer on top, there is a marked tendency to a more concentrated type of organization and the supersession of the old industrial autocracy. Inside the Conservative Party the movement is slow. Here the old ways are still very strongly entrenched. But the more advanced spirits look to the association of employers in large combines, partly of a kind with State participation, partly purely private – such employers' associations then to treat with the parallel organizations of workers. It is on these lines that Lord Melchett (Sir Alfred Mond) has recently been negotiating with the General Council of the Trade Union Congress (1928). On the Liberal side, too, there is undoubtedly readiness for large measures of reform; here indeed, more insistent voices are audible: for instance there is energetic opposition to the idea that the landlord has a prescriptive right to ground-rents. In the Labour Party, again, there are two currents of opinion. As to the broad general aim – the establishment of a thoroughly organized and organic State, in which the worker has his fair share – there is complete unity. On methods, however, there is difference. There is a right wing which would make terms for the moment with capitalism, demanding merely State protection against unemployment, high wages and heavy taxes on the possessing classes, in order to finance far-reaching schemes of social betterment; and toys with the notion of guaranteeing such a system by high protection. This group more or less accepts the Australian Labour programme. At the farthest remove from it stands the extreme left which looks only to the dictatorship of the proletariate, on the Moscow plan. Between them is the great body of the party, with its programme of progressive socialization.

§ 8

The mind of the industrial workmen of to-day is a strange medley of modern and mediæval elements. In his robust claims to comfort and pleasure, he is a definitely modern creature, a man of here and now. He can calculate, pretty exactly, the purchasing power of his wage, and its movement up and down. He shares with his fellow-denizen of the big city, the employer, quickness and mobility and swift responsiveness to any and every sort of baseless panic. But he is far less capitalist in mind than his master. Money, for him, is not an end in itself, but a means to an end: as a rule, the satisfaction of some quite primitive instinct – drink in so far as he is not influenced by the strong Temperance movement, the cinema, a noisy ride in a motor-car or steamer. For him, the struggle for money is ennobled by the struggle for the simple, natural enjoyment of life, as, for his employer, by the effort after consideration and influence. The love of power, one of the outstanding characteristics of modern man, hardly developed in him until the present generation. He is good natured, his individualism being mainly negative, and expressed rather in a desire to be left alone than to impose his will upon others. Nor is the contrary demonstrated even by the tense obstinacy with which he throws himself into a strike, since the workman is invariably convinced, with an often child-like *naïveté*, that he is being attacked. (The industrial *Conquistador* is a phenomenon that only appears, among the more advanced sections, in the last two decades, under the influence of French Syndicalist propaganda.) His understanding of money is limited to its translation into immediate needs: he has little head for thrift or management, even when his wages permit such. Like most small folk, he has little or no power of grasping sums beyond those he is accustomed to handle himself, and feels an almost boundless confidence in the financial capacity of his employer and the State. The strenuous resistance he offers to every attempt, real or imagined, to limit his independence, in no way diminishes his instinctive belief in the old class hierarchy. His tendency to blame the wicked employer for everything he does not like arises out of a tenacious, if subconscious belief that the State and the employer are the guardians of the welfare of the worker. Class consciousness, however vigorous its expression at a given moment, is not natural to him; at heart, he is only a rather discontented *petit bourgeois*, enchanted by a smile from a nobleman, and finding a sort of personal satisfaction and even a personal participation in the glamour of rank and wealth. There is a hidden but constant conflict, therefore, between this instinctive snobbery of his and the idealism of the contemporary Labour movement. For his class, the British workman is ready to make any sacrifice of time, comfort, and money: his Union contributions represent an enormous sacrifice, laid on the altar of the class idea: without a murmur, he will produce vast sums for the support of a strike on the part of some other group of workers; however hard-up he is, he will do without, for himself, in order to come to the aid of the widow and children of a comrade. With truly mediæval *naïveté*, he peoples the world with men either perfectly good or perfectly bad: witness any popular family newspaper, any cinema in a working-class suburb: and this black and white division to him practically coincides with the division into workers and exploiters. His political instincts are absolutely simple and primitive. While suspicious of noisy patriotism, he shares with other Britons the proud sense of *civis Romanus sum*. During the World War, the majority of the working class showed a readiness to sacrifice themselves for their country no whit inferior to that of any other class. Small trace of modern International feeling is to be discerned in him. Only in the last generation has he been affected by modern materialism, either in thought or action. The older men still read their Bible, and are strict in matters of conduct. They are apt to belong to some Nonconformist denomination, whose primitive Christianity satisfies their child-like religious sense. At the same time, the Puritan aversion from this world hardly appears in them – a point of differentiation from the class above them. One has but to observe the British workman on Bank Holiday, giving himself up to a frank enjoyment of boisterous pleasures, unmelodious noises and a good-natured, primitive love-making very reminiscent of his Germanic ancestors, whether on Hampstead Heath, or in the gallery of some music-hall or cinema, to realize how far he is from submitting to the drab ideal of Puritan respectability and self-control that confines the middle classes. Proud as he may be of his school education and attendance at some University Extension course or other, he still retains the lively temper and keen sensations of an earlier world.

But about the turn of the century, and notably after the great wave of unrest that began in 1911 and did not die down completely even during the war, the workers began to reveal a challenging aggressiveness, the lack of which had previously been the specific mark of the British proletarian. The younger generation is almost wholly aloof from religion: the Anglican parson is regarded as, obviously, the priest of the exploiter, while even the Nonconformist pastor makes little or no appeal. The new workman feels himself the authentic force in the State: he may be a pariah at the moment, but he means to retrieve his strength. The revolutionary temper, long in the ascendant in France and Germany, has, as usual in Britain, taken several generations longer to arrive there. Its Continental counterpart, that faith of the dispossessed in a future state which shall banish all evil from the world, which is the idealistic and reconciliatory aspect of the revolutionary *credo*, finds little response; the average British workman is too little imaginative, too much of a realist, to accept this dream. He knows, or thinks he knows, that in 1832 he won the franchise for the middle class only to be cheated out of it himself; that in the war he gave his life for the State and sacrificed his sacred Trade Union conditions, to get nothing in return but unemployment, housing shortage, falling trade, and falling wages. This is the background of the great mining struggles of 1921 and 1926: and defeat has only deepened and darkened the temper they expressed.

§ 9

Even the most cursory sketch of British social and economic conditions must note the existence of a group below the land-owners and labourers in the country, the employers and workpeople in the towns, comprising the 'unclassed' who inhabit the grisly slums of the cities.

These slums are the price Britain has paid for her freedom. With or without the forms of purchase, the British landlord robbed the peasant of his land and drove him into the towns, no king having the power to restrain his greedy thefts. Unrestrained selfishness, on the part of landlord and urban jerry-builder alike, compelled wretched men and women to huddle in quarters and dwellings that beggar description, without any interference on the part of the police. Unrestrained selfishness on the part of capitalism enabled them to scratch up a miserable existence at some pitiable wage, always on the verge of destitution, diversified at intervals by the poor house and prison. Christian charity has done an immense amount to lighten the lot of these hapless souls: great philanthropists have built tolerable houses for them: in Birmingham, for example, a social leader like Joseph Chamberlain cleared whole quarters of their plague spots: Christian Socialists like Charles Kingsley exposed the horrors of sweated industry, in *Alton Locke* (1850): the Salvation Army brought some sort of primitive religion to the poorest of the poor: here and there, as for instance at Toynbee Hall in London, men of rank and academic distinction founded settlements which brought some touch of ethical and intellectual life into the drab waste of human misery. But the root of the evil remained. In 1886, Charles Booth estimated that no less than a third of the population of London was living on wages below a decent subsistence level, and without any prospect of steady and satisfactory employment.

These facts explain why care for the poor, nowhere else a political issue, has for more than a hundred years occupied the forefront of public interest in England. The question whether poor relief shall be given only in institutions or in the houses of the poor themselves, is a still unsolved problem. During the first third of the nineteenth century, the burden of poor rates did more than anything else to ruin the old feudal State. If, ever since the turn of the century, the workers have tended to stand, more and more, for a legal minimum wage, and since 1911 have preferred a system of old age pensions for the poor to one of insurance against old age, the reason is that up till now, there are large strata of the population who have no regular employment and from whom therefore no regular contributions can be expected. That the workers should have carried two such fundamentally Socialistic demands as old age pensions and the minimum wage, in the teeth of the individualist State, is a landmark in British social history. After casting a section of its people into a condition more disgraceful than the whole rest of the world can show, the individualistic Capitalist State has been unhinged by the resistance of the same people, the very poorest of its citizens.

§ 10

Nothing has been said, so far, of university, official, or artistic groups, for the reason that in Britain they do not constitute separate sections of the population. There is of course an increasing number of civil servants, local and national. But they do not constitute an independent group, with distinct ideals and a characteristic form of life. They are respectable members of the middle class, but enjoy no special consideration. The same is true of artists. Here and there an individual will break over the traces of bourgeois respectability: instances of personal style in dress, dwelling, and demeanour are frequent enough. The great wave of after-war mental pathology that is at present passing over Europe makes these instances rather conspicuous now. But they are mainly confined to London and to a group which preaches birth control, and therefore means little or nothing for England's future.

The clergyman, who in most continental countries represents a distinct special type, is far too indistinct a figure in Britain to deserve special study. We shall see, later (p. 154 *seq*.), that this relative lack of differentiation, this tendency to an immensely potent development of one single type, is one authentic source of Britain's formidable power; but that the same singleness of type makes England inferior, by comparison with other nations, in variety and subtlety of civilization.

CHAPTER VI
NATIONAL CHARACTERISTICS

THE essential traits in the English character are those of the peasant of Lower Saxony and Friesland, who has kept his old mentality with very little change in his new abode. Fundamentally, he is like the peasant of all climates, a creature of rather materialistic bent, fond of money and the pleasures of the table, matter of fact, conservative, energetic, and tough. Admixture of Scandinavian Viking strains, partly from Scandinavia direct, partly through France, has raised the naturally strong will of the primitive stock to a Berserker force such as is found in no other people. The qualities of fineness, tenderness, and intuition, hidden everywhere under the hard shell of the Lower Saxon peasant, are in constant danger of being strangled by this harsh egotism and love of strife. In the same way, the profound sense of religion, native to the type, is in perpetual conflict, here as in the homeland, with the defiant arrogance of the peasant who cannot admit a fault, sees himself invariably as a model of piety, and looks down upon all who differ from him with a sublime self-assurance. At every period of English history, as in almost every Englishman, wide as are the psychological differences between them, this typical character appears, with astounding uniformity. Some of its outstanding traits deserve closer study.

§ I

The Englishman is an individualist. Such is the traditional view, which requires more precise definition. He will submit to no order, save of his own creation, and is at all times prone to revolt against compulsion, whether governmental, military, or sacerdotal. The State he does not understand. The world for him is a wide plane, occupied by many other Lower Saxon peasants all at appropriate distances from each other. Social feelings, when they appear, take the form not so much of respect for the community, as of respect for the individuality of others, of a man's wife, and of his young child, who has a right to existence like that of the adult. Life, to him, is composed of the activities of individual men. When he takes interest in the world outside, it expresses itself as a desire for contact with human beings. History, for him, is not the story of the development of economic, social, or historic tendencies. Despite Darwin and Spencer, he regards every kind of evolutionary formula with deep

147

suspicion and mistrust. Biography, on the other hand, he likes, since it enables him to establish some sort of personal relation with great men. A personality of any significance can hardly die in England without a biography appearing within the shortest possible period; there is a ready market even for the poorest type of biographical gossip. The interview, like the ubiquitous Kodak, which tracks the great man down to the intimacies of his home, is, despite the contrast in which it stands to the English ideal of the sacrosanctity of the home, an Anglo-Saxon invention, which of course has developed further and faster in the great Anglo-Saxon democracy across the seas than in England, inveterately aristocratic still.

Comparatively rare in English literature is the novel or play thoroughly exploring some ethical, political, or social problem. What interests the Englishman is the story of personalities. A typical Englishman like Charles Dickens makes a great show of artistic analysis of such a social question as is presented by the workhouse or the debtors' prison, only to go off, both in *Oliver Twist* and in *Bleak House*, into a regular romance of character and adventure. An author who pursues Meredith's course of subtle psychological analysis does so at the cost of popularity of appeal. A great landscape artist like Turner had to wait long for recognition because he did not give the average Englishman the two things he understands in painting – portraits or anecdotes. Even the highly educated reader dislikes real literary history which is an analysis of tendencies, and prefers instead an analysis of personalities plentifully interspersed with anecdotes. An election is not a conflict for or against this or that idea or programme, but for or against this or that individual, some great leader or local magnate, whose personal merits and capabilities matter far more than his political views. What counts, too, is not his election address but canvassing. The largest possible number of electors has got to be visited personally, either by the candidate himself, or by persons the higher in social status the better. Enthusiasm is roused, not by any abstract idea, but by a person – not by the League of Nations, but by President Wilson. In times of great national conflict, the enemy has got to be personified in some Satanic opposing figure, some Napoleon or Wilhelm II.

It would seem as though this dissolution of the world into a collection of personalities and personal relations must smash social life. Actually, the reverse is the case. The Englishman, like his Lower Saxon peasant ancestor, is an individualist only within traditional limits. He is an individualist who desires to be left alone. Within the limits of tradition, he desires to express a highly definite and self-willed individuality. But he is far from being the complete individualist, who seeks to be different from the rest. On the contrary, he is very much the herd man. He wishes to be left alone, lord in his castle, but inside that castle exactly like every one else. His schools are devoted to the creation of a dominant type, not of individuals whose independent thought and action might be dangerous to that type. True, England has produced men widely different from the norm; at periods, like the Romantic Age, when the idea of individualism was in the ascendant, quite a number of them at one time, for instance, Blake, Shelley, Byron, and, at a later epoch, Swinburne, Wilde and Shaw. But none of these men was hailed with the kind of national enthusiasm that greeted Goethe, Heine, Nietzsche, or Ibsen. Rather, their variation from the type was just the thing that made success slow and difficult at home.

§ 2

Like the Lower Saxon peasant, again, the Englishman has a penchant for the obvious, the prosaic, the practical and the useful. His grammar is matter of fact: all superfluities have been shorn from it. The more delicate shades on which any æsthetic quality in the spoken word depends have gone. The sole formula of address is 'you,' whether the nearest and dearest person, or the most matter-of-fact object, is in question. Inflection has almost completely disappeared, grammar has been simplified, syllables are cut to the minimum necessary for understanding: the language is almost wholly unadorned, yet everything can be expressed with remarkable clearness and precision, and the smallest possible expenditure of effort.

Of theory, the Englishman has always had an innate mistrust. Compulsory education was not introduced until 1876, and University teaching, brilliant exceptions notwithstanding, has always been much less intellectual than on the Continent; modern technology did not take any root till shortly before the war, and the highly-trained engineers thus produced have, despite all its lessons, a hard fight to keep their end up with the merely practical man. There is a hatred of any mental process that is lucidly and severely carried to its logical conclusion. In legislation, general maxims are avoided and all special points are preferred. A thorough and comprehensive juridical system makes no appeal. In a manner incomprehensible to the

Continental, the veritable bases of modern constitutionalism, penal and civil codes are dispensed with and substituted by a tissue of individual enactments which still bear traces of their mediæval origin but can be adapted to all modern needs by practice and precedent.

This turn for the practical and obvious is reflected in British learning, partly to its advantage and partly to its disadvantage. English philosophy is not, like German or French, mainly metaphysics; but it is great in psychology which gives a handle for the treatment of men, great in ethics which regulates the behaviour of men, great in giving a philosophical foundation to sciences so eminently practical as politics and political economy. The greatness of Bacon lies in the fact that he believes only what he can prove, and exposes all general preconceptions as unscientific prejudices. An Englishman, Locke, was the first to reject the old accepted notion that a man entered the world with a certain furniture of innate ideas, and declares that all general ideas were products of experience. A Scot, David Hume, with the Radicalism of his narrower racial type, went further than his master, and rejected all general ideas, including the notions of substance and causality, while, at the same time, declaring scepticism to be superfluous and unnecessary. Another Scot, Thomas Reid (died 1796), simply swept aside all difficult metaphysical inquiries, positing a human common sense as the source of every metaphysical, logical, ethical and æsthetic concept. Reid thus let philosophy end where it begins, and for many generations of his countrymen he seemed thereby to have uttered the last word of wisdom. It was, again, an Englishman, Darwin, who banished teleological questions from the theory of evolution, and saw all development as a product of two great English activities, struggle and adaptation.

Even more characteristic and even more momentous for civilization in general is the attempt of British philosophers to devise an ethical code on the basis of utility. The old Epicurean ideas, revived in England in the eighteenth century, became a sort of popular scientific gospel there. Utility, as conceived by its philosophic exponents, Francis Hutcheson (1694–1746), and, above all, Jeremy Bentham (1748–1832) and John Stuart Mill (1806–73), is of course not any mere usefulness to personal comfort and personal gain. For most of them it is, rather, a thoroughly serious attempt to detach some greatest common factor in the diverse impulses of human action, and so reduce them to a calculus. Utility, as they understood it, is, further, not the good of the individual, but the greatest possible good for the largest possible number. Inevitably, however, such a philosophy led to the most fatal confusion in the minds of the mass. Bentham was himself largely responsible, in so far as he cited human selfishness in all his philosophic disquisitions as the one really reliable motive on which to base the State. Not the selfishness of an individual, say the King, or of a class, say the nobles, must be considered, but an organization such as to give to the selfishness of each class or group free play, subject to the limitations set upon it by the selfishness of other classes, groups, or individuals. Thus, when a Member of Parliament exclusively pursues his own selfish desire to become a minister, and the individual voter exclusively pursues his own selfish desire to pay as little taxes as possible, the diagonal between these two selfishnesses will give the desirable end, i.e. careful and economical administration. Minds of much deeper insight, like Herbert Spencer and the American founder of Pragmatism, William James, followed in the footsteps of Bentham. There is really nothing but a refinement of Utilitarianism in Spencer's deduction of all morality from the individual's experience of the good or evil of this or that action, his derivation of religion from fear of the dead and of the idea of the State from fear of the living, or his notion that children should be educated, in the first instance, to recognize the good or bad consequences of what they do by doing it. Despite loud protests from men like Carlyle, Dickens and Matthew Arnold, a highly vulgarized form of the philosophy of Bentham and Spencer has become the philosophy of the mass of Britons. That good is commensurate with what promises a tangible advantage – health, wealth, economic advance, or, in the last analysis, personal profit – this is the tacit conviction of the British Philistine man in all classes, though, for public consumption, it is wrapped up in pseudo-philosophic Utilitarian phraseology. The effect is the more painful that thanks to a genuinely English passion for compromising the most opposed notions in the mind, it is apt to go hand in hand with a solemn mouthing of lofty ethical principles, derived, uncritically, from the arsenal of English Calvinism.

§ 3

Further, the Englishman transplanted to his new home the Conservative instincts of the peasant of Lower Saxony and Friesland.

They continued, in him, with enhanced strength, since no rapidly changing course of history challenged his Conservatism with new events of the first order. As a matter of fact, England has never embarked upon a course that represented a sharp break with the past. It experienced the Wars of the Roses in the fifteenth century, and the Puritan Revolution in the seventeenth (the bloodless revolution of 1688 hardly counts as such), but there is no comparison between the Wars of the Roses and the Thirty Years' War, or the Cromwellian Period with the Continental struggles of the Napoleonic era. The last battle on British soil – a trifling fight against the Pretender at Culloden – took place in 1746. And Culloden was a battle of purely dynastic significance. England alone of all nations does not know what war on one's own soil really means.

No other country in Europe shows so steady a cultural development. In Germany and France, the great epochs of civilization broke over the country with revolutionary impact. When Humanism discovered the Classical world, the Middle Ages suddenly sank in ruins; Plato and Cicero remitted the Nibelungenlied and the Roman de la Rose to the shades. But in England there were living links between Shakespeare and old Chaucer or even such an insignificant figure as Lydgate; the sixteenth-century Reformers tried to find supports for the new teachings in Anglo-Saxon homilies and chroniclers. The rise of the Romantic school in Germany put the eighteenth-century writers in the dustbin, but an English Romantic like Byron prided himself on being a follower of Pope, whom he regarded with passionate admiration. Nowhere is the mixture of styles in architecture so general as in England, where Gothic and Renaissance, and even Gothic and Baroque are found together; nowhere have the forms of the past so tenacious a hold upon the present. To this day, old French formulæ are used in the solemn prorogation of Parliament and the opening of the Law Courts; judges and barristers still wear eighteenth-century wigs, and professors and students the gown and mortarboard of the seventeenth century. Every youngster in the schools, every clerk in an English counting-house, still practises the late Roman and Frankish system of $L(ibra)$, $s(olidus)$ and $d(enarius)$ and grapples with the vagaries of an impossible old Germanic system of weights and measures, which the Englishman alone considers superior to the metric system. The Englishman alone dates his laws not by years A.D., but as his ancestor in Anglo-Saxon times did, by the years of the reign of the monarch which will never coincide with the years of the Christian era. There is still a civil Warden of the Cinque Ports (Dover, Hastings, Sandwich, Romney, and Hythe) who supervises the non-existent fleet of what were once important coastal points. Because, in mediæval times, Members of Parliament were often anxious to get rid of their uncomfortable position as representatives of the nation, no M.P. may resign his seat; if he really wants to give it up, he must get himself nominated to the Stewardship of the Chiltern Hundreds. There is no such office now, but this nomination is a royal favour that carries with it the extinction of membership of the House. At the accession of a new monarch, the herald still calls upon all who dispute the succession to come forth to single combat, and the mob of the English capital listens with devout respect without the slightest temptation to utilize the occasion for a grand practical joke.

But there is another side to this. Conservative as is this people, it never ossifies. True, an ancient institution is not reformed until it has sunk into complete chaos, but then it *is* reformed, and both thoroughly and well. The franchise was allowed to fall into a condition such that places which had long ceased to exist sent members to the House, while great populous industrial centres had none. But the reform did come in 1832 and did its work well. London government had to reach such a point of confusion that there were no less than some 400 independent and irresponsible authorities in mutual conflict, before reform took place; but, in 1855 and 1899, it did take place. The conservative spirit remains, however, even in the case of the most thoroughgoing reform. Old forms are generally preserved, while the spirit of reform turns them to absolutely new uses. Thus, there is still a Chancellor of the Duchy of Lancaster, although Lancaster has long been assimilated to the rest of the country for the purposes of government. But the office has become a ministry without portfolio, and so provides for the case where an influential statesman is wanted in the Government but not to act as head of one of the great State departments. The post of Lord Privy Seal, now quite superfluous, is another case in point. In the same way the Lord Mayor of London is elected on a franchise that, from one point of view, is ridiculously out of date, but, from another, is most skilfully adjusted to meet contemporary facts. As in the Middle Ages, he is still elected by the old Merchant Companies of goldsmiths, brasiers, fletchers, broderers, cordwainers, and loriners, whose very names the ordinary citizen does not understand. In form and name they are mum-

153

mified survivals of mediæval Guilds: actually, they represent modern Capitalism organized for specific purposes, and, as such, a thoroughly rational electorate for the symbolic head of a great city. Here is a typical instance of the characteristic talent of making some reasonable use of what might appear mere archæological curiosities. 'Old' England is often looked upon, by friend and foe, as no longer an effective factor in the new order of things, but it has again and again astounded the world by its undiminished vital force. In a nation so conservative and at the same time so strong, the pathological after-war modernism of a certain London group can hardly constitute a grave national danger.

§ 4

To the great surprise of the Continental student of England this matter-of-fact, practical and conservative English character appears wherever the Anglo-Saxon is met with: the differentiation between different geographical sub-types of the race is astonishingly small. Germany is the country of the most marked local variations – between the old Prussian, the Bavarian, and the citizen of the Hanseatic towns. On top of these local are professional differences: the clergyman, the professor, the officer, the merchant, the high-school teacher, the elementary-school teacher, the peasant and the artist are, in Germany, special species of the genus man, and differ in outlook as well as often in speech, manner and physiognomy, even in ethics. The absolutism of many petty German princes kept all these types pretty well apart. It created a great deal of caste snobbery, but it also served to train certain hereditary qualities of immense value for modern life – the sense of honour in the officer, idealism in the clergyman, duty in the official, love of knowledge in the teacher. In England, *per contra*, a much older royal absolutism, that of the Norman kings, prevented the development of territorial powers. The result was that racial differences could not well develop on a large scale. Here and there they can be dimly discerned: the peasant, in the South, is more refined, more lively and relatively more tractable than the rough, dumb Yorkshireman, capable of breaking out into flames of love or hatred, as described by Emily Brontë. But its range is small compared to that presented in Germany. Where real variations from the type appear in Britain, they are to be attributed to the influence of a State developing outside of England and the Norman sphere of influence. Thus, the Scot was affected neither by Norman centralization, nor by a civilization based upon the Anglican Church. So, under Calvinist influences, he developed a profound habit of thought and a one-sidedly religious character, while the wildness of his nature, half-English and half-Celtic, never fully submitted to the surface polish of an Anglo-Saxon court. The Irish, even after the loss of their language, went their own way. Visionary dreamers, capable of swift passionate excitement, prone to swift weariness and disillusionment and richly endowed with artistic gifts, they also have their full share of the peasant inheritance of coarse materialism, and, at the centre of their inner life, in the sphere of religion and national feeling, are capable of an amazing toughness of endurance, that centuries of disappointment proved powerless to break.

In England itself, royal absolutism welded the various races into a homogeneous national character, and excluded the development of class types, such as exist in Germany. True, the landed proprietor, the employer and the industrial worker, present three well-marked categories, but the minor class stratification, created or at least fostered by absolutism in Germany, does not figure in England. The second wave of absolutism, under Tudors and Stuarts, was broken even before a royal administrative system had been established which might have kept the classes apart. The novel and the drama in the seventeenth and eighteenth centuries recognize only two distinct class types; the coarse, roisterous, drunken landowner and the clergyman, learned, devout, and often poor as a mouse, Squire Western and Parson Adams. Any tendencies there might have been towards clearer differentiation of types were bound to die away with the substitution for absolutist efforts of the mild oligarchy of the 'good old families.' While absolutism in Germany attempted to maintain itself by keeping the productive forces of the country neatly compartmented and separate from each other, the method of the British oligarchy was to hold down the masses while drawing the upper section to itself and assimilating it. The London merchant could look forward, at the end of a successful career, to possessing a country house, marrying his daughter into the aristocracy, and seeing his son returned to Westminster to represent the nearest borough to his own estate. All he needed was plenty of money, a speech and attire the same as those of the aristocracy, a fine contempt for the populace and the chapel, the possession of a stable, and, incidentally, attendance at the Anglican church. Every successful merchant was connected with families which had risen in the world, which were looked up to by the mass of middle-class people as dazzling models to be imitated in everything, from the shade of their Church views to the hour at which they ate dinner and the cut of their clothes. Early in the eighteenth century, English essayists poked fun at the merchant who would copy the late midday meal of the landed gentry and try to set up a residence for himself outside the town, as much like an aristocratic abode as might be. The middle classes began to employ men-servants like the nobility, their ladies would withdraw after dinner, and have a drawing-room for constant use, instead of the bourgeois 'best room,' opened on special occasions only. In many middle-class families, the eldest son, like the heir to the title, has all sorts of little advantages over the other children, and the eldest daughter is universally Miss Smith, a little superior to her younger sisters, who add their Christian name to that of the family. In towns, the ordinary English house is separated from the street by a ridiculous little strip of ground, useless in itself and only to be explained as a pathetic survival of the ideal to have a park surrounding the mansion as the nobleman had. Similarly, the 'hall,' even if it has room for coats and umbrellas only, pays tribute, at least in name, to the hall of the baronial castle. Whereas in Germany everything was done to separate classes from each other, in England the eyes of the lower orders are yearningly raised to those above them. In Germany, again, distinct and separate ideas of life have been worked out for various classes, with appropriate codes. The officer puts first a notion of honour, incomprehensible to wide circles in the nation, while sometimes regarding debts rather casually; for the merchant, on the other hand, to live beyond his means is the worst slur on his honour. For men of learning yet another clause of the ethical code stands foremost: the sin of sins is any disregard for scientific truth, or the self advertisement of the windbag. In England, on the other hand, there is one standard for all and this one standard only the ideal of the gentleman. This ideal originally is a product of the court, but has now, subject to certain middle-class modifications, become the ethical ideal of all classes alike.

§ 5

In so far as modern civilization cherishes the belief in an ideal human being, this ideal is derived from a blend of mediæval chivalry and Renaissance humanism. Humanism first proclaimed the ideal of an equal development of all human faculties, and of a philosophic penetration of the whole of life. This ideal is a Renaissance heritage. But the Renaissance had also consciously taken over some of the chivalric ideals of the Middle Ages – absolute loyalty to the Sovereign, personal honour, even at the cost of life, reverence for women, and elegance in dress and demeanour.

Distinctly, and more strongly than with any other people, the traces of this old knightly ideal live on in England. There, however, it has submitted to a characteristic attenuation. When the entirely non-military elements of the English middle class began to penetrate into the nobility, the old ideal was adapted to the comprehension of the bourgeoisie. The knight attaches great importance to physical development. The gentleman of to-day hardens his muscles through sport, but the skill in weapons special to the knight has completely vanished. The old monarchical ideal persists, visibly. Even in Walter Scott's day, more than a century after the expulsion of the Stuarts, there were Legitimists in Scotland and even in England; moreover, the absolute fidelity with which the Briton sticks to a leader, once he has chosen him, is nothing but the monarchical instinct in a modern guise. It is one of the most potent factors in political life. Thanks to it, men like Gladstone, Chamberlain and Lloyd George could treat the party programme with a sovereign arbitrariness; in the same way the workman goes on re-electing his Trade Union secretary, even when dissatisfied with his work and policy. Throughout, indeed, this chivalrous spirit in the nation acts as an effective counterpoise to the notorious flightiness of modern democracy. The knightly notion of honour still persists, likewise, quite generally. The duel, of course, is gone; even in the eighteenth-century novel, gentlemen are to be met with who honourably refuse to take part in it, and since 1850 it has even disappeared from the Army. But English law has pains and penalties of a Draconian severity for the violator of honour, which afford at least as much protection as the duel (i.e. to the man who is in a position to pay the costs of a lawsuit; but this is the standing limitation set everywhere by the plutocratic character of contemporary English society). Nowhere does woman enjoy so much respect as in the two Anglo-Saxon lands. Here the connexion with mediæval court ideals is patent, for all this honour paid to women is by no means an original feature of Anglo-Saxondom. Tender consideration for woman is native to the Anglo-Saxon peasant only to the highly limited degree in which it is found in all the Germanic peoples. In the economy of the English peasant or working-class house, the woman is just as much a beast of burden as in other countries. Mediæval law is no more favourable to women in England than elsewhere among the Germanic peoples. Until 1923 England, unlike other countries, had a dual divorce law – simple adultery on the part of the wife gave the man grounds for divorce, but adultery on the part of the husband required to be aggravated by cruelty or wilful desertion. Woman in general is not better placed in England than elsewhere, only the lady. Early in the Middle Ages, the wife of a knight possessed the right of inheritance, both of lands and feudal title, in the event of the male stock dying out; there are to-day twenty-six peeresses in their own right. Gradually, this respect for the lady spread to the middle classes. In the cities of sixteenth-century England, the well-to-do burgher's wife had won a social freedom unknown on the Continent at the time. By 1700 the lady was making her claim heard to a certain degree of higher education; the essayists like Steele and Addison began to write for female readers. In 1848 F. D. Maurice founded, in Queen's College, in London, the first educational institution of university type for ladies, at a time when their elementary education – that is to say the schooling of women of the lower classes – was in a pitiable condition.

The wife as such was dependent upon her husband in all financial questions. Her property was his, even her earnings. But from a very early date, the lady was independent because it had become an early custom for the nobility to secure by skilful marriage contracts to its daughters what the law did not allow to women generally. Very recent legislation only (in 1870 the first Married Women's Property Act was passed) gradually admitted mere woman to the privileges of the lady. Women's rights in England derive, not from respect for the sex as such, but from the knight's devotion to his lady, whence they passed, at first very slowly, to other classes. This knightly attitude appears in the consideration shown to the lady – by no means always to the woman as such – in the thousand and one details of daily life. The lady – again, by no means always the woman – is spoken of with all the forms of deep respect. Follies, blunders, even breaches of manners, morals and decorum on the part of the society lady – though not on that of the woman of lower rank – are accepted with a sigh, as natural events, which cannot be helped. This is chivalrousness, the spirit of the gentry. In its turn this spirit, like the rest of the gentleman ideal, is constantly percolating down through the lower orders. The automatic way in which popular feeling reacts to the slogan 'Woman and children,' and springs to their defence when they are, or are supposed to be, in any danger, proves the degree to which the old knightly spirit is entrenched in the popular mind.

It is part of the knightly tradition to show a certain splendour of address in good clothes, a splendid house and an open hand. This part of the mediæval code has become second nature to the Englishman. The Scot, who has had to struggle with an unproductive soil, and who keeps out of the knightly tradition in other ways also, does not possess it, but it is evident as early as 1400 in the burghers of Southern England, when they appear in Chaucer's works. With the mercantile spirit of Puritanism, there came a certain tendency to honour a matter-of-fact thriftiness. But so soon as the Englishman seeks to be more than the mere merchant, so soon as he strives after social recognition, he displays a luxurious standard of dress, diet, travelling and personal service without parallel in the world, save in Anglo-Saxon America. Petty thrift is regarded as ungentlemanly; the average Briton views the arts of the German *Hausfrau* with a pitying smile. When the mildest of war restrictions with regard to food became necessary in England, they were completely ineffective, except in so far as they could be made compulsory, since every one regarded them as a social declension. In spite of the very real declension in buying power of the pound after the war, everybody affects a certain extravagance of living so long as he possibly can, all the frequent exhortations towards a simpler life are without avail, and the very first thing the social upstart can do is to show by an affectation of luxury that he wants to be classed as a gentleman.

Another characteristic point of the knightly ideal is the inviolable force of the code, the ethics and the forms of the social order, and this, too, is characteristic of the modern English gentleman. Every Englishman recognizes Church, State, and Society, and conforms to their customs, however much he may doubt them in his heart; opposition is bad manners, and a sin against the spirit of the knight. It is 'not done.' One goes to church – the Established Church, of course; one votes for one or other of the two parties that stand for the existing order, Conservative or Liberal; if, in the marital relation, individual temperament brings one into collision with the moral code, any external breach will be avoided, and any scandal quickly covered up. There has been a certain relaxation of the code immediately after the war, but it is not probable that it will have a far-reaching effect.

Humanism did not materially affect this class ideal of the knight. In Germany, it created something entirely new, the idea of the 'educated' man (*Gebildeter*), a new, intellectual knighthood, recognized by everybody as supreme. The gentleman ideal, on the other hand, lacks any sort of contact with mental power. Theorists like Ascham and Elyot did demand humanistic learning of the gentleman, and did secure it. In no country in the world is a knowledge of classical authors so widespread as in England. Parliamentary speeches, between 1830 and 1850, whether from great landlords or distinguished jurists, abound in classical quotations and show an almost philological comprehension of the ancient world. Nowhere in the world are there so many agreeable gentlemen, with charming manners, who have tasted all branches of knowledge and, with modern eclecticism, made the best of the Stoics and the best of the Epicureans their own. Even to-day, when the study of the classics is sadly declining, they can be found in many a country parsonage, in many a country house, in the common room of the Colleges, and in many an English authors' club. Thoroughly typical, too, is the man who unites eminent success in practical affairs with a high degree of scientific activity – the philosophic statesman and jurist, Francis Bacon; the Scottish Lord John Napier of Merchiston (d. 1617), who managed his estates and also discovered logarithms; John Milton, fighter for religion, poet and pamphleteer; John Stuart Mill, civil servant and philosopher; Gladstone, Prime Minister and student of theology and the classics; Arthur James Balfour, and Richard Haldane, both statesmen and philosophers. And so on.

In so far as Humanism means general classical education and the rounding off of the human personality, no people has been so strongly interpenetrated by it, in its ruling classes, as the British. On the other hand, but a faint echo is to be found of the even more important humanistic ideal of life, which means over and above even classical learning, some definite individual intellectual achievement, the adoption of a personal angle to some great general human problem. There has been no Goethe and no Nietzsche in England. Like most of the other great civilizing forces, Humanism worked differently here and in Germany. In Germany, it was revolutionary – its first fruit was the Reformation, bringing in its train the Thirty Years' War. The more developed nationalism of England simply assimilated it. The old knightly ideal of the gentleman remained, but received a classical substructure; discipline and morals, instead of being based on the teaching of the Church and the conventions of the troubadours, were based on Cicero and Horace. But the revolutionary germs of the new ideal, so potent of fruit in Germany, did not develop in England. Knowledge became the supreme grace of life, never its content or the substance of a life and death struggle. A philosopher like Edward Herbert of Cherbury (d. 1648) is a cavalier, a diplomat and a statesman, and, quite as a side-line, the father of Deism; he wrote an autobiography which hardly contains a word of philosophy. A philosopher of the rank of John Locke can draft a model educational system, in which philosophy is no more than a fine accomplishment for the drawing-room.

There is only one tendency of Renaissance philosophy which is accepted early and strongly in England. This is its practical side, which, in contradistinction to Ascham and Elyot, rated the inventor and the statesman above the man of learning or the poet. Spenser's friend, Gabriel Harvey (d. 1630), and the great Francis Bacon regard knowledge not as the fruit of speculation, and as an end in itself, but as something eminently practical, which gives power to its adepts. This train of thought never died out in England. Knowledge and art were prized, ever since the advent of Humanism, but their professional representatives were never the really great men of the nation. Always they had to give precedence to the nobleman and were apt to be treated as pedants and pushed politely into the corner of the drawing-room, or still further. An echo of this neglect seems to be perceptible in Shakespeare's Sonnets. In the eighteenth century a great man like Lord Chesterfield is terrified by the idea of his son's playing the violin in company; aristocratic poets, until Byron, were apt to treat their artistic efforts with deprecation as a mere hobby; the gentleman may be the patron of art and science, hardly their apprentice. The aristocratic outlook of the Englishman was dignified by Humanism, but not changed.

The Age of Rationalism, in its turn, merely strengthened inherited traits. Its influence coincided with that of the rising bourgeoisie of Puritan origin. The edge was taken off the extreme demands of the ideal of chivalry; the duel was looked upon as superfluous or even as godless; the King ceased to be the object of hereditary, feudal devotion, while remaining as the revered representative of the nation. Tolerance of the opinion of others counts as gentlemanly, since the enlightened man, who knows that civil war arose from religious passion, has grown sceptical.

The religious atmosphere in which the rising middle classes were living contributed little or nothing to the modification of the knightly ideal. Under Puritan influences, the knightly canons of honour and truthfulness were carried over into the domain of commerce and industry, where they created the notion of 'fairness' and set the world a brilliant example. But this was no innovation in principle, and this was the only contribution of the religious atmosphere. It would really be more accurate to say that Puritanism falsified the knightly code of absolute truthfulness, by importing into this area its own questionable doctrine of the saint's adjustment to this world and its individual standard of morals. No gentleman can 'tell a lie,' but a 'fib' is a harmless way out of many a difficulty, which plays a disastrous part not only in the contingencies of daily life, but even more harmfully in politics. A typical feature of political and religious controversy, henceforth, is the tendency to support one's own position with assertions not absolutely false, but distinguished by a notable economy of truth. When political struggle reaches a high degree of tension, the desire for power is never frankly and honestly admitted as the motive of personal action, but invariably decked out with a plenitude of threadbare ethical wrappings that have nothing to do with the facts. To honour truth, in such a case, would be positively ungentlemanly. If a nation fights its adversary in open war, it ought not to be done without shedding pacifist tears at the same time. To speak the full truth would be barbarous and uncivilized. When Bethmann-Hollweg, in 1914, openly admitted the wrong done to Belgium by Germany, the accuracy of his statement was disputed in Germany, while in England it was looked upon as a piece of brutal cynicism. In any conflict between the love of truth and the other great human impulses, the religious instinct of the Puritan is far too weak to secure it the victory. Human salvation, and the sanctification of all life, both private and public, while providing the pivot of Puritan thought, have never achieved the independent force that could make it a national ideal. The gentleman conforms to the demands of Society and observes the Ten Commandments; he will even go to church; but no one asks whether or no he is religious at heart. In the relations of the sexes almost everything was, in the eighteenth century, permitted to the gentleman, as the novels of Smollett and Fielding are there to show. Not till the Victorian age did Puritan views acquire any real hold over the nation in this department of life. The gentleman's code never has the moral rigours of the Puritan's ideal. That code never quite coincides with the teaching of Christi-anity; it includes the degree of Christianity that has become the common inheritance of European civilization, but silently excludes all the more exigent Christian claims. Christ Himself, as the son of a 'tradesman,' would not have been a gentleman.

That the moral code of the gentleman has no sort of absolute character is evident by the fact that it begins to waver so soon as the foreigner comes into question. All class ethics invariably refer only to its own community. Relations to those outside it may be settled by a general ethical code; but there are no items of conduct, here, to which the class code applies the irresistible pressure of its social censorship. Irish policy in the eighteenth century certainly did not comply with the most modest provisos of the gentlemanly code, yet, outside Jonathan Swift, there was hardly a protesting voice against it. The slave trade ought to have touched a most tender spot of the knightly ideal – the protection of the defenceless – but throughout the eighteenth century criticism was confined to a tiny minority, and its voice, when it found one, was not that of the gentlemanly feeling of the well bred, but of the religious compassion of the pious. It was not till the nineteenth century that the gentlemanly instinct began to operate in relation to the foreigner. All admixture of political shrewd-ness notwithstanding, it is a feeling of this order, and one that goes down to the lowest strata of the population, that has made England the asylum of the political refugee from all over the Continent. But it is weak enough when there is any conflict between it and the predominant instinct of the Anglo-Saxon: his love for power. The sections were small that protested loudly and energetically against the South African concentration camps. Nor did gentlemanly feeling rouse any effective protest against the conscious and system-atic use of lying in the World War. No question, here, of the sort of transitory lie that may develop out of the fumes of the battlefield in any nation, and then passes away; a compaign of systematic and artistic lying this, like the brutal stories of the chopped-off hands of Belgian children, the Canadian crucified to the barn door in France, or the German factories which extracted fat from the bodies of dead soldiers. These were no evanescent fallacies, but were kept up for months by the skilful innuendo of Ministers of the Crown, by clergymen and distinguished artists, and spread all over the world, and notably in the Orient, through indignant references by Indian and Chinese statesmen, at the time when China was being pressed into the war, and the country of gentlemen did not protest.

The gentleman is, in fact, the mediæval knight with certain modifications of a rationalistic, middle-class kind. The name still preserves the class character of the ideal. The gentleman is the nobleman, and not merely verbally; good birth and good social position are essential parts of the idea, unwillingly as the Englishman may admit it. True, it has been gradually spiritualized, from an early date in the Middle Ages. Birth and position no longer count as they did originally, but they still count a great deal, in spite of the protests of ethical theoreticians. Writers of the sixteenth to the eighteenth century, like Harrison, Peacham or Defoe, use the most comical devices in the effort to secure the title of 'gentleman' for the middle-class physician, lawyer, or official, or at least (!) for his son. They want to spiritualize the ideal, but cannot break away from its class character. The attempt of Addison, Steele and Defoe, about 1700, to rate the merchant as a gentleman, was positively revolutionary; here and there, a novelist would endue a man of inferior position with the feelings of a gentleman, but anything of the sort was felt to be quite exceptional and consequently emphasized to a ridiculous degree. To-day, of course, members of learned professions and great industrialists are gentlemen, *sans phrase*, but the conception is far from an ethical one: popular psychology still regards a certain fortune and certain connexions with 'good' families as inseparable from the gentleman.

As the middle-class Puritans pressed up in the social scale, they accepted, with a few minor qualifications, the class ideal of the aristocracy. Not that this is an inevitable incident in social advance. In Germany, for example, where the knightly ideal was represented by the Army officer and most of the student corporations, a great part of middle-class opinion rejected the knightly duelling code on principle, and, despite occasional conflicts, maintained this view, even after they had moved up in the social hierarchy. Outside of the Guards regiments, moreover, the prevailing mixture of middle-class and aristocratic officers meant that the sound middle-class ideal of simplicity of life penetrated right into the officer class, even in cases of men of considerable means. In England, on the other hand, the conflict between the class ethics of the well-bred and the absolute, religious ethics of the Puritan middle-class ended, in the main, in the victory of the former. English society is still dominated by the spirit of the old chivalry. Even the aspiring workman seeks to make himself a gentleman, and includes in that not merely the ethical code, but the bearing and exterior manners of the type. So long as this is so – and it seems to be part and parcel of the specific character of the race – England can never be a pure democracy. All democratic forms notwithstanding, the old gentry still rule, for they have conquered the soul of the people.

Among the things every Englishman is proud of is the fact that the idea of the gentleman is peculiar to England. It is a fact – but does it demonstrate any ethical pre-eminence? The gentleman is a class ideal; before it can become the norm for mankind, it must shed its purely class attributes – a process sufficiently remote. Nor, as an ideal, and measured by its distance from the common, workaday world, is it even the highest of existing class ideals. Infinitely higher above this earth stands the ascetic monk, ignorant though he may be of the breeding of the gentleman. Higher, too, the Calvinist, who seeks to mould the earth to the likeness of Christ, or the Protestant pietist, absorbed in God, and indifferent to the world and its demeanour. Higher, again, the student who, often hard put to it for his daily bread, nevertheless devotes his life to the search for truth; or the Prussian officer or official who thinks of nothing but his duty, and moderate though his means, lives an honourable life, often rich both from a spiritual and from an intellectual standpoint. All these ideals, making loftier demands on human nature, stand higher in the ethical scale than that of the gentleman. Further, a nation containing within itself a variety of ideal life, and of high human types, must be richer than one that can train up a single such type only. England is alone among modern nations in having permitted its ethical outlook to be confined within the limits of a single one. But this ethical idea, though not the highest, is certainly high; the type has been developed to the utmost of which it is capable. With characteristic common sense, conflicting and impossible claims have been cast overboard; nothing is absolute; the mean is always struck when rigid or disputable points come up. For the rest, every social force that can be used to back up a moral code is then brought into play, to carry the idea into action. Hence the immense effect produced by the English gentleman all over the world.

The level of English morals is hardly higher than that of other nations. Needless here to inquire whether there are not black spots on the others, since none of them attempts to impose its specific ethical standard upon other people or hold it up as a model to the rest. For instance, the Englishman is probably no more truthful than the Frenchman or the German. If he makes that impression, it is because there are certain areas of conduct, above all in the daily transactions of 'mine' and 'thine,' which English Society regulates with an insistence on absolute truthfulness. On the other hand, in other instances, both of daily intercourse and of politics, an elaborate appearance of truthfulness is taken as sufficient. In the limited area over which social sanction is given to the ethical demand for truth, the individual Englishman meets it with an automatic readiness which makes it difficult to the observer to find out how much of this is spontaneous and how much actuated from the dictates of Society. The Englishman tends to see in his fellow-man another gentleman, and shows a confidence that only the ethics of chivalry can sustain; his courtesy, to the weak and the helpless is unfailing; within the limits prescribed for him by the knightly code (foreign policy is under the ægis of Christendom, but the social compulsion of the knight's code plays no part there), he refrains from pursuing his own advantage to the full extent, as from promoting it by means he does not regard as decent. All ethical action is, further, performed as though it were something quite obvious. There is no struggle against temptation, no sense that this 'good form' constitutes a burden, as is apt to be the case with the rigidly disciplined German, or that it is a mere empty formalism, as is apt to be the case with some Frenchmen. In depth and in absoluteness the British code certainly gives no final answer, because, quite consciously, it covers only a part of the area of human morality. The ultimate question about any ethical code, namely how far does it constitute a universal standard of universal application, and how far special rules must be made to meet the special case, is one that it simply does not put, nay consciously rejects. But this, while it may lower its status, gives it an incomparable practical effectiveness within its own limited sphere. All controversial issues, all awkward individual cases, are simply left out; the code works, like everything English, with the vast potency of the type. And it is a fact of vast importance for the world that the Englishman, wherever he comes as a conqueror, should not merely demand subjection, but should, in addition to the economic advantages he brings in his train, spread an ethical code of high value in itself and with all the magic of a sovereign type behind it. But the finest flower of human development, the highly developed individual, finds no place in this code. Thus, although the world would have lost something very precious if the English gentleman had never existed, he does not represent the final word in ethical life.

§ 6

Within the average Englishman there is a constant struggle between his gentlemanly instinct and the natural passion of his temper. Passion is the last thing a foreign observer is apt to expect behind the cold assurance of the gentleman's manner, but this is, nevertheless, one of the basic traits in the English character. Observe the masses on some popular holiday; watch how the traveller of the lower class, or the British soldier, lets himself go when he is out of his own country; note the fearful force of passionate love and hate that spring to life on any occasion when social compulsions are, for the moment, withdrawn; and it is impossible to withhold profoundest respect for the tremendous disciplinary achievement concealed behind that mask of calm self-mastery. In the gentleman, the slowly gathering tide of passion that breaks out in a rush of Berserker rage, has been mastered; but the instinct lives on, unbroken. The trace of this Viking passion is everywhere legible in English literature. The popular hero of the cheap novel or cinema is not the gentleman, with his cool self-assurance, but the strong man, thoroughly kindly at bottom, smiling and humorous, but more than ready to let fly, both with tongue and fists, if he is roused to real anger. The choleric squire of the eighteenth century, of the type of Fielding's Squire Western, long played a leading part in literature, to reappear in the nineteenth century in the guise of the somewhat grim paterfamilias and normal Briton of the comic papers. It can hardly be an accident that only in the literature of one people, and that the British, is the Renaissance man of passionate will fully represented, as he is by Shakespeare and all his contemporaries. Even to-day, after a long and far-reaching process of educating gentlemen, the choleric man suddenly breaks out again, with all his old Berserker violence, in Emily Brontë's *Wuthering Heights* or Thomas Hardy's *Mayor of Casterbridge*.

The British will to power shows this passion in its tremendous potency. It has made him conqueror of worlds, discoverer of unknown regions and of the Pole, inventor and technician. Of all the prisoners of war, the British were the most difficult to handle. The typical Briton knows only one form of relaxation: sport. He can hardly understand gymnastics – i.e. athletic exercises for their own sake, as practised in Germany, or the German *Wanderlust*, as a combination of exercise with intellectual, artistic and social pleasure. He cares only for sport, the trial of strength between two men or two sides, to show which is the stronger and more skilled; conflict, whether in the form of tennis or football, horse-racing or cock-fighting. Historically, the Anglo-Saxons appear as rude, ruthless and cruel conquerors. The story of their kings is richer in ambitious violence, crafty murder, and fratricidal war than that of most of the Germanic stocks. The Danes in Viking days, and the Normans in the eleventh century, brought a second and third dose of these qualities to Anglo-Saxon soil. Inherited consciousness of power found exercise, in the course of the Middle Ages, against Celts and French, from behind the secure protection of impregnable cliffs beyond the green sea wall. The later fifteenth century down to the Battle of Bosworth sees a new orgy of cruelty, heartless ambition and unprincipled lust go through English history again, and it awakens anew in the time of Henry VIII. At this period it begins to be tamed and disciplined by the sea, where the Englishman learned again audacity, endurance and power. Foreigners began to be painfully aware of their arrogant sense of superiority in the fifteenth century, and, from the seventeenth on, this instinctive bent received its religious consecration; in the Puritan camp Milton taught his countrymen that they were the chosen people, selected to serve as model to the less enlightened nations of the earth – in other words, to rule over them. When the Puritan middle classes gradually penetrated into the gentry, they brought this idea with them, though it became good form not to brag about it. The eighteenth century completed the process by developing a conception of the State and of civilization which the Englishman of to-day still considers as the only one possible. It is characterized by freedom for the individual citizen – that is to say, of course, of the privileged aristocrat and his allies from the camp of the wealthy employers; by the doctrine of the golden mean and a nervous evasion of all deeper problems of theology, politics and philosophy, by the substitution of a high ideal of gentlemanliness for any definite Christianity and by protestations of sanctified shrinking from war, which is constantly being waged. Such is the British state in the eighteenth century, and such the sole form of state that the Briton of to-day can conceive. Deviations from this norm he regards with simple contempt. Even when a philosopher like Spencer made an effort to dig down to the roots, he could see nothing in Continental monarchy but a militarism, based on sheer compulsion. He relegated it, without qualification, to the lowest level among state forms, while seeing the 'industrial society' of Britain with its Free Trade and individual liberty as the highest, the one towards which the development of others must tend. And Spencer spoke what millions of Britons only think.

The religious consecration which Milton gave to the elementary instinct for power, certainly is a grave danger to other nations. But it also has its redeeming qualities. English patriotism never expresses itself in merely rhetorical phrase: rarely, and only in the passion of a dangerous war, as a brutal appeal to mere force. The chivalrous gentleman imposes his will, if necessary with pitiless sternness, but then spares the defeated; precisely so does the British nation force its enemy to his knees, using every resource of cruelty and intrigue for that purpose, and then, provided only the said enemy has become quite harmless, offer a hand and spare neither generous recognition nor self-sacrificing assistance. This recognition can rise to the finest and most magnanimous enthusiasm. After peace was made in 1902, the Boer Generals received impassioned admiration in London, and, in 1914, the real hero with the British public was von Müller, the captain of the *Emden* – though this, of course, was at the beginning of the war. This sense of being the first of nations, with a civilizing mission to other races, and a final responsibility for any evil that happens anywhere in the world, has, at critical epochs in history, more than once rescued the nation from the bondage of inactive comfort. Thus, it found itself again in the nineteenth century, when, after long quiescence, it began to think Imperially. When in 1914, it drew the sword to treat Germany to the same fate it had prepared for its earlier rivals, France, Spain, and Holland, it felt that it was embarked on a missionary enterprise on behalf of world civilization. That note echoes through all the speeches of British statesmen at the time. The moving verses, in which Rupert Brooke hailed the war as a release from arid egotisms and mammon-worship, roused many an echo throughout the Anglo-Saxon world.

§ 7

The softer traits of the Saxon peasant survive, too, in his descendant. For there is a tender inner life concealed within the hard-shelled, grossly materialistic Germanic peasant, shamefacedly though he is apt to hide it from the view. For everything non-rational, he may have an occasional contemptuous sneer, but cherishes in his inmost soul the profoundest respect. This reappears in the strong religious instinct of the Englishman, absolutely genuine and deep, to which we shall recur (p. 396 *seq.*). One aspect only need here be noted. The religious fervour of the Germanic soul will break out occasionally in deep mysticism and passionate words. Prophetic spirits like George Fox, John Wesley, Carlyle, and Ruskin, singularly un-English as they seem to the foreigner, derive from this deeper substratum, as does the mysticism of the Oxford Movement. Here, there breaks across the moral dead level of materialism a responsiveness to beauty of form in worship, to music in its loftier aspects, to the non-rational element that lies behind a universal Church. In literature, too, a sense of form constantly appears, despite the marked tendency of the bulk to vulgar didacticism and empty fluency. Epic poetry, for instance, almost completely dependent on form, which seemed to be dying out everywhere in the nineteenth century, was in England revived vigorously by William Morris, Tennyson and the Brownings. English literature instinctively retreats before any form of extreme naturalism. The drama of bourgeois life emerges in English literature early in the seventeenth century, well ahead of other countries, but it remained a short-lived episode; England's greater dramatists, for example Shakespeare, found their material and their problems in the highest sections of society, where form plays an important part. Matter-of-fact as is the English of ordinary conversation, the prose employed in the pulpit and parliamentary debates, in leading articles, and in scientific books, has far more claim to form than is the case with German prose. Here the plain, predominantly Germanic locutions of daily use, with their contracted vocabulary, are suddenly reinforced by a speech of extraordinary flexibility, loaded with French and Latin admixtures, and with a definite melody which raises it high above the speech of the vulgar. Life, in this highly matter-of-fact country, is dominated by conventional forms preserved with a positively religious zeal, and applied to the Church, to art, to the law, to the Constitution and to Society. The colour fantasies of a Turner, the ethereal figures of a Burne-Jones, the imaginative visions of Shelley, Blake and Coleridge, the heady love of form of a Spenser or a Shelley, the stylistic design of English furniture, ceramics and book-production – all these are as typically English as the dull didacticism of a Richardson or the dreary gossip of an English drawing-room. If some infusion of the Celt is here working through the Germanic strain, it has been so completely nationalized that it is no longer felt as in any sense alien.

In the lower classes, whose drab and dreary existence leaves their irrational instincts no scope, and for whom the non-rational elements in religion, the arts or poetry mostly are a sealed book, this impulse ever and anon will break through with the primitive force that characterizes everything English, and will spend itself on some worthless object; whether it be in the passion for alcohol, the delight in crude tales of crime and murder, or of the fortunes of some abandoned heir of a princely fortune, in the nervous apprehension of some 'hidden hand,' some secret enemy who, according to the prevailing fashion, may be a Jesuit, a German spy or a Russian Bolshevik. Dickens' Uriah Heep – that strange and secret being, all the stranger and all the more secret because shown against the sordid background of daily life – is the highly artistic embodiment of this ill-regulated and non-rational need of the English masses. Out of kindred soil spring the many queer prophets who claim to redeem mankind by vegetarianism, occultism, etc., and all religious revivals from Wesley to the Salvation Army. Unless this irrational instinct is taken in, there is no understanding English life. It is everywhere the counterpoise to an appalling bareness of daily life, and, co-existing as it does with the crudest commercialism and brutal domination, with no attempt made at any fusion between them and it, is apt to strike the foreigner as hypocritical. It appears again and again in English life, as reverence for unwritten law, as respect for the legal and social order, for everything which is, with all its imperfections on its head. It is the force that makes it possible for the Anglo-Saxon to pursue material pleasures and the lust for power without losing himself in them, and to organize his common life in democratic forms such as would lead to a complete dissolution of the social order in any community where there was less reverence for non-rational values.

With the great mass of the people, the instinct for the non-rational has been so completely driven under by their business and sporting instincts that it comes out only rather shyly, and on rare and ceremonial occasions. It is substituted, in daily life, by a singular emotional softness. Of this the average Englishman is as much ashamed as was his Continental progenitor on heath or marsh, but it is one of the real factors in Anglo-Saxon life, and breaks through its dead level even more constantly than does either mysticism or sacramentalism. This sentimentality must be immemorially old. In the best poetry it rarely appears, but on the borderline between literature and the 'best seller' it flourishes prodigiously, and often intrudes into writing that possesses some æsthetic quality. As early as the tenth century there are astonishingly moving touches in Anglo-Saxon literature on the relation between master and servant, between man and wife. The emotional life of woman is early explored, not only by such a master as Shakespeare, but by the crowd of poets of average rank; that of the child appears in literature with Defoe, long before it was touched on in other literatures. Popular ballads of the fifteenth and sixteenth centuries contain a mixture of harsh masculinity and sentimentality; they speak of wives waiting, in vain, for their husbands whom battlefield or sea has swallowed, or of the bold outlaw Robin Hood, who is a far better man than the legitimate powers of Church and State. When the ballad passes from the county into the metropolis, the bounds of æsthetic possibility are crossed – the noble King Cophetua marries the virtuous beggar-maid. Nowhere else in the world do we find anything comparable to the sentimentalization of the criminal, initiated about 1830 by the novels of Harrison Ainsworth and Bulwer Lytton.

This sentimentality is not confined to novels and popular lyrics; it is a potent force in public life. Britain is the home of modern social legislation, of prison and asylum reform, of protection of animal life, and of the fight against alcohol. The contrast may be a grotesque one, between the sentimental philanthropist, man or woman, and the fox-hunting, game-shooting squires and the Stock Exchange speculators; but the former are quite as genuinely English as are the latter; in the United States, where everything British is exaggerated to gigantic proportions, sentimentality also often attains preposterous forms. Every cinema, every music hall proves the strength of this vein in the lower classes; the feeblest sort of sentimental clap-trap in the novel and the pictorial arts is the sole æsthetic form which produces any reaction in the average English Philistine. This trait must be common to the Germanic and the Celtic temperament. Inhibited by the rigorous conception of knightly will and Puritan self-discipline, it will find an occasional outlet, with the force of something elemental. The national character inclines to ruthless oppression of the weak, exploitation of the worker, insensitiveness to the sick or the prisoner, and crimes of violence of all sorts. But over-developed will-power has not spoiled that national character, and since there was neither a tradition nor an organ for the expression of its higher sensibilities, its emotional life seeks to redress the balance by sporadic and undisciplined outbreaks, that, too often, waste an unproductive sentimentality on the least worthy objects.

§ 8

The Anglo-Saxon, further, took with him to his new home the Saxon peasant's love of liberty. All the great events of English history contributed to strengthen this feeling, and make of it the determinant factor in English history itself. While the story of the Reformation, in Germany, is one of doctrinal conflict, in England, in so far as it rises above the unexhilarating scramble of private court interests, it is a struggle, at first for liberty as against the hierarchy, and finally, against absolute monarchy and the establishment of some sort of free democracy. The development of the idea of liberty is conceived of by the Englishman as his specific contribution to civilization. Magna Charta, wrested by the barons from the tyrannical John, was, quite unhistorically, exaggerated by the Puritans into a democratic document, supposed to have established the liberties of the later middle class as far back as the thirteenth century – a view that seems ineradicably fixed in the public mind to this day. Actually, English freedom was the achievement of the seventeenth century. It was the Puritan revolution that, once and for all, disposed of the monarchical claim to dispense with law and impose taxation without consulting Parliament; the second revolution, in 1688, formally precluded the use of these two weapons by the Declaration of Rights of 1689. That England broke the power of absolutism at a time when it dominated the whole of the rest of Europe, is its capital contribution to modern civil liberty. Religious freedom for the individual was worked out, not in England, but in Germany, mainly as the outcome of the Thirty Years' War. In England it existed only under the Puritan regime, and then subject to the very important limitation that it was confined to the various Protestant sects. Catholics did not achieve civil equality till 1829, and, indeed, not fully till 1870, when they gained admission to the older Universities. In other departments, however, England led. Thus, towards the close of the eighteenth century, the press began to be a power, and, in the course of the nineteenth century, a remarkable degree of freedom for the press was established, on lines actually laid down by John Milton.

The development of civil liberty, in its modern form, was the work, first of the eighteenth-century aristocracy, arfd then of the democratic tendencies of the last three generations. The protagonists explain the limits of what was achieved. When the Whigs and Tories defeated the Crown, the country received as much liberty as suited the purposes of those then in power; thus Parliament became, in practice, supreme authority in taxation and in legislation. This was an advance on the personal rule of Charles I or James II, but the ideal still remained remote. On any question touching the private interests of the new rulers, such as the Poor Law or Protection, those interests prevailed, without let or hindrance; there was no scope for efforts after freedom on the part of other classes, if their claims conflicted with these interests. Toleration of Dissenting sects had to be accepted in principle, since Dissenters had a certain power in the State: but nothing was left undone to make this toleration practically inoperative. No one thought of extending it to Catholics, on grounds of principle. There was freedom for those in possession and, as time went on, for those who were able to wrest it from them – the middle classes and Nonconformists, first; then, workers and women, Irishmen and Boers.

English liberty really consists in the limitation of the power of the State as against the individual. This is the natural consequence of the conditions of 1688. Absolutism had never succeeded in organizing anything like a centralized administration in the country, and the aristocracy saw no reason to make good this defect. The great lords sat like so many little kings in their mansions in country or town, taking part in politics, paying taxes, but feeling no desire to have the State bothering too much with smaller matters, which – as the new Liberal doctrines put it – were the sole concern of the individual. Thus, local government was no concern of the State; it was carried on by the lords and gentlemen, acting as J.P.s, entirely to their own satisfaction. It was no concern of the State that the last of the free peasantry was being expropriated, that a dangerous town proletariate was growing up, or that almost all the forests in the country were falling under the axe. The landlord could do as he pleased on 'his' land. With the development of large industry at the close of the eighteenth century, the industrialists naturally claimed the right to fix such wages and conditions in their factories as seemed good to themselves. The building contractor in the cities took the same view; he was free to pack in as many hapless proletarians as he could on one plot of land at the highest rents he could extract. Since the State did not maintain any schools, but left education entirely in the hands of Church organizations and private benevolence, it could impose no professional qualifications. Anyone was free to preach, to treat the sick, to instruct the children, or practise for fees in the Courts – subject only to a proviso that he did not come into conflict with privileges in the possession of the Church, and of specified medical, legal and other corporations, that made this freedom somewhat illusory in practice.

English liberty, up to the beginning of the eighteenth century, was the prerogative of the then ruling upper class, and signified, in practice, the disfranchisement of the middle and lower classes. For these last, conditions were decidedly better in Prussia, where a strongly organized Central State saw to it that the little man could enter successful complaint against a great landlord – who, in England, was a J.P., while any application to the ordinary Courts was practically out of the question, on ground of the cost and elaboration of the procedure there. Prussia to a large extent protected the peasant from the doom of expropriation by the landlord and compulsory proletarianization; the occupation of its share of Poland was followed by a colonization and systematic development of the area, at a time when England was grinding Ireland under its heel. In England, the advance to anything like general liberty dates from the struggles of the hitherto excluded elements in the population to force a way in for themselves. Thus, gradually, the Dissenters wrested their recognition as full citizens, the Catholics followed in 1829, the middle classes in 1832, and later in the century, Irishmen, working men, and women did the same. Since the essence of full citizenship was to be let alone by the State, English liberty thus achieved its perfectly negative character. Every one separates himself from the State, and so from his fellows, sits in his own little castle and asks, 'Am I my brother's keeper?'

The gradual extension of freedom is accomplished, however, not merely by means of the extension of privileges to other classes, but by a gradual approximation between lower and higher, inevitable in a community where the oligarchy was steadily taking up the top layer of middle and lower class into itself. Thus, the idea of the gentleman gradually filters down, bringing with it the delicate and tactful reserve of the well-bred man in interfering in the private affairs of another, and his avoidance of conversational reference to politics or religion. The English official of all grades is a past master in the art of treating each man as an individual. The drill-sergeant voice is practically unknown and bureaucratic insolence very rare and confined, as a rule, to isolated cases in the inferior grades. Official failures are not covered up under a cloak of official secrecy. If anything like a scandal occurs, public opinion insists – it did so even in the middle of the war – on a thorough investigation of the offence and punishment of the offender, such as is not approached in any other country in the world. The average Briton has no sort of respect for the State, as the merely traditional order. He has an inexpungable mistrust of all government, not excluding the democratic. Revolution, according to British ideas, is not only the justified *ultima ratio* of the oppressed, but almost a necessary means of keeping the State within bounds. Despite knout and pogroms, Russia, after 1905, counted as a 'free' State because it had won liberty by revolution; Germany and Austria, on the other hand, remained till 1918 reactionary, although their franchise was far more democratic than the British, because their constitutions had been peacefully imposed upon them by monarchs.

The process of assimilation, by which liberty was achieved, had another result, namely a renunciation of many aspects of liberty itself. The Philistine of the middle classes, who aspired to belong to the gentry, began not only dressing himself more carefully and adopting a more choice diet, but also associating himself with the Anglican Church, instead of the Congregationalist or Methodist chapel, voting not for a democrat like Wilkes but for some Whig candidate of consideration in the world, and acquiring a carriage and men-servants like an aristocrat. This imitation of the higher by the lower went to positively servile lengths. And so it is, still.

Freedom is only possible within the type. Society prescribes the school to which a man must send his children and regulates his Sunday churchgoing. It decides his choice of a summer holiday or health resort. It sets definite limits to his political thinking; to vote Labour or profess Republicanism is not gentlemanly (in spite of recent Labour Lords). The liberty of the individual is allowed to develop only within the type.

But it is precisely the union of a rigid type with complete individual freedom that constitutes the driving force of British civilization.

So far, Britain alone of modern European lands has accomplished the dual task of creating a world dominion and within it a civilization of a distinct type. Since Roman days, the world knows no other case of this combination. There is a British fashion in clothes, a British method of hair-dressing and cutting, both for men and women, a British type of dwelling-house, a British hour for meals, British table manners and British delicacies at table. In sport, there is a specifically British kind of amusement. In the eighteenth and nineteenth centuries, a British school of philosophy grew up; Anglicanism is a form of religion that occurs only among the Anglo-Saxons; Eton and Rugby, Oxford and Cambridge, with peculiar methods and ideals of education, are products as completely national as are the forms of indirect rule by which Britain imposes its will on foreign peoples. Moreover, these types of civilization, unlike French art style or German learning, exist not only in given areas of the world, they are to be found almost universally; in the heart of Africa football is played according to Rugby rules; under the burning Indian sun, men dine in high collars and boiled shirts; the short British pipe is smoked in distant Australia. Moreover, all these peculiarities have spread far beyond the limits of the Anglo-Saxon world. The Anglo-Saxons have built a dominion that, more nearly than any other, approaches the ideal of a self-sustaining, self-sufficient State. It is not an association between a homeland and colonies supplying it with raw materials, but an Imperium, whose centre has surrounded itself with a series of daughter States, essentially like it. Each of the Dominions strives to imitate its motherland by developing industry as well as agriculture, establishing colonies of its own, and becoming a reflection of the home country in all its scientific, literary and artistic efforts. It is an empire so extended and full of so many diverse interests, that only force could have founded it, but force cannot maintain it; it is held together by the free voice of all its members. The fact that it is so held together derives partly from political and economic reasons, but partly from the force of the Anglo-Saxon idea.

This Anglo-Saxon idea rests upon the premise that, within the Empire thus founded by force, every citizen who recognizes its power is a free man. He can express any opinion he likes, in the press or on the platform, he can profess any religion that he chooses – Hinduism, Buddhism, and Islam enjoy the protection of the State. Unlike the citizen of every Continental State, he is free from conscription, though exceptional legislation may impose it upon him, in exceptional circumstances. No official interferes in his private life, he can move from place to place, clear of any police regulation. The State makes no demands of him, and imposes no compulsion upon him; it merely invites him to co-operate with it. In principle, the Briton is subject to no authority but the one he recognizes. He obeys the law so long as it seems just to him, pays his taxes, in so far as he approves the purposes for which they are levied, and has the moral right of refusing obedience, tax payment, military service, and even of overthrowing his Government, when it seems right to him so to do. These same rights belong to every constituent State in the Empire, *vis-à-vis* the whole. None of the Colonies of to-day is ever compelled to pay tribute to the Home Country either in money, men, ships or goods; whatever they have done, was voluntary. Should any one of them ever decide on turning its back on the Mother Country, there will be regret, but no slur cast on the rebellious one. Despite all this freedom, the Empire holds together – a fact which proves that this State, unlike any other in the world, has a moral basis. On no other can a State be erected. In principle, the Anglo-Saxon world-confederation is the only complete State (the American offshoot is silently taken to be a part of or a parallel to it). It is an advantage for any nation to belong to this State. When the British missionary seeks, conscientiously, to provide not only for the spiritual but also for the worldly welfare of his flock, he can desire nothing better than to have them taken into the British Empire. When the Briton, talking of the Balkans, desires Serbia, Greece or the Armenians to be free to develop on their own national lines, the best method seems to be the creation of a State that relies as closely as may be on Britain, and has the closest possible political and economic relations with the centre of modern civilization. If there is to be world progress, the Anglo-Saxon idea must continue its missionary work in the future. It is the strenuous but glorious task of Anglo-Saxondom to stand for freedom all over the world and to draw the sword in the cause of small and oppressed nations; the development of the world will one day bring it about that the entire earth is filled with the Anglo-Saxon idea, when the Anglo-Saxon dominion (with which the United States will be associated, in some form or other) will transform itself into a league of free nations, whose defence – in so far as this may still be necessary – will be undertaken by Britain.

We have here more or less set out what no Briton would think of setting out systematically, or even, disliking systematic thought as he does, arrange for himself as a logical sequence of thought, but what dominates the feeling of every Briton with the force of a Gospel. The roots of this convinced faith in freedom and empire go back to Milton and his Puritans; they were renewed by an Imperially-minded Puritan like Carlyle, and given an idealistic gloss by the whole Imperialist movement associated with the names of Seeley, Cecil Rhodes and Chamberlain, and issuing in the World War. Cecil Rhodes, indeed, expressed them in his will (cf. p. 73), with a singular blend of the instincts of the beast of prey and the idealism of the devotee.

The whole of this train of thought is utterly incomprehensible to the Continental European. Nine-tenths of its contents are a mere travesty of truth. English liberty, being liberty only within the bounds of a certain well-defined type, is not what the Continental understands by that name. There is something preposterous, too, in the complete ignoring of all non-Anglo-Saxon civilizations that speaks in such a confession of faith, since Anglo-Saxon culture is unthinkable without the German Reformation and Romantic Movement, or without the manifold influences that have come across the Channel from France in every century. The idea that Britain brought liberty to other nations and that a voluntary bond holds the Empire together is, when looked at coldly, a grotesque perversion of history. Canada, India, South Africa, and the Sudan were acquired by the sword. Colonies are administered intelligently and humanely, though always in the British interest, until they resist. India is to send its cotton to England, but not to spin it at home; Egypt shall grow cotton, not corn, such is Manchester's will. If India attempts to become independent, the answer is not a sad farewell but the deportation of Indian patriots. Irish history shows no trace of the attractive force of British civilization; prison and the scaffold reappear at every turn.

Is then the whole thing a mere verbal construction, which the world has somehow been induced to accept, thanks to the vast power of the British press and the British cable monopoly? By no means; there is more in it than that; like any untruth in which people believe passionately, there is a certain, significant kernel of truth in it, which is more important than the cover of untruth around it. British liberty is, in origin, the liberty of a certain noble caste in the eighteenth century, and as such was real enough. But this caste was the solitary oligarchy of history to refrain from shutting itself off from all other social classes in petty self-esteem. Instead of that, it had the brains to missionize, on a limited scale. Even the working class is moving towards assimilation to the world of the gentleman. Other nations are treated in the same way. Sir Roger Casement goes to the gallows; but the Boers, in so far as they submit to British overlordship, have golden bridges built for them on which they may pass to wealth, consideration, and the free use of their own language. The kernel of truth within the great historical distortion is the fact that Anglo-Saxon civilization is the privileged community of mankind. Those who belong to it, enjoy a freedom that the rest of mankind knows not, and the duties connected with it are trifling – they amount to little more than recognition by the individual of the dominating position of this community. It is, to-day, as little exclusive as was the oligarchy of the eighteenth-century nobles. It is always ready to take in other white brothers, Irishmen in Europe, Boers in Africa, or Frenchmen in Canada. There is but one condition attached – the new entrant to the community must recognize the rule of the Imperium. Apart from that, he may keep his peculiarities, his language and his religion. British propaganda even extends to the non-European races. Since Macaulay launched the momentous decision to give English culture to India, the effort of British administration has been directed to making civilized brothers of the Indian, the Egyptian, and the negro. In proportion as they mentally accept the ideals of British civilization and forget all their dreams of retrieving their old native freedom, they are gradually equipped with all the freedoms of the British citizen. These two groups – the full citizens and the protégés – are completed by a third, composed by the friends and admirers of British civilization throughout the nations who may be hoped, in course of time, to give the Anglo-Saxon idea the ultimate mastery within their own people. To all of these, British freedom appears the high light of civilization; that it can only be purchased at the price of British supremacy is naturally not stressed: the Briton himself is apt to be vague in his mind about the connexion.·

If the Anglo-Saxon idea of the free world State be taken as a description of something actual, it is a crude falsehood. But if it were no more than that it could not exercise the magnetic force it does on the world. It is the same with other great historic falsehoods. False, too, was the statement that Protestantism is a religion of merely faith and not of works, that the Puritans are the chosen saints of God, that Socialism brings fraternity and equality. Yet these lies have a greater vital force than any matter-of-fact truths, since they express an idea, and state in the indicative mood what really can only be stated in the imperative. The Anglo-Saxon idea can only be understood as the confession of faith of a community, organized like a Church, which demands from all the faithful the absolute acceptance of this faith and the recognition of its own ecclesiastical authority, and, for the rest, leaves them quite free. It is the confession of a community of faith that presents a high ideal as though it were a reality, and finds in the shameful contrast between the 'is' and the 'ought to be' the spur to approximate the real to the ideal. The outsider may find it hard to credit that this confession of faith, despite the crude falsehoods contained in it, and the crass ignorance of the whole of non-Anglo-Saxon actuality that it reveals, is nevertheless sincerely believed in by millions of people. Such, however, is the case. Perhaps a key to understanding may be found when we examine Anglo-Saxon religion. There is a vast danger here, of course, for all non-Anglo-Saxon peoples. For the British idea is not the programme of a few Chauvinists and enthusiasts, but the faith of a civilized world. In it the utmost freedom – for the chosen ones – is combined with the silent ignoring of the whole of the rest of the world, with an obstinate incapacity to recognize the value of any other form of civilization. It affords a formula for approaching the world in the guise of a redeemer, while ruthlessly subjugating alien states and forms of life. It is this that made it so mighty an engine of propaganda in the war. Germany told the world that it merely wanted to maintain itself. The world was not interested; it watched its struggle for existence with bleak impatience. Britain set out to conquer half the world, with the declaration that it brought peace and freedom to all. And the world believed it, since it desired peace and freedom, and is used to paying an infinite price for an infinite good.

BOOK II
THE CONSTITUTION

INTRODUCTION
GENERAL PRINCIPLES

THE British Constitution cannot be measured by the ordinary Continental standards. There is no written constitution, delimiting the functions of the various factors in the State, King, Lords and Commons. It is a construction of custom and precedent. For day to day purposes, rights and duties are fixed, with sufficient definiteness; the limits of constitutional authority are so firmly lodged in the mind of the people that, in the normal course of things, friction does not arise. Any alteration in the balance of forces in the State, which is the real basis of any constitution, carries with it an instant modification in their respective delimitation, with the result that there is, without any conflict, still less revolution, a progressive shift as between them. Cromwell's short-lived Instrument of Government (1653) apart, no British legislator has ever attempted to reduce the mass of principles, rules, established traditions and mere emergency provisions to a series of paragraphs. For that very reason, the machine of government possesses an elasticity which has permitted the greatest changes in the balance of forces – for instance, the substitution of the middle classes for the aristocracy in 1832 – to take place without upheaval.

There is another reason why the normal Continental constitutional framework does not fit the British case, and that is the fact that it has only three recognized constitutional powers – King, Lords and Commons. A hundred years ago, this arrangement was not only a theoretical construction but it reflected actual practice. Then, the State was ruled by the upper classes, consisting of two groups, the great territorial magnates (Lords), the lesser landowners and merchants (Commons), whose resolutions required to be sanctioned by the King. The government was carried on by nominees of the King (ministers), who had to possess the confidence of the Lower and Upper Houses. Of the people as a whole there was no question in this scheme; it was, to all intents and purposes, dumb.

To-day, however, the constitutional structure presents a very different face. Power rests with the people. Every five years, at least, the policy of the Government has to be submitted to popular vote, in the shape of a General Election. But this vote can only take one form: it determines which party shall carry on the government. The people either decide for the Government at the moment in

185

power, in which case they are confirmed in office for a maximum period of another five years, or for the Opposition, which then forms a Government. All the leading offices in the State are then filled by representatives of the governing party, and all acts of government devised and defended by it. The other party, the Opposition, endeavours to criticize these measures, and make it impossible for the Government to carry on. It achieves its object when the Government feels that it no longer has the confidence of the people. In this event, the Government must either give way, or appeal to the country, either getting from the electorate a vote of confidence, which returns it to office, or give place to the Opposition, whereupon the old duel between the thorough defenders of the measures of the Government and its thorough opponents begins afresh.

Such is the British Constitution of to-day, stated in its simplest terms. The picture has been intentionally made schematic, with a view to giving salience to its structural lines. As such, the focal points are clear enough – the people, as ultimate sovereign, and the two parties contending with each other for the confidence of the people, as the organ of government. Neither the King nor the Lords call for mention in this simplified statement, since their rôle in the living constitution of present-day Britain is merely subsidiary. Any picture of contemporary Britain must therefore deal with forces that hardly figure in any Continental constitution. It must deal with:

1. The parties that alternately exercise power as representing the people.

2. The machinery through which they exercise their functions, i.e., the House of Commons, with the House of Lords as organ of control, and the King, as expedient for dealing with emergencies and unforeseen conflicts. We shall find that the mandate committed by the people to the House of Commons is actually exercised by a sub-committee of that House, the Cabinet, and, in the last resort, by a single individual, the Prime Minister.

3. The machinery through which the representatives of the popular will (House of Commons, Cabinet, Prime Minister) endeavour to keep in touch with public opinion. They endeavour strenuously to present their own policy to the people as the only right one, in order that, at the great assize of the Election, they may receive a fresh mandate; and, to this end, keep a constant watch on the movements of opinion, with a view to adjusting their policy to meet it.

The channels through which this occurs are so various, and to a very large extent so ill defined, that they defy any intelligible summary. There is the party Whip with his staff, the party Conference, dinners of the faithful at some club or other, deputations from the constituencies, by-elections and local elections, great social functions arranged by the social leaders of the parties, and speeches made by political chiefs in the country. And there is the Press, which can be examined and described, the most potent instrument for the influencing of opinion and preparing the way for electoral swings.

We shall therefore have to speak, in the following pages, not only of King, Lords and Commons, but of the Parties, the actual pillars of the constitutional machine, and of the Press, its barometer.

But we are dealing with the country of gradual and slow historic development. It cannot be understood by the airman who sees it only in aerial perspective, but only by the historian who takes into account the features of earlier periods in his attempted picture of the twentieth century. The development of the Constitution of to-day, with its four focal points – Party – House of Commons – Prime Minister – Press – out of the older tripartite system of King-Lords-Commons, must be kept in mind in the discussion of each particular aspect.

CHAPTER I
POLITICAL PARTIES

§ 1

IN most States political parties wear a hybrid aspect. They have a political programme, which binds their members and seeks adherents in all sections of the population. At the same time, they are the representatives of special interests belonging to specific groups, classes, or nationalities, within that population. The Conservatives stand for an intelligent maintenance of established tradition, and at the same time for the interests of agriculture, officialdom and the craft-worker. In the same way, Liberals and Socialists in most countries have a political programme which is as characteristic as their representation of the economic interests of trade and industry in the one case, and of the working-classes in the other.

This is also the case in Britain. The basic assumptions of Conservatives and Liberals, there, are the same as on the Continent. At the same time, the parties stand for a division of a more or less professional kind – the core and stronghold of the Conservatives being the landlords and the Anglican Church; that of the Liberals, trade and industry. But the division is by no means clean. In either case, there are a series of subsidiary groups, associated with the central one. Large sections of heavy industry, high finance and the exporting trades are associated with the landowning aristocracy of the Conservative Party, because, their interests being mainly abroad, they expect a strong foreign policy and think that the Conservatives are most likely to come up to their wishes. Opposition between the workman and the Liberal industrialist has always been driving a certain section of the workers into the Conservative camp; the land-worker has an inveterate habit of voting as his master does, either voluntarily or under some form of mild social pressure. The Liberal Party, too, has allies outside the merchants and industrialists, who form its nucleus. From the time when the Whig lords played the first part in the State, it has had a certain section of landowners among its supporters. A powerful central section is composed of Dissenters, mostly in the ranks of the lower middle class, which gives the party a strongly lower middle-class character. And they still have a considerable working-class following. Until quite recent times, the enfranchisement of fresh sections of the population has, with a single exception – that of the Irish – not led to the formation

188

of fresh parties, but to the strengthening of one or other of the existing ones. The narrowly class outlook which has overtaken almost every political party in Germany has thus been avoided in England. The ranks of the Conservative and of the Liberal Party include members of the aristocracy, of the middle class and, to a certain – though to-day to a diminishing – extent, of the working class. Land, trade and industry are – of course in varying proportions – represented in both.

The fact that the element of class is much less important in the formation of parties than it is in Germany would lead one to expect a sharp distinction in their programme. The reverse, however, is the case: Conservatives, the protagonists of Protection, in 1846 introduced Free Trade; Liberals, passionate for disarmament, began the World War in 1914; Conservatives stood for a 'firm' policy in Ireland and against any extension of the franchise, yet the most far-reaching reforms in Ireland and the introduction of the democratic franchise in 1867 were the work of Conservative ministers. A great Liberal statesman like Gladstone began as a Conservative, while the two outstanding Conservatives of the nineteenth century, Disraeli and Chamberlain, won their spurs as extreme Radicals. Thus, parties, in England, are to-day primarily neither class formations, nor the organs of a clearly determined political outlook, but in the main opposing groups contending for political supremacy. Political conviction, of course, will help to make a man a Conservative or a Liberal, but at least as potent is the force of habit, the fact that parents or school-mates belong to the one party or the other. In the main, people incline more to one political party than to the other by class, origin and political conviction, yet every five years there comes the great day of reckoning and no party can be absolutely sure of its hold on the bulk of its adherents: it always must look to the possibility that the mass of the electors, which has hitherto supported it, may go over to the other side.

§ 2

How has this state of things come about? The roots of the English party system of to-day go back to the period after 1688, when the Stuarts were overthrown and (in 1714) the House of Hanover took their place. Then, the determinant voice in the State was that of the *Whigs*, a clique of nobles which, since it dominated Parliament, found favour with the theory of the omnipotence of the people and its representatives as against the hereditary monarch. In opposition to this group and its inclination to 'liberal' ideas stood the *Tories*, another clique of nobles, which would have welcomed the return of the Stuarts, and therefore inclined to the Conservative notion of the omnipotence of kings. There was nothing of party fanaticism in either group: that indeed was hardly to be expected in a political situation so peculiar, when the representatives of the revolutionary principle, being in possession, were averse to any kind of change, and the representatives of conservative theory could realize their ideas only by revolution. Further, both parties were mere cliques of nobles, opposed to one another, but united on the maintenance of the privileges of their class. Thus, while at this early stage a distinction between party programmes existed but was by no means marked, any class division between them was altogether lacking. Soon, however, it began to develop. The Whigs, representing the existing order, succeeded in associating to themselves the heads, first of big businesses and then of developing industry, who were naturally opposed to any sort of upheaval; thereby this new connexion gradually weakened the landowning interest among the Whigs. Further, since their new middle-class allies in the main belonged to Nonconformity, at that time still fighting for the elements of civil equality, the Whigs gradually became the champions of a – very modest – religious toleration for the sects and of a certain degree of freedom of opinion. True, when the modern ideas of liberty, equality and fraternity, were blown over to England on the wings of the French Revolution, the great majority of Englishmen, without distinction of party, rejected them out of hand. Nevertheless, to the great mass of the middle class, hitherto completely excluded from political life, these ideas acted as the stimulus to the construction of a grandiose idealistic programme on which they effected an entry for themselves into the political arena; the Whigs, in their turn, took advantage of this new tendency to overthrow their Tory opponents. 1832 saw the passage of the great Reform Bill, admitting the well-to-do merchant and manufacturer to the franchise. They achieved power and held it, with interruptions, essentially unbroken down to 1886: their position as representatives of specific middle-class interests and Liberal outlook was thereby fixed. And as the Whigs gradually developed into a party of Liberal reform the Tories drew into their fold all the conservative, agrarian and feudal elements. Whigs and Tories became Liberals and Conservatives.

POLITICAL PARTIES

§ 3

Throughout the nineteenth century, the Liberals were the decisive factor in the whole of England's domestic policy. It is they who transformed the old aristocratic State into a modern State-organism, a free citizen State: tore down all the barriers that impeded the free play of economic forces, and cast the doors wide to untrammelled individualism. Their greatest statesman, William Ewart Gladstone (1809–98), is, if not the actual founder, at least the most brilliant architect of the new British State as based on trade and industry. Energetic, constructive, clear-headed, with a realism however constantly crossed by a strain of authentic ethical passion which swept the Englishman off his feet, Gladstone, first as Chancellor of the Exchequer (1852–55, and 1859–66), and then as Prime Minister (1868–74, 1880–85, 1886, 1892–94), had a larger influence on the history of his country than any other statesman of the nineteenth century. The great reforms which modernized administration in every department, put English finances on a sound footing, encouraged trade, and strove to secure equality for Dissenters and to solve the Irish problem, were, to a large extent, his personal work; at the same time, they typify the ideals and outlook of Liberalism. Whether they concerned a new tax, the removal of some ancient burden, or the extension of the franchise, Gladstone's political proposals, while invariably resting on a foundation of hard and realistic thinking, equally invariably were presented with the trailing clouds of glory about them of some lofty humane or ethical principle. This combination of hard fact with the most exalted moral motives fired the Englishman with enthusiasm, and has continued to characterize Liberal policy to this day. Moreover, Gladstone knew how to use his extraordinary powers as an orator to bind the great mass of the middle class to the Liberal Party, whose backbone they in fact became. So the course of the nineteenth century saw the aristocratic section of the Whigs, whose authority had been unquestioned in its opening years, and who had actually been responsible for the 1832 Reform Act, sink more and more into the background. Within the party the selection of a middle-class man, like Gladstone himself, as official leader in 1867 was, at the time, a significant innovation. This development continued in the Asquith Cabinet which entered upon the war: the only representatives of the old Liberal aristocracy were Sir Edward Grey and Winston Churchill. Its social stronghold is now the middle class. Geographically, they rule Northern Wales and Scotland, where Anglicanism plays no part. In Ireland they used to be strongly represented, but after the Liberal Party committed itself to Home Rule, Nonconformist Ulster went right over into the Conservative camp. With a following thus constituted, it was natural that Liberal administrations should tend to be matter-of-fact and economical, and that Liberalism should tend to be faintly hostile to parson and squire (although Gladstone personally stood well on the right in all Church questions), while, up to 1914, it took little or no interest in the Army or the Navy or in questions of power. To general social betterment, its contribution was notable; they reformed English education (though the final steps, the Acts of 1876 and 1902, were the works of the Conservatives); the reform of the Universities, the reform of municipal government, legal reform, the establishment of the political equality of Dissenters – all these things stand to the credit of Liberalism. These reforms implied a constant though gradual movement of the party centre towards the left, the more so after the second (1867) and third (1884) Reform Acts had extended the franchise to great new sections of the population. From 1880 on, indeed, Liberalism visibly drew more and more from the spiritual fountains of Philosophic Radicalism, from Jeremy Bentham, James Mill and John Stuart Mill, who had created a strong under-current within the party even in the first half of the nineteenth century. These Radicals stood for constitutional reforms far more drastic than the timidity of official Liberalism could face: for nothing less, indeed, than a complete reconstruction of the State along lines of a scientific centralization, in place of the eternal patchwork which is the sign-manual of reform in England. They had great difficulties to contend with. To the average Englishman there was something positively abhorrent in their very thoroughness, the logic of their thought, and their readiness to learn from foreign examples, German or French. Never more than a tiny handful in the House of Commons, they were never strong enough to found a party of their own. Yet their influence was great; their little group is the parent of the much maligned Poor Law of 1834, of the introduction of universal suffrage in towns (1835), of all the educational reforms and the introduction of compulsory attendance at school (1870–76). From about 1880 on, Joseph Chamberlain, until he leaves the Liberals on Home Rule in 1886, pushes this Radical programme more and more into the foreground, and the shift to the left grows with the growing importance for the party of the great new working-class electorate. From 1874 on there is a sort of tacit alliance between the Liberal Party and Labour, whose Members of Parliament, up to 1892, act with it: the Newcastle Programme (1891), in its emphasis on reduction of working hours and increased responsibility of employers for accidents, goes a long way to meet the demands of the workers. Now, however, a double tendency begins to be marked within the party. On the one hand, the Radicals press further and further to the left, demanding the disestablishment of the Church, a bold agricultural programme, far-reaching social reforms, Temperance, Disarmament and Pacifism. On the other hand, the manufacturers and merchants who constitute the right wing succeed for a space (1894–95) in getting Lord Rosebery, an Imperialist of the right, elected as Premier, while their spokesman, Lord (then Sir Edward) Grey pursues a definitely Imperialistic line in foreign policy from 1905 to 1915. Within the party, however, the right loses ground steadily, and those who adhere to this angle of vision tend more and more to pass over into the Conservative ranks.

From round about 1905 on, Lloyd George leads the Radical left wing within the party and begins another reform era full of the boldest and far-reaching measures. As Chancellor of the Exchequer (1909, 1911), he carried an unprecedentedly heavy taxation of large fortunes, in particular in land (1909), and began to create a new English peasantry (1907) by his new agricultural holdings. He was responsible for a degree of interference by the State in the private concerns of the individual (the 1909 and 1911 Insurance Acts, the Mining Minimum Wage Act of 1912) which runs quite contrary to the hitherto most sacred traditions of Liberalism. In 1918 universal suffrage and votes for women followed, and war-time legislation in industry – through tried only as a temporary emergency – showed that the Liberal Party is not afraid of measures which come dangerously near Socialism. In the domain of domestic policy, Liberalism, right down to the present day, has shown that it has ideas, energy and the capacity for development.

Its record in foreign policy is much less distinguished. Here, Liberalism tried to follow liberal philanthropic principles concurrently with carrying on a policy of British ascendancy. Typically Liberal, thus, is the foreign policy of Lord Palmerston (d. 1865), who was, with minor interruptions, Foreign Secretary between 1830 and 1841, and again between 1846 and 1865; and, as such, championed every Liberal movement in every small country against real or imaginary oppressors. Everywhere he would pose in the rôle of universal judge, and extolled everything English in vociferous speeches, while, as a rule, beating a hasty retreat whenever – as happened with Bismarck over Denmark – he met any substantial resistance. Palmerston succeeded in making Continental Liberalism everywhere the moral ally of England and set up Belgium as a bridgehead against France, a Liberal policy which did not prevent him from acting as Turkey's ally in the Crimean War against Christian Russia, from giving tacit support to the American Slave States against the North in their war of secession, or from opposing the building of the Suez Canal, since – before Disraeli had begun to influence Egyptian policy – the new waterway might be mainly to the advantage of France; or from waging a disgraceful war on China in the interest of Indian exports of opium thither, which ended in the cession of Hong-Kong to England. (1840–41). The same obscure mixture of a policy of national interest and a policy of fervid ethical enthusiasm reappears with Gladstone. His 'object all sublime,' in whose support he constantly invoked the loftiest ethical motives, was to pursue a policy of peace, to keep England clear of all foreign entanglements, to reduce or, at all events, not to increase its Colonial possessions, and to act with perfect equity towards all alien races, whether Egyptians, Chinese or Boers. But when it came to a decisive act, like the occupation of Egypt, he was sufficiently the British statesman and man of affairs to discover, almost invariably, some turn that would leave England in possession of substantial advantages which, at the same time, would constitute a specially humane dispensation – for the benefit of Boer or Egyptian. The uncertainties and contradictions of Gladstone's foreign policy have become characteristic of the Liberal Party. It everywhere proclaims its pursuit of humanitarian ideals; in point of fact, it long refused to envisage the possibility of war, and fatally neglected army and navy for a long time. At the same time, there is no case where Liberal peace policy has sacrificed any real British interest; when the Liberals came back to power in 1905, they simply carried on the Imperialistic foreign policy of the Conservatives, which led straight to the World War.

§ 4

By way of contrast to the party of lofty ethical principles, the Conservatives have always pursued a matter-of-fact policy of might.

POLITICAL PARTIES

After a brief period of opposition to the House of Hanover and of coquetting with the idea of a Stuart restoration, the Tories made their peace with the dynasty. They represent the English landed aristocracy – hard, energetic, pleasure-loving, capable, not burdened with excessive thought – and their natural ally the Church. They fight for the interests of landed property and of the Anglican establishment, and turn but a cold eye on the claims of Dissent, of the Irish, even of manufacturers and artisans. In foreign affairs, they pursue an ascendancy policy, and either waste no time on discovering arguments to defend it or simply borrow the humane phraseology of their Liberal opponents. They tend to lack that large command of word and gesture which even the Englishman asks of his statesman; they have never produced a man who captured the soul of the nation as Gladstone did. Yet their contribution to English history is actually even greater than that of the Liberals. They have possessed the longer view of what is politically possible, the greater art in the management of men, and a capacity, impeded by no theorizings, of learning from their Liberal adversaries. Always the Liberals have had a greater plenitude of political ideas, the Conservatives a greater art in directing the State. Further, the Conservatives are in intimate touch with the things that every Englishman in his heart of hearts adores, with the Court, the Church and the nobility; hence, however often and for however long they are driven into opposition, they are, in the long run, politically the strongest element and the one that tends to attract the strongest political heads. In the region of foreign policy, they were the soul of European resistance to Napoleon. True, they offered the most exasperated opposition to the 1832 Reform Bill, and for long carried on a policy of absolutely selfish agrarianism on the question of the Corn Laws. But they have always had the *savoir faire* not to lose contact with actuality. It was their leader, Robert Peel, who carried through Free Trade when it had become inevitable: it was their leader, Disraeli, who introduced the second Reform Bill of 1867. Irish land reform, begun by Gladstone, entered its decisive phase under the leadership of a Conservative Irish Secretary, George Wyndham. Above all, thanks to their great leader, Disraeli, the Conservatives rediscovered the track of an energetic foreign policy – a fact that won them a permanent place in the heart of the Englishman who worships power. Benjamin Disraeli (1804–81), the most significant undoubtedly of English Conservative leaders, who succeeded in becoming England's most successful statesman, remained to the last an alien figure to the average English mind. The gentlemanly instincts of the Englishman frequently revolted against this Jew, for whom any and every political means was justified, against his lust for power and Oriental unscrupulousness; the narrow orbit of the Tory had neither words nor comprehension for the perfervid glow of an Oriental imagination which, as early as 1847, in *Tancred*, foreshadowed a British Empire in whose structure Asia and above all India were to be more important than England itself. There was something positively painful to the tactful gentlemen who conducted England's ascendancy policies in the recklessness with which Disraeli loudly proclaimed the primacy of England to the world. At the same time Disraeli's contributions to England's world dominion are prodigious. He is responsible for the proclamation of the Empire of India (1877) – sneered at in England as an empty decoration, yet of great significance in winning over India, where, from this time on, the English King was no longer an alien ruler in the land, but the legitimate heir of the Mogul dynasty. About 1880, moreover, Disraeli took two steps, both decisive in setting English policy on the path of world dominion: at the Berlin Congress he baulked Russia's designs on Constantinople, and, by the acquisition of the Suez Canal shares, secured for England the shorter sea-passage to India, at the same time manœuvring France out of Egypt. In his footsteps followed a Conservative Colonial Secretary, who, like Disraeli himself, had a Radical past – Joseph Chamberlain. He was responsible for the acquisition of the Boer States and of the Sudan. Although his attempt to bind Canada and Australia more closely to the Mother-Country by a Tariff Union failed, he did succeed in taking the steps that made their military aid available for Imperial purposes. Although the actual signal for the World War was given by a Liberal statesman, in the policy that led to that war – the Treaty with Japan in 1902, the Entente with France in 1904, and the preparations for the Russian Entente in 1907 – the determinant steps were taken by Lord Lansdowne, the Conservative Foreign Secretary from 1900–5. The Liberals were rich in men of ideas: the Conservatives in statesmen of long views. When the 1832 Reform Bill was carried, after the Tories had fought against it in the last ditch, it looked as though they were condemned to sink into a helpless and disgruntled reactionary clique. From that fate Robert Peel and Benjamin Disraeli saved them. In home politics, the great merit of the Conservatives has been that they knew how to turn round in time. When they get back to power, they leave reforms passed by the Liberals on the statute book; Disraeli, indeed, overdished the Liberals by granting the vote to the lower middle classes and so re-establishing the hold of his party in the middle and lower middle sections of society. In this direction they were further helped by the fact that the Liberals, under the influence of the Nonconformist conscience, gradually inclined towards temperance legislation, which drove the brewing interest – most powerfully organized and highly influential in all classes – into the Conservative camp; further, important groups in commerce, the exporting industries and high finance, were being alienated by Gladstone's foreign policy which, often weak, was always incalculable. The provincial middle classes are held in the Conservative camp largely by the attraction of the great galas of the Primrose League, which give the small man the opportunity of being invited to the mansions of the great and sniffing the perfume of rank and breeding; the small provincial shopkeeper, utterly dependent on the favours of his 'betters,' often fears he might lose, were he known to have favoured the Liberals. Moreover, the far-sighted social endeavours of the Church, particularly its right wing, has tended to keep part of the masses within the Conservative camp; the labourer in the agrarian districts generally votes – either voluntarily or under social pressure – as his landlord does, and the natural opposition between workers and factory-owners has kept a not inconsiderable part of the former in the Conservative fold in spite of all persuasion from Labour circles.

So, the party which once seemed in danger of dwindling into a mere reactionary agrarian fraction is once again firmly planted in every section of society: absolute in Church and landowning circles, it is represented in every other group. In proportion as the Liberals are pressed, by their own left wing, along the path of Socialistic experiment, the Conservative party will become the haven of refuge for timorous Liberal capital. Jewish world capital grouped round the London Stock Exchange which, on the whole Continent, tends to be Liberal, is Conservative in England. Since the Conservatives have more capital, they have the more influential Press: *The Times*, first of world newspapers, supports them, as well as journals like the *Morning Post*, *Daily Telegraph* and *Observer*, whose political influence far exceeds that of any Liberal sheet. Even in areas where Conservatism seems to play no part, the leading papers (e.g. *Scotsman*, *Irish Times*) enable them to influence the upper classes.

§ 5

The World War seems to have brought about a re-grouping of parties which is still far from being completed. There was a previous period – 1886 – when such a far-reaching re-shift of party affiliations did take place. An important section of the Liberals, under Chamberlain, revolted against Gladstone's Home Rule policy, and created the Liberal Unionist Party, which, after acting with the Conservatives for awhile, finally assimilated with them. The Liberals – so ran the charge – intended to break up the unity of the realm for the sake of the Irish; they were not sufficiently Imperialist; they neglected the Army and the Fleet. Liberals like Lord Rosebery might strive to stem the tide, but high finance and the great exporting industries, once pillars of Liberalism, but now Imperialists heart and soul, threw their weight more and more on the Conservative side. Now, during the World War, the feeble policy of Asquith, the Liberal leader, was held responsible, on all hands, for the disasters and disappointments of the early period of the conflict, and in June, 1915, the Conservatives, with the aid of the Liberal Imperialists, forced the reconstruction of the Liberal Government as a Coalition Cabinet, in which they increasingly called the tune, thanks largely to the fact that Lloyd George, the best brain in the Liberal ranks, openly inclined to them, despite his Radical antecedents. The Lloyd George Cabinet (December, 1916) had a definitely Conservative complexion, and by 1920 the Liberal Party openly split into a Lloyd George group and an Asquith group. The split ended in 1926 with the retirement of Asquith; the supporters of the fallen leader, however, organized themselves as a Liberal Council within the party, under Lord Grey. Whither Lloyd George is now steering his party no one knows. In the Coalition Cabinet he had his definitely conservative period. He was in a close alliance with high capitalism whose leaders were by him frequently ennobled and contributed largely to his ' war-chest,' which was long kept apart from the official party funds. Then, all the signs seemed to point to his taking himself and his party capitalists over to the Conservatives, while leaving the leadership of the social reform section to Asquith. More recently, however, there has been a re-awakening of the old Radical in him, and he has made a semi-State Socialist land reform programme his rallying cry at the General Election of 1929. A programme like this if carried through must bring

198

about a sharp line of demarcation; it must unite in the Liberal camp the more ardent reformers from both of the old parties and make the Conservative Party even more strongly than it is to-day the stronghold of the old Manchester spirit. Equally unclear, at the moment, is the position of the Conservatives. Baldwin, the official leader of the party, is working with one hand towards a Protectionist policy of the Chamberlain type, and with the other towards a large social reform policy to be financed out of tariffs, motived, that is to say, to secure a reconciliation of Capital and Labour. How far he will get with this programme is open to question. He has against him the representatives of pure capitalism in his own party, the big landlords and industrialists who smell Socialism in every social reform proposal, and are ready to defend the old capitalist system in the last ditch (Diehards). Which wing wins in this struggle will determine the history of England for the next decade.

§ 6

The development of a distinct Labour Party came surprisingly late in England. 1874 saw the return, for the first time, of two working-men M.P.'s, but they were elected on a Liberal programme; not till 1906 was a Labour Party formally constituted, which, however, was markedly different in outlook from any Continental Labour Party.

While the German or French workman was enthusiastic about the Socialistic millennium of the future, the English Trade Unionist, instinctively averse from theorizing, was occupied with cool realism on dry practical work. Once, in 1832, he had fought in alliance with the Liberals for an extension of the franchise. When, the battle won, the spoils all went to the middle classes, the workers, about 1840, plunged into the turbid sea of the Chartist movement. The movement failed; bitterly disillusioned, the workman withdrew to his workshop. Parliamentarism had nothing to give him; for all its grandiose democratic phrases, it seemed to him the tool of a reactionary capitalism. Agitation inside the factory and the strike seemed the only weapons that could give him anything. In no country was it so hard for him to make his political influence felt as in England. True, 1867 and 1884 had given him the vote. But English elections cost money that the workman simply cannot pro-duce. Up to 1918, parties had to meet the heavy costs of getting the names of electors officially entered on the voting Registers. Elections further entail a personal and a Press campaign; until 1919 when the

Daily Herald reappeared regularly, the Labour Party was without an organ in the Press. For these reasons, up to 1892, workmen only made their way into the House of Commons as henchmen of the Liberal Party. Their real strength was in their Trade Unions. This Trade Union movement expressed the mind of the socially and politically active workman; it comprised an aristocracy of relatively well-paid workers, closely tied up with things as they were, most of them individualist Liberals in outlook, who hoped either by conflict or by peaceful negotiation to achieve a steady and progressive improvement in their standard of life without Parliamentary action. In the same way, the Co-operative movement, here as elsewhere, originated in fantastic Socialist experiment, but in this country of matter-of-fact practicality, early accommodated itself to the existing order. Its spiritual parent, Robert Owen (d. 1858), regarded his associations as the embryonic cells of the State of the future; but when the Rochdale Pioneers in 1844 revived his long-shattered plans, they only limited instead of trying to eliminate profits. The Co-operative Societies· with their prodigious development – they included, in 1927, 5·4 million members – effectively trained an upper section among the working class to raise themselves, by associated effort. But a working-class movement dominated by Trade Unions and Co-operative Societies offered no very favourable ground for party politics in any Radical-Socialist sense.

About 1889, however, a change took place. In this year the great London Dock Strike brought the unskilled labourer into politics. It marks the emergence of a social class which, reaching down among the unclassed, is too weak economically to carry on a steady wages struggle on the Trade Union model, and therefore has to look to legal action by the State in the shape of Insurance legislation, measures of social hygiene, the establishment of minimum wages, etc., to better its conditions. For it the acquisition of a share of political power is the first objective, and a more effective one than the strike weapon, since the latter can only now and then be used to effective purpose. Out of these groups arose the radical Independent Labour Party (1893), which, in the course of time, became more and more definitely Socialist, and during the war took up a Pacifist position, under the leadership of Ramsay MacDonald, its chief intellectual exponent. For many years, Keir Hardie was the chairman of the party; he founded its organ, the *Labour Leader* (now the *New Leader*). About the same time as the foundation of the Independent Labour Party, under the stimulus of

Henry George's *Progress and Poverty*, and with the co-operation of German Socialists who had taken refuge in London, a whole series of Socialist groups came into existence – with one of which, the well-known Social Democratic Federation, the great artist and craftsman, William Morris, was closely associated. In 1911, most of these groups united in the British Socialist Party (organ since 1884, *Justice*; leader for many years, H. M. Hyndman, who died in 1921). A third political group was represented in the Fabian Society (founded in 1883), a group of middle-class Radicals of the J. S. Mill school. They present Marxism in a thoroughly English dress, rejecting everything revolutionary, everything theoretic. The class war, the Marxian theory of value, ideology of any kind are neither here nor there. Waiving all talk of socialization in principle, they strive, with the slow caution of Fabius Cunctator, for the transference of land and minerals, mines and transport to State control, and while leaving ultimates to look after themselves, carry on an energetic and tireless immediate propaganda. They support all the demands of the Trade Unions, no matter how extreme. They have been the protagonists of municipal action, and stand for an extended system of State inspection and control, including therein the restriction of profits. Their chief representatives are Sidney and Beatrice Webb, the great historians of the Trade Union movement, and Bernard Shaw. Their principal organs are the *New Statesman* and the *New Age*.

Since 1900, all these various bodies have been united in the Labour Representation Committee, and since 1906 in the Labour Party, which thus comprises both the Trade Unions and the Socialist societies. This division between the two wings has never been completely overcome. Before the war, the Moderates, broadly speaking, were the Trade Unionists, while the Socialists and Fabians represented the left. The Trade Unionists had always been the men who had learned caution through industrial fighting, practical people who were averse to any mere programme-making and visionary dreams. Their identity was not sunk in that of the Labour Party, since, independently of it, they were a power in British industrial life; moreover, the whole party organization was built up on their contributions. Since by no means every Trade Unionist was a member of the Labour Party, but quite a considerable number continued to vote Conservative, the Unions were bound to be on the moderate side at all Labour conferences. This meant that the overwhelming majority of the Labour Party was cast against any extremism. But the non-Trade Union wing has always had far more influence in the party than its small numbers measured. The English workman, in addition to belonging to his Trade Union, which in turn will be part of a great craft association, organized as it were on vertical lines, is associated, through another, horizontal organization, with the members of other unions and societies in the place in which he lives, which are there grouped in a Trades Council, including the branches of the local Socialist and Co-operative societies, and so fills the rôle of a local section of the Labour Party. In these local parties resides the strength of the I.L.P. and of the Fabians; they have succeeded in capturing the leadership in them to a degree out of all proportion to their own numbers. Their work in the localities explains the steady Radicalization – or more properly, Socialization – of the Labour Party, as registered in its new constitution in 1918 and such resolutions – definitely Socialist both in substance and form – as passed, for instance, at its Conference at Liverpool in 1925. The 1918 Constitution, admitting individual 'workers by hand and brain' as members to be grouped in local constituency organizations, was designed to put the party on a broader basis; and since it was adopted, the increase in the non-Trade Union element has proceeded rapidly.

The war showed the workers their strength. It gave them the Ministry of Labour, universal suffrage, an acceptance of Trade Union wage-scales throughout the country, the extension of the principle of the minimum wage to the rural worker, and the development of agricultural Trades Unions. The right to strike, nominally abolished under the 1915 Munitions Act, was recovered after the war. During the war, the workman's exemption from military service depended on the word of an influential Trade Union leader. Men who enjoyed such power were not inclined to return to the factory as the servants of some rich capitalist.

This explains the very marked movement toward radicalism conspicuous after the war. The British Socialist Party openly passed over to the allegiance of Moscow, and even the Trade Unions, from of old the conservative wing of the party, became gradually more and more radical. The Labour Party enjoyed a short spell of power (1923-4), to the great disappointment of the radical wing – for practically nothing was achieved. Two great strikes in 1926 further strengthened the radical tendency.

The question therefore whether the advanced or the moderates will gain the upper hand is still undecided. In the last resort, the extreme left is hardly to be distinguished from Moscow and Communism; its programme already is one of practically naked force. The official programme of the party stands for a peaceful and progressive Socialization, and on that knows that it enjoys the sympathy of a powerful strain among the Liberals. Its present programme is the nationalization of the mines with heavy taxation on capital – immediately after the war in the form of a single heavy impost (a Capital Levy) now in the simpler form of a steep rise in the income tax on unearned incomes. The decision, as always in the British Labour movement, is in the hands of the Trade Unions, which have greatly been affected by radicalism. Possibly the Swansea Trade Union Congress (1928) marks the end of the phase. At any rate it registered its approval, by heavy majorities, of the effort, between representative bodies of workers and employers, to reach a new basis of social peace, somewhat on Whitley lines (cf. also pages 134 *seq*.).

§ 7

In England, as has been already noted, parties are responsible for carrying on the whole business of the State, and political power derives from the fact that one or other of them accepts responsibility and carries on government, while the other criticizes and tries to drive the party in power out of office. Since, however, the country at present has three parties, not two, this schematic picture does not fit the facts. The present state of things is a compromise between two political views, originating in different stages of evolution.

The older conception is that of the eighteenth century. Then, the King directed the country's policy through his Ministry, and principally through his Prime Minister. Ministers were the executive officers of the King, and at the same time of the majority in Parliament. At that time public opinion still was apt to view Opposition as something slightly indecent, factious, even rebellious. The Opposition party, on the other hand, saw itself as the custodian of traditional English liberties, against the King and his ministers. A wealth of invective was directed – in public – against the Government for filling offices with its own creatures and spending State moneys on party purposes; in private the Opposition had every intention of doing exactly the same, so soon as it got the chance. The Opposition was made up of various groups, which did not necessarily require to be fused into any sort of unity. Whenever it succeeded in bringing down a Ministry, the King had to form a new one; whom he entrusted with that task was entirely in his discretion: the new Prime Minister had to produce a majority, no matter where he found it. The younger Pitt was the last Prime Minister to govern in the light of these conceptions.

Very soon, however, even in the eighteenth century, the Englishman's marked political instinct taught him that an Opposition can only function effectively when its enjoys the greatest possible cohesion under a single leader. When success comes, the King ought to have no choice but to entrust the Opposition leader with the formation of a government; and since he has his majority ready behind him, the Opposition more or less automatically takes its places on the Government benches. The prospect of this contingency is bound to influence the policy of the minority in its fight for power; wild and irresponsible opposition is excluded when those who conduct it may be taken at their word and called upon to carry out the measures for which they have even now been clamouring. Thus, dignity and realism are imposed upon the Opposition and it loses its demagogic character ; the Leader of the Opposition, who very likely has already been Prime Minister and may be so again, is the second citizen in the State, second in consideration only to the Prime Minister himself. In some of the Dominions, the logic of this is recognized in the payment of a salary from the State to the Leader of the Opposition. During the debates of various Imperial Conferences it has frequently been proposed to have each Dominion represented not by its Prime Minister alone but by the Leader of the Opposition also, in order to make any resolutions more binding; the Leader of the Opposition has clearly become a kind of junior partner in the government of the State.

This point of view prevails to-day. Its complete realization posits the existence of two parties and only two in Parliament, both loyal to the State, differing only on individual and specific issues of greater and lesser magnitude, and alike willing and capable of serving the State with more or less equal capacity and disinterestedness. This condition was realized, until the Irish constituted themselves a third party in 1874. They were by no means disposed to accept duties as part of the function of an Opposition party. They desired merely to oppose; they never filled any ministerial position; their single object was to extract all that they possibly could out of the detested English State. They supported whichever party promised them the most, but were invariably highly unreliable allies. Their fierce opposition, frequently degenerating into mere obstruction, time and again came near to laming the parliamentary machine. The Labour Party, in its turn, at first did the same, coldly rejecting any share in the Capitalist State. Entering the House in 1874 in alliance with the Liberals, it constituted itself an independent fourth party as soon as, in 1900, it was in a position to do do. In 1906, one of its members, John Burns, did become a Minister, but the party never regarded itself either as a part of the Government or of the Opposition. Only after the World War (in 1919) did it constitute itself a formal opposition. As such it took the responsibility of office in 1923. But the shortlived Labour Ministry plainly showed how much the British Constitution stands in need of the two-party system. The Elections of December 1923 had resulted in no clear majority and no possibility of a working coalition. Ramsay MacDonald, the new Premier, could command a majority with the help of the Liberals only. He never was a Prime Minister with great driving power, but he held office so long with Lloyd George's consent. At the first occasion when he endeavoured to pursue a distinctive policy of his own in the making of a Treaty with Russia, he fell. It was felt as a general relief, that for the following five years, a clear Conservative majority held sway. But the situation has arises again in 1929: after the fall of Baldwin's Conservative Government MacDonald has come into office again under the conditions of 1923. It is yet too early to expect a result. At any rate the British public has not yet accepted the three-party system as something permanent. The two-party assumption may not always be realized to its full, it is nevertheless generally regarded as the normal condition of things, which tends, despite manifold temporary interruptions, constantly to return. So, the Prime Minister is, as a general thing, the leader of one of the two parties, and the power he has over its machine both inside and outside the House is the normal basis of his position in the State. This power really is in his hands, not, as in the United States, often in that of a group of bosses and wire-pullers behind the scenes. Prime Minister and Leader of the Opposition really are the big men in the State. True, in 1873, Joseph Chamberlain built up a Liberal machine with local groups, a county and national organization, and the Conservatives followed this example; yet in either party, attempts by ambitious party-chieftains, like Chamberlain himself or Lord Randolph Churchill, to mobilize the organization against the leader have invariably broken on the deep-seated monarchical instinct of the Englishman. The only case where a party machine has overthrown a leader is that of Lloyd George's defeat by Sir George Younger in 1922.

From this identification of the head of the Government with the party which finds itself at the helm certain consequences follow that at first sight seem surprising. The head of the Government being at the same time the head of a party, the interests of Government and party are, for the time being, one and the same. So, no one sees anything strange in the fact that the Chief Whip, the chief organizer, that is to say, of the party which is in government, is paid by the State. Nominally, he is one of the Junior Lords to the Treasury – a post that recalls the fact that in the eighteenth century his principal function was to employ the State funds in bribery for the party interest. Since the party in power fills the main offices in the State with its adherents, every change of government means the distribution of desirable plums. In the eighteenth century this involved a veritable scramble for place and pelf; but the merciless criticism of the Radicals reduced anything of the kind to very modest limits. The spoils of office are nowadays confined to a series of ministerial offices and certain positions about the Court, all of which are changed when a new administration comes in. The Civil Service is not affected; these administrative posts are very properly regarded as non-political, with the result that Civil Servants have to abstain from any active part in politics. At the same time, the party in power is traditionally permitted to reward its followers with certain dignities; from time immemorial, the grant of a peerage has been a means of encouraging influential members of the party, who are thus elevated into the House of Lords. This sort of thing has been going on from time immemorial under the mildest of protests from the Opposition. Only when Lloyd George between 1916 and 1922 elevated to the peerage no less than eighty-seven captains of industry, brewers and Press magnates and was accumulating a party-fund at the same time, loud protests were heard in all political camps, and a Royal Commission was instituted in 1922 to establish more stringent rules for the distribution of Honours. During the war, too, the reproach was frequently levelled at Mr. Lloyd George of creating unnecessary ministerial and under-secretarial posts in order to attach complaisant or rebellious followers to his policy. Even the administration of justice is not wholly clear of this reproach. The practice of appointing none but members of the party in power as Justices of the Peace dates from the period when they were not merely legal but administrative officers; it is employed to-day as a most handy instrument for rewarding party services, but it is rarely used in a way that could arouse criticism. Moreover, the highest Judge in all England, the Lord Chancellor, is invariably a political personage and the member of a party Cabinet, and no one sees anything odd in the fact. It is further stated that politics come in in the nomination of Judges; a barrister who is a distinguished member of the Liberal Party cannot look to be raised to the Bench by the Conservatives; and even the nomination of Bishops is said to be not entirely free from party considerations. Of these survivals of the old eighteenth-century spoils tradition, only the use of peerages can be said to represent anything like a danger. Broadly speaking, national interest proves stronger than mere party interest. Nor is there any real peril that swift changes of government might upset the ship of State. An unwritten and unexpressed tradition has withdrawn foreign policy wholly from party strife. In domestic policy too, fundamental decisions, when once taken, such as the extension of the suffrage, the introduction of Free Trade, the disestablishment of the Anglican Church in Ireland, or the support of denominational schools from rates, are, as a rule, accepted by successive governments. The Englishman is neither a fanatic nor an ideologue in politics. Every now and then people deplore the fact that every English Government is a party government and that there is no superior controlling authority with the power to make the interests of the State prevail as against those of party; but in the long run they accept things as they are, and find comfort in the fact that parties alternate more or less regularly. After all, the diagonal of forces, which Bentham saw as conditioning the progress of the State, is most readily realized by a process through which each party in turn uses its strength in its own interest.

CHAPTER II
PARLIAMENTARY GOVERNMENT

§ 1

FROM modest beginnings has Parliament reached to its present plenitude of power. Customary law of immemorial date imposes on the King the obligation of calling together his nobles for all important decisions, and prescribes that extraordinary taxes be not levied without the consent of the taxed. For both purposes the Anglo-Saxon king had his Witenagemot, the Norman his Magnum Concilium of the dignitaries of the realm. For any extraordinary demand, such as might be likely to call forth passive resistance, representatives of those mainly affected by the new charges – i.e. the towns and lesser knights – would be called together in the form of a great national assembly, a Parliamentum, the vote of the representatives there being binding on the whole. In these deliberations, the towns and the lesser nobles felt a certain community, as against the mighty great vassals of the Crown; they formed a 'Lower House' in contradistinction to the 'Upper House' composed of the latter. From the fourteenth century on, the centre of political gravity moves more and more to the Lower House. It makes the grant of taxes depend, more and more, on redress of grievances, which it takes this opportunity of bringing forward. It feels – sometimes in combination with the Upper House, and sometimes by itself – that it is the representative of the nation. In 1399–1400 we find Parliament claiming the power of deposing the King, and causing the new King, Henry IV, to confirm this right. By 1583 it is possible for a jurist, Sir Thomas Smith, to speak of the omnipotence of Parliament. In the seventeenth century it came to a last decisive fight with absolutism. In 1688 the fight was settled; by the Bill of Rights, in 1689, the new King had to recognize that he could not dispense with the laws, that he could not levy any taxes without consent, that he could maintain no troops without parliamentary sanction, and that no special Royal Order might dispense from the law of the land. In the eighteenth century the King renounced, in fact if not in form, his right of veto on parliamentary resolutions – and the supremacy of the popular assembly was thereby established. Meantime, inside Parliament itself, the Upper House was pushed more and more into the background. By the fifteenth century the Lower House was claiming to be the authentic representative of the nation. The fact that it represented the poorest of the three Estates, the bourgeoisie, entitled it to claim the right to be heard first in all questions of taxation. Side by side with the burgesses in the Lower House sat the lesser landlords, who had no desire to see the great landowners wax too powerful. From 1678 it claimed precedence over the Lords in all matters of finance, inasmuch as the latter might throw out but not amend a Finance Bill – an arrangement which meant, in practice, that there was nothing left for the Lords to do but pass such Bills without alteration. A further and momentous consequence was that all legislation requiring financial provision is set forth in one single comprehensive enactment, the Finance Act (1861, 1894) which, of course, no one desires to reject, so that the Lords are deprived of any influence on the general economy of the State. Their influence on legislation is still further restricted through the practice, developed in the nineteenth century, of 'tacking' more and more important legislative changes on to the Finance Bill, with the object of removing them from any attack by the Lords. In 1911 the Parliament Act made further great inroads on their authority, since it provided that the Lords' Veto could only be twice applied to one and the same measure; any measure which has been passed, in three successive sessions, in the Lower House, and thence sent up to the Lords, is submitted for the Royal assent, without their agreement if need be. By this means the House of Lords ceases to be the determining factor in legislation and the Lower House governs, through alternating parties. The King entrusts the leader of the party which has a majority with the task of forming a Cabinet; who proceeds then to form his administration out of members of his own party in the Lower and Upper houses. The other party becomes the Opposition, electing a leader. The Cabinet directs the entire policy of the country, and every member of it is jointly responsible for the policy of each of the ministers of whom it is composed. For example, any one of them must be ready to answer, in the Chamber, for a colleague who happens not to be present. The Government is supported by a majority in the House of Commons, and remains in office until the majority either dissolves within the House or is superseded as the result of a General Election. When that happens, the Leader of the Opposition comes into office as a new Prime Minister: the forces of attack and defence change rôles.

The object of this system is to give the Lower House the greatest possible power as against the King and the Lords. The King can only make a member of Parliament Prime Minister. So long as he remains in office, he is supported, on every measure, by the influence of each of his colleagues, and knows that the majority of the

House of Commons is behind him. Since this majority is the outcome of a popular vote, the Prime Minister and every other minister
knows that he has the support of the majority of the people of England. Since 1918 the House of Commons has become, in fact, representative of the people. Right down to the eighteenth century it was
representative merely of the feudal upper class. Although the representatives of the towns were in a numerical majority in the Lower
House, the influence of the landlords was so supreme that it was possible, in 1710, for a resolution to be passed prescribing a minimum
electoral qualification of £600 per annum in the agricultural areas and
£300 in the towns. There is a record of the actual sale of a seat in
1594.[1] The franchise was rigidly restricted, by all sorts of legislative
devices, and extraordinarily complicated, the one object being to keep
voters, whether in urban or rural areas, entirely in the leading-strings
of a small clique of aristocratic families. To such lengths was this
carried that the number of electors returning a member was only
seven in Gatton, only ten in Tavistock, and in Bute for several years
a single individual combined the functions of sole voter and returning
officer. Dissenters were, in practice, excluded from election; Catholics
by an express enactment, not repealed till 1829; not till 1858 were
Jews admitted to a seat in Parliament. The 1832 Reform Act admitted the upper middle classes to the franchise, which was extended
in 1867 to the lower classes in the towns and in 1884 to large sections
of industrial and agricultural labourers. This meant a considerable
degree of democratization. But the franchise was still very far from
being equal or universal. Since it had never been organized on broad
general principles, each extension of the franchise, while adding new
groups of electors, also left out considerable groups, especially in the
lower classes, especially those who moved from place to place.
The regulations governing the placing of names on the Register
worked in the same way. The Register was made up by the agent of
each party entering claims on behalf of as many members of his own
party as possible, while the agent of the other side contested as many
of these claims as he could. Under this circumstantial and costly procedure it could happen that on one occasion – in 1893 – no fewer than
13,000 names out of an electorate of 84,000 were challenged.[2] While
the old historic Tory and Liberal Parties could afford to charge the
expense of getting every possible man on to the Register to their party
funds, the Labour Party was in no position to do this. In another
direction, too, the old franchise worked in the interest of the pluto-

cracy. It was traditionally based upon landed property, and consequently wherever a man had property, there he had a vote. The English landowner generally had more than one residence in the country, as well as a house in town; the property basis of the franchise therefore worked out as a system of pluralism, which was of no small advantage to the historic governing class. Nor was its significance merely theoretical. Contests did not take place on the same day in all constituencies; on the contrary, the Royal messenger who traditionally brought the writ declaring a fresh election, took longer to get to Newcastle from London than he did to get to Oxford, with the result that the election was spread over several weeks – a fact that enabled the possessing classes to make full use of their plural votes. In debates in Parliament, the number of these property-owning pluralists was estimated to amount to a round half-million; in 1905 it was reckoned that they gave the Conservative Party some forty seats – or an eighth of its entire number. Since, in addition, M.A.s of Oxford and Cambridge, London and Dublin, and certain representatives of the four Scottish Universities return University M.P.s, some 55,000 representatives of education were thus endowed with a plural vote. Further, it was not till 1911 that payment of members was restored. It had existed in olden times, but was abolished in the seventeenth century. Under the guise of a desire for complete disinterestedness, the upper-class oligarchy had, here, an admirable device for excluding any but men of private means from membership of the House of Commons. When the workers founded a party of their own, they paid salaries to their M.P.s out of Trade Union funds, until they were stopped by the Osborne Judgment in 1909. In 1911 this old injustice was remedied, by the allowance to every M.P. of a salary of £400 per annum from the State.

Finally, in 1918, the principles of a thoroughly democratic franchise were at last established in England. True, equality is still not secured: education still has its privilege – the University vote has been extended to the graduates of the newer Universities, and there are altogether fifteen University M.P.s; the graduate has the right to vote for a second representative in addition to his local M.P. The privileges of property have been largely limited, but not abolished; no one may vote in more than two constituencies,[3] and voting now takes place in all of them on the same day; but the elector may still vote once where he resides and again, in virtue of his occupation of business premises – an arrangement that is occasionally advantageous to the supporter of the Labour Party, but works, in the main, to strengthen the pull enjoyed by the well-to-do suburban supporters of the powers that be. These two exceptions apart, however, the franchise is now throughly democratic. The 1918 Act gave votes to all males at the age of twenty-one on a six-months' residential qualification, with arrangements for sailors and soldiers. The Register has been simplified, and the expense of its preparation, instead of being cast upon the parties, is borne as to one-half by the State and as to the other by the authority in the constituency. Proportional representation, once strongly urged by John Stuart Mill and a section of Radicals, is admitted in theory, but restricted in practice to University representation. The number of members, now the Irish members have withdrawn from Westminster, is 615. Further, the franchise was by the 1918 Act extended to women. Female suffrage had been on the programme of Radicals like Bentham, and demanded by the champions of the Rights of Women, like Mary Wollstonecraft, ever since 1792; it had been in effect for some time in Australia. Under the pressure of an unremitting and ruthless agitation on the part of women themselves between 1911 and 1914, it at last became law in England. The limitations as to age and property of the 1918 Act were swept away in 1928.

§ 2

The whole power of the State is concentrated in Parliament – i.e. in the House of Commons. Parliament can depose the King and determine the succession. Its legislative authority is unlimited; it can, in the words of an oft-quoted saying, do anything short of making a man into a woman, and vice versa. There is no constitution which might protect certain fundamental institutions as the Monarchy, private property, etc., by demanding a qualified or repeated vote for any change. It would be quite possible for a strong Labour majority in any given Parliament to do away in the forms of ordinary legislation with any sacred rights of any part of the nation. Moreover, the authority of Parliament over administration is also unlimited. The theory of Roman law, placing all administration under the monarch, though favoured by the Stuarts, has never obtained in England. Parliament can supervise every detail of administration, through its power to have all official acts submitted to it, and to call anyone – whether an official or no – to appear before it and give evidence. Consequently, there is no *lèse-majesté*: only offences against the

PARLIAMENTARY GOVERNMENT

privileges of Parliament. There is no Government ordinance that cannot, at any time, be superseded by parliamentary resolution; no military jurisdiction outside the ordinary courts of law, and no, or only a very limited, protection of officials. For the Englishman, this omnipotence of Parliament constitutes 'liberty': every other form of constitution is for him synonymous with 'slavery.'

Parliament works by Bills which, after three readings, become Acts. A Bill is introduced for its first reading by a member, generally a minister. This first reading is purely formal, and there is no discussion. Conflict begins on the second reading, when the principles underlying the proposal are debated by the leaders on either side. If the Bill is then rejected, it is dead for the session. If, on the other hand, it has a majority, it is referred to committee. Since all members are entitled to take part in the discussion, this Committee of the whole House simply enables debate to take place without certain restrictions. (Real committees, in the sense of Continental practice, are gradually becoming more frequent but are still the exception rather than the rule.) Now, the debate proceeds paragraph by paragraph, and every detail is fought. This detailed discussion is then, as it were, summed up in the Report stage, when the assembly has the Bill reported to it and there is a second opportunity for the House to debate details. The Report stage decides the fate of the Bill; the third reading as a rule produces only small modifications. The Bill, as passed, then goes up to the Lords. If it is passed there, it is finished with; at the close of the session it receives the Royal assent and becomes an Act of Parliament. If the Lords amend it, it travels for a time to and fro between the two Houses, until, finally, either agreement is come to, or the Commons either drop the measure or pass it again in the form that enables it to dispense with the Lords' veto.

A peculiar tradition governs Budget discussions. There is no general Bill which comprises all income and expenditure of the State in a single perspicuous statement. Rather, a considerable portion of State expenditure is charged to the Consolidated Fund, which is voted *en bloc*, and is considered as a grant made to the King for the period of his lifetime, like the Civil List, interest on the National Debt, and the salaries of the Judges. In the same way, about half the State income, the Permanent Grants, are voted once and for all. The balance comprises merely the sources of the year's income which have to be voted, notably income tax and indirect taxes – the annual fixation of his income tax is the one part of the Budget that interests the

213

average citizen – and the fresh expenditure to be voted for the year, which is either of a temporary nature or such as the House has hitherto refused to accept as permanent. The expenditure of each separate Department is laid before the House in the form of annual Estimates, voted separately, and then, after the conclusion of the Budget debates, gathered together in one great proposal, the annual Finance Act. At the close of the debate, the provision for new taxation is set out in an Appropriation Act.

The Budget is, in Germany, the favourite battle-ground of the most efficient and best informed among the members; in England, however, the private member finds himself more or less in the background, when it comes on. Budget debates, comparable to ours, take place only in Committee of Supply, which corresponds more or less to our Budget Commission. Time presses – the discussion begins on March 1, the financial year on April 1. The imposts proposed can be rejected or reduced but not increased (for it is the duty of the member to defend his constituents against the rapacity of the King's counsellors); the way is therefore effectively barred to the satisfaction of any small local claims; the Government, not the private member, is the important factor. Finally, and most important, the Government has a wide latitude in the distribution of items; within the same expenditure section, it can apply sums voted for one purpose to no inconsiderable extent to another. Its power to do this is always contested in principle but always condoned, since Parliament is far too overburdened with business to undertake anything like a thorough examination of the Budget. It becomes more and more evident that Parliament has little or no voice in matters of finance; on this, the terrain *par excellence* of parliamentary authority, the Government is slowly becoming everything and parliamentary control over finance is breaking down. It is hardly possible to stop this development. If Parliament should make real use of its theoretical right of cutting down estimates, an adverse vote might easily lead to the overthrow of the Government at a time when nobody would want to throw it out.[4]

In legislation, too, the private member has astonishingly little say. He is, however, independent of his constituents. He is not a delegate; the central office of his party had, as a rule, much more to say than the local branch in his selection. The M.P. has to figure prominently in any local celebration and put his hand deep into his purse for local activities; in Parliament, however, he represents no merely local interest. He is the spokesman of his party, not of his constituency.

He is not, as is apt to be the case in other countries with parliamentary government, the man whose business it is to see that the wishes of his constituents are met as far as may be in the matter of light railways, fine buildings, and honours for local magnates. He may secure the nomination of outstanding men among his supporters as J.P.s, but he has little or no power to meet the special grievances of his constituency, since they can only be dealt with through Private Bills, where his scope is apt to be straitly limited. Moreover, the M.P. is tied to the head of his party. If he belongs to the Opposition, he has to vote against the Government on every occasion; if he belongs to the Government, he has invariably to vote with the Cabinet, no matter what his own opinion may happen to be. Every question is, for the Opposition, an opportunity for bringing the Government down; that end is attained if, on a single issue of little or no intrinsic importance, there is a majority against the Government. *Per contra*, the supporters of the Administration are under compulsion, for good or ill, to follow it on every question, even on those where individual convictions point the other way. Nor is it at all easy for a member to build up a position for himself, locally, behind the scenes, against the head of his party, since the local organizations are apt to be in the hands of the party leader.

To win a personal position in the House of Commons is not easy. The new M.P. first discovers that his daily attendance is not considered as very important; for there are only 476 seats for 615 members. Outside the handful of influential members, it is hard for a man to find much opportunity either for speaking or for doing any real independent work. The rule of the Speaker is well-nigh autocratic; he can, if he choose, handle the Orders of the Day with almost despotic authority; he can decide that a resolution is out of order, shut up a speaker guilty of wandering from the point or of tedious iteration, without any right of appeal on the part of the individual in question; he can propose the suspension of anyone who resists his authority; above all, he has complete freedom of choice in calling on members to speak – although, in practice, the party leaders generally arrange a list of speakers with him.[5] The private member is free to introduce as many Bills as he likes, but his chances of having them discussed or ultimately accepted are exceedingly small, since Government measures always have priority. On the Budget, it is only on a topic at once important in itself and also interesting to the public, that the individual member with special knowledge has the opportunity of making himself dangerous to a minister. Every year sees votes for entire Departments passed without any debate, because the date for financial discussion has passed by.

During and since the nineteenth century, indeed, the burden of parliamentary business has become so enormous that it simply cannot be coped with. Since the sole division of the country is that into counties and there are no administrative districts or provinces, all sorts of petty questions have to go straight up to Parliament. For the smallest of them – tramways, gas-works, etc. – a highly ingenious abbreviated form of procedure has been devised in the shape of Private Bill legislation, which enables such issues to be handled moderately speedily and on more or less non-party lines. But this is far from meeting the difficulty. Since the committee system is most imperfectly developed, and the Irish in the eighties proved that the most important Bills could be successfully obstructed, recourse has had to be had to legislation by time-table and the use of the closure. Nowadays hardly any highly controversial Bill is put through without a ruthless use of the 'Guillotine' procedure, which makes grave inroads on the opportunities of the private member, while giving the minister responsible for the measure the right to speak as often as he likes and to wind up. This never happens without loud protests on the part of the Opposition – but *au fond* no one takes them very seriously, since the Englishman regards Parliament as a fighting ground rather than as a legislative commission or organ of financial control. In 1832, when the magnificently extravagant administration of the aristocratic dilettante was made an end of by a Parliament of thrifty manufacturers, the controlling functions of the Commons were taken seriously. But as the mass of legislation grew year by year, decade by decade, and Parliament seemed in danger of being submerged, a decision had to be made: Did Parliament seek to be a court of audit with legislative functions, or a political arena? German development pursued the former line, the powerful fighting instinct of the Englishman pushed him along the latter. The more active the part the English man of business takes in politics, the more does he tend to become a political gentleman – complaining, of course, about his taxes, but never really putting them first. Thus, the pivot of the English parliamentary machine is not quiet, objective work, but the thrilling game of bringing down a Ministry. Leadership does not go to the men who understand figures and keep a keen eye on the Bills, but to the fighting spirits who want their country to forge ahead.

In these circumstances, Parliament offers very little scope for the private member; he is lost in the machine. He may make himself useful, nay indispensable, to his leader by skilful fighting when something unexpected turns up; he may, either at party conferences or as leader of a 'cave,' attempt to force the party machine to adopt some specific line of policy – but that is all. On every issue of any importance, his vote must be given along party lines; a man has to be very strong to risk defying the Whips. Two lines of activity alone are really open to him. He can put questions to the Government; and these questions, put to Ministers directly after the opening of each day's work, do enable a certain check to be kept on the Government's political – though not financial – activities. Further, he can do all sorts of work behind the scenes, and so make himself sometimes so indispensable, sometimes so dangerous to his party that they find it desirable to draw him into the inner circle of its control.

§ 3

The fact that the private member is pushed into the background saves the English system from the democratic deterioration that has taken place in Germany, France and elsewhere. The Government, instead of being merely the executive instrument of a many-headed majority, is a powerful office with some hundreds of parliamentary servants whom it really commands. The bow must not be stretched too taut; there is always the possibility of a palace revolution to be reckoned with, should loyalty be pressed too hard; but direction is in the hands of the Government, all the time. Without anyone's being fully aware of what was going on, a long course of peaceful evolution has presented the nation with a choice between an interfering if thrifty democracy and a politically large-scale rule by the few, and, instinctively, it chose the latter alternative. By a process not recorded in any definite legislative enactments, the historic supremacy of Parliament has been superseded by a well-nigh complete supremacy of the Cabinet. In practice the most vital organ of the life of the State, the Cabinet has no juridical existence. In the seventeenth century, it arose, gradually, as a sort of secret cabal, composed of the most trusted advisers of the King, who settled matters with him and progressively superseded the real State department, the Privy Council.[6] From the Restoration on, the Cabinet became the effective Ministry, which directed the fortunes of the country. It still retained, however, something of the character of a non-legal, secret conclave. Even to-day, by no means all ministers are in the Cabinet. Nor is there any regulation as to who is and who is not a member of it. Actually it is composed of the heads of the great political administrations, i.e. the ancient Secretaries of State (Foreign Office, Home Office, Colonies, War, India), the Chancellor of the Exchequer, the First Lord of the Admiralty, and, as a rule, the Secretary for Scotland, the President of the Board of Trade, and, more recently, the President of the Board of Education, the Minister of Health, the Minister of Agriculture and often one of the Law Officers, generally the Attorney-General. The Postmaster-General and the First Commissioner of Works, like the Law Officers, may or may not have a seat in the Cabinet. It invariably contains the holders of completely fossilized offices – the Lord Privy Seal and the Lord President of the Council, and often the nominal chief of a practically imaginary provincial administration, the Chancellor of the Duchy of Lancaster. The Prime Minister, who is himself equipped with an ancient historic office which no longer has any real significance – he is the First Lord of the Treasury – fills these posts with ministers without portfolio – men whose co-operation he desires but who for one reason or another are not available for one of the great offices of State. To the Continental theoretician, an English Cabinet is a rather confusing medley of responsibilities; there are ministers responsible for the whole Empire (Foreign Secretary, Attorney-General, First Lord of the Admiralty), others for Great Britain and Northern Ireland (Secretaries for Trade, Agriculture) or for England alone (Education), or for another part of Great Britain alone (Scotland) or even part of England alone (Lancaster) or a very important part of the Empire (India). No Englishman complains, or is even aware of such anomalies. He is quite accustomed to important matters being settled by an inner clique, while the Cabinet as a whole is presented with a *fait accompli*. Cabinet meetings have no regular agenda; until very lately, no minutes were kept; nor was it considered good form even to keep notes of what took place. Down to quite recent times, the most powerful political machine in the world worked with complete, nay wilful, freedom from all rules and regulations. Complaint is rife that the members of the Cabinet, who are also heads of great State departments, and normally must be in the House in the afternoon of the day of the Cabinet's meeting, can give neither sufficient time nor attention to Cabinet business. In such circumstances, real power is concentrated in the hands of the man who gives direction to the otherwise unregulated play of Cabinet machinery – i.e. the Prime Minister. A hundred years ago, the centre of the life of the State was in Parliament as a whole; since then, it has concentrated more and more, first in the House of Commons ; then in the Cabinet, which really is a part of the Commons; and finally in a single statesman. Cabinet oligarchy has a tendency to change into a dictatorship.

The day-to-day work of legislation is entirely in the Cabinet's hands. Minor matters, for which the House has no time, are settled by Orders in Council. Formally, these are orders of the Cabinet, issued by the King with the sanction of his Privy Council; they are swallowed by Parliament by the dozen, without any sort of examination. It must pass them – i.e. the majority on which the Government depends must be there, or the Government will fall. The number of these Orders, through which the Government actually governs the country, without effective parliamentary control, steadily increases; during the war, issues of the very first order like the Blockade regulations were simply put through by Orders. The Cabinet reigns supreme in the same way, as it has almost complete control of finance. Even legislative measures are hardly altered in Parliament, unless the Opposition succeeds in detaching sizable groups from the Government's majority there. Amendments of substance, if made at all, are as a rule concessions rather to an agitation in the Press and public than to the campaign of the Opposition. The Government is thus doubly entrenched. On any vital issue, its supporters must vote for it, whatever their opinions on the issue in dispute. Further, the Government as a whole is responsible for all the measures it introduces. Thus, to attack an individual member is impracticable. If successful, it would mean the fall of all the rest, whose fall may not be desired. Only the Prime Minister can, if he chooses, drop a colleague who is the subject of attack, and so save his administration. So, the path of English constitutional development is plainly set towards a sort of limited dictatorship, under which the dictator, while enjoying full autonomy in detail, remains subject to a general political control, which may elevate any trifle into a great political crisis rife with danger for the Government as a whole.

For dictatorship has not ruled out opposition. The real object of parliamentary fighting is not to convince the Government's majority of the obnoxious character of its Bills; party discipline makes any such effort futile. They can, however, be delayed; they can be greatly modified by amendments; opinion both in the House and in the country can be so roused against them that the result may be to break up the Government's majority. A party in power comprising say 400 members naturally consists of very different elements, of groups whose particular political aims are widely divergent, and whose wishes can only be met, as it were, in rotation. This fact – that every majority in England is made up of groups – has been one of the main forces which have trained the people to be politically competent citizens, ready to make compromises. If, however, on a governmental programme consisting of four main items, the Opposition succeeds by skilful tactics in delaying legislation under the first three heads, the members of the Government's majority who are primarily interested in the fourth will grow increasingly chilly as their chances of getting any part of what they want dwindle away. Ultimately, the members in this group may break away from the majority; on decisive divisions they will not be there. The Leader of the Opposition will devise topics and proposals of his own to put the Prime Minister in a dilemma, then exploited by the Opposition forces, who will use every available device of parliamentary strategy for the purpose of embarrassing him. The questions with which each day opens serve the same end. They may not be used as excuses for debate: the questions must really be questions. But there is scope for parliamentary skill in the putting of supplementary questions, leading on to more and more difficult ground; the minister, on his part, tries to say as little as may be in words so definite as to make further interrogatories impossible. This highly exciting and often amusing form of parliamentary guerrilla warfare does give opportunity to the private member to shine, though not to settle anything. The real fight is between parties, between leaders – those in the Cabinet and those on the front Opposition bench, most of whom have been ministers and hope to be ministers again; and, in the last resort, between the Prime Minister and the Leader of the Opposition.

§ 4

In the previous pages, no mention has been made of the most important chapter in politics – Foreign Affairs. This is a region in which the operative forces can be described more easily in the negative. The individual Member of Parliament may talk as he pleases about foreign politics, his influence upon them is as good as nil. Even ministers are in the main powerless; the issues are in the hands of the Foreign Secretary and the Premier, with, possibly, a few other members of the

Cabinet, who make their voice heard by sheer weight of personality. It is, of course, also possible for some non-parliamentary outsider, like a great banker or journalist, to intervene, or for the Monarch to exert a decisive influence, if he be a forceful person. But the really decisive force has generally been the permanent officials of the *Foreign Office*.

In the department of foreign affairs, the old absolutism of the kings has changed its person, and, fitted externally into the schematic parliamentary form, goes on very little altered in practice. Once the King decided in his Privy Council, now the Foreign Office decides, and on the Foreign Office one or two great personalities may exert an influence as they would in any constitutional form, but Parliament cannot do so. Parliament has never exercised continuous control over foreign policy. There is no parliamentary Foreign Affairs committee. Public opinion may count a great deal, though negatively rather than positively; there are unpopular measures which adroit political leadership will either not attempt at all or only after long and careful preparation; Parliament will reflect public opinion here to a certain extent. But neither the majority in Parliament nor the party in power will ever succeed in getting the direction of foreign policy into its own hands. The popular assembly has the decisive voice in the making of treaties, in military preparations (military and naval estimates, naval bases, etc.), and in the declaration of war and peace – but on the broad lines laid down for it by the Foreign Office, and in a situation which in most cases leaves it no option. Ministries do not fall because their foreign policy does not command a majority, but at best when they fail in carrying out a policy – which has already been approved by a majority. The main lines of foreign policy are laid down by the Foreign Office, with the co-operation of such official and unofficial advisers as know how to make themselves influential enough to count. If Prime Minister or Foreign Secretary – either or both – have sufficient personality they can, with the Foreign Office, actually settle the country's foreign policy, and it hardly matters whether the majority in Parliament belongs to one party or another. The most momentous decision in the last generation – the ranging of Great Britain with France and Russia against Germany and Turkey, in 1902–7 – was carried through without the cognizance of Parliament; the secret military pact with France of 1906 (which meant an alliance) was throughout withheld from its knowledge, in flat disregard of the majority there. In foreign policy, so many diverse, nay divergent, aims have to be pursued concurrently; its substance is composed of such small, nay infinitesimal steps – the particular turn of a letter of congratulation may be more important than the text of a Commercial Treaty – that judgment upon them is possible only to the single individual who holds all the guiding threads in his own hands. In an assembly which protects the fighter at the expense of the expert, the mastery will always belong to the permanent official who hides his inner knowledge from the world and then, when the moment comes, will smash his ill-informed critics into a recognition of their own utter powerlessness and ignorance.

§ 5

A constitution in which there is nothing regulated, but substantive matters as well as personal questions are remitted to the individual decision of a Prime Minister, would be perfectly intolerable to most continental minds. There is something revolting to every lover of logical clarity in a machine of State whose perspicuity diminishes as one advances from periphery to centre. The rights and duties of the elector are clear enough; so is technique of debate and division, although here many points instead of being formally established are left to the authority of the Speaker. But when we come to the question of ultimate rule – whether it is the Cabinet, a committee of the Cabinet, or the Prime Minister – nothing is laid down. For instance, a question so vital as under what circumstances a Cabinet is bound to resign is far from clear. Gone is the old theory under which the Cabinet is held to have lost the confidence of the House if it is defeated in a division on any subject, no matter how paltry. This theory was incidentally an instrument of party discipline. Effectively as this apprehension served to hold parties together, it did not serve to avoid snap divisions, in which the Ministry found itself in a minority on some trumpery issue. Then, instead of resigning, it caused the division to be taken again, and gaining a majority, remained in office. In the case of the Labour Government of 1924, Ramsay MacDonald actually stated, on taking office, that he should not resign as the result of a Government defeat in the House unless it took place on some vital item of the Party programme: and his Party did, in fact, sustain numerous such defeats before one on a major issue – that of the Russian Treaties – caused it to go to the country after nine months of precarious tenure of power. Has Ramsay MacDonald established a precedent which is to hold for all the future, or did he make use only of a temporary device, the force of which has gone with the disappearance of his Cabinet? Nobody knows.

But this whole organization is unintelligible unless certain fundamental conceptions which we take for granted are abandoned.

We have seen that Parliament is no longer primarily an organ of financial control, nor even, now, a legislative machine. The day is gone for good when each township and each county sent two representatives to Parliament to vote as little by way of taxes as they must and get as much relief for local burdens as they could. To-day, it is not the interests of Cardiff or Nottingham that are represented in the House of Commons. The fact that the 615 members are returned on a territorial franchise is a mere historical survival: a functional franchise would serve the purpose equally well. The House of Commons allows its ancient budgetary rights to be taken from it by the Civil Service: less and less does it take any real part in legislation. But it settles who is to rule the British Empire. It has become a sort of electoral college, which chooses the ruler and can at any time depose him, if either the electors or their constituents cease to approve his policy. More than that – it is an assembly of 615 plenipotentiaries, to whom the British people has delegated its sovereignty for a period of five years.

Within this electoral college, there is a continuous combat for mastery between the parties, and within the parties themselves are other combats, between the different sections which constitute them and the different leaders and sub-leaders at their head. The prize of the combat is a virtual dictatorship for five years.

The supreme ideal is not the silently working machine, but the discovery of the ablest man to fill the office of leader in the State's business. The English system is based mainly on the egotistic impulses in man. True to Bentham's description, the statesman in power obeys his ambition to rule and realize his own ideas; leaders of Opposition, in their own interest, seek to overthrow him and reign in his stead. Neither of them need be thinking very much of the welfare of the State; it will be promoted, automatically, by their mutual and opposing efforts. The English system gladly makes use of any ideal forces in mankind that come its way, any disinterested creative activity, any loyalty on the part of the lesser man toward the great; but it is built upon the egotism of opposing parties and of the parliamentary careerist, just as it was at the time when Whigs and Tories wrestled for supremacy, and Robert Walpole ruled the land with the aid of an army of purchased M.P.s. Only the forms of the conflict have become more amenable to general decency.

Yet the leader can never become the sheer despot. He is dependent on the good will of his supporters in Parliament. His personality may win him that good will: the loyalty of the member to a great leader has always been a real force in the House of Commons. But the system reckons expressly with the egotism of the average man. The individual member of the majority party has an interest in attending assiduously and voting regularly behind his leader; the lack of his vote might bring all his glories suddenly to an end. At the same time, the system reckons with the imperfect operation of this motive. When a Government falls, as the result of a parliamentary division, the reason is apt to be that party discipline has failed to work, one or more groups having broken away from the majority and either gone over and joined the minority or – more frequently – abstained. The motives of such rebellion may be entirely disinterested, but they tend to be largely rooted in a petty form of egotism, in thwarted personal ambition and disappointed vanity within the ranks of the leader's own party. The fact that the earlier legislative tenure, seven years, proved too long, and that five years has been taken as the limit for a party's power to hold its own majority together, is *pro tanto* a proof that petty intrigue and the disgruntlement of small minds have to be counted as normal phenomena in English politics. Even a Gladstone enjoyed nothing like Bismarck's twenty-eight years of uninterrupted rule. There had to be pauses, in which the small mind could enjoy the exalted sense that the great were no greater than himself.

In such circumstances, there is perfect logic in the arrangement whereby the Cabinet, if suddenly put in minority by a vote of the House, itself decides whether it will resign or no. Such an event invariably signalizes the break-up of its majority. If the statesman at the helm is confident of his power to reassert his shaken authority, to guarantee that the disagreeable event will not be repeated within the next few days, it is open to him to do it. To re-establish a shattered front has always been the most difficult feat in politics: the man who can accomplish it is just the man worthy of being leader.

Why, moreover, should the leader be trammelled by elaborate prescriptions in handling his own Cabinet? Absence of friction in the working of the machine is not the supreme consideration as it were if quiet legislative work or financial control would stand foremost. The question whether or no a given Member of Parliament is taken into the Cabinet is not settled by his competence as a departmental minister. For purely departmental questions, however important, there is the permanent secretary. In making up a Cabinet, the vital qualifications are parliamentary ability, readiness as a speaker, and, above all, the number of absolutely safe men the minister has behind him. To tie a dangerous rival to one's own policy by taking him into the Cabinet may be at least as strong a motive as the desire to secure an efficient colleague. From this point of view, questions of prescriptive right lose their importance: that form of handling business is the best which is most serviceable to the party – and party, according to English ideas, is synonymous with the country. This unwritten constitution which throws all power upon the leader, moreover, contains all safeguards against the possible despotism of the great man. He is not tied to paragraphs, but he is to a large extent tied to tradition, and that means something in a deeply conservative country. Tradition is represented and voiced by the Speaker[7] of the House, who in his domain is a monarch as absolute as the Prime Minister. On his election to office the Speaker ceases to be a member of any party: as First Commoner of the realm he enjoys an almost princely status and a salary on the level of a minister. His decisions are not open to discussion: they have often served to develop constitutional law. So long as the Prime Minister has to have the Speaker behind him on any question of the extension of his own authority, he can never be a despot.

Even in the formation of his Cabinet, the statesman is bound by the practice of his predecessors. Tradition constrains him to include, so far as he can, those of his colleagues who have been ministers before. Tradition settles all questions of precedence and competence – although never with the binding force of law. Any deviation from it will raise a dangerous storm from among the ranks of the disappointed. If, however, a statesman has force enough to ride the storm, he may; and in that event he has created a fresh precedent, binding on his successors.

A further and most important limitation of the supremacy of the Prime Minister is the constant regard he has to take of public opinion. At the end of five years, the Cabinet must submit its policy to the judgment of the electorate – this is the writing on the wall, which warns him against overstretching the bow. Public opinion is the haven of refuge of the disappointed in his own party, who spin their webs against him in the clubs, in society, and in anonymous articles in the Press. If the Prime Minister really is a big man, he can count as a rule on rousing that strong sympathy among the masses which the Englishman feels for every dominant personality: but the critical opinion of the thinking classes, better informed and longer-sighted, tends, as time goes on, to turn more and more against him. Public opinion is, indeed, the main weapon on which the Opposition relies. Its attacks are dangerous not in the House, but outside in so far as they awaken a powerful echo in the Press and in public meetings. Here, too, forces not represented on the floor of the House may come into play – provided (and the qualification is significant) they are served by some newspaper. Unfavourable Press criticism of a measure, and revelations of scandals in the Government, have in course of time become the really effective checks on the constant growth of power in the hands of a dictatorial Prime Minister.

At the same time, this public opinion gives him his most potent lever for controlling opinion within his own party and forcing on it measures unacceptable to party conferences. His ultimate strength is that it is in his hands to appeal to the ultimate tribunal, the verdict of the Nation, both against rebellious supporters and a menacing Opposition. This fact makes it vital for him to keep on good terms with the Press. If, historically, Mr. Lloyd George, during the war, came very near to being a dictator, the person who limited his dictatorial authority most effectively was Lord Northcliffe, the Press magnate.

§ 6

In view of the supremacy of the Lower House, the Upper has sunk more and more into the thankless rôle of a mere controlling body. Its position is aptly characterized by the fact that it is denominated, not the first but the second chamber. Up to the seventeenth century, it still possessed equal powers with the House of Commons. During the Puritan revolution, it was abolished for a time: subsequently, although there was an immense increase in its numbers, its influence slowly declined. After 1678 it had no say on money Bills, including everything that could be classed as such by skilful tacking (cf. p. 209), and thereby lost all its influence in day-to-day policy. It still retained, however, the power to reject Bills, and made the amplest use of this power. The preponderance of Conservatives in the Lords was however so great that the whole institution fell into discredit with all non-Conservatives. If the Conservatives are in power, so it was said, the Lords are superfluous, for Conservative measures go through without amendment. If, on the other hand, the Liberals are in power, one important reform after another is thrown out by the Conservatives there. In 1911 opposition to the Lords' powers reached such a pitch that their right of veto was restricted. Under the Parliament Act, it can only be used twice in relation to the same measure: a Bill that has passed three times through the Commons is sent straight up for the Royal assent.

Certainly, the Upper House is overwhelmingly Conservative and feudal to a degree, vastly surpassing the feudal character of the former Prussian *Herrenhaus*. It consists at present of three Royal Dukes, twenty-six ecclesiastical dignitaries (Archbishops and Bishops), and 690 representatives of the nobility.[8] The gentry, which formerly in Prussia was the most preponderant element, is completely absent. Naturally, apart from the descendants of a handful of old Whig families, all these Lords are Conservative. The middle-class element – representatives of cities or universities – is altogether lacking; as is the element of life-peers, with the exception of the five Law Lords (Lords of Appeal in Ordinary). This means that one of the principal uses of an Upper House – that of affording scope for service to men of distinction who neither can nor will fit into party harness – is cut out. There is much talk in Conservative circles of reform of the House of Lords. In July, 1922, and about the same time in 1927, a proposal was brought forward, designed to transform the ancient bulwark of aristocracy into an institution more like the Prussian *Herrenhaus*. Membership was to be cut down by about half and the hereditary element drastically curtailed. Instead of every peer having a seat in the Lords as of right, only a certain number of representative peers were to sit there. In addition to them were to be the Princes of the Blood, the Bishops and Law Lords, together with an elective element. To this reformed House an influence on legislation was then to be secured by the provision that any further restrictions on the powers of the Lords should only be made with their consent. But such a reform could only be carried through by a strong Conservative majority. The more advanced Liberals and the Labour Party regard the House of Lords simply as an obsolete institution which arrogates to itself unjustifiable class privileges, to the detriment of the country as a whole, and therefore deserves not to be reformed but to be abolished altogether. Actually, the House of Lords has not been reduced to absolute impotence, even by the legislation of 1911. The hereditary head of every noble or ennobled family, being a member of the Upper House, is *ipso facto* eligible for every ministerial office. And since (with one or two exceptions) the Prime Minister may fill every

Cabinet position indifferently from the Lords or the Commons, membership of the privileged Chamber opens to the English peerage the opportunity of a political career without any of the uncertainties of an election. Moreover, the delaying veto of the Lords is still an important instrument in their hands. The huge amount of business which the Commons have to get through, in any session, and the fact that every party contains a number of groups, each one of which is eagerly pressing forward its own pet Bill, mean that it is never easy for a Prime Minister to get one and the same Bill put thrice through all its legislative stages within a five-years period of office. At every stage in that process there is fresh opportunity for opposition, both in the House and in the country: at every stage the want of interest in it felt by many sections in his own camp has got to be overcome afresh. There are possibilities here which have not yet been exploited, but may have a certain value in a future crisis.

§ 7

The King has, in the course of time, sunk from being the most important to the least important factor in legislation. Stuart misgovernment in the seventeenth century filled the English mind with deep distrust of personal monarchy. After the 1688 Revolution, real power was in the hands of the great aristocratic parties. After 1714, when the foreign Hanoverian dynasty had a difficult part to play between them, the King ceased to preside at meetings of the Cabinet, and did not venture to make any use of his right of veto on parliamentary resolutions. The King cannot even defend himself against ministers whom he does not happen to like; George IV was the last monarch to make the attempt to exert this very modest Royal right. The King has become the honoured symbol of State supremacy. Personally unassailable and immune, he can intervene politically only when he nominates a Prime Minister. Theoretically, the selection of his leading statesman is entirely in his hands, and there have been cases when the King has imposed his own wishes in such a choice. But the opportunity for this occurs but seldom. It presumes a division in the governing party so marked that the King's favour extended to one among the rivals is a decisive factor on his side. Should the two-party system in future disappear, and England be governed by three or more parties, the case might easily arise where the King would have the choice between several candidates for the leadership. Moreover, his action may find a way out of an impasse

– such for instance, as arises when power is almost equally divided between Government and Opposition. The King thus represents a sort of residuum of power, constitutionally undefined, which can, in combination with other factors – but never alone – help to direct the ship of State in one course or the other: a technical aid, available for unforeseen contingencies. Therefore, his prerogative must not be defined in detail: indeed, it is necessary to have him clothed with a theoretically almost absolute power, normally never employed, because it is impossible to be sure that future circumstances may not arise in which this still reserve of power might not be serviceable. And since during the last years, the Dominions have become entirely free from English command, and are united with England only through the person of the sovereign, there is another direction from which an energetic and skilful king may expect a resuscitation of dormant power. Who is to serve as the last arbiter in a serious conflict between Ireland and Canada, or more probably between South Africa and India, the Dominion of the future? More probably than the English Prime Minister or the League of Nations the common monarch of both, if he should be personally fit for the part.

The King has his significance in day-to-day politics, too. He is the one Englishman who has access at any time to the Prime Minister. This may sound like a travesty of monarchical theory, but it is profoundly significant. The King's opinion is of importance to the leading statesman. It will penetrate through countless channels into court and aristocratic circles and the political clubs. The opinion of the Sovereign – when the throne is occupied by a personality, like Victoria or Edward VII, who refuses to be gagged by the convenient theory that the King can communicate only with the Prime Minister – is bound to be one of the factors with which the Prime Minister has got to reckon. This is notably, but by no means exclusively, the case in relation to questions of foreign policy. So long as monarchies and family relationships between them exist, an intelligent Sovereign will be earlier and better informed on many things than even a clever Ambassador. It is well known that a skilful diplomat like King Edward VII knew how to use this Royal freemasonry to win for himself a position in English policy that went much beyond its constitutional theory.

There is another circumstance, too, unknown to constitutional theory, of the last importance in English political life. Public opinion, the last resort of all English public life, is largely formed by English

Society, whose acknowledged head is the King. Any social group or individual whom the King distinguishes with his notice receives thereby a social *cachet* that disarms all criticism in the country of Snobbery. English politics was deeply affected by the fact that Victoria's court, under the influence of the Prince Consort, took an interest in social questions, and that the Queen imposed bourgeois morality on her court. The duel disappeared from the Army and from society: the laxity, in matters of the Seventh Commandment, characteristic of such novels as Fielding's, was replaced by the lofty moral tone of Dickens: the coarseness and obscenity that had been universal in caricature since the days of Hogarth, vanished away. A new era of capitalistic influence was opened when the then Prince of Wales set up his own household in Marlborough House (1883), introduced Jewish and American financial magnates into the most exclusive clubs, and, as King, chose his associates more and more from among them. The fact that in the nineteenth century no personage of Royal blood showed any interest in art or literature largely contributed to the ineffectiveness of the author and the artist in public life. In a country which puts less emphasis on the passing of examinations or the possession of knowledge than on bank balance, pedigree and social connexions, a Royal invitation to Sandringham or Osborne gives a social *cachet* that really means more than even the ownership of millions. Here is a region where a determined and gifted wearer of the Crown may reap a future harvest such as he cannot be deprived of by any growth in the dictatorial powers of a Prime Minister.

§ 8

English Parliamentarism has two great achievements to its credit. It has given a great people a political education and presented it with leaders of singular competency.

In the first place it trained the people to be law-abiding. Every section of the population knows that every advance for which there is a majority in the nation can be accomplished by peaceful parliamentary methods. The reconstruction of practically every department of public life since 1832 amounts in its effects to a revolution, but in this revolution not a drop of blood was shed. This, a great national achievement, England owes to its parliamentary constitution.

Further, the two-party system represents a school of comprehension of what is attainable such as no other country possesses. The pull of tradition is so strong that each new section of the population admitted to the franchise showed a tendency from the first to join one of the existing parties. New political tendencies, when they arise within an already established party, are much less apt than in France or Germany to lead to the formation of new, independent groups. True, there is the Labour Party and there was the Irish Party; on the other hand, the Tariff Reformers remained as a group within the Conservative, as the Nonconformists, the Land Reformers, the Temperance advocates or the Welsh Nationalists within the Liberal Party, instead of splitting off into independent fractions, foredoomed to political sterility. This, of course, makes it more difficult to get any new idea established. Such ideas have little or no chance, indeed, unless their champions succeed in capturing one of the two great parties as a whole – which is difficult, but not impossible. Each period of office, each parliamentary session even, has its fixed programme of measures for which the party stands, in its fixed order; each group, of course, endeavours to affect the plan in the interest of its own proposals and to push them forward as far as may be, while it is sufficiently disciplined, politically, not to waste its limited strength in unprofitable efforts at independent action.

The two-party system, secondly, trains parties in responsibility towards the State as a whole. The Opposition, in England, does not bring forward vote-catching but impracticable proposals. It knows that victory may put parliamentary power in its hands and call upon it to carry out its promises. The purely demagogic tone that is apt to appear in Continental assemblies is out of the question in a Chamber in which the leaders of the Opposition are past or future ministers, and where the word 'opposition' by no means suggests rancorous and unprofitable criticism. His Majesty's loyal Opposition is set up, in every Anglo-Saxon country, as an obvious and necessary institution; it is taken for granted that parliamentary business will be determined by discussion between Prime Minister and Opposition Leader, that both are co-operating in every great national pronouncement and give expression to the general will of the nation through this co-operation. Every party is committed to the maintenance of the State: every party in its turn provides ministers, and, in so doing, undertakes its share of responsibility.

Thirdly: English parliamentarism has till now known how to set limits to Democracy. The single M.P. is a glorious hero only to his electors; in the House and in the Government offices he does not count for much, unless he really is something. All the petty officiousness by which even the smallest deputy in Continental assemblies knows how to obtain a light railway or a new school for his constituency or a decoration for this or that small light in his native town, is absolutely and ruthlessly excluded. In its freedom from graft and all its accompanying evils, English parliamentarism is unique in the world.

Fourthly: parliamentarism is a machinery for sifting out men of effective will, men with the natural gift of leadership, which is quite unique. It provides certain traditional limits within which a powerful will may operate – limits that, far from acting as fetters, give free scope to a man's creative energies and his ambition. It opened the way to a plenitude of power such as no other system could have afforded to men of supreme gifts, like the younger Pitt, Gladstone, or Disraeli, while they were still young: it enables a man from the lower orders, like Lloyd George, who, in Germany, could in all probability have been no more than a brilliant orator without any real power, to rise to the highest position in the State.

§ 9

Does this mean that it is therefore the ideal system of government for every nation? As a system of selection of men of potent will it may, undoubtedly, work everywhere; but this is not to say that it is the sole system by which such men can be found. The Prussian General Staff, working on quite different lines, devised a totally different method of training men for swift and effective action that reached the same end in its own sphere. Moreover, the State does not require men of will alone: it also requires men of brains who can achieve a true balance between the interests of the various classes in the population, and give each group its place in the sun. For such men, English parliamentarism does not afford free scope.

Parliamentarism is not the absolutely ideal system of government, but simply the system which the English race has constructed in accordance with its own psychological premises. It works well, because two premises are fulfilled in England – the supremacy of the Prime Minister and the two-party system. It is because it offers him something like unlimited power that it brings the really outstanding man to the top in the State; it is that fact which makes a political career more attractive to ambition in England than any prize that can be offered by industry, trade, the Press, the Army or the Civil Service. Where Parliament does not offer this semi-dictatorial power to the leader: where power is not in his hand but in those of mutually contending climbers in kaleidoscopic party groupings, the man of real greatness is not attracted to it. In such event, the man who takes the helm is not the strategist of large and high ideas, but the tactician, whose skill is in devising working compromises and who cannot help pandering to the petty ambitions of demagogy at the State's expense. Parliamentarism is possible with a people of strongly monarchical instincts, and therefore succeeds in Anglo-Saxon countries, hardly in Romance ones. It is impossible where a nation is composed of strong individualities inapt for submission, but is the foreordained outcome of Anglo-Saxon civilization, which tolerates individuality only within the limits of the fixed and essentially uniform type (cf. p. 154 *seq.*, p. 176).

Again, parliamentarism stands and falls with the two-party system. It can function only when each party is ready, at any moment, to take over responsibility for the State; when, that is to say, the Opposition feels that it is a sort of junior partner in a common concern. The nation must be uniform. It must not contain fractions of other nationalities, who feel their nationality more important than the State. It must not be divided in religion. The man whose life is set in an atmosphere of passionate religious controversy tends to have two vital centres - a national and an ecclesiastical - and then Church parties will arise almost inevitably side by side with political, and cross them. For long, English parliamentarism was gravely endangered by the existence of the alien Irish body in its midst. More than this, the nation must be made up of men in whom national and political interests are stronger than any other; men so inspired by the struggle for power that they will put every religious, social or other difference behind them in their desire to win a share in the governance of the State. The Anglo-Saxons are like this, and only they. In the case of more normal human beings, whose lives admit more than one centre, parliamentarism works badly. It has been tried as a kind of political panacea wherever old absolutism was swept away by democracy, in France and Spain, Italy and Germany: it was given to the new nations of the East, like Greece and Poland. In no single country of Europe outside England has it worked really well. In most of these countries it is felt as a plant of foreign origin and tolerated only because the national spirit has not yet had time to work out something more congenial to the soil. Parliamentarism is the natural outcome of the Anglo-Saxon spirit, which cares for the strong leader much more than for a really just and efficient administration. Parliamentarism, far from being a natural institution, is simply an Anglo-Saxon anomaly, which may yield great results on Anglo-Saxon soil, but, if slavishly imitated elsewhere, nothing but harm.

§ 10

English parliamentarism imposes on the whole development of life and of the State the form of fight. It cannot be said that this is invariably beneficial to the whole. There are important strata of the population who cannot fight or will not fight, who have no voting power, and who therefore, in England with its parliamentary system, are pushed to the wall, while a strong monarchy most probably would have preserved them from exploitation. Who, in England, is at all concerned about the dire poverty of the small curate? Who paid the smallest heed, in war and after-war taxation, to the numerous class of small investors, male and female, of good family? Who, in England, will release the mass of suppressed humanity out of the slums? They have no political influence; they are not organized and have no voting power: and every political organ in England has one eye, if not two, riveted on the ballot box. The administration is bound to be more lax than in Germany, since in England Parliament has no time for the mass of Bills, merely necessary detail work in all departments, which are passed every year by our legislative corporations. A necessary Bill for altering the administration of Health Insurance or some provisions of Liquor legislation is considered by everybody concerned as an unmitigated nuisance with no chance of getting through, unless a section of influential supporters succeed in making a loud clamour about it. A Bill, in England, is a measure with a certain intrinsic utility, but chiefly advisable because it gives the party in power the hope of detaching some fifty or twenty votes from its opponent and extending its lease of life for another year or two. Very few things are done on their own merits. In practice, it is impossible to do anything effective in the way of combating alcohol without attacking the Conservative Party. Who wants to promote drink legislation will probably attack the Conservatives on their land policy or their educational programme, since then there is some prospect of bringing their Government down. There may be political shrewdness in attacking the opponent on his weakest side, even against one's own conviction – but an element of falseness and unreality is thereby imported into politics which often tends to keep the very best elements in the nation remote from the field of operations of the mere man of will.

This unreality runs all through parliamentary life. In most debates, fighting is not directed to the Bill which is its nominal subject, but to getting a blow in at the other side; and is conducted not on reasons but on arguments of a mainly rhetorical character. If the Conservatives bring in a Land Bill on lines formerly advocated by Liberals, it may happen that public opinion is now so unanimous for the principle that resistance is out of the question. Much more likely, however, is it that the Liberals will now eat their own earlier demands and oppose the Bill with might and main, because, though the principle is good, the method is false and objectionable: the circumstances have changed: other measures are more urgent, etc., etc. This sort of sham fighting is hardly resented by public opinion. It is perfectly aware that all these words are only the counters in a struggle for power: it does not mind that every apparently cogent argument really serves a manifold purpose: it is designed to detach this group or that from the other party's majority, to import disunion into the opposing camp, and silence some dangerous champion among their ranks. People are accustomed not to expect objectiveness in political fighting, but the arts of the advocate: they take it for granted that the *argumentum ad hominem* should play a determinant part there. Only, the personal must always be masked behind the disinterested; the combat with the opponent must always appear in the guise of combat for great moral principles. Parliamentary life has taught England the cant that every Continental regards as a mote in its eye. A tendency to that may be part of the Lower Saxon-Friesian peasant strain. Even in Milton's political pamphlets the voice of the tribune of the people is as loud as that of the passionate servant of God. It can hardly be accidental that, at a time when Continental literature had barely taken cognizance of the demagogue, an English poet, in his Mark Antony in *Julius Cæsar*, or Jack Cade in *Henry VI* should have already represented him in a classical form.

English party fighting is as unreal as possible. Yet there are limits to its unreality. The Opposition cannot put forward absolutely impossible demagogic demands, because it may be forced by some turn of the wheel to carry them out. In practice, however, it enjoys all the freedom that is desired, inasmuch as its leader can let the firebrands in the party do the demagogic talking, while he remains carefully in the background. The bold freebooter in his own ranks

235

is part of the system; he may pass the bounds of decorum in his personal attacks on the leaders of the other side, and, provided only he does not raise such a storm of public opinion as to affect votes, his well-bred leader may drop a conciliatory word, but will not do anything to restrain the ardours of his firebrand. No one familiar with English parliamentary methods was astonished by the campaign of lies against Germany of 1914–18. To destroy the enemy from within and brand him before the world was merely to do *en grand* what has been the daily practice in Parliament *en petit.*

§ 11

Undeniably, however, parliamentarism does contain within itself strong and operative checks on the defects of the system. Unreal as are the debates, their external form is irreproachable. It is not permitted so much as to mention an opponent by name – lest he be injured: and the effort to dislodge the arguments of the 'honourable member for X' by counter-arguments is not addressed to him direct, but always to the Speaker. Courtesy is further safeguarded by the rule which permits any inaccurate statement to be immediately contradicted by interruption. On great occasions, such as the death of a prominent statesman, tributes to him are paid not only by his own party but by its opponents. At elections it was for long the rule to put up no candidate in opposition to party leaders – a habit now abandoned. The external forms of parliamentary fighting derive from the period when the chamber was occupied by the nobles and their friends. To this day, the influence of aristocracy and gentry in public life is uncommonly strong. This influence not only gives Parliament its perfection of form, but also much of its ancient knightly spirit – that spirit which keeps the stark contest of wills within well-bred bounds, and, throughout, interpolates certain imponderabilia proper to the gentleman as effective ethical forces to control the sheer diagonals of force. Where no such aristocratic tradition operates to curb the nakedly instinctive will of the race, as happens in the American Congress, we find the diagonals of force naked – not to the world's good.

Can English parliamentarism maintain its old level? It depends on its success in assimilating to the ancient aristocratic surroundings the democratic elements that have to a large extent found entry since the 1918 Act. This was accomplished, with no great difficulty, in 1832, 1867, and 1884, but the aristocratic basis is by no means as substantial as it was then. Capitalist elements in Parliament and politics generally have grown stronger every decade since 1832, and notably since 1901, with the accession of Edward VII. The number of members drawn from trade and industry has grown, as has the influence they exert in virtue of intermarriage with the peerage, membership of influential clubs, and as the financial power behind the Press. That a Liberal leader of Jewish descent like Sir Rufus Isaacs (Lord Reading) should become Lord Chancellor of England, would have been impossible in Gladstone's times; even more impossible that he should go to India as Viceroy as a successor to a long line of British aristocrats. Equally impossible would have been the discussions about Lloyd George's war chest. There may have been earlier instances where large sums suddenly flowed into the coffers of the party manager with some vague expectation of a peerage. But never before has the leader of the party kept such sums as a private political fund which was given up to the party only under strong pressure when his claim to undivided leadership was completely accepted at last. Moreover, the lower orders in society are now pressing into Parliament and carrying on politics on their own lines there. In the Labour Party there is a strong left wing group that rejects all middle-class co-operation on principle, although no practical Labour policy for the moment is possible on any other terms. Even more dangerous, perhaps, is the growth of extra-parliamentary democratic influence in the last decade or two; and the fact that the man in the street, rather than the Prime Minister, still less Parliament, has taken to settling things on more than one occasion. It was the influence of the street that forced the miners' minimum wage on Asquith in 1912 – and with it a complete break with the traditional old individualism of the English economic system. The Irishman in the street, from 1912 on, was a powerful factor in English policy too. In the war, free play was given to the instincts of the street. Mass emotion was exploited to the highest possible pitch, and there was a standing fight not between Lloyd George and Parliament, but between him and the rebellious workers of South Wales and the Clyde. It was they who forced food control on him, the limitation of war profits and the semi-socialization of production, all of which Parliament had to accept. One episode in this struggle is especially deserving of notice.

Everything in the Englishman resisted conscription – his old proud sense of freedom, his love of comfort, his conviction that England was in no immediate danger, and a kind of naïve egotism that likes to shove the disagreeable job on to other men and other nations. The appeal to patriotism brought out students and a great number of individuals of all ranks; but it was not sufficient to stir the masses. Therefore mass suggestion, such as the world had never seen before, pressure from employers, Trade Union leaders, comrades, wives and sweethearts, was then tried – naturally without result – to cajole them into the trenches; every device of persuasion was exhausted, at home, in trams and trains, outside the factories; there were speeches, posters, letters from the great; all to no avail. Finally, Asquith and Lord Derby devised a cunning ruse whereby to storm the fortress. Public opinion was against conscription, but it was angered by seeing hundreds of grey-haired fathers of families volunteering while thousands of young men would not budge. Amid the thunderous applause of the multitude, Asquith in the autumn of 1915 threatened to introduce conscription, if the nineteen-year-olds could be got for the Army in no other way. Lord Derby, then Minister for War, set through one more campaign, with an unparalleled use of moral pressure and an incomparable organization behind it. He enlisted even those who had justifiable personal or business claims to exemption. Their claims were to be benevolently tested, the whole body of these volunteers being divided into age groups, and those entitled to exemption then remitted to a higher age group. Since calling up took place according to age, a higher age group meant a longer time to wait before being called out. The whole system was voluntary – but if, as was hardly to be imagined, more old married men should sign on than young single ones, then the Government would refuse to tolerate a state of things so shameful to the nation, and proceed to introduce conscription, which would take every man fit for service, irrespective of any exemption claims.

In these circumstances, conscription, as a moral purification-bath for the nation, suddenly became popular, and the plan thus skilfully laid went through without a hitch. No one really wanted to volunteer: the enthusiastic volunteers were already in the Army. Those who signed on, did so in the hope of being assigned, on some personal ground or other, to the highest possible age group, so – since the war could not possibly last for ever! – that they might never be called up, in fact. By promising extraordinarily liberal exemption grounds (marriage, for example, and 'serious personal hardship'!) the Govern-

ment got every one who had any such ground to cite, to sign on –
i.e. every father of a family – in the hope of avoiding the threat of
compulsory mass enlistment. But the majority of these 'volunteers,'
whose self-sacrifice was telegraphed by the Press in sensational head-
lines all over the world in descriptions of how they stood half the
night, in storm and rain, outside the signing-on offices, were bent
on not serving! Completely absent of course were the young un-
married men, who had no claims of exemption to put forward, and
however the scheme was worked, must be the first to be called up.
National shame was there; the grey-haired fathers of families had
rolled up, but not the young lads; and this shame could be wiped
off only by making conscription law. Once it was passed, those who
signed on and those who had not signed on were taken with equal
strictness; what difference did it make whether a man was assigned
to a higher age-group or a lower? True, the earlier ages were drafted
sooner than the later; but within three months the whole of the
human spoils was in the net!

§ 12

It was a serious experience that a period of extreme national stress
should have found England unable to master its own masses: that,
ready to wrest an excess of bread and circuses from the State, they
had to be swindled by the old tricks of the coney-catcher, into finally
giving the State what belonged to it. Are masses, dominated to this
extent by the coarsest selfishness, capable of being so far aristocratized
as to learn to use the aristocratic forms of English parliamentary
government? Or does the 1918 Act mark a transition to American
shirt-sleeves politics, from which every decent, patriotic and well-
bred person holds aloof? Is public life in England to be governed
merely by the crude diagonals of cunning and force in the nation:
to degenerate into a prize-fight in which capitalism, decked out in
the trappings of democracy, exploits the instincts of the masses for
its own ends? Or will England's ancient civilized forces have the
strength to set up, side by side with the democratic chamber, another
organ of power, which can afford effective scope to the fine, the
aristocratic, the truly civilized elements in the country? An institution that represents not parties, but the nation as a whole, and
includes those incommensurable forces that do not enter into the
parallelogram of interests at all? Will a reformed Upper House, or,
perhaps the monarchy, come to the rescue, and save the country

from being submerged under the flood of capitalism and democracy? Is there perhaps yet to be significance in the fact that the King has not really surrendered anything of his old historic rights, but represents a reserve of aristocratic force that is still available?

CHAPTER III
ADMINISTRATION

THE history of administration is the same as that of the constitution. Originally, matters great and small were determined by the Royal will, limited here and there only by traditional authorities. From the eighteenth century on, the picture is changed. In Westminster, the Royal power of the House of Hanover shrank decade by decade – temporary reversals of the process notwithstanding – while its place was taken by the servants of the aristocracy who filled the Upper House. So, in town and county, it yielded, at the same period, to an administration that was overtly or covertly entirely in aristocratic hands. At the time when Whigs and Tories enjoyed unlimited ascendancy in Parliament, they also ruled the country absolutely, as Justices of the Peace. The organs of Royal administration became the instruments of aristocratic control: since it was their idea to reduce government to the minimum, they developed no bureaucracy. From 1832 the system was changed; the bourgeoisie pressed into Parliament, occupied the towns through the new Municipal Government enactments of 1835, and took a firm hold of local government. To-day the will of the people prevails in administration, too. The forms are similar to those of the constitutional sphere; administration is in the hands of elected representatives of the people, chosen at statutory intervals; they then proceed to elect one of their number to act as chairman or mayor. This democratization has been accompanied by an energetic but thoroughly generous and non-bureaucratic centralization. Under the aristocratic dispensation, each town or county was a little independent kingdom of its own. The bourgeoisie has restored influence to the nation. Ultimate decision rests not with the fraction of the population resident in a given town or county; on the contrary, the part is subject, there, to the whole. In the last resort the sovereign people of the land, as represented in Parliament, determines. But this ultimate reference only takes place on issues of principle; the local authority is responsible for details. This development has proceeded *pari passu* with a steady growth in administrative activity. Without being aware of it, democracy feels after the ideals of the absolutist State, and seeks to intervene by way of regulation, control and assistance, in every possible direction by means of its newly established bureaucracy.

Here, too, change has for the most part been quite gradual. The old absolutist machine of the Royal Lords-Lieutenants and Sheriffs survived the transition from monarchical to aristocratic administration, and exists to this day, although it has long lost any real significance. Both in the towns and in the country certain other survivals from oligarchic days persist, which gradually grew up side by side with the Royal machine and superseded it at last, such as the Mayor and Aldermen, and the Justice of the Peace as an administrative officer. Democracy has incorporated a part of this oligarchical machinery – e.g. the Mayor and Aldermen. It has taken over from the oligarchical State the method of using powers of State supervision, where necessary, in individual instances – e.g. the Private Bill. At the same time, it has created essentially new forms of administration, like the democratically elected Councils in town and county, the new Ministry of Health and the peripatetic Inspectorate. By this means, a certain degree of centralization and bureaucratization has been effected, which has a tendency to proceed further. Many Englishmen regard this innovation as an alien growth. But it will hardly be possible to oust it again because it constitutes the one efficient counterpoise to the tendency of English individualism to run to excess.

§ 1

In the Middle Ages the King had immense powers in administration – sufficient first to restrain and then to extirpate particularism. By the end of the mediæval period, the old Palatinates on the Welsh and Scottish Borders – Chester, Shrewsbury, Hereford, and Durham – have lost their significance. The county of Cornwall has become a fief of the Heir-Apparent; the special administration of the county of Lancaster still gives its name to a ministerial portfolio and survives in certain secondary local government regulations. Henry VIII deprived Wales of its separate administration. Only Scotland still has a special position. True, it is subject to the Parliament in Westminster. But Scottish Common law still obtains in so far as not substituted by English; Scottish Courts are entirely independent: Scottish administration has, since 1885, been under a special Scottish Department, with its Secretary of State in the Cabinet, and its offices in Edinburgh.

The organs of Royal authority in the Middle Ages were, locally, the Sheriff as head of the county administration, and centrally, the

Curia Regis, which after the sixteenth century became the Privy Council, dealing with various departments of the realm through its sub-committees. As intermediate bodies, the Tudors set up Provincial Councils or Presidencies, which however did not survive the Puritan revolution.

Only fossil remains of all this survive to-day. The Sheriff is the executive officer of the Assizes, and acts as returning officer at the election of Members of Parliament. Even less important is the Lord-Lieutenant, who appears in the seventeenth century as commandant of the Royal forces in the county, but to-day is hardly more than a symbolic figure. The old central organ, the Privy Council, with its Lord President, still exists; nominally it is still the highest department of government, and exercises its authority in diverse rare cases, not otherwise provided for. It further has inherited the function of the mediæval *Curia Regis* as Supreme Court of judicial appeal. This judicial function is still alive. The Judicial Committee of the Privy Council is the Supreme Court of the British Empire and has especially to deal with appeals against the higher Courts of the Colonies. Otherwise the Privy Council has little to do. Of its one-time status as supreme governmental department little remains but the fact that all ministers of the Crown have to be members of the Privy Council. So, the Cabinet is, in theory, a committee of the Privy Council. In the same way, executive modifications of laws, issued by the Cabinet, and all provisional decrees – in other words, a very important and continually growing part of the legal fabric – are called Orders in Council (cf. page 219), and thus are still, in theory, what they were in Tudor times in fact: decrees promulgated by the King at a session of his Privy Council. Further, the tradition that it is the Privy Council and its committees that govern the country, still lives on in bureaucratic technique. Thus, the favourite method of creating a new office is to create a new committee of the Privy Council to meet some fresh administrative requirement. This was done for Trade (in 1706), Education (1839), Agriculture (1889), and Local Government (1871). Subsequently, the committees developed into new ministries. So, the Privy Council is the fount of new departments and governmental powers, and since every minister is a member of it, it still retains, in theory, its old control over all the business of the State. So, the old absolutist machine, with the Sheriff as its local officer and the Privy Council as its central department, still exists. In practice, however, decision rests not with it but with the multiform offices that have developed out of it. Further it has been completely pushed into the background, nay, superseded, by the mass of organs of modern self-government.

§ 2

A younger organ of the administration of the State is the Secretary of State, who first appears in the sixteenth century as the confidential servant and Privy Councillor of the Monarch. As absolutism was gradually transformed into parliamentarism, he developed, for a time, into the first minister of the Crown, until this rôle was gradually transferred to the First Lord of the Treasury. It is highly characteristic of the actualities of aristocratic rule in the eighteenth century that this latter individual, originally the head of the Exchequer, should have risen to the head of the entire State machine and pushed the State Secretary and Lord Chancellor, originally far more important than himself, into the background; since it was the head of the Exchequer who had all the secret funds and 'patronage' at his disdisposal – who was, therefore, lord of all the 'spoils' available for greedy politicians to snatch. This gave him a power the Secretary of State could not match. Through distribution of functions, the latter's office was finally split up into five permanent State Secretaryships – Foreign Affairs, Home Office, War, Colonies and India; that they were originally part of the same office is shown by the fact that any one of the Secretaries of State can take the place of the others if need be. In more recent times, the number of Secretaries of State has been further increased by the addition of a Secretary for Scotland (1885) and for the Air (1918). (The First Lord of the Treasury, on the other hand, continues to be a minister without portfolio; charge over finance is assigned to his one-time subordinate, the Chancellor of the Exchequer.)

The essential change of modern times, however, consisted in the removal from the King's control of the old bureaucratic offices of the absolutist epoch. The Tudors and Stuarts attempted, quite in the spirit of enlightened absolutism, to create a set of officials competent to get the utmost out of the country by way of taxes and economic results generally. But before achievement could crown their efforts, the process of clearing out the king sets in, bureaucratic departments are transformed into boards, parliamentarians are put at their heads, and the learned official disappears; the determinant voice in the official hierarchy is no longer that of the King but of the Prime Minister; in local government, the old Royal officers are gradually entirely superseded by self-governing bodies.

§ 3

The substitution of boards for bureaucratic departments frequently implied a marked limitation of one-time executive authority. Even the absolutist State had shown a tendency to group administration. Under the Stuarts, this organization was applied to the Treasury and Exchequer (1612). During the Puritan revolution, almost every department was transformed in this sense: the Board met the Puritanic distrust of anythingreminiscent of absolutism, and its machinery had already been found useful in the presbyteries. No fundamental change in this respect was introduced by the Restoration; the Board became the normal English administrative organ. Then, bit by bit, the Royal administration weakens; Parliament occupies the key positions. Under the Tudors, the effort to be as free as possible of the Royal influence had taken the form of a refusal to permit officials to sit in Parliament; now, the contrary movement sets in; Parliament fills the most important offices with parliamentarians, in order to curb the will of the Monarch.

So we find the Board system in the Commissioners of Customs (1671), in the Board of Inland Revenue (1849), in the National Debt Commissioners (1786), in the Ecclesiastical Commissioners (1836), in National Health Insurance (1911), and in the departments responsible for national defence. Since 1708 the Admiralty has conformed to this model; the new Army Council followed in 1904. But in both military organizations the Board is little more than an advisory body, whose real head is a single individual, the Minister. His power is not so much restricted by the Board as such, but by the High Command, represented in the Admiralty by the First Sea Lord, and in the Army Council by the Chief of the General Staff.

To this day, the principle of parliamentary heads for all the more important offices of State is maintained, and introduced wherever a new department is founded. (Certain exceptions were made in war-time – any special talent from outside Parliament might be called to rule an administration, but a Parliamentary Under-Secretary was usually added.)   But the Board system is not universal. It has been resisted in most of the offices which grew up out of the old State Secretaryships – the Home, Colonial and Foreign offices and that of the Postmaster-General. Some of the newer offices, while organized nominally as boards – e.g. the Local Government Board, predecessor of the present Ministry of Health, had no less than seven ministers on it in addition to the President; but practice did not conform to theory, and the actual administration was bureaucratic.

At the present day, the organization is as follows:

1. The centre of the administrative machine is the *Treasury*. It is the finance ministry and has the usual extensive powers *vis-à-vis* the other ministries. At its head is the First Lord, who, however, has hardly any influence on administration, but as Prime Minister directs policy as a whole. His subordinate Junior Lords of the Treasury, again, are not financial officers, but his political adjutants. They are the secretaries of the party – though paid by the State – and whips, whose duty it is to look after, protect from shocks and keep together the party, the parliamentary basis of the ministers' power. Of the Prime Minister's ancient patronage rights, certain valuable political items remain: he proposes new peers to the King, fills ecclesiastical benefices including bishoprics: and, as final relic of his once extensive control over sinecures, has power under certain circumstances to grant pensions to distinguished representatives of art and letters. The administrative work of the Finance Ministry is now assigned to the former Under Treasurer. Since the Middle Ages, he has presided at sittings of the Treasury at a table covered with a chequered tablecloth (Fr. *échiquier*), whence his name, *Chancellor of the Exchequer*. He is responsible for the Budget, and therefore has a determining voice in every department of administration. Directly subordinate to him are the Board of Customs and Excise, the Board of Inland Revenue, the National Debt Commissioners, etc.

2. The old Secretary of State (cf. page 244) has disappeared, but out of his administration the following offices have developed:

(*a*) The *Home Secretary*, or Minister of the Interior, who controls police, Factory and Mines Inspection, naturalization, etc., and exercises some of the powers assigned in other countries to the Minister of Justice – e.g., control over prisons and the prerogative of mercy, etc.

(*b*) *Secretary of State for Foreign Affairs*, who controls Foreign Affairs with practical independence (cf. page 220 *seq.*).

(*c*) *Secretary of State for the Colonies:* responsible for Colonial affairs with the exception of India (*g*). The Dominion affairs are under a special department of this administration, though the Dominion ministers write to the British Premier directly.

ADMINISTRATION

(d) *War;* (e) *Air;* (f) *Scotland;* (g) *India.*

3. The *Admiralty*, with the First Lord of the Admiralty at its head. With him as a parliamentary layman is associated the First Sea Lord, a naval officer.

4. The *Lord Chancellor* as head of the administration of justice. No one in England seems to object to the fact that he is at one and the same time a minister, and therefore a definitely party-man, and, as President of the Upper House and of the Chancery Division of the High Court of Justice, supreme head of an impartial Judicature. He nominates the majority of Judges, from the Justices of the Peace to the Judges of the Supreme Court. In the selection of Judges merit is still the determining point, but in that of J.Ps., party membership comes in as well. The Lord Chancellor further exercises a large amount of secondary ecclesiastical patronage, and must therefore be a Protestant. As representatives of the Crown in important cases, both civil and criminal, he has, associated with him, though quite independent, the Attorney and Solicitor-General.

5. Offshoots of the Privy Council are:

(a) *The Board of Trade* (Patents, Trade Statistics, bankruptcy, harbours, railways, canals, shipping and mines). Jointly dependent on it and on the Foreign Office is the Department of Overseas Trade, set up in 1917.

(b) *The Board of Agriculture and Fisheries.*

(c) *The Board of Education*, controlling Elementary and Secondary Education (but not the Universities) in England. There is a special Scottish Education Department in Edinburgh.

(d) Since 1915, the Department of Scientific and Industrial Research for food investigation, geological survey, chemical and physical research, etc.

6. *The Ministry of Health*, which developed out of the Poor Law Commissioners of 1834 and the Board of Health 1848. This office has gradually reformed the administration of rural England and the administration of the small towns. In 1871 it was named the Local Government Board, in 1919 the Ministry of Health. It exercises supervision of all self-governing bodies, principally in matters of finance, it administers old age pensions and various acts for the welfare of children, etc.

7. *The Postmaster-General:* and the First Commissioner of *Works.*

8. In the war, in addition to the Air Ministry, already referred to, there were set up a large number of emergency ministries. Of these

there still survive the Ministries of Transport (Roads and Railways) and Pensions. There is also the new *Ministry of Labour*, primarily charged with Unemployment Insurance administration.

§ 4

The modern official derives from the mediæval 'clerk.'[1] The clerk is a cleric with a benefice to which certain emoluments and certain duties attach. He bears the responsibility that the duties – e.g. the collection of the King's revenues in a certain port – are performed, and he has in consideration of this the right to certain emoluments, e.g. a certain percentage of the duties collected. His responsibility need not imply personal attendance: so long as the King's revenues are collected and delivered, either by himself or somebody in his name, the clerk has performed his side of the contract. Under this system, a clerk might hold a dozen offices, have badly-paid substitutes to do the duties of every single one, and himself pocket the major part of all the salaries without doing any work at all. For centuries this system satisfied mankind.

This mediæval system has been reformed so thoroughly all over the world that it has become hardly intelligible to the modern mind. Reform came from the absolutist king who made an official out of the clerk and substituted the ideas of chivalry for those of the canon law. The official is the highly honoured, though perhaps sparsely remunerated, personal servant of the Monarch. Duty and the spirit of personal devotion come first, remuneration will follow, but it must never be the major consideration. This is the modern conception, brought into prominence in France and with especial vigour and success in the Prussia of the eighteenth century. It still persists even in states where the Monarchy has collapsed, the idea of responsibility to the State having gradually taken the place of devotion to a personal ruler.

In England, the mediæval idea of the beneficed clerk has survived with an astonishing tenacity. There was no absolutism to reform it. Down to the nineteenth century highly paid sinecures with few duties or no duties at all survived; during the eighteenth century they even were one of the pillars of the aristocratic state. They were part of English liberty. Sinecures and pensions were freely distributed among the younger sons of aristocracy and gentry, and all their henchmen in every walk of life.

And just as the right of presentation to ecclesiastical benefices was

248

long the bone of contention between King, Papacy, Bishop and a whole series of inferior authorities, so protracted strife raged over the question of appointment to civil offices. Practically everywhere throughout the Continent, the Kings emerged victorious in this struggle; but in England the prize fell to the First Lord of the Treasury, the representative of the aristocratic clique and helped further to strengthen its power.

Eighteenth-century Prussia made the official the vehicle of enlightened absolutism, the instrument of the Royal will, the selfless guardian of the public weal. Such an ideal waked echoes in the hearts of subjects; to be an official was a distinction, and with the weal of the State as object, the best man was not too good to be an official. The English aristocratic State, on the other hand, made the official a petty benefice-holder, whose object was to get as much pay as possible for as little work as possible; since he was offered nothing very important to do, it was small wonder that the best men did not become officials. Sociologically, the value of the service was really limited to its providing, from time to time, means of subsistence to such worthy men of letters as the poet Gay, the dramatist Congreve, and Romantic poets like Scott, Southey and Wordsworth. From the eighteenth century on, the official, regarded as a mere survival of earlier days, was, as far as possible, dispensed with.

In the course of the nineteenth century, however, a new officialdom was created – by English Liberalism. From about 1800 on, the sinecures were swept away, with negligible exceptions. There are still ministerial sinecures, which permit of the inclusion of an outstanding personality in the Cabinet, without putting him at the head of a Departmental ministry: there is the 'office' of Steward of the Chiltern Hundreds, to which a M.P. gets himself nominated when he desires to retire, since it automatically extinguishes his membership; the office of Poet Laureate, which secures a distinguished poet a pension; or such an incomprehensible survival of the forgotten past as the Wardenship of the Cinque Ports.

The Liberal view of the bureaucracy has never been single or clear. For the Manchester men, the genuine official is an evil, to be guarded against as far as possible. For them, he is suspect; he smells of the French police state. He is a will-less creature of Authority, whose final object must always be to rob others of their liberty; the more talented, the more dangerous is he. He cannot be wholly dispensed with, since there must be people to carry out instructions and cope with legislative material. But that is the limit of his functions. He should have no ideas of his own, and no wider outlook; all that belongs to the 'free citizen.' He is an almost inevitable but ultimately unproductive member of the State machine, the 'free citizen' alone being designed for genuinely productive work. According to John Stuart Mill, it is not in the State's interest to have specially efficient officials; the active and most ambitious forces in the country should not cling to the ledges of the Government, but select free professions. Whence it follows that the status of the official should not be too high. There is no reason for giving him any special social position or any very high rate of pay. Political activity he must not exercise, since as a Government servant he is not a free man. There should be no development of an official caste; the field of selection of officials should be wide; to demand any special preliminary education – e.g. in the law – is entirely false. Liberalism so far is the sworn foe of the official.

At the same time, Liberalism, wherever it reigns, will create new officials. Liberalism was energetically bent on reforming the State. The more far-sighted men in its ranks were freeing themselves from the narrow Manchester conception of the mere watch-dog, do-nothing State. The view gains ground that it is the business of the State not merely to supervise, but to stimulate and direct. Theoretically, committees of free citizens ought to exercise this function, but the idea proves increasingly impracticable. It is simply impossible to get on without officials. So, Liberalism, while deprecating their existence, constantly adds to the number of official posts in town, county and national administration. Officials grow more and more numerous, though the Englishman never likes to admit that his principles have gone by the board. By 1855 the number had become so great that a special career, the Civil Service, had to be established, with an entrance examination. By the turn of the century, under the stimulus of war-time legislation, the army of officials had swollen to a point that made England almost a bureaucratic country. Present conditions reveal an interesting compromise between the two streams of Liberal thought, one bent on reduction, the other on increase, in the number of officials.

This compromise carefully maintains the pretty façade of self-government. The leading posts in the State are occupied by ministers, popularly elected Members of Parliament, each of whom acts as a head of department. The leading posts in the municipalities are occupied by elected Mayors; in the counties, by elected County Councillors. The appointed officials are certainly numerous, but in theory they are everywhere assistants only. They cannot form a caste, since they have no uniform training. The entrance examination for the highest grade of the Civil Service is certainly liberal. It demands on the face of it, no University career, merely a high standard of proficiency in a group of subjects selected by the candidate, classics being as eligible as the law. Even the Civil Servant in the lower grades may (so bland theory affirms) rise to the higher by passing this examination. The Civil Servant cannot rule the country, for he is debarred from political activity; he may vote, but cannot be a candidate. So much success has been attained by the Liberal tendency which desired to keep down the official.

Yet mere growth in their numbers has given them far more weight than was at all desired by Liberal theorists. Practice has nearly reversed theory. An official caste does exist, although the methods of training are more various than under the German system. Practically all the higher officials are University men, since the Civil Service examination presumes that standard of education. Cases of a second-grade clerk or an outsider rising into the higher grade do occur, but are very rare indeed.[2] The characteristics of the modern bureaucracy, security of tenure and a pension, though not universal in theory are so to all intents and purposes in practice. There is a retiring age between sixty-five and seventy. Even the Prussian 'conflict' in favour of the official – the State protecting its servants from legal punishment, in certain cases of slight offences, substituting disciplinary for legal punishment – is possible, though it occurs only in a very modified form.[3] Pay in the lower grades is not high; in the higher grades, however, it is on a far higher standard than the German. Above all, the influence of the official is immense. It is simply not true to say that his work consists in carrying out obediently the directions of the enlightened representatives of the people. A quite different division of labour obtains as between the apparatus built up by popular election (Mayor, Town and County Councillor, Minister, Cabinet, Prime Minister) and the nominated bureaucracy. If public opinion is specially interested in an issue – no matter what – the bureaucracy will obey its wishes. In all other cases – and they cover nine-tenths of administration – the bureaucracy governs with the autocracy of the clever man who knows his job and knows what he is aiming at. And since Parliament has long ceased to have time for details, an increasing volume of highly important business is transacted by Orders in Council, i.e. by the autocratic official with only a nominal supervision of Parliament. The bureaucracy of the Foreign Office tends to be independent even of this formal control. And where the power of the bureaucracy is threatened at some vital spot, it generally has withstood even the pressure of public opinion. There was general consent all over England after the war that ruthless economy had to be practised in the State. All the newspapers were in favour of it, Parliament proposed the most drastic measures, but very little was done. The silent, energetic and dogged resistance of the omniscient Offices which loudly praised economy but refused it in every single case under discussion, with a wealth of detailed argument that silenced the ignorant critic, successfully weathered the storm. Bureaucracy is slowly, imperceptibly but effectively gaining ground in free England also. The decisive brain, which settles things in nine cases out of ten, is not that of the popularly elected minister but that of his chief official – the Permanent Secretary; and, in the Town, not the elected Mayor but his bureaucratic aide, the Town Clerk.

Nevertheless, there are certain important differences between the English official and the Continental. One-sidedness, formalism, and superciliousness, rarely develop in the English bureaucracy, although the over-sensitiveness of the freedom-loving Englishman is always prone to detect these foibles.

The official approaches the public with no trace of superiority or excessive correctness; the fact that he addresses all his communications over the formula 'your obedient servant' is something more than empty words. And there are two important main differences in organization: (1) The whole organization is much less centralized than in Germany or France; the tasks of the official in the capital do not include any detailed supervision of local administration nor the decision in individual cases – on the contrary, the individual case is left to the body which has made the decision, unless it has in so doing exceeded its functions or contravened clear orders from the central body; excessive red-tape is thus excluded; (2) In general, the preparation of extensive plans of fresh legislation does not fall to the officials. Such large-scale tasks as have been carried out by Prussian officials, for instance in the organization of German Insurance laws with practically no models in the whole world, or the introduction of the German State railway system, hardly come within the scope of their English colleagues, although there are traces, in recent times, of an extension of bureaucracy in this direction also. Parliament, petitions, the Press, published books – these are the sources whence legislative ideas derive; all points of moment are settled by discussion between leading ministers, party leaders and M.P.s. This, of course, does not prevent some official or other from having a decisive voice in the actual work of Bill-drafting, but when this occurs, he does it not in virtue of his office, but of his personality and his personal influence with ministers, and because practical experience has given him a better knowledge than any of them of the subject in hand. The official can influence the minister and will generally stress the intrinsic merits of the question, while his chief will be more preoccupied with what, in England, is the decisive aspect – how to make the matter palatable to public opinion, how to gain for the Bill the maximum support in Parliament and do the maximum damage to the other side.

When it comes to new and really far-reaching proposals, especially such as are not of a party type, English distrust of the official tends to lead to the employment of the device of a Royal Commission. In such cases, the best practical men that can be got together, associated with members of the various parties and an official or two, will be gathered to form a Commission under the chairmanship of some well-known individual, often a nobleman; they sit, they sift all the material available, they examine witnesses, and then work out recommendations. If the Commission is unanimous, its recommendations are, as a rule, put into a Bill; if, on the other hand, as is more common, there are one or more minority reports in addition to the report of the majority, the decision is either taken on party lines or nothing more is heard of the matter – a result that is by no means unusual. (Sometimes also the nomination of a Commission is a clever subterfuge to shelve a difficult matter; some awkward topic is remitted to a Commission composed in such fashion that numerous official volumes but no clear Report will emerge.) Such a Commission has statutory rights. It can decide to hold public session; its papers and reports are publicly printed. When war broke out, such Commissions were sitting on Canals, on Irish Railways, on Delays in Legal Procedure, on Oil Fuel for the Navy, Tuberculosis, Venereal Diseases, etc. The Royal Commission is a typically English device for bringing the best brains in the country to bear on great legislative tasks in their very earliest stages; for making self-government effective over topics for which there are as yet no self-governing organs. True, it is seldom that this is done without some admixture of politics. The statesman who nominates the Commission can almost always determine the course that it is going to take, since he will have a pretty good knowledge beforehand of the minds of the experts whom he puts on it, while, of course, avoiding any appearance of 'packing' his team. And there is certainly much waste involved, when one thinks how all the talent thus assembled for some piece of legislative preparation is afterwards dispersed to the four winds.

§ 5

Rapid as the progress of bureaucratization has been, the normal form of administration in England is still that of Self-Government, though self-government with a marked official support. Only a trace, here and there, remains of the mediæval and early modern apparatus of Privy Council and sheriffs (cf. page 243). From the end of the seventeenth century on, there was a powerful development of self-government which gradually almost entirely replaced the centralized system.

Even in mediæval times, the King could never be quite sure of his actual instrument of Royal power in the counties, the sheriff. He was a representative of the territorial aristocracy, bound by ties of blood and marriage to those whom he was supposed to govern, and there was always the danger that he might regard himself rather as the confidential adviser of the barons than the representative of the King. It was, therefore, to the King's interest not to let his sheriff grow too powerful. For that reason, he inclined to permit more and more independence to the *conservatores pacis* or *justiciarii*, the Justices of the Peace (cf. page 296), who had originally merely been the sheriff's assistants, and even allowed them gradually to take over from him not only judicial but administrative functions. But his new supports served the King no better than his old: the Justices became more and more independent; by the eighteenth century the Justices were actually the representatives of the territorial aristocracy whence they sprang. They were able to exclude anybody who was not somehow of their kin from pressing into their ranks, first by a very high property qualification, and after the Test Act by the proviso that any nominee had to be an Anglican communicant. Within their own area, the Justices were judges in all matters, great and small, and also administrators; county government was in the hands of the Quarter Sessions of J.P.s, whose resolutions required no further sanction. Administration was, in general, benevolently patriarchial, but devoid of any wider point of view, incompetent for larger tasks and completely selfish on questions touching the landlords' interest; under its ægis, the free peasantry was gradually destroyed, without a single representative of the general interest of the community raising a finger to save it.

Development in the towns was similar. There, despite all their privileges, the Royal influence continued strong throughout the Middle Ages. Only to a very small extent did the towns form themselves into confederations of the Continental type; there are traces of this development in the Cinque Ports (Hastings, Hythe, Sandwich, Romney and Dover and, later, Winchelsea and Rye) of the south, the Convention of the Royal Burghs in Scotland. But the power of the Royal administrator – the bailiff – was pushed more and more into the background. The town would buy either the right of nominating him, or of replacing him by a mayor of its own selection. From the fifteenth century, towns began acquiring charters which specified their rights against the Crown. In the seventeenth century the towns had completely escaped from the power of the kings. The Stuarts attempted to win back their lost influence by casting their weight on the side of a smaller and smaller group of persons (which might the more easily be controlled through intimidation or corruption), and by doing all they could to restrict the influence of public opinion. Thus, 'open' corporations were transformed into 'closed'; the number of electors was reduced to a minimum, or co-option substituted for election. Later, when the influence of the Crown declined, that of the territorial aristocracy took its place. The towns were completely dependent on the landlords, and the lesser boroughs served to send the largest possible number of tame members to the House of Commons (rotten boroughs). Administration was not merely backward, as in the countryside, but absolutely dishonest; the huckstering and bargaining that went on was an open scandal, decade after decade, until finally the whole system collapsed under the problem of the relief of the poor.

When the 1832 Reform Act brought the middle classes to power, the first work of the new Parliament was reform of municipal administration. After Poor Law had been put on a modern footing in 1834, the hold of the oligarchy over the towns was broken by the introduction of universal suffrage in local government elections (Municipal Corporations Act, 1835). The form of municipal self-government then introduced persists to this day. County administra-

255

tion was more gradually reformed; the change, there, was not completed until the establishment of County Councils in 1888.

Not that the reformers set to work in any revolutionary spirit. True, a small minority among them – Jeremy Bentham, James Mill, and Edwin Chadwick, the father of the new Poor Law, may have dreamed of ultimately establishing a bureaucracy of the French stamp, interfering everywhere to regulate and control. The majority mind was set in precisely the opposite direction. In principle, they wanted as little administration as possible. Where it was unavoidable, self-government was the only form it could take consonant with the dignity of the free Briton. Since, however, everything must be harmonized with a broad general conception of the State, there must be State inspection.

Nothing like a systematic reconstruction of administration now took place. Where offices or fragments of offices had historically grown up, with no real connexion between them, they remained wherever no serious inconvenience seemed to accrue. To this day there are a large number of offices whose existence is entirely in the air. Continental ideas would cause one to expect to find Museums, Observatories and Archives subject to the Ministry of Education, and that of Lighthouses and Pilotage (Trinity House) under the Admiralty. But every Museum is an independent centre, formally on the same footing as a vast administrative department like the Post Office. Post-eighteenth-century attempts to co-ordinate the various lesser offices under an organized administrative centre have never got any distance. Tendencies exist towards the development of the administrative centres normal on the Continent, but only tendencies. A great fund, set up by Queen Anne to eke out insufficient clerical stipends (Queen Anne's Bounty) exists, but it is entirely independent of the Ecclesiastical Commissioners, who administer the property of the Church. There is no connexion between the Charity Commission and the Friendly Societies Registry; a movement towards the creation of a Ministry of Public Works may be discerned in the Port of London Authority, the Thames Conservancy, the Lee Conservancy Board, the Road Board, and the Commissioners of Works and Public Buildings – but so far there has been no move to co-ordinate them. The inevitable result is much duplication and overlapping, as well as neglect of work that falls through the meshes of the net. The English have never had much feeling for the economies of labour and money realizable by organization. In trade and industry they have always been the sworn foes of modern forms of organization, and in public administration they have an almost superstitious dread of anything like a French or German omnipotent bureaucracy, which might attempt to limit their freedom.

The State leaves everything as far as possible to private initiative, subject to certain supervision. The mines are entirely in private hands and the State only insists on certain hygienic regulations and shares in their yield through taxation. What remains of the woods is privately owned, with trifling exceptions. State concern with the railways is limited to the grant of powers of construction, a voice in the fixing of rates, and the right to claim their services as carriers of postal packets. The lighthouses are under Trinity House, a highly respected private corporation with a nominal supervision by the Board of Trade. Similarly with harbours, although the State is gradually acquiring a larger share in them. Schools were left to private initiative as long as possible, receiving subventions over whose expenditure a certain watch was kept. A Public Prosecutor (with very limited powers) is a very recent institution; down to the end of the nineteenth century private bodies concerned themselves to prevent the exploitation of child life, cruelty to animals and other offences, and bring those guilty to punishment. Right down into the nineteenth century, the supply of gas, water, and, later, electricity and trams, was left exclusively in private hands. It was not till near the close of the century that municipal enterprise began to take them over, since when progress has been so rapid and thorough that even the provision of working-class housing and meals for school-children at the State's expense is now taken for granted. Yet, to this day, such forms of activity are looked askance at by the law. Every parish, every county, has to get parliamentary sanction through the machinery of Private Bill legislation, before it can embark on any department of economic activity. Private enterprise is everywhere assumed as the natural and desirable method of doing things. The State encourages, subsidizes, provides models and advice where such are desired, but it plays an independent part only where there is no alternative, and then along the line of transforming existing self-governing arrangements into a section of the general administration.

The first department to be reformed was that of the Poor Law. Here, the lack of any kind of control, and the absence of clear governing principles, either as to title to relief or its administration, had led to such complete breakdown that reform was unavoidable. It was the more urgent that he collection and administration of the Poor-rate is the basic function of parochial government in England, and both direct taxation and the parliamentary franchise are founded on the Poor-rate. The following were the main principles of reform:

1. The distribution of relief remains entirely in the hands of the Guardians of the Poor, elected in each parish. They have absolute powers of decision in the individual case – there is no recourse to any higher authority.

2. At the same time, the principles in accordance with which the self-governing body may spend its funds are determined centrally by the Poor Law Commissioners who, now, after many changes, have become the Ministry of Health. This central authority originally laid down what was known as the 'workhouse test'; and can make very thorough and national regulations as to the method and scale of relief, whose execution is secured through inspectors. The officers of the local authority are nominated by itself, but are subject to dismissal, under certain circumstances, by the central body.

3. The entire accounts of the local body are tested centrally by the Audit Department, which can surcharge the responsible persons at law for expenditure contrary to regulations.

These principles have gradually been applied, not to Poor Relief only, but throughout the whole English administration in town and country, with the result that the entire system has been reorganized. The same principles as here find expression reappear in the new educational administration and in the system of Workmen's Insurances. In the upshot, there is developed an organized self-government which entirely replaces the State over the whole range of direct administration.

In Germany the two systems, State- and self-government, exist everywhere side by side. In town, district and province, there is self-government, but in countless cases it is dependent on State confirmation of its own decisions. And, side by side with this self-government, there exists a hierarchy of State organs and offices, in which, step by step, each is subject to control by the one above it. In England, on the other hand, the State has no say at the lowest stage at all.[4] Self-government has it all its own way. Communal obligations, like the relief of the poor, sanitary legislation, licensing and education, and even the maintenance of the Territorials – elsewhere an obviously State concern – are handed over to it. Even the police are in the hands of the town and county councils, subject to a few survivals of

an older system: thus London – the metropolis, not the City – had a
State police imposed upon it in 1829 by Sir Robert Peel, after the old
local police had become a laughing-stock. In the provinces, the
Chief Constable, though nominated by the County Council, has to be
confirmed by the Home Secretary, and is subject to a Standing Joint
Committee, composed of equal parts from the Council and Quarter
Sessions. In the towns, an analogous arrangement obtains, the Head
Constable being, although not subject to Home Office confirmation,
under a Watch Committee of the Council and (nominally) the J.P.s.
Since the J.P.s can be removed by the Lord Lieutenant, and the
Home Office pays half the costs of the police and is therefore entitled
to lay down general principles for their administration, there is a
certain degree of central influence here. Inasmuch as these self-
governing bodies have taken over the duties of the State in their
localities, it is but logical that they should receive grants-in-aid of
considerable dimensions, e.g. half their expenses under police and
education.

Further, the local authority has complete administrative freedom.
In practically all cases its decisions need not be confirmed by any
higher authority. If the town or county council does a foolish thing,
it has the sole responsibility and will bear the consequences. If the
town of X decides to purchase a site for a new town hall at a fantastic
price, or rejects a proposal for the building of a new high school, there
is no means of staying them. Initiative and responsibility belong to
the place where the resolution comes from. Sanction from the
Health Ministry is only required in cases where resolutions have an
important bearing not only for the present but for the future; as for
example, where a municipality desire to issue stock or raise a loan.
In other cases, a resolution, once passed, is practically unalterable.
The fact that the Ministry of Health can proceed by Order in Council,
by writ of *mandamus*, or prohibition, has a mainly theoretic significance. On the other hand, recourse to the courts is open to the
ratepayer, not only theoretically but practically. The individual's
protection lies with the courts rather than with the Government.
Every ratepayer can enter a complaint against illegal expenditure of
his rates, and can challenge the legality of the action of any official or
administrative corporation; more, he can submit any by-law to the
courts on the ground that it is 'unreasonable' or vexatious. This
provision keeps the activity of councils within bounds.

But the State has not altogether resigned its functions. It can intervene – but not as a rule in individual cases. The central body has the right to issue general instructions, which must be applied universally, and whose application can be compelled. For instance, the State can remove a recalcitrant official, even of a self-governing authority, though it tends, as a rule, rather to rely on the milder methods of reducing or refusing grants-in-aid: a practice that has often been employed even against important towns who had jeopardized the purposes for which the said grants are made, either by lax administration or by disobedience to the fiat of the State Inspector. The State cannot compel a given authority to pay an individual teacher at a higher rate, but it can so direct its demands for the attainment of a standard of teaching efficiency – on which grant depends – that the authority has, in practice, to carry out its will. This standing danger, of seeing its grants cut off, does actually work out as an effective instrument of State supervision. So, State supervision exists, and in a tolerably stringent form; complaint indeed is frequently made by local authorities that the general prescriptions of the central authority gradually become so far-reaching as gravely to contract their freedom of action. With a view to lightening the legislative machine, the central authority has, moreover, been given the right to issue Provisional Orders on its own account, a right of which it makes increasing use. These are valid in so far as no objection is raised to them by any authority or private interest; in the event of such being entered, recourse has to be had to a Private Bill.

A peculiar form of State supervision over local administration is the Adoptive Act. Here, as elsewhere, it is to be noted that neither negatively nor positively does the central authority ever intervene in the individual case, and there hardly ever arises a condition of latent conflict between State and local authority such as to induce the latter to make use of its power to resist interference by the State. Nowhere do we find, either in legislation or in administrative practice, any ill-concealed suspicion of the local authority's making a show of abusing its power against the State. Even when – as constantly happened in Ireland – a municipal body shows a definite political bias, whether by the grant of its freedom, the issue of addresses, resolutions and what-not, such overstepping of its formal limits is not taken too seriously.

Throughout the whole of English municipal legislation, there runs the fear lest local authorities could use their powers selfishly, in the interest of their own members, and limit the political and economic ilberties of the citizen. The memory of the old pre-1835 unreformed corporations is still alive, as well as the Manchester theory of that date, which regarded communal politics as at best a necessary evil. Hence, the sphere of self-government is strictly limited. Whereas in Germany a town is free to undertake any activity within its sphere of operations, that is not contrary to its constitution, in England these functions are strictly prescribed by statute.

Every new form of municipal enterprise, every new tramway or gas-works, requires a Private Bill (cf. page 276), with all the expenditure of time and money it entails. It also requires exhaustive inquiries by officials of the Health Ministry, as well as a vote on the part of the local electors to give an opportunity to local opposition to make itself heard. Further, it is not open to a local authority to purchase land for future use, though this obviously makes any far-reaching town-planning policy impracticable. Its power to provide amenities is restricted; it has acquired powers to provide libraries, and a good deal has been done in that direction, but in others, the theatre for example, nothing. There are too many Puritans among the voters, and nothing can be done without a vote.

On the principles described here, first, the Poor Law was re-organized, both in towns and country. Then, in 1835, the towns were given a new constitution. In 1848, a Board of Health was set up, which laid down strict regulations for the dreadful sanitary conditions, both urban and rural, then prevailing, and saw that they were carried into effect. In 1902 the duty of making provision for education was laid upon all municipal areas. An Act of 1871 combined the Poor Law and sanitary authorities under a Local Government Board, which, in 1919, was transformed into the Ministry of Health. In 1888, subject however to marked deviations in the Conservative interest, these principles were applied to rural areas, by the establishment of County Councils.

We must now examine how these administrative principles work in detail.

§ 6
CITIES, MUNICIPAL AND COUNTY BOROUGHS

Officially, towns are 'boroughs'; in Scotland, burghs. Certain towns, of ancient status, generally the seat of a Bishop, are cities; when a town reaches a given size, it will frequently apply for a charter as a city. But, administratively, there is no distinction between a town and a city.

The duties and rights of a municipality are prescribed by its charter and further by the Municipal Corporations Act of 1835 and the amending Act of 1882. They include the maintenance of order, the administration of police, the carrying out of sanitary legislation – i.e. food-control, housing, street-cleaning, the control of noise and smoke, the provision of free libraries and, since 1902, elementary education. In addition to these general tasks, individual towns have, by Private Bill, obtained powers to run trams, carry on water undertakings and all sorts of communal activities.

The administrative organ is the Town Council. Councillors are elected by direct suffrage, which, though almost universal, gives certain privileges to property. Women have since 1835 enjoyed the franchise as well as men. The conditions are that the elector shall be of age, that he shall have resided at least one year in the area, that he is a ratepayer and an occupier – a somewhat difficult expression which in practice gives the vote to the occupier of a flat or shop within a building, but not to the person who merely rents a room. This interpretation prevents town administration from falling into the hands of the rabble; but it also excludes the younger workman and a large section of the property-less. The elector is not required to live in the town itself, but anywhere within a seven-mile radius of it; further, he has a vote even if he is not an occupier, but only the owner of land rated at more than £10 per annum, within the town boundaries. This prescription again favours the upper class; it is obviously designed to give a vote to the influential landowner or financial magnate dwelling in the environs, who is apt to be worth more to the town than hundreds of mere inhabitants. A man with an income of £1000 per annum or over is eligible as councillor, even if he lives only within a fifteen–mile radius of the town. (Contractors are not eligible.)

A notable survival of the old town government is represented by the Aldermen, constituting a third of the entire Council; they are not elected by the general body of citizens, but co-opted by the Councillors themselves, for a term twice as long as that of the elected representatives – six years instead of three. They are a sort of aristocracy within the Council, though their rights and duties are identical with those of the other members. The advantage of retaining this ancient form is that it makes it possible to enlist the services, by cooption, of outstanding men, who might be unwilling to submit to the bustle and uncertainties of popular election. It is usual, to-day, to elect as Aldermen only such men as have been frequently re-elected to the Council and done a long term of service upon it.

ADMINISTRATION

The Town Council is presided over by a Mayor, elected for one year by Aldermen and Councillors, generally from among their own number. As a rule, he receives a salary, but one that is quite inadequate to meet the heavy expenses he has to bear in the way of entertainment, etc.

The Mayor (in London, Birmingham, Leeds, Liverpool, Manchester and other great cities he bears the title of Lord Mayor; in Scotland, that of Provost or Lord Provost) tends more and more to become a merely symbolic figure. His year's period of office is generally too short to permit of his doing much; rarely does it happen, as with Joseph Chamberlain in Birmingham, that a mayor is the leader of a new and considerable departure in town policy. Actual administration is in the hands of the various committees of the Council – Tramways, Education, Street-lighting, etc., which have the power of co-opting non-councillors to serve upon them. Administrative unity is safeguarded by the provision that all resolutions passed by committee have to be endorsed by the Council as a whole. This is, in most cases, purely a matter of form; but the Council as a whole retains in its hands the power of decision on all vital issues in civic life. The highly characteristic office of Town Clerk further makes for unity. It dates from the oligarchic period; the Town Clerk was originally a legal assistant to the Mayor. To this day he is still, in theory, a mere subordinate, under the orders of the high and mighty authoritative members of the Council, and, as such, is not entitled to vote at meetings. He is a 'mere' official, with no defined functions, who has to concern himself with every department of civic administration, attend all committees, and represent, in his own person, the connecting link between the various activities of the Council. With him there enters into a sphere of activity based exclusively on the free action of far-sighted citizens the trained lawyer, the paid official – and that in an almost directive capacity. With him, too, other officials came in; we find everywhere a Treasurer, a Chief Accountant, a Medical Officer, an Education Officer, and a Surveyor, and, in the larger municipalities, each one of them will be at the head of an administrative department with many ramifications. Everywhere, however, the experts are only the advisers, the subordinates; decisions are in the hands of the citizen members of committees, who alone are 'free'. But the picture which we have encountered in the central offices of the State presents itself again in the municipality. In the central offices the Permanent Secretary, who outlives the changes that overtake his chief, the Secretary of State, though inferior in consideration, really is the directing master mind of the administration. In the same fashion the Town Clerk – unless some very remarkable personality happens to be Mayor in a given year – is the indispensable controlling force in the activity of every one of these separate branches of administration. He is the most powerful man just because he has no definitely limited sphere of action and can therefore make his influence felt everywhere. Of course, only a first-rate man can make himself paramount in a position which bristles with opportunities of friction; but the high salary (£2000–3000 in the larger towns) is an attraction, and the Town Clerk, as the solitary man permanently in touch with civic business, soon acquires the natural superiority of the expert over the merely well-intentioned. The Englishman feels, instinctively, that it is more important to get something done than to stick strictly to the limits of one's own function.

This lack of specific prescriptions appears elsewhere in English civic life, in surprising forms. Thus, the municipality is entitled to issue by-laws, as a rule without any need to apply to the superior authority for sanction; and such by-laws can only be suspended after a very cumbrous procedure – Order in Council or Court decision. To prevent any formalism in the application of the by-law, it is laid down that it can be deviated from, in any individual case, if the Council votes to do so with a qualified majority. The same purpose is served by the arrangement under which it is prescribed that, in the event of legal proceedings against any trespasser, the costs must be voted in advance. Here is a very effective safeguard against any excess of zeal on the part of the police and minor officials.

But this flexibility of the apparatus at the same time often works in favour of Capitalism. A great magnate of the town – who may not have strictly observed in his factory some necessary by-law about some hygienic question, might easily escape prosecution. On the whole, English municipal government is clean; corruption, in the American sense, is not characteristic of it. Nor is it conducted on party lines, although the elections are run by the local political organizations, and fought, more and more, on purely party issues. The election once over, parties sink into the background in the work of the Council. But administration is far less thorough than in Germany. The appalling slums of London, Dublin, Glasgow, or Edinburgh may be, in the main, a heritage from a time before the Act of 1835, but that they should persist after nearly a century of universal franchise is a sign of the potency of the evil side of Capitalism in municipal life. Enormous difficulty is met with in taking over tramways, gas-works, electricity undertakings and the like and putting them under public ownership or even securing a share in their profits and management for the community; as in fighting the vested interests of the Liquor Trade, which is apt to play a very important part in municipal politics. Again, the regulations and police rules about food adulteration, hygiene in bakeries, housing standards and the like, which are for the most part admirable, are often but feebly carried out in practice. Public opinion guards against the graver abuses; in addition, the influence of the Labour Party (whose outlook on municipal administration has largely been created by the work of the Fabian Society, which has borne notable fruit in London and other great cities) is a factor of growing significance. So far, however, Socialism in its cruder form has been almost completely resisted; only in a few of the smaller boroughs of London has it played an important part.

On the whole, the administration of English towns is honest and clean, but conservative and always apt to favour the interests of the town magnate, who generally will be the exponent of some capitalistic interest. By law and by tradition, the sphere of municipal government in England is confined within very narrow traditional limits. Any additional powers can only be sought by the Private Bill machinery (cf. page 276), which is not only extremely expensive and slow, but also very difficult to set in motion. A big majority of taxpayers must be in favour of the enterprise in question before a start can be made; everything is done to favour the opposition – which, in the great majority of cases, naturally comes from capitalists, whose personal interests will be injured by a new municipal undertaking.

The opposition is, further, assisted by the antiquated rating system[5] which sets the mass of middle-class voters against any municipal enterprise involving a rise in their rates. The said rates have nothing to do with the citizen's income; they are determined entirely by the rateable value of his dwelling; that is on the visible standard of comfort of the burgher, as displayed in his house. This system suited the landowner, since it hit not the owner of the land and site but only the occupier, the man who paid rent. The landowner's assessment was fixed on the value of the house he inhabited himself, not on the income coming to him in rents of all sorts. His ally in the oligarchical period, the capitalist in the town, was equally benefited; he was rated on what he spent for his dwelling, not on the income coming to him from trade and industry. The full weight of the rate fell on the small middle-class man, who spent a large proportion of his income on rent. And so it is to-day. The scholar, teacher, or lawyer for example, who lives in some modest but rapidly developing suburb, sees his assessment put up every five years. Even if the rate is not raised it hits him harder at each re-assessment. The amount he has to pay rises as the value of his house rises, although the ratepayer's income may have actually sunk in the interval; for him the enhanced value of his house is a purely fictitious quantity, unless he can let off a portion of it to someone else. In the same way, every lawyer or doctor who has to have a consulting room of some sort or other, has not only to pay more and more in rent, but is in a much worse position so far as his rates go than the miser who may have a big income from investments but lives in some tiny apartment in a poor part of the town. Often, especially among the poorer classes, the owner of the house pays the tenant's rates for him (of course raising the rent in proportion). The town favours this system of compounding because it saves its officials trouble in collecting; and the landlord who collects the rates receives a rebate. Under this system, the poor man pays his rates only in the shape of enhanced rent, that is, without being aware of them. Certainly he is hardly aware of the fact that a town tramway that fails to pay its way comes back to him in the shape of rates and so reduces his real income. These circumstances naturally make the poor enthusiastic for more town parks, libraries, free meals and so on; at the same time, they make the middle-class voter, for whom every welfare activity on the part of the corporation translates itself automatically (even if the rates are not raised) into a larger rate-payment from him, excessively sceptical of all forms of municipal enterprise.

Everywhere, therefore – except in the working-class quarters of modern industrial towns – the backbone of municipal life is the rich man with a strong civic consciousness. And such men are to be found everywhere in England. Let the franchise be never so democratic, there are ways and means of enlisting his co-operation. He can be co-opted to the Council as an Alderman, without going through the efforts of a contested election. He may even be elected, if, as so often happens in the land of princely industrial magnates with motor-cars, he lives outside the town.

It is part of the ideal of the wealthy citizen in England to play in city government a part analogous to that played in the county by the great landowner – despite all the sacrifice of time involved. No other country has anything like the supply of outstanding men of business, competent, in their clearness of vision, energy and turn for affairs, to replace the expert to a very large extent and render intensive State supervision superfluous. Moreover, business life in England has not grown so intensely absorbing as to exhaust the last drop of energy possessed by the men engaged in it. True, it may be questionable whether it would at this day be possible to repeat the achievement of Joseph Chamberlain, who reformed the rotten civic administration of Birmingham through years of embittered guerrilla warfare, thrice serving as Lord Mayor of the city, and, at the same time, be one of the directors of a great industrial concern. Nevertheless, these great captains of industry are the backbone of English municipal government. The obverse of the medal is the fact that, in governing, they are very tender of capitalist interests, even where they involve over-crowded slums and factories whose standard of hygiene is anything but perfect. So far, it is only in a comparatively few industrial areas that the working-class element has won anything like a determinant voice. Until recently, the urban workman tended rather to vote for the richest man in his town than for his trade union secretary. But there are signs that this is changing.

§ 7

LONDON

That the position of London in municipal governments should be unique is natural. The capital grew up gradually out of its kernel the old City of London, the equally ancient City of Westminster, and a group of adjacent parishes on either bank of the Thames, like Marylebone, St. Pancras, Whitechapel, Southwark, etc. At the time of the reorganization of municipal government, each of these parishes had a completely independent constitution, generally very different from that of its neighbour; certain parishes – but in no case all – had entered into common agreements for specific purposes, such as water, parks, etc.; but these agreements never prescribed any clear delimitation of functions. The entire London area belonged, politically, to the four surrounding counties of Middlesex, Kent, Essex, and Surrey, with the result that there were incessant conflicts between city and county authorities. The whole was a helpless confusion of some 400 municipal and county authorities and special bodies, whose principal occupation was fighting against each other in the law courts. The only really active organ of government was that of the City, dominated by time-honoured trading wealth; the lesser bodies were given over to the most devastating Philistinism. The petty stall-keeper and artisan ruled the roost. The description of the election of a beadle in one of these rookeries, as given by Dickens in one of his early works, determined not by any merit in the man but by the number of his children, gives a good picture of the futility of this so-called administration.

For decades it was a subject for caricaturists. To get rid of it, however, was not so easy. On the one hand stood the famous City, guardian of civic freedom, whose domain, to this day, may not be entered, even by the King, unless the Lord Mayor has solemnly cut the ribbon that bars his ingress to the area of the City; its vast revenues were administered on absolutely traditional lines by the ancient Liveries; a municipality whose wealth must be made to serve London's purposes, but at the same time one that could not be merely assimilated to the suburban mass. On the other hand were the swarm of hole-and-corner little parishes, where the better-class people had to be induced, somehow, to take part in local government, and the powers of the Vestries, chosen haunt of the rampant Philistine, had somehow to be broken in the interest of a Greater London which had yet to be created.

Half a century of abuses had to be endured before, in 1855, a provisional scheme could be put through, under which, while the City retained its independence, the other parishes were, at least so far as public building went, put under one department, the Metropolitan Board of Works. More and more extensive functions were assigned to it, until, by 1888, the whole of London, with the exception of the City, could be given the status and the functions of a county of its own. Complete unity was still not achieved. To this day there are various Londons. There is the Administrative County of London, with $4\frac{1}{2}$ million inhabitants in 1921; the Metropolitan Police district with $7\frac{1}{2}$; while the area of the Postal district is again different, as is that of the Water Board.

Above all, the separation of the City from the rest of the metropolis is maintained. As regards all the major tasks of City administration – Fire, town-planning, education – it is subordinate to the county. But it has its own Lord Mayor, with more than Royal pomp, its own Aldermen, its own Common Council, its own Watch and Police administration. Moreover, it has retained its old constitution. The universal equal suffrage of all inhabitants on which the Municipal Corporations Act was based would have been ridiculous in the City, whose inhabitants are caretakers and porters – in 1921 it had only 13,706 'inhabitants.' Therefore, what seems at first a grotesque anomaly, the election of the Lord Mayor by the ancient Guilds, was preserved to this day. And this is quite sensible. London's City ought to be represented by those who embody its dignity, its wealth and its trade. And since the heads of London firms tend to belong to one or other of the ancient Guilds, they can, despite seeming paradoxes, still serve as representatives of London trade and banking interests. Thus, as so often in England, new wine comes to its own in old bottles. The Lord Mayor has behind him his Common Council, his Town Clerk, and a notable staff of lawyers and technical officials.

The rest of London is organized on the county model. At the same time, any sort of false centralization has been avoided. No effort is made to govern the vast aggregation from a single centre. Even after the introduction of the county constitution, in 1888–9, the little local administrative units of the old parishes – the forty-two Vestries and District Boards – continued in existence. The London Government Act of 1899, however, finally brought order out of chaos, by combining individual districts into boroughs. Of these boroughs there are twenty-eight[6] (including the City of Westminster), each being an independent town with a mayor and town clerk at its head. Each is responsible for street repairs, lighting and cleansing in its area; for minor drainage, etc., and the lay-out of lesser streets, as well as for certain amenities, like libraries and public baths. The fact that there must be a great difference in such respects between a rich borough like Kensington and a poor one like Islington is taken for granted. For all larger and important purposes, such as really concern its citizens as a whole, London forms an administrative unit. Main street and drainage works are undertaken by the County; likewise bridges and transport, water and electricity, housing and factory inspection, building of working-class dwellings, and education. This expenditure is financed by rates, levied by the County Council; by grants-in-aid from the State for police and education purposes, and, since the war, for housing also; and by the proceeds of loans and returns on productive undertakings. A county rate is collected from the boroughs in proportion to their population; for the rest, the boroughs levy their own rates. Communal burdens naturally fall with varying weight in the various areas; some provision is made for the equalization of rates, but one that is regarded by the poorer areas as wholly inadequate. Administratively, the centre of the system is the London County Council. Its vast and wide-ranging activities attract the services of those citizens who are ambitious for the common weal; the boroughs, on the other hand, serve mainly as political training grounds for the lower middle classes.

The problem of administration in a gigantic city like London, which is at the same time the capital of the realm, is undoubtedly the most difficult that can well be presented to legislative technique. Government from a single centre is impossible, at the outset; and yet a high degree of uniformity in administration is absolutely essential; the whole must not be permitted to fall into separate areas, some of which might be too poor to meet the elementary tasks of street-lighting and repair, while others were so rich that any demands would represent but a bagatelle in relation to their resources. At the same time, provision for the capital of the country, for the greatest port and the financial centre of the land, cannot be left merely to the caprices of the electorate of a great city. For this complex problem a workable solution, of considerable dignity, has been found in England, but not one that is absolutely superior to that found in Berlin, Paris, or Vienna. Broad general matters, like fire, tramways, and lighting, have been handed over to the L.C.C.; minor matters are left to the Borough Councils; but the delimitation is by no means so clear that there is no friction. For instance, in 1921, Poplar refused to pay its county rate because it held that the individual areas were being sacrificed to the county. In general, there are so many conflicts between the county and the boroughs that the administrative machine suffers. Further, the county area is far too small. The town has grown so far that the tram and bus terminals lie far outside the L.C.C. boundaries. The establishment of the L.C.C. was intended to end the difficulties and the awful waste of time and energy caused by endless conflicts and adjustments with neighbouring authorities, all eager to get the maximum for themselves from the wealth of London, but in fact they have merely been pushed to the periphery from the centre, and there continue, in a very unexhilarating fashion. Even within the L.C.C. area there is no real uniformity. Thus, the water supply of the gigantic city is under the control of the Metropolitan Water Board, which levies its own special rates; the docks and harbours of the Thames are under the Port of London Authority; the small river Lee is administered by the Lee Conservancy Board; a large number of hospitals and similar institutions are under the Metropolitan Asylums Board; a large part of the Parks and the Police under the State. Above all, the division of the area as between the City of London and the London County is a serious defect; it is only to be explained by the powerlessness of modern ideas to cope with traditional and capitalistic usages. Not only is it an absolute source of difficulty and a block to progress; what is more important is that, in a land where historical tradition is so strong, the City, and only the City, affords a field of activity attractive to the important and wealthy man who has civic ambitions. We have seen how, despite its democratic forms, municipal government depends for efficiency on the co-operation of some rich capitalist (cf. page 266 seq.); here, while such a man may become an Alderman or a Lord Mayor, he will hardly be attracted by the prospect of being an Alderman or even Chairman of the L.C.C., which affords him hardly any real publicity. So, the supplies of civic wealth and civic energy flow into the City, not into the County of London, where they are much more urgently wanted. The fantastic wealth of the City is most imperfectly tapped for the general purposes of London as a whole. The result is that the body which has to cope with the gigantic tasks of a population of millions is perpetually short of money and short of the necessary number of first-rate civic helpers. The average elector takes local elections, whether for Borough Councils or L.C.C., with the greatest apathy, broken only occasionally when some Socialistic experiment enables a great cry about raising the rates to be launched.

English municipal administration affords full scope for democracy, while at the same time setting certain quite definite limits to it. Anyone who feels himself called to service in the administration of his native town has no great difficulty in becoming a Councillor, no matter what his origin may be. Actually, municipal government has proved a great school of working-class talent; it is there, and in the Trade Unions, that the working-class Member of Parliament most often wins his spurs. But the limits of democracy are clearly drawn. Inasmuch as votes are not possessed by the great masses of the floating population of any big town which rents some furnished room, or merely cubicle, the danger of mob-ocracy is guarded against. A great capitalist who is also a great citizen, like Joseph Chamberlain, can rule a city, even if he does not live in it (cf. page 262). In London, in particular, an extremely powerful – to our ideas far too power-

271

ful – bulwark of the old capitalism has been erected. London's vast historic wealth has maintained its separate organization in the City, and so far no democratic assault upon it has prevailed. The financial treasures of the ancient City of London are intact; universal suffrage has not been able to touch them. They are administered by the old merchants with the sense of *noblesse oblige* that belongs to them. The City maintains, in exemplary fashion, certain benevolent institutions, a school like the City of London School, the Guildhall Library and Museum. The City's rulers give generously to all sorts of worthy objects; but they, and not the officers of the masses, are to determine what these objects are. When a foreign potentate is welcomed in London; when the King, after his coronation, shows himself in his capital; when the Premier delivers his annual allocution at the Guildhall in November, amid the attention of the world at large, the distinguished guest, be he who he may, is received, not by the representatives of London's millions, but by the chosen of its thousand or two capitalists. The Chairman of the London County Council – such is the austere title of the man chosen by universal suffrage – stands modestly on one side, while the representative of High Finance and Big Industry, clad in royal ermine, surrounded by the Justices, the City Sheriffs, the Sword-bearer and the Sergeant-at-Arms, gives and receives homage with mediæval pomp and mediæval dignity. With the old legal corporations, the City of London constitutes, even in this age of universal suffrage, a Conservative residuum within the metropolis such as no capital city of the Continent can even begin to parallel. We shall see that county administration has to an even greater extent remained a citadel of Conservatism, all democratic forms notwithstanding.

§ 8

COUNTY COUNCILS

What is an English county?

England, unsystematic and haphazard in all matters, does not even give a clear answer to a question so simple as this.

I. There is an old, historic division of the country into forty counties which goes back to the earliest Anglo-Saxon times. Anglo-Saxon tribal nomenclature still lives on in the names Sussex, Essex, Middlesex; as in Norfolk, Suffolk, Northumberland. On its basis England is divided into parliamentary constituencies. Often the boundaries of a county coincide with those of a bishopric. But so far

ADMINISTRATION

as administration goes, the old forty counties have no longer any
meaning. They are part of an older administrative system of which
only a few fragments survive. The Justices of the Peace who once
administered these counties are still mostly nominated for the entire
area of the old county; in other respects the old counties have lost
their meaning. For modern purposes of administration, England is
divided not into forty, but into fifty counties, called administrative
counties.

II. Actual administration rests on the basis of the new fifty
administrative counties which have been made out of the old counties
by frequent subdivisions, and are governed, not by nominated J.P.'s
but by democratically elected bodies. The Local Government Act
of 1888 has put an end to all sorts of tentative divisions and subdivisions of the country and divided England into fifty administrative units. Further, Wales provides twelve counties, Scotland
and Ireland thirty-three each – with the result that the country
as a whole was divided into 128 administrative areas, outside of the
largest towns, which were cut out of their adjacent counties and
made into County Boroughs. In size and population the counties
vary enormously. The largest, Lancashire, has 4·9 millions; Kinross
in Scotland, only 8,000.

The administrative machine as set up by the 1888 Local Government Act and the 1894 Parish Councils Act is organized as under:
1. The smallest unit is the Parish with its Parish Meeting and
Parish Council, with very limited functions and financial powers.
In all larger tasks, as for financial operations like the raising of loans,
the parishes are subject to county supervision. They can extend their
functions by applying Adoptive Acts (i.e. Skeleton Acts, provided
by Parliament for draining, cemeteries, etc.), which a parish or town
may adopt, if it thinks fit. The Parish, can for these and other purposes, combine with other parishes; in which case a lasting union
often results, with the creation of a new district unit. Gladstone, who
was responsible for this Parish Act, hoped to see arise an active life
in the rural community independent of the landlord and the Church.
This aim has not been realized. Since the majority of the dwellers
in any village are apt to be agricultural labourers, economically
entirely in the hands of their landlord, and with no opinions of their
own, the Parish Councils vegetate rather than function.
2. The next unit is the District. Districts are either Rural Districts
– i.e. compulsory unions of rural parishes for sanitary, police, market,

273

road, slaughter-house, food-control or other purposes; or Urban Districts, i.e. lesser townships, with somewhat more extensive functions. In either case they are administered by District Councils, subject to the general supervision of the County Councils. The District, like the Parish, seldom shows a strongly developed communal life. They seldom contain any influential leading personalities, and are apt to be slack and lethargic. Finally, the main administrative unit is the Administrative County, to be described below.

3. This schematic construction was up to 1928 crossed everywhere by a totally different division of the whole of England into Unions, set up in 1834 for the administration of Poor Relief. They were run by elected, voluntary Guardians of the Poor. The Guardians administer either Indoor relief, in the Workhouse – as established by the 1834 Act – or, as is now more general, Outdoor relief, administered to the applicant in his own home. The costs of this are met by the ancient Poor Rate, which is in fact the basis of the whole system of direct taxation in England. The Unions were not supervised by the County Councils, but directly by the Ministry of Health. This administrative anomaly has at last been abolished by the 1928 Local Government Act (Derating Act), which devolves the functions of the Unions upon the County Councils, and at the same time equips them for these, and other new purposes by extensive new block grants from the Exchequer.

4. All rural administration is now based on the Administrative County with the County Council as its organ. Excluded from their ambit are the towns, in so far as they have their own administrative functions. What is really admirable in English communal organization is the care with which, instead of making a merely mechanical separation between town and country, it sticks to the real facts of life and recognizes the existence of manifold transitional forms. Thus, towns with more than 50,000 inhabitants constitute counties; they are County Boroughs, independent administrative units, subject only to the general supervision of the Ministry of Health. The other towns, in accordance with their size and efficiency, enjoy much or little independence of the County Councils. They may lay out and maintain their own streets, their own police – as a rule this happens only with towns of middling size approximating to the status of a county borough – etc., while they remain, for all functions not specifically committed to them, parts of the county and to that extent have to contribute to the county rates. The whole system is extraordinarily elastic. It is

exceedingly well designed to stimulate individual efficiency, where such is in existence, and does not tend to weaken an efficient county by cutting too many small and possibly weak units out of it.

The tasks of the County Councils are manifold. They are responsible for communications – bridges, roads, rivers and light railways; for police, in conjunction with the J.P.'s – the Chief Constable, for example, is under a Joint Committee composed of Councillors and J.P.s; care of the sick and insane, in so far as it is not carried out by private benevolence; the provision of small holdings (in theory: in practice most County Councils do all they can to prevent it); education; and the Territorial organization of defence. The Council is elected on the basis of a franchise [7] that, like that of the towns, is democratic but riddled with a few provisions to the advantage of the well-to-do, and functions like the Municipal Council, its Mayor, called simply Chairman, having a legal Clerk and a staff of officials, and the work being done in the main through smallish Committees.

Although the County Council franchise is democratic, administration has been till now mainly in the hands of the local territorial magnates. Socially, they dominate the countryside; there is no influential section of the population, there, that is not economically dependent upon them. There is a modern tendency on the part of the new farming population to make its voice heard; up till now, however, they have not yet done much more than endeavour to keep rates down. As a rule the landlords are still paramount. As, in mediæval times, the landowning interest bent the Royal sheriffs and J.P.s to its service, so to-day it has conquered the County Council which was supposed to break its power. The nominal head of the county, the Lord-Lieutenant, who survives from the days of Royal authority, and still enjoys a high degree of prestige and ceremonial pomp on occasions, is a landowner. The Chairman of the Council, who, owing to the fact that he is constantly re-elected, has far more real power than the Mayor, is almost always a landowner. The Clerk of the Council, the legal assistant who turns up again here, counts for less than his urban colleague. So, all changes in form notwithstanding, the power of landed property persists to-day, as strong as in the eighteenth century, nor has the spirit of administration greatly altered either. When the essential interests of the landlord are in question it is narrowly selfish; every effort is made to put obstacles in the way of the creation of small holdings or the establishment of Trade Union organization among agricultural workers, although, since the war, there has been a marked weakening in this direction. In other matters, it is intelligent, thorough and honest. Real skill is shown in the development of combined organizations, with other counties or with towns, for the maintenance of asylums, secondary schools, hospitals, canals, waterworks and transport arrangements generally. Such joint bodies take the place for many purposes of the Provincial bodies that are lacking in England.

§ 9

County Councils, with their subsidiary organs, and the corresponding municipal authorities, complete the picture of local self-government. The Government, functioning through the Ministry of Health, supervises, controls and occasionally checks through its inspectors (cf. page 258 *seq.*). The State contributes by regular grants towards the expenses of the County Councils; its position has been strengthened by the new system of block grants (1928) for purposes which formerly were laid upon the rates alone. There is nothing between the counties and the national government. This lack of intermediate administrative authorities is a source, often, of real difficulty. True, *ad hoc* bodies can be set up, with functions extending over a larger area, but this device hardly secures either the needful length of vision or freedom from special interests. Thus a mass of concerns, like municipal or county enterprises in electricity, gas, or tramways, all of which require some central policy, have to go to the House of Commons for decision. There they are handled through the Private Bill machinery, a kind of legislation hardly found outside England. From time immemorial, Parliament has passed special legislation in the interest of individuals; it was, indeed, for long the sole body competent to deal with change of name, divorce, naturalization, while a parliamentary Bill of Attainder was the method by which an individual could be charged with high treason. A Parliament which can legislate on individual matters, can therefore also pass a 'Private Bill' in the interest of an individual county or municipality. For such Private Bills, an intelligent and speedy machinery has been devised, which enables the matter in hand to be lifted out of the area of party controversy and makes its settlement irrelevant to the fate of parties. The procedure, further, is designed to prevent the representative of a given constituency from merely promoting the wishes of his own locality. On the other hand, Private Bills consume time, weary members, and

are a very imperfect method of distinguishing justifiable from unjustifiable objects. The most trifling little local concern may, in fact,
be raised, by this device, into the arena of real parliamentary fighting.
True, that fighting will not be conducted along ordinary party lines;
the opposition will be between the section in a given town which
wants a tramway, and the interested parties there who fear to be
injured by its construction; but the interests of the town as a whole,
in such a case, are apt to be very imperfectly and indirectly considered. The procedure, moreover, is fearfully costly and tedious.
A single Private Bill cost the city of Birmingham no less than £44,750.
It has to take place in London, in a court that is in vacation for at
least half the year, although the nature of the case demands close
acquaintance with local needs. The authority promoting a Private
Bill has to confide it to a London lawyer, to subpœna endless witnesses, and arrange for the necessary number of local hearings – an
infinitely costly and circumstantial business when the question
concerns an authority, say in Northumberland.

All this has caused a certain movement in favour of some scheme
of Devolution, by dividing England into larger districts or provinces
on the Prussian model. Since Chamberlain in 1893 first vented the
idea, it has been recommended again and again by persons of rank
and influence. But it is merely a matter of expediency – no fighting
measure; no Government could hope to gain votes or smash opponents
by it; it therefore belongs to the category of merely useful things for
which in England no Prime Minister has time. And any Government
which would propose such a measure would meet with the silent
but efficient resistance of the legal profession, which draws a considerable income out of the constantly recurring needs of the towns
for more Private Bills. So it seems safer to leave the matter alone.

§ 10

What are the prospects for the continuance of the administrative
system thus described?

Indubitably, the next few decades must see a great extension in State
activity. Under the old oligarchic state, this activity was reduced to an
absolute minimum; but ever since the 1834 Poor Law and the 1835
Corporations Act, State activity has been everywhere on the increase.
The mere recognition of the creation of a healthy people as a desirable
aim has caused the establishment of an endless series of regulations
affecting the ordinary citizen at every turn, in the conduct of the

factory, in building, in the lay-out of streets and canals. And this development is by no means at an end. Still every big town has its slums, with a population in them hardly able to lift themselves out by their own unaided efforts. They can hardly be helped, or the chronic burden of Poor Relief lightened, save along the lines of an extension of the Minimum Wage principle, in the form of some sort of State regulation of wages. With the introduction of compulsory attendance at school in 1876 the State further undertook the responsibility for education, in principle. Primary education is so organized; for secondary, much still remains to do, which private enterprise cannot accomplish. It seems that State assistance to and supervision over both secondary and university education must become much closer in the future.

Certainly the pressure from Labour is in this direction. The war produced a great heightening of working-class consciousness, and the workers are no longer willing to be mere hewers of wood and drawers of water for the capitalist. They feel that they are the servants of the nation and are demanding a right to be consulted in the conduct of the concerns they work in, and to share in their profits. If it is as yet far from clear in what form these desires can be realized, it is matter of universal admission that some sort of limitation of private control has got to take place.

The nineteenth century, though the era of economic individualism, was forced to create bureaucracy even in England. The country has grown used to the Factory Inspector and the School Inspector and State control over workmen's insurances. The old idea that the official must be confined to the central body and, at best, travel thence to exercise control, is going by the board. Factory Inspectors have their districts all over the industrial areas, and this tendency is bound to grow.

Further, demands for communal and State aid are constantly on the increase. Even one-time haughty defenders of independence, like Oxford and Cambridge, are now in receipt of subventions from the State. But State subvention means State supervision, and with it a tendency, bound to grow, for the limitation of self-government. The increasing flood of Provisional Orders (cf. page 260) shows which way the tide is flowing.

Further, the official is bound to play an increasing part. Ireland and India are two countries, one of them among the greatest in the world, which England has ruled by means of a bureaucracy, and one that has rendered brilliant service in both. It certainly possesses the material out of which a first-rate bureaucracy, at once energetic and tactful, can be constructed. Everywhere, the course of development is through the rule of the many to the rule of the single competent person. At the top, the Prime Minister has pushed his colleagues to the wall; in the realm of administration, the Board has grown into a purely personal instrument; in the cities, the Town Clerk is the man who counts. There can be no doubt that the efficient official has a great future in England.

A great future – but not the whole future. The official will, as before, work with self-government, rather than instead of it. It is far too deep-rooted in the Englishman's heart. That government should be good is desirable; that it should be self-government is, to his idea, simply necessary. Even in the war, there was no case of complete control given to a bureaucracy; that the mind of the nation rejects. So, though State supervision may become more marked, and its administration more thoroughgoing, the principle of self-government will remain intact.

People talk in England of a danger of 'Prussianization' of public life, meaning, by that, a growth of officialdom and officialization. But there remains a profound difference between the spirit of English and Prussian administration. Both attempt to be benevolent, far-seeing and just, but the special qualities of the German bureaucracy are just as little articles of export as the special qualities of English parliamentarism. The distinguishing mark of the old Prussian system was its extreme objectivity. This is incapable of translation to a country under parliamentary government, where a nervous regard for the shifting sands of a parliamentary majority must enter into every decision. Essential to the Prussian system is the power of the official, in most cases, to put through a decision he feels to be right in the teeth of resistance from the malicious and the self-interested; the necessary safeguards imposed on error and excessive zeal on his part work, as a rule, effectively. True, the English official has this power in many cases too – but only when he or his chief enjoys the support of public opinion. That is to say, he can force a recalcitrant landlord to give allotments to his villagers, or prevent abuse of the work-house; but he is powerless against workmen on strike, practically powerless against a Town Council that makes no provision for higher education, or against a local magnate who disregards regulations about night-baking, and snaps his fingers at local efforts. And the English official has practically no defence against a press that may at any moment launch a campaign against him and his chief. Nor is this state of things likely to be altered in the future. The spirit of *suum cuique* behind the Prussian official is alien to the Englishman; he is too much of a fighter. He does not ask that every one shall get his own, but only fair play – in other words a fair chance to use his own strength, which means something entirely different.

The remedy for his egotism, and one that in practice is at least as effective as the Prussian, derives from the same source as his fighting instinct, from *noblesse oblige*, the gentlemanly code of the fighter and the knight. Important it may be whether the new officialdom arising in England turns out well or ill: not decisive. What is, however, vital is the question whether the old aristocratic instincts that, hitherto, have to a large extent dominated both Parliament and administration, can survive capitalism and permeate the working-classes. For it is on the ethical content of these forces, and not on the efficiency or inefficiency of officials that the future of English administration depends in the last resort.

CHAPTER IV
THE LAW

§ 1

THE basis of English law is the old Germanic law, profoundly influenced however by the old Norman administrative law. Roman law affected it far less than was the case either in France or Germany. True, certain princes of the Church, and, from the twelfth century on, the Kings, attempted to transplant Roman law into England, because it seemed to be more favourable to their own pretensions. But the traditional common law successfully resisted its introduction. From the seventeenth century this common law came to be regarded as the bulwark of English freedom as against the absolutist law of the Roman jurists. It became the specifically English (and Irish) law, and the foundation of the legal system both throughout the Colonies and in the United States, while Scotland, unable to work out any such complete code of its own, was more amenable to Roman law. To this day, English and Scottish law are distinct, both in principles, formulation and jurisprudence. Roman law, of course, influenced common law in many details. It further, in its late development of canon law, forms the ultimate basis of the law of wills, marriage and inheritance. Over the area of international relations, too, Roman law is predominant. Certain courts, such as the Court of Requests (up to 1642), and the Admiralty Court for long, were primarily governed by it. But the juristic world of England always and successfully opposed any extension of Roman principles in England. The Universities of Oxford and Cambridge may at times have shown an inclination towards it, but the Inns of Court, which were more powerful than the Universities, became the guardians of the common law.

Any attempt to outline the principles of English law would carry us far beyond the limits of this book, and of the competency of its author. All that can be done here is to mention certain outstanding points, characteristic of England, where England differs from ordinary Continental usages.

English law knows no principle of codification. The common law of the land is unwritten, but absolute; statute law is only a special form of this common law. Far from regarding unwritten law as an exception, requiring special declaration, for the Englishman it is statute law which is in this position. The law is the sum of what has, from time immemorial, been viewed as customary and – for the primitive conception of law the two are absolutely identical – as right and equitable. It is the sum total of the unformulated sense of right of living generations and the generations that are past, felt as a vital force, a spiritual possession in the mind of the man of to-day. To try to express this sense of right fully in words is impossible: any attempt at codification must, therefore, destroy what it seeks to define. Unwritten law is felt as sacred, in proportion as it is felt to be indestructible, immutable and immediate, but this aura must perish for any generation that seeks to confine the unnameable in words. Actually, this sort of law is absolutely sufficient; for convenience, however, certain excerpts from case-law are set out in statute form, and there appear, side by side with the Law Reports in which legal judgments are recorded and the Statute Book containing the laws as formulated by the legislative authorities of the land. Ever since the unremitting agitation carried on by Jeremy Bentham, who pressed for codification on Continental lines, the portion of English law actually fixed in written form has steadily grown. For example, commercial law is now to a large extent codified (Bills of Exchange Act 1882, Partnership Act 1890, Sale of Goods Act 1893). On the other hand, departments as important as Contracts and Torts are, to the larger extent, still governed by unwritten law. Again, a fundamental fact in real property law like the law of entail is not only not incorporated in any legislative enactment but actually in contradiction to written law.[1] So strong is this disconnexion of law from enactment, that old Scottish legal tradition actually contains no legislative definition of a crime. If a Judge declares an action punishable and a jury condemns the doer thereof, the action thereby becomes a crime!

§ 2

The Englishman has an exceedingly strong sense of law. It is perhaps the stronger that, by comparison with the feeling for law of other nations, it is so thoroughly primitive. Law, for him, is not an abstraction, nor something common to human beings, as such: he has little or no understanding of the general rights of man; he has little or no use for abstract legal principles; in England, there has never been a system of jurisprudence in which definite legal principles run like a consistent thread through all the turns and twists of varying circumstances. On the other hand, his respect for every concrete legal instance is absolute, as for every concrete legal relation between individuals. The Englishman is slow to pick a quarrel, he observes agreements as to 'mine' and 'thine' with the utmost fidelity, even where they are unwritten – indeed respect for unwritten law reappears in his respect for the unwritten contract. Strikes are far more seldom accompanied by violence than in any other country; revolutions of any notable extent are a rare exception in English history.

At the same time, the Englishman has small respect for the letter of the law. He regards the text of a measure which emerges often in a carelessly drafted form, from debates in Parliament and after party compromises, as deserving no particular reverence; nor is his attitude very respectful to the small change of legislation, as, for instance, the police regulations of his town or county. Them he will break, whenever he has a chance. He simply does not understand that a social life, comprising millions, has got to have its details organized. On the other hand, his sense of law is governed, to this day, by two quite primitive yet still vital ideas – (1) that there must be the utmost freedom for himself, but also for everybody who shares the law with him; (2) that things as they are are good and should as far as possible continue.

The Englishman demands freedom. Not freedom for any definite or higher purposes, but freedom in itself, the old freedom of the Germanic peasant, who wants to rule in his own farmyard and will tolerate no interference from anybody. This is the root of the Englishman's opposition to the State and his disinclination to any team work. As probably the governor of the State will always incline to restrict the rights of his fellows, rebellion on the part of subjects is entirely natural. The Englishman does not take readily to this *ultima ratio* of the ruled. On the contrary, it is one of the distinctions of English history that revolutionary change has so often taken place without revolution – e.g. the rise, first of the bourgeoisie and then of the working class in the nineteenth century. But resistance, from time to time, is inevitable, and the average Englishman is always on the side of the resister. In such case, injury to the *lex scripta*, the letter of the law, is readily forgiven, provided the result is to establish the *lex non scripta*, which guarantees liberty. Open if occasional resistance to the law is not only no disgrace, but something absolutely pardonable and normal, since it is a sign of the existence of force and independence of spirit in the individual or the people who resist. Occasional revolution serves to push on the history of the world.

If the great events in English history are the revolt of the Barons, which led to Magna Charta, the great Puritan revolution and the lesser revolution of 1688, there is hardly a great political question where progress has been purchased without open resistance on the part of some group or other to the statute law of the day. The history of Ireland is a long chain of risings on the part of the oppressed Catholic majority; and from 1913 on, rumblings of revolution from the Protestants of the North. Canada would never have acquired self-governing status if Papineau had not raised the standard of revolt in 1837, nor could it have put its Pacific Railway through half as quickly as it did, had not British Columbia threatened to secede. The history of Australia, New Zealand and Cape Colony is full of similar examples. English Dissenters would have been hard put to it to get free of Church rates, had not the Chelmsford shoemaker, Thorogood, simply refused to pay in 1839. Respect for the law of the land, simply because it is the law, seems to the Englishman nothing but weakness. The fact that it was in England, where the law made every form of strike illegal, that the industrial strike developed and thence spread all over the world, is among the results of this English contempt for 'mere' statute law. The Englishman's heady sense of freedom no doubt plays an important part in this, but it is not the sole root of this phenomenon. How great a part in it is played by indifference to written law is proved by the existence within the Statute Book of ponderous laws that no one bothers to repeal although they are completely out of date. It suffices that no one heeds the law: formally to kill what is dead would be waste of energy.

This unrestrained love of liberty is at first based upon unrestrained egotism and must – unless restricted by other powers and motives – lead to ruthless oppression of all who are too weak to defend themselves. The early history of every English Colony affords proof of this. French, Portuguese and even Spaniards tried, according to their lights, to achieve the salvation of the Indians' souls, but neither the Puritan of Massachusetts nor the Anglo-Indian merchant took the slightest interest in doing anything of the kind: for him the 'nigger' at the outset was a mere object to be exploited, without either a soul or rights. He became something more as soon as he began to resist exploitation. By resistance he rose in status. And this is quite in keeping with primitive Germanic feeling. The primitive Germanic warrior recognized those belonging to his own horde as having equal rights with himself, but about others he did not trouble very much. This very limited sense of right is the basis of the whole elaborate superstructure of the sense of law, right up to the stage of international law. In England, these extensions of the primitive, highly exclusive, sense of right have also taken place, though more slowly and gradually than in other nations. They have throughout been dominated by the primitive warrior conception of right as inhering simply in the man who is able to defend himself. True, Christianity, with its mighty missionary idea of the equal worth of every human soul, made a wide breach, extended again and again with the centuries, in the barbarian exclusiveness of the old warrior pride, but only very gradually and imperfectly does it succeed in breaking down the distinction between men of absolute and men of lesser worth – a distinction positively sanctified in the Puritan doctrine of election. Under eighteenth-century aristocracy, the great mass of the middle and lower classes obviously did not possess full citizen rights: the right of self-government and free enjoyment of all State institutions was, of course, confined to the landowning Anglican: he was entitled to purchase and enclose common land to any extent, and convert woods into money and political influence: he was free to dissolve marriage contracts and protect the estate of his daughters from the clutch of an extravagant husband: he was permitted to preserve his game by the most savage devices[2]: and in none of this had he any sense of trampling on the rights of his inferiors. The nineteenth century saw an alteration in the picture. The anti-social legislation of the previous era was repealed: Dissenters achieve equality before the law: women have their property protected and even receive the franchise: the small man is given a vote as the result of the overhauling of local government: divorce and facilities for education in all its stages are thrown open to him. But in England the emancipation of the lower orders and groups in the population is not ushered in by any great night like August 4, 1789. No solemn flame of patriotic or humanitarian enthusiasm sweeps away the misdeeds of centuries of feudalism and burns them on the altar of humanity. All that happens is that the workman learns how to resist authority. In so doing he acquires respect, shows that he is a full member of the community and worthy to be treated as such. In proportion as the small man fights for his rights contempt is exchanged for respect; and it therefore becomes easy for the peer to share power with his inferiors. In the same way, women won citizen equality for themselves: so did the Irish, and, among outsiders, the Americans and the Boers. Anyone who wants to be respected by the Englishman must resist him. Let a class or a race allow itself to be exploited, and no sense of right in the English will protect it. In proportion, however, as it resists, there awakens in the Briton the warrior sense of right, which recognizes the stout foe and, if with no very good grace at first, ultimately accedes to him, with ready respect, the right to freedom which the Briton himself enjoys. Along this line the aristocratic State has developed into the democratic. So far, the sense of the equal right in the foreign nation has not yet become part of the universal sense of right. For the meantime, it tarries still in the forecourt of ethical and religious claim: is not yet accepted as a matter of course by the national mind. At any time of national crisis, it is still possible to rouse the old Berserker instinct, and obliterate any sense of the opponent's right in a darkness as dense as that of primitive epochs.

There is another source of the Englishman's slowness in recognizing the rights of others – his incomparably strong sense of the sacredness of what has always existed. This prevents him from ever admitting another to new rights without a struggle. For him, the existing order of society and the State is holy simply because it has been so from time immemorial, because the history of some thousands of years has set its seal upon it. For the deeply conservative peasant strain in the English the new is *ipso facto* suspect. That is why his law still moves within ancient forms, such as have long been superseded elsewhere. This is no question of mere externals, like the barrister's wig or the old French terminology: the attitude to the law that underlies all this is old-fashioned. It moves within a narrow and traditional gauge; it is crude, cumbrous, and grossly materialistic. England has never developed a science of jurisprudence, working out new legal concepts and giving new expressions to the sense of right. On the contrary, English law operates through ancient, outworn, primitive Germanic and Norman concepts, and attempts very often with an astonishing success, by feats of forensic skill, to force new conditions into the old moulds.

For example, no general right of supervision of a higher court over a lower has ever been recognized in English law. There are, however, certain mediæval formulæ which can, in any individual case, be used to permit a court to intervene in proceedings elsewhere, or stay the judgment of a lower court; and by the extension of these forms, originally designed for quite limited and specific purposes, under *mandamus, certiorari, procedendo* and *prohibition*, something like an unlimited right of intervention on the part of the higher courts has developed in the course of time. Or another instance of this: there is in England no constitutional protection of the individual against illegal arrest. But a highly ingenious interpretation of an ancient formula of arrest (*Habeas Corpus*) has, while preserving the ancient form, translated it, in practice, to its exact opposite – a comprehensive guarantee of individual liberty. Primeval conceptions, with all their cumbrous crudity, have been carried down into the legal outlook of quite modern times. The existence of corporal punishment for young offenders is hardly felt to be an anachronism. The injured husband still has the right to claim damages against a co-respondent – chivalrous respect for woman has not availed, in a case where questions of mine and thine are concerned, to supersede a primitive view of a wife as an assessable piece of personal property.[3] Closely analogous is the right to claim compensation for breach of promise: or the right possessed by the husband, down to quite recent times, to appropriate any earnings on the part of his wife. Equally materialistic conceptions come to light in the relations between the individual and the State. Down to the nineteenth century, State offices were regarded as purchaseable,[4] loanable and taxable, while advowsons were in this category until a generation ago. In practice, however, the evils of this survival of the crude outlook of an earlier date are much less than might be expected. If written law has not kept pace with the development and refinement of the sense of equity, judicial interpretation has softened many of its reactionary features, nay, often transformed them, in practice, into their opposite.

§ 3

The Judge is, in fact, the pivot of the English legal system. He is the traditional guardian of the common law. In deciding the application of a former individual case to a new individual case, he practically becomes the dictator of the law. For the precedent hardly ever corresponds exactly with the case in dispute; everything turns on his determination how far the divergence is fundamental and which, out of the wealth of existing precedents, has got, here, to be applied. Almost equally great is his power in application of statute law; since only a small proportion of laws is ever formally repealed, it is for the Judge to determine whether or no a given law is or is not actually in force. He can thus declare quite a recent law to be obsolete; on the other hand, so late as 1916, an English Judge condemned Sir Roger Casement to death under a statute of Richard II. Everything, in the last resort, turns on his sense of equity and his sound common sense and knowledge of men. Not that the English Judge will ever appear in public as the dictator he virtually is. His interpretation of the law always hides behind precedents. But an amazing audacity is displayed in the development of principles and concepts that have once been established. Take, for instance, the crime of Contempt of Court. This comprises naturally (1) offences against the Judge or jury; but also (2) offences against the discipline of the court, improper behaviour on the part of parties or counsel, failure, without due cause, to appear, unpunctuality or refusal to take the oath on the part of a witness; (3) failure in duty on the part of any officer concerned in the case. This would cover corruption on the part of any servant of the court; neglect of duty on the part of a J.P. or inferior magistrate who fails to make proper inquiry into any aspect of the case; illegal arrest of an innocent person by any police officer; the giving of advice contrary to the law by any solicitor. Further contempt of court (4) is committed by a newspaper which, while a case is *sub judice*, makes attacks on an accused person, speaking, for instance, of him as 'the murderer,' although this is a matter to be determined by the court; or (5) by anyone who hinders the execution of the sentence of the court: e.g. a dilatory official or anyone who stays summary execution; under this category, too, falls (6) the party who does not conform to a judgment of the court, for example the debtor whom it orders to make payments monthly and who neglects to do so: the father of an illegitimate child who does not carry out the duties laid upon him, etc. Here is an example of the way in which an apparently quite limited offence is continually being extended, so that what is in origin a matter of court discipline ultimately comprises the regulation of debt and the rights of the illegitimate child.

The famous *Habeas Corpus* formula[5] has proved at least as elastic. Originally issued by the court to some police station or prison officer, it commanded the delivery of X.Y. before the hereinmentioned court; it is a formula for arrest and summons. It can, however, be used – and to-day is so used exclusively – to compel a police officer, suspected of having illegally arrested X.Y., to deliver him up at once to the courts in London, with a statement of the grounds on which he has been arrested. Should these grounds not appear sufficient, the court will at once order his release. In Puritan times, when the courts were concerned to check the spread of Royal absolutism, the original formula for arrest was converted into its opposite, an order of release. So, the tenor of the formula itself is a matter of complete indifference; the Judge's will to equity prevails, and he finds a way of making it prevail that serves, although it may be logically impossible.

It is even possible in English law for a Judge to tolerate the presentation of a case in an absolutely distorted form, including clear violations of the truth, in order to do justice more efficiently and more quickly. The famous 'legal fictions' (now obsolete) are a case in point. A man sues another for not paying his debt. This is done in the form of complaining that the defendant had maliciously hindered the plaintiff from paying his taxes to the King. By bringing forward this (absolutely fictitious) allegation that an interest of the King was involved, the case could be wrested out of the jurisdiction of the usual civil court and brought before another court which might work more quickly and expeditiously. English Judges would tolerate this perversion of the truth in the interests of justice. More famous still are the notorious two gentlemen (neither of them existent) John Doe and Richard Roe, who figured in numberless English lawsuits of olden times. A dispute on land was always a difficult, lengthy and dangerous proceeding. The difficulties would be lessened if the dispute had arisen out of another already pending in which case the law would dispense with various disagreeable formalities. It had therefore become customary for a plaintiff to assert that certain rights of his were injured by the action of John Doe and Richard Roe – neither of them existing – which was being fought in this court, and that his action against X.Y. was the outcome of this previous (non-existent) case. Any English Judge would smilingly wink at this absolute untruth in order to expedite justice. Mere words are nothing if higher interests are involved.

But on the other hand, words may be everything, for they might protect human life or human liberty. When the Judge happens to see some needful protection in the precise wording of a given formula, he can adhere to that wording in a fashion very hard for outsiders to understand. The meticulousness with which the English Judge insists that a prisoner can only be charged with offences cited in the indictment is renowned. If the facts are varied in the course of proceedings, he must be released. Renowned – or notorious – is the good old joke of the man, accused of stealing a young cow, who was saved when his counsel succeeded in proving that the *corpus delicti* was not a young cow but a calf – and there was no word in the charge about the theft of a calf! Thus we find, in combination, violence done to formulæ in interpretation on the one hand, and, on the other, the most meticulous regard for the text of formulæ!

Typically English is this sovereign freedom and energy of action, united with the most meticulous respect for traditional ancient ways. We came across it in parliamentary life. A useful man is taken into the Cabinet, even if there is no office available for him – and then some window-dressing post like that of the Lord Privy Seal is there, ready for just such a contingency. It is this same force which presses through in politics, often revealing the full nakedness of national egotism, while covering everything up with high ethical generalizations. It explains how it is that the Englishman always has religious and pacifist tears ready when he goes to war· ever since the days of William the Conqueror, his fighting has pursued this form. The continental is apt to take this to be hypocrisy; for the Englishman, it is merely the necessary stylization of action. It enables him to feel the gentleman: without it, he would feel a brute. The want of correspondence between form and action troubles him no more in a declaration of war than it does when his judge uses an antique formula for arrest as a guarantee of personal liberty.

Intelligent application of precedent and intelligent selection of written law are the founts of English justice. The result is a thoroughly national compromise between subjective extemporization and rigid adherence to precedents. This compromise has not been reached without crises; common law, originally, was rigid enough. The need of deviating from the dead letter in the interest of equity early led to reform. This was not done in the old Roman fashion, by giving the magistrate authority to let considerations of equity prevail in the place of the dead letter of the code; the fourteenth-century Equity procedure court was developed under a special court, the court of the Royal Chancellor (Chancery Court), with rules and a form of procedure often diametrically opposed to that of the other courts of law.

For centuries these two systems continued to exist side by side, cases of minors, mortgages, and others going as a matter of course before the Chancery Court, which however further developed into a general court in competition with the other courts of law. This dual system became the more superfluous in the course of time, that the English tendency to have recourse to precedents penetrated the Equity court too, driving out any freedom of interpretation there, while common law judges on their part inclined to make more and more use of ordinary common sense in their judgments and to treat precedents as non-existent. In the first half of the nineteenth century, this dualism led to a complete chaos of jurisdiction and of justice. A decision might be given in one sense in the Common Law court and in the opposite in the Equity court, on one and the same matter. To reach an Equity decision, it was often necessary to carry a case right through all the Common Law stages and then begin afresh on the other side. The delays, red-tape, and cost of this procedure made the Court of Chancery the mock of the whole world, especially after the ridicule poured on it by Dickens in *Bleak House* (1852). A Lord Chancellor, Lord Westbury, went so far as to say: 'We have two series of courts, one of which exists to create injustice and the other to put it to rights again.' Nor did confusion stop there. In addition to common law proceedings in the Court of King's Bench, and equity proceedings in the Court of Chancery, there was another court administering Roman law, the Court of Requests: under the Great Seal: to say nothing of a more or less independent Court of Exchequer, as well as a whole series of local courts attached to certain towns and certain districts (Chester, Lancaster, Durham, Wales). An end was finally made of this chaos by the Judicature Act of 1873, which assimilated Chancery proceedings with the common law and made the court a Chancery Division of the new High Court of Justice.

The sovereign authority of the Judge is not exhausted by the description of his independence given above. There is, in England, no other authority, except the Judge, competent to lay down the law. There are no special laws or privileged codes: every tendency in that direction was stamped out in the Middle Ages. Even special courts like the military and ecclesiastical tribunals have never succeeded in becoming effective factors in the legal system; their application has been confined to a highly restricted class of cases. There is no special law for administrative cases, no special court for determining issues between the executive and the judicature. Certain relics of former judicial authority still inhere in the House of Lords and the Privy Council of the King, which are the final court of appeal in a limited number of cases; but even here, the process of assimilation to the ordinary law of the land has long been accomplished: the special jurisdiction they possess is entrusted to the highest ordinary Judges, who are, for this purpose, members of the House of Lords and of the Privy Council.

So extensive are the powers of the English Judge that he even practically shares the Royal prerogative of mercy. He can, in a civil action, award the purely nominal damages of one farthing, or bind over a person charged with breach of the 'King's peace' to keep it or to 'be of good behaviour'; or he can quash a suit by solemnly binding over the accused to 'come up for judgment if called upon' (which never will be the case). Or, with the formula 'that this motion stand over,' the Judge will exercise a certain prerogative of mercy in the case of youthful or first offenders.

Such powers naturally carry immense consideration with them. The Judge is something like the representative of a privileged caste. He mostly is of good family. In practice, he is always an Oxford or Cambridge man – though, of course, there is no rule on this. After that, he will have studied in one of the ancient Inns of Court – Lincoln's Inn, Gray's Inn, Middle Temple, Inner Temple – where, and, if he so chooses, at London University likewise, he learns the law of the land. After three years at an Inn, followed by at least two in some barrister's chambers, his period of study is complete; he can be called as a barrister, and, after seven years' practice may be made a County Court Judge.

This career of the Judge is influenced by the State only in so far that the Lord Chancellor will ultimately issue his appointment. But the State in no stage of his career examines or accepts the candidate. English lawyers are a privileged caste with the monopoly of carrying out the law. The State may change the law, but does not determine who is to administer it. The Inns admit whomsoever they think fit, and a Committee composed of their representatives, the Council of Legal Education, regulates the course of study and examines the candidate. No University has a say in this, nor has the State. Who is not passed by the Inns of Court can never be barrister or Judge.

This course guarantees one thing – the Judge is much more carefully selected than if he had to pass a State examination, and all sorts of imponderabilia besides his intellectual attainments are given full consideration. Admission to an Inn generally demands good family and in most cases considerable means. There is the usual number of free places and scholarships to keep the caste barriers from becoming too rigid. But recommendation by two barristers is indispensable for admission to the Inn, and this would hardly be attainable by the mere clever upstart.

While every effort is made, in the case of this as of every other profession, to avoid anything like a visible caste system, the Bar is a corporation, confined to all intents and purposes to men of good family, into which, without that advantage, only the man of exceptional talent can make his way in the exceptional case. The poor German Judge of modest origin is impossible in England. A further noticeable point is the emphasis laid on practice. The budding barrister does not merely study the theory of the law and then gradually get his initiation into practice. At the university, he has had an all-round humane education, but as often as not has not studied law at all. At his Inn, he has the opportunity of hearing lectures on the law, but whether he does so or no is his own affair. He must, however, work in some barrister's chambers, or read up the subject-matter of his profession. His real education in the law is acquired through concrete cases: the degree to which he learns to connect isolated cases and comprehend their articulation, is a matter of chance or his own gifts. This want of theory explains much in English law. The ordinary lawyer, without special theoretical gifts, simply does not learn how to follow a fundamental principle of law through all its ramifications; it makes him prefer a rigid adherence to precedents, to be broken, at will, by some carefully veiled autocracy of interpretation, if need be. Competent observers even doubt whether jurists capable of a work like the German civil code, or practitioners who could apply a system founded on general principles, exist in England.

§ 4

The chief limitation of the absolute authority of the Judge is the marked co-operation of the layman. This, again, is typically English. The Englishman may trust his great man, but very rarely (only in the Church and in the School) does he permit him to be all-powerful or irresponsible. But the usual English remedy is not to subdivide his authority and substitute a series of half-gods for his god (on the collegiate system), but to compel him to work in harness with a body of plain citizens, on whose love of freedom and sound sense he relies to provide adequate protection against the concentration of power in a single hand. The great statesman has to face a plebiscite at least every five years; the Town Clerk has to work through well-meaning councillors with no special knowledge of the matter in hand.

So, the veritable palladium of English freedom is held to be the association, with the Judge, of a jury – to establish facts, and pronounce the verdict; the judgment remains in the Judge's hands. Historically, the jury system did not arise for the defence of English liberties. It arose out of the effort of would-be absolutist kings, in mediæval times, to preserve their jurisdiction, at all costs, against the rising tide of particular courts, notably those of the nobles and of the cities. The King sent his own Judges through the country to gather into their own hands all outstanding cases; since they were entirely ignorant both of the circumstances of the cases and of their personnel, they enlisted the services of twelve local inhabitants to assist them in passing judgment. Not until Stuart days, when absolutism made its most serious challenge of citizen rights, did the jury system become the pillar of civil liberty. Then, the Star Chamber, the great court of absolutist jurisdiction, tried to keep suits as far as possible out of the hands of juries, made juries responsible, in any case where an accused person had been acquitted by them, and attempted to restrict their competence even in the determination of fact. The attempt was vain. The result was that, from the seventeenth century on, the jury was so firmly rooted in the popular mind that it seemed impossible either to restrict or remove it, although grave doubts of the jury system are felt to-day by serious politicians as well as by legal opinion. The admission of women to serve on juries is of quite recent date.

The activities of the jury are twofold:

(a) Preliminary investigation by the Grand Jury. In this case, the jury consists of between thirteen and twenty-three persons, and has to determine whether the grounds of suspicion against an accused person are sufficient to enable a charge to be brought against him. They have to 'bring in a true Bill.' If they say no, the proceedings drop: if they say yes, they pass on to the ordinary courts.

(b) In the courts as petty jury or simply jury. In this case, twelve persons are empanelled, and have, at the end of the proceedings, to answer the question, Guilty or Not Guilty. In Scotland, a verdict of 'Not Proven' may also be brought in.

The prime sphere of the jury is the criminal court of first instance. In questions of life and liberty, the popular sense of justice demands the presence of a jury, whether the proceedings take place at Quarter Sessions before the Justices of the Peace or in the Court of King's Bench or Assizes. The jury system is not employed where issues which even the layman can perceive to be strictly juristic are concerned. Juries do not appear in appeal cases, and though frequently by no means invariably in civil actions. They hardly ever occur in the civil cases handled by the J.P.'s who are already laymen-judges. Parties in County Court cases can, generally, ask for a jury, and the same procedure is available in the Court of King's Bench. At the same time, civil actions are so largely technical, and the citizens at any rate in the Metropolis so much occupied with their own business, that the jury is the exception rather than the rule. There is an established practice of summoning a Special Jury for a large number of civil actions that come before the central courts in London: and for this the panel is drawn from the upper classes, largely merchants and bankers, who have clear views as to *meum* and *tuum*; this type of jury has proved very efficient. Further, old-established custom provides for a jury of twelve in coroners' cases, and in such cases (as indeed in many others) the jury is apt to take advantage of the opportunity to utter opinions on matters of general public interest, and voice criticism of defects in legislation or other faults in the conduct of affairs.

A diversity of opinion prevails, both in English and in Continental legal circles, as to the value of this large use of the lay element in complicated criminal cases, and even, at times, in civil actions. Already Bentham sharply expressed the doubts which are shared by most professional lawyers in all countries now; in addition two further points must be stressed with regard to England. The Grand Jury is gradually becoming superfluous, as its task of preliminary examination is, in most cases, already performed by the Justices of the Peace. If it continues to exist, the main reason is that it is drawn from the upper classes, and its assembly in a town where Assizes are being held is apt to be something of a social function. The common jury, on the other hand, owing to the fact that the upper classes for one reason or another get exemption from it,[6] tends more and more to be so exclusively composed of small men that it is gradually becoming a caricature of its original principle. Whatever criticism of the system there be, however, no one in England contemplates either superseding or modifying what is so thoroughly regarded as a palladium of national liberty.

§ 5

The specific English method of introducing the lay element is, however, the Justice of the Peace. This institution relieves the learned

Judge of the great mass of minor litigation about mine and thine, and lesser offences such as petty larcency, assault, breach of the peace, etc., on which he is compelled to spend his time in Continental countries: thanks to it, the number of Judges can be reduced to a minimum, and their quality kept at a maximum. The J.P. system arose in the twelfth and thirteenth centuries, when the King felt the need of erecting some counterpoise to the power of the Sheriffs, both in administration and in jurisdiction, which was gradually slipping out of his control. The Justice of the Peace had to seize the criminal and hand him over to the King's proper Judge, the Sheriff. Gradually, however, the justices extruded the Sheriffs from both their original spheres of action, and developed into a special authority on their own, which came into collision with the central authority as the prime defender of local interests in administration and in justice. In the sphere of administration, a system of government by J.P.'s developed which gradually superseded the sheriffs altogether (cf. page 254); in that of justice they constitute, again, a system that even now is not completely fused into the ordinary judicial arrangements of the land.

In the seventeenth and eighteenth centuries the Justices of the Peace constituted the backbone of aristocratic influence. No one could be a J.P. without a certain fortune; they had in their hands the entire administration of all the smaller civil cases, and, in addition, the whole of county administration. In the course of the nineteenth century, the greater part of their administrative functions were taken from them. But they retained judicial power and the consideration attached to it; whoever can send another to prison is the great man in the district. All democratic tendencies notwithstanding, this remains a privilege of the possessing class, and one of their social bulwarks, in England. For this reason, access to the ranks of J.P.s is one of the active demands of every section striving for political control.

The hold of the landowning nobility on this office is notably strong; in the country the J.P. is generally an aristocrat. When the Liberals are in power, they therefore tend to appoint members of other groups – clergymen, doctors, and barristers, who are almost always Liberal – to be J.P.s in the country; since 1919, women have been eligible. Since 1884, working men's leaders have been appointed as J.P.s in the big towns, though with little practical result; in daily life, the freedom-loving British workman would rather go to the man with the well-polished tall hat, than the man who has been chosen in accordance with his party programme.

The association of the J.P.s with law takes a dual form:

1. *Petty Sessions.* These are the lowest courts in England, and before them come disputes arising out of day-to-day matters of rents and wages, small debts, food adulteration, legal separation (as distinct from divorce), and such minor offences as assault, petty larceny, drunkenness, etc. They further serve as an investigation court for the majority of cases that go up higher for judgment. Nominally conducted by the whole body of J.P.s, they are actually, as a rule, composed of not more than two and in quite minor cases by only one J.P.

2. *Quarter Sessions.* Here we have the historic organ of administration by the J.P.s – an administrative and judicial office, which originally assembled all the J.P.s of the county or lesser district, quarterly, for the business of administration and of justice. To-day, Quarter Sessions have been shorn of almost all their administrative functions; they only retain the right of granting licences. Their juridical competence, too, has been straitly limited. At the same time, they continue to be the court of appeal from Petty Sessions – in so far as appeal is available – while almost all offences not expressly reserved to a lower (Petty Sessions) or a higher (Assizes) Court, are dealt with by them; in practice, that is to say all offences of middling gravity. At Quarter Sessions, justice is in the hands of all the J.P.s who are present, under the guidance of a chairman of their own selection; the minimum number is two. In the cases of offences of first instance there is nearly always a jury: on other cases this is exceptional.

The forms employed before the J.P. are of the utmost simplicity and very speedy. The preliminary investigation which, in Germany, takes place even in the most trifling contingency, with a thoroughness often in strange contrast to the insignificance of the case, is non-existent here; as a rule, the accused is dealt with at a single session at which judgment is pronounced without any further formalities.

The difficulties presented by the assimilation of this lay jurisdiction to the regular forms of justice are met in a fashion that may be open to juridical exception, but works tolerably well, thanks to the existence of good general common sense. Even a people more disposed to systematic thinking out of problems than is the English might well have felt it hard to devise a clear line of demarcation between the cases suitable for handling by the J.P.s and those more adapted to expert handling. It is therefore left to the accused to decide whether, in a given case, he will or will not accept the jurisdiction of the J.P.: a matter as to which he is seldom in any doubt: since the procedure in that case is both cheap and expeditious, and the worst penalty to be expected is three, or, in exceptional cases, six months' imprisonment. So, it is generally to the interest of the accused party to have his case dealt with by the Justices. The apprehension that may be aroused by assigning cases of a complicated juridical character to lay judgment has also been dealt with intelligently and fairly. In the first place, there are almost always two J.P.s – a fact that excludes extreme partiality. In the second place, the law expert has been introduced by the back-door into this lay system: the J.P.s always have a legal clerk at their service in the working out and declaration of sentence. He is a mere adviser, with no voice in the delivery of judgment: but, if he has the personality for the task, he may actually hold all the threads of business in his hands, just as we have seen it done by the Town Clerk in municipal administration.

From of old, the system of J.P.s has been exposed to very lively opposition. Jurists bewail the far-reaching transference of legal powers to laymen, while Liberal circles opposed the system as a bulwark of the old aristocracy, especially in the rural areas. In novels from Fielding's day to that of Dickens, the J.P. is invariably presented as the typical drunken, profane, tyrannical and uneducated landlord. But the dislike felt by Liberals for the J.P. system has not availed to shake the pride with which the average Englishman regards this lay justice as a characteristic national institution. While the J.P. has been practically deprived of his administrative functions, there are only two points at which this has been accomplished in connexion with justice:

1. A law of 1839 gave larger towns power to have Stipendiary Magistrates nominated by the King to take the place of Petty Sessions. So far, the number of towns which has taken advantage of this is small – London, and seventeen others including Birmingham, Leeds, Liverpool, etc. The J.P. is not wholly dispossessed under this arrangement: he may relieve the Police Magistrate by acting with or in substitution for him.

2. In the place of Quarter Sessions, more than a hundred towns have appointed a barrister to act as Recorder and judge cases which would otherwise come before the higher J.P. courts. Juries co-operate here on the same lines as in the case of Quarter Sessions.

Finally, by way of legal guarantee and of drawing a clearer line between ordinary and J.P. jurisdiction, the entire system of J.P. jurisdiction has been made subject to the general supervision of the ordinary courts. Not in the form of granting appeal to the latter in all cases. Appeal to a higher court is legally limited and takes place only in exceptional cases. In other cases, however, the J.P.s, if the matter does not seem to them quite clear, or if the case is of such importance in principle that a determinant judgment by the higher court seems to them desirable, can, at the request of a party to the suit, hand it over to the ordinary courts. For such a case, specific forms are laid down legally for the various stages of procedure. On the other hand the High Court of Justice in London may instruct any J.P. to handle a case which he has waived aside; while the said court also has, in almost every case, the right to remove an important case from the J.P.s and deal with it itself. So, the unity of law is hereby successfully safeguarded, and in a characteristically English fashion. It seems to be impossible for the Englishman to work out a principle to its end and establish an organization that clearly would bring the two systems of jurisdiction, that of the J.P.s and of the ordinary courts into one organic whole. But he follows his own line, by letting things go as they please, never asking more of human beings than they can accomplish, sparing the self-respect, always, of the man on the spot – but, at the same time, giving to the higher court such powers of supervision as make it almost invariably possible for it to deal energetically with any slackness or incompetence on the part of a local body. This is the English way of organizing things. We have seen the same principle at work in municipal administration, and shall meet it again in education.

§ 6

Side by side with the administration of justice by the J.P.s, crossing it at many points and supervising it, is the system of ordinary jurisdiction. Even here, however, we are dealing not with a clear and unified structure, but with two principles, operating side by side – the central and the local. True, the old Norman kings did strive to unify the whole body of law and bring it under the control of the central Royal courts. The system of local jurisdiction – both the time-honoured sheriff courts and the later courts of the great nobles, cities, etc. – was ruthlessly smashed by them. The old principle, according to which there is no law but the King's law, was firmly introduced. To force it on the provinces, Royal Judges were to hold the so-called Assizes throughout the country, which, with the aid of juries, were to administer law, both civil and criminal, in all cases. But the competency of the Assizes was by no means clearly distinguished from that of the standing Royal courts which gradually found their seat in London. A large part of jurisdiction continues to be centralized in the metropolis, and compels the parties to pay heavily for the privilege of going before the central courts. In such circumstances, the attempt to suppress the jurisdiction of the J.P.s can hardly succeed, obvious as are their defects. Thoroughgoing reform did not take place until the nineteenth century: then, while the competence of the J.P.s was gradually diminished, a system of County Courts of national scope was set up, with a procedure at once expeditious and inexpensive, with the High Court of Justice in London as court of appeal, but not such as to deprive the lower courts of their status as courts of first instance. Further, there is a court of Appeal in London to which, in many cases, recourse can be had against decisions both of the High Court and, upon occasion, of those of lower courts. Thus ordinary jurisdiction reveals a triple system:

(a) County Courts with the High Court of Justice in London as appeal court.

(b) The High Court of Justice in London as the real court, competent, in principle, for all cases. It is at once the court of first instance and the court of appeal, against the decisions of County Courts as well as of J.P.s. Modern tendencies try to delegate all cases of first instance as far as possible to the County Courts, making the High Court an appeal tribunal simply. The High Court resides in London normally, but also sends its judges into the provinces to hold Assizes there.

(c) The Court of Appeal in London.

b and c together constitute the Supreme Court of Judicature.

The mutual relations of these courts are not systematized in any unified way. At the same time, there is a well-marked tendency to leave ordinary civil suits to the County Courts, and confine criminal proceedings, almost without exception, to Assizes. The High Court in London, on the other hand, is and remains the court of final instance in all cases, both civil and criminal, and at the same time a court of first instance for civil cases of primary importance. There is no regulation, in detail, of the relations between the J.P. system and that of the ordinary courts: the tendency is, however, to make the County Court the court of appeal from the J.P.s' jurisdiction, while leaving to the High Court a general supervision which entitles it to intervene in jurisdiction whenever it may seem good to it so to do. Competence is distributed as between J.P.s, County Courts and Assizes through a mass of detailed prescriptions which tend, in general, to se⁻d minor criminal cases to the Justices, major to the Assizes, while assigning civil actions to the County Courts. Many points remain quite unregulated, and as usual in England, the gaps of theory are apt to be pieced up by practical wisdom.

§ 7

In detail, then, something like the following picture emerges:

1. *The County Courts*, founded in 1846. In general, they cover all cases concerning property up to a value of £100. England is divided into 552 Districts, which are from time to time distributed among the available Judges (legal maximum 60). The districts assigned to any given Judge constitute his circuit. In each district of his circuit – i.e. in practice, in every largish place – he must appear officially at least once a month. He is paid the high salary of £1,500 per annum. Associated with him is a Registrar, a solicitor by profession, who, originally a mere clerk, has gradually become an assistant to the Judge, with competence in all minor matters. A jury may be constituted if the Judge think fit, and, in most cases, on demand by the parties to the action: but in practice it is the exception rather than the rule. In all actions of more than £20, appeal may be laid to the Court in London, which can, further, on request from either party take cognizance of a case, while the Judge also has the right, in accordance with the proper forms, to remit the case to the said higher court. Modern legislation tends more and more to push forward the County Courts as the relevant instance for civil actions.

2. *The Assizes*. Although these constitute, properly speaking, a sub-division of the High Court (cf. next section), they are more conveniently treated independently. They are not courts with a fixed location, but periodical (as a rule thrice a year) sessions of the High Court of Justice in the provinces. England and Wales are, for this purpose, divided into eight circuits to each of which the High Court is wont to send a Judge, who then, in the capital of the said district and in other localities of importance, sets up a court of justice, with a local jury. The Assizes, like the J.P.s, represent a national institution which, despite their shortcomings, the English-

man regards with a certain pride. In the Middle Ages they have had grounds for this feeling. It meant much for the legal unity of the land that the central Judge should 'bring law to every man's door,' that he should thereby supervise local jurisdiction and plant the legal practice and legal principles of the capital throughout the country. But under modern conditions there are other ways by which these benefits can be more conveniently realized. To-day it is a strange anomaly that the highest Judges in the land should have to waste a good part of their time on travelling, and that grave criminal cases should, in the majority of places, only be tried twice or thrice a year. Yet, this clumsy, circuitous and costly machinery is still popular. One of the reasons certainly is that the Assizes represent the great social event of the year throughout the province. Wherever he goes, the Judge is received with mediæval pomp and Royal honours. The Grand Jury – unlike the ordinary jury – is recruited from the first circles who stream to the county town for the Assizes and celebrate all sorts of social and commercial functions at that time. Without the Assizes, there is many a non-industrial English town that would sink into a tedious and often poverty-stricken provincial hole.

The competence of the Assizes extends, formally, to all cases within the ambit of the High Court in London; that means all cases whether civil or criminal. At the same time, a large, nay the preponderating part of civil actions is transferred by various methods to the County Courts. On the other hand, the Assizes constitute the ordinary court for all major criminal cases; the latter are handed over to them partly by the J.P.s and partly by the interposition of the High Court: in major cases, they alone are competent.

In London – where criminal cases accumulate and the periodic Assizes cannot constitute a social event – Assize Courts are substituted by a standing Central Criminal Court, of which the Lord Mayor (purely in theory) is president.

3. The first division of the Supreme Court of Judicature, the *High Court of Justice*. The High Court is the highest court in England. It is not merely a court of appeal, but to a considerable extent a court of first instance (officiating mainly in London, and, in the form of Assizes, also in the provinces).

The High Court was set up by the Judicature Acts of 1873 and 1875, by the combination of various, previously separate, courts. It is itself divided as follows: into three divisions with two to fifteen Judges, each of whom receives £5,000 per annum.

(a) The *Chancery* division, with the Lord Chancellor at its head, takes the place of the old equity courts. Its competence extends to all cases of trusteeship and wardship, to the law of companies, charitable foundations, etc.

(b) The *King's Bench* division – the largest, most distinguished and oldest court in England, with the Lord Chief Justice at its head – takes the place of three earlier courts: the Court of King's Bench, the Court of Common Pleas (for civil actions), the Court of Exchequer (for financial claims on the part of the Treasury).

Like the older King's Bench Court, it is the court of the country, competent, in principle, in all actions not expressly assigned to other courts. The tendency, to-day, is to limit this extensive competency in matters of first instance, and to make the King's Bench division rather a supervisory and appeal division. Associated with it is a Commercial Court, a Bankruptcy Court, for London only, and a Court of Criminal Appeal, to which in certain cases appeals against judgments of inferior courts can be made. The courts from which appeal can lie to the Court of Criminal Appeal are the Quarter Sessions, Assizes and the King's Bench division itself, in so far as it is a court of first instance.

In principle, the system of the individual Judge is supreme in the King's Bench as in the other divisions. Certain matters, however, notably of a criminal character, are handled by Divisional Courts with two Judges. In civil cases, a Special Jury, of gentlemen, generally takes the place of the ordinary common jury of lower middle-class persons.

(c) The Probate, Divorce and Admiralty division (with a President and two Judges) is competent in will cases, divorce actions, and most matters concerned with sea law.

4. The second division of the Supreme Court of Judicature is the *Court of Appeal* (not to be confused with the Court of Criminal Appeal, which is part of the King's Bench division). It is composed of five ordinary Judges, while the Lord Chancellor (the active Chancellor and the ex-Chancellors likewise), the Lord Chief Justice and two other high Judges have likewise the right to vote. Judgments are generally issued by a quorum of at least three Judges.

5. The final legal court is the House of Lords, both in criminal and in civil cases, although its functions in regard to the first have almost disappeared in practice. In the Middle Ages, Parliament claimed to possess supreme judicial authority; the opposing claims

of the two Houses were finally settled on terms that provided that while it is for the Lower House to impeach, it is for the Upper to decide their charge. A procedure under which Parliament by legislation makes a certain action a crime and passes a Bill of Attainder is also conceivable. In either case, what is involved is some act of force, scantily clothed with the forms of justice, like the ostracism of the ancients or the outlawry of old German law: a political opponent who cannot be got at through the ordinary forms of law is dragged by his enemies before some political tribunal which then proceeds to declare him an enemy of the State and even to execute him. In the seventeenth century the royalist Strafford (1641) and the Jacobite John Fenwick (1697) were made away with by Bill of Attainder: an effort was made to deal with Warren Hastings (1787–95) by Impeachment: and the last attempt in this direction was that undertaken in 1805 against Lord Melville. Analogous, too, was the Bill of Pains and Penalties attempted in 1820 against Queen Caroline.

Very little now remains of the powers of the House of Lords in criminal cases. It has competence in criminal cases against its own members. It went on much longer acting as a court of first instance, notably in regard to divorce. The reforms of 1873–75 took these functions away from it, leaving only a small fragment of its old powers as supreme court of appeal. Here, in normal cases, the Court of Appeal has competence. As against its verdicts appeal to the House of Lords can only lie if the Court of Appeal gives its consent thereto; and the enormous costs of such a proceeding mean that it is only taken advantage of in cases of the very first importance. In criminal cases, the practical competency of the Upper House is still less: in such case the consent of the Attorney-General, as chief representative of the Crown in legal matters, is requisite for the presentation of an appeal to the Lords against a decision of the Court of Criminal Appeal. At the same time, there are cases of great importance in which the rôle of the Upper House as supreme juridical body is still retained. But there Parliament has been fitted in to the general juridical structure; the juridical functions of the House of Lords are not assigned to the whole body but to a small legal committee, consisting of those Lords who have held or now hold high legal office: the most important of them, the Lords of Appeal in Ordinary, are high jurists who sit in the Lords for this very purpose. So, it is no longer possible, strictly speaking, to talk of the juridical function of the House of Lords, but only of a supreme legal tribunal which is composed of members of that House. That this is so is proved by the fact that the Judicial Committee of the Lords is not bound by the sessions of Parliament, but sits quite independent of them.

6. During the sixteenth and seventeenth centuries absolutism made its last attempts to curb the ordinary courts under the will of the King. The King's Bench and the other ordinary courts which laid down the law in the King's name, had become independent of the King's will. Against them absolutism endeavoured to force the Privy Council on the country as supreme legal tribunal, and so win back for the King that immediate influence on jurisdiction which he had given over to his high courts. A committee of the Privy Council, the 'Star Chamber' of Henry VII's creation (apparently so-called after the decorations on the ceiling of the chamber in which it sat) was, during the sixteenth and seventeenth centuries, the principal instrument of Royal absolutism: it attempted to bring before itself all cases, whether criminal or civil, in which the Crown was interested, and to settle them in accordance with Roman instead of common law. With the fall of absolutism in the seventeenth century, the Star Chamber disappeared. The judicial powers of the Privy Council have been steadily contracted ever since. But a last, but highly significant remains of them is retained, inasmuch as the Judicial Committee of the Privy Council is the court of appeal for the ecclesiastical and consular courts and also against the decisions of the Supreme Courts of the Colonies. It is, therefore, the court which upholds the legal unity of the Empire, one of the last links of the Mother Country with the Dominions. True, the latter are by no means completely satisfied with this limitation put upon their freedom of action; every case where a Privy Council decision goes against a colonial court arouses the most lively opposition. Indeed, the major Dominions, Australia and Canada, have made appeal to the Privy Council largely conditional on the approval of their own Supreme Courts. Even this special jurisdiction of the Privy Council's is fitted into the framework of the ordinary legal system – in such cases it is not the Privy Council as a whole which exercises juridical functions, but, apart from the Lord President, there *pro forma* in virtue of his office, only those members of the Council who hold or have held high legal office, as well as five Colonial Judges. So the old Cabinet justice is maintained in form, but in substance completely adjusted to modern demands.

7. Outside the system above described there is the *Coroner*, who

dates back to early mediæval times. Once always a landowner, now more frequently a doctor or solicitor, appointed by the town or county, the Coroner has, with the assistance of twelve jurors, to inquire into any case of suspicious death (and, in London, of arson) and, if suspicion falls on anyone, to hand that person over to ordinary justice. From the legal point of view, the Coroner is a Royal official who is there to watch over the interests of the Crown in case they are jeopardized through breach of the Royal peace.

8. The old judicial powers of the *Sheriffs* has died out save for a few cases in which the Sheriff has to decide on the amount of damages. His administrative functions have also been limited to the preparation of lists of jurors, the supervision over prisoners, and the conduct of parliamentary elections. In Scotland, on the other hand, the Sheriff, either alone or in association with a jury, still exercises important functions in relation both to civil and criminal justice.

9. Independent of this whole system there are (*a*) the Industrial Court of London for the decision of industrial disputes; (*b*) a system of Ecclesiastical Courts in London and the cathedral towns; (*c*) the Scottish Court of Session in Edinburgh, with the Sheriffs' courts in the Scottish counties.

§ 8

One result of the surprisingly unsystematic character of English law is that it is almost completely in the hands of lawyers.

England has neither a civil nor a criminal code, neither a statutory civil or criminal procedure. Nowhere any kind of clear systematization between the duties and prerogatives of its various courts. In the majority of cases, the court of reference, though often probable, is by no means clear; again, the status of the various courts is dubious and settled by no fixed rules – in spite of all the sound work of the last three generations to bring order into former chaos. The consequence is that the few persons who can master all these difficulties, simply rule the law, i.e. the lawyers. In no other country is the litigant public so entirely in the hand of the lawyer as in England. He alone knows what precedent is raised by a given case and what court is available; whether, and if so in what form, action is admissible and would be advantageous. However trifling the matter, and however clear the claim, the ways of the law are so impenetrable to the individual that his steps must be led through them by the lawyer. This means, of course, high costs, a protracted procedure, and again high costs. But the law reforms of the nineteenth century proved powerless to touch this effective legal monopoly.

§ 9

The impartiality of English Judges is renowned; yet dread of a possible misuse of the power of the Judge runs like a scarlet thread through the entire criminal procedure. Every possible device is employed to obviate such a possibility. The idea of criminal justice as designed to protect the State or safeguard the peaceful citizen from attacks by the undisciplined, is entirely subsidiary to that of protection against wrongful arrest and condemnation. To the English mind, the freedom of the individual matters more than the order of the whole; nay, more, the sole purpose, according to English ideas, of any public order is to secure the freedom of the individual.

In no country is it so difficult to arrest a criminal. Domiciliary visitation and apprehension require not only the warrant of a Judge or a J.P., but, in addition, the fulfilment of certain extraordinarily precise conditions. The citizen can make complaint of improper arrest by a policeman or J.P. before the High Court in London and there obtain a writ of *Habeas Corpus* which causes his immediate release. At the preliminary examination that then takes place, before the Justices of the Peace, the officer who has made the arrest lies under suspicion of having taken an innocent person into custody, and has to clear himself by a full account of all the circumstances which have given rise to suspicion. This preliminary investigation is hedged about with every conceivable precaution for the protection of the accused; he may be defended by counsel, and the proceedings are open to the public. At no stage in the proceedings is he subject to interrogation; on the contrary, the presiding magistrate will draw his attention to the fact that he is not called upon to commit himself, and that silence on his part will not be used against him. If this preliminary investigation before the Justices leads to the formal establishment of the charge, it is, in any serious case, renewed in summary form before the Grand Jury at the Assizes, nor can proceedings proper begin until they have found a true Bill.

Further difficulties are imported into the prosecution of a criminal by the fact that, as a general rule, there must be a plaintiff to present the charge, who must retain counsel to act for him. In earlier times, indeed, the personal risks run by anyone who assumed the rôle of complainant – whether on ground of personal injury or moved by his feelings as a citizen – were so great as to amount to an encouragement to crime, since the criminal could remain at large unless the injured party made up his mind to take proceedings. Gradually, private associations developed and took over what in other countries is considered the duty of the State; thus associations for the prevention of cruelty to children or animals, of adulteration of food and obnoxious trade practices, would bring into court cases that interested them. Only on certain capital crimes did the police appear in the rôle of accuser. Not till 1879 and 1884 was recourse had to the method (always existent in Scotland) of establishing a Director of Public Prosecutions, who, however, only for certain serious offences (murder, coining, etc.) is compelled to prosecute. Obviously, the lack of adequate machinery for entering complaints represents a definite and serious injury to the poorer classes, who are constantly unable to prosecute offenders with skill, means and social position. Moreover, police action must often fail where public opinion happens to be on the side of the accused, since the local authority must first vote the costs of a prosecution before taking action against the accused.

After the case has been opened the same sort of precautions in favour of the prisoner reappear. The accused is again protected against any kind of inquisitorial examination. Neither in relation to the accused nor to the witness does the Judge conduct the case; it is a contest between counsel. The counsel for the prosecution calls witnesses to prove his case; the counsel for the accused, witnesses for the defence; both are cross-examined, but the prisoner need not go into the box unless his counsel chooses to put him there. In his interest, further, questions as to his mode of life, his past, etc., are generally disallowed. Suppositions on the part of witnesses, any questions to them as to whether they believe the accused to be guilty, are forbidden. The counsel for the prosecution has to establish his case by compelling evidence. In this the Judge does not in any sense support him; he is present merely as an interested auditor of the proceedings, only interposing to clear up some answer that is not perspicuous by question; although at the close of the case he gives a judicial summing-up of the facts before the jury. This summing up is, in form, merely informatory and elucidatory, but actually the Judge will, by his emphasis on certain points for or against the accused, frequently guide the jury's mind in a definite direction. At the same time, the English judge invariably exercises this power of his in a moderate manner and in any case of doubt gives the accused the benefit of it.

The protection of the accused is developed, under English law, in absolutely model fashion, such as is secured in no other law the world over. Here the negative individualism of the English mind finds its sharpest expression. The fact that the accused lies under the suspicion of having, it may be, injured the community by the worst of crimes, is here a secondary consideration. What does signify is that an individual is here in conflict with the machine of the State, and, in such case, the English mind assumes that the individual is likely to be right. That a murderer should be at large is an evil, but nothing like so serious an evil as that a Briton should be illegally deprived of his freedom.

This intensive development of guarantees for the protection of the accused is entirely comprehensible to anyone who has grasped the nature of the Englishman's legal sense. In him, the abstract sense of law is but feebly developed; but his sense of the necessity of safeguarding the right of anyone whom he has recognized as his equal before the law is exceedingly strong. The damage done to the community by a crime is something abstract; it appeals far less to him than the concrete fact of a man in the dock. Every man who is in trouble with the law, challenges the Englishman's feeling of justice. It was not always so. English law is, originally, the law of the land-owning male of English (not Irish!) nationality and his dependants, developed through constant fighting against royal absolutism and its organs, and against all sorts of oligarchical coteries. Participation in the full protection of the law has been won, again by constant struggle, by sections of the population once legally inferior. The struggle is now over; the law works admirably; the Englishman's sense of law is to-day extraordinarily sensitive to any injustice – but it was not always so. On the contrary, the pervasive and often excessive precautions against partiality and similar oppressions which permeate English legal procedure represent the hard-won inheritance of times when they were a bitter necessity. They are precautionary regulations against the Berserker strain of passion which, though to all appearance stifled under the well-bred forms of gentlemanliness, burst out now and again with volcanic force. Superb impartiality has not always characterized the English Courts. In the times of fierce clash of political passion, the innocent accused was by no means safe in the hands of English justice. The Star Chamber, instrument of absolutism, has the worst possible reputation in history, and English Judges made themselves the tools of this perversion of justice. Impeachment and Bills of Attainder were terrible examples of the tyranny of the inflamed majority—like *lettres-de-cachet* on the other side of the Channel. After every rising in Scotland or Ireland, all legal safeguards were suspended by England, and courts-martial or special legal Commissions sent its opponents to the gallows or prison. Ireland in the year of grace 1920 is the latest example. Even where the forms of ordinary justice were maintained, the opponent of the authorities was by no means sure of impartial treatment; it is hard to find any parallel in modern history to the Bloody Assize of Judge Jeffreys. English legal history is full of complaints of the 'packing' of juries. Out of the devices of this period there survives the very dubious employment of 'King's evidence' – i.e. the pardon of an accomplice in return for his testimony against his associates. Protection of the accused was, for the most part, worked out in the seventeenth and eighteenth centuries, as the outcome of a thoroughly justified suspiciousness. It is suggestive that, even after the fall of absolutism, the popular imagination never gave birth, in England, to even a single story on the lines of the *Miller of Sans-Souci*, whose motif is that rock-like confidence of the people in the justice of the King's Judges. In popular memory, even the justice of the eighteenth century was the justice of the tyrannical, wilful and partial Justice of the Peace – in a word, class-justice. The novel may be a poor witness to reality, but at least it shows us what people thought.

§ 10

Even to-day, despite its superb impartiality to the accused, English justice cannot be quite freed from the reproach of class-justice. Not in criminal proceedings; there the last traces of one-time one-sidedness have vanished completely. But class-justice exists in connexion with all the cases – that never come to court. Even in criminal cases an injury to the poor is involved in the imperfect development of anything like a public prosecution office; the poor man often cannot afford to bring an action. This injury is much more marked in the case of civil actions. In matters that can be handled by the Justice of the Peace, all is well. But in all major issues, the unintelligibility, dilatoriness, and expensiveness of the process amount to a denial of justice to the lower and middle classes. The degree to which these drawbacks are felt even by the English themselves is sufficiently demonstrated by the fact that the trading commuuity – i.e. that body of citizens for whom a satisfactory functioning of the laws is most important – avoids the courts as far as possible. To an extent un-paralleled in any other country, arbitration has been substituted in England for the machinery of the law. Chambers of Commerce and other trading corporations have erected arbitration facilities for the use of their members, which are gradually becoming competitors with the Courts of Justice, and it has become almost normal practice to include in any contract binding on both parties a clause under which they undertake to submit any difference of opinion to arbitration, not to law.

The only people who are interested in the maintenance of the present unsatisfactory state of things are the members of the legal profession. Public opinion demands the utmost decentralization. That means more Judges, and, probably, fewer Judges at the status and salary prevailing under the present system, which concentrates jurisdiction in the hands of a very small number of men of royal consideration and princely income. A more speedy, cheaper and simpler legal system must dissipate something of the nimbus surrounding the Judge. It would also injure the barrister. For this reason, there is no change. The lawyers are more powerful than the law.

England has two sharply differentiated classes of lawyer: barristers and solicitors. (Since the war, women have been admitted to both.) The barristers are the aristocrats. They are almost exclusively recruited from the good families, educated in the imposing and dignified Inns of Court, and constitute the pillars of the English legal hierarchy. Solicitors are recruited from various obsolete legal categories – from the solicitors proper (lawyers in the Chancery Courts), attorneys (in the Court of King's Bench), proctors (in the Ecclesiastical Courts); all of whom stood far below the barrister both in social status and birth. To-day solicitors can only appear in County Courts, barristers in any, and notably in the High Court, where all the great cases are settled. The solicitor enjoys considerable status and may make a very good income. The legal assistants to trade and industrial undertakings are generally solicitors, as are most Town Clerks and the great majority of State legal officials and judicial officials without the title of judge, such as the clerks at Petty and Quarter Sessions and the Registrars. But in all proceedings before the High Court the solicitor may be indispensable, but he is secondary. He prepares the case, collects the material, assembles the witnesses, and acts as intermediary with the public; his place, however, is in the background. It is the barrister who presents the case in court, enjoys the honour, the glory, and most of the pay; only the barrister, no solicitor no matter how competent, can become a Judge, a Lord Chief Justice or a Lord Chancellor.

Solicitors have long been asking to be admitted to the privileges of the Bar. Certainly, this would represent the most immediate relief to the litigant public, who could then enter on a case with one lawyer, instead of two, to fee, and one who would have to be paid a good but not a princely honorarium. The interest of the barristers is of course set in quiet but obstinate opposition to any such change. Often in the past the private interest of the legal profession has been a powerful factor, generally of a reactionary type, in the history of English jurisprudence. There is a classic satire upon it in the pages of Dickens. The egotism of the Inns of Court was a powerful instrument of defence of the old unreformed common law against the Romanizing law courts. To this day, this egotism has prevented, nay, made to all intents and purposes impossible, any such clarification of English law as would render it accessible to the common man. So long as law is a secret doctrine, the adept is all-powerful. A long fight was put up by legal intransigence against the fusion of the two separate legal systems, Common Law and Equity. In the same way, it stands to-day in the way of the needful decentralization, acceleration and cheapening of litigation, and is mainly responsible for the aversion of the litigant from civil actions, which contrasts so markedly with the impartiality, humanity and decency of criminal procedure.

The fact, that even in these democratic days barristers have been able to maintain their privileges at the expense of the general good, shows how strong the influence of birth, breeding and property still is in England. What makes the present state of things possible is that the barristers, like high finance, the clergy and the landowning aristocracy, belong to the real rulers of the country. They are a closed corporation, localized, with insignificant exceptions, in the metropolis, and enjoy the closest contact with the real possessors of power, the members of the House of Commons. Barristers, indeed, constitute a notable proportion of these members (an eighth in 1906) and the most efficient and talkative section; while the solicitor, lower in social status, is much less strongly represented (only a twenty-fourth in 1906). In both the older parties they play an important part; every local authority, every corporation comes to Parliament, at some time or other, with a Private Bill, and then has to have recourse to a barrister to present it. This gives them all sorts of contacts with socially influential circles; money and social status do the rest. Most important of all – England does not possess the independent State organization, acting and judging on purely objective grounds, that could cope energetically with their privileged position. There is a party complexion to every great political tendency or movement – and there is not likely to be any use of the barristers' privilege as a stick to beat the party in power with, so long as the attack on that party has to be largely recruited from the ranks of the barristers themselves. An English Prime Minister rarely has the time to undertake a reform of purely practical significance which holds out little or no prospect of detaching a hundred votes from the other side. So, judicial questions are, from time to time, investigated by Commissions; but the realization of reforms has to wait till a condition of things develops so patently intolerable that both parties are compelled to unite in finding a way out of the impasse. Chaos has not yet reached the pitch which, in its day, produced the reconstruction of local government, the creation of a single London, or the fusion of Common Law and Equity in one jurisdiction; meantime, the mere middle-class taxpayer, who has no millions to pour into the party chest, and does not know how to strike, is used to waiting.

CHAPTER V
THE PRESS
§ 1

THE English Constitution of to-day, no matter what its historic origin, rests upon two pillars—the power of the leading statesman, and its control by public opinion. The Prime Minister, more or less independent so far as day-to-day issues are concerned, is nevertheless subject to the recurring verdict of public opinion. He seeks to carry it with him, to rouse it to enthusiasm for his policy. At the same time, he submits to a certain guidance from it. A perpetual interplay goes on, between leader and led, in which the pull is ultimately exercised by the stronger. The mediocre statesman has his ear constantly to the ground, trying to hear how any little step he takes will affect the public. But even the strongest is not strong enough to disregard the echoes of public opinion.

In a thousand different places the formation of this public opinion goes on. Every political meeting contributes to it, every occasion when men gather together, in the evening or at the midday meal; so does the music-hall, the theatre, the church, every opportunity when politics are talked or impressions received that react on politics. It is therefore capable of being affected along a thousand lines—through a sermon, an election meeting, a great Party congress, the political clubs, the great reunions, for sport or social enjoyment, that take place in the mansions of the aristocracy. Most potent, however, is the influence of the Press. What counts to-day is not what the leading statesman or his opponent says in the presence of a few hundred Members of Parliament or a few thousands in the provinces. A hundred years ago, when politics was an affair of the few, that might have been so. But to-day what matters is what the Press puts before its millions of readers. The statesman loves the sense of using personal power over men that he gets when he speaks in the breathless atmosphere of some packed hall, crammed with human beings who alternately break out into ejaculation and loud applause; but this method is no longer necessary. What is necessary is that his speeches should be broadcast to the million; what cannot be effected by the popular meeting or parliamentary speech can now be done through an interview with a single reporter.

In the course of the nineteenth century, the part played by the Press in politics has steadily grown. Up to 1832, politics were confined to a small group of gentlemen who sat in the House of Commons.

The plebs had no right to know anything of such matters. For Addison and Steele, the upholsterer in politics is still a figure of fun; and right down to the close of the eighteenth century the Commons rejected any suggestion of opening their debates to the public. In the reform struggle, however, the leaders began talking to the electorate outside the House of Commons, and this sort of political activity comes more and more to the fore. Cobden's great fight against food taxes (1838–46) was carried on almost entirely outside Parliament; by means, therefore, of reports in the Press. Gladstone chose his constituency, Midlothian (1879–80), and not the House, for his great campaign against Disraeli; after the Boer War, in the same way, Chamberlain carried on his tariff propaganda by means of mass meetings all over the country; throughout his career, from the very start, direct appeal to the masses has been the characteristic technique of Mr. Lloyd George, and the real support of his Government a Press to report his ideas, underline them, drive them home by iteration, now from this angle and now from that. The modern Press is a great deal more than a mere instrument for reporting. Its function is the formation of public opinion. Its main business is, not to tell its reader what is, but to create something that ought to be. So the journalist will, as far as possible, put before his public only such news as is calculated to influence it in a certain direction. His ideal is to present not everything, but whatever he or his proprietor regards as important. He still adheres to the time-honoured reportorial form, and writes in the indicative mood, but all the time he seeks to make that indicative work as an imperative. Professional tradition and a certain moral compulsion, accepted by every journalist of standing, make a considerable part of his work a simple narrative of what has been; but the more important part of his paper is that where the imperative prevails. It has become an indispensable part of the machine of every democratic State because here the larger part of public opinion is made, which is the basis of all democratic government.

The Press is, further, necessary as an instrument for controlling the executive. The individual Member of Parliament has the right of keeping the Government on the *qui vive* by a standing flow of minor questions addressed to ministers. But whether this method will have any results or not, depends on the newspapers. Only in rare cases of unusual importance can the House begin a formal debate upon a minister's replies to questions; the Press, on the other hand, can do so at every moment. If it merely faithfully records question and answer, the effect is nil: if, however, they are made the subject of excited comment in leading articles and correspondence, a first-class political affair may develop. The same political result can be achieved, without troubling Parliament at all, by the publication of some article that gets widely talked about. Indeed, the centre of gravity, the controlling point of the machine has, to-day, shifted from the House of Commons to the Press.

The political Press consists of party organs, which represent definite points of view. A large part of their work, however, in England, is devoted to the fulfilment of a duty to the State. As a matter of course, speeches by leaders are impartially reported in the newspapers of either party. Party complexion only comes in in the reporting of spokesmen of the second and third rank, where, of course, considerations of space also play their part. The good form of the House of Commons is reflected in the Press. Errors in an opponent's speeches will not only be readily corrected: he will also be given the opportunity of replying in his own defence – which is not always the case outside England. Blankly false statements are never made; errors are at once corrected, in decent fashion. The Press, on the other hand, has established for itself the respectful consideration appropriate to the organ of an important function in the State. Representatives of the great newspapers have access to ministers, irrespective of party, and expect, up to a point, to receive confidential information. The refusal of Government information to Lord Northcliffe, at the height of his feud with Mr. Lloyd George, in 1921, was an event hitherto unprecedented.

The Press, in addition to having its public function in the State, is – and this is its primary outward concern – also the representative of the private interests of certain groups of politicians and capitalists. Up to the last quarter of the nineteenth century, capitalist influence on the Press was still confined within modest limits. Many of the best papers were still the property of wealthy individual proprietors, or family concerns carrying on a policy of their own, dependent on no party but inclining to one or the other and so exerting a determining influence over it. John Walter, founder of *The Times* (1785), and his successors afford the outstanding example of the absolutely independent, politically immensely influential journalism unknown outside England; here, politics on the grand scale were conducted by means of a strong will and ample capital, without binding party affiliation. *The Times*, at first outspokenly Liberal, moved more and more to the right, and is now a thoroughly Conservative organ. A similar basis in family capital existed in the case of the Edinburgh *Scotsman* (founded by the Ritchie family in 1817), and still exists in that of the *Manchester Guardian*, the property of the Taylor-Scott family (founded in 1821). The Quaker families, Rowntree and Cadbury, own a whole group of periodicals, the London *Daily News* and *Star* and a series of provincial papers. But in this case, we are no longer dealing with a family business. The proprietors are industrial magnates – here, cocoa manufacturers – who combine, in a fashion typically Quaker, the making of profits by trade and manufacture with the pursuit of lofty ethical aims. The vast majority of British newspapers, however, are to-day owned by great politico-capitalistic groups who are in close touch with a political party though not absolutely identified with it.

They are in the hands of great concerns, which will in general represent a given political tendency but lack that personal note that used to characterize the older newspapers. Such concerns generally control a whole series of papers. The most important and outstanding newspaper combine – the Northcliffe Trust – will be dealt with more fully below (page 323 *seq*.). This trust was the great mainstay of power for Conservative and Imperialist tendencies in the last generation before the war, doubly powerful because it always kept clear of any too close connexion with the official Conservative Party. Northcliffe's rival was Cyril Arthur Pearson (1866–1921) the owner of the three Conservative papers, *Standard, Evening Standard* and (at one time) the *Daily Express* and a whole series of provincial and harmless family newspapers. Pearson proved the commercial advantage of combining the ownership of a great metropolitan paper with that of periodicals of the other two types; and his example has been followed more and more frequently and with capital flotations reaching into gigantic figures. During the war, a considerable part of the provincial Press passed under the control of a combine organized by Sir Edward Hulton, of Manchester, which also acquired the London *Daily Sketch* and *Evening Standard*. Subsequently the Hulton papers were in 1923–4 acquired by three other powerful concerns, which now between themselves control the larger part of the English newspaper world – the Rothermere, the Beaverbrook, and the Berry Trusts. The concern headed by Lord Rothermere, the brother of Lord Northcliffe, represents what was left of the latter's gigantic newspaper trust after the death of its founder, the *Daily Mail, Daily Mirror, Evening News*, and several lesser papers. Lord Beaverbrook's chief organ is the

Daily Express, founded in 1900 by Pearson, which has always been the chief organ of crying sensationalism and loud imperialism. The trusts of the two chief competitors (Rothermere and Beaverbrook) are closely allied through interlocking shareholding. The third and apparently most powerful of the three newspaper trusts is that headed by Sir William Berry with heavy industry in South Wales behind it. Its chief organ now is the *Daily Telegraph*, which, founded in 1855 as a Liberal organ, has long since passed into the Conservative camp. The Berry papers have, however, a less pronounced Conservative tone than those of the Rothermere and Beaverbrook group. They are definitely anti-Socialist, but otherwise of a more coalition character. Business with them comes before politics. All this process of evolution of the last generation, by which one paper after the other passes, is a very ominous sign of the times. It means that the independent newspaper owners and editors who have long represented a real force in the country are going to disappear. It means that newspapers, whatever their professed political aims may be, are becoming more and more the executive organs of big capitalism.

There is close contact between the great newspapers and the political parties, but none of them is an official party organ. A paper like the *Morning Post* or *Daily Telegraph* is externally quite independent of the Conservative Party. Each of them has a complexion of its own. The latter is of the mildest Conservative, the former of the most uncompromising Die-hard type. Equally different are the chief Liberal organs, the *Daily Chronicle*, generally the mouthpiece of Lloyd George, and the *Daily News*, the old Manchester School organ, now the mouthpiece of mild Pacifism of the Quaker type. Within general party lines, the editor, with as many outsiders as may influence him, will pursue an independent policy of his own, for which the party will not assume responsibility. But editors will sit on the committee of the party, party magnates will hold great blocks of shares in the paper – so that in the upshot the party can exercise as much influence as it likes on the conduct of the paper. This influence, in its turn, is used with perspicacity; forcibly on big political issues, seldom in minor details. Englishmen do not like to be dragooned. That the Press should be relatively – not absolutely – independent, is actually altogether an advantage to the party leader. It is to his advantage to have in his reserve forces the greatest possible variety of organs: some being correct, others moderate, others advanced; to have papers with different circles of readers: the industrial world, the educated classes, the lower middle classes, the masses. The papers of either great party will vary in their attitude on issues that have not as yet become matters of party politics – like the League of Nations, Protection, Land Settlement, or Nationalization – and the party executive has neither the power nor the will to compel them to toe the line on such issues. On the contrary, a paper's commercial success serves to test how far the editorial policy, on this issue or that, attracts circulation; when a great variety of papers exists, a *ballon d'essai* can easily be launched in one or other of them, or a covert attack engineered; then, if convenient, paternity in such a child of the pen can be avowed or repudiated later at will. Variety of papers further permits the various groups, sections and tendencies within a party to express their views, and, not infrequently, engage in conflict. Then, the editorial will often be less significant than the Correspondence columns, which echo the opinion of the led upon the leader's policy, often with striking force. Press criticism of a Bill largely takes the place of debate in the House, where the time allotted is apt to be too sparse for adequate discussion. It is by no means uncommon for an important Government measure to be radically altered or even withdrawn by the ministry that has brought it in under a sudden hail of criticism that descends upon it from all quarters; every big swing of the political pendulum is apt to be heralded by an outburst of protests against the Government from its own supporters, in the columns of the party Press.

It is to the interest of everybody concerned that this machinery should work with the greatest possible freedom. Since the latter years of the seventeenth century a censorship of the Press has ceased to exist. Press offences, under the Libel Bill for which Charles James Fox (1792) was responsible, are exclusively jury matters, and very seldom occur. An attempt was made, at the period of the French Revolution, to make newspaper reading a privilege of the educated, by imposing a heavy stamp-duty on each issue and so raising its price to sevenpence; in 1853–5 Gladstone abolished the duty. To-day there is complete liberty of the Press. It acts as a political thermometer, registering every change in the political atmosphere. In the last resort, the Press machine works pretty much in the same way as the Parliamentary one – the pregnant, ultimate words of command are uttered by a small handful of persons, and the mass of the led see their own opinion expressed in them. Political opinion is made by a few leading politicians in the political clubs, subject always to constant watchfulness for the echo of public opinion. It is not always easy to convert the party Press to their views, and at times splits within the party have got to be faced. Then, powerful pressure will be exercised, behind the scenes, on recalcitrant editors; as often as not by the big shareholders in the newspapers who are apt to be identical with the wealthy capitalists in the party. Such contests behind the scenes are apt to mark the decisive stage in the approach to a new political measure. The fight will often have begun in the Commons by then, but even so, what really counts is not so much the arguments adduced in debate as the sort of reception they are finding in the country, the letters of support or protest that appear in the Correspondence columns of the papers, the communications addressed to Members, and the deputations of constituents that suddenly present themselves in the metropolis. If, nevertheless, despite the storm of opinion that seems to be blowing up in the country, it proves possible to mobilize a united front in the party press in support of the Government's policy, it has carried its point, and the protesting voices among its own parliamentary adherents will soon fall silent. Even in the country, opposition will tend to die down, since arguments that are put before readers once or maybe twice a day in different forms have a suggestive power which the average Briton is too little disciplined intellectually to know how to resist.

Naturally, the Government is in the closest touch with the Press. In England, however, there is no official Press. This is one of the points that is always specially emphasized on English press dinners as a specifically English trait. According to the traditional Liberal view, which still bears traces of ideas natural enough about 1770, every Government is a tyrannical force, and the Press, the refuge of the persecuted, exists to oppose it. Hence, a Press in alliance with Government is suspect; a newspaper which has connexions with authority that are not openly admitted, is guilty of treachery. The existence, at most times, of an official Press in Germany and in France, is the plainest signal of the fact that these countries were not free. Ethical arguments, however, are hardly relevant to explain the lack, in England, of one of the less attractive by-products of modern democratic government. Without some organization for influencing opinion, without the possibility of privy attack on its enemies and of sending up *ballons d'essai*, modern democratic government is impossible – the ethical flaws in the process are only side phenomena of the problem presented by a Government whose main instrument is conflict. If a Press dependent on the Government of the day does not and cannot exist in England, the simple reason is that in England government always coincides with the machinery of a party, and that no English government is thinkable without control of at any rate a considerable part of its own party Press. It may not be able to give orders to this Press, but it always has enough influential supporters to enable it to influence it. Thus, every one in politics used to know that pronouncements by Mr. Lloyd George were first and foremost to be found in the *Daily Chronicle*, but this did not expose that newspaper to the reproach of venality which attaches to every Continental sheet which is credited with being in close touch with the Government. But in 1920–1, Lloyd George's Government was known to maintain a wireless Press service which telegraphed the views of that Government on all important issues all over the world, without indicating that its news was inspired – in other words, a semi-official news service, differing in no respect from Continental semi-official news services. Since at that time Asquith was at the head of the great party machine, Lloyd George, as Prime Minister, had got slowly to construct for himself a machinery of publicity like the one which the former already controlled. Thus, at the moment when problems of government, as presented on the Continent, arose in England, where they are not as a rule found in that form, they were solved on entirely Continental lines. Protests against such methods – which certainly are open to exception – remain confined to the Opposition, exactly as was once the case in Imperial Germany.

§ 2

We can best study the methods of modern English journalism by casting a glance at *The Times*, its greatest achievement. *The Times* owes a position unique in the newspaper world to the brilliant business ability with which, from 1785 on, it was managed, as a private concern, by the Walter family. The sole paper with a European position, it was, from the first years of its existence, entirely independent of the governmental news service, and consequently, a power in itself. From the time of its great editor, John Delane (1841–77), it often, nay generally, supported the Government in foreign policy, while frequently imposing its policy on the Government of the day. *The Times* further maintained its independence of great telegraphic news agencies like Reuter and Dalziel. Its policy was to have a correspondent of its own, on a princely salary, in every key position abroad, supported, when war broke out anywhere, with a whole staff of outstanding war correspondents. Sums well-nigh fabulous would be spent by it on such occasions on telegrams and travelling expenses. This absolute independence, both of all other public news services and agencies and of the Government, made *The Times* a power, able, on occasion, to direct home as well as foreign policy in accordance with its will. Often *The Times* correspondent in some European, Asiatic or American capital was a more powerful personality there than the English Ambassador, since he controlled a news service, almost invariably directed by certain political views, that influenced the entire globe. In addition to its staff of foreign correspondents, *The Times* has its experts on all economic, scientific, religious and social topics, often the first men in the subject. It is informed in a way that puts all other sources of information in the world in the shade. No statesman in the world can afford to leave *The Times* unread. This is the real source of its power. On all matters which are not at the moment the subject of political controversy – and this covers a large part of the contents of any newspaper – it is absolutely reliable and objective in its handling. The result is that an equal degree of objective trustworthiness is imputed (by at least nine-tenths of its readers, who have no opinions of their own on politics) to the great mass of news which is presented with a very definite political angle. Colonel Repington's famous reports on the German army manœuvres, in the years before the war, were, in detail, a model of correct and objective criticism. Nothing that he said was false; there was no ground on which objection could be taken. Yet those *Times* articles were thoroughly tendentious, partly in their skilful omission of essentials, partly in the suggestion of polite suspicion on the part of the writer with which they were suffused. Like a scarlet thread there ran through the reports a subtle doubt, growing more definite as year followed year, of the quality of German armament at the crucial points (artillery, aircraft, generalship, mobility of the individual unit), and it was these reports that bred in France and Russia that belief in a sudden collapse of Germany which did so much to bring about the outbreak of the war. During the course of the war *The Times* regularly published absolutely true reports of economic conditions in Germany, pictures of the steadiness of popular opinion there, and true accounts of the administration of the occupied areas, weaving into them reports, true and invented, of atrocities and pictures of despair with such skill that its accounts were swallowed alike by optimistic and pessimistic readers, by those who judged according to their feelings and by those who tried to use their heads. The internal contradictions in these reports were hardly noticed in England. Unpalatable news items and reports which did not fit into the picture people wished to see, were not suppressed, but quietly recorded, for the most part without any malicious commentary calculated to offset them. But they appeared only once and were accordingly speedily forgotten by a public accustomed to react only to opinions and to facts hammered into their heads day after day with perpetual variations on the same string.

Nine-tenths of *The Times* news was perfectly accurate, even under Lord Northcliffe's management. But all the skill of the journalist is confined to spreading that part of the news only which was convenient and desirable; inconvenient truth comes still-born to the light. And the part of *The Times* that counted in those years was the small tenth that was not truth but the creation of opinion, in the service of British ascendancy; the creation of opinion which, often enough, was the thing that is not. An organization of wonderful genius disseminated this throughout the globe. In this organization, the key idea is the assembly of papers designed for the most various groups in the population in Britain and outside it, all subject to the unifying control of a single political will. Such was the organization created from 1908 on, by Alfred Harmsworth, who died as Lord Northcliffe in 1922; and used by him for a systematic anti-German and pro-Imperialist propaganda.

In 1916 the circulation of *The Times* itself was but 200,000 copies of a single edition. But what counts is that it is read throughout the world, and everywhere by the educated upper classes, by the people who matter politically. What was even more important, under the Northcliffe regime, was that this high-standing publication served as news-feeder for his other mass-publications. Lord Northcliffe ruled the millions through the *Daily Mail*, with a circulation, in 1922, of a million and a half. In addition, he reached classes barely accessible by the printed word with the *Daily Mirror*, owned by his brother Lord Rothermere. These sheets, designed for the breakfast table of the upper and middle classes, were brought thither, even to Birmingham and Manchester, by a mighty system of special trains, and, more recently, by air service. For the workman and all those who read their paper as they come home from the office at night Northcliffe had his blatant *Evening News* ready. On Sunday, when the ordinary newspaper does not appear, he catered for the workman through the *Weekly Dispatch* and the shrieking sensationalism of the *Sunday Pictorial*, made up mainly of pictures and sporting news. For the woman reader and readers who took no interest in politics, he ran a series of sheets of a family kind, designed, in ordinary times, merely to feed an infantile curiosity, but serviceable enough, when any crisis was on, since they could contain 'stories' with turns of great propaganda utility.

The Times, both under Northcliffe and since, further meets the needs of special professional groups through special supplements – the weekly Education, Engineering, Literary, Imperial and Foreign Trade Supplements, and Law Reports; the Reports of Commercial Cases, appearing at irregular intervals; and the half-yearly reprints of Prospectuses of Public Companies – all of which have to be separately subscribed for, and are of a very high type indeed. These carry with them the advantage of equipping the newspaper with à staff of technical experts in the various classes, available, when need arises, for *The Times* itself; *per contra*, articles from *The Times* are frequently reprinted in the supplements. Moreover, it is then possible, at a relatively small cost, to compile books, like *The Times History of the War* or the very useful *Daily Mail Year-Book*, from material that has already appeared in one form or another – a fact which has the further advantage of accustoming the public to regard *The Times* as the final impeccable authority on everything.

Northcliffe's journalistic activity also had a notable foreign side. For consumption abroad, *The Times* appeared in a weekly edition that has a large circulation. For the purpose of trade propaganda in South America a Spanish Supplement is issued. Further, the *Daily Mail* appears daily in a French edition. Lord Northcliffe also established the closest contact between his own Press and the *Matin*, *Corriere della Sera* and *Novoje Vremja*, the great exponents of anti-Germanism in France, Italy and Russia – a contact mainly shown in the permission to these foreign papers to employ the Northcliffe telegraphic news service, which thus put behind them the support of millions of capital and gave them an advantage over all other papers in their respective countries. A similar tie existed between Northcliffe and the Amsterdam *Telegraaf*, the Buenos Aires *Nacion*, and the Sydney *Sun*, as well as, apparently, with various United States newspapers.

In its day the Northcliffe Trust was at once the most successful and the most sinister fusion of political and commercial organization that the world had yet seen. It collapsed after the death of its founder, but it is still worth studying its methods, in the day of similar gigantic newspaper trusts which must try more or less to work on the lines of their great prototype. Northcliffe's various papers retained their special identities, and were designed, each of them, for a special type of public. Independent of one another, even engaged at times in mild controversy and competition with each other, they had to be at the Dictator's beck and call on all ultimate questions of policy. The expensive cablegram, sometimes also the highly-paid leading article, would normally appear not in one paper only, but in a whole series. The undertaking as a whole was rendered practically self-contained by the possession of its own telegraphic service, its own fleet of trains, and its own forests in Newfoundland which supplied it with wood pulp. And the whole giant organization of economic, scientific and political talent was devoted to using all the arts of persuasion and conviction, all the technique of a savage sensationalism, to influencing the public opinion of England and the world to a single end. Among Northcliffe's helpers were the most distinguished students, the most exemplary philanthropists and patriots, the most unscrupulous demagogues, the lowest political adventurers, and the dirtiest scaramouches on earth. Sublime enthusiasm for exalted purposes, self-sacrificing patriotic devotion, consuming personal ambition, boundless egotism, national and individual – all were to him means whereby he might make himself rich and Britain great. Nowhere, over the entire area of public life, is an equally salient mixture to be found of brilliant gifts for organization, perfect breeding in regard to most questions of first, and all questions of secondary, importance, and ruthless and unscrupulous force of will in the final, decisive questions. The Catholic Church and the Prussian army have been called the only two complete organizations in the world; but as an instrument for influencing day-to-day politics at any given moment, the Northcliffe organization undoubtedly surpassed them, in so far as it knew how to harness not only the idealistic but the most material, nay, the lowest instincts of mankind to its chariot and to use them to achieve its influence.

The head of such an organization need not be, strictly speaking, a journalist. Whether he can dictate leading articles is entirely irrelevant. But he must be able to read all his papers from A to Z, which certainly is a more difficult task. For in a great newspaper of this type everything is politics, not only the leading articles. There is political significance in the amount of space a sub-editor will give to a news-item; whether it is merely inserted once or hammered into the reader's mind with a constant stream of fresh detail; the kind of type it has been set in; whether it is being followed up in a succession of leaders and so used to create opinion, or merely lost amid the mass of other news-items. When political agitation, on the grand scale, is being carried on, this propaganda purpose must inspire not leaders only but every line that appears in the paper. If, for instance, as was the case between 1907 and 1914, opinion is to be influenced in favour of Russia, in addition to a leader on the point there will be a full report, in the local news, of some celebration organized by the Russian colony in England; the picture pages will have photographs of the last ball given by the Russian Ambassador and portraits of a whole series of Russian notabilities of the day; the Home-reading section will contain an account of a religious festival in Russia and describe the strange customs of the Russian peasant; 'fill-pars,' dotted about, will stress the advantage of learning to speak Russian; the foreign pages will suddenly be crammed with carefully selected and sympathetically arranged Russian news; there will be long notices of Russian books in the literary columns, while the spiritual activities of other nations are treated with discreet economy or complete silence. All the outlying provinces of the concern will be pressed into the service; experts of the first rank will suddenly emerge in all the technical, economic and literary supplements, extolling everything Russian to the skies; their contributions, which are very often little masterpieces of journalism, thorough in substance and most appealing in form, will then, later, be collected and reprinted as a Russian Supplement. Behind this there need not, as the person unschooled in journalism may be apt to fancy, be any question of bribery. All that is required is a certain knowledge of men. In our age of Relativity, there is no conceivable opinion which is not held, with genuine enthusiasm, by some expert or other; they only have to be found, flattered a little, and paid at a rate a trifle above the normal. In this art Northcliffe possessed a perfect mastery; he had hardly anything in common with the journalist, a great deal in common with a leading statesman.

And during the World War this was very nearly what he became. He was responsible for elevating Kitchener and Lloyd George to the positions which they held, and was about to bring the former down when he suddenly perished on his journey to Russia. He had conscription introduced. He set up food-control and the first minister to work it. It was he who, in the final crisis, got Foch made General-issimo. It was primarily his Press rather than the House of Commons which secured public inquiries into the Mesopotamian and Gallipoli failures, in the teeth of the natural endeavour of the War Office to conceal unpleasant facts and shield responsible officers. So, he made war history; and the facts brought out on the occasion of these inquiries enabled him to override the attempt of certain strategists to seek decision in the Orient alone and to leave France more or less to herself. Whether these bright ideas were the off-shoots of his own brain or he merely ventilated the ideas of others is entirely irrelevant here. At any rate, they achieved actuality from the moment of his taking them up; throughout the war, there was no question on which Northcliffe was on the beaten side. After the war, he broke with his one-time hero, Lloyd George, because the Prime Minister would not obey the behests of the newspaper magnate. But in so doing he overstretched his bow. The Welsh Wizard proved too strong even for Northcliffe. Here we see the limits set to the most comprehensive and intensive journalistic activity, if it is merely demagogic. Its immense weight may crush any opposition that bars the way to an end, provided that a considerable section of public opinion is already set to this same end. Journalism may transform a minority into a majority, if it has behind it the capacities and the machine of a Northcliffe. But, demagogy is not creative. Once Germany was defeated, Northcliffe no longer had any political pro-gramme to support. Even the most brilliant demagogy cannot live by the personal squabbles of petty politics. When Northcliffe died, he was already played out. His Trust collapsed under the dearth of ideas of the post-war period. His brother, Lord Rothermere, saved a part of the concern, and re-built it, round the *Daily Mail*. But its most important portion, *The Times*, has been bought back by its pre-vious owners, the Walter family, and handed over to the trusteeship of a board of eminent men with no financial axe to grind, whose duty is to see to it that *The Times* remains the possession of the British nation, and is not primarily run on merely commercial lines. Since then, the tone of *The Times* has markedly improved.

§ 3

To judge the English Press fairly is no easy matter. In sheer journalistic quality, fullness and reliability of reporting – objective

327

accuracy in presentation, as against subjective evaluation – *The Times*, its supreme achievement, occupies a position unique throughout the world. From a technical point of view, all English papers of any standing are admirable. Printers' errors are hardly ever met with. Telegrams, letters, etc., are not merely stuck in mechanically; names and references, unintelligible to the reader, are explained; important events occurring in unfamiliar regions are at once elucidated by maps; long and complicated speeches, Bills and official documents are illuminated by summaries and cross-headings. In this respect the English standard is very high indeed, certainly higher than the German. But a different picture is given by a comparison of the contents of the newspapers of the two countries. While, in this respect, the better-class English newspaper, like the *Morning Post*, *Manchester Guardian* or *Daily Chronicle*, certainly does not give its readers any more than the *Deutsche Allgemeine*, *Vossische*, the *Frankfurter Zeitung* or *Hamburger Fremdenblatt*, the great mass of English newspapers, even in the metropolis, are incredibly thin and empty. Most of them, in sharp contrast to the half-dozen or so papers with an international reputation, have practically no foreign news, little or no literary or general information, and no magazine page; they are made up of leaders, telegrams, local gossip and a mass of sporting news. In the provinces, there is the *Scotsman* and *Glasgow Herald* in Scotland, and, in the industrial areas, the *Birmingham Daily Post*, *Liverpool Daily Post*, the *Yorkshire Post* and the admirable *Manchester Guardian*; but outside this half-dozen there is an almost unbelievable dulness. No one who has not been condemned to read a local sheet of that sort regularly can understand the empty chatter that does duty as the average play or the popular novel, or the idiotic war-lies which English politicians dared to serve up to their unsuspecting public.

The Press is the indispensable foundation of the life of the English State. It creates and directs public opinion. It is becoming more and more important, the more modern States are becoming democratic. Newspapers of the older stamp, like the *Manchester Guardian* to this day or *The Times* a generation ago, addressed themselves to the educated reader, to the comparatively few who then held political decision in their hands; they sought to convince and to persuade, and to this end, employed the same weapons and methods as had been used by Addison in the *Spectator* or Jeffrey in the *Edinburgh Review*. The newspaper of to-day seeks to capture the masses; it agitates. The

Daily News (1846) was the first attempt at capturing the lower middle classes. It was followed by the Conservative *Daily Telegraph* (1855) and in 1895 appeared the *Daily Mail*, the first halfpenny sheet openly aiming at a mass circulation; in 1900 the *Daily Express* followed suit. The distinguishing feature of all mass journalism is that it does not appeal to intellect, but to blind instincts. The mass believes in men who are either wholly noble or wholly debased; to the first category belong the members of one's own class, one's own religious persuasion, one's own nation; to the second, those in a higher social station, religious opponents, and most foreigners. Press technique works upon these primary instincts, it takes them for granted, hardly ever tries to correct them. It further works upon the constant wants of the human mass for sentimental emotion or general excitement, and tries to stir up these moods, day by day, to such a pitch that there is simply no time left for quiet consideration or any other faculty of the intellect. Suppose, for instance, that the political wirepullers decide to come out in favour of protective tariffs – whether on grounds of selfish class-interest or on those of general political necessity. It then becomes the business of the party Press to translate the intellectual motives of the leaders into the language of instinct of the led. By way of flattering the mass-mind, a feint is made of employing the intellectual apparatus of argument and demonstration; but the real arguments presented are that the champion of the new policy is a man of the exalted character of Chamberlain, or that it will keep out the wicked foreigner, or that it will save the wives and children of the British worker from the workhouse. Altruistic motives must never be lacking, since they are strong in the lower orders, but they must always appear with a definite egotistic admixture; there were Roman crowds weeping for noble fallen Cæsar and waiting with bated breath for the dead man's testament; and eighty years ago Free Trade agitation was irresistible, because it promised universal peace and benevolence throughout the world, plus cheap bread and mountains of money.

Even the educated Englishman seems hardly to appreciate the degree to which public life is degraded, both intellectually and morally, by the methods of mass-agitation. Fondly imagining that he, personally, is unaffected by Press suggestion, he is satisfied with the parts of the contents of his newspaper that are reliable, and leaves the rest – the part devoted to writing important political personages or measures up or down, as the case may be – with a shrug of the shoulders. It is good enough for him to know that the British Press does not absolutely lie or falsify. Yet sensitive as he is in social life on all questions of truthfulness, he has a strange moral latitude for political warfare. There never must be a positive lie: on this point he is firm. But falsification of the motives of an opponent is a high game which the connoisseur in any political camp relishes with gusto – this is politics. It certainly is not confined to Anglo-Saxon countries: it is the approved democratic method of dealing with the masses, but it is Anglo-Saxondom which has ushered it into the world and uses it on the broadest international scale.

This is one method to influence the masses: the other is continuous reiteration of all the slogans of the market-place to darken counsel and stifle independent thought in the bud. The Press always boasts that it educates the masses intellectually: it certainly does so in many small questions of the day; in all the big issues, however, it does exactly the opposite: it repeats – with the most skilful variation in detail – the same argument so often that it becomes an axiom and makes the reader's mind absolutely inaccessible to any arguments from the opposite camp. English love of truth has imposed equal treatment for the other side in the world of sport; but in politics, where the conflict of wills is a serious matter, the mere outward show of decency passes muster. And when it comes to ultimate life and death questions – for example in a struggle for political supremacy – the gentleman very often yields place to the prize-fighter. Controversy with the Cavaliers reduced a great and divinely-inspired humanist like John Milton to a raucous zealot, by no means concerned about the finer points of truth; and the lies employed a century ago against Napoleon, and recently against Germany, are a tragic sign of the ethical depths to which a great nation can descend. War-lying, of course, has existed at all times and in all countries. There are myths about the wicked enemy engendered in the trenches and in the hospital. They will die quickly, if let alone; they do not permanently poison the atmosphere. But there is a difference between temporary outbreaks of elemental hate and a huge campaign of world-wide lying, systematically conducted against the better knowledge of those who started the game. There is no analogue, in the annals of any country, or any time, to the story of how the Germans melted down the fat of their dead, and fed themselves upon it; a story which filled the Press for months in 1917, was authenticated by an alleged facsimile document, was referred to in Parliament and in indignation meetings the length and breadth of the land, was telegraphed, for obvious reasons, to India and China, and publicly commented upon by Indian and Chinese statesmen, was a subject for distinguished painters and the lowest of penny-a-line scribblers. Not far behind it stand the tales of the crucified Canadian and the Belgian children with their hands hacked off. The possibility of such stories is plain proof that even a Press of a high status is perfectly compatible with a perilous ethical irresponsibility and an outlook so barbarous that even in the epoch of universal education an European adversary can be credited with cannibalism. Nor is this ethical degradation confined to foreign politics; in home politics, a type of scandal-mongering sheet has appeared within the last decades such as was unheard of a generation earlier. During the war the *Financial News* (founded 1884) and, above all, *John Bull*, subsisted on fomenting panics and outcries, not only against the enemy but against all sorts of politicians of standing, notably such as had the backbone to stand out against some mass-instinct. Nothing could be more eloquent of the danger with which this type of demagogy threatens English life than the fact that, during the war, *John Bull*, with a circulation of 1·5 million (in 1917), was the most widely read of English periodicals.

§ 4

Two forces dominate England to-day – the old aristocracy and newer capitalism, which, thanks to the Press, is everywhere more and more dangerously in the ascendant, though there are already signs on the horizon to show that it will not last for ever.

In the last thirty years – and since the accession of Edward VII at an increasingly rapid rate – the infiltration of the old nobility with new capitalists has gone on so fast that the aristocratic spirit is in serious danger. Money is beginning to be so important a factor in politics that the old nobility, their strength undermined by Lloyd Georgian finance, begins to withdraw from the game. Modern election expenses,[1] with meetings, advertisements and canvassing, are so enormous that only a wealthy man can meet them out of his own pocket. The man of modest means – who still fortunately is to be found in Parliament – has therefore to rely on substantial assistance from the party funds – a fact that gives the big capitalists in the party a dangerous influence behind the scenes – always denied, but certainly real – on the choice of candidates. Fortunately, the member, once elected, tends to be more dependent upon the party Whip than

331

upon the party capitalists, but since he always wants to be re-elected, regard to the wishes of the financial magnates always threatens his independence. It is, however, more on the other side of the machine that the influence of the capitalist really tells: on public opinion. Obviously, a concern like the Northcliffe or Berry Trust is unthinkable without immense capital resources behind it; competition with the Trusts forces all other papers to spend more and more capital; anyone who seeks to capture the public ear without millions in his pocket is like a man who tries to fight siege artillery with a child's sword in his hand. And it is difficult to raise capital and fight against it at the same time.

A new policy directed against a powerful industry is not only a serious matter to the political editor but to the financial manager as well: it may lose him big advertisements which he cannot well spare. And if he must lose advertisments, he must make up the loss – if it can be made up – by more readers, that is, he must cater for the masses even more than he actually wants and gradually lower the tone of his paper to meet their wishes. This means continuously less intelligence and more suggestion, with the result that it is becoming more and more difficult to resist its methods. Nobody can resist it, least of all the workman who may hate Lord Rothermere but goes on reading the *Daily Mail* and *Evening News* certainly not for their politics, but for the sporting news and other sensational matter which he finds there in a much better quality than the *Daily Herald* can supply. But he will read the political news as well and be influenced by it without knowing it – just what Lord Rothermere wants. It is not an accident that the Conservative attitude always has the wider appeal in England as well as abroad than the Liberal, for all the really great London papers are Conservative (*The Times, Morning Post, Daily Express, Daily Mail, Daily Telegraph, Sunday Times, Observer* – as against *Daily Chronicle, Daily News, Star*), and the more powerful provincial papers as well (*Scotsman, Glasgow Herald, Birmingham Daily Post, Yorkshire Post, Irish Times* – as against *Manchester Guardian* and *Liverpool Daily Post*), and behind Conservatism is big Finance. And one of the chief reasons for the slow growth of a Labour Party in the most highly industrialized modern State is certainly the poverty of its Press apparatus. Up to the war there were only poor weeklies to represent the Labour attitude, while even now it boasts of one daily paper only (*Daily Herald*). It is capitalism which gives the Englishman, practically without distinction of party, his daily intellectual bread. The more democratic the forms of political life became, the more completely the outward influence of the old upper classes waned, the more potent has grown the power exercised by the possessing classes through the Press. Their control over the Press enables them to form the minds of the masses to love and to hate what their newspaper tells them. Nor is this state of things entirely a matter of regret. If this had been otherwise, the fabric of the State would have collapsed long ago. When the authoritarian State, which can compel the individual, is resolved into the libertarian, which can only lead and induce him, the State would become chaos if it could not find ways and means of directing the individual selfishness with an absolute certainty approaching to a command. The methods of doing this have been to a large extent the appeal to higher motives: love of country, religious enthusiasm, rational recognition of the mutually interdependent interests of all mankind; nor have they been quite unsuccessfully summoned for the fight against sheer selfishness. But, with the mass, they operate only at certain great moments. In their day-to-day moods men can only be appealed to through their instincts. The greatest instinctive appeal is the imitative – and that is employed in England to the blessing of the nation. England is not lost so long as the example of the upper classes – set, in the last resort, by the nobility – retains its ethical effect. But the one method, which is sure never to fail with the masses, is the art of suggestion, and this has become the approved form of rule in the democratic State. So far no other force has been found equally effective. The preacher in the pulpit, the teacher in his class, the professor in his chair, will exert their influence within their sphere and it will be an influence to the good. But their sphere is restricted by the fact that their appeal lies only with a certain set of human motives: the higher and idealistic. They lose power when they begin to preach hate. But the demagogue is – for all day-to-day events – more powerful than they, because he has all the scale of human emotions to choose from: love and hate, enthusiasm and fear, admiration and malice, all the self-sacrificing and all the sneaking instincts of mankind. He works through an apparatus of extreme costliness, the Press, and makes it the real instrument of power in the land. And those circles of the nation who control this instrument, including the demagogue who works it, are the really powerful. Through the Press capitalism reigns paramount, all the democratic trappings notwithstanding.

§ 5

But not all the English Press is sensational or threatened by sensationalism. There is the rich gallery of magazines, monthlies, and quarterlies which is a credit to English culture. The crude sensationalism of part of the London Press is an unsavoury by-product of the English school system, or rather lack of school system.

The education of the masses had been shamefully neglected for generations. At last education came, but it produced a mass which just knew how to read, without any stock of ideas or facts, a mass educated enough to be accessible to the demagogue, but far too little educated to withstand him. This explains the success of the *Daily Mail*. On the other hand the high level of the English magazine of the *Edinburgh Review* type, which has no parallel in other countries, is one of the finest by-products of the Public School and the University of the old type. Both, as we shall see, did not try to develop the instinct for active specialized work in science and literature. But they tried to develop and have developed minds fresh and receptive for intellectual work of no mean order in all departments; they trained, if not so much the independent scholar, at any rate the gentleman at once well informed on and interested in everything. In these conditions, England has developed a range of publications unique in extent throughout the world. Their origins go back to the Liberal *Edinburgh Review* (1802) and the Conservative *Quarterly Review* (1809), still the leading periodicals of their class. In their columns, every aspect of public life – politics and literature, finance and shipping, philosophy and science – is handled in articles (nominally reviews of books), which are often absolutely first-rate in quality and thoroughly scientific in tone. They are, however, not the work of experts for experts; they are written by scholars who are at the same time men of the world, for men of the world with scholarly tastes. They find their public in the Universities, in the country rectories, in the homes of lawyers and doctors, and also in many a household where, despite very limited earnings, a rational limitation of the working day leaves a certain time for mental reflection. There are several high-standing papers for economic interests: the *Economist* (Free Trade) and the *Statist* (Protectionist), *Fairplay* (Shipping paper), the *Journal of Commerce*, the *Financial Times*, – the first of them of really outstanding importance – which deal with their particular interests against the highly-toned political background,

inseparable from all British culture. It is not much different with
religious periodicals like the *Church Times* and *Guardian* (Anglican),
Tablet (Catholic), *British Weekly* (Nonconformist). Frankly political
are, of course, the imperialist magazines like *Empire Review*, *United
Empire*, *Round Table*, the last of which is really remarkable for the
richness of information and food for thought it supplies. That there
should be no less than three magazines for this particular political
strain amply shows how deep the roots of Imperialism lie in the
English mind, while the *National Review* represents the more turbu-
lent and sensational aspects of the movement. Only Literature proper
seems not to prosper. The leading paper of several generations, the
Athenæum, was compelled during the war to amalgamate with the
Nation, the *London Mercury* has not fully supplied its place; *The
Times Literary Supplement* has become the leading critical organ.
But no literary paper can compare in England with the success of the
political magazine.

So far as domestic politics are concerned, most of these magazines
have a definite political line, which varies, of course, in the intensity
with which it is followed, but is nearly always followed in pretty
complete independence of party leaders. Thus the *Spectator* and the
Observer, while Conservative, take a line of their own; and the very
fact that they are thus independent, very influential and high-
standing, gives them a great hold on thinking Conservatives,
notably in academic circles. And in these organs new or contrary
tendencies within the party find an expression which is often
denied to them in the daily Press. It is here that the *ballon d'essai* is
sent up which the party newspaper might find too risky; here, too,
internal fights between personalities inside the party can be fought
out under the safe cloak of anonymity, whereas in the daily they might
rouse an undesirable amount and kind of notoriety. The Liberals,
whose Press is very much weaker in this camp also, have the weekly
Nation, inspired by J. M. Keynes; to the left of it, inclining to
Socialism, is the *New Statesman*, founded by the Fabians; further to
left still, and at one time the main organ of Guild Socialist theory,
the *New Age*.

More specifically characteristic than any of these, however, are the
periodicals that, quite loosely connected with one party or the other,
seek to be a forum of all the talents, and thanks to a great variety of
contents and a high scale of payment to contributors, do largely attain
this end. Among them, on the Conservative side stand the *Quarterly*

335

Review, the *Fortnightly Review*, the *English Review*, and the *Nineteenth Century and After*; on the Liberal, the *Edinburgh Review* and the *Contemporary Review*. The *Review of Reviews*, originally founded by W. T. Stead, was, under him, a definitely Pacifist organ, with a lower middle-class appeal in the main.

All these papers represent something like a platform which gives the man of intellect the opportunity of speaking to the many. In papers relatively free of close party affiliations, the events and problems of the day really are handled by men of differing points of view: they constitute a political and spiritual arena such as the daily Press always professed to be, but hardly ever was and certainly is not now. Here are papers, not read by the masses, which still retain the well-bred detachment from traditional party controversy. During the war, nearly all of them used sharp weapons, but in a spirit of chivalry. If the arid depravity of the Northcliffe and Rothermere Press were to incline one to despair of the intellectual future of the British race, here are periodicals of a calibre to remind one, if literature and scientific work had not already done so, that the nation still has great reserves of character and spirit to bring into the field.

BOOK III
RELIGION AND THE CHURCH

CHAPTER I
THE CHURCH OF ENGLAND

§ 1

NOTHING in England is quite so hard for the Continental observer to understand as the Anglo-Saxon attitude to religion and the Established Church. The Continental from a Catholic country will, perhaps with a little difficulty, find certain points of contact which will help him to approach it. The Continental Protestant, on the other hand, will find strange difficulties, anomalies, obstacles everywhere. What he sees is, first of all, extremely near Catholicism. Moreover, all the points which are important on the Continent mean little in England. He knows that Protestantism is full, even down to the twentieth century, of discussions of dogma and dogmatic conflicts. Such discussions play certainly no great part in the Church of England. What does matter there, are questions about the Church, its functions, its necessity, its government by Bishops who descend in an unbroken line from the apostles, its relation to the State. All those questions which to a Continental appear to be at best of secondary importance if not futile and shallow, seem to be unduly stressed in the Church of England. And should the Continental observer not be one of the inquiring spirits, he will easily be satisfied with having come across another instance of English hypocrisy.

The first point to be noted, therefore, is that English (or, better, Anglican) religiousness is something different from the *individualistic* type of religiousness which has found its strongest expression in German Lutheranism. It is *communal* rather than individualistic religiousness.

For the average Englishman religion is not, first and foremost, an individual life, an individual sense of responsibility, an individual happiness: it is a cult, distinguished, primarily, by the sense of reverence and worship of the Highest; a participation in and common enjoyment of the service of God, rather than an individual concern. As religion is something communal, it finds its strongest expression in the Church. That is why controversies about dogma, arising out of the effort of the single Christian individual to find a more adequate formula for his own experience than that of the official doctrine of the Church, have played but a secondary rôle in the history of the English Church. The principle of division between creeds, sects and religious parties was in Germany a question of dogma; it is, in

339

England, one of organization. Whether an organized Church is necessary to personal salvation? what should be the position of the priest in the Church? whether he, or the layman, should conduct and direct the religious life of the community? – such are the issues that have, for centuries, divided minds in England. English Protestantism has never made any notable contribution of its own to theology. But the Englishman always was extremely sensitive when a question of Church organization was touched. When John Wycliffe started an heretical movement, he was the idol of the whole people, so long as what he fought was the Papal claim to raise tribute; for, on this, English love of liberty flared up. But when he began to dig deeper beyond this mere question of organization, when he uttered doubts about the Romish doctrine of the Communion, the English people left him to pursue such useless inquiries in solitude. When, in *King John*, Shakespeare deals with the attempt of Innocent III to bring England under his temporal supremacy, he shows no gleam of comprehension of the sublime ideal underlying such a claim, nothing but the outraged sense of national independence. in arms against the pretensions of a foreign potentate. Of the practical side of Christianity, the Englishman has always had a ready understanding: of the theoretic, but a limited one. The doctrine of the Communion has never been a real dividing issue in the English Church. Predestination, again, while its appeal to the hard and masculine elements in religious life fell on fruitful soil both in England and, notably, in Scotland, never acted as a main principle of sectarian division in England; it only helped to stress existing differences on questions of organization.

English Church service is thus entirely different from that of German Protestantism. It is a great communal cult, which will deeply move those who are accustomed to it; to others, who may want their intelligence stimulated or their conscience deeply stirred, it is apt to appear like empty formalism. To the Protestant German there is something suspect in this excessive emphasis on church attendance, sacraments and good works. All this, however, is the result of the great root fact that, to a degree incomprehensible to the German, worship is for the Anglo-Saxon the main form of expression of the religious sense. The German Protestant goes to church because he seeks to derive some spiritual benefit from the service of God: the Englishman, in order that God may receive from him His due service, honour and gratitude. The English point of view is intelligible enough to the Continental Calvinist: not to the Lutheran. To his religious consciousness, there is something repulsive in having service conducted, with preaching and hymn-singing, in the open street. His heart could not be stirred amid the noise and bustle of a great city. Not for the Englishman. Why should one not praise God everywhere? Where individual piety is the determinant impulse, the German is superior to the Englishman: mysticism, the old, pre-Methodist pietism, modern Biblical criticism – all are German. In the organization of piety, on the other hand, the German's contribution is negligible, that of the Englishman supreme. Every conceivable form of external Christian activity has been tried out in England and realized in the practice of Anglicans, Presbyterians and Independents. And Christian ideals of conduct have – though all fulfilment always implies a certain coarsening of the ideal – been realized in Anglo-Saxon hands with a fullness to which the whole rest of the world can show nothing equal or even comparable.

§ 2

The ultimate explanation of these differences is, then, a natural difference between the racial characters of the two peoples. But these differences were, moreover, strongly accentuated by differences of history. Every aspect of the relations of Church and State had to be worked out in Germany, where the claims of the King to the world dominion of a Holy Roman Empire brought him into continuous collision with the Pope and his spiritual claims. This collision, again, was the central fact of mediæval German history. It involved the whole people, for there was hardly a problem on which it did not impinge – Imperial and territorial power, even the relations of the German King to the adjoining States. Of necessity it drew into itself every spiritual force in the country. For England, on the other hand, the conflict between State and Church was a relatively subsidiary problem; far less important, for example, than that of relations between England and France. In Germany, questions of conscience were involved, which made the limits to the authority of Church and State problems of burning immediacy about which the most apathetic person had to make up his mind; in England they remained, essentially, theories, on which the learned might exercise their skill. And there was something else. In Germany, the struggle between temporal and spiritual authority ended in a compromise, in which the most important item, from the point of view of religious history, is

341

the fact that the State did not succeed in establishing its claim to rule the Church. A spiritual power remained independent of the State and able, on occasion, to turn against it – this is the most significant outcome of the protracted struggle; more significant than its other side, the incapacity of the Church to realize its dream of a State of God. In England, the Church has achieved no such freedom from the State. True, the English mediæval Church was, too, subject to the Papacy and there were plenty of complaints against the flow of money to Italy, and the overweening privileges of the clergy. But the Curia never interfered in the spiritual life of England to anything like the extent that it did in Germany. The Papal Legate, who called all Church matters, and many others besides, before his judgment seat, was the exception rather than the rule. Above all, while the Pope did lay claim to temporal supremacy over England, and did, at times, assert it – under Henry III the Papal representative was for many years the actual ruler over the country – nevertheless, in the long run, the Church was unable to maintain its claims even in such purely spiritual matters as the nomination of Bishops. Even in Anglo-Saxon times, and, definitively, in Norman, the Bishops were nominated by the King, and were, essentially, State functionaries; the co-operation of spiritual powers which, in Germany, gradually became a reality, was, in England, in the long run, the merest form. Administratively, the Church in England might be independent; it might have its own canon law, and at times challenge the rights of the State; but the leaders of the Church, on whom the maintenance of these claims depended, were selected by the King. Even the parish priests were only here and there nominated by spiritual patrons: in the vast majority of cases by temporal ones. In such circumstances, it was inevitable that the average Englishman should look upon the Church, not as a spiritual power independent of the State, but as, in essence, another manifestation of the State. The result was that when the State altered the forms of worship, the great mass of people saw no more in that than the exercise of a natural authority on the part of the State.

§ 3

These preliminary observations are necessary to an understanding of the English Reformation and present-day Anglicanism. Temporal rulers changed the organization of worship; in 1534 Henry VIII intro-

duced his private Reformation to suit the needs of his own dusky
Cæsarism and matrimonial exigencies, but with an acute comprehension of the religious temper of his people; so far as dogma went (to
the English mind the unessential part of reform), concessions were
made to Continental Protestantism; worship remained mainly what
it was, the organization remained absolutely hierarchical and Catholic;
only the Church was transformed into a national institution, completely subject to the King, and every bond with Rome was severed.
In 1547 the Regents for Edward VI, a minor, swayed over to pure
Calvinism; in 1553 Mary reverted to Catholicism; in 1558 Elizabeth
turned back to a type of Protestantism corresponding more or less
to her father's model. At each turn there was loud opposition in
certain quarters, and a certain number of heretics burned; but at no
time was there any lasting resistance on the part of the people as a
whole. This is a fact incomprehensible to the German Protestant
mind of all centuries. To the average Englishman it was quite
within the rights of the State to alter the forms of worship and religion
– which, according to English ideas, is very much the same. The
dependence on the State of the Church of England as founded under
Elizabeth has remained unaltered to this day. True, the English
Church is freer in relation to the State than was the Protestant Church
in Germany before 1918. The State has no influence in the ordination
of a single priest. As a rule it makes no payments for the Church
(apart from a few relief measures in times of emergency[1]). The
income of the Church is derived, rather, from the immense ancient
Church property, originally constituted by tithes and Church dues,
and increased by pious benefactions. This freedom of the Church in
all matters of detail, however, co-exists with a complete and organic
submission to the State in all fundamentals. The two Archbishops and
twenty-four Bishops (two-thirds of the whole Episcopate) sit in the
Upper House. The Archbishops and Bishops of dioceses, the
Suffragan Bishops, the deans and many canons of cathedrals, are
nominated by the King, as *Summus Episcopus*. His responsible
adviser in Church matters is not an Archbishop, but the Prime
Minister, the head of the State. Scottish Presbyterians like Balfour
and Campbell-Bannerman have nominated Anglican Bishops, as has
a Welsh Dissenter like Lloyd George. (Only a Catholic minister,
under the Catholic Emancipation Act of 1829, is forbidden to exercise
any influence in the English Church.) Many hundreds of benefices
are filled by the Prime Minister or Lord Chancellor, even if he hap-

pens to be a Dissenter. The basic laws of the Church are the Thirty-nine Articles, the Prayer Book and certain rubrics dating from the time of the Reformation; they are all State laws and can be altered not by the Church, but only by legislation, in which members of the Lower House who are not Churchmen enjoy their full right of voting. The Church in itself is not a corporation (though the individual incumbents, cathedrals, etc., are so). A Commission set up by the State in 1835, the Ecclesiastical Commissioners, has most far-reaching powers of interference in the administration of Church property; it has drastically interfered with the revenues of bishoprics and cathedrals and used the surplus to improve the stipends of old livings and establish new ones; further, it administers a considerable Church revenue. Of this Commission, a majority of members were originally lay; the episcopal majority is of quite recent date. In 1869 the Irish Church was disestablished; in 1920 the same thing happened to the Church in Wales. Disestablishment in England, with the diversion of the greater part of the revenues of the Church to Dissenters, would be an entirely possible procedure. Church jurisdiction, further, is restricted within narrow limits. The Court of Arches for the South, and the Chancery Court of York for the North, exercise disciplinary powers over the clergy; the Consistory Courts of the dioceses have certain rights in Church buildings. But the Court of last instance for all questions of canon law is the Judicial Committee of the Privy Council, that is to say one of the highest tribunals of the State. The Church's right to levy rates on its own behalf is severely limited by the fact that, ever since 1868, a suit for Church rates does not lie; since the introduction of Marriage Registry Offices (1836) the Church form of marriage is no longer the only one; divorce is granted by the State only. The only concession made to the Church is that no clergyman can be compelled to re-marry a divorced person.

Even the Church's power over its incumbents is limited. At least half of the livings are still in the gift of patrons who fill vacancies according to their fancy. This right of presentation is in part an inherited privilege of the owner of the soil, in part derives from old feudal rights over abbeys and Church lands, and in part goes back to purchase or thinly-veiled robbery. The other half of livings are filled partly by the representatives of the King, as *Summus Episcopus* (the Premier, the Lord Chancellor), partly by University authorities, partly by Cathedrals and Bishops. Patronage was the strongest bond between the Church and the old noble class. Generally, the patron was some landowner of high rank, who filled vacancies with the junior members of his own family, or tutors and other dependents, and, through the control over such appointments, acquired no inconsiderable influence in the academic world. The right of presentation is a legal entity; it can be bought and sold (though this privilege is gradually dying out); it inheres in the proprietor, so long as he is an Anglican; although the Bishop may object to a given nominee, cases of abuse are frequent. True, the parson of the older novel, distinguished rather for his breed of pigs and his prowess in the hunting field than as a spiritual guide, is extinct; nevertheless, the Bishop's power of veto is so restricted that the nice young fellow, with decent manners but devoid of any real interest in things of the spirit and of any spark of authentic Christianity, is not only a casual exception. There is no sort of co-operation by the congregation in the selection of their pastor.

Nor is any real power secured to the Church by its own Convocations and National Assembly. The two Convocations (of York and Canterbury) dating back to the Middle Ages, had become nearly extinct in the eighteenth century, when the power of the State over the Church reached its zenith, and were revivified in 1852. They consist of two Houses, the Upper being composed of Bishops, the Lower of the Deans, Archdeacons and elected representatives (called Proctors) of the Clergy. The Church of England Assembly (Powers) Act of 1919 combined the two Convocations into a common body, the National Assembly of the Church of England. The two Upper Houses are here fused into a House of Bishops (thirty-eight members), the two Lower Houses into a House of Clergy (251 members), and a House of Laity[2] (357, including many women) was added. It was hoped that the influence of an Assembly as broad and representative as this would be strong enough to make it practically independent of State influence, that a measure proposed by this Assembly would have no difficulty in finding the assent of Parliament. When, however, the first controversial matter, the Revision of the Prayer Book, was brought before Parliament, it was twice rejected by the organization of the State (1927, 1928). This event plainly showed how strictly the Church of England is still fettered to the State.

Even the Bishop's authority over his own clergy is limited and depends entirely on the force of his own personality. Except in

345

extreme cases he cannot rely upon the State arm to carry out his decisions, and, in the interests of the Church, he will certainly refrain from invoking it. There can be no question, in such circumstances, within the Church, of the kind of intense life that might affect political decisions or even, on occasion, set the Church in conflict with the State. The presence of Bishops in the Upper House of Parliament does not alter this fact.

Thus, when the Church desires to influence public opinion, it does not rely upon its inadequate official organization, but on modern forms of association. One of these, the Church Congress, which ever since 1861 has annually gathered both clergy and lay persons interested in the Church together in some English town or other, is among the powers in English spiritual life. By modern forms of organization the Church has learned to extend her influence even beyond national boundaries. Since 1867, the Bishops of the Anglican world have met in periodical Lambeth Conferences (so called after the place of meeting, the Archbishop of Canterbury's London Palace) for assemblies that, though they may have no legislative power, enjoy the consideration that belongs to a council of all the leaders of Anglicanism. This Conference was originally called to deal with a very ticklish schism. John Colenso, Bishop of Natal, had been dethroned by the Bishops of South Africa on grounds of heresy (1863), and appealed successfully to the English Courts against their decision. But the importance of the Conference extends far beyond cases of discipline. It constituted, for the first time, a union of Anglicanism outside England with the homeland. The Central Consultative Body of the Conference, set up in 1908, may prove to be the parent cell for an international Anglican organization. The Conference, further, strives, with the utmost circumspection, for unity among Protestant Churches throughout the world (cf. page 391). So far, without success, it is true, it has endeavoured to find a basis of common work and possible reunion among the English sects. The Old Catholics and the German Protestants have been recognized as spiritual brothers, and since the war, increased energy has been put into the effort to bring world Protestantism together under Anglican leadership. A movement like this, though absolutely disinterested in itself, would certainly have consequences of more than spiritual importance; it would provide Anglo-Saxon world dominion; resting hitherto on battleships and banking, with a spiritual basis which might prove far more effective than either of these.

§ 4

A further sign of the close relation between Church and State is the claim put forward by the Anglican Church to be the sole Church in England. In practice, there is complete toleration for Catholicism as well as for the numerous sects that account for at least half, if not more, of the church-going population. At the same time, Anglicanism in England is not one religious body among many, but the single religious body to which every one belongs who has not expressly declared the contrary. Nor is this a merely theoretic claim. The King (or Regent), the holders of certain high offices, the Lord Chancellor, and, up to 1921, the Irish Viceroy, must be Protestants. Where religion enters into any public ceremonial – the laying of foundation stones, the opening of Parliament, etc. – the Anglican Church's claims are, as a rule, the only ones considered at all. When the State takes cognizance of religion, whether in the form of spiritual provision for soldiers or prisoners or the education of rescued children, it is the Anglican clergyman who is first called in, and generally only he. In the Colonies, the professional representative of religion is – despite protests entered here and there by Dissenters – everywhere the Anglican clergyman. Since 1868 compulsory Church rates have been abolished; at the same time, whenever a Dissenter moves to a new locality, he is there, in the first instance, assumed to be a Church member unless he gives intimation to the contrary. The fact that, in England, questions as to a person's religion are, officially, not asked, arises in the main out of consideration for the Anglican Church, since exact statistics might show that its privileged position is hardly justified.

The primacy of the Anglican Church is contested, bitterly, by all Dissenters, but it exists in practically undiminished force. It is the source of the power of the Church, which, in turn, acts as a buttress of the State. With Parliament, hitherto the stronghold of landlords and capitalists, the City of London, and the privileged corporation of the Law, the Church constitutes the fourth and strongest bulwark of a governing class which knows how to make the forms of democracy practically inoperative. Not that the clergyman necessarily comes from the governing class. Since, however, the middle and lower classes are, in the main, Dissenting, the main recruiting ground for the clergy is the upper and upper-middle classes. The clerical profession is, in England, mainly what it was in the Middle Ages – to a small extent,

347

the ladder by which the gifted young man of the lower orders may mount in the social scale; to a larger one, a means of providing for the younger sons of the higher classes. Right in to the nineteenth century, the self-interest of the then dominant landowning class acted as a barrier to every reform of the Church. Pluralism, which makes any real cure of souls impossible, denounced as far back as mediæval times, is rare to-day, but still exists. It is still quite common to find one vicar drawing the stipends of several livings, whose care he devolves on to wretchedly underpaid curates.

Not that the Anglican Church is *merely* the Church of the upper classes. Its *strength* is essentially in the squirearchy and the higher grades of the middle class, but its *influence* extends from the highest sections in the population to the lowest. Like the Conservative Party, it has lost its hold on the majority of the lower class. But among the rural workers, accustomed from time immemorial to go where their masters go, it is still strong, and it still has a following among the industrial workers, at least in areas where the employers are Dissenting. Thus, all opposition notwithstanding, it has countless points of contact with Dissent: and to-day, when the sects really have no grievances of any substance, the relations between Church and Chapel are plainly improving.

The theological education of the clergy is still quite perfunctory. University training is not compulsory though it is practically universal. There, however, the education is not theological, but general; theological training is provided in an episcopal seminary, where a brief course is followed by an examination, of a purely formal character, conducted by an official of the Bishop's but not by professors of theology. The cleric is not, as in Germany, a member of a learned profession, but of a class of gentlemen. As such the clergy have a proud tradition. Like the German Protestant pastorate, it has given a large number of leaders to the political and spiritual life of the nation – Addison, Swift, Young, Goldsmith, Wesley, Coleridge, Sterne, Crabbe, the Brontës, Kingsley, Tennyson, Samuel Butler, Cecil Rhodes, came out of the Anglican parsonage or were themselves clergymen. But, despite the shockingly low pay of a considerable proportion of the minor livings, the structure of the English clergy is decidedly more aristocratic than the German, and its influence on national life markedly greater. Something like half the elementary schools are to all intents and purposes under clerical control; the Grammar Schools, as they rise in the social scale, endeavour (now less so than formerly) to secure a cleric as headmaster; the Church may be subject to the State, but the individual Churchman has possibilities enough to make his influence felt. Resolutions of the Lambeth Conference, speeches at the Church Congress, the speech of a Bishop in the Upper House mean something. Moreover, in a country where at least as many political decisions are taken behind the scenes as on the stage, the personal acquaintance with political leaders possessed for instance by a Bishop in virtue of his seat in the Lords, and the consideration shown to every wearer of the cloth in public life, is worth pretty nearly as much as any direct intervention could be. The influence of the Church upon public life may have notably declined during the last generation, but it still exists as one of the great conservative powers upon which English life rests.

§ 5

The Anglican Church is a peculiar half-way house between Protestantism and Catholicism. Dogmatically, it is Protestant. The basic law of the Church, the Thirty-nine Articles, have been profoundly influenced by the Augsburg Creed and other Reformation formularies. But, to the English mind, dogma is of secondary importance. Richard Hooker (d. 1600), the most influential English theologian of the Reform era, is always lenient and mild in all questions of dogma. But Church and Episcopacy – just the things which would seem secondary to German Protestantism – are essential to him, though they may be essentially not *iure divino*, but only *iure humano*. Emphatically, if under protest from its left wing, the Anglican Church describes itself as a Catholic Church, governed by Bishops who, through the laying on of hands, have received the Holy Ghost in unbroken succession from the Apostles. Where this unbroken succession of Bishops is wanting, there is no Church. It insists that it continues, not replaces, the mediæval church. It has never accepted the Bible with Lutheran rigidity; reference to the Bible plays far less part in Anglicanism than does the tradition of the Church.

Bishop Jewel of Salisbury (d. 1571) formulated the position of Anglicanism thus: The Church of England is *the* Church, the only pure continuation of the primitive Christian Church. Roman Catholicism as well as Continental Protestantism have gone astray. In the course of time there have been periods where the right wing of the Church of England which is leaning towards Romanism had

E.   z preponderating influence: in other periods it was the left wing which would have preferred closer spiritual community with Continental Protestantism: in all periods the Church has refused to give to Jewel's, or any other formula, its official backing. But even to-day the average Anglican thinks mainly on the lines of Jewel and later developments. There are three great Churches in the world: the Roman, the Greek, and (purest of all) the Anglican. All the rest is not Church but Dissent. Individually there are all sorts of qualifications to this statement in favour of the Scandinavian, very occasionally even in favour of other Protestant Churches, but as a general average Anglicanism feels itself to be *the* Church with no recognition but only toleration for other creeds.

The entire organization is Catholic. The Church is sacerdotal; the lay element, despite the existence of a House of Laymen in the Church Assembly, has little or no real influence. Not on the dogmatic side, but on that of organization, the power of priest and Bishop is strongly emphasized. The priest is distinguished by a special garb, which carries over into social life his separation from the laity. The Bishop is a lofty prelate, who sits in the Upper House, enjoys a princely salary, and represents, everywhere, the claim of the Church to be heard even in temporal matters, notably in the schools and the care of the poor; a small, but characteristic symbol of his position is the fact that official documents are signed by him, not with his surname but, like a mediæval Bishop, with his Christian name. All this is Catholic. Catholic, above all, is the entire spirit of the Church. Its piety is not individualist-Protestant but collectivist-Catholic. The object, in its services, is the worship of God, not the cure of the individual soul. Therefore the sermon plays but a secondary rôle. Every liturgical and ceremonial device is, however, employed to raise the soul into communion with the divine. Worship is an end in itself, not a means to piety, in accordance with the Catholic model and in sympathy with national traditions. Attendance at service, participation in religious exercises, count as good in themselves. Only one thing – but a very essential one – is Protestant: there is no celibacy. That means the priest is not a being apart, with a special divine function and special duties towards God. He remains, in spite of all consideration shown to him, definitely human, a citizen, a fellow-man. So long as this line of demarcation exists, Anglicanism, with all its leanings towards Rome, will hardly become definitely Catholic.

§ 6

The combination of Catholic organization and Catholic spirit with Protestant dogma, as it appears in Anglicanism, is bound to give rise to perpetual difficulty and conflict. The dogmatic connexion with Continental Protestantism must constantly drive powerful groups within the Anglican fold to a closer contact with genuine Protestantism. The Catholic spirit of the organization must, equally, feed contrary tendencies, working for a yet nearer relation with Catholicism. Even in Reformation times, the more radical Reform wing felt so dissatisfied with the Church as a whole that it founded its own religious associations, which live on in the powerful organization of present-day Dissent or Nonconformity. This radicalism which threatened the dissolution of the Church, naturally drove the right wing, the High Church, into the opposite tendency: it dissociated itself sharply from every Continental-Protestant tendency and stressed the relationship of the Church of England with Catholicism. In the sixteenth and seventeenth centuries this High Church section bent all its energies to the suppression of all non-Anglican sects (with the exception, of course, of Catholicism, which it viewed as kin to itself). When the leading representative of this party, Archbishop Laud, went so far as to attempt to compel the Scots to Anglicanism, the undertaking cost him and his King, Charles I, their heads, and, for a few years Anglicanism was superseded under the Commonwealth and Cromwell.

In the second half of the eighteenth century, the opposite strain came uppermost in the Low Church or Evangelical Party. The reformer, John Wesley, was driven out of an Anglican Church, then worldly and completely in subjection to the State. But the effort towards a more spiritualized Church life, founded by him, in close sympathy with the German Pietists, was carried on by a number of Anglicans who remained in the Church and became a powerful force there. Their originator and most distinguished representative was George Whitefield (d. 1770). Clergymen like John Newton (d. 1807) and Thomas Scott (d. 1821), carried on the movement. Wilberforce, the emancipator of the slaves, and William Cowper, the poet, belonged to it. Its headquarters was in the London suburb of Clapham, with Exeter Hall as its main rallying platform. These 'Evangelicals' were a group of earnest pietists who accepted nothing but the Gospels – the word and deed of Christ. To the official Church they opposed

351

an inner, individualistic piety, analogous to German Pietism, professing a deep distrust of all theological and every other learning; relying, with the simple faith of the pious, on the power of the Holy Ghost to reveal the truth; displaying a complete indifference to all disagreements on doctrine, questions of government, and church tradition, they read and expounded the Bible. Their influence on the life of the Anglican Church was profound and beneficial. At a time when the ruling party within the Church, contributing little or nothing of its own, was bent merely on crushing the Dissenters, they held aloof from controversy, and recognized the Dissenters as equivalent brothers *in Christo*. Together with the Quakers and the Dissenters, the Evangelicals secured the abolition of slavery in the Colonies and so, indirectly, throughout the world. By the foundation of the Church Missionary Society (1799) the mission to the heathen was raised, by them, from the work of a few enthusiasts to an organized international movement. They made the religious tract (Religious Tract Society, 1799) a form of religious mass-propaganda of immense potency, at a time when the older forms of spreading the Gospel were proving inadequate to the new conditions produced by industrialism. Theirs, too, is another Society, created to meet similar needs – the British and Foreign Bible Society (1804). In all these efforts, these evangelical Churchmen worked with Dissenters in common faith and common zeal. Out of their circles there arose, in 1846, the Evangelical Alliance, with the reunion of all Protestants throughout the world as its aim. But the great title to fame of the Evangelical Party is the social activity of its leader, Lord Shaftesbury (1801–85), the tireless protagonist of Factory legislation and every possible form of protection for the worker. He, more than anyone, filled the Church with a sense of responsibility for the social problem in all its vast extent: an achievement that gives him a significance extending far beyond his own party or even his own nation. Kingsley's Christian Social movement is profoundly influenced by him; nor were Shaftesbury's High Church opponents able to hold aloof. Of course, Low Churchmen have the defects of their qualities. They often show an excessive, one-sided piety, which results in a dry matter-of-factness, a hostility to culture, and a narrowness of a peculiarly unexhilarating kind. In many of them, their excessive religious individualism prevailed also in temporal matters and there showed itself as a callous and unimaginative highly irreligious Manchesterism. While Shaftesbury found in the Gospels a call to social responsibility, many Evangelicals clung to an untenable economic individualism, hypocritically shutting their eyes to a distress that, from their standpoint, could not be remedied. They produced no leader of mark after Shaftesbury's death, but exhausted their energies in protests against the High Church Party. In figures like Mr. Stiggins and Mr. Chadband, Dickens caricatured a type of Low Church pastor (and his nearly related Dissenting brother) which is not yet quite extinct.

The High Church Party, in contradistinction to the Evangelicals, stresses the Catholic aspects of the Anglican Church. While the Low Church seeks affiliations with the Dissenters and Continental Protestants, the High Church looks to Roman Catholicism as an ally against infidelity and Radicalism. In Protestantism it sees something negative and unsound. It prefers to speak of the Anglo-Catholic, or even Catholic, Church of England. In the seventeenth century Anglicanism was dominated by the High Church: in the eighteenth it (the High Church) had almost died out; in the nineteenth, thanks to the Oxford Movement (1833 on), it began to spring up anew and became the most influential reforming agency of modern Church life. Modern Liberalism tried to reduce the Anglican Church to a mere religious corporation (one among others), but the poet S. T. Coleridge (d. 1834) entered a powerful plea for the necessity of a great State Church, emphasizing, at the same time, the need of its coming into line with the modern social conscience. In the thirties, the Liberal Reform movement began to interfere in Church matters. Church property was brought under State supervision by the establishment of the Ecclesiastical Commission in 1835, and Disestablishment and even Disendowment were talked of. Effective resistance to all this was organized by the High Church movement, which, after 1833, found leaders in three Oxford clergymen, John Keble, John Henry Newman, and Edward Pusey. Their programme included first the maintenance of the privileged character of the Anglican Church: resistance to Dissent: support of the Church's rights to its own property and schools as against any and every Liberal inroad. Secondly, however, they fought Liberalism itself, seeing in its indifference or hostility to the Church the firstfruits of a materialism that challenged every spiritual value. It inveighed against the shallow rationalism which made the Church Service a kind of ethical exercise, and the Church itself a convenient pillar of established order in the State. Its campaign against Liberalism was notably successful.

Church building was stimulated by the foundation, as early as 1848, of the Church Building Society, to which the State, despite the fact that it makes no legal contribution to Church funds, on various occasions granted large extraordinary subventions. The number of episcopal sees and of parochial livings was increased. Convocation was stirred to fresh life (1852). Above all, the empty, routine formalism into which the Church service had ossified during the eighteenth century was broken up completely. The emotional appeal of fine architecture, ritual observance, incense, genuflexions and the wearing of ceremonial vestments, was enlisted. The influence of the Church was thus carried far outside its own sphere and made a factor in general culture, everywhere serving its nobler, reverential and artistic aspects, and so constituting a much-needed counterpoise to the dry common-sense quality of English life elsewhere. High Churchmen supported Augustus Pugin (1812–52), and later Ruskin, who gave a powerful new stimulus to the feeling for architecture in general and Gothic in particular. By way of hiding the revolutionary character of their innovations, and connecting them with early Christian or even Reformation practice, the men of the Oxford Movement were potent advocates of the study of the history of art and of the Church. All this gave them a contact with Catholicism which was strengthened in various directions. Where their influence was strong, the Church became more and more sacramental; the communion from a kind of extra service became the central service of the Church; it was celebrated daily, and, what is more, fasting, and in forms absolutely similar to the Roman Mass. The host was reserved and – it is impossible to deny it – adored in truly Roman fashion. Saints' days and holy days, including those of the Blessed Virgin, were celebrated, auricular confession was practised, even the Pope – as the oldest Christian Bishop – appeared in prayers. In vain did Dissenters and Low Churchmen invoke the aid of the State: the Public Worship Regulation Act, which Parliament passed in 1874, remained a dead letter. The Bishops were unable to suppress the High Church zeal of the more advanced clergy, gradually High Churchmen began to become Bishops themselves. At last in the new Prayer Book of 1927 some of the most hotly contested High Church practices – including the Reservation of the Host, if only for the use of the sick – were openly allowed as an alternative formula. This new scheme was disallowed by Parliament and has therefore not become law, but the force of the movement is hardly broken by this check.

354

For the Oxford Movement has gradually accomplished something else. It has regained for the Church of England some ground among the lower orders, which before 1833 seemed to have fallen a prey to Dissent. There has been a very important social movement in the High Church ranks which has gradually superseded the Low Church activities of the same kind. It is social work of a distinctly clerical character: the work is social, but its ultimate aim is not humanitarianism or social welfare in itself, but by social activities to promote the cause of the Church. There are now Anglican convents, brotherhoods and sisterhoods of all kinds; and 'retreats' have held their ground despite the embittered opposition both of the Low Church and the Dissenters. The High Church is organized in the English Church Union (founded in 1844), the Low Church in the Church Association (1865) and the National Church League (1906).

The German Protestant finds the High Church, as a rule, extraordinarily unsympathetic. He is apt to see nothing in its service but empty ceremonial. He is put off by the markedly clerical tone of its social work. Its hierarchical pretensions for him reflect the spirit of an outworn century. There may be force in all these objections. There may be higher forms of religious life than the High Church offers. But it remains the fact that, for the English people, Anglicanism, and particularly the High Church, have, so far, proved the one congenial religious form. The external pomp of the High Church and its historic aura satisfy a strong leaning towards ceremony, native to the people, and not otherwise fed. No one who has witnessed the furore of the lower classes for a spectacular piece in the theatre: the naïve enthusiasm of the man in the street for a Lord Mayor's Show or a Royal wedding procession, can believe that the romantic strain in the English mind, which once blossomed forth in the Elizabethan stage, is dead to-day. Romance, driven out of daily life by Puritanism, has found a refuge in the service of the Church. English mysticism finds food in two directions only – in an almost superstitious reverence for the presumably unchangeable, unwritten constitution, and in the religious exercises of the High Church. External pomp, thus, is not an end in itself, but a means to religious emotion. The great poets of the Anglican Church, George Herbert and Richard Crashaw in the seventeenth century, John Keble and Christina Rossetti in the nineteenth, belonged to the High Church. What strikes the German observer as the lack of individual forms of piety, is a lack not peculiar to this form of life, but one characteristic of the English mind in general, with its emphasis on the typical and aversion from nonconformity in all matters. This same trait appears, markedly, in education. It is undeniable that, of the two ruling tendencies in the Church of England, it is the High Church that in the last two generations has made progress and produced important results, not only in its own sphere but in that of social work of all kinds – far more than the Low Church. Impossible, to-day, to maintain the old thesis that the High Church is lost in externals; one might rather charge the Low Church, since Sháftesbury's death, with having occupied itself, more and more exclusively, in fruitless protests against the High Church.

§ 7

Theological Liberalism has never played a great part in England. Christianity, for a people with such a passion for deeds and want of comprehension for dogma, is an action and an organization dedicated to the glory of God, and, as such, certain mystic needs, common to the Germanic peoples, find in it their satisfaction. In the development of dogma, England has hardly co-operated. Its eighteenth-century philosophers shook the dogmatic structure of the Church to its foundations. A few outstanding theologians, like John Spencer of Cambridge (d. 1693), anticipated certain fruitful modern lines of thought. University scholars and the Oxford Movement made important contributions to Church history. But England has contributed nothing original to the erection of a modern dogmatic structure, nothing to the reconciliation of old theology and new philosophy and science. The history of English Liberalism, in this connexion, is that of a struggle over the achievements of German theology and philosophy – over Kant, over the Tübingen school, over Strauss and Baur. Ever since Coleridge, there has been an impassioned eagerness for a reconciliation of old faith and modern science. This was always the prime object of Broad Churchmen such as Frederick Denison Maurice (d. 1872), James Martineau (d. 1900), and Frederick William Robertson (d. 1853) in their effort to make the way into the Church as broad as possible. And there have been plenty of fine minds, like Charles Kingsley, Robert Browning and Alfred Tennyson, the Arnolds, Arthur Stanley (Dean of Westminster) and F. W. Robertson, whose lives afforded the model of a Christian life at once deep and open to every scientific and artistic impulse. Anything like a systematic theology, however, is altogether wanting. Either the real points at issue are casually evaded, or modernism exhausts itself in questions of nomenclature, designed, more or less skilfully, to conceal the fact that the old conceptions are maintained practically intact. Coleridge, the most freethinking of English theologians, can, as truly, be called a complete reactionary. Public opinion, in England, has never thrown itself into this controversy with anything like the fervour that marked the same contest in Germany. True, his rationalist attitude to the question of Eternal Damnation cost Maurice, in 1853, his professorship at King's College; *Essays and Reviews* followed in 1860; in 1863 Bishop Colenso's publication of ideas on Wellhausen lines led to a schism in the South African Church. But the publication in 1865 of *Ecce Homo*, an essay in Liberal ideas by the Cambridge historian, John Seeley, produced only a moderate storm. Liberal Biblical criticism, after a stiff fight, gradually won for itself a place within the Anglican Church, but it was and is represented by a handful of scholars and some Bishops who have striven in vain to rouse any general interest in the average Churchman. True, the old dogmas are widely challenged nowadays, but the challenging spirit rather represents modern materialism than a new religious attitude. Churchmen take far more interest in a new incumbent's putting or not putting flowers on the altar, in the garments in which he intones the Liturgy, in his employing the Sarum ritual or one with Romish glosses, than they do in any such question as 'What think ye of Christ?'

CHAPTER II
ROMAN CATHOLICISM

JUDGED by the number of its adherents, the Roman Catholic Church in Great Britain is an insignificant body. There are one or two great Catholic families, like the Dukes of Norfolk, who pride themselves on having stood staunch, ever since the Reformation, all persecutions notwithstanding, in the faith of their fathers; and they take the dependants and workers on their estates with them. Further, parts of the Scottish Highlands, like the Hebrides, are traditionally Catholic. In the large towns everywhere there are considerable bodies of Catholic workers mostly of Irish origin, though they do not always belong to the settled portion of the population. The English census, unlike the Irish, asks no questions as to religious profession: the number of Catholics can therefore only be estimated at round about 2·08 million in England and 0·6 million in Scotland. The organized Catholic Church, broken by the Reformation, was re-established, in 1850, by Pius IX. The Government contented itself with loud protests: it passed certain restrictions on Catholic worship which were never enforced. The head of the Catholic hierarchy is the Cardinal Archbishop of Westminster.

Ireland, on the other hand, with 3¼ million Catholics in 1911, is an overwhelmingly Catholic country; Ulster alone, where, ever since 1605, English and Scottish immigrants were settled in definite districts, shows a Protestant majority and complete Protestant ascendancy. The English State in Ireland, originally purely Protestant, has had to accommodate itself to Catholicism. After it had been proved that Catholicism was not to be extirpated either by barbarous penal laws or savage persecutions, concession was tried. There was protracted search for a formula which might allay the deep-rooted dread of the Protestant State of Papal interference in temporal matters. From 1774 on, there were negotiations about a special oath to be taken by every Catholic before he could be recognized as a citizen; all sorts of forms of State control over Bishops and Episcopal election were devised as preliminary to official recognition of Catholicism. Finally, however, all these restrictive efforts had to be abandoned and three offices only – that of Viceroy, Lord Chancellor, and, eventually, Regent – confined to Protestants. Ultimately, the fact was recognized that no smallest concession in principle could be extorted from Catholicism, but almost everything secured in the way of a practical understanding on questions of the hour. On this basis, a reconciliation was reached between England and the policy of the Vatican. In 1829 the Emancipation Law admitted Catholics to the enjoyment of practically every civil right; in 1869 the disestablishment of the Irish Church removed the crying injustice of taxing the poverty of Ireland to support an alien Church with a tiny congregation. The Catholic Church of Ireland is wholly independent of the State, except in so far as it is subject to the general law of the land in such matters as marriage, etc. In 1869 a single grant was made to the Seminary at Maynooth; otherwise the State made no contribution to the Church and, in return, takes no part in the nomination of priests and bishops. Popular education has been handed over entirely to the Church, which has also got higher education almost completely in its hands, as well as, in practice if not in law, the University of Ireland. Financially, the Church is wholly independent of the State, and subject only to the general law of the land. That rates cannot be compulsorily levied hardly matters in view of the overwhelmingly religious character of the population.

This arrangement with the Catholic Church has also served the purposes of the State. The tacit *quid pro quo* of the Church consisted in the fact that it took over, in Ireland, the rôle of solid pillar of the State assumed in England by the Anglican establishment. Time and again have Irish Bishops, and even Papal Legates, damped down the fires of revolution in Ireland. The Church – following, in this, the line of its own interest – set itself against the excessive Nationalism of the Irish, when, for instance, there was talk of a national Celtic University in Dublin.

To the Church as a whole, though of course it had to make occasional concessions to Irish nationalism, it was a matter of supreme indifference whether three million Irish, of whom the overwhelming majority will remain Catholic in any event, achieved national autonomy or no. Indeed, from the Catholic point of view the continued representation of Ireland at Westminster was desirable, since Ireland's eighty Catholic M.P.s acted as a powerful, often as an overpowering, representation of the tiny number of British Catholics, impotent to return even a single member on their own. Without the Irish Catholic M.P.s it would never have been possible for the two million Catholics in Great Britain to secure State aid for their schools. It is not in the Catholic interest to have the national Irish University in Dublin dominated by the Celtic language, which only a minority even in Ireland understands, and no one at all outside of it; it is rather to its interest to have Dublin develop as a University for the whole of English-speaking Catholicism. The determining consideration, for the Vatican, has always been not Ireland but England. For, puny as the rôle of Catholicism is in England to-day, Rome still cherishes the hope of seeing the world-wide Anglican Church brought back to the bosom of the Mother Church. What a feather in the scales against this vast possibility are the nationalist aspirations of three millions of people, without political influence and faithful sons of the Church!

Rome hopes much from High Church Anglicanism, and not wholly without reason. Its spirit is Catholic; its emphasis on organization, on emotional appeal, on vestments and exercises, has reawakened an understanding of Catholicism within the Anglican Church. The most important of the three founders of the Oxford Movement, John Henry Newman, died in 1890 as a Roman Cardinal. Edward Pusey (died 1882), who ranks after him, regarded it as part of his life-work to reunite the Anglican and Roman Churches. It was natural enough that Pius IX should have felt, in 1850, that the hour had struck when the hierarchy destroyed by the Reformation could be restored by the re-establishment of Catholic Bishoprics.

Nevertheless, it is to the last degree improbable that the hopes of the Vatican will achieve any substantial realization. The groups in England favourable to reunion contemplate fitting Anglicanism into the grand framework of Catholicism, subject, however, to the maintenance of the independence of Anglicanism, and its recognition as a form of Catholicism on a parity with Rome. (There have been tentative negotiations on the possibility of reunion in the years 1921–25, at Malines between Anglicans and Roman Catholic dignitaries.) Rome, on her part, may perhaps, without violating her tradition, find a formula to cover dogmatic differences, but must insist on recognition of Papal Supremacy. And that the Englishman's sense of liberty cannot tolerate. In the realm of dogma, less important to Rome, he could make concessions, but he will never submit to a foreign power. Even in the Middle Ages, every attempt, no matter how constitutional, on the part of the Pope, to interfere in the affairs of the English Church, was looked on askance.. To-day, the feeling, on this point, of the English people is hardly changed from what it was in the time of Wycliffe or of Shakespeare. Rome is a foreign power. Every concession to Rome is felt as a national disgrace, and greeted with the battle-cry 'No Popery!' under which the Low Church goes forth to combat against the High. The refusal of Parliament to sanction the new Prayer Book in 1927 and 1928 was a striking last instance of this. In the last analysis, the Reformation of Henry VIII and Elizabeth is more than the accidental result of Cæsarian temper: there is something that truly expresses the instinct of the English masses in the combination of the Catholic character of the whole structure with an energetic repudiation of foreign church authority. The hour of reunion has not struck, so long as Rome on the one hand, and the High Church in England on the other, are prepared only for concessions on points of no real significance to each other. Perhaps, indeed, it has passed. Certainly, the Oxford Movement brought Anglicanism very near to Catholicism. But one result of its great achievements within the English Church is that all those English-speaking Christians who feel and seek a mystic impulse and a mystic ceremonial no longer need to drift to Catholicism in search of the religion of their hearts. They can have Catholicism at home: they can feel Catholic without having to make up their minds about those aspects of Catholicism unattractive to the Germanic spirit – the politics of the Curia, Jesuitism and the Index.

CHAPTER III
THE FREE CHURCHES
§ I

THE roots of opposition to Anglicanism go back to pre-Reformation times. Wycliffe fought for the independence of the English Church from the Pope. He appealed to the higher authority of the Bible against that of Church tradition. Under his influence, little conventicles of laymen gathered everywhere; the so-called Lollards who had their own conception of Christianity, made revolutionary social and political demands, spread their views through lay preachers, and supported all their claims on the authority of the Bible which, they said, every layman was called upon to read, in accordance with his own, God-given inspiration. The Lollards were actively persecuted by the Government, which however failed to extirpate them. The Opposition movements that all at once sprang up everywhere in the sixteenth century are, despite their manifold diversities, so closely related to Lollardy that it must be regarded as a very vital root of modern Dissent. Under Henry VIII, this opposition began to appear. Under Elizabeth it began to take an organized form. Under Charles I it grew to a revolution, and, for a brief period after the fall of the monarchy, actually dominated the whole religious life of the country. Even the Restoration did not succeed in crushing the manifold forms of this religious community life outside the Church. The sects of the Reformation era survived the Restoration. More than that, in the eighteenth century, they were reinforced by a new one, more powerful than any of them, the Methodists. Something like a half of the professing Christians in England belong to the Free Churches.[1]

The opposition to the Church of England, however – and this is its fatal weakness to the present day – has never been united, never proceeded from a single dominating common point of view. For this reason it has inevitably split into multifarious organizations. Common to them all is their final point of departure – the strong sense of independence and personality; that is all. The English feeling for the type finds its expression in the Church of England; Germanic individualism, naturally not absent in English life, in Dissent. All the sects oppose the claim of the Anglican Church to sovereignty in matters of religion; all resist the demand of the Anglican clergyman for authority and obedience. They comprise all those whose piety the Church does not satisfy: drawing, mainly from the middle, and, in part from the lower classes of society, men and women whose minds are not apt to be exalted by the æsthetics of worship, whose outlook is too literal for the mysticism of transubstantiation, and whose imaginations are too bounded to be stimulated by the ideal of a universal Church. Here one finds the harsh piety of a warrior race, determined to set up the Kingdom of God and put the Devil under His feet, fighting, with relentless self-discipline and merciless severity, against whatsoever does not seem to their narrow understanding to be the will of God: with harsh intolerance against any dignity in the service of the Lord, as well as against any form of secular pleasure like dancing and music, the theatre and the arts. Men rigorous to the point of asceticism in their lives, often however of such a crudely materialistic outlook that they expect piety to be rewarded here on earth, and view success in business as a sign of the well-earned favour of Heaven. In the storm and stress of the seventeenth century, the seeds of many earlier religious cults sprang to life again in the singular soil of a section of humanity limited by no sort of critical faculty and no profound knowledge – Lutheranism, Calvinism, Anabaptism, early Christian Gnosticism, Plotinian Mysticism, Oriental ecstasy. They threw off a number of ephemeral sects, few of which survived the Cromwellian century. Dogmatic differences accounted for but a small proportion – the doctrine of the Real Presence, the Augustinian doctrine of grace, etc.; far the larger number of sects arose out of some question of organization, some question of the relation of the individual to the minister and to the Church. With time, the multiplicity of the sects diminished somewhat. To-day three main types of Dissenters can be distinguished.

(a) *The Presbyterians.* The Church is Calvinist, both in organization and doctrine. In contrast to the lay character of Independency, the idea of the Church is strongly emphasized. The Church is holy, established by God, necessary to salvation. It is above the State, and exists in order to build the Kingdom of God upon earth. The Sacraments are necessary, and there is a pure doctrine, upon whose uncorrupted diffusion the greatest weight is laid. The Presbyterian, like the Anglican, regards his as the true Church, and dislikes being described as a Dissenter. The Church, however, is not merely priestly: rather every form of hierarchy is absolutely dispensed with. Still less is it a lay Church. There are in the Church two God-appointed offices – that of teaching, belonging to the minister, and that of ruling, to the elder, the presbyter: who is therefore by virtue of his office, no longer a layman though he may follow some ordinary business or profession. The other members of the congregation are laymen, and, while possessing the right of electing the presbyter, have no other voice in the Church. A Church realizing these ideals has been built up in Scotland and in Northern Ireland.

(b) *The Independents* (Congregationalists). They derive in part from the Lollards, in part from Baptist theories of the sixteenth century. They want not to be a Church but a sect. The Church is in the grip of Antichrist, but the few true believers may be gathered together that they may flee the wrath of the Day of Judgment. The State is as corrupt as the Church. Hopeless, any dream of controlling it. It too must be rejected. In the little flock of the chosen there is no distinction between priests and laymen. Since, really, there is no Church, the Sacraments are not of decisive importance: what is important is to seek out God's will in the Bible. Here, however, the greatest freedom of choice rules both in the interpretation of the text and the exposition of dogma, since every individual in whom the spirit moves is alike called and entitled to interpret what is written. Germanic individualism, subordinated to the idea of an organized Church both in the Establishment and with the Presbyterians, here finds an unlimited field of action. Reformation ideas of universal priesthood and the unlimited authority of the Bible are here carried to their logical conclusions, indeed often distorted to the point of travesty. Clergymen are really superfluous: they may have a certain practical utility, but any layman can take their place. It is quite logical for clergymen of any sect of the Independent type to wear no gown, but sit, at service, among the congregation in lay attire, and for extempore prayer to take the place of any rigid liturgy in the service. It is in the State of Massachusetts that the Independents have developed most strongly. Their ideal has also been adopted by the Quakers, the Irvingites, and (in part) the Unitarians, who are associated with them only in form of organization, in all other matters entirely distinct.

These two groups were at first mutually hostile. Where the one is in the ascendant, the other is found in open opposition to it. Where however, as in England itself was normally the case right down to the nineteenth century, both were persecuted by Anglicanism, numerous contacts and a certain reciprocal influence took place. Calvinist doctrine took its rise among the Presbyterians, but spread from them among the Independents and similar sects. On the other hand, Independent influences helped to soften progressively the extreme rigidity of Presbyterian aristocratic sacramentalism. Originally, the Presbyterians repudiated the idea of the lay church since the few elevated, under it, as ruling elders above the mass of laymen ceased thereby to be laymen. In the course of time, however, this sacramental notion was profoundly modified under the influence of Independent ideas. The result was that a certain approximation between the two types took place everywhere. To these two older groups there was added, in the eighteenth century:

(c) *The Methodists*. They are outside the Church not on any internal ground, but simply and solely because their founder, the great John Wesley (1703-91), was driven out of it in the eighteenth century. Actually, they constitute an organization parallel to the other Church formations, democratic in government, Calvinistic in dogma, in which every shade of religious life is represented, from something very near to Anglicanism on the right, to something quite Independent on the left. Within themselves, they are again subdivided into a large number of separate groupings, among which the Salvation Army may be mentioned. They are distinguished by an exceedingly energetic, methodical (hence the name) and most skilful organization, which owes some of its successes to periodic 'revivals' during which their adherents are worked up to a kind of religious ecstasy.

§ 2

Presbyterians and Independents represent the two oldest types of opposition in the Church. Under Cromwell they dominated the English Church for a brief period. The Restoration led to their complete suppression, and even the expulsion of the Stuarts was of advantage only to the Church, not to the Dissenters. The Conventicle Acts (1664, 1670, etc.) forbade every non-Anglican form of worship; the Corporation Act (1661) excluded all those who accepted the Presbyterian Covenant and all Puritans who recognized a right of resistance to the Throne from participation in local government; the Test Act (1673) excluded all non-Anglicans from every civil office; the Act of Uniformity (1662) placed the entire educational system under the Bishops, and strove thereby to abolish Dissenting schools. This civil outlawry of the religious opposition remained practically unmodified by the expulsion of the Stuarts. The Anglican Whigs absorbed all power to themselves, and the Puritan middle classes remained excluded from political life. Since, however, they constituted an economic power which the territorial magnates could not ignore entirely, they succeeded in getting the rigour of the law averted from the Puritans, on condition that, oblivious of their most vital tenet, they silently recognized the existing State. In 1721 they received a sort of State subvention – the *Regium Donum* – at the hands of the all-powerful Premier, Walpole. Charles II had handed it over to the Irish Presbyterians for the maintenance of the orphans of Dissenting ministers, and it was now extended to the other sects. The effect of this was profoundly demoralizing, since it meant an apparent recognition of the supremacy of the State amounting to a betrayal by Dissent of its own Holy of Holies. (It was not abolished till 1857.) The political ban on Nonconformity was further, if not abolished, practically circumvented. Nonconformists were barred as Mayors or Councillors by the Corporation Act. But a habit grew up of shutting an eye to this, so long as the Puritans were willing to compromise by 'occasional conformity'[2] – i.e. partook once of communion, according to the rites of the Anglican Church, and adhered for the rest to their own sect. This solution is highly characteristic of the English conception of an established Church: thus, the rebels showed their respect for the Church, and, that done, were left in peace. By such devices adaptable spirits among the Dissenters sheltered themselves from persecution; those, however, with strong characters and a high sense of honour, were ruthlessly held under. In the eighteenth century, anyone with pretensions to culture or consideration belonged to the Established Church; the genuine Dissenters dwindled, gradually, into a wretched and helpless group of people absorbed in sterile controversy on petty points and mutual recrimination and heresy hunting. From this creeping paralysis, John Wesley rescued the whole religious opposition. The movement he initiated rehabilitated the essential principle of all Dissent: religious individualism, as against mere sacerdotalism; religious action, as against mere cult; holiness of life, as against mere orthodoxy. He did this by founding a sect of his own when the Church turned him out. And in so doing he forced the Church to enter into most salutary competition for the souls of middle- and lower-class Christians: while, at the same time, he breathed new life into the body of Nonconformity, by revivifying its basic principles.

In the course of the nineteenth century, the civil disabilities of Nonconformists were gradually removed. They began to be a political power, and this although the process by which a considerable proportion of the wealthy upper section passed over into the camp of the Establishment was still going on. By degrees, first the Whigs, and then the Liberals, made themselves the mouthpiece of Nonconformist grievances. The Reform Bills of 1832 and 1867 enfranchized the majority of Dissenters: all limitations on their freedom of worship were removed; in 1828 the Test and Corporation Acts were repealed; the establishment of Civil Registration in 1836 broke down the Church monopoly in relation to baptism and marriage; the various Burial Acts of 1852 and 1880, that in relation to interments; in 1868 they were relieved from tithe and Church rates; between 1854 and 1871 the Universities were opened to them. It is now possible for Dissenters to breathe freely and erect an individual type of religious community on the basis of their own principles.

Two points characterize their historic mission. First, they have saved Protestant individualism from annihilation in a State Church in which external organization must rank first. This is not contradicted by the fact that, in Scotland, one of the strongest of the Nonconformist Churches, Presbyterianism, is a State Church; nor by the fact that, with the Methodists, organization is apt to be fatally rigid. For in both these Churches there is enough individualism to have, time and again, burst the bonds of organization, and to have forced upon the original association a thoroughly healthy fight for existence against the opposing developments within itself.

Second, if the Established Church of Scotland and the Unitarians are, for the moment, left out of the picture, Nonconformity is the small man's Church. Anyone who rises from its ranks to wealth and position tends to find himself attracted, with surprising swiftness, to the respectability of the State Church. The solid strength of Dissent lies among the middle and lower classes. Here, in the smaller religious communities, small men can feel that they have something to say. They may choose a minister of their own class; they can play a part of their own, as elders, lay preachers, and holders of various honorary offices. This lower middle-class atmosphere, proper to almost all Nonconformity, gives their piety its distinctive note. Save for the Unitarians and the Presbyterians, they have developed no theology of their own. Questions of dogma may have played their part in the foundation of a sect, and have been taken up with the one-sided enthusiasm of the layman. But the lasting force which makes for the foundation of a sect is the enthusiasm of the small man for a great leader. The force that has drawn Englishmen into sects is to be found in the personal force of some such truly great and genuinely inspired individual as Wesley, Spurgeon, or William Booth, or even of some enthusiastic cobbler or half-crazy fanatic, rather than in the dogmatic formulas with which they happened to adorn their sermons. Dogmas tend, as a matter of fact, to appear suddenly, and, as suddenly, disappear again, often subsequently to be picked up by some other sect and elevated into a fashion. Bitter as sectarian strife may be from time to time, and loud as is the din of battle, the sects are not really dogmatic opponents. They resemble, rather, political parties, contending for the mass of souls floating now this way now that. Just as the difference between Conservatives and Liberals is not so much a question of programmes as the pull of some great leader's name, so is it with the Free Churches. True, most Nonconformists belong, by family tradition, to a particular religious affiliation, to which the majority adhere throughout their lives. At the same time, any great revival, whether initiated by a Baptist, like Spurgeon, or a Methodist, like General Booth, will at once attract adherents from the other sects. In the same way, a Congregationalist, removing from London to Liverpool, may easily follow the friends he finds in his new abode to the Baptist chapel. There is a perpetual interchange of souls as between the various denominations – a fact which does not in the least prevent individual Nonconformist groups from competing violently among themselves. Their various colleges, schools, charitable institutions, and home and foreign missions are, almost invariably, separate, and often, as a result, condemned to wretched penury. In one point only are they united – the struggle against the Established Church. For, although there is now such complete toleration of Dissent that substantial grievances hardly exist any longer, complete equality is not yet attained. Since 1844 they have striven for the disestablishment of the Anglican Church. They desire to have it reduced to the status of one among the other denominations. They seek to have the vast property inherited by the Church distributed among all denominations. Above all, they desire the supersession of the primacy of the Church in education. A large portion of the Liberal Party, which gets the bulk of the Nonconformist vote, is pledged to this.

Self-preservation, as against the Establishment, has been, from of old, the one bond of union among sects that would otherwise have split into helpless atoms. As far back as 1727, a Board of Three Denominations was set up, through which the Presbyterians, Baptists and Independents came together for common action. Since 1894, Free Church Councils have existed, designed to present a common front to the activities of the local Anglican incumbents, with, behind them, the National Free Church Council (1892) – a great conference for the representation of Nonconformist interests. Noteworthy is the fact that this Council is composed not merely of delegates from the various denominations, but from local Councils, so that it may happen that a Methodist represents the Congregationalists in his area. Such signs of co-operation indicate that Nonconformity is by no means identical with a dissolution of organization. The power of Nonconformity, when it acts together, was displayed in the electoral compaign of 1905; the fall of the Conservative Government was patently due to the revolt of Dissenters against the favour shown to Church schools in the 1902 Education Act.

§ 3

Calvinism had a greater influence in Great Britain than Lutheranism Luther's influence is visible in the Articles of the Anglican Church, and the English Bible is impregnated with it; but in the vital question of organization Lutheranism could give the Anglo-Saxon no aid. For a brief period, under Edward VI (1547–53), and, later, under Cromwell, England was a Presbyterian – i.e. Calvinistically organized – State; in Scotland, Calvinism rules unchallenged to this day. In 1560 John Knox introduced the Calvinistic system of Church government, and the Scots accepted its spirit, with the immense and obstinate enthusiasm native to their character. When Charles I attempted to force Anglicanism upon them, the entire people rose and, on March 1, 1638, signed the Covenant – an outstanding example in modern history of an Old Testament bond with God entered into by a whole nation, filled with religious zeal. The Covenant finally cost the King his throne and his life. After the accession of William III (1688), Presbyterianism, on the Calvinistic model, became the Established Church of Scotland. To this day, Calvinism in Scotland interpenetrates the whole people. Here alone in the world the Protestant has the feeling that something like an Evangelical state is really possible.

Calvinist dogma dominates Scotland. The idea of Predestination is still a living force there, though perhaps less so in the present than in earlier generations. Here is the solitary Anglo-Saxon country where a Christian dogma plays a genuinely dominating part in religious life. Not, of course, in the sense in which this is the case in Germany, as the starting-point for a host of individual dogmatic expressions, but as the vital faith of a people. Every soul is called to eternal blessedness by God, and the Scottish people – and, consequentially, the whole fabric of Anglo-Saxon culture – is elected to the rôle played in the early history of religion by the People of Israel. In defiance of every form of rationalism and Liberalism, this dogma has maintained itself in all the rigid force with which it can animate religious life. Vain was the eighteenth-century effort of the 'Moderates' (with whom the poet Robert Burns was associated) to soften the harsh outlines of Calvinism by rationalism or sentimentality: the modest attempt was drowned in the wave of Methodism that swept over the whole of Britain in the wake of Wesley. It is only in our own generation that Scottish dogmatic exclusiveness shows any sign of softening. In the big cities, at any rate, lukewarmness and indifference in religion are common both among the upper classes and among the workers.

§ 4

The organization of the Scottish Church is Calvinist. It is dominated by two main ideas. First, the world must be won over for God, and organization, consequently, made as comprehensive and intensive as possible. Second, everybody must be enlisted in that fight, priest and laymen as well. Since the close of the sixteenth century, there have rallied round the standard of Presbyterianism all the groups in England and Scotland who found Elizabeth's Reformation too hierarchical. The non-theologically educated man whom we should call a layman, is, in Scotland, as ruling elder the holder of a God-appointed clerical office. Together with the ministers, these elders rule the Church, and administer its finances in kirk session. This same organization reappears on a higher stage; above the kirk sessions are the Presbyteries, provincial synods, and the General Assembly, led by its elected Moderator. The laymen proper – those, that is, who are not elders – had, at first, little or no say in the Church. They had to elect the elders for the kirk session (i.e. on the lowest step of the hierarchical ladder) and can also elect their ministers, subject always to approval and nomination by the synod; for the rest they are merely the object of Church administration. Under the influence of Methodism, however, whose impact upon Presbyterianism was to intensify, notably, a care for the soul possible only by the active co-operation of the lay element, a change took place. There exists to-day a mighty lay organization which assists the preacher in the cure of souls. By the side of the minister stands a whole army of parish officers and voluntary helpers, who work with and under him in Sunday school, Church business, care for the poor, and missions. The whole work of missions, at home and abroad, like the whole range of humanitarian institutions, from the campaign against drink to the provision for cripples and epileptics, are here associated in some way or other with the Church or actually subordinated to it. Not Christianity only is a power in Scotland, but the Church. The old ideal of the interpenetration of the State with Christian life is, in Scotland, realized to an extent to which no other evangelical country affords a parallel. The rigorous observance of Sunday, accepted by the people rather as a natural thing than as a burden, is but one small sign of this. (During the last generation, especially after the war, there has been a visible relaxation in this.)

In such circumstances, the relations of Church and State have a greater importance in Scotland than anywhere else in the world. The religious ideal of the Calvinist is the transformation of the evil, unchristian State into a State of God. This can only come about when the Church rules in the State; to permit it to be ruled by the State would be to sin against the Holy of Holies. The Church's complete freedom from the State is, for the Presbyterian, the preliminary condition of any religious life. It was the fact that the Anglican Church is bound to the State and ruled by the State that, in conjunction with its episcopal constitution, made any union between Scots and Anglicans impossible in the seventeenth century. Since the seventeenth century, the history of the Church in Scotland is, essentially, a history of the progressive emancipation of the Church from what remained of State or worldly influence. The main issues were the State's demand that ministers should take the Oath of Supremacy, and its right, or that of certain landowners, of presentation to certain livings. After every conflict in which the Church failed to secure the complete liberty it demanded, a split in the Church took place. Thrice, between 1690 and 1800, was there a secession from the State Church, generally led by the poverty-stricken Highlanders, whose principal property was the fervour of their religious beliefs. In 1690 a large number of individual parishes seceded, uniting, in 1743, to form the Reformed Presbyterian Church. The foundation of the Secession Church by Ebenezer Erskine followed in 1747; of the Relief Church by Thomas Gillespie in 1752. These small Church bodies proved, in the long run, incapable of maintaining themselves: they had, in the end, to reunite with other sects which had left the Church on grounds of similar fanaticism. One such division, only, had a more solid significance – when in 1843 Thomas Chalmers took more than a third of the total number of ministers with him, and left the Established Church to found the Scottish Free Church, which, in 1900, took in the older eighteenth-century seceders to become the United Free Church. The event was one that could only have happened in Scotland. Not on any question of doctrine, but on a conflict arising out of the right of presentation, such as would have been called of very minor importance in any other country, one-third of the whole number of ministers went out, literally into the wilderness. All the churches, all the manses, all the funds, all the widows' pensions, all the theological faculties, remained in the hands of the Established Kirk. The new Free Church had to create all this out of its own resources. And it did it. But two generations later, the Free Church was as important and as efficient as the Established.

In Scotland, to-day, therefore, two great Church bodies exist side by side:

1. The Established Church (Kirk of Scotland). About half the population belongs to it. Its creed is formulated in the Westminster Confession of Faith, together with the Larger Catechism, Shorter Catechism, and Directory for Public Worship, the work of the Westminster Assembly of 1643–48, designed to supply the religious basis for Cromwell's Puritan State. It is bound to the State in so far as its Church laws have to be sanctioned by Parliament, and the monarch is represented on the General Assembly through a High Commissioner, though the real head of the Church is the annually elected Moderator; for the rest, it is entirely free. It enjoys the ancient funded revenues of the Church. In 1925, by the Church of Scotland Property and Endowments Bill, the State renounced its last rights of control. In 1928 the Church claimed 759,797 communicants.

2. The United Free Church, in 1928, had 536,380 communicants. This is Chalmers' foundation. It is 'United' since, in 1900, the original body which split off in 1843 to form the Free Church of Scotland united with the United Presbyterians who, in their turn, represented an amalgamation of the earlier secessions under Erskine and Gillespie (page 371). Identical with the Established in doctrine and constitution, it is distinct from it through the fact that the Free Church

never had any connexion with the State, with the result that the Church is wholly dependent for its revenue on its members. In no other country of the world would it be possible for two Churches, separated by a merely theoretical difference, to maintain a separate existence side by side, with the result that in almost every parish there are two churches and practically every major form of Church enterprise – home and foreign missions, homes for cripples, etc., theological faculties – to be duplicated. On both sides there is a growing feeling of the unreality of this division, and the reunion will probably be effected very soon.[3]

The Anglican Church in Scotland, known there as 'Episcopalian,' is the Church of a minority, but an important one socially. It is at once the Church of the numerous English people resident in Scotland, and of the greater part of the Scottish nobility, and a proportion of the upper middle class. Nothing shows the supremacy of class distinctions in Anglo-Saxon countries more clearly than the fact that even in Scotland, despite every nationalist and religious prepossession, pride of place belongs to the Church of the governing class. Only 59,657 communicants belong to the Episcopal Church in Scotland (1928), distributed among seven Bishoprics. Other religious minorities that may be mentioned are the Catholics (some 600,000, in all); the Congregationalists (50,000 communicants); Baptists (21,000 communicants), Methodists of various denominations (13,000 communicants); and all sorts of fractions from earlier splits, mainly to be found in the Highlands, poor, uneducated, and given over to the most rigid form of Calvinism. Among these the 'Wee Frees,' that section of the Free Church which resisted the union of 1900, are the most important, with some 32,000 communicants.

Presbyterianism outside Scotland plays only a subsidiary part. Scots domiciled in England naturally tend to belong to their native Churches. The old English form of Presbyterianism, which gave Elizabeth so much trouble, and, in the time of Cromwell, ruled over almost the whole of the country, was reduced to a sect by the Act of Uniformity (1662), and subsequently fused to some extent with the Independents (although the basic principle of the latter is in sharp contradiction to the Presbyterian ideal of the state of God), and to some extent with the Unitarians. The official representative of Presbyterianism in England is the Presbyterian Church of England (84,764 communicants in 1928), which is affiliated with the United Free Church of Scotland. In Wales, a fusion of Presbyterians and Methodists formed the Calvinistic Methodist (Presbyteran) Church of Wales, whose services and Sunday schools are, in the main, conducted in Welsh (1928: 189,132 communicants).

In Ireland, the Presbyterians, with 709,748 communicants, are the most important body in the province of Ulster, where the population consists in the main of immigrants from Scotland. In the Colonies, and especially in Canada, they are also strongly represented, again through Scottish immigrants.

§ 5

To build the kingdom of God upon earth and impose it upon the State is the religious ideal of the Presbyterian. To this, towards the close of the sixteenth century, a diametrically opposed conception was presented by the Independents. The world is corrupt: the Church, as it exists, an accursed idolatry, incapable of reform. For the true Christian, flight from the world is the only solution. As so often in Church history, we have here the sect fighting the Church, and rehabilitating the will to strenuous religiousness which tends to be broken by the compromises inseparable from an organized Church. In 1580–90 the Independent, Robert Browne, gathered his followers in autonomous little groups, that would have nothing to do with the State. Protection was the utmost they asked from the State: neither support nor subvention; they therefore refused to permit any interference by it in matters of religion. Persecuted by Elizabeth, the Independents emigrated, about 1600, to Holland, where they entered into the closest relations with the extreme reformation tendencies of the Continent, notably the Anabaptists. In 1616, English Independency was re-established in Southwark, and in 1620, under James I's persecution, the historic voyage of the Pilgrim Fathers to America transplanted it thither.

The Independents have played a prominent part in the history of England and the English Church. They were Radicals who followed the basic idea of Christian freedom with inflexible logic to its extreme limits. In religious matters they recognized no power of the State over the citizen and rejected any claim on its part to supervise the Church, just as they rejected every financial contribution from it, or any assistance on the part of temporal power in the fight against false doctrine. The Independent, Roger Williams (d. 1683), repudiated by his own sect in Massachusetts on grounds of heresy, went so far as to deny to the State the right of demand-

374

ing membership of a Christian body, the observance of the Sabbath, or the taking of an oath by its subjects. He founded the State of Providence, the first in the world to extend complete tolerance even to non-Christians. He was the first to contemplate the holding of State office by an atheist, the first to utter a serious doubt as to whether Christians had the right to take the Indians' land from them. The great service rendered by the Independents to civilization is that they raised the idea of tolerance from a dream of humanists to a reality in the State. During the brief regime of the Commonwealth, Oliver Cromwell established it, at least so far as the mutual relations between the Protestant sects went: while the writings of John Milton handed it down to the eighteenth century, which then, gradually, brought it towards effective operation.

The Independents, who to-day call themselves Congregationalists, are still fighting for the complete religious liberty of the individual. Their point of view found expression in the famous Savoy Declaration of 1658; the *credo* adopted in 1833 by the Congregational Union of England and Wales has no compulsory character. Further, they allow complete freedom to the individual parish; since, in contradistinction to the Presbyterians, they have not the ambition to erect a Kingdom of God which is to cover the whole earth; questions of organization are, with them, secondary. They recognize the individual parish, but instead of presbyteries, have only free conferences of parishes, which, in their turn, cannot arrive at majority decisions, of a compulsory kind. For extreme and exceptional cases only, they reserve the possibility of turning a parish out of the Union. The distinction between ministers and laymen, which appears strongly even with the Presbyterians, is with them practically non-existent. Their leader, Henry Barrow (d. 1593), inclined to an aristocratic type of parish government, on Calvinist lines; to-day it is customary to give to the pastor certain directive functions, always however as the mouthpiece of his congregation, while the more radical sections dispense with the office altogether, and give every member of the congregation the right to preach if and when the voice of the Holy Ghost should prompt them.

The very existence of Congregationalists in Anglo-Saxondom is a fact of great significance in any estimate of the character of English piety. For this is no tiny handful of people, but among the most considerable of the Free Churches (1928: 415,083 full members). It proves that English Christianity is not, after all, so closely chained to an organized Church as might be suggested by Anglicanism and Presbyterianism, but includes a notable minority of evangelical individualists. Moreover, since these individualists have not been compelled for any length of time – the Commonwealth period, after all, constitutes but a brief exception – to face the problem of organizing the majority of a great nation in terms of their ideal, they have been able to carry the individualistic idea of Continental Protestantism through to its ultimate implications. Not that the Congregationalists deny their Anglo-Saxon inheritance. They are religious Individualists, of a type as authentic as any Germany can show, but Individualists who lack any strong doctrinal interest. Especially in the seventeenth century, the history of Independency is a story of schisms and splits, going far to divide the parent stem into infinitesimal filaments: but all these conflicts did not rage round the great doctrinal controversies of the theology of the time, such as the Real Presence and Predestination. Some enthusiastic member of a congregation advocated a new and strange ritual, declared that the Kingdom of Christ was arrived, or to be expected immediately, and at once a swarm of adherents followed in his steps and founded a new congregation. Or, no less often, the impulse came from some wretched personal difference. Pettiness and sectionalism were painfully rife in a body that, at any rate for the first century of its existence, was recruited almost exclusively from the lowest classes in the population, while the middle classes went with the Presbyterians. (In more recent times, the stress laid by the Independents on the idea of Tolerance has won them friends of all sorts from among the higher social grades.) It has also been proved, abundantly, that there is a bad side as well as a good to the absence of any sort of State organization, any central supervision, any check on the hasty formation of new foundations. Independency has assuredly shown that it is an important and splendid form of realization of the Protestant ideal, a wholesome antidote to an overweening sacerdotalism or the abuse of the Church as a mere buttress of the State: its history, however, also shows that it is not the one ideal form of Protestant organization.

§ 6

Almost every sect that arose out of the welter of Reformation radicalism has struck root in England. At first, the Dutch Independents were in close contact with almost all such tendencies. Impossible, therefore, to say, with any precision, how many sects developed in the soil of Independency, later branching off from it, and how many were fed directly from the spring of German reform. Certainly, the link between the Independents and the *Baptists* is a very close one. Here, at last, is an English sect actually building itself upon a dogma – the rejection of infant baptism. Characteristically enough, however, this dogma could not maintain itself there as the basis of congregation-formation, in face of the different orientation of the English mind. The specific dogma of the sect plays no part in the writings of the most famous of Baptists, the tinker of blessed memory, John Bunyan. And the split among the Baptists arose not on the issue of infant baptism, but on the Calvinist dilemma, Free Will or Grace? In the seventeenth and eighteenth centuries, there were bitter fights between General Baptists (Arminian and Unitarian) and Particular Baptists (orthodox Calvinist) which led to far-reaching divisions. The question of infant baptism itself amounted to no more than a discussion as to whether those who had not been re-baptized could be admitted to full communion in the Baptist Church, or whether the latter must be limited to the close communion of the re-baptized, which would have grouped all others in a wider circle of adherents round the nucleus. In the nineteenth century, open communion was victorious all along the line; only a few isolated groups of Strict Baptists adhere, now, to the former type. To-day the Baptists are a denomination with the tolerant ideas of freedom and the loose organization of the Independents, and, like them, have experienced continual splits and reunions. Their central organization is the Baptist Union of Great Britain and Ireland. They were strongly influenced by the missionary spirit of Wesley, the great Methodist; one of the greatest 'home missioners' of the nineteenth century, Charles Haddon Spurgeon (d. 1892) came from their ranks: they have also done pioneer work in the foreign mission field. William Carey's Baptist Missionary Society (1792) was the first really successful English Missionary Society. The number of adult Baptists in England is (1928) 415,083; in the United States there are estimated to be some 7·8 millions.

§ 7

The Unitarians are a sect founded by Fausto Sozzini (d. 1604) in Poland, which denies the divinity of Christ.

In the seventeenth and eighteenth centuries they made converts from among Anglicans and Presbyterians; grew by adhesions from the Baptists; and finally shared in the collapse of English Presbyterianism. The organization of Unitarian parishes is partly Presbyterian, partly Independent. In 1842 came a threat to their very existence, since án immense fund, bequeathed to them by Lady Sarah Hewley (d. 1710), which had provided finance for their chapels and the salaries of their incumbents, was taken from them by the House of Lords and assigned to the orthodox Presbyterians. A special law of Sir Robert Peel's (1844) did, however, rescue a portion of their property for them. In the eighteenth century, the greater number of their adherents deserted them for other sects – especially for Congregationalism. There remained a small band of outspoken Rationalists, who, like the scientist, Joseph Priestley (d. 1804), and the Radical reformer, Harriet Martineau (d. 1876), found satisfaction in a subtle and somewhat dryly intellectual form of Christianity. Under the influence of German theology, and, above all, of James Martineau (d. 1900), the rationalism of such groups was developed into an intelligent but not very original system of modern Protestant religiosity. The Unitarians are now the solitary English sect recruited mainly from the upper classes. They support Manchester College, Oxford, which provides undenominational theological training, and are, further, responsible for the foundation bequeathed by the merchant, Robert Hibbert (d. 1849) – the Hibbert Lectures and the *Hibbert Journal*, designed to promote religious education in a comprehensive and wholly undenominational form. To-day, when Unitarian views are no longer taboo even in the State Church, and Congregationalists, with their complete freedom of belief, have won for themselves a certain social position, such attraction as the Unitarian sect ever possessed in a country where their definite and dogmatic programme was temperamentally alien, has dwindled away. They claim some 80,000 adherents. Since 1882 they have been loosely associated, rather on the Congregationalist model, in a National Conference of Unitarian, Liberal Christian, and Kindred Organizations.

§ 8

The mystics of the Reformation, too, left their mark on England. About the middle of the seventeenth century appear the Quakers, founded by George Fox, whose singular personality shows English democracy and primitive Christian mysticism in most original blend. The Quakers are opposed to any kind of Church organization, condemned by their radicals as superfluous and dangerous, by their moderates as superfluous and irrelevant. They oppose both Anglicanism and Presbyterianism, and even Independency, on the ground that the Independents still recognized the parochial idea, failed to take the equality of mankind seriously, and, at any rate in the seventeenth century, still took the strict Protestant attitude to the Bible. The Quakers form no organized congregations: they are a 'Society of Friends,' united for mutual edification. Their service has no set form: any man or woman among those assembled for worship may speak (or, more rarely, sing) as the spirit moves them. They have no creed, and for them the Bible, though treated with reverence, is in no sense indispensable to piety or the knowledge of God. Sacraments are of no primary importance with them. They do not expect any return of Christ, in the body: the historical Christ to them means little. But they hold that the spiritual Christ, whom alone they recognize, is constantly in their midst. In the beginning, they often testified their objection to all forms of Church organization by open disturbances, and sought to distinguish themselves by the use of a special old-fashioned garb of extreme simplicity, and the disregard of all forms of class distinction. Thus, they would not uncover in presence of the King, and addressed everyone as 'thou.' They would not take an oath, pay tithe, or have anything to do with military service. For this they had to endure persecution by the State under the Restoration and far into the eighteenth century. To-day these exterior differences have been practically dropped. After the usual contests and splits, the Quakers have finally settled into a loose association, without a regular ministry, but with occasionally a brother or sister specially appointed for conducting missions[4]: they have made peace with the State; they allow their members to be married in Church; they no longer insist on complete non-resistance; in the World War (and before that, in the American War of Independence) some of their members even served in the army although the vast majority and the official organization of Friends stood firm in maintaining the Fifth Commandment and were staunch opponents of conscription; the only point on which they have been absolutely rigid is the refusal to take the oath, and on that the State met them by permitting them a special form of affirmation.

In English Church history, the Quakers are a phenomenon of immense significance. Their number is very small; there are only (1928) 398 'meetings' with 19,044 members. But over the whole area of

Christian charity, they have played a part out of all proportion to their tiny membership. Since they have been in a perpetual minority and therefore had to rely on their power to stir others to common action, they have, further, always stood for a highly spiritual and constructive toleration. To them belong John Woolman (d. 1772) who even before Wilberforce preached against slavery, John Bellers (d. 1725), the father of Christian Socialism, Elizabeth Fry (d. 1845) the reformer of the prison system, and Joseph Lancaster (d. 1838) the founder of the elementary school, as well as William Penn (d. 1718), the founder of the tolerance State of Pennsylvania in America. A special kind of continuation school for adults of the working class, with a strongly religious tinge, the Adult School, was established by the Quakers. At the same time, they were certainly no unworldly pietists. From the very beginning, they played a prominent part in trade and industry, as witness such men as the cocoa manufacturers, Cadbury and Rowntree, founders of modern garden cities and owners of newspapers: like the semi-pacifist *Daily News*. Above all, during the war, the Quakers took the commandment, 'Love your enemies,' seriously; their care for German military and civil prisoners during the war and, too, their mighty works of charity for the defeated foe have brought home even to the greatest sceptic that English Christianity is a reality.

Similar principles – the rejection of creed, liturgy, and Church constitution, and an ascetic temper – combined with the sternest rejection of all unbelievers, are found in another sect formed round the Anglican clergyman, John Darby (1800–82), in Plymouth and Dublin, in 1827 as Darbysts or Plymouth Brethren – a sect that soon split off into a large number of smaller ones. During the war they, with the Quakers, formed the backbone of the conscientious objection to military service.

A chiliastic sect, proclaiming the immediate return of Christ on earth, was formed round Edward Irving (1792–1834), a Scottish minister and friend of Carlyle, under the name of the Catholic Apostolic Church. Its officers (bishop, presbyter, deacons, apostles) aim at reconstructing the primitive form of Christianity. After the death of the last of the 'apostles' (in 1901) who were to witness the return of Christ, it has tended to vanish away, so far as the public are concerned. A similar sect, found here and there in industrial areas, is the Christadelphians, founded by a clergyman, John Thomas by name (d. 1871).

§ 9

The outstanding figure in the history of the English Church, the only one who in force of personality and range of effect can stand with the great Continental Reformers, is John Wesley (1703–91). He founded Methodism, the Church of the lower middle class, at a time when Anglicanism, absorbed in a narrow sense of its own dignity, was dying, when Dissent had sacrificed any kind of freshness or life of its own to the mere struggle for existence: when religion in England seemed to be no more than the mechanical continuation of a traditional Christian form. Wesley, in founding Methodism, restored to the Dissenters faith in their own principles. On the Church he forced, to its own incalculable advantage, a real fight for life, inasmuch as Methodism threatened to deprive it of its last adherents among the lower orders. Moreover, he discovered new methods of organizing a Church for the masses, and showed that, inside modern society, it is possible to fill a whole people with Christian spirit, without the help of the State, nay in opposition to it. Actually, his foundation of Methodism as a denomination is the least important part of his work. Rather is he the grand organizer of Protestantism itself, inasmuch as he saved the Evangelical Churches from either sinking into powerless little sects or withering up in sterilized obedience to the State.

Christianity was to him a reality. As a young Oxford fellow of markedly High Church tendency, he founded a 'Methodist' conventicle in Oxford in 1729, with definite activities – frequent communion, set hours for prayer, visits to the sick and to prisons, education of deserted and neglected children. He fell under the influence of the Moravians, and learned from his intercourse with them to expect a specifically Christian life to begin in a sudden conversion, whose onset is marked by weeping, wailing, and ecstatic pangs, such as can be prepared and encouraged by methodical penitential exercises and the stimulation of dread before the imminent day of judgment. He brings the Gospel to all those whom the Church has neglected – to the settlers in Georgia, to the Welsh, to whom he preaches in their own language (he revived the Celtic tongue in Wales, and made Methodism the national religion of the Principality), to the sick and the prisoners, to the proletariate in the big cities, and the men and women of the country-side, whose alienation from the Church was none the less real that they often dwelt in a dim darkness of superstition with a superficial varnish of Christianity on the top of

E. 381 B B

it. Bursting all the bonds of dogma, bidding defiance to all tradition he preaches not only in the churches but at the cross-roads, in the crowded squares of the cities and in the market-places of the country. For he sees that the old formulas of the hierarchy are inadequate to the new mass-problems of the present: and acts on his insight. He sends out lay preachers, as John Wycliffe once did: organizes the hordes of the newly saved in tiny groups meeting regularly for mutual instruction in Bible classes, led by an experienced layman: builds up, out of these trained lay helpers, an organization of overseers and elders to aid in missionary work and provide for the carrying on of the church by intensive propaganda among the children. Gradually, he rises to be a figure in the international history of the church almost as great as Luther or Calvin. The whole of the contemporary structure of home mission work, the whole Sunday-school system, the whole of the provision for drunkards and fallen girls, the whole of the organized crusade against alcoholism, begging, and immorality, derives from Wesley. Methodism is the parent of every effort to organize the Christian masses in groups for special action or treatment – in associations of young men, young women, or parents. Methodism is, again, the parent of the employment of wordly activities for Church purposes, as in bazaars and social teas. Notable, too, is Wesley's influence on the Church in Scotland. The stamp of Wesleyan intensity is deep on an organization that, to-day, is still able co reach the individual, even in the big towns.

Wesley, however, is also a figure in political history. He is one of the most significant parents of the democratic organizations of the new State.

Methodism has shown that it is possible to hold together masses and direct them to one great political aim. Methodist ministers worked in the Chartist movement, and many leaders in the rising Labour movement were Methodist lay preachers. In the last resort, it is from the Methodist 'class' that the technique of modern democracy was learned, the formation of gigantic parties which, for all their colossal size, are adaptable tools in the hands of small leading groups. The 'class' gave the key to Methodist organization and its discipline. Wesley introduced into it the appeal to instinct and the stimulation of the human joy in battle. And his class became readily adaptable to political organization. Every party has now its local party unit; the lay form of the Methodist class. The paid peripatetic preacher has in politics become the official propagandist, and the Methodist conference the party congress, which nominally is there to give the leaders their policy, but in normal times is merely a body for registering decisions already arrived at by the controlling caucus.[5]

In itself, Wesley's organization was compatible with the Church; but, in fact, it split it. The well-bred Anglican mind could only see with horror the unusual, loud and often positively screaming methods of the great evangelist, and even more so, of the disciples who outdid their master. The fact that he preached not only to churchgoers but to all Dissenters, made him doctrinally suspect. His adherents were excluded from communion in the church, and his preachers excluded from the pulpit. Thereupon they celebrated the communion themselves, and, from 1784 on, were ordained priests by Wesley himself. This made a complete breach with the Church. From that time on, Methodism was a sect.

Intrinsically, it is the very reverse of that. No Church lays more stress on organization, or emphasizes more strongly the necessity of making all men members of the Church of Christ. But the narrowness and externalism that constitute the shadow on every hierarchy are alien to Methodism. Vital in it, too, is the Free Church spirit of the Independents, for whom forms, in themselves, are worthless, and to be judged only by the extent to which they do or do not promote the main end. Methodism is a Revivalist movement, tied to no particular form of Christianity, but exerting a lasting influence both on the Church and the sects.

The organization Wesley created is a brilliant amalgam of Independent, Presbyterian and Catholic strains. It is by far the most striking instance, in the history of the Church, of the English genius for handling men. From the Independents, Wesley took the small congregation, with a well-marked lay element, which alone ensures effective Christian life. Nor did he stop there. The smallest cell in the Methodist organism is not the congregation but the class, in which twenty to thirty persons of the same sex meet at least once a week for mutual religious edification under the direction of lay local preachers or other religious individuals (leaders, exhorters). Every Methodist must belong to such a class; it is the backbone of the whole organization. Classes are then associated in societies, and they in turn unite to form circuits. These circuits were originally conceived of as largish territorial units; as the organization has grown, however, they have gradually become parochial. In the quarterly circuit assemblies lay members, in so far as they are concerned in the leadership of classes, both sit and vote, as workers in Christ. The executive, however, is monarchical: the superintendent rules like a little Catholic Bishop, nominating both pastors, stewards, and class leaders. Over the whole rules the Methodist Conference, modelled on the Presbyterian General Assembly, but recording Wesley's strongly hierarchical will in that it was originally conceived as an assembly of ministers only. No place in Wesley's Church-State for the logic-chopping democracy of any inspired tinker.

After Wesley's death, however, Methodism became involved in the great struggle between clerical organization and the lay urge for liberty. Methodism resounded with the contest between hierarchs and democrats, degenerating only too often into personalities, and finally split under the strain. The air buzzed with controversy: doctrinal differences were frequently employed to mask personal incompatibilities. Wesley himself was an Arminian, and would have nothing to do with the Calvinist doctrine of election. In 1797 the first split occurred, when the Methodist New Connexion broke off. They accept the democratic organization of the Independents; their classes choose their own leaders, and laymen are represented in their Conference. In 1810 came another big schism; the Primitive Methodists, under Hugh Bourne and William Clowes, founded a new Conference in which the lay element was strongly represented. Their strength was principally in the Midlands. In Cornwall, about the same time, William O'Bryan (d. 1868) gathered the malcontents in the small community of Bible Christians.

Finally, official Methodism had to yield to democratic pressure. A sort of two-chamber system was introduced into the Conference: Pastoral Session and Representative Session (i.e. Laymen): under which all spiritual questions, as before, are in essentials decided by the pastorate, and the effective influence of the layman is confined to matters of business and finance. With the clearing away of the main issue, it would seem as though the reunion of the divided Methodist sections were only a matter of time. At present, however, the following separate organizations exist (figures for 1928):

1. Wesleyan Methodists (Wesley's church) with 1,376,964 adherents (members and Sunday scholars).

2. Primitive Methodists, 609,156.

3. United Methodist Church, founded in 1907 by a union of the New Connexion of 1797 with a series of insignificant offshoots from the years 1815-49. Membership 384,071

4. Independent Methodists, organized quite independently, without Wesley's stages: 35,397; and Wesleyan Reform Union of similar strength (35,857) and principles.

Further, the Methodist movement which revived the old Cymric speech in Wales also gave birth to the purely Welsh Calvinistic Methodist (Presbyterian) Church of Wales, with 84,058 adherents, which has gone over to the Presbyterians.

The Methodist seed has produced a mighty harvest in America. The number of its adherents there is far greater than in Europe, and the development of the organization there has followed lines of its own. The Methodists claim some 32 millions of adherents all over the world. The reunion of the different bodies seems to be imminent.

§ 10

Methodism's most modern offshoot is the Salvation Army, the creation of the genius of a Methodist preacher, William Booth. Wesley went to the lowest of the low, and spoke to them in their own language: he was a masterly organizer and could hold recruits to his flag as well as make them. A hundred and fifty years later, William Booth addressed himself to the old problem along new lines. The destitution with which he had to cope was more formidable than that Wesley had to deal with: the slums now held tens of thousands instead of hundreds, and the human beings in them were sunk in a deeper misery, bore a heavier burden of hereditary wrong, and represented stocks more tainted with the degeneration of the life of the great city than their predecessors in Wesley's day. To reach these people, Booth had to employ means more crude, more vociferous and more hysterical than Wesley's. Cheap mass-suggestion, violent assaults upon the nerves, banal theatricality, the exercise of religious hypnotism through dancing, shrieking, and barbaric music reminiscent of the religious orgies of primitive peoples – all these instruments were employed by him with the skill of a virtuoso. In addition, he revived the old devices of the popular missioner for bending to religious ends those images and instincts that cannot be broken; Christian texts were set to barrel-organ tunes; the various corps of the Army competed against each other, with all the apparatus of modern sport, to bring the largest number of saved souls to the stool of repentance within the shortest possible time. Booth's genius, however, showed itself most conspicuously in his using the primitive human need to feel oneself part of a great mass: this instinct he utilized in the creation of his 'Army.' Its immense success proves that there is much more than a mere trick in its underlying idea: Booth was able to rouse in the town-bred degenerate the very same instincts that once inspired the Crusader and again proved their force in the Order of Jesuits. With the aid of his Army, ruled by him, like a Jesuit general, with the autocratic authority of the founder of a religion, he built up a mighty edifice of social activities. It ranges from shelters for the homeless and homes for the magdalenes of the great cities and institutions of all kinds for the young, to agricultural settlements in Canada; a special form of salvation has been worked out for every form of social misery – juvenile crime, alcoholism, prostitution, vagrancy, and so on. Natural enough that the more sensitive should avert his eyes in disgust from a Christian propaganda which at first used the low pothouse and the doubtful ballet advertisement for Christian purposes; certainly, the adjustment of Christendom to the existing facts, which began with the elevation of the teaching of a Jewish sect to a world religion, has never produced more questionable results. (The most unpalatable of those devices have long been abandoned.) What William Booth and his successors offered to the East End pariah was hardly Christianity, but, at best, a nameless religion which, by devious routes of fear, horror, and mass-suggestion of the most varied kind, created a bridge back to Christianity. In the long run, the Salvation Army has adopted milder methods and is now slowly developing into a kind of lower-class dissenting body. To the student of English life, however, just the crudest of its forms of propaganda were interesting; they show to what extent unredeemed primitive life and crudely primitive instincts still exist in England, beneath the veneer of culture and education.

CHAPTER IV

IMMEDIATE ISSUES OF ENGLISH CHURCH LIFE

§ 1

A GENERAL picture of the organization of religious life in England has been given in the preceding pages. Almost every possible variety is there represented. To the extreme right stand Catholicism, and its Anglican twin-brother the High Church party; to the extreme left, Quakerism, essentially mystic, with a minimum of organization; between them, every conceivable variation, from rigid to loose: Low Church Anglicanism, Presbyterianism, Methodism, Anabaptism, Congregationalism. The content is as varied as the form: on the one hand, Presbyterian groups lay strong emphasis on Calvinist Predestination: on the other, Quakers waive dogma altogether; although orthodoxy is almost universal on Christological questions, the Unitarians altogether deny the Sonship of Christ.

It is habitual to note this multiplicity of form with regret only. Certainly, it has results that are serious, and some that are positively grotesque. There is an immense waste of effort, when every tiny village in Scotland has at least two national churches, and, as often as not, a Congregational, a Methodist, and possibly a Baptist chapel in addition, where one minister would amply suffice for the needs of the population. There is an immense waste of effort when every enterprise, whether it be the rescue of inebriates or a mission to the heathen, is conducted simultaneously from half a dozen centres at once. If, for every purpose, the number of workers has got to be multiplied by six, there must inevitably be a lowering of the standard of work – a result patent in the case of the Theological Training Colleges, which every denomination tries to maintain if at all possible. Something, too, is lost when organized Churches, of nearly identical doctrine and form, are so far from mutual recognition that their adherents carry on the most stupid heresy hunts and internal feuds. Again, the financial reactions of competition between denominations are often distressing. A rich man, of unknown Church affiliation, may and often does find himself the object of most painful solicitation when he takes up his residence in a new place, since his adherence may decide the very existence of an entire parish.

All this is true, but there is another side to the picture, and one

387

frequently overlooked. Keen competition among the denominations produces a wealth of religious life, such as is hardly known elsewhere. No Church, not even the Established, can rest on its laurels. It must strive to influence the children. It must offer something to the individual at every crisis of his existence: must take up a position on the question of Temperance, Housing, Hours of Labour, Strikes, Education. The pastor has to endeavour to reach the individual by domiciliary visits. The result is small parishes and a close-knit organization, in which the individual is not merely a receptive object but, within certain limits, a co-operating subject in spiritual life. All this, of course, is particularly true of the sects which, possessing no ancient property, have to rely wholly on voluntary gifts: but it is true also, in very large measure, even of the Church of England. Ever since Wesley forced competition upon it, it too sees the believer as a human being, of intrinsic worth, who can and must be drawn into co-operation.

Each individual, moreover, can find a religious form to suit him. The obstinate insistence of the Establishment on being the one and only Church of England has this one good side that no solemn act of State is required before leaving it to join, say, the Methodists or the Congregationalists. One ceases to pay Church rates – which are not legally enforceable – and pays subscriptions to the denomination that happens to suit one better: that is all. There need be no secession, no painful scene in the presence of judges or priests. True, every one is, by heredity and education, member of a certain Church and, even in England, such a step cannot be taken without the severing of strong bonds of association: but it is infinitely easier than the corresponding action in most Continental States. The fact, too, that every one can select the religious group whose doctrine, form of organization and general religious type (to say nothing of its social grade!) best suit him, makes the number of lukewarm uninterested and refractory spirits in the Church infinitely smaller than in other countries, where every one is born into a Church which he cannot easily leave, and where his finding spiritual satisfaction is often a dubious risk. Had England nothing but one State Church, the alienation of the masses from the Church might have occurred to a much greater extent. But though to a very large extent the Church has lost the workers, the denominations saved them for Christianity. And in the course of its contest with the denominations, the Church itself has learned ways and means of winning new territories for itself among the lower classes.

§ 2

Is there any possibility of a reunion of the Church and Dissenters? For one whose eyes are fixed on the differences between them, and on the unexhilarating spectacle of daily strife, the question may seem hardly worth discussing. The entire Anglican right wing, which gives tone to English religious life, insists on the necessity of an episcopate going back, in unbroken succession, to Christ. Without such an episcopate and an ordained priesthood, there can be no Church. With such views, how can there be any possible union between the exalted prelate of the right, and the Methodist lay preacher, who may earn his bread by peddling herrings? How can a Church with such views find place for the direct access to God of the Quaker?

So long, however, as the spirit of Christ moves in His Churches, the apparently impossible must be pursued; nor is it perhaps wholly vain to work for such an end. Hard as it is to find any point of contact of the extremes on right and left, there are groups between for whom such contact does exist: groups which, meeting daily in common social and political work, have learned the mutual respect of allies. Among a people as gifted politically as the English, politics itself is bound to force to the front the question: Has the Church, has organized Christianity, no part to play in the solution of contemporary political problems? And where such questions are put seriously, the answer is bound to be that the solution can come from no one Church, but must come from a union of all Churches.

All the Churches are painfully aware of the fact that their influence is declining, and the modern generation turning from them. Already evident at the turn of the century, non-attendance and indifferentism have reached alarming dimensions since the war. Gone is the old tradition of Sunday observance; in the big cities, Sunday is the most convenient day for all kinds of worldly pleasures. Churchgoing has ceased to be the normal national habit. The war and the post-war period have seen a grave decline in public morals. Entries to the clerical profession have fallen off seriously. Indifference or even open hostility to the Church prevails both among the workers and the educated; patent in London, it is penetrating into the provinces and even into Presbyterian Scotland.

Yet the position is far from hopeless. At bottom, the modern coquetting with Eastern wisdom, Spiritualism and Occultism merely is a yearning for religion, that has lost its way. The powerful Catholic tendencies in the Anglican Church, the increasing power of Catholicism, and the religious bent to be found in many groups of younger men and women, prove that it is not religious sentiment that is lacking, but merely that the Churches have no answer to give to the religious questionings of the day. Can the old message suffice, in a period of class war and of the rise of the oppressed against the capitalist organization of society throughout the world? Have the Churches nothing to say on the issue of Imperialism versus Pacifism? must they always be merely the guardians of the old? is it not their task to help the incoherent new to achieve form and life?

The spirit of Christian Socialism, which found its most powerful exponent in Charles Kingsley, is not yet extinct, in the Broad Church party and all its affiliations. The more the worker turns his back upon the Church, the more insistent must be the query whether the Church is not in part to blame. Has she really nothing to do with the social order? True, in principle she can neither oppose nor support any given social order, whether the capitalist or the Socialist; but can she, must she not demand of any social order with which the Church can co-operate a certain minimum of Christian conditions? Must she not condemn certain forms' of money-making, certain ways of treating other human beings? must she not demand for every human soul a certain minimum of leisure, of opportunity for recreation and self-development? Cannot, must not the Church, here and now, adopt some Church-social, or Christian-social programme, which while avoiding any and every partisan formulation, at the same time perhaps condemns absolutely every form of economic warfare, whether strike or lock-out, and insists on the payment for every kind of work of a legal minimum wage?

Further, must the Church see herself as the loyal servant of the State, and approve or at best pass over in silence any and every expression of the policy of might in international affairs? Is it not her task, as an international spiritual force, to influence the public opinion of all nations to see in her a moral counterpoise to the ruthless nationalism of State power? Is it not possible to organize a movement of revolt against the oppression of small nations by a great, against the open breach of a solemn treaty obligation, a movement that, supported by Press and in Parliament, might be strong enough to arrest the violence of the violent, even in his own country? Is it not the duty of the Church to brand as un-Christian and immoral some of the methods of colonial Imperialism, and above all, war in every form?

even, in case of necessity, to call for disobedience to the State? Is not the present epoch, when the naked brutality of economic interests seems to rule the world, expressly designed to call for the resistance of spirit against matter, of the eternal against the temporal, of Christendom against the international Cæsaro-papism of capital? What hope is there, for the higher values in life, save the reassertion, in modern terms, by the Church, of the mediæval Cluniast-Gregorian ideal of the primacy of spiritual values, expressed in modern terms, but expressed with the utmost definiteness? In view of this life-and-death struggle, in which the Christian idea is actually involved, are not all the things, which actually divide the Churches, ridiculous trifles? not only differences like those between Wesleyan and Primitive Methodists, but even the differences between Roman Catholics and Protestant Independents?

Such a line of thought is widespread among the intellectual leaders of English Christians everywhere; it is the strongest proof – if proof were necessary – of the vitality of Christian ideas in modern life; it is, in part, the spiritual parallel to the political Imperialism that dominates the English mind.

In 1920, the Lambeth Conference issued its famous report on Christianity and the Problems of Industrialism; and 1924 witnessed, in Birmingham, the Conference on Christian Politics, Economics and Ethics (shortly known as Copec), which was attended by representatives both of the Established and of the Free Churches, and, unofficially, by many Catholics. At this, questions of the day like Divorce, Prostitution, Gambling, Drink, the Cinema, Capital Punishment, Wages, Nationalization of Banking, Nationalism and War, were handled carefully and definitely, from a Christian standpoint. The Conference rejected economic capitalism as un-Christian and came out in favour of progressive nationalization, adequate wages, and the removal of the grosser inequalities of wealth – subject to a recognition of class distinctions – a programme that must have struck all those who, consciously or unconsciously, are in the habit of regarding the Church as the guardian of the existing order, as positively revolutionary. Politically, the Conference accepted democracy based on thorough political education as the highest form of State, and worked out, in connexion therewith, a programme for the international relations of States, which, while recognizing the right of every people to its own independent form of State, laid stress, in particular, on the view that the national rights of States are accompanied by duties towards a higher inter-

391

national community: condemned exploitation and forcible Europeanization in colonial policy; hailed the League of Nations with enthusiasm, and, without going so far as to condemn war without exception, promised support to all organizations pledged to working against it. A political programme for the Churches of this character, representing, as it does, not a few isolated idealists but the most influential representatives of the entire Church life of England, is a noteworthy sign of the times.

In this spirit, churchmen of every camp have, ever since 1900, been seeking some kind of union among the various Church organizations. However impossible as it may appear to sweep away, at a stroke, the differences between Church and sects, ever since about 1900 leading men on either side have been actively engaged on an effort to clear the air. Broadly speaking, the ideal at which they aim is that of an organization, for the Anglican Church, comprehending both the Establishment and the denominations, with the strongly knit State Church as its kernel, surrounded by a series of loosely affiliated Free Churches. Any sort of practical formulation of such an idea is still quite beyond the bounds of possibility. Conferences of Churchmen of the left, and Free Churchmen of the right wing have reached, however, the point of exchanging respectful greetings. More and more frequently, leading Nonconformists preachers are invited to preach from Anglican pulpits, and co-operate with Anglican prelates in Festival services. True, there are loud protests from the Ultras on either side, who, so far, have still the majority of the people behind them. Nevertheless, the effort after a genuinely English form of compromise, leaving the issues in dispute to sleep while co-operating in practical work, goes steadily on, and, it would seem, not without success. What is in a country like England, perhaps the sharpest line of demarcation between Church and Dissent, the social gulf, begins to lose its importance. In November 1918, the King, the official head of the Church, took part in a thanksgiving service of all the London Free Churches, the one-time rebellious heretics. An event like this cannot fail to leave a deep impression upon the English mind.

At the same time, there is no remission of the effort of the right wing of the Church for an approach, first to an Anglican, then to a Protestant, and, ultimately, to an œcumenical Christian union. Ever since 1867, the Lambeth Conferences have aimed at an increasing unity of Anglicanism throughout the world.

In 1845–46 an Evangelical Alliance movement, originally with a very strong anti-Catholic bias, started among the Scottish groups associated with Thomas Chalmers; but, despite the vague enthusiasm with which it was greeted by Frederick William IV of Prussia, it completely missed the tide. A new epoch in the international activity of Anglicanism was marked by the Hague Peace Conference of 1907, when English pacifists like Allan Baker and W. T. Stead, then editor of the *Review of Reviews*, placed themselves at the head of a pacifist movement on a Christian basis. Out of this developed the peace efforts made by English and German pastors in 1908–9. At the time of the outbreak of the World War, their work had resulted in the formation of a World Alliance for Promoting International Friendship through the Christian Churches. At its conference in Beatenberg, in the summer of 1920, the Archbishop of Canterbury became President of this league, which thus constituted an important parallel to the International peace efforts being made by American and Scandinavian Protestants.

An effort is, further, being made under the pacifist neo-Gregorian flag, to achieve the apparently impossible, i.e. the reunion of Protestantism with Roman and Greek Catholicism. What is in question here is, of course, rather a patient endeavour to create a favourable mental atmosphere for co-operation, than any Quixotic dream of inducing the policy of the Vatican to recognize the equality of other Churches. Ever since the days of the Oxford Movement, there has been a persistent effort to arrive at some measure of practical, if not of theoretical, understanding with Rome; an effort greatly encouraged by the secret arrangement entered into between England and the Vatican in relation to Ireland (cf. page 359). An association of Free Catholics has recently launched a plan for uniting all who, whatever religion they profess, believe in the necessity of a visible Church of sacramental character, in an effort to carry a programme of an undenominational kind for the reconstruction of human society. Despite its Catholic name, this association numbers not only Anglicans but prominent Nonconformists among its adherents. Efforts of the right Anglican wing to negotiate with Rome at Malines since 1921 have already been referred to (cf. page 360). When the effort at a *rapprochement* with Rome broke on the obstinate resistance of the Vatican, the Lambeth Conference, in course of time, established relations both with the Old Catholics and with the Greek Church. Old Catholic priests are recognized by the Anglican Church. In 1888, moreover, German Protestants were admitted to Anglican communion. At the same time, the Lambeth Quadrilateral laid down the principles on which a reunion between the Anglican Church and the world outside it could be effected. In 1908, in association with the Lambeth Conference, a Pan-Anglican Congress was held, for which the widest publicity was secured by the admission of simple clerics and laymen from the entire Anglican world. Since 1908 an Eastern Churches Committee has been addressing itself most seriously to all Greek-Catholic questions. In 1915, for example, it arranged that all the Serbian theological students who had fled before the German invasion of their country could continue their studies in England. In August, 1920, the Lambeth Conference addressed a great Manifesto to the world, designed to lay the bases for Church reunion. What was contemplated there was not a reabsorption in Anglicanism of the Free Churches or any Continental sects, but the erection of a World Church, in which the Church of England would be only one among a series of equivalent Churches. Invitation was extended to every Church based on the Bible and the Apostles', or Nicene Creed, on baptism and communion, and accepting an authoritarian priesthood – i.e. Roman and Greek Catholicism, German Protestantism, and the greater part of the English sects. For a speedy success for this step no one can hope. But the issue of such an invitation by the head of the English Church, at a time when the shouts of victory in war were resounding in the air, constitutes a landmark in the history of civilization.

There is a tendency, on the Continent, either to ignore this spiritual Imperialism of Anglicanism, or to dismiss it with a shrug of the shoulders as one more sign of English hypocrisy. It is pointed out that none of the friendly gestures of the English clergy prevented the campaign of vilification that did more than the blockade or the Peace of Versailles to erect barriers between the two nations, nor the extension of the blockade long after the conclusion of the Armistice. The English missionary is recalled, with his Bible draped with the Union Jack, and all clerical efforts after unity are put down as spiritual variations on the tune of Rule Britannia. This is both exceedingly unjust and exceedingly short-sighted. There certainly are camp followers of the movement, notably in the Press, who are more concerned with politics than with Christianity; many of them. There is much in the professions of friendship issued by the clergy and others, both before and since the war, which reveals a blank ignorance of any point of view but the British. Further it is obvious that a real success in this

394

spiritual Imperialism would be of the greatest possible utility to the political Imperialism of England. But none of these objections touches the fundamentals of the neo-Gregorian idea. Every powerful Church in the plenitude of Christian life must strive for world acceptance. That is what it is for. As to the impregnation of the entire movement by authentic Christian fire there can be no doubt, however many political beggars may warm their hands at it. A movement, beginning in 1845-46 with the Evangelical Alliance, and reviving in 1867 with the Lambeth Conference, is no mere by-product of war emotion, but a slowly ripening fruit of the dawning sense of responsibility and power of the Anglican Church itself. It is a phenomenon strictly parallel to the renewed strength of Roman Catholicism in the nineteenth century, a movement that dates back, in the last resort, to the Oxford Movement. There is, further, nothing hypocritical in the translation of the new Imperialism of the Chamberlain era to the religious sphere; on the contrary, the fact is but one sign among many of the healthy interrelation of political, spiritual and economic forces in English national life. As to the future of the movement, opinions will differ. If to-day, as was the case two generations ago, the world is still dominated by the questions of food and shelter only, then it will dissolve into thin air, as the Evangelical Alliance did in its time. If, however, those are right who hold that our age is yearning for new spiritual leadership after the pernicious drought of a materialistic age, a movement with the leaders of a world-wide Church behind it must be rated very seriously indeed. Any Church or any nation which stands aloof from world tendencies, condemns itself. Mere negation will not help: the task is rather to see to it that a stream rising from spiritual springs is not muddied from political swamps.

CHAPTER V
ENGLISH PIETY

§ 1

Two types of piety contend for supremacy in modern England – the Catholic mystic, and the Calvinist.

The purest expression of the Catholic mystic type is to be found in the High Church right wing of the Anglican Church. An elaborate and æsthetic ritual of worship: a technique of other-worldiness, practised by a priestly caste that, while not compulsorily celibate, is elevated by every legal and sacerdotal device, and supported by orders, male and female, grouped in loose associations of modern form: exaltation, atmosphere, the creation of moods of mystic vision – such are its ideals. This type is seldom as fully realized in the Anglican sphere as in the Roman, but the ideal is everywhere dominant there, though, of course, it is that of a minority of the nation, and of one practically confined to the upper classes. Its voice sounds clearest in the lyrics of the Caroline poets, Crashaw and Herbert, and, more recently, in the poems of Christina Rossetti.

The other, Calvinist, type, is sterner, more masculine, cruder. Native to the Puritan sects, it extended its influence even to the Anglican left wing when, after the Restoration, the top layer of the denominations passed into the ruling class. The religion, this, of a harsh and militant race, which sees ethical progress as a fight between Christ and Satan, victory as the subjection of the world to the Lord of Heaven. Life, for it, is a pilgrimage, a constant struggle with the Powers of Darkness, as described by Bunyan in a book that every Englishman knows almost by heart. Little, here, of rapturous feeling, of ecstasy, of problems for the soul; the one question that really troubles is, 'Do I belong to the Elect who are to conquer the earth for the Lord?' the one dogma that has really taken root in the popular mind, the issue of grace and predestination. The great question, for this strenuous generation, is the establishment of the Kingdom of Heaven upon earth: far more importance, therefore, attaches to the questions of Christian organization, than to 'What think ye of Christ?' or the doctrine of the Real Presence. Battle rages over the constitution of the synod and the question of State patronage; on these men go out into the wilderness, while Transubstantiation and Christology are left to the experts. Harshly and churlishly do they wrestle with their God. They give Him honour, make endless sacrifice for the fulfilment of His law, build up a structure of Christian charity to which no other Protestant country affords a parallel; and, at the same time, harbour a crass materialism that regards every flourishing business enterprise as a sign of His favour, and justify their instinctive identification of the rich with the good by the tacit Calvinist assumption that worldly success is a sign of Heavenly grace. This type of Christianity is rooted rather in the Old Testament than in the New, and derives in the last analysis from the Jewish doctrine of the holiness of works as interpreted by Saxon peasants. From the Old Testament, too, comes the doctrine, peculiar to all forms of English piety and tingling them all with what the Continental observer feels as a repulsive hypocrisy, – the idea of the English as the chosen people. Isolated observers drew attention to the intolerable arrogance of the English attitude to other nations even before 1500. Sharp periodic reactions against every kind of foreign influence have already been noted above (page 46 *seq.*). Native from the very first must have been some degree of this proud, wilfully ignorant, obtuseness; it is a family trait in the peasants of Holstein and Lower Saxony. But it was the Puritans who gave it an ethical basis, formulated by Milton – the English are what the Jews were, God's chosen people. The British Druids constituted a philosophic Cathedral for mediaeval France: the English Constantine – he was by descent a Roman of the East, but commanded the legions in Britain, when he became Emperor! – baptized the Roman Empire: Alcuin brought culture, Wycliffe religion, to the Continent of Europe![1] God, according to Milton, made a second revelation of Himself to His servants, 'and, as is His custom, first to His Englishmen.' Cromwell's court poet, Edmund Waller, held that Heaven had created this island in order to promulgate laws, hold the balance in Europe, and instil respect into the peoples of Europe. For the Republican, James Harrington (d. 1677), it was England's plain duty, in opposition to Venice, the merely selfish State, to shed the blessings of its free constitution over the entire globe, as once Rome had done.[2] Even the angels, in the most aggressive National Anthem ever composed, sing 'Rule, Britannia, Britannia rules the waves . . .' Though most Englishmen, of course, do not take these assertions more literally than national anthems are wont to be taken, there still are some, not only among the lower classes, who revel in a crass literalness and take modern Englishmen to be the bodily descendants of the old Israelites: from the Kingdom of Judah came the Jews who did not recognize

Christ and therefore have forfeited salvation; now all the blessings of the Old Testament remain with the descendants of Israel proper, the lost tribes, who once upon a time mysteriously found their way to the British shores and have ever since thrived there under the special blessing of the Lord and shall rule all the Gentiles.[3] The educated Englishman may smile at this, but the voice of the humble often utters what is there in the heart of the nation never uttered, but persistent with all the tenacity of the subconscious. It cannot be denied, that this sort of national pride has developed to a danger to all other nations, and that thus a religious sanction has been given to every form of nationalist egotism.

Moreover, a mantle of Christian love is thus cast over every national failing. The Puritan knows that even a sinner may belong to the chosen of God. Inevitable that crude materialism and theological casuistry should pervert this profound doctrine to mean that whatever the Saint of God may do, can be no sin, however evil it may look. The English Philistine subconsciously translates this into a dogma of English Puritan infallibility, which has believers more impassioned than the Papal. Puritan literature is full of the question how a man is to know whether he has the grace of God and is among the elect predestined by Him to eternal bliss, despite their sins. There is no safe mark of election, but a strong presumption of it is created by the visible blessing of God on a man's earthly doings.[4] Popular ethics, further vulgarizing this dubious interpretation, identifies the blessing of God with worldly advancement, and makes a saint of the smart salesman. Of course the position is never stated in anything like this crude fashion; on the contrary, it has been passionately attacked by every genuine English teacher, for instance, Carlyle, Dickens, and Ruskin. But the very fury of their onset shows how deeply the morality of sheer success has eaten into the English – and even more, American – soul as a dangerous by-product of Puritanism. In the sphere of foreign policy, an Imperialism, devoid of any sort of ethical or cultural fig-leaf, is, by it, provided with a cloak, which, to the Continental, remote from the *naïvetés* of Puritan materialism, is nothing but a repulsive piece of hypocrisy. In the literature of no country is national greed so mercilessly exposed. The oppression of the Irish, the exploitation of India in the early stages of colonization, the raid on the Danish fleet (in 1807), the extermination of the Australian natives, the Chinese opium war, the faithless policy of England towards Frederick the Great, the Boer War – the heaviest cannon are turned on all these actions in English political literature, some of it even contemporaneous. But such judgments, outcome as they are of an honourable repudiation of national excesses, do not alter by one iota the deeply-rooted assumption of the faithful Puritan that the English people, despite certain smirches on its escutcheon, is, after all, chosen by God and designed by Him for lordship. Even the most impassioned opponent of Imperialism seldom dares to draw the logical conclusion that English rule over Ireland or India should cease. He is generally satisfied with intensive benevolence to oppressed races as a form of penitence.

At the same time England's pity for a defeated foe ought not to be dismissed as mere hypocrisy. There is an element of genuine good in the fact that England never permanently pursues a policy of brutal repression, but makes serious efforts to reconcile the vanquished to their lot. Nor is this mere self-interest; it often contains an element of genuine admiration, and a sense of atonement to be made. But ethical considerations are straitly limited to that. Once the fight is won, historians may display a gentlemanly frankness in calling things by their right names: a broken people may even be fitted out with the halo of martyrdom. That does not alter the facts, and the victorious nation remains the chosen people of the Lord.

§ 2

Puritanism dominates the English soul. Once, it was the dogma of a party, the creed of the middle and lower classes. But the persecution of the Puritans in the Restoration period brought large numbers of these people back into the Church of England, and they brought their Puritan spirit with them. Even linguistic changes indicate a steady infiltration of the upper classes from below between 1650 and 1700. The present-day pronunciation of vowels in 'mine,' 'house,' 'up,' 'bird,' like the silent consonants in 'write,' 'gnat,' and 'knot,' are vulgarisms that penetrated educated speech at that time. Throughout the eighteenth and nineteenth centuries, the process went on, by which the wealthy Puritan, rising into the upper classes, infiltrated them with the Puritan outlook. Puritan influence degraded music and the theatre from the much higher position they once occupied. Public life in England to-day is still overwhelmingly Puritan. The boisterous heroes of Fielding and Smollett, who, in their lordly egotism and sexual irresponsibility, faithfully represented the seventeenth-century Cavalier point of view, have been replaced in novels by the virtuous heroes of Dickens, who must earn money and have the most correct outlook on all questions of love and marriage. Only the lowest social grade is non-Puritan. Down among the masses whom Puritanism has never touched, the passions of the natural man still rule untamed in love and hate, drink and violence. And as this lowest class gradually pushes its way up, Puritanism is being gradually outworn. Its zenith, it would seem, is already passed. And after-war pathology is largely contributing towards its decay.

§ 3

Whether Puritanism has been a blessing or a curse to English culture it is not easy to say. Certainly it has lent the Britons a religious force of incomparable intensity, which is not the possession of a few religiously gifted spirits, but practically of an entire nation. When ten thousand clergymen found a new Church for conscience sake, going out with wife and child into an uncertain future, as the Scottish Free Churchmen did at the time of the Disruption under Thomas Chalmers in 1843, and thousands of clergymen and laymen did before them: and, within a couple of generations, build a new Church in every respect equal to the old, the world bows in admiration before so grand an act of religious idealism, however incomprehensible it may find the basis of such martyrdom. Puritanism has enriched the British people with a lofty conception of uprightness and decency in questions of mine and thine, a highly-developed sexual morality, and a deep religiousness that victoriously survives all its Pharisaism. During the war England presented not only the odious spectacle of a campaign of vilification and slander, but the passion of the conscientious objectors, a by no means negligible body of men and women who, alone in the entire Western European world, had the courage to refuse military service and hold to their convictions, despite mockery and scorn, imprisonment and calumniation. Whether they were right or wrong in their attitude to the war does not signify; what does is that they dared, in the Anglo-Saxon world, to be different from the rest.

With equal force could one call Puritanism the bane of English culture. Except where it broke against stronger forces, it has clothed English life in a universal matter-of-factness and joylessness which insists on looking at every issue, no matter how remote, from some religious or ethical angle: presents the same blank face to scientific problems and artistic ideas: and is in constant danger of withering up into a dreary worship of Mammon, under the most superficial of ethical overlays. And Puritanism again and again fosters an aggressive Mission to other nations, reconciling as it does a total want of understanding of every civilization but its own with a harsh spirit of domination, upon which the Puritan then hastens to set the stamp of 'the will of God.'

Finally, and most important – Puritanism is the parent of English cant. Its roots may lie deeper still; kindred phenomena appear in the peasant of Lower Saxony. It is a somewhat complex phenomenon, a mixture of presumptuousness and ignorance which declines all correction and an incapacity to understand or accept anything new and foreign, all of which traits are common to the peasant stock. But whereas religious forces, everywhere else in the world, are engaged in fighting this perversion, Puritanism sanctifies it, with its doctrine of the chosen people. Many deductions have to be made from the Continental attribution of English hypocrisy. The ethical motives that impelled leading Englishmen to fight slavery or protest against Armenian atrocities, to struggle for Free Trade, Church unity and the brotherhood of nations, are indubitably genuine, however they may be combined with grotesque blindness to the feelings, desires and sufferings of non-English people. Dishonesty comes in, however, when English statesmen, instead of plainly and candidly justifying their actions on the basis of interests of their nation, invariably clothe them in the garb of an abstract humane idealism. Cant cannot always be translated as hypocrisy; a Pharisaical mental slackness often describes it more accurately. Cant, in this sense, once justified sending ten-year-old children to work a fourteen-hour day in factories, on the ground of the moral advantages to them of an early familiarity with work; even to-day it is quite usual to find an English publicist, M.P. or minister of the Crown glossing over a plain evil at home on the ground of some infinitesimal ethical benefit which the microscope of human selfishness has been able to detect in a mountain of wrong. Cant is often moral cowardice, which dare not call evil by its real name; often a criminally easy-going ignorance, which refuses to take the trouble to probe the unpleasant charges of an opponent. In the upshot, cant has produced a blunting of the sense of truth that is a moral danger to the entire nation.

For no unprejudiced observer can accept the national claim that the English are the most truth-loving people on the earth. The basic condition, respect for fact, is lacking. Beneath the mask of the disinterested observer, the Englishman is far too much the man of emotion and will to be able to look at anything in detachment from his personal wishes. An accuracy for facts is the last thing the Englishman cares for, if several conflicting virtues have to be reconciled. So, we find the English judge distorting ideas to their opposite (see pp. 287,289), or acquitting after formal condemnation (see p.292); and no Englishman seeing anything questionable in this. His passion for performing some apparently good action causes him to wrap it up in such a profusion of lovely ethical phrases and formulæ, that its dubious aspects are quite hidden from him. Any objective presentation of facts outside the domain of science is apt to strike him as pedantic, senseless, or brutal (p. 290). It does not in the least upset him to have meaningless old laws still in existence. Any attempt to use them to fetter present action would rouse him to opposition, but his sense for the actual fact is so feebly developed that he finds no inconvenience in the continued existence of the old and unmeaning, as such. His attitude may be quite harmless or even right, but such faulty understanding of the value of objective facts is not the soil in which the love of truth for itself can flourish. The bitter and unavailing struggle of a man of such rare objectivity of mind as Jeremy Bentham against the vague generalities on which his countrymen feed, or the similar fight of Bacon against 'idols,' shows how poorly developed, in England, is the sense of fact without any admixture from the sphere of the will.

And yet the Englishman does really love the truth, when it comes to him under the aspect of the duty of the chivalrous gentleman, with an admixture from other ethical spheres. He does not care for truth in itself, but he sees in truth a right which every gentleman may claim. Demanding truth as his own right, he grants an equal right to it to anyone whom he encounters as partner in business, co-operator in politics, or respected opponent – though not to an opponent, as such. His love of truth, that is to say, originates not in the sense of fact, but in the fighter's feeling of right: it is based not on understanding but on will: it possesses the strength and the weakness characteristic of the English sense of right (cf. p.285 seq.). Upon this peculiar, English expression of a common human trait Puritanism has set its religious seal, giving a definite home in the English heart to a tendency probably existent before. The subconscious feeling that truth is due to the gentleman explains the singular phenomenon of absolute truthfulness in business co-existing with a mere similitude of truth in politics, and above all in foreign politics, which may amount, in essence, to absolute untruthfulness.

§ 4

A German author may perhaps be pardoned if he tries to compare, at the end of this study, the religiousness of England with the type prevalent in his own country. One great difference has already been set out: the prevalent mark of English piety is communal worship: of German religiousness, individualistic piety. Puritanism carries that difference a stage further. English piety, inasmuch as it is Puritan, seeks to save the world; German piety seeks to overcome the world.

German piety recognizes one form of religion only – the union of the soul with God. That and that alone is religion. Church attendance, the ten commandments, charity, missionary effort – these in themselves are not religion. Religion is the religious spirit, and all the rest but means to that end. All official piety had always a tinge of suspicion attached to it, because there might be something insincere in it. The Church – in the opinion of the deepest religious minds of Germany – was apt to share in the same suspicion. All good habits of churchgoing, of almsgiving might equally be a mere cloak. Sincerity alone counted, and even the fanatical sincerity of the atheist or moral degenerate was apt to be preferred to the average Christian of good churchgoing habits. The danger of this lofty religious attitude is obvious. It kills the religiousness of the average man, who is no saint, but will be a faithful soul, if he is not exposed to the strongest of temptations, if he can have some prop and hold on externals, on social and religious habits, on a good moral code, on a strong Church. An overstressed ideal of sincerity will develop a highly religious life in the religious and leave the average man to the temptations of crudest materialism. This is where German Protestantism fails.

It further fails by thinking of religiousness alone. It develops a state of mind which acknowledges no bond between the ideal and the actual; it leaves the world to take care of itself. It has no religious demands for everyday life in the sphere of politics and social relations. The political pastor has always been suspect in German Protestantism. He could not touch politics without soiling his gown. Many other powers care for political and social progress, religion is far too lofty to have anything to do with it. The day will come when God's hand will bid the dark waters recede.

RELIGION AND THE CHURCH

The prevailing type of English religiousness is the opposite of all this. It cannot see that a mere good habit should not be encouraged because there may be some irreligious motives behind the prompter. It cannot see that religion has nothing to do with the world, on the contrary it sees that a good environment is better for religion than a bad. It opens its eyes wide and sees with religious pride and joy how Christian culture is gradually gaining ground in the missionary field abroad and at home and enlists the service of every true Christian in this work. All this is true, but danger lurks even here. The care for the surroundings may detract interest from the real field. A highly-developed ethical code may insensibly take the place of religion, mere good form may be fostered more carefully than inner religious life, the gentleman may take the place of the religious man, the social order, private property, law, all that exists, may intrude into the Holy of Holies from outside. There may be in this type more of external religion, more religious action, a more perfect moral life and less religiosity.

There is more in Christianity than can be embraced by the prevailing religious type in one nation, there is more than can be found even by a fusion of the best in both. Who has been brought up in one of these types will more easily see the depth that is there, but will never forget that in matters of religion, all depth is only shallowness compared to what should be.

BOOK IV
EDUCATION

CHAPTER I

THE UNIVERSITIES OF OXFORD AND CAMBRIDGE

§ 1

ENGLAND possesses two Universities, Oxford and Cambridge, dating back at least to the middle of the thirteenth century, and possibly even earlier. The oldest Colleges are University (1249) and Balliol (1262) in Oxford, and Peterhouse (1284) in Cambridge. They were 'bursae' or inns, designed to provide poorer students with a decent abode, which developed gradually, as teaching was given in them, into centres of University life. The lectures of the colleges became, bit by bit, of more importance for the great body of students than those of the Professors appointed by the University itself. In the fifteenth and sixteenth centuries both Universities were put upon a broader basis, by the foundation of great numbers of colleges, and the introduction of humanistic teaching; they are the great centres of culture and learning for the nation as a whole. The history of both is closely bound up with the Reformation. The founder of the movement, John Wycliffe, was an Oxford teacher; Cambridge was the centre of Presbyterian resistance to the ecclesiastical policy of Elizabeth; an atheist (or what his contemporaries were wont to call by that name), Francis Kett, was burned at the stake there in 1589. In course of time, however, the Government succeeded, partly by gentle inducements, partly by severe pressure, in making both Universities instruments of its own ecclesiastical policy. In the civil war of the seventeenth century both, and more particularly Oxford, were centres of the Royalist cause.

The Stuart Restoration strengthened this conservative character. In the standing quarrel between the rights of the separate colleges and those of the University as a whole, the Tudors had taken the Colleges' part; the Stuarts did so, much more energetically. It was easier for reaction to get hold of a small group, like the college, than of the whole; the effort, therefore, was to strengthen the colleges (compare the contemporaneous tendency to transform open into close boroughs). Puritan leanings were ruthlessly suppressed; the Act of Uniformity made the Thirty-nine Articles obligatory on every teacher. Further, students of Nonconformist bent were driven entirely out of Oxford and largely out of Cambridge. This produced a radical change in the character of the Universities. Hitherto, they had been open to all. Now they became bulwarks of the ruling class. Not that there was anything harsh in the process. The door stood open to anyone who would sign the Thirty-nine Articles; he had no need to fear any examination of his inner mind; the ruling class, with notable far-sightedness, opened arms to all who desired to join it. But the great mass of middle and lower-class folk would not sign the Thirty-nine Articles. The Nonconformists preferred sending their young men to their own poor little Training Colleges to having them submitted to the Anglican and often very High Church, influence of the Universities. The Universities became the bulwarks of a caste; the majority of the middle class was excluded not only from the clerical but also from the legal profession. They became the aristocratic High Schools of the world. Not that every young man of rank attended a University: very much the reverse. But the aristocratic admixture was potent enough to give the tone. It was set by the lordling, with his golden tufted cap, who sat in Hall at the High table, not among his fellow-undergraduates. Complaints were loud, in the nineteenth century, that the Universities, once designed as seats of learning, and the colleges, intended to assist the poor, had become resorts of well-bred indolence, while the poor student, though eligible in principle, was to all intents and purposes in practice shut out from collegiate life.

For the moment, the State did nothing to interfere. So long as the gentry were in the saddle, its interest in the Universities was mild. While non-interference passed as the last word in statesmanship, no one thought of asking for any contribution from the Universities to the welfare of the State as a whole. In Germany, absolutism concerned itself more and more with these matters, founding professorships, supervising curricula, lest they should contain too many 'soft options,' and setting up special courses and State examinations in medicine, law, theology and philology. There is no parallel to any of this in England. True to old Guild principles, the education of the student was regarded as the exclusive concern of professional bodies. Thus, from the sixteenth century, the education of lawyers was supervised by corporations of barristers in London, and the Universities had no more to do with it. That of doctors, carried on for centuries on a system of apprenticeship, and sunk to a very low level, was in 1858 made subject to a professional body, the General Council of Medical Education. The old apprentice tradition still lingers here. Practical training is still given in recognized hospitals, with their own teaching staffs, and in the Universities only so far as these hospitals are affiliated to them (which now is becoming the rule). Ordination is in the hands of the Bishop, when he or his archdeacon is satisfied about the candidate; attendance at a University is almost invariable, but not prescribed. There is, to this day, no recognized course of training that leads into the higher teaching profession.

The Universities, that is to say, are educational institutions, enjoying high respect, not specialist bodies. In the eighteenth century, while the gentry ruled, the country had practically no officials; the Church and the Law were allied powers, for whom conditions neither were nor could be laid down. The Universities, accordingly, developed, on lines convenient to the ruling caste, as seats in which the youth of the country could acquire a modicum of classical learning; they gave an intellectual sanction to the domination of the gentry, and brought up the young men to be gentlemen, accepting and exemplifying the ideals of a class. And such, despite the far-reaching reforms of the nineteenth century, Oxford and Cambridge remain, to this day, to a very large extent. They have gradually bent to modern conceptions and have become schools for promoting the development of freedom of thought and independent research, but at the same time and even more prominently, they have remained bulwarks of a specifically English culture. Whereas the German Universities, first of all, train scholars and members of learned professions, Oxford and Cambridge, first of all, train gentlemen.

§ 2

The primary influence of Oxford and Cambridge is to make the vast majority of its young men, contrary to the tendencies natural to the early twenties, Conservative. The undergraduate is surrounded by tradition on every side. In the hall of Merton, the portrait of John Wycliffe looks down from the walls, for it was here he once dwelt and worked; Balliol owes its name to a thirteenth-century claimant to the Scottish throne; memories of Christopher Marlowe, John Milton, Isaac Newton, and Lord Byron are about you, as you walk in Cambridge. Marvellous mediaeval architecture, and lawns smooth with centuries of careful tending do their work on the impressionable mind of youth; in such surroundings buildings of nineteenth or even eighteenth-century date look like upstart intruders.

EDUCATION

Undergraduate and teacher alike wear mediaeval cap and gown. The Vice-Chancellor at the head of the University recalls the fact that the old High School was attached to the Bishop's Chancellery. The forms of life are mediaeval, nay, cloistral; in most colleges the day opens with chapel; meals, eaten in common, are preceded by a Latin grace; by twelve o'clock at night every undergraduate must be *intra muros*. University discipline makes allowance for youthful high spirits, while keeping the undergraduate well within the bounds of good old tradition; after dusk he may not be seen in the streets except in cap and gown, and any offence against the seventh commandment counts as a grave sin against academic discipline. In addition to study – and, in many cases, instead of study – life is occupied with games of various kinds, rowing, cricket, football, etc.; the great event of the year is Inter-University Regatta, and the Boat crew the real heroes of the University. Since the nineties there has been an O.T.C. on a voluntary basis, which played its part in providing officers in the war. Interest in the political questions of the day is stimulated by the Union, a luxurious club, joined by most undergraduates who can afford an annual subscription of £4; it includes a fine service of daily papers and a good general library, and, once a week, a debate, conducted with all the parliamentary forms and a vote at the end, on some burning question of the hour. In this atmosphere of sport, friendship, discipline of the will, patriotism and luxury, the young Briton learns to use his strength to take his part in the life of an organized community, to handle and rule men, to think politically, and to regard himself as a civilized being, a Briton and a lord of creation; if, in addition, he desires to train his mind, ample opportunity is afforded him, in the shape of lecturers and tutors. The Universities are held to have done their part so long as they create and promote the type of man by whom the country desires to be governed. That, not learning, is the point. It was for that Cecil Rhodes founded his scholarships at Oxford.

For the creation of gentlemen, two main instruments exist – corporate life in the colleges, and games. Living in college, under the constant observation of young men of his own age, the undergraduate acquires the Oxford (or Cambridge) manner, and with it a blend of charming amiability in trifles and reserve in most big things, together with self-consciousness, energy and love of his country. Any personal idiosyncrasies he may have brought with him are rubbed off, and the perfect picture of the gentleman emerges, as desired. Games have a similar effect. They are not, first of all, an affair of bodily training for the individual. As a matter of fact, the forms of sport which most systematically make for individual prowess – gymnastics, throwing the spear, running and jumping – are here either quite secondary or not developed at all. Archery, that old national sport, still practised in the sixteenth century, has nearly died out. Boxing kept its place longer, and, after being looked down upon, for generations, by the well-bred, is reviving to-day, under the hardening experiences of war. The truly English form of sport, however, is that of a contest between sides – between rowing crews, cricket or football teams. These teams are not casual, but strictly representative sides, selected after severe tests. Thus one school class will meet another, Balliol will play against Christ Church, Oxford against Cambridge, Ireland against Scotland, England against America, and so on. For this form of sport the English have a passion, and it is the great school of Englishmen. Its first effect is to strengthen and harden the body, and train it, through the medium of a Spartan discipline, to such a point that every power of mind and body can be concentrated on a given purpose. Team fighting teaches a man to respect his antagonist and, while putting out every ounce of strength, not to take any kind of mean advantage, not to rejoice with unmeasured arrogance in victory, and to accept defeat with unruffled calm. Its second effect is even more important. It is to teach the young Englishman, as nothing else could do, to take part in corporate action, to feel not as an individual, but as a member of a group. A player in a team must not play his own hand, but serve as a member of a whole: what is at stake is the honour of college, University, town or country. The man who has learned how to play in a team will, later on, be a useful member of a parliamentary party, of a Town Council, of a Ministry, or of any one of the thousand and one Committees that play so large a part in English life. Success, however, depends on one condition – a leader with the capacity to gather together the best elements to form the team, to place the stronger and weaker members of it in their appropriate places, and then rule, with dictatorial authority, over the individual. So the Captain prefigures the omnipotent Headmaster, Bishop, or Prime Minister of the future. The qualities England needs in the State are disciplined on the cricket and football field and in the boat race path; here the leader reveals himself, and the individual learns to serve as a member of a whole. The leader, too, who may be a dictator but never a despot, learns how to get the utmost out of other people and, at the same time, how to study their personalities, their weaknesses and even their vanities. That is why the University is precious even to the average Englishman without intellectual culture; instead of bringing up men of learning, whom he would have no idea how to use, it produces men who know how to lead and how to co-operate: men who enable England to dominate the world.

§ 3

Something like two-fifths of the students of Oxford and Cambridge seek and find in the University the training of a gentleman and little more. He is the passman who is not hard put to it for science, who will see very little of the professors; but does some not very exhaustive work under a tutor, who will direct his reading. After three years he will take his final examination and be a Bachelor.[1] If he cares for the title of M.A., which makes him a life member of the University, with a vote in its business, in Congregation or Convocation, he can receive it, after a few years, in return for the payment of certain fees, without passing any further examinations. None of the ordinary degree examinations assumes any specialized knowledge. At the end of his three years, the graduate possesses a certain body of general knowledge, but he faces no larger problems; he has received no specialized instruction. Generally, after taking his degree, he goes into business, or then begins his specialized training with a solicitor, at one of the Inns of Court, or at a Hospital. He does not bring much knowledge with him, but he is generally a good character, a decent fellow and a gentleman.

§ 4

Public opinion was satisfied, on the whole, for centuries with this training of young men of good family as gentlemen; a University which accomplishes this was held to have done its duty. Nevertheless, Oxford and Cambridge had, as the result of the Royal Commission of 1850-52, to submit to far-reaching changes. Public criticism addressed itself to two main points: (1) The exclusively Anglican and aristocratic character of the Universities was resented by the whole middle class, which was predominantly Nonconformist; (2) Their intellectual sterility was felt to be a disgrace, by a small minority of intellectual leaders. To this small class belonged men like John

Stuart Mill and Matthew Arnold, and, in particular, scientists like Herschel the astronomer, Huxley the anatomist, and Sedgwick the geologist, while the mass of the public took little or no interest in this aspect of the matter. There were, therefore, immense difficulties in the way of scientific modernization, and, although the reformers did achieve remarkable results, their aim is not fully attained to this day. Thanks, however, to the reforms of the second half of the nineteenth century, the Universities were transformed in three directions: (1) The removal of all tests threw them open to the whole nation; i.e., to the Puritan and Methodist middle classes; (2) Teaching was modernized; and, (3) Carried to a much higher point.

§ 5

In 1871 all tests were abolished, and the Universities thrown open to Dissenters. They thereby lost their specifically Anglican but not their religious and Protestant character. College chapel is still obligatory on all Anglicans, though often evaded; the clerical element is still very strong among Heads of colleges; professors are apt to be Anglicans, if only because drawn, in the main, from social groups of that complexion. The theological faculties at both Universities are Anglican, although, since 1920, Anglicanism has ceased to be indispensable for a theological degree, and since 1899, Mansfield College (Nonconformist) has been loosely attached to the University, and, since 1889, Manchester College, as a Unitarian foundation for undenominational religious teaching. Catholicism has no status at either University, though there are Catholics among the professors and even halls for Catholic priests among the students. Reform has cleared the Universities of their intolerance, but left them in the closest touch with the prevailing national religion. The purely secular University, of the German, French or American type, cannot be the ideal where piety and respect for ecclesiastical authority are part of the make-up of the gentleman.

Closely connected with the break-down of the Anglican monopoly is the effort to throw the Universities open to middle- and lower-class students. The tests represented one obstacle here: the luxurious and costly life another. Attempts to meet this latter difficulty have been made along various lines; special colleges have been established for students of limited purse, like Selwyn (Cambridge) and Keble (Oxford), and unattached students have been permitted to reside outside college, subject to rigid discipline on the part of the University authorities. These, however, are mere makeshifts which can, at best, secure the admission to academic professions of competent young men from modest homes. Unattached students are apt to be isolated, and little affected by the aristocratic spirit of the place. But they ought to be drawn into it: this is the demand of the English snobs as well as of the far-sighted reformers who desire to keep the Universities aristocratic but not exclusively so. What is desired is that from them a broad current of aristocratic feeling should flow out to the nation, and so educate democracy in the British tradition. Thus, in recent times, the efforts of reformers have been directed more and more to getting men from the lower classes planted inside the aristocratic majority, as a minority on an equal footing. This can be attained only by the establishment of such a scholarship system as may permit the existence, within every college, of a considerable number of young men without means. On these lines, no small success has been accomplished.[2] There are a number of such scholarships, amounting, in total, to a very large sum. On the basis of attainment only, without any questions being asked as to means, the gifted, hard-working lad can win a school, town or country scholarship. Notably since the war, State scholarships have filled in the gaps to a large extent. The system is so comprehensive and well organized that, to-day, the lower orders are, to no small degree, pressing into the old citadels of the aristocracy. Once again, the upper classes are revealing their immense powers of assimilation. Just as the small group of real old aristocrats in the House of Lords inoculated brewers and cotton-spinners with upper-class ideas and outlook, so the University, the intellectual bulwark of the gentry, is influencing the rising mass below it. Far from democratizing it, the scholarship system serves to diffuse the aristocratic point of view through ever widening circles. Great as is the number, to-day, of undergraduates from simple homes, no one could call the spirit of Oxford democratic.

Women, too, have now made their way in. In 1873, Girton was founded as an outgrowth of a women's college established in Hitchin in 1869, and in 1871 Newnham followed, both in Cambridge; in 1879 Lady Margaret Hall and Somerville were founded in Oxford. The University as such was still closed to women, but teachers were available on the spot who gave them an education fully of University standard. Gradually, teachers of progressive mind admitted women to their lectures, and, at last, the University admitted them to lectures and examinations. By 1921 the fight was won, so far as Oxford was concerned: there, women are now on an equal footing with men, being granted degrees and eligible for membership of Congregation and Convocation, with consequential rights to participate in University administration. Cambridge still lags behind women have been admitted, in 1921, with a fine Socratic distinction to all the *titles of degrees*, whereby they may call themselves B.A., but not to the *degrees*, so that they have no voice in University business.

§ 6

Wide sections of general opinion supported both the abolition of tests and the democratization of the Universities; far greater difficulties were met with in the effort at modernizing them. For such an attempt there was no general sympathy. Moreover, the old, easy-going, hand-to-mouth aristocratic administration was so firmly entrenched that something like a revolution was required to make room for modern scientific requirements. Since 1850, both the constitution and the curricula have been thoroughly overhauled. The old system, concerned only with the making of gentlemen and contemptuous of scientific problems, was by no means abolished. Only, a new University was superimposed upon the structure of the old. The old, with undergraduates absorbed in football and rowing, and the pass degree as ultimate aim remains; one day, it is hoped, it may die out. Within its fold, a new has been created, with a truly scientific ideal. Side by side with the old pass course, which converts the ordinary undergraduate into a gentleman, with some scientific varnish, an Honours course has been set up, which implies a thorough and scientific course of study. The degree taken, in either case, is the B.A. The visiting card marks no distinction. But the object aimed at, and, in large measure, attained, is to have only the Honours degree taken seriously. The pass degree is a hall-mark of gentility: the Honours degree, at least so far as first- and second-class honours go, is a genuine credential of scientific training. Some 60 per cent of Oxford men now take honours.

The construction of a new university within the old necessitated a complete transformation of its constitution. The pillars of the old system were the colleges, which had practically monopolized both teaching and revenue, leaving the University powerless. Reform, therefore, had to aim at:

EDUCATION

1. The modernization of the constitution, so as to give the University power as against the colleges.
2. The reorganization and improvement of teaching.

§ 7

The modernization of the constitution was thorough. The task was Sisyphean, since fundamental change had got to be accomplished in an atmosphere in which the most modest programme was regarded as revolutionary, and in the absence of any compulsory powers with which to counter obstruction.

The root difficulty was that, by the opening of the nineteenth century, there no longer existed a University in any real sense of the word, but only a loose agglomeration of colleges. Every college had its own, generally ample, revenues, its own administrative system, its own scholarships, and its own staff of tutors and lecturers. Its government was conducted by a Head, often a man of striking personality, whose autocracy was limited only by a circle of colleagues and friends with no defined responsibility. Somewhere in this system the University was vaguely located, with professors who gave lectures attended by a mere handful among the students, and ideals quite incomprehensible to the great majority among them. It was responsible for examinations, but their conduct was in the hands of special functionaries, and the professors had nothing to do with them. A very small number of men read for the higher examinations,[3] and so provided the professors with a certain voice in the University, though a very faint one.

The basis of this organization remained intact. To this day, the colleges are comparatively rich, the University poor. The most important, influential and best paid persons are the Heads; it is from their number, and not from that of the professors, that the Vice-Chancellor,[4] the Head of the University, is chosen. The Senate (called Hebdomadal Council in Oxford, Council of the Senate in Cambridge) contains an equal number of Heads of colleges and professors. Many colleges are enormously rich: at Oxford, Magdalen and Christ Church have each of them nearly one-third of the income of the University. In a country like England, the power of vested interests of such strength simply could not be swept away.

Nevertheless, the reforms did substantially curtail their privileges. On the basis of the Royal Commission Report (1850–52) reform was instituted on the lines already applied to municipal government. In

416

the towns, power had been taken out of the hands of the few and transferred to a democratic electorate, on a wide franchise. So, here, the power of irresponsible Heads of colleges was reduced, to the advantage of that of the University. Substantial contributions were exacted from the colleges for University purposes. They now form about one-sixth of the University's revenues. A democratic element was introduced through the body of M.A.s who, in mediaeval times, had taken considerable part in University government; the right was given to Congregation, in Oxford, and the Electoral Roll in Cambridge, to elect members on to University Boards, from among the Heads and professors, and even to fill places on them by ordinary M.A.s.

To-day the University comes first, not the colleges. Large portions of the revenues of the latter have to be paid over to the Common University Fund, founded in 1877, which provides University (in contradistinction to college) lecturers and professors; as a result the direction of teaching is now entirely in the hands of the University. The College Fellowships are now more and more placed at the disposal of the University. They are, in origin, administrative posts; the passage of time has made them mere sinecures. In the eighteenth century they afforded a means of providing the favoured protégés of the aristocracy with an agreeable and easy existence. Now, though still attached to the various colleges, and filled, in part, by them, they are, in the main, in University gift. A fellowship serves to improve a poorly-endowed chair; above all, it serves to assist men to stay on after the close of their three or four years undergraduate course. So the young B.A. can support himself for seven or ten years and, by this means, a long step is taken towards the solution of the problem of training the next generation of academic teachers, so arduous in other countries.

§ 8

The constitution of the Universities, as established by the Royal Commission of 1872–4, the Universities of Oxford and Cambridge Act of 1877 and an analogous Act of 1923, represents the outcome of a generation of strenuous reform. Its main principles are as follows:

1. The University remains a privileged corporation, in whose concerns the State has no right of interference. Up to the war, the State only made grants for specific purposes; it now gives large permanent grants, which have become absolutely indispensable.

The State, of course, has the right to appoint Royal Commissions from time to time, to inquire into University affairs. But the State neither founds professorships for purposes of its own choice, nor takes any part in the selection of professors: it has no control over examinations, and nominates no curators. The University in fact enjoys a degree of autonomy impossible outside Britain.

2. Within the University, the colleges continue as privileged corporations of a markedly independent type. Their Heads continue to be important persons, with a determinant voice in many questions; the Vice-Chancellor is still chosen from among them. In general University business, however, decisions are not in their hands, but in those of bodies like the Senate and Faculties, in which professors have an equal voice.

3. Ultimate decision in University matters rests with the general graduate body. The M.A.s form a democracy in University matters corresponding to the democracy of universal suffrage in local and national administration. They decide all constitutional issues, on the basis of proposals emanating from Senate and Faculties; they elect Senate and Faculties and determine the appointment of junior teachers.

University democracy comprises two organizations, one more, the other less, limited in scope. First, in Oxford Convocation, in Cambridge the Senate, composed in either case of the whole body of M.A.s irrespective of abode or occupation. The commission of influence over University affairs to a body of this type has proved a complete mistake. Interest in University matters, or in educational and scholastic questions, is in most cases confined to the small proportion of M.A.s actually in residence; the great bulk of the non-residents make no use of their votes unless some issue arises like the abolition of compulsory Greek or the admission of women to degrees; then they troop up to their Alma Mater to renew old acquaintances and save it from any suggestion of reform, or to elect a Chancellor, in most cases a Conservative statesman. This form of University democracy that consigned the most vital decisions of policy to men who take neither interest in nor responsibility for them, has been, actually, the strongest barrier to every kind of progress. Its abolition can only be a question of time.

On the other hand, the modified form of this democracy illustrated by Congregation at Oxford, works well. Since 1913 this body has been composed of those M.A.'s who are concerned, in one way or another, with University teaching or administration. Of these there are some 500. In Oxford all business save matters of constitutional change and the election of Chancellor is transferred from Convocation to Congregation, whose work is generally regarded as satisfactory. It does not interfere at all in the routine work of Faculties and Senate; its vote generally confirms decisions already arrived at by experts in all everyday matters. At the same time it has proved useful to have a body of men, free to make suggestions and willing to do work who, while connected with the University, are not, like most professors, exclusively concerned with academic matters and routine work.[5]

The administrative organ of the University is, in Oxford, the Hebdomadal Council; in Cambridge, the Council of the Senate. The members are, in the main, elected: only a very small number are *ex officio*. A certain number must be professors or Heads, but there is no limitation of status on the others. Next come the Faculties,[6] comprising the whole body of teachers in any department, who by an elected body, the Faculty Board, supervise teaching and examinations. Matters of greater importance come before a General Board composed of members of all Faculties.

The method of filling teaching posts is peculiar. The Faculties have nothing to do with it. For each professorship there is a special body of electors, statutorily determined, of whom many but not all are professors.

§ 9

The second object of the reformers – the modernization and improvement of the curriculum – has been pursued energetically for two generations, and with considerable success. More and more, Oxford and Cambridge are becoming similar to the Continental University type, but without completely losing their old essential character. To this day, the most conspicuous and most highly valued subject is Classics, although Cambridge since 1919, and Oxford since 1920, have abolished compulsory Greek for entrance examinations. University education is humanistic, by tradition, and because a humanistic education belongs to the gentleman. The classics are the mark of good breeding; the banausic mind values them, because they cost time and money and give a *cachet*; the thinking minority, because their study disciplines the mental powers and is clear of any narrow vocational limitation or premature specialization. To the English mind there is something inferior in any kind of specialized education. In the eighteenth-century novel, the man of learning is invariably a pedant. It is the same in administration; over its entire area, from the tiniest local authority up to the highest positions in the realm, personality is what counts: the specialist is always the assistant. The sole expert rated high in England is the barrister, trained in the law schools of the Inns of Court. What concerns the University is the training of gentlemen; hence the emphasis on the classics – once the sole, and still the central subject there. The disproportionate number of classical scholarships, and the excessively high marks allotted to classics in some of the examinations, serve, to this day, to force them on the undergraduate, often against his inclination. A classical degree, pass or honours, is still regarded as the best preparation for a vocational study or for the Civil Service.

Only after long and arduous struggles have the non-classical schools established themselves at the two older Universities. They have won their way in, gradually, but have not yet attained a position of full equality. History and theology fare relatively well, the theoretical study of law is well provided for (especially by All Souls' College, Oxford), though all the more practical branches are left to the Inns; and the same is true of medicine. Since 1835, modern language teaching has been amply endowed, thanks to the bequests to Oxford of Sir Robert Taylor (d. 1788), but the larger developments of this study date from about 1900.

Natural science, which presented in the past the most striking deficiencies, shows to-day the most remarkable advance. The men of science were the life and soul of the movement for reform. Moreover, the middle-class students, then fighting for admission to the Universities, came in the main from homes where the outlook was strictly practical; where a piece of chemical research was rated above a treatise on classical philology; which saw the advantages being reaped by German trade and industry from scientific research, and therefore were ready to encourage expenditure on chemical and physical laboratories. Cambridge took the lead, followed, at a considerable distance, by Oxford, in establishing scientific chairs and laboratories on a level absolutely comparable with the German.

But this change, accomplished mainly within the last generation, involves a great deal more than a mere increase in tutorial and academic activity. The old methods had proved incompatible with scientific advance. The pass man was a mere schoolboy, who could translate a passage of Homer, and repeat a few historical dates and mathematical formulæ. The best work done in Oxford and Cambridge certainly need fear no comparison with the best of the German Universities. But a different verdict must be passed if the comparison is between the average level of scholarship at one and the other. Here, the English system is still on a lower plane. Study is still over-directed. The subjects open to the student's choice are confined to a definite group, and within that chosen group there are prescribed lectures he must attend, prescribed authors and prescribed works or parts of works – certain books of Vergil, certain plays of Shakespeare, and so on – that he must have read; there is his tutor always at his elbow; there are intermediate examinations to assist his progress, with the result that the number of those who do anything substantive of their own is relatively small. Yet it is in the direction of increasing their number that development is obviously tending. Side by side with the pass and honours man a new type of student, the research student, has arisen, who has already passed his B.A. with honours and is now working for his Ph.D.

The type of the Oxford professor also is undergoing a change. The professor of the older type was not exactly overloaded with work at an English University. He would deliver a few lectures – but there was no one to ask whether his lectures covered the whole subject in any sort of regular sequence. In addition, there would be a small handful of men studying some special subject, with whom he would carry on more serious work, as much or as little as happened to suit him. With examinations of any sort he had nothing to do. He was not the pivot of his department, but rather its very distinguished outside patron. Its working really rested on teachers of secondary rank, the readers, lecturers and tutors. This system, under which the professor enjoyed genuine academic leisure, is gradually dying out. It still exists in connexion with subjects where the number of students is small; but, where it is large, lecturing takes more and more of the professor's time, and he is even called in increasingly to take his share in the work of examination, which used to lie quite outside his ken. So, the difference between the English and the German University, once so marked, is gradually losing its importance.

§ 10

But the difference has not disappeared. The German University is one-sided. It endeavours to give its students an intellectual grasp

421

of life, and directs the whole of its energy to that end. That the student should strengthen his body is certainly desirable. That he should, in association with groups, large or small, achieve some training in citizenship, may be necessary; but it is not the task of the University itself to make provision for these things; it has done its part when it equips its students to cope mentally with the problems of existence. This consciously limited, consciously one-sided aim the German University has hitherto achieved. (This is not the appropriate place for examining the question whether the conception of life behind this ideal is gradually changing and whether the mass problem, now threatening the Universities and likely to continue to threaten them, may not compel them to adopt quite other aims, much more on English lines.) But the aim of the German University is not that of the English. In England what is desired is the training of the whole man, not merely as a brain, but as a being who is physically sound and also a citizen. Where the aim of endeavour is so wide and comprehensive, there can be no concentration of energy on securing what is merely a single part of it. This comprehensive aim is still being pursued by the English University, with the applause of the nation, although the place allotted to the intellect in the picture of what is desirable is somewhat larger now than it was.

The University has never had a monopoly of learning in England. In Germany, in the nineteenth century, it was taken as a matter of course that great philosophers, historians, scientists and theologians were at the same time University professors; in England, with its much greater wealth, it was quite common for the rich man to have his private library and his private laboratory. True, the nineteenth century produced a distinguished series of University professors, but no University harboured either of its two great philosophers, John Stuart Mill and Herbert Spencer, or such historians as Macaulay, Lecky and Gardiner, or such scientists as Darwin, Faraday, Davy, or Huxley: while Froude and Ruskin sojourned but for a brief space in Oxford. On the other hand, the influence of the Universities extends far beyond the limits of their academic work and academic teaching.

At a time when the State did nothing for higher education, and there was practically no system of State inspection, the Universities began inspecting schools and conducting examinations. First came the Local Examination Board, in Oxford, founded in 1857, with a parallel organization in Cambridge; later, in 1873, the Joint Schools

Examination Board of the two Universities; both organizations, especially the latter, have established a system of graded examinations for the entire country. Schools are thereby tested both from the point of view of general efficiency and from that of efficiency in special subjects. There was no obligation on any school to submit to these examinations, but educational reformers gradually secured for those who passed them exemption from the entrance examination for the Universities, the Services and the Bar. This gave these examinations a rising status, and they were finally accepted even by the Public Schools. University professors have little to do with these examinations save in so far as a few of their number co-operate in the general organization; but they presented welcome opportunities of ekeing out their incomes to a host of younger lecturers and tutors and provided many a graduate with a profession. By this system the Universities have acquired a decisive voice in education, both at home and in the Colonies.

Moreover, Oxford and Cambridge exert their influence over other places of academic learning in England. They co-operate in the M.A. and B.A. examinations of the newer Universities; some of the professors of the older Universities examining side by side with those of the locality. This system was introduced in order to guarantee that a high teaching standard should be maintained in the newer Universities and no undue favour shown by any professor to his own students. As it worked well it was maintained even after the original cause had disappeared, and professors of the newer Universities begin to co-operate in the examinations of the older. The supreme administrative organ of the University of Wales, founded in 1893, includes representatives of Oxford and Cambridge, while a large number of University colleges, like Lampeter, Nottingham, Southampton, Monmouth, Exeter and Reading, are affiliated to them – i.e., students of the lesser colleges, after a year's study there, may complete their course at Oxford or Cambridge – a privilege confined to institutions at a definite academic level. Thus, Oxford and Cambridge dominate education throughout the Anglo-Saxon world.

They are, moreover, the great nurseries of Imperial sentiment. Here again, what counts is not their academic distinction so much as the hall-mark they confer. To have been at one of the older Universities opens all sorts of doors for the young student from the Colonies. Youthful Indians come thither to prepare for the Indian Civil Service Examination, the royal road to high administrative posts at home.

Cecil Rhodes tried systematically to transplant the gentleman ideal to the Colonies, by scholarships bringing great bodies of young men to Oxford year by year. Association with Colonial Universities is assiduously fostered; since 1912 there have been quinquennial inter-University conferences, and a Universities Bureau of the British Empire exists in London. Imperialism has always found a lively echo in the undergraduate mind. J. R. Seeley (d. 1895) in Cambridge; J. A. Froude (d. 1894), for a short time in Oxford, were the most powerful intellectual exponents of the new spirit; from 1905 on, the voluntary Territorial movement was more active in Oxford and Cambridge than anywhere else; a new chair of American history, founded in 1920 by Lord Rothermere, the most active propagandist of Imperialism in the Press, points in the same direction.

§ 11

The intellectual and political influence of the Universities extends far beyond the somewhat narrow limits of their undergraduate body. Cambridge is the parent of University Extension. The idea of securing some share of higher education to men unable to attend a University dates back to the Humanistic epoch; to this day Gresham College in London still exists, founded by Sir Thomas Gresham (d. 1579) for people of the merchant class. The Rationalistic epoch has similar efforts to its credit, and the idea revived in the nineteenth century, under the influence of the Benthamites; it was with them that the attempt to create a bridge between primary and higher education, to be described later, originated. In 1873, James Stuart, a Cambridge professor, founded the University Extension movement, which ultimately became national in scope, for the universal dissemination of University education. Thanks to his enthusiasm, the scepticism of the Universities was gradually overcome. The University now bears a portion of the cost, and a University Board of Extra-mural studies organizes the courses, though the lectures are given, not, as a rule, by professors, but by the younger men, some of whom take up this as a life's work, while others regard it mainly as preliminary to academic or scholastic employment. The courses are organized in a very thorough fashion; generally there is a series of lectures (twelve or at least six) followed, if successful, by a second series on some cognate topic. This systematic lecture-course serves, as a rule, as the starting point for serious work on the part of the students themselves; the lecture being followed up by a discussion class, the recommendation of books for further study, the writing of essays on the subject-matter of the course, and, at its close, an examination with the grant of certificates. The class held after the lecture is the groundwork of the whole system.

The new system soon established itself, but its success was greatest among those for whom it had not been intended primarily. The audience very largely came from the lower middle class and the women; a great many teachers used it as a means for enlarging their poor modicum of training, but the workers only came as individuals, certainly not as a class. The average workman had neither time nor inclination for mental exertion; the cinema rather than a lecture attracted him, or, at best, the fiction shelf of the popular library. Political difficulties also came in; the best of the workers, being 'class conscious,' distrusted a culture offered them by middle-class Danai. Only when, in 1903, Albert Mansbridge, one of the few working men active in the Extension movement, gathered his fellows into the Workers' Educational Association, the movement grew to be a real power among those for whom it was intended. Here the workers, instead of being merely the object of education, co-operate in drawing up the courses and the choice of teachers, with the assistance of a University Committee. In contradistinction to University Extension of the old type, the new organization is actually in the hands of the Trade Unions and other working-class bodies in close co-operation with the Universities. Inevitably, therefore, in spite of the stress repeatedly laid on its non-party character, the trend of the whole organization is somewhat Radical in tendency – a fact that often puts a strain on the good sense and knowledge of the University lecturers who work side by side in it with Trade Union leaders and workmen. But these difficulties tend to disappear when the workman has once acquired confidence in the new system; he tends to be more amenable to the new academic influences, and to acquire also an interest in subjects which have nothing to do with political and social problems.

The movement now seems to have passed the stage of experiment. All Universities have now fallen in with Cambridge and regard University Extension as part of their normal activities. Though the type of the old University Extension lecture still persists, the main stress is now laid upon the new Tutorial Classes. These are lectures given by University men to a small number of workmen, two lectures a week, extending over three successive winters, supplemented by discussions and essays. The costs are borne by local organizations of all types, by the local Education Authorities and by the Universities; since 1924 the Board of Education makes substantial contributions, provided its rules and conditions of efficiency are fulfilled.[7]

It would be very unjust to judge the success of the movement by the number of workmen whom it has sent to the University. Their number is infinitesimally small. But this must be reckoned to the credit of the movement. It has made the University and its academic honours accessible to a few and thus has shown to the many that the University is not a class institution. It has further shown them that intellectual work is extremely hard work, and that the many will do better if they remain fully trained members of their own class. The Tutorial Classes have transferred a very small number of workmen into the higher walks of life, but provided the workmen with leaders to a large extent. The danger that these Tutorial Classes may produce a kind of semi-scientific intelligentsia with all the dangers of hasty, half-crude knowledge is not so easily to be brushed aside; it exists, but would be very considerable only if less exacting work were required. Neither University Extension nor Tutorial Classes is the ideal system of bridging the gap between the elementary school and the University. The best system, and one which is being tried to a very large extent in England, will always be to select the promising few at the earliest possible moment and help them to pass the curriculum of the normal secondary school. But so long as this better method of selection is not yet fully developed, the path indicated by University Extension will also retain its importance. Further, University Extension has helped to close painful gaps in the education of many a school-teacher, male and female. And the seed it has scattered so profusely has found other fruitful soils. There is hardly a town where it has not played its part in educational development. In many the movement has grown into a college (Nottingham, Exeter) in others (Sheffield, Reading) it has developed into a University. Everywhere University Extension has become a powerful antidote against that dreary matter-of-factness and bleak materialism which crops up everywhere in English life, not least among English workers; the cheap books and popular libraries which have been scattered over the country in the nineteenth century, have largely, through University Extension, been made a living force in the land.

§ 12

It is this combination of academic and, strictly speaking, non-academic work that gives Oxford and Cambridge their lasting influence upon the English nation. To the Continental observer who only thinks of lectures and degrees, the English University seems to be failing in many things. Enormous sums are spent in the luxurious life of students, an enormous staff is needed for purposes which seem to be wholly irrelevant to the proper functions of a University, while the cry for more money for research, for salaries, for laboratories and equipment goes incessantly through the land. All this is true, but hardly the whole truth. It is a question what the nation wants the University to do, whether it shall foster thought and thought alone or whether it shall influence life as it is. In the former case, the outlook will be into the future and University influence will be enormously strong, though it will take time to make itself felt, and though periods may intervene where that influence may seem to be nil. In the second case, the influence may spend itself sooner, but it will be felt at once and permeate the whole of life. In Germany the national ideal has hitherto tended to lie in the former direction, in England in the latter: just as religious ideals in Germany are more far-reaching, in England more practical (cf. p. 403 *seq.*). In neither nation is the tendency quite one-sided, quite definite, so as to exclude altogether the other possibility, and one century may stress just those points which the other has missed. On the whole, Englishmen being what they are, the English University ideal must also embrace the practical side of life, it must also tend to develop the faculties of the human body in its students, it must also do something for human life outside the walls of the University. It makes its influence felt everywhere.

No one who knows English history can forget the great movements that have taken their rise in Oxford. Every contemporary current finds fruitful soil in this close association of gifted young men. Oxford in the fourteenth century was the domain of Wycliffe; in the eighteenth century it was the cradle of Methodism, in the nineteenth of the High Church movement; it was there that Ruskin taught. Cambridge is the birthplace of University Extension, and the social settlement; it was there that Seeley taught Imperialism to his generation. Above all, Oxford and Cambridge breed the sort of leaders that the nation wants – men not always of learning, but always of will; men furnished, too, with an adequate supply of correct ethical

427

notions, with knowledge of their fellows and of the world: men who are keen, well set-up, and of perfect manners.

Nor would it be just to underrate the purely intellectual significance of these Universities. Pure study may, for the mass of undergraduates, be little but a name; but there are others in whom moves a genuine impulse to study, and for them Oxford and Cambridge have an enormous importance. Here, in one spot, are united professors of distinction most of them, not ground down by dreary routine; libraries of incredible range; a life of ease and culture; every advantage of the small town plus all the glories of historic associations! To every individual here multiform activity is open. There are men of learning. There are also men occupied, either as teachers or examiners, with every topic under the sun – from the school system of New Zealand to the mental yearnings of a Welsh miner. The number of men upon whom all these treasures are wasted may still be great, far too great after two generations of strenuous reform. But there is also an unusually large body of persons who live in and for the things of the mind, in the spirit of the purest classical models. Side by side with the aristocracy of gentlemen, spread throughout the English-speaking world by Oxford and Cambridge, is an aristocracy of humanism, also of their breeding, small in numbers but extraordinarily fine in quality. It dwells, for the most part, within their walls; but representatives of it are also to be found in many a solitary vicarage, many a rich country house, and may, perhaps, be found in the House of Commons. And it has saved England, so far, from sinking altogether into the morass of materialism. The great mass of the nation can neither understand nor appreciate the pure learning of the don, but they can understand and appreciate his fostering care of schools at home and as far away as South Africa and New Zealand, and what he has done to give the woman and the working-man some sort of contact with culture. And this gives to every University resolution, every professorial lecture, a resonance throughout the country stronger than in any other country of the world.

§ 13

Has the war had lasting reactions on the life of the University? No one would venture to answer this question as yet. There is an increase in the dependence of the University on the State: the State makes large grants; in Oxford it contributes a quarter of the present total revenue of the University. There is an increase in academic strenuousness; side by side with the pass and honours man has appeared the research student, who, after taking an honours degree, goes on, quite on German lines, to work of an independent character. The philosophic doctorate on the German model has been introduced. Thus, the effect of the war has been to strengthen the tendencies already noted above. But it has had another effect, which is entirely new – in Oxford, Conservatism is no longer 'the thing'; now, the 'best people' coquet with Socialism and come out as unsparing critics of Society and the State; they are no longer Imperialists but incline to pacifism, and many seek to establish contacts with Germany. Nowhere is the blast of realistic scepticism blown over England by the war and its aftermath so sensible as in the Universities. This certainly is a proof that the nation's pulse still beats in them: that every spiritual movement in England finds its strongest echo within the walls of the University. But it would be rash to assume, on the evidence of such momentary disturbances, that anything like a real breach with the past is preparing. The problem of this after-war pessimism in contemporary Britain must be discussed more fully at the end of this book.

CHAPTER II

THE SCOTTISH UNIVERSITIES

THE type of University, as represented by Oxford and Cambridge, is by no means the only one in Great Britain. In Scotland, a type developed similar to the German, both in premises and in results. The desire for learning, from the time of the Reformation on, was far stronger here than in England; Scotland was Presbyterian and Calvinist, and the discovery of truth, knowledge of the Bible, and with it, of the classical tongues, were questions of life and death for every one. The roots of Scottish zeal for education lie even deeper; in pre-Reformation times, the little country had three Universities – St. Andrews (1411), Glasgow (1450) and Aberdeen (1494). In 1582 Edinburgh, now the most important of them all, was added, and in 1880 the University College of Dundee, affiliated since 1897 with St. Andrews. The social and religious difficulties that made the University, in England, the citadel of the gentry and barred any access to it to the middle-class youth, never existed in Scotland. Broadly speaking, the whole country was Presbyterian and democratic. As a matter of course, the professor was a member of the Kirk, and every University represented on the General Assembly. After the split in the Scottish Church between the Kirk and the Free Kirk, the Free Kirk had to set up theological schools, equipped as small faculties, in Aberdeen, Edinburgh, and Glasgow. The split was a calamity for Scottish theology. The equipment, from its own resources, of four theological faculties, in a country of five million inhabitants, would have been impossible except in a nation where every man is half a theologian; seven, even here, could only be maintained at a sacrifice of quality. Colleges, in the English sense, do not exist in Scotland; such foundations as do exist are mere hostels, which do no teaching of their own, and have no suggestion of luxury about them. Since the Universities (Scotland) Acts of 1858 and 1889, administration has been more or less on the German model, although the head of the academic Senate is a Principal, who need not have been a professor. Above the Senate is the University Court, on which professors, graduates, and, to some extent, the city and donors are represented. The General Council, the organization of graduates, has the right of making proposals to the Court. The Lord Rector is elected by the whole student body and tends to be some distinguished politician. Important endowments are received from the

THE SCOTTISH UNIVERSITIES

State; further, £50,000 annually is distributed to the Scottish Universities from the fund created by Andrew Carnegie for the promotion of Scottish education. From Reformation days, the City of Edinburgh has enjoyed the right of nominating four of the seven curators to its University, in whose hands lie the appointments of professors.

The curriculum differs, in many respects, from that of Oxford and Cambridge. The predominance of classics is much less marked; modern languages, however, are hardly developed sufficiently. Glasgow, with its professorships of mining, engineering and shipbuilding, has something like a Technical faculty; Edinburgh has lectureships on Forestry, and Banking; Aberdeen on Veterinary medicine and Fishery. The medical faculties are highly developed in all the Universities; the reputation of the Edinburgh Medical school is world-wide. In Glasgow and Edinburgh there are, in addition, independent Technical Schools – the Royal Technical College and Heriot Watt College.

Here, too, however, the level of much of the teaching is quite elementary, as at Oxford and Cambridge, from other causes, however. Owing to the lack of a sufficient number of really good secondary schools the students come up very young and spend their University time in learning what they ought to have learned in school. The degree – always M.A., not B.A. – does not perhaps quite rank on a level with that of the English Universities, but its academic content steadily improves. The students are drawn almost exclusively from the middle and lower classes. Since the upper circles have long been Anglican, they tend to send their sons to Oxford and Cambridge. The effect of the Carnegie grants in providing bursaries to all necessitous students has greatly increased the total numbers, but definitely impressed upon the Scottish Universities a kind of lower-middle-class stamp which is no advantage from any point of view. With all these handicaps however, Scottish Universities have become an important factor in English cultural life. Their democratic and highly intellectual character gives to the nation a powerful and beneficial stimulus which Oxford and Cambridge could hardly have supplied from their own resources.

CHAPTER III
LONDON AND THE NORTHERN UNIVERSITIES

§ 1

THERE seemed, in the first third of the nineteenth century, small hope of the abolition of tests at Oxford and Cambridge. With the aim, therefore, of securing, at least for Dissenters, an equivalent academic training, University College, London, was founded, in 1827, and endowed, by a group of Liberals, among them Lord Brougham (d. 1868), the jurist, George Birkbeck (d. 1841), the educational reformer, Joseph Hume (d. 1855), the Liberal M.P., James Mill the philosopher, and George Grote, the historian of Greece. Something on the lines of Berlin was in their minds; the new University was to be neutral in religion and no questions asked of any student as to his opinions on that head. Out of their foundation London University developed, as a model for all subsequent Universities established in England. There was, at first, sharp opposition; the University felt the repercussions of the embittered struggle between Radicals and Churchmen over the schools, raging at the time between the partisans of the undenominational system associated with the name of Lancaster and the strictly religious one, associated with that of Bell; in 1829–31, Church circles set up, in competition with the 'Godless' University College, their own King's College, with exclusively Anglican professors and an overwhelmingly Church tone. In 1836 University College was associated with King's College to form London University under an arrangement which, while permitting it to carry on its teaching activities, compelled it to conduct its examinations and grant degrees in combination with the denominational body. It was a meagre result, but the main thing was accomplished: the University was no longer the monopoly of the Anglican and the rich. A generation later, a new important step followed. By the new charter of 1850 and subsequent legislation of 1858, London acquired the right to admit to its degrees any fit candidate, no matter where he had studied. This very singular development can only be understood by a glance at the educational situation of the time.

The first half of the nineteenth century was a period of experiments in pedagogy and the establishment of more or less unsystematic lecture courses of all kinds. Thus, George Birkbeck founded Mechanics' Institutes all over the country, partly to give to the artisan the general education then almost entirely lacking in England, and partly to give more advanced education to those who already possessed this degree of training. These Institutes gradually developed into centres used by the middle as well as by the working class for continued education. Steps in the same direction were the Rev. R. T. Bagley's Peoples' College in Sheffield, and the Working Men's College in London, founded by the Christian Socialists, F. D. Maurice and Henry Kingsley. London University, then, provided something like a fixed standard for all this more or less unsystematic philanthropic activity; matriculation there opened the way in to one or other of the two London Colleges to the small number who succeeded in getting anything in the nature of a systematic training out of the mass of institutions available for the purpose. Meantime, all over the country, organizations came into being designed to provide something in the nature of university education, to improve the technical training of merchants and industrialists, or give women an access to higher education; such as Owens College in Manchester (1851), Mason's College in Birmingham (1875), and, in London, Bedford College for Women (1849). At the same time there was a rapid development of training colleges for dissenting ministers. This diversity of courses and needs was, gradually, systematized by London University. It could give or refuse official recognition to the courses of any institution. By exempting students from 'recognized' institutions from its matriculation examination, it stamped them as having achieved a certain level. London University is by these means an institution for the education of colleges. It further has become an institution for helping the self-made man. It admits to its examinations for degrees any one who has passed matriculation, whether the subsequent study has been accomplished through Extension courses, home work or correspondence classes – a method greatly used in the nineteenth century to compensate for the deficiencies of the public educational system in England. London was primarily the institute which tried to stop all the gaps in the then existing educational web. The tendency is the same which we encountered in our description of Oxford and Cambridge. The University is not regarded primarily as an academic body giving a specific education in an organized form, but as a national institution for the raising of the general level of culture of the nation. Oxford and Cambridge endeavour to do this by giving a high general education – and specialist training, if desired – to the upper classes. The aim is

433

extended to include the provision, through school examinations and University Extension, of a measure of higher education to a wider range of persons. London, on the other hand, sought in the first instance to meet the needs of the middle and lower classes by direct instruction in its two colleges, and further, by means of its examinations, to promote any and every educational effort throughout the country. It was left to private initiative to endow all sorts of foundations and call colleges into being absolutely without plan or co-ordination; it was the task of London University to attempt to bring order into this chaos through the gentle but definite pressure of its examination system. And as, in Oxford and Cambridge, University examinations give a sort of unity to the multifarious colleges, here there are colleges too, King's and University, fully developed, but besides them all sorts of sister institutions in London which, when they prove their competency, may be recognized as constituent colleges of London University. Such sister institutions have also arisen in the provinces. Partly as a result of the Extension movement and gently fostered by the requirements for the London degree, colleges sprang up in various localities, e.g. Reading (1892), Exeter, Southampton, Nottingham (1880), etc. Their teaching includes the usual University subjects, and their students are educated men and women of all classes, who, for the most part, have come up through the elementary schools; and, after a series of years' study, are eligible for a London degree.

§ 2

The London method has been widely imitated. In Ireland, from 1591 on, there was one strictly Anglican University in Dublin, naturally avoided by the Catholics – Trinity College, a classical and aristocratic institution, on Oxford and Cambridge lines. In 1845, however, the Government founded undenominational colleges: Queen's Colleges, at Belfast, Cork and Galway, united, in 1850 to form the Queen's University – and equipped with an examination system on London University lines. But the Catholics, by no means satisfied by this concession, replied by founding a Catholic University in Dublin, with Cardinal Newman as its first Head. It proved a complete failure however; and in 1880 the Government attempted to meet the Catholics by setting up a free Royal University of Ireland – an examination, not a teaching body, to which anyone, whether trained in the Protestant atmosphere of Queen's Colleges, or in the Catholic atmosphere of Dublin, might present himself, and if worthy, receive either the B.A. or the M.A. degree. Finally, in 1909, Protestant Belfast was made an independent University, while the Queen's Colleges in Catholic Cork and Galway were united with the Catholic University of Dublin – all under the name, now, of University Colleges – to form the National University of Ireland. Teaching is carried on in the constituent colleges; the University does not teach, but only examines, and is responsible, thereby, for keeping the academic level of the different colleges at an equal height. From an academic point of view, the Royal University, as a whole, lags behind Trinity College, with its well-established reputation; this is markedly the case with Cork and Galway.

London University has, further, been relieved by the foundation, in 1884, of Victoria University, as an examining body, then composed of Manchester (Owens College), Leeds and Liverpool, all of which have subsequently become independent Universities; and of the University of Wales, constituted in 1893 from the University Colleges of Aberystwyth, Bangor, Cardiff and Swansea.[1] In India, the Universities of Bombay, Calcutta and Madras were founded, in 1857, on the London model, followed, in 1883, by Lahore and, in 1887, by Allahabad, all these being examining bodies which supervise the teaching given in a very large number of constituent colleges.

§ 3

London still continues its work as an examining body for the mass of men and women with more or less irregular training. But its main importance now lies in its teaching. By gradual incorporation of other teaching institutions it has become the great academic centre of the Metropolis. It now consists of:

1. The old teaching bodies, University and King's College, each of them a small university in itself, with faculties of philosophy, natural sciences, medicine and law, and, in King's College, theology also, although the insistence on all the professors being Anglicans, which was part of the old dispensation, has dropped. From the outset, instruction here has been more modern than that of the older Universities; the study of English has always been strongly accentuated, the same is true of science and technology.

2. A series of women's colleges – Bedford (founded in 1849); Westfield College (1882), and Royal Holloway College [2] (1886).

3. A large number of theological Seminaries for Dissenters – New and Hackney College (Congregationalist), dating back to 1696;

Regent's Park College (Baptist); Wesleyan College; as well as St. John's Hall, Highbury (Anglican).

4. (*a*) The widely famous London School of Economics and Political Science, (*b*) The South-Eastern Agricultural College at Wye, (*c*) The School of Oriental Studies.

5. The London Day Training College. There is also a women's Training college, affiliated to Bedford.

6. The Imperial College of Science and Technology, at South Kensington.

7. Thirteen London Hospitals, with their own University classes; the Lister Research Institute, and the Royal Army Medical College.

8. East London College and Birkbeck College.

Immense difficulties were, obviously, presented by the task of welding into some sort of unity institutions as different, in their educational aims, their teaching staffs and in their student bodies, as these, and combining them with the others which stood in some sort of loose association with the University; difficulties all the greater in a country where the authority of the State is lax, where everything depends on the good will of those concerned. Nor has complete success been achieved as yet. Each of the institutions mentioned above counts as a separate school of the University. Each retains its own teaching staff, its own conditions of admission to study, its own curriculum (often with a distribution of faculties quite peculiar to itself), its own teaching methods, its own budget and financial arrangements generally. The result is bound to be a wide range of diversity. Since, however, none of these institutions has a really adequate staff of its own, all are bound to supplement their own 'recognized teachers' by 'appointed teachers' nominated by the University, and the existence of this centrally appointed part of the staff helps to raise the general level. A similar effect is produced by the examination system: the University fixes standards both for matriculation and degrees, and in this way its sphere of influence is immense. Its kernel, the two old colleges, King's and University, provides courses in the faculties of theology, philosophy, law and natural science equivalent to the Honours Schools of the older Universities, if not indeed here and there superior. A London M.A. represents a degree of genuine academic achievement, and still more so the new doctor's degree, which may follow upon it. University examinations further set the standard for the courses given in other, special, institutions, e.g. medicine, agricultural science, economics, theology, etc. Its influence further extends to all sorts of extra-mural institutions in London – e.g. technical institutes, training colleges, institutes of music, and the Hospital medical schools – through the recognition it extends to effective individual teachers by making them 'recognized teachers' of the University. As the number of such teachers increases in any institution, and, as a result, the general level there rises, the prospect opens of becoming a constituent college within the University itself.

The administration of this mass of institutions, so diverse in type, is a gigantic task, and one that cannot be accomplished by professors alone. Irrespective of the institutions in which they work, all professors are grouped in eight faculties – theology, arts, law, medicine, music, natural science, technology, economics. Thus, for example, in the theological faculty of London University the teachers in King's College, which is Anglican, sit side by side with those of the three Nonconformist schools. The ultimate governing body is the Senate, consisting of fifty-two members, the grouping of which represents all the interests comprised in the University. Sixteen members are appointed by the Faculties and four by the old vested interests, University and King's Colleges, with four or five from the Medical and Legal Associations of the country. The State has the right to nominate four, in view of the very considerable grants it makes to the University, and, for the same reason, the City and County of London send three (as well as the representative of a particular Technical Institute). A third group of sixteen, elected by the Convocation of graduates, is intended to secure the representation, on the Senate, of men of distinction as educationalists, whether or no they are professors or graduates of the University. At the head there is, in addition to the Chancellor (who is apt to be some great nobleman, e.g., Lord Rosebery) and Vice-Chancellor, a permanent Principal, who is the life and soul of the entire University. Thus, the constitution borrows Convocation from Oxford and Cambridge, as the organ of University democracy, while following the Scottish-American practice in the status of the Principal, as in the large influence given to practical men in the general government of the whole. This last idea reappears in all the more modern foundations.

§ 4

A similar development, from the tiny educational institute, through the great examining centre, to the complete teaching university, took place in the great industrial areas of the North. The point of departure, here, was Owens College, Manchester (1851), which, by 1880, had developed into Victoria University, as an examining body, with teaching colleges in Manchester, Leeds and Liverpool. In 1903 Liverpool and Manchester, and in 1904 Leeds, became independent Universities. In 1900 a University was established in Birmingham (out of Mason's College, founded in 1875); in 1909 in Bristol, and in 1905 in Sheffield. In Durham a small theological (Anglican) University had existed since 1831, now combined with the medical school founded in Newcastle in 1851, and with Armstrong College (1871) also there, to form the University of Durham. The newest foundation is the University of Reading (1926).

These new Universities arose in response to the needs of areas mainly occupied in trade and industry. They have no desire to compete with Oxford and Cambridge; they serve a section of the population with other ideals. In their curricula, classics no longer have pride of place; modern languages are on an equal footing with them; medicine is everywhere a strong, separate faculty; law tends to occupy a subsidiary position, and theology to be lacking altogether – only in Manchester is there a separate theological faculty – but natural science, economics and technology are very important, indeed predominant. Faculties (or at least departments) for technology and engineering occur everywhere, so do medical schools. There is a faculty of commerce in Birmingham and teachers' colleges everywhere. Arts have a more difficult standing in the atmosphere of modern industry; in one place, Liverpool, difficulties have been overcome with remarkable success; here, besides a renowned medical school and remarkably good provision for modern languages, there is an Institute of Archaeology, provision for Egyptology and Oriental languages.

Most of these newer Universities are strongly scientific in bent. A comparatively high academic level is assured through a matriculation examination common to all the Northern Universities (with the exception of Durham), for which the Scottish Universities Entrance Board examination may be substituted. Their M.A. degree, if taken on the Honours level, implies serious study; here and there (for example, in Liverpool) Honours requires the submission of a thesis. In addition, the Universities carry on active Extension work, and almost all have teachers' training colleges.

In organization, too, these newer Universities are quite different

438

from the old. Their constitutions are modelled, not upon Oxford and Cambridge, but upon the Universities of Scotland and the United States. They receive considerable State grants, although the State exercises no control, and has no voice in the selection of professors. All it does is to nominate some man of public distinction – generally a peer – as Chancellor, and some man of academic attainments as Vice-Chancellor or Principal. The latter, appointed for life, is, like the American University President, the soul of the whole; he sits and speaks on all University governing bodies and has far more influence than the German Rector, appointed annually; with him, as usual, one comes back to the monarchical principle, everywhere operative in England beneath the forms of democracy. Current business is dealt with by the Faculties and the Senate, comprising them all. Above this purely academic body is the Council, in which the determinant voice belongs to donors and municipal representatives, not the professorate, of which only a certain number of members have seats. The Council controls University finance and is also the ultimately deciding body in the appointment of professors. The Senate makes proposals, but the Council can exert pressure on the professors to submit a new list. This, of course, implies the danger that University policy may be directed along the lines laid down by economic and financial interests. Above the Council itself there is a Court of Governors, a great body of some hundred dignitaries, a sort of blend of the idea of Convocation with that of a meeting of shareholders. It comprises representatives of the graduate body, of the professors, and, above all, of the donors, chosen, naturally, in accordance with their wealth and consideration. Formally, the Court must approve the resolutions of the Council; its real business is with the collection of new pecuniary resources – a task of enormous importance, in view of the constantly growing needs of the Universities.

§ 5

There is much that is extraordinarily characteristic in the development of the English Universities out of such mediaeval scholastic institutions as Oxford and Cambridge still were, in the first half of the nineteenth century, to a University of the type of Liverpool. The older Universities have been most thoroughly overhauled; their ecclesiastical character has been swept away, and modern scientific studies introduced; they have been thrown open to women, and have put themselves, to a very large extent, at the service of general popular education. Yet, despite comprehensive reforms, the class pyramid on which the whole of English society is based is only modified. A great scholarship system has cast wide the doors of the older Universities to the less well-to-do, but the old spirit of the gentry is still in possession within the house. The education offered, though no longer exclusively classical, is still largely so; the ideal of learning is still secondary to the main ideal of the training of gentlemen. Middle and lower-class demands for access to more knowledge have been met by the foundation of new Universities. The excessive specialization of Germany has been avoided: there has been no rigid separation of what is good in the new from what is good in the old, such as resulted, there, in the foundation of Technical and Commercial High Schools. Moreover, instead of pushing the whole crowd of young persons, pressing eagerly up from below, into the old seats of learning, there has been a skilful selection from among them of just such a number as could be easily assimilated. In mass they might have been a danger to the ascendancy of the gentry; a few have been accepted in the older seats of learning, the mass has been provided with educational institutions of their own. In specialist Germany, the organization of University education is based upon subject matter – the University, the Technical Institute, the Commercial High School; in political England, the grading is social. First, there are the new Northern schools, often called contemptuously mushroom Universities, because they shot up so suddenly round about 1900. More 'respectable' are the Scottish Universities, which at least have a notable pedigree. At the top, beyond competition, are Oxford and Cambridge. From a purely academic point of view, the new Universities may beat the old on this or that point. It makes no difference. The average Englishman rates them far below Oxford and Cambridge. If a post is to be filled, the academic qualifications of the M.A. of Liverpool or Leeds will not prevail against the social status of the Oxford B.A., which bears no mark of coal dust and the fumes of brewing vats.

The task of the Northern Universities is no easy one. They have to serve science, they are supported by capitalism and frequented by the lower middle class, and have, somehow, to find a *via media* between these three interests. Their students, born in the lower social grades, seek the education of the higher. Their parents, like the capitalists who founded the University, conceive of science as a useful instrument for winning a large income in a short time. They

will produce money for laboratories, but less easily for libraries: for
brewing research, but hardly for philosophy. Greek, over-emphasized
in Oxford, has a stiff fight for existence in the North. It is the University's business to emphasize the fact that scientific study is an end
in itself, and that practical results are to be counted on only when there
is no attempt to force them like hot-house plants. That is not easy.
Even more difficult is it to care for the students' needs outside the
lecture-room and utilize the great opportunities of this time of life for
general educational purposes. By founding hostels for those students
who do not live with their parents on the spot, the University seeks
to transplant college life, in a simplified form, into the ranks of the
bourgeoisie. Sport, social contacts, and debates, according to parliamentary forms, are promoted. Social service, in the form of University Extension, is encouraged, as well as active co-operation with the
W.E.A. But all this is not easy to accomplish among students of a
big town who have very little in common outside the lecture-room.
Further, these things are not cheap. No small tact and skill are
required of the Vice-Chancellor or Principal of a new University who
has to make a case for these requirements before a Council of big
capitalists.

Capitalism has a large say in the Northern Universities. The
alliance between capitalism and aristocracy, existing in other departments of national life, reappears in this. In Oxford and Cambridge
the aristocratic spirit rules; there, the plebeian has been kept well in
the minority, while humanism gives the tone. In the new schools of
the North, trade and industry dominate. The English conception of
the State as consciously partisan forbids its being allowed any strong
influence over the University; it is generally feared that a party tinge
might enter into the appointment of professors if it were in the
hands of a Minister of Education. *Per contra*, it seems obvious, to the
English mind, that the capitalist donors should govern 'their' University. Not that this is done in any narrow-minded spirit. There is
no trace of that in any Englishman who counts for anything in public
life. In the details of day-to-day administration, the Universities
are perfectly free. In the vital matter of the election of professors
academic influence is strong. If it should not be sufficient, the power
of the Vice-Chancellor or Principal, again academic persons, ought
to be strong enough to hold capitalistic influences on the Council
in check. Yet, considerations have to be kept in view, here, on a
thousand points, great and small – such as the grant of honorary

degrees, and now and then the appointment to chairs – that do not occur in the older Universities, and cause grave searchings of heart to professors of strong individual convictions. The way the wind blows was shown, plainly enough, by such a dispute as arose in Bristol in 1913, when the University had been too free in granting honorary degrees to the merchants and industrialists on its Council. So far, the dependence of the newer Universities on capitalism has not proved dangerous, but their position is hardly strong enough to be viewed with entire satisfaction – in England as well as in other countries.

CHAPTER IV
ELEMENTARY AND SECONDARY SCHOOLS

§ 1

PROTESTANTISM is the parent of the modern elementary school. In his concern for his soul's salvation, the Protestant had to seek the will of God in Holy Scripture. For him, therefore, reading and some degree of intellectual training were religious demands. Luther exhorted the Protestant princes to found schools. From the eighteenth century on, Protestant Prussia was the pioneer of elementary education.

In Calvinist Scotland, a parallel development took place. The Reformation (1560), here, too, caused the foundation of schools all over the country; to a nation of natural theologians, Bible reading, and consequently the spread of some degree of education, were matters of vital importance. In England, the case was quite different. Although the Church had adopted Protestant dogma, it was frankly opposed to the individualistic piety of the Continent; too much knowledge might lead to Deism or to a sectarianism perilous to Church and State. A perfectly blank face was presented to every effort at improving popular education; the Church's interest was confined to preventing the foundation of Dissenting schools which might prove hostile to it. The reactionary Act of Uniformity (1662) attempted to nip all such attempts in the bud by making it impossible for anyone to teach except by permission of a bishop. Since the lower orders were, in the main, Nonconformist, there were almost insuperable difficulties in the way of establishing schools, and the level of popular education remained appallingly low. The children whom the mighty industrial developments at the turn of the eighteenth and nineteenth centuries swept into the factories, grew up, as a rule, without any sort of education. The intentions with which Robert Raikes, the pious printer (d. 1811), founded his Sunday Schools (in 1780) were admirable, but the most they could do was to give the children some scraps of useful knowledge in addition to their Scripture lessons; any kind of real education was out of the question.

This continued to be the position until the Quaker, Joseph Lancaster (d. 1838), established his free school in a London working-class area – Southwark, in 1801. His genius, both for education and organization, enabled him to surmount all the obstacles presented by the apathy and greed of parents, the complete indifference of the mass, and his own lack of means. He taught children of varying ages and stages in a single room; those who had learned something were at once set to teaching the others; the older scholars served as monitors. There were no slates, so they used a board sprinkled with sand; there were no books, so they pinned a page from the primer on to the wall. Corporal punishment was taboo, but although his pupils came from the most degraded section of the urban poor, Lancaster succeeded in rousing some sort of sense of honour even in the worst of them by a skilful plan of rewards and punishments.

Lancaster's immense success led to the foundation, in 1808, of the British and Foreign School Society, designed to ameliorate the wretched condition of the youth of the great towns, along his lines – the employment of great bodies of monitors or pupil-teachers, who taught as they learned. About the same time, Andrew Bell, an Anglican clergyman, transplanted to England the analogous system employed by him in an Orphan Asylum in Madras – the same system, in effect, as that used by Raikes in his Sunday Schools. In 1811, Bell (d. 1832) established the National Society for the Education of the Poor. The distinction between the two societies was religious: Lancaster's, founded by Quakers, other Dissenters and representatives of the left wing of the Church, aimed at building up undenominational schools; the National Society, supported by the Right wing of the Church, stood for a strictly Anglican education. This fatal opposition (the counterpart of the foundation of King's College, on an Anglican basis, in 1831, by the side of University College, founded in 1827 on an undenominational one) was for decades to prevent any progress in education in England, and to this day dogs the advance of educational reform.

The State, dominated by the ideas of Manchesterism, for long did nothing, thus abandoning the most important field of State activity entirely to private philanthropy. Philanthropy, in its turn, proceeded, in the main, along two lines. On the left were men like Lord Brougham, a Liberal minister, and, notably, Radicals like Jeremy Bentham, the two Mills, Harriett Martineau and George Grote; on the right, a small group of reformers within the Church, like Coleridge and later Lord Shaftesbury, who were quick to see that the cause of the Church itself would be lost if a matter so fundamental were left to its enemies. Under their dual pressure, the State, in 1832, had reached the point of making grants of £200,000 to the two societies – a sum multiplied more than twentyfold within the course of the next forty years. This subsidy was originally given only for buildings. 1839 saw the establishment of the first official education department, in the form of a department of the Privy Council, with James Kay-Shuttleworth at its head. Originally a physician, Shuttleworth had learned to know the plight of the young through his work for the poor in Manchester; his tireless and far-seeing devotion entitles him to be called the veritable father of popular education in England. In so far as the State made grants, it acquired a certain right of supervision; the grants were based on the quality of the schools, as tested by an elaborate system of examination. Thanks to the self-sacrificing energy of the societies, school-attendance rose notably, although there was no sort of system of compulsion; a Royal Commission, under the Duke of Newcastle, which sat from 1858–1861, reported that the standard of teaching in the schools was lamentably low, hardly ever comprising more than the three R's, but that something like one-seventh of the population was actually going to school. So far as attendance went, then, England was not so far behind Prussia, where the proportion at this time was one-sixth. The quality of instruction, on the other hand, was of the poorest. Under the new code promulgated by Robert Lowe, the vice-president of the Committee on Education in 1861, all the contributions of the State were graded according to proficiency of the school in the most elementary subjects and these alone. This first meant, in practice, neglect of any higher aims in education. And further, since the very existence of the school depended on examinations, it led to a soulless grinding of youth for examination purposes, the traces of which are not yet vanished. In 1870 a decisive step was taken at last. W. E. Forster, a member of Mr. Gladstone's Government, introduced a Bill imposing the obligation on parishes of providing schools where the existing provision was not adequate, with the option of making attendance compulsory. In 1876, Disraeli's Cabinet added universal compulsory attendance. In 1899, the Board of Education[1] was set up, as an independent ministry of education. At first, the schools were maintained by the parishes or by *ad hoc* bodies (School Boards) composed of the combination of several such parishes; in 1902, County and Town Councils were substituted for School Boards as education authorities. Now, local resources are supplemented by State grants (which are not, however, given in respect of denominational religious instruction). The State has the right of inspection of the teaching of all subjects towards which it makes grants. Administration, instead of being entrusted to local officers on the spot is, in the characteristic English fashion (cf. p. 258), directed from a central office in the capital, which issues a mass of circulars and orders and controls their execution through peripatetic inspectors. State interference is confined to matters of principle: the Department has nothing to do with individual cases (the appointment of a teacher, the dismissal of a pupil, the choice of text-books, etc.).

The development, here, is typically English. At first, the gentry direct the State. They care nothing for general culture. In 1832, the wealthy middle classes take the helm. At first, things are not much better. The captain of industry cares as little as the landowner about the education of the proletarian child. 'Knowledge only makes people restless and disinclined for useful work.' 'Parents are the best judges of how much education their children need' – such was the profound reasoning employed to oppose compulsory education. The result was a condition of chaos that was a disgrace to England. But in England, such a chaos is the necessary preliminary to anything thorough being done, as we have seen in relation to municipal government, and to conditions in Ireland or in Canada. But, in England, such chaos is never fatal. There are always enough powerful individuals to seize hold of things and establish some voluntary association which, after performing an immense work, ultimately compels the State to take over a burden that has become too heavy for it to carry. Popular education was not created by a Ministry of Education from above, but by a couple of private individuals, Lancaster and Bell – just as the transformation of the horrible English prison to a humane institution was the work of a single philanthropist, John Howard, and the reconstruction of administration was due to the powerful impetus of publicists like Edwin Chadwick and Jeremy Bentham.

§ 2

Sectarian disagreement was the great problem, and one that, to this day, has been bridged rather than solved. The Education Act of 1870, introduced by the Liberal Gladstone Ministry, favoured undenominational schools. True, grants were still paid to Church schools, and the State left them free in their religious teaching. At the same time they had to guarantee free entry to children of all denominations, and, under the so-called Conscience clause, exempt

446

any from denominational religious instruction, on the wish of the parent. Further, so far as non-religious teaching went, denominational schools were subject to State inspection: only religious teaching, and the appointment of the teachers, remained entirely in the hands of the religious bodies maintaining the schools. The intention of the Government in all this was that the denominational school should become, more and more, the exception, the normal type being the undenominational school, managed by a communal body (at first a School Board), supported and inspected by the State, with religious instruction of an undenominational character [2] (a clause proposed by W. F. Cowper-Temple, a former vice-president of the Committee on Education) on broadly Christian but not specifically Anglican lines, the Conscience clause permitting anyone who objected to withdraw his children from these lessons.

Undenominational education might thus have seemed to be established as normal. Although Church schools continued in existence, their dependence on subscriptions (with the aid of the State grant) meant that it was difficult for them to compete with undenominational schools, solidly based on local rates and taxes. Anglicanism, however, was not so easily dislodged. In 1902 it acquired rate-aid for Church schools, for all purposes save denominational religious teaching. There was a great agitation throughout the country, with Passive Resistance, in the shape of refusal to pay taxes, on the part of large bodies of Dissenters. Nevertheless, to all intents and purposes, the Church held on to what it had won; to this day this is the chief grievance of Dissenters. The so-called voluntary or non-provided schools continue to be under the control of religious associations, although the local authority is represented on their governing body, and the teaching, in all but religious subjects, like the appointment and dismissal of teachers, subject to control by the local education authority. That authority may not interfere with religious instruction, nor can it refuse sanction to the appointment of a teacher on religious grounds. The cost of buildings has to be borne by the religious bodies themselves. Any child may be exempted from religious instruction on the application of his parent. Considerable concessions, these, to the opponents of denominational schools. Against them, however, must be set the countervailing fact that there has been, since the 1902 Act, a marked revival of schools giving religious instruction along Church lines and animated – all paper restrictions notwithstanding – by a definitely Anglican spirit. This type of school the 1870 Act was designed to eliminate; it is now being subsidized by the State and by the rates. The 1902 Act was a decisive victory for Anglicanism.

For this reason, the Act is a thorn in the flesh of Dissent, of part of the left wing in the Church, and of those who stand aloof from religion. Not that either these people, or any substantial portion of the English nation, desire to have the schools completely secularized. There is religious teaching in the undenominational schools. What does trouble Dissenters, who are about half the population, is that the majority of the schools in the country are not undenominational; what they complain of is that a majority of children are being taught in schools of an Anglican stamp by teachers who, whatever the law may say, are, in fact, overwhelmingly Anglican. The standard of teaching in Church schools is lower, but they are more numerous; in 1926–7 they outnumbered the provided schools by 11,553 to 9,170, and almost all of them are Anglican. Theoretically, both Catholics and Dissenters can found schools of their own. Catholics, thanks to the wealth they still retain, have done so to a very considerable extent. Dissenters, on the other hand, are so subdivided that they can do very little in this direction. For them, the provided school is the only type that serves, since the dogmatic distinctions between Dissent and Anglicanism being trifling, undenominational teaching provides a groundwork which can either be completed by special sectarian teaching, or avoided altogether through the working of the Conscience clause. As it is, however, they have not only to pay rates to support the Anglican school they dislike, but, to a large extent, to send their children to it, since in many country districts, the Anglican is often the only school; local government is in the hands of the gentry, who do not bother to meet the wishes of Nonconformists who may happen to dwell in the area. The Conscience clause is then their sole resource, and it, at best, merely enables them to withdraw their children from religious instruction in school, and take upon themselves the obligation of providing for it somehow from their own usually very slender means. With most of them, the religious instinct is so strong as to compel this; anyhow, the Conscience clause is seldom employed to withdraw children from religious instruction altogether, since social pressure in England is so strong that (outside the bohemian set of a few great towns) any kind of 'free thought' requires more courage and conviction than is at all common. For this reason there is a fervid demand for the abolition of denominational teaching in schools, organized since 1903 in the National Education Association (not to be confused with Bell's National Society).

Church circles, on the other hand, are far from satisfied with the religious teaching offered them in provided schools. Such teaching has difficulties of its own. Any unconsidered, obscure, or misapprehended word used by a teacher may bring down the wrath of some exasperated parent or school governor upon his head. Safety lies only in the reading without comment and memorizing of Bible texts and stories. And this is what undenominational religious teaching generally amounts to. The result, in countless cases, is a teaching that is ethically dead: a mere exercise of memory, without any, or but a very small, religious stimulus. Since the financial position of the Church makes it impossible for it to make good these deficiencies by its own teaching, it seeks to achieve the universal establishment of popular State-aided denominational schools, in which it will have the power of appointing the teachers and so be able to infuse religious and secular subjects with its own spirit. Thus, the latent conflict between the Church and Nonconformity lives on. To understand the sharpness of the antagonism between the two types of school, it is necessary to remember that, like everything else in England, they reflect a social conflict. The Church school, though indubitably inferior from the educational point of view, has a higher social status, because it is dominated not by the teacher, but by the clergyman with his higher social standing, who very often acts as an attraction which cannot be counterbalanced by the superior educational achievement of the County Council school.

§ 3

Although the religious difficulty was not removed entirely by the Education Acts of 1870, 1876 and 1902, they produced an immense reform. An outlet was at last found for forces long pent-up. There was a sharp and progressive rise in expenditure on education by State and County. Popular education became a national concern, and the bodies responsible – at first School Boards, later Education Committees of local authorities – frequently led by experts of wide experience and keen mind, became centres for every kind of social work and general culture. When the London School Board was set up in 1870, it had the audacity to take immediate advantage of the clause in the Act giving it the power to introduce universal compulsory education in its area, although it was obvious that the schools could, at best, accommodate half the children, apart from the fact that not more than a bare third of existing schools could be regarded as useable. Nevertheless, the curriculum was at once planned on lines of positively grotesque amplitude – popular education was to comprise, in addition to elementary subjects, physics, economics, English history and manual training, while algebra, geometry, and domestic science were instituted as optional subjects. No one was prepared to wait to have school buildings to accommodate the 100,000 children for whom this splendid programme was devised. On the contrary, the impossible programme was boldly proclaimed, for the guiding mind on the School Board, the great scientist, Huxley, knew that the criticism of the disappointed, far from destroying what was started, would help its development. Actually, educationalists were soon able to rely upon the voluntary help of a great body of assistants, largely women. The social side of school activities is actually carried out in quite masterly fashion. If a child fails in regular attendance at school, that is not treated, in the first instance, as a crime to be punished, but as a symptom of social malady, to be investigated by School (Board) Attendance Visitors. The provision of free meals to school-children has, in many areas, developed into a definite branch of public assistance. Almost everywhere, the supply of school-books, paper, pencils and pens is free. There is an elaborate system of medical inspection. In many areas, visits to museums, galleries and theatres, and expeditions that may extend over several days, to the neighbouring country or even seaside, are frequently provided, at the public charge. The social activities of education authorities in many of the larger cities are of a model character; here and there, indeed, they perhaps go so far that there is a certain danger that education to-day, like the Poor Law system a hundred years ago, may degenerate into a sort of amateur Socialism.

A strait limitation is, however, set to the activities of education authorities by the fact that the number of schools is still insufficient. A loop-hole, here, is found in the numerous exceptions, in practice, to the 1870 and 1876 Acts making school attendance compulsory from the ages of 5 to 14. As to the quality of the education provided, the impression conveyed to the mind of the non-expert student of conditions in England is that the standard achieved in the great rich cities is extremely high, whereas any comparison of country districts in England and Germany must be very favourable to the latter. An efficient central authority like the German sets a pretty high general standard; English freedom, while giving scope to the stronger spirits to accomplish the most splendid results, has little power against slackness or ill will.

In the up-building of the educational structure, the main impulse came, from the first, from Radicals like Bentham and Mill. This group regarded the largest possible amount and the greatest possible intensity of education for the largest possible number of people as the panacea for every evil, and, at the same time, the indispensable prerequisite to the new democracy they desired to substitute for the old feudal aristocracy. These men were by no means satisfied with a popular education confined to reading, writing, arithmetic and religion. From the start, therefore, we meet an effort to introduce economics and natural sciences into the curriculum sometimes before more necessary subjects are suitably provided for. Since the Board of Education's influence upon the curriculum makes itself felt only very slowly, the schools of the great cities often offer a curriculum that extends far beyond the usual subjects of popular education. Keenness on the part of some local magnate or enthusiastic teacher will cause the inclusion of all sorts of optional subjects, and build up continuation courses that bring the school very close to the *Realschule* type. Thus in the big provided schools in London, there are such optional classes in French, algebra, mechanics, chemistry, physics, botany, physiology, geometry, trigonometry, hygiene, typewriting, book-keeping, and, more rarely, German and Latin. On top of this are the Continuation classes, generally held in the evenings, and including both technical and general instruction. Here, again, there is less system as yet than there ought to be; the results attained are more or less haphazard, and the product of vision, energy and organizing genius on the part of a handful; the general picture presents a mixture of insufficient average with here and there brilliant individual successes.

§ 4

The time, however, seems to have come in English education when the State must interfere to create some sort of order out of the chaos of variations. At first, State supervision was limited to the insistence, prior to grants, on certain minimum conditions, both as regards the standard of instruction, the proportion of certificated teachers, and the condition and upkeep of buildings. The 1918 Education Act, the work of H. A. L. Fisher, marked a definite step in advance. Under it, State grants to town and county authorities are contingent upon the preparation, in conjunction with the Board, of organized schemes of education. Since the local education authorities would be bankrupt without State contributions to primary education, the Act, without any definite prescription on the point, contemplates a great compulsory organization, carried through by the parties concerned, but supervised by the State through its establishment of certain general standards. Attendance at school is fixed at from 5 to 14, under the Act; the whole complicated system of exceptions being swept away and the penalties on child employment being notably tightened up. Further, it is open to local education authorities to raise the school leaving age to 15. The following institutions are to be maintained:

1. Nursery schools[3] for children from 2 to 5.

2. Elementary schools from 5 (or where there are not enough children, 6) to 14, optional classes being permissive for the older children.

3. The possibility is envisaged of the substitution, for the Elementary system, of one of Junior and Senior Central Schools. Junior schools being the ordinary elementary schools, which all children must, in the first instance, attend; at 12, however, the more gifted children in any area are to be gathered into a Senior school, where they will stay till 15 or beyond, receiving an education of a higher type. Thence the more gifted children will be transferred, by the aid of scholarships, to the secondary schools.

4. Those children who do not pass on to a higher type of school (i.e. Senior or Secondary) are to pass into the (free) Continuation School, where they will stay till they are 18 (after a transitional period, up to 16) at classes normally taking two afternoons a week. Existing institutions for continuation education may be amalgamated for this purpose. The State will relieve localities of the major part of the cost of this.

The 1918 Act is the foundation on which the future development of education in England is based. For it aims at no less than the extension, throughout the whole country, of the educational practice of the most progressive authorities. This applies not only to the schools themselves, but to all sorts of subsidiary organizations. Thus the local authority can be called upon to provide, over and above its Elementary school, Continuation school and Nursery school, all sorts of playgrounds, swimming baths, gymnastic halls and 'other

facilities for social and physical training,' as well as to make arrangements for housing children whose parents do not live on the spot, or
who have to walk long distances to school, and, further, institute
scholarships of all sorts. Were the Act to be fully carried out, England
would possess the most advanced school system in the world.
Mobilized against it, therefore, one finds all the backwoodsmen and
all the opponents of what they call 'Municipal Socialism,' who regard
the new Act as a call to pillage the possessing classes. Against all this
opposition thé Act had to fight its way with some difficulty. But the
thick of the fight seems to be over. Since about 1925 there is progress
all round. The Board has made school attendance compulsory up
to the age of 14 and now even thinks of extending it as far as 15.
It is even contemplating far-reaching measures in order to bridge
the gulf between Elementary and Secondary education by new
legislation (cf. p. 459).

§ 5

The development of the training of teachers in England followed
in the tracks of Lancaster and Bell. These ardent reformers were
animated by a conception of efficiency which the modern capitalist
would respect; they contemplated educating millions of children at
a minimum of cost, without trained teachers, by the simple device
of employing those children who had already learned something to
instruct those who did not know their A B C. The English world
of their generation loudly applauded. Only very slowly did it penetrate to their minds that this system, trumpeted to the world as a
panacea for all social ills, was at best but a poor makeshift; that
England, far from being in the van, was actually lagging behind other
civilized nations in the matter of education. It was long before any
higher notion of training teachers penetrated. Progress was barred
by the disastrous contest between denominational and undenominational teaching. In 1840 a private training college was founded by
Kay-Shuttleworth in Battersea; then the State came in with subventions for all sorts of clerical and Nonconformist foundations and
one or two secular ones on the part of the British Society – the aim
in every case being extremely limited. Since 1890 the Universities
have developed training colleges. Women teachers had for long
to depend on private initiative: the Maria Grey Training College in
London was founded shortly after 1870. Secular institutions were
gradually taken over by Town and County Councils. State support of

training institutions follows the lines of its support to schools generally; it meets up to three-quarters of the cost, makes ample scholarship provision (Queen's Scholarships since 1846), examines teachers and gives them a certificate (since 1847). Intending teachers, before they go to the training college, are first trained as pupil-teachers at 'Centres,' now generally in association with the secondary schools. The 'Centre' is to give them a somewhat higher instruction than the elementary school: the Training College, the advanced knowledge necessary for their profession; and instruction in the art of teaching is going hand in hand with the progress of studies. Not that the traces of the old monitor system have disappeared altogether. Pupil-teachers teach while they are attending their Centre, not occasionally but regularly during half the working week, and that at an age at which intelligent instruction can rarely be expected from them. Their own intellectual training is bound to suffer gravely; the demands upon their time and strength thus involved mean that they can have but a superficial and perfunctory grasp of the mass of material comprising their own course. At the training college, again, they still learn too much and too fast; most of them only do a two years' course there; only the exceptionally gifted can stay for a third or, in rare cases, a fourth year. Worst of all, even this inadequate training is not obligatory. So far, efforts to give the 'certificated teacher' a monopoly have failed, in a country where individualism is overwhelmingly strong. The Elementary school statistics of 1926–7 show that about a fifth of English teachers is still uncertificated.[4] Of those who have a certificate, a very large number had not attended any training college, but merely prepared for the State examination for the Teacher's Certificate by some form or other of unsystematic training, frequently through private correspondence classes. The educational standard of the women (who are nearly three-quarters of the teaching profession) is especially low. In London and Scotland the untrained teacher is more or less a thing of the past, but in Council Schools (and especially in the poorer Church schools) they are still in the majority.

Even the best type of English school-teacher gets no training comparable to that of his German colleague. Hence a concession of questionable wisdom was made to the claims of the teachers for social consideration and higher education, when all the Universities, within the last few decades, agreed to admit those of them who had passed Matriculation as fully qualified students. In such case the

454

State pays the whole cost of education, outside of University fees. Intending teachers pursue the same course of study as other students, take the B.A. like them, and in their fourth year do a course in pedagogy at a teachers' training college in connexion with the University. Although the average course at an English University has much more of the purely school character than is the case in Germany, these training college students are so ill-equipped that, although they have managed to pass their Matriculation, they constitute a heavy ballast in most of the faculties they attend. Their B.A. is a doubtful gain to themselves: it is generally no gain whatever to the elementary school, for few of these University-trained teachers go into the Elementary schools; most of them get posts in Secondary ones.

From a human point of view, one can understand the enthusiasm with which the teacher has fought for his admission to the Universities, since in few countries was his social status so low as in England. The attempt to create anything like a teaching profession with common aims and objects was for long blocked by the wretched country teachers, most of whom had drifted down from all sorts of other occupations and taken to teaching simply as a last resort. A general recognized organization of teachers is the product of quite recent times: the Teachers' Registration Council was not founded till 1912. The Council has an official register,[5] and imposes certain conditions on new entrants that will undoubtedly be progressively raised, as the dead weight of those admitted in the first instance, merely on the ground that they had been teaching for three years, is gradually reduced. Something in the nature of a trade union organization for all the branches of the teaching profession is thus in process of creation, which, ultimately, will exclude the non-registered teachers altogether. It has further been of great practical advantage to the National Union of Teachers (the association of teachers in elementary schools) that, in the absence of any teaching profession in the academic sense, the Government and public opinion have to come to them, as the single organized representative body, on all questions of education.[6] In spite of this their advancement has been slow because it took a long time for them to develop that sort of strength which alone counts in England, i.e. the solidarity which would have made it possible for them to exercise influence on the electorate in the choice of a government. It was not until the disgruntled younger teacher showed a tendency to move into the Socialist camp that the Government was impelled to cope with the problem of improving the material conditions of the teacher.' The 1918 Act disappointed their hopes; in 1920, however, a step towards improvement was at last achieved. A Committee presided over by the then proprietor of the *Daily Telegraph*, Lord Burnham, worked out a scale of normal salaries, which is now being forced on local authorities through the agitation of teachers and pressure from the Board of Education. It is a kind of Adoptive act, in which the State assumes the costs of teachers' pensions and which is gradually being forced upon the country.[7]

§ 6

England, especially in the larger towns, possesses a great range of intermediate stages between elementary and higher education. Between the elementary school, on the one hand, and the University on the other, there is a multiplicity of institutions for adult education. Most of them date back to the mighty, but more or less unorganized, wave of enthusiasm for education which the Philosophic Radicals did so much to promote. Sweeping over a nation which possessed almost nothing in the shape of an organized educational system, it expressed itself in the most varied forms of well-meaning haphazard foundations. In 1823 the activities of George Birkbeck, Professor of Natural Sciences in Glasgow, gave birth, there, to a Mechanics' Institute, designed to open higher education to the artisan. This example was immediately imitated in London, and all over the country. Starting, in the main, with the teaching of science, these Institutes developed into schools for more or less advanced technical education, and, as such, acquired a measure of Government support. Another group is the Polytechnic, of which the foundation endowed by Quintin Hogg, a successful merchant, and located in Regent Street, London (1880), is the most important. They, again, are mainly technical schools, designed to assist the economic advance of the student and serve purely practical ends. General, humane education, with institutes of this type, tends to fall more and more into the background. Often its sphere is limited to a minimum of practical ethics; the encouragement of sociability, through common outings, dances and other pleasures; or of political education, in the form of evening debates; and the provision of lending libraries and reading-rooms.

Social reformers on the Right had a much more far-reaching conception of what they wanted in the shape of popular education:

nothing less than the transplantation of the college idea into the life of the masses. The object of the Mechanics' Institute was to subserve economic ends; the new Working Men's College, in 1854,[8] in London, founded by Christian Socialists like Maurice and Kingsley, was designed to promote ethical culture, and rejected, on principle, any notion of narrowly practical training. Here the guiding ideas were such a close and constant contact between students as might give birth to a sense of real comradeship among them, and frequent meetings between students and teachers, who for the most part gave their services as a piece of Christian work. Similar principles inspired the foundation, in 1899, of Ruskin College at Oxford, by an American, Walter Vrooman: since supported mainly from Trade Union funds. The aim, here, is to make the free intellectual atmosphere of the University accessible to the working class, and bring it as near as possible to the student body – an aim that, though it may reach only a limited number of students, does give them something that enriches the whole of their lives. The students who go to Ruskin are selected and maintained there by the Unions; the intention is not that they should rise out of their class to higher professions, but that they should be educated as Trade Union leaders and learn to conceive the interests of their class from a higher standpoint than that of mere selfish immediacy. Ruskin endeavours to keep its teaching clear of any party-political bias: an effort which brings it into collision with a strong tendency of an opposite kind, in certain sections of the workers themselves. In 1909 a Left wing group of students broke away and founded a Central Labour College in London ; another group, even further to the Left, called the Plebs, also carries on teaching courses of its own. The Conservatives have founded a parallel organization of their own: Philip Stott College at Northampton. Mention might be made also of the Home Reading Union, founded in 1889 by an Independent minister, John B. Paton (d. 1911), which tends to foster the reading of good books, and of the mass of correspondence colleges which well-meaning educational reformers spread all over the country for the enlightenment of the unenfranchised; they have now sunk to merely commercial undertakings, to cram up would-be teachers and others for all sorts of minor examinations.

From yet another angle, the University Settlement seeks to bridge the gulf between the upper and lower classes. Young men of University training, inspired by social idealism, there live for several years in the poorest working-class districts, among the slums, where they work in close association with the Trade Unions and other institutions, and take part as instructors in all sorts of educational courses, doing this, always, not as members of a different class who come to improve the less fortunate, but as co-operators who learn as well as teach. They belong to no political or religious affiliation, and are bound by no sort of vow; during the day they attend to their profession or studies; their effort is to get into the closest possible personal touch with the workers and so form a real community, and bridge the gulf between rich and poor, not by missionary work, whether political or religious, but simply and solely by personal contact. The most striking example is Toynbee Hall, founded in 1884 by Samuel Barnett, then rector of Whitechapel, in memory of Arnold Toynbee (d. 1883). Also in the East End is the People's Palace, founded by the novelist, Walter Besant, which seeks to give some sort of access to culture to the dispossessed who inhabit London's slums, by means of lectures, concerts and educational courses of various kinds. Or men of different trades and from different denominations and social positions combine in little groups with friendship and social work as their aim, under a quaint ceremonial with religious tinge, as is for instance done in Toc H (i.e. Talbot House, founded in 1915), called in memory of a soldiers' hut in Poperinghe, Flanders. The efforts of such institutions are backed up by a well-developed system of free libraries, mostly rate-supported, and the University Extension Movement, to which reference has already been made (p. 425 *seq.*).

§ 7

Admirable as may be all these efforts, they are of secondary importance only, from the point of view of a national educational policy. Much more important is the systematic provision for facilitating the rise of gifted children from the lower classes to the upper through the medium of the schools. And in this direction a great deal has been accomplished in the last decade. In characteristically English fashion, the procedure has been experimental, the attack being made at many points at once, and the old as far as possible spared. No one thinks of the democratic tyranny of the unitary school; there are some hundreds of preparatory schools (for the public schools), and where preparatory classes exist in the higher schools, the latter receive the usual State grant in respect of them. What is, however, now being attempted is to draft children systematically from the lower classes into the higher schools. Thus, every school receiving State grants must reserve a quarter of its accommodation as free places; in addition, there are scholarships to cover the cost of the scholar's maintenance, while at school. Similar scholarships – County Council, Town Council, and recently State, as well as, in Scotland, the vast Carnegie Endowment (cf. page 431) – carry the capable scholar on to the University. This scholarship method is the most usual, and for this purpose there are always funds forthcoming.

The time seems to have come now for bringing all these sporadic attempts into a kind of system, and to create a type of *post-primary school* with the double aim of preparing the brighter Elementary scholar for the Secondary school and of giving to those who will stay in the Elementary school a better training for life than the old type of school can afford. The post-primary school is to cover education from about the eleventh year, as far as, if at all possible, the fifteenth. During the last two years a practical bias is to be introduced by some sort of schooling in accountancy, housekeeping, stenography and the like. Senior classes to be added to the Elementary school will be devoted to this work in smaller places, while special modern schools will arise in the towns to cover the gap between the two systems.

§ 8

There is, of course, a close kinship between efforts of this kind and the attempts made by religious and other bodies to look after the young. This is, for instance, the primary concern of George Williams' foundations, the Young Men's Christian Association (1846), and the parallel organization for young women. Designed to meet the needs of adolescents of the lower middle class, they provide hostels, libraries, gymnasia, and recreation grounds, and are notably active in the organization of holiday camps. During the war a large part of the spiritual and material provision for the army was assigned to the Y.M.C.A. The combination of an ethical aim and a more or less military form, which had by 1878 developed into the Salvation Army, was also taken up by all sorts of Church organizations for the young; thus, in 1883, the Boys Brigade[9] was founded, and in 1891, the Church Lads Brigade, in both of which the camp is the centre. Both of these were overshadowed by the Boy Scout Movement, founded by General Baden-Powell in 1908, which aims at training lads to be gentlemen, giving them bodily discipline and the sense that they are patriotic Britons. The effect of the Boy Scout Movement was prodigious: through it, Imperialism – in a very refined and non-aggressive form – with the naive international plank in it, so characteristic of the British Imperialist, has captured the youth of England, and a large part of the young people abroad.

When young people, at the most impressionable age, spend some weeks in the company of young Englishmen whose very shyness makes the heart-felt kindliness behind it all the more affecting, and who address them, throughout, in the language of international comradeship, they are apt to feel that England is the first among countries. At eighteen one is not fit, fortunately, to probe very deeply into the problems arising out of the possible conflict between national and international ideals.

Since the war, too, there are signs of the development of movements closely akin to the German *Youth Movement* in the stress laid on all that is simple and natural and the avoidance of alcohol and tobacco and often of sport, and in the feeling for the romantic side of the life of woods and fields (though there is much less of this than in Germany) as well as for Folk songs, dancing and handicrafts; in all this the Youth movement is rich in possibilities for the future. Hand in hand with it there is apt to go a marked political tendency towards Socialism and Pacifism, to the ideas of William Morris and Ruskin, and a definite repudiation of the militarist and Imperialistic tone and the bustling activity of the Boy Scout movement. The direction of the activities of the young by adults, found there and in Church circles, is likewise abjured. There are a variety of smallish associations, working on these lines, by no means comparable in numbers with the Boy Scouts, but free, at all events, from the atomization of the German movement. Among these Kibbo Kift, a definitely pacifist group, founded by John Hargrave, and devoted to all kinds of Anglo-Saxon romantic lore, and the Order of Woodland Chivalry, which cultivates Indian nomenclature and natural symbolism, may be mentioned. In addition, the Labour Party, the Quakers and other associations, endeavour to organize their young people in groups. Some of these groups are federated in the British Federation of Youth.

§ 9

Have these efforts of Education to bridge the gulf between classes succeeded? Superficially, the answer may well be an emphatic, 'No.' Actually, many, perhaps most, of the available institutions are used not by workmen, for whom they were intended, but by artisans, commercial employees, and women of all classes. Actually, the antagonism between classes has become more embittered in every decade. The mind of the average workman shows small sign of the sort of comprehension of the other fellow's point of view which education is supposed to impart. Yet such a verdict fails to touch the roots of the matter.

In the first place, exaggerated hopes should not be attached to the diffusion of education. Only short-sighted Rationalism, an outlook naïve as that of Harriet Martineau, could hope that the class struggle would be abolished by intellectual training. Such training may lift struggle to a higher, nobler plane, but not eliminate it. The World War has afforded ample proof of this. In all countries the vast majority of the leaders of thought shared the national feelings of the masses. And the same applies to the class struggle. Not education can bridge it, only the gradual establishment of a conscious communal feeling within the whole nation. From this point of view, the elevation of a workman to rule over the upper classes as a Cabinet Minister, the establishment of a consumers' co-operative, the smooth working of profit-sharing and industrial councils, are worth more than all popular lectures on Shakespeare. So, among all the efforts described above, the only ones that can have any real influence in this direction are the scholarships which enable a considerable number of Council scholars to go to the Universities.

Lectures on Shakespeare, however – and all similar educational attempts – do something quite different. They are a link in the chain of efforts – religious and social – whose object is to make the two-legged, breathing and toiling machine, to which modern Capitalism has reduced the workman, back into a *Man* – a man who, though he pursue his own advantage energetically, nevertheless is aware of altruistic motives in himself, and may, step by step, gradually be led to see that they are operative in the heart of his antagonist likewise. Education has already brought the workman to the point of not smashing up machinery any longer, of carrying on intelligent negotiation with his antagonist, of having a mind open to the patriotic and even to the internationalist appeals addressed to him in times of political stress. The fact that, despite grumbling and cursing, the British workman not only accepted military service but gave up his sacred Trade Union regulations, fruit of three generations of bitter struggle, represents a great achievement in this direction. The crafty machine-smashers of 1816 have by 1923 become capable of administering England. In so far as they helped to teach a minority of workmen how to think, the Church and the primary school and all the other educational institutions have played their part in bringing this result about.

If they did not do so in fuller measure, the reason lies not in the faultiness of the educational system, but in the national aversion of the English people to systematic thinking. The lack of intellectual interest characteristic of the nation, which makes possible such an ideal as that of the gentleman, irrespective of intellectual demands, is bound to be reflected in those strata of the population whom such educational efforts as we have described were designed to reach. The workman or bank clerk, who carries on his education after his day's work is done, may be rare enough in any country; in England he is a vanishing exception. The worker's own desires for education could never have brought such a movement as University extension into existence. It has arisen, rather, out of the zeal of a small body of well-meaning men of high intellectual status and views partly Radical partly Christian, who ascribed to education a saving potency which it cannot possess. The fruits of their amiable exertions have fallen short of the gigantic expectations of the early apostles, but that is no reason for saying that their work has been vain.

CHAPTER V
HIGHER EDUCATION

§ 1

THE beginnings of higher education in England were the same as on the Continent. The Middle Ages had the cloister and cathedral schools. At the end of the fourteenth century, William of Wykeham founded at Winchester a preparatory school for New College, Oxford; in 1441 King Henry VI founded Eton, designed to occupy a similar position in relation to King's College, Cambridge. The Renaissance brought a notable number of new foundations: St. Paul's in 1509, Westminster in 1560, Merchant Taylors in 1561 – all in London – Harrow in 1571, and Rugby in 1567. All these institutions were designed for the middle classes, for the 'pore scholar' of past days, since the nobility either despised the new culture altogether or maintained a private tutor for its sons. Schools thus stood on a high level at the time when the Reformation and the dissolution of the Monasteries gave opportunity for the endowment of new educational institutions out of monastic funds. Had such Anglican reformers as Cranmer had their way, this would have taken place, as it did in humanistic Germany. Actually, however, education was to suffer, right down to the nineteenth century, from the fact that Royal rapacity and private greed of gain cared nothing for its needs.

In the seventeenth century there gradually took place that silent revolution which gave the English school system its characteristic stamp. Bit by bit, the nobles began sending their sons to school and to the University, though as late as 1700 their doing so was by no means a matter of course. Even in 1693, Locke, in his famous Treatise, was advocating the system of private tutors, and Defoe in 1729 devised, for his Compleat English Gentleman, a realist training such as could only be achieved outside the University. Gradually, however, the nobility began to concern themselves about education, and, contemporaneously, the middle-class element withdrew – grammar school and University gradually became pillars of Anglicanism. The middle class, being predominantly Puritan, loses its hold on the schools (cf. p. 408). Numerically, its sons might be in the majority in school and college, but the social tone at both was aristocratic and the Bishop was in the background to check any possibility of Puritan tendencies. The type of the Public School came into being, first represented by Eton, Harrow, Rugby, Winchester, but gradually

imitated by newer foundations, so that it became the normal type for
secondary education. They are all boarding-schools, all classical
schools with the training of gentlemen as an ideal as high as and
even paramount to the ideal of humanism. Both aims are pursued
concurrently. But wherever a choice has to be made between the
humanistic ideal and the ideal of training, training prevails, generally
in the form of its primary discipline – i.e., athletic sports. If a choice
has to be made between two teachers, of whom one is more learned
and the other more athletic, the athlete will carry it off every time.
When any conflict arises between the claims of physical and mental
training of boys, the latter gives way. If a boy behaves in such a
way as to damage the spirit of the school, he is removed, irrespective
of any brilliance in class.

§ 2

The main instrument of training is games. This fact we have
already noted in dealing with the Universities. Athletics of this kind
have nothing to do with record-breaking. Games are designed to
stimulate the utmost efficiency of body and will, to develop the
quality of leadership in boys, and to teach the young how to obey
where they cannot command. Games breed corporate pride; one
house of a school plays against the other, school against school; and
there is no prouder moment in the boy's life than that at which he
leads his own side in football or cricket to victory in contest against
some other team of equal standing.

Second to sport is the corporate life of boys, as worked out, with
notable pedagogic insight, by the famous Headmaster of Rugby,
Thomas Arnold (1828–42). The outstanding personality in the
school is the Headmaster. His primary concern is not with teaching.
He may teach, in so far as his more important duties leave him time
to do so, and in so far as he regards teaching as a means for getting
in touch with his boys. But he must, first and foremost, know boys
and how to mould them: must possess the gift of rousing and
inspiring. He has to create a Sixth Form that can inform the whole
school with his spirit. The English mind measures a school by the
quality of its head boys. They are responsible for order in dor-
mitories, at games, on outings and half-days, and further possess a
certain limited power of chastisement, subject to an (almost nominal)
appeal to the Head on the part of the poor sinner. Chief of their
tasks is to prevent the congenital vice of boarding-schools, the bully-

ing of the weak by the strong. The system includes fagging (much reduced in these days), but the fag is not to be permitted to become the slave of his fag-master. It is not the master who can prevent this happening, for, except in very grave cases, a boy must not take grievances up to his master. It is for the head boys to keep an eye on it, to cope with the evil, or, if they fail in this, themselves to bring the sinner against the sacred spirit of the institution to book.

Such are the principles of the English system of training. The boy, placed betimes in a corporate life, is thereby to be trained to be a citizen rather than an individual. This close and cloistered association of young people, with its ready scorn of everything contrary to their own ideals, tends to transform the individual who might seek to rise above the type into the prominent representative of the community. Every opportunity is taken of bringing home to him the honour of belonging to *this* community. The dining-room is hung with tablets commemorating distinguished former pupils. On Speech-Day, the great day that closes the school year, when the best pupils come forward with recitations in English or Latin and a rain of prizes descends on all but the veritable dullard, parents and relations come up in swarms to their ' old school'; as often as not, some 'old Boy,' now occupying a distinguished position in the State, will make a speech, found a prize, and 'tip' the boys who happen to please him. Anything that does not fit in to the spirit of the community is suppressed: here, again, we meet the ruthless energy with which the Englishman repels whatever seems to him dangerous. A potent instrument is corporal punishment, from which only the elder boys are exempt. Although sparingly employed in the better schools, for lying and similar faults, it is part and parcel of the English system of training. The boy is to be made a gentleman, and that ideal does not comprehend the code of honour of the Continental officer, which feels any blow as an insult. In this atmosphere, the standard of values is not what the boy himself thinks good or bad, but what the community regards as right or wrong. There can be no appeal from the verdict of the community to the verdict of an individual, whether that individual be a master or the boy's own conscience. To lead the community, not by bringing in new values and so transforming it, but by oneself becoming the embodiment of all that is lofty and ethical in the community, is the ideal of the English school. Throughout the system there exists no stimulus to individuality, to being in any respect distinct or different from one's surroundings. Here is trained the dyed-in-the-wool Conservative gentleman, who has never heard of Ibsen, who crosses himself at the mention of Bolshevism, who thinks, as his newspaper tells him from time to time, that Lloyd George is either the greatest of Englishmen or the scum of humanity, who treats women with unfailing tact and politeness, who resents any infraction of his own sense of right, and who, in some remote Indian court, will rule millions without any external power, simply by his skill and energy as Resident. It is a type that everywhere rules men and knows them; despising any sort of problem as mere moonshine, and compels even the unwilling outsider to recognize its great relative efficiency.

§ 3

Immense stress is laid, in this system, on the autonomous powers of the Head. He is all powerful. There is no regular teachers' conference with statutory rights. There are trustees, but their functions are normally confined to electing a Headmaster, and finding and administering finance. The Head, being a gentleman, will make no great display of authority as against his staff, but responsibility belongs to him, and to him alone. He alone chooses teachers, settles the curriculum, the text-books used, the internal organization and all details of the life of the institution; he decides the admission and dismissal of pupils. Very often, he is an Anglican clergyman of good family. Appointed, as a rule, while still tolerably young, he is exceedingly well-paid. A capitation grant in addition to his salary gives him a direct interest in the success of his institution, without making him dependent upon it. Once again, the tendency to develop the autocratic personality breaks through the forms of democracy and freedom – and the school gains by it.

In the high schools, too, the general character of the teaching staff is fixed by the Head. Broadly speaking, he succeeds in gathering a group of men about him who know how to handle the young. The teacher has got to be good at games – not that he may train up athletes but because games create a bond between teacher and taught, while the teacher's intellectual achievements generally leave his boys cold. This teacher always knows how to convey at least the surface culture of the gentleman to the up-growing generation. In the average school, a certain body of external facts is also willy-nilly driven into the boys' heads. Where the Head and his staff are mediocre, the entire curriculum is apt to be subordinated to passing

University examinations with success. To this end, there are annual school examinations, often deplorably dull and mechanical, and apt to wear out any real mental energy the teacher retains. This, however, is the minimum accomplishment. The more competent the Head, the more successful is he in gathering men about him who possess the power of the real teacher and can infuse their pupils with the inner reality of the idea of the gentleman: and, in the best schools, there are masters who intellectually and ethically stand on a very high level.

Here, in addition to proficiency in games, an honours degree is invariably insisted upon, and, almost invariably, an honours degree of one of the two older Universities. Immense stress, here, is laid on the personality of the master. He is not merely the teacher in certain classes and subjects, but the tutor, and this latter aspect is the more important in his work. As such, he has a certain number of boys under his supervision throughout the time they spend at school, to whom he is not merely teacher, but a human friend and counsellor.

In this system of training, which turns on the development of the will, and, as means to that end, on physical efficiency, mental instruction has long played a decidedly secondary part. Moreover, the majority of educated English parents regard this side of the matter with complete indifference. Before the University examinations were set up, there was a danger lest education should degenerate into a business of learning by rote a more or less meaningless Græco-Latin ritual. The reforms of the last decades have saved the schools. The classical education given at the great public schools is on a high level. It is assisted by every stimulus that can be given to ambition by a mighty system of prizes, which sometimes, indeed, suggests the question whether the material value of the distinctions does not actually outweigh the glory that they bring. English, history and science are secondary, but have been greatly stressed in the last generation. In the highest class, the Sixth Form, boys tend to remain for two years, and here there is a considerable measure of specialization, according to the gift and inclination of the pupil.

§ 4

In the above pages, the ideal English school has been described and it certainly is one of the finest types in our day. But in actual fact it is represented, at best, by perhaps a couple of dozen of outstanding Public schools. The rest of the picture shows an attempt, more or less – generally less – successful, to carry out this ideal within the limits set by mediocre staffs, indifferent parents, and City Fathers definitely hostile to education. The English system has four pillars – the autocracy of a Headmaster with a touch of genius: the cultivated teacher as House tutor: the Sixth Form: and the boarding-school system. It begins to totter, so soon as control over it falls into the hands of a man of mere average outlook and average knowledge of men, who may choose the wrong teachers as house-masters, who may be firm and mild in the wrong way and at the wrong time with boys and masters, or simply lacks courage to take a line of his own. In this case, boys and masters alike will tend to have as little to do with the Head as they can; bullying will develop among the bigger boys, crushing out all that is decent and fine in the little ones: sport will be overdone, and instead of serving the honour of the school, degenerates into mere individual swank. Nor can the individual case be met, or the Head got rid of, either by State inspection or teachers' conferences.

The English ideal is further attainable only through the boarding-school system. Nothing but living together, from morning to night, can give the close contact, the real mutual knowledge that can be used as the basis for building up a definite and strong human type, if, perhaps, to the detriment of the finer individual shades of humanity. It is of incalculable worth for a nation to be governed by a dominant type, represented throughout all professions, of men who are bodily sound, full of energy, and animated by a reasonably limited idealism – and this type is trained by the boarding-school. But the inferior boarding-school and the day-school dominated by the boarding-school ideal, lack what is good in the English ideal – and also what is good in the German. They are mere machines for grinding boys into men of a certain social type.

The view is widely taken in England that the public school, despite its immense merits, is seriously one-sided. An admirable system for the development of the will, its product lacks the individual counterpoise of an equally developed intellectual life. The full development of human personality would require a strong emphasis on the study of philosophy or history, and necessitate such a familiarity with the civilization of some other nation as would enable the student to distinguish what is lasting from what is transitional in his own mental life. Actually, this was aimed at in the intensive study of the classics, and in the case of a small minority of boys at a small minority of institutions, with success. Where a man of the force of character and dominant cast of mind of a Thomas Arnold is Headmaster, a type of schoolboy may be bred that ranks with the very best in the world. But the cases where the system in fact achieves anything of the sort are exceptional. This is fully recognized among thinking people in England; for three or four decades there has been an active school reform movement, whose object is somehow or other to combine the spirit of the English public school with the humanistic – not necessarily in the classical sense – spirit of the German higher school.

§ 5

The impulse to reform came, again from the Utilitarians, who regarded the public schools as a mere class preserve. As against this form of aristocratic one-sidedness they set up, with equal one-sidedness, the German ideal of intellectual training, an ideal wholly alien to the mass of their fellow-countrymen. Between 1861 and 1868, there were two Royal Commissions on Education: Lord Clarendon's Commission and the Schools Inquiry Commission. Their labour revealed an almost incredible picture of neglect and inefficiency. In many schools, the curriculum and methods generally were exactly as they had been at the time of their foundation in the sixteenth or seventeenth century; teaching confined in the main to Latin and Greek, the number (and, often, the salaries) of teachers what they had been a hundred years earlier, the arrangements for the pupils bad, the teaching methods and text-books antediluvian; frequently, there was no division of classes, only one big schoolroom, in which various groups of scholars of similar age repeated their lessons aloud at the same time, their progress being encouraged by praise or blame and stimulated by canings and the imposition of hundreds of hexameters to be written out. Here was the crass conservatism of the average Englishman *in excelsis* – in a sphere in which the nation as a whole had taken no interest.

Since the Clarendon Commission, there has been progress in every direction. True, the reformers' effort to have higher education subjected to the State on the same lines as primary, did not succeed. The reforming zeal of the average man could not face the bogey of an all-regulating State with the power of making Robots in its own image out of the free Englishman. All that was done was to set up an Endowed Schools Commission in 1869, with powers to supervise the financial administration of the foundations out of which

EDUCATION

schools were maintained, to suspend foundations no longer suitable to modern conditions, and extinguish a certain number that were insufficient. Under the gentle pressure of this Commission, which, in the course of time, examined the whole of the public schools, improvement and modernization was universally carried out. Where the terms of its foundation did not prescribe a definitely sectarian character, liberalizing reform was directed to making institutions undenominational, while their plutocratic character was also greatly lessened by the increase in the number of free places and sensible arrangements for filling them. (In 1874, the Commission was amalgamated with the Charity Commissioners; their functions now are relegated to the Board of Education.) For the rest, the public schools remained, unaffected. They receive no sort of State support, and therefore are subject to no inspection, provided there is no doubt that their funds are being expended in accordance with the provisions of the foundation-deeds.

§ 6

Even more urgent than reform in existing schools was the extension of educational facilities. This was first secured, to any large extent, by the provisions of the Technical Instruction Act of 1889, which gave power to the newly constituted County and Town Councils to levy a rate for technical and craft training: in 1890, a considerable subvention was granted to local authorities for this purpose, in the shape of the so-called 'Whisky money.' General supervision over this new branch of higher education was committed to the Department of Science and Art,[1] a section of the Privy Council. The conception of 'Technical' education gradually widened, until it comprised not only drawing, but also music, mathematics and the natural sciences, and even – as indispensable to technical progress – modern languages, so that, ultimately, classics alone were excluded from the purview of the Department. In 1899 a new Ministry was set up, the Board of Education, and supervision over all branches transferred to this centre; in 1902, the new Education Act gave power to Councils to include in their activities the provision of primary and higher education, in the widest sense. Thus the foundation stone was laid for a perfectly new establishment.

The picture of the New Secondary Education system is still fairly complex. The existing schools form a bright mosaic of private management, old foundations and public control. There are private

470

schools that are purely commercial undertakings. Many of these are so-called Preparatory Schools, and take boys only up to the age at which they pass on to the public schools. Then there are remnants of the old Proprietary School type, for example, the institutions of the Girls Public Day School Company.[2] Besides these older types the (town or county) Council school grows more and more numerous: it is now indeed the standard type. Since the 1902 Act increase in higher education has been along these lines. The County Council and Borough Council School has gradually become the real instrument of English higher education. It is attended by the overwhelming mass of children of school age, and its success will determine that of the English school as a whole. Here, what is being coped with is the extremely thorny problem of at once transplanting to the day school the ideals of the public school, which have grown up under the boarding-school system, and combining with them the satisfaction of the need for a more thorough and intellectual form of training characteristic of the middle class. The nature of the problem is universally recognized, and ample means and sincere idealism are being brought to its solution. These schools are subject to State supervision. It takes the form, first of a demand that they shall be directed, or at least definitely influenced by public bodies; second, that they shall give higher education with at least one foreign language up to not less than 16 years of age; third, that a quarter of the places are reserved for ex-elementary scholars; fourth, that State supervision shall be accepted, notably in the form of working out the curriculum in close consultation with the Board's Inspectors. If these conditions are fulfilled, the school becomes a recognized secondary school, and half its costs will be met by the State. Other schools – e.g., public schools and certain Catholic institutions, which do not fulfil the first condition, while not earning grants, may be recognized by the State as efficient secondary schools, which carries with it a solid recommendation.[3]

The curriculum is, in the first instance, left to the school itself; State supervision is introduced very slowly and cautiously, lest private initiative be stifled.

Schools of the distinct type of the German *Realschule*, *Real-Gymnasium*, and *Gymnasium* have not, so far, developed. A large proportion of the schools are really primary schools plus one or two years' higher classes, or with some sort of continuation course attached to them. In schools of this type there is some sort of vague idea of preparing scholars for trade. There is a very large number of 'higher' schools, hovering vaguely in a sort of intermediate stage between the continuation school and the secondary school, and laying emphasis rather on the acquisition of vocational aptitudes and the study of practical branches than on anything that could be called higher education.

There is yet another type of school, which addresses itself, more or less vaguely, to preparing its scholars for the University, for the Army, engineering or the law. Here a higher education in the true sense is provided. Half a century ago, it was still almost exclusively classical: nowadays, non-classical subjects are coming more and more to the fore.[3] Not wholly without effect have been the moving plaints constantly uttered by leading men in all walks of life of the English technician's lack of sound scientific training. They led, in 1916, to the establishment of a Neglect of Science Committee, promoted by leading men of science with the object of encouraging practical and natural science teaching. By way of reply, the classicists formed, also in 1916, a Council of Humanistic Studies. The decline in classical study is shown by a questionnaire undertaken in February, 1920, among secondary schools; only 44·3 per cent. of scholars were then learning Latin, and only 4·4 Greek (the figures for girls were 27·5 and 0·4 per cent. respectively). With the abolition of compulsory Greek in the Entrance examination at both Oxford and Cambridge, it seems obvious that the classical type of education, once taken for granted, will disappear more and more. Most secondary schools now have modern sides in addition to their older classical ones. So far, however, there is no trace of any sort of system either as to the manner in which classical and modern, language and scientific subjects are grouped, at what stage the study of any of them ought to begin, or what place any of them occupy or ought to occupy in education.

State inspection does not concern itself with any of this. As in local administration generally, its concern is merely with the larger questions of principle. Certain hygienic and pædagogic conditions must be fulfilled by any institution which seeks to be recognized as a high school. By a process of gradual screwing up of its demands for certificated teachers, both as to their number and their quality, the Board exercises a thoroughly salutary pressure. The State inspectors visit the schools, and, through careful discussions with their Heads, make proposals for improvement and development; they seek to develop something of an organic kind, out of praiseworthy individual initiative. The endeavour, throughout, is to appear, as far as possible, in the rôle of well-meaning counsellor merely; any suggestion of a desire to impose a standardized uniformity is avoided. There is no interference in personal matters like the removal or punishment of a pupil or the personal relations of a teacher; on all such matters the first word, and the last, is with the Headmaster. At the same time, the well-meaning counsellor has his authority. An institution which permanently turns a deaf ear to the official admonitions of the inspector may find its State grant reduced or cut off – the latter being tantamount to closing down. From time to time, official demands are consolidated in general circulars applicable to all schools eligible for State grants, and these circulars extend, progressively, to cover every department of school life – school materials, teaching methods, school hygiene, the number of hours of instruction, the scale of salaries, and, recently, the general educational provision made by municipality or county. Thus, the Board demands a certain ratio between expenditure on elementary and higher schools; designates certain categories of expenditure – e.g., medical inspection – as urgent, while recommending economy in other directions; and behind such a recommendation stands the power of the purse. Thus, little by little, the entire area of school life is being enclosed in a tighter and tighter network of State regulation, in such fashion, however, that the Headmaster never appears merely as the executive organ of the State circulars; rather, it is only in the event of a failure to function on the part of those immediately responsible that the State employs its authority. (In other words, the picture is the same as we have already met in local government.) By this skilful policy, the Board of Education has already achieved remarkable results.

Very slowly and gradually the Board has also helped to introduce into the schools a system of *Examinations*. It did not take the initiative, for in this department they were just the best and most progressive educational experts whose distrust of bureaucracy was most insuperable. But the initiative came from the Universities.[4] The Examinations of the Joint Board of the two older Universities, set up in 1873 (cf. p. 423), are a voluntary system voluntarily accepted by the schools – even, latterly, in increasing measure, by the renowned public schools. Gradually other examining boards, set up by the newer Universities, came in, and it became increasingly the fashion to pass the University Entrance examinations during the school curriculum, so that these

University examinations began gradually to become the standard to which school life and work had to conform. At last – in the usual English fashion – some sort of chaos resulted from the multiplicity of these examinations and the State stepped in. Since 1917 there is a Secondary Schools Examination Council, composed of the University Examination Boards, and two examinations are offered by it: the First Examination for scholars of 16, the Second Examination for pupils of 18; the first intended as a general leaving examination, the second (more specialized) as a more specialized test in specific subjects, for advanced pupils who have stayed longer than the normal. The whole system is voluntary. There is no obligation on any school to conduct the examinations, or on any scholar to take them. They are optional, and do not mark a particular stage in the school life of the examinee: do not, that is to say, necessarily imply his leaving school so soon as he has passed. In all probability, however, they will develop into a system of leaving examination.[5] At present, the first examination is regarded as normal: for those who are going into commercial life or the teaching profession, it generally constitutes the normal close of the school period. The second is already regarded as the prerequisite to obtaining a scholarship; later it will probably constitute the normal way in to the University.

§ 7

Through the co-operation of County and Municipal Councils with the Board of Education, a new type of school is gradually developing, which is much nearer to the German school than the old English public school. Modern languages, history and natural science are emphasized at the expense of classics; the aim being to give a good all-round education and stimulate the pupil's intelligence. Great efforts are also made to promote the boarding-school spirit even in these day schools. Thus, on public school lines, different sections of the institution meet each other at games, with the idea of rousing a healthy spirit of mutual competition; for instance, the school will be divided into two groups, from different parts of the town, which then play against each other. In the same way, common meals, and school performances of all sorts are used to give the sense of communal life; and the attempt is made to transfer the strict supervision, exercised by boys in the upper forms over the smaller ones, from the boarding-school, where it is natural, to the day school. Obviously, this can only be imperfectly achieved. The admirable spirit of the public school

474

is rooted in the fact that the boys live, eat and sleep together, receive common impressions, great and small, at the time of life when their minds are most receptive, and, during their school life, have all their experiences centred in the school. The day boy's tie with his school is bound to be looser, because in his case the school has to share its central position in his experience with the family and other circumstances. The new kind of school now arising in England can never equal the old boarding-school as an organization for disciplining the leader type. It will be bound to attempt some sort of compromise between English and Prussian school ideas. The directing minds in the Board of Education and on the Education Committees of great and progressive cities like London and Birmingham have a clear aim in view, which is being pursued with the blend of skilful energy and cautious tact that habitually characterizes English progress. Experiments of all kinds are encouraged: here on the American Dalton system, there on modern German lines – as for example in the renowned old Perse School at Cambridge, where William Rouse made his pupils converse, question, versify and act plays in Latin, Greek and French, teaching history through all kinds of group performances, and natural sciences through the cultivation of the school garden. Between fanciful reform notions and the old jog-trot, between the pushful energy of a small number of local authorities and the anxious economy of the majority, the Board is slowly endeavouring to push its way to the creation of something new and distinctive and the establishment of some sort of unity in the method of instruction. As yet, the line of advance is still undefined, and there is no clear goal on the horizon: but the will to advance is everywhere present.

At the moment, the most urgent reform seems to be the creation of a uniform teaching status for the higher schools. The new county school cannot possibly afford to attract the first-class teachers, at princely salaries, who are apt to fill the post of Head at the best of the public schools: neither the men nor the money is available. They can only try gradually to attract a good average, the type of the good University man who has, moreover, received careful professional training. This type does not yet exist, but it is being gradually developed. At the present moment the elementary teacher plays still a far too prominent part in the secondary school. And the University graduates, among the teachers, generally have received a professional training only if they were originally trained for the elementary school.

So far the supply of really competent secondary teachers is yet insufficient.

§ 8

If the main line of present development runs to the building of new State and county day schools, there is also a revival of the idea of the boarding-school, of a type which owes its immediate spiritual parentage to Ruskin, but ultimately derives, through him, from the ideas of Rousseau and Salzmann. The modernized boarding-school seeks to retain the great educational value of the public school while clearing it of the excessive emphasis on games and the atmosphere of luxurious exclusiveness that is always threatening it. Work on the land and in the garden is at once to harden the pupils bodily and give them a contact with nature such as the pampered boarding-school boy knows nothing of; at the same time the character building and truly educational elements of regular manual work are greatly emphasized. The first school of this type was founded by Cecil Reddie, in 1889, at Abbotsholme near Rocester in Derbyshire. His work is being imitated at Bedales in Sussex and has greatly influenced modern educational experiments in Germany.

CONCLUSION

CHAPTER I
ENGLAND AFTER THE WAR
§ I

ENGLAND's gains from the World War were immense. The German fleet, against which the war was waged in the first line, lies beneath the waters of Scapa Flow. For the moment, Germany is hardly a factor in world politics: for some time to come it can hardly trouble English political circles, even if it desired to do so. German trade and German industry, against which the war was waged in the second line, has received the heaviest blow dealt in history at a nation's economy. Almost the whole of German property abroad has been wiped out, while Germany's pre-eminence in a whole series of most important branches (dyes, chemicals, potash) has been broken. Germany no longer possesses any considerable supplies of iron ore. The British flag now waves over what were its important colonies (German South-West and German East Africa). The Indian Ocean is now a British sea. The Peace of Versailles has given the British Empire nearly as much as did the peace concluded after the downfall of Napoleon.

Yet in England a profound pessimism rules, a feeling of dissatisfaction with what has been accomplished, a mood of uncertainty and oppression, as though England had lost the war. A general idea prevails that the objects of the war have not been attained. And war, with its gains, has also brought losses so heavy that it is a question whether they do not offset all that has been won. Most menacing of all, it has produced internal transformations so perilous as to exclude any sense of tranquillity.

Germany is overthrown but not destroyed. It was broken only after four years of resistance and the alignment against it of an entire world. Such a combination can never recur. Germany's long resistance proved that, against any normal combination, it is an enormously powerful force, and will be so again as soon as post-war political pressure is lifted.

Circumstances enabled victory to be won and a great but momentary advantage to be secured; but, so English pessimists fear, there has been no lasting settlement of the balance of political power. Above all, Germany proved far stronger economically than was ever thought possible. Immediately after the war, it reappeared in world markets as a formidable competitor, and Nemesis has made of the Dawes

CONCLUSION

Settlement the means of setting it upon the road of economic recovery by forcing it to produce with feverish intensity and capture markets at all costs. The Peace of Versailles injured Germany deeply; but was the war worth while?

Its immediate reactions have been most unsatisfactory. France and the United States have been strengthened politically in a way that is by no means to Britan's interest. Versailles, the League of Nations and separate treaties have built up for France a position of power in Europe that is most unwelcome. Whether France, with its dwindling population, can maintain this position may be doubtful: for the moment, it is the leading Continental Power, and, after a period of attempts at playing off other Powers against it, it would seem as though, in 1928, there were nothing for it but to bow to the accomplished fact. Economically, too, where Germany has been successfully competed with on the Continent, the profits have gone to France, not to British industry. Even more striking is the post-war ascendancy of the United States. It is the great gainer by the war, financially, industrially and politically. It has gathered in Europe's gold, in payment for war supplies: it is the creditor of the States of Europe and takes ruthless political advantage of its financial superiority. It is using the burden of war debts to prevent the nations of Europe from increasing their armies and navies in accordance with their own wishes. Britain has had to be contented with a fleet that instead of being the first in the world is merely the equal of the American, and even this equality is being threatened. The effort to present the loss of English naval superiority as a sacrifice on the altar of international reconciliation is hardly convincing, even for home consumption. Financial power has further immensely increased American commerce; while British exports to all parts of the world have fallen, American have gone up. Where Germany has been driven from the field it has been to the advantage, not of Britain, but of America – and Japan. While American industry expands, British industry, in its vital sections (coal, cotton) contracts. America has become the greatest financial magnate in the world.

Moreover, the war has shaken British dominion precisely in those quarters where it seemed to be most secure – in the Far East, in India and in the British Dominions. No doubt new forms will be worked out for the association of the Dominions and the Mother Country, but it is abundantly clear that the larger colonies must be regarded rather as a burden on British foreign policy than taken for granted as a support to it. No doubt India will be held and the vast trade of the East not lost, but there will have to be a far-reaching writing down of assets in all these regions. Was the war worth all this?

The war cost Britain heavy sacrifices in human blood. The toll of blood is not so high as that exacted from Germany (Germany, killed, 1,611,104; Britain, 706,726; British Empire, 848,133), but far higher than that ever paid before for any victory. The National Debt has risen from £661 millions, in 1914, to £7,631 millions in 1928; in the 1928–29 Budget, the service of the debt accounted for £369 millions out of the total of £760·2 millions. The war imposed grave financial burdens on the middle classes. True, their loss is small by comparison with the complete extinction of the savings of the corresponding social grade in Germany, but the sharp rise in the prices of all necessaries, between 1916–21, accompanied as it was by heavy war taxation, made serious inroads on their funds. The landlords were burdened by Lloyd Georgian death duties, which, though not in origin connected with the war, were aggravated during its course and subsequently, with the result that in England as elsewhere the older aristocracy of birth and education was replaced by war profiteers who had come up from below: the vulgar parvenu flourished like the green bay tree, while the finer culture of the older social order collapsed under the combined pressure of prices and taxes.

Further, the moral looseness that swept through the world like a destructive plague on the wings of war was felt in its full force in England. The discipline of the Church disappeared, the observance of Sunday died out, Puritanic rigour in sex relations was replaced by a licence bordering on shamelessness. The effects of officers' leaves in Paris began to travel homewards; England was drawn into the post-war dancing carnival, and there, as elsewhere all over the world, an alarming proportion of young women began to imitate the gestures and behaviour of the *demi-monde*. Now, self-expression is the cry: the old moral code is scorned as prudery. There is a deterioration in manners everywhere: men's dressing becomes slack – dress clothes, once obligatory for every evening function, are, as on the Continent, the exception rather than the rule. In literature, a similar change is perceptible. The erotic note, so timidly handled ever since the opening of the nineteenth century, is now pervasive: sex problems and situations are dwelt on with a delight that was wholly un-English; all at once, birth-control became a chief topic for open discussion.

CONCLUSION

The Church has nothing for the rising generation; everything Puritanic is dismissed as ridiculous hypocrisy: it is hard to get young men to train for the ministry. For the first time in its history, it would seem as though England has broken with Christianity. In so far as any sense of religion does survive, it finds its satisfaction in Socialism, or in all or any of the crude forms of charlatan occultism. Small wonder if serious minds begin to see in all this confused welter of a post-war world signs of the impending doom.

Is all this merely the witches' sabbath of a time of upheaval, or does it really presage the downfall of a civilization? England's young men went into the war with enthusiasm, because they believed they were fighting for the victory, throughout the world, of liberty, self-government, individualism and Liberalism, which was what English civilization meant to them. But it is precisely this form of civilized life that seems to have gone under in the war. True, the Continental monarchies were broken, but there is little hope of comfort in what has taken their place. And ten years after the victory of Western civilizations, three-quarters of Europe is dominated not by Western Liberalism but by dictatorship. The greater part of Southern Europe is under military or Fascist rule: Eastern Europe is partly under the Polish sabre, partly under the Russian proletarian dictatorship. England itself is the scene of a struggle for mastery between profiteering capitalism and the crude egotism of the working-class – with the spectre of Moscow brooding in the background. The hand of Moscow is discerned in the nationalist agitation in India; in China, Russia has obviously been working against England; and the English world, which ought to be closing ranks in the face of the dangers that menace it, threatens, instead, to break in sunder: the Dominions are no longer to be relied upon, and even at home the English soul is infected with Bolshevism. Can England be said to have won the war, when its victorious gospel of liberty is no longer current in the world? Has Imperialism not been an utterly vain dream? Is not war under all and any circumstances a mistake? Is not politics a dirty business? Would it not be saner to devote oneself to the better things life has to offer – to art, to poetry, to music? For the first time in its history, the youth of England is consciously anti-political, anti-Imperialist, anti-Conservative.

Wide circles in England to-day are filled with doubts of civilization, and deep pessimism. Among Conservatives of all kinds this appears as a bitter criticism of the lack of power and want of discipline of the present day; in the Labour Party as Revolutionism. Has England become powerless? is it moving towards dissolution?

§ 2

The answer to this question can only be a decisive No. The pessimistic criticism of civilization, universal at the moment in England, does not go very deep even there. Essentially, it is confined to London, and to the younger circles at the Universities. It represents the utterance of men of letters and of learning, of theologians, and of many politicians – in other words, of thinking England. But England's greatness does not rest with its thinking minority, but with the great mass of men of instinctive action and powerful will. All of these want England to be somehow different, but despair does not occur to them. And the distant observer, comparing England's troubles with those of other countries, while finding that England will have to cancel many hopes, as other less fortunate countries have already had to do, sees no ground for despair in that fact. What England is now experiencing is a grave crisis in which a new state and a new type of society are coming to birth. The old has to a large extent lost its justification for existence, and must now yield place to the new. There is at the moment 'an inhuman dearth of noble natures.' But this is equally true of the rest of the world. Nor is the present crisis really new, but rather a century old; the war has not created it, but only accelerated the *tempo* of the decline of the old and the upgrowth of the new. The old state of unfettered individualistic capitalism, the form under which England rose to economic mastery of the world, is doomed to destruction. Decade by decade, its bad side – the atomization and dehumanization of the masses and even of great groups among the upper classes – was becoming more glaringly obvious. England entered, more than a century ago, on the road to a new form of state, in which capitalism was gradually interpenetrated and transformed by the Socialist idea; Factory legislation (from 1833) and Trade Union recognition (1824–5) were the first stages on this road. With the extension of the franchise to the masses (1867, 1884, and 1918) a fresh and vital step was taken in the same direction, for then a certain share in power was placed in the hands of the unorganized and, so far, politically almost useless mass. True, capitalism at once found in the mass-newspaper [*Daily Mail* 1895, etc.] an instrument for prolonging its domination, by wheedling and guiding the still infant mind; with the result that, for another generation, the masses continued to live under the spell of capitalism and its individualistic-liberal ideology, and, in the war, willingly lent their service to capitalism against Germany, then relatively less under capitalist control and still largely in the patriarchal feudal stage. Nevertheless, even before the outbreak of the war, the miners (1912) succeeded in making a notable breach in the capitalist state by exacting the payment of a minimum wage to a large section of the working-class. Thanks to war, again, the system of economic individualism was, under pressure of necessity, converted into a sort of temporary Socialism; capitalists might protest, but the mass had felt its power, and saw its aims on the verge of realization. Impossible now to go back permanently to unfettered, individualistic capitalism. The Asiatic solution worked out in Moscow runs counter to every Anglo-Saxon sentiment. The *via media* of the possible has not yet been discovered; hence the unrest. It is to this uncertainty that fears of revolution in England to-day must be referred, and equally, all indignation with the demagogic demands of the masses, the blatancy of the profiteers, and the insincerity of politics. But certain broad lines of advance begin to appear on the horizon and are perceived by politicians of all camps as well as, notably, endorsed by the leaders of spiritual life and to an increasing extent by the Churches. They include the limitation of profits, State supervision of great capital amalgamations, the liberation of the worker from wage slavery by the establishment of a decent living minimum, special taxation on all unearned gain, limitation of luxurious and non-moral expenditure of money; at the same time they reject, firmly, both Bolshevist and Socialist dictatorship. The practical working out of these main lines is still matter of hot dispute, but their more or less general recognition is visibly going on. Where there is such a growing clarity of aim, destruction is not in sight.

The contemporary moral crisis is likewise old; the war merely accentuated it. Economically, nineteenth-century society rested on the unfettered egotism of the business man, morally on the righteousness of Puritanism, pious, but narrow and wall-eyed to modern problems. For the industrial middle classes, there was nothing real but religiosity and business: they had no use either for philosophic problems or for æsthetic enjoyments. For intellectual thought and for artistic sensibility, two of the most potent human traits, there was no place in the ordinary Victorian *credo*. But here, too, the counter tendency was already operative long before the war. The

Oxford Movement brought into the poverty-stricken aridity of English Philistinism the feeling of wonder and the elevated mood of soaring poetry: Ruskin was the prophet of artistic perception to his generation: the Irish in the nineties brought a new popular romanticism: William Morris a new art in house decoration and dress. Historical, scientific and ethical doubts of the validity of traditional views flow from Carlyle and Darwin in ever-widening streams to Bernard Shaw, who was acting as a sort of English Ibsen as early as the nineties. Here, too, war heightened the *tempo*, carrying doubts of old dogmas to extending circles, and above all, tending, with its inevitable undermining of all standards, to restore to sexual life something of its natural right of which Puritanism has sternly deprived it. The immediate result of all this may be exaggerations and temporary aberrations that are certainly not attractive, but, when taken as a whole, and in its larger bearings, there is nothing specially dangerous in it. Danger would only arise were the blank materialism which is preached from Moscow to-day to penetrate deeper than it has done into the heart of the younger generation among the lower classes, and were the Church, at the same time, to prove unequal to the tasks set it by the hour. Since, however, there are signs of new and potent life stirring in the domain of the Church, the hope seems justified that the crisis of to-day may prove of brief duration.

Less simple is the question whether the war has improved England's position in the world. Here those who doubt would seem to have right on their side. The elimination of Germany would seem to be a gain of dubious term, while the political expansion of America would seem to be a factor of lasting significance for the future. Further it is probable that England's economic importance in the world must decline, at least for a generation to come, and that its relations with its Colonies will be at best passive and hardly such as to strengthen its international position. This situation must have a double consequence for the next decade. Politically it would seem that England has no alternative but to share world dominion with America, and strive, through the League of Nations, for the imposition of an Anglo-Saxon regimen of world peace – which, however, it is doubtful whether Europe would accept. From the economic point of view, on the other hand, America is the rival, open and apparently superior. It is highly questionable whether anything like a unified, all-British economic association can be brought into being, against America and against the continent of Europe. It is much more probable that economic

CONCLUSION

pressure may force England to a *rapprochement* with the continent of Europe, which would mean a partial, but surely not a complete re-establishment of its political influence. This is the situation for the next decade; nobody will venture to prophesy further ahead. To a nation with its ultimate powers unimpaired – and that is the case with England – any new development is possible out of the present political and economic chaos of Europe. The deciding factor here would seem to be whether or no England can succeed in putting itself at the head of a European coalition to save Europe from Bolshevism. The country that can do this will for long be leader of the West. So mighty an achievement, however, implies the realization of two conditions: a country which is to fight Bolshevism with spiritual weapons must have cast off from its own economic system the fetters of an outworn and predatory capitalism, and must be in a position to fuse Europe into a really coherent entity – an enterprise only conceivable to a policy sufficiently long-sighted and sufficiently strong to have substituted a genuine system of European peace for the regime of force of the Versailles Treaty.

CHAPTER II
ENGLAND AND THE WORLD
§ 1

VARIOUS, indeed, are the manifestations of the English mind surveyed in the preceding pages. We have studied the Englishman in his political capacity, at home, in his Colonies, and in the larger world; in relation to his economic and juridical system. We have acquired a certain insight into his Churches, his Schools and his Universities. It remains to connect these various strands: so to collate the observations gathered in these different spheres as to clarify and complete the slight, empirical sketch already attempted in the chapter on the English character (page 147 *seq.*).

In the history of social development, England represents a quite peculiar national type. The old peasantry, groundwork in every country in Europe,[1] lives on to this day in England, in an unusually definite form. In many respects, the country is still thoroughly mediæval. The modern idea that the relations of the millions of human beings must be regulated by law, that there is a communal life above individual life, that the State has paramount rights over the individual, is much less developed in England than in Germany, France, or any other modern community. The relations between Englishmen are governed, not by written law, not by a constitution or a civil code, but by unwritten tradition, handed on from generation to generation: constantly changing, no doubt, but felt to be immutable and, therefore, sacrosanct. There is no paramount right of the State as such over the individual; there are rather innumerable single and private rights, of which various rights of the King, representing the State, are a certain category. Every individual has his own special right – the King, the University professor, the clergyman, the barrister, the taxpayer. The (nominal) Veto of the King on Acts of Parliament is an instance of such a right; it is not a right vested in the representation of the State as such, but the personal right of a certain exalted individual; the average English citizen sees no distinction between this and the private right of Mr. X to fill a vacant living, the private right of the Bishop of Y to a seat in the House of Lords, the right of the barristers to fill a vacant judgeship, the right of every Briton to be exempt from military service. Right down into the nineteenth century, the State was, like the mediæval State, a mere bundle of private rights and duties. In vain did Tudor and

CONCLUSION

Stuart absolutism endeavour to impose upon England the more modern conception of the State as an entity with rights transcending those of the individual. When, first in the Civil Wars and then in the American War of Independence, the citizen refused to pay taxes he had not directly or indirectly sanctioned, the old mediæval conception of the State triumphed over the more modern view. In the nineteenth century, the battle was renewed, but the issue, this time, was different. Round about 1800, the State was on the verge of dissolving into a series of privileged groups: the landowning aristocracy passed laws: the industrial capitalist laid down such conditions of work, wages and housing as seemed good to him: the Church dominated spiritual life: a series of privileged Gilds – Inns, Corporations, Universities, Public Schools – possessed rights nobody might infringe. Every great reform of the nineteenth century – Franchise, Local Government, Factory Inspection, Housing, Ecclesiastical Commissioners, Compulsory Education – made a breach in this mediæval conception of privileged groups. The total effect was to create a new conception of the State. This new conception has at last in the nineteenth century conquered England as it did other countries in the sixteenth and seventeenth centuries, but with a characteristic difference. In England it is not, as everywhere else in Europe, based on absolutism. This new State, on the contrary, is a quite peculiar combination of modern democratic forms with the aristocratic spirit of the gentleman. The most recent instance of the old struggle was that presented when the Briton in 1915 passionately asserted his right to refuse the elementary citizen duty of fighting for his country. Conscription was accepted only as an emergency provision for the duration of the war; the fundamental claim of the individual to freedom from State compulsion stands intact. In the last analysis, English freedom is the *liberum veto* of the individual against the collectivity: if it is innocuous, the reason is that there is, in the Englishman, a combination of dislike for logic and sound political instinct that saves him, except in very rare cases, from drawing the logical consequences of his own principle.

The Spirit of mediæval peasantry survives, further, in the Anglo-Saxon's naïve assumption that his State, his culture, his conception of honour and morals are the only ones in the world. All his religiousness further is primitive and mediæval, composed of the two main ideas, that God must be worshipped and the world made his. There, too, is the root of the cant which regards everything English as sacred and God-appointed, simply and solely because it exists (cf. page 401): the root of the religious primitivism which identifies piety, formal observance, respect for property and the Monarchy, and regards them all as equally holy and deserving of honour: the root, too, of unscrupulous war-time propaganda, which weighs no heavier on the national conscience than did the half-naïve falsification of documents by pious men in mediæval times.

This ancient peasant strain, which is still part of the make-up of the present-day Englishman, has submitted, however, in the course of time, to all sorts of modern influences. There is first mediæval chivalry: it produced all over the world a complex fighting code, which has survived in the Englishman's subconscious mind longer than anywhere else in the world (cf. pages 284 seq., 309): outsiders belonging to another race or even to another class of men, have no rights worth mentioning: to despoil them may be a virile virtue, to lie to them a venial offence. Insiders, on the other hand, are protected by a rigid code of fine aristocratic forms and observances. For the insiders, mediæval chivalry gradually built up an ethical code of a very lofty order, which still dominates the English mind in the form of the idea of the gentleman and is one of its greatest possessions (cf. page 156 seq.). As the centuries passed, the ethical content of this idea deepened and its ambit became more comprehensive: its narrow class emphasis was progressively softened, and, after gradually widening so as to take in all the members of the nation, it is now on the way to losing its exclusively national character. But the mediæval strain lives on: good form is at least as important as any ethical prescription: the appearance and garb of good breeding are not sharply differentiated from the equivalent of the thought and action it should connote. And the difference between insiders and outsiders, well kept under in normal times, will strongly accentuate itself in any national emergency.

Humanism, the second great civilizing movement in Europe, produced a relatively feeble reaction in England. It did little beyond impressing a strong classical stamp on education. It could not dislodge the class ideal of chivalry. Just as in the Middle Ages, the man who counts is not the man of profound and penetrating intellect but the man of good family. Humanism founded Grammar Schools and Universities: the English transformed them into hot-beds of chivalry (pages 408, 463). A lofty Humanistic ideal is proclaimed, often enough, but it failed to make any deep mark on the mind of the nation.

CONCLUSION

The peasant substratum is as evident in English philosophy (page 150) as in the English constitution; empirical and objective, believing only in what can be apprehended by the senses, English philosophy inclines either to eliminate the non-rational altogether, or to leave it in a sort of mist, without any sort of attempt at scientific analysis. Hence, one of the most significant of English philosophers (Hume) regarded the soul as a collocation of disconnected concepts, just as the typical English citizen regards the State as a collocation of disconnected rights. So, too, life is conceived as a mere product of struggle, and truth not as an absolute but as a means (Pragmatism). The effort to understand life as a whole in its entity, on Humanist lines, has been less assiduously made in England than in other countries.

The second great wave of the time, the Renaissance movement, penetrated England too, but again the primeval groundwork of the national character remained unaffected. It had a potent effect within a comparatively small group of distinguished men, and, through one of them, Shakespeare, influenced succeeding centuries profoundly; but the inartistic outlook of the peasant continued, after as before, to characterize the nation as a whole. Only one of the currents of the Renaissance movement had a strong echo in England, its appeal to strong action. It bred a group of great individuals, like Drake, Raleigh, Henry VIII, Elizabeth and Strafford. The nation responded to their rallying cry in so far as it roused them to seafaring and national defence, but the old peasantry proved too strong for them when they strove in true Renaissance spirit to create a new state on the groundwork of the mediæval community. It was the mediæval conception of the State as composed of privileged individuals and estates that defeated Charles I.

The third great strain of the time, Reformation, in the specifically English form of Puritanism, had a more potent effect. Here, an English variety of Protestantism impressed its religious stamp on the life of the mediæval peasant. It gave the English the sense that their inner life, in spite of all its faults, was the work of God, and called by Him to the highest destiny. Puritanism sanctified the powerful will to action roused by the Renaissance, and dedicated it to religious uses. From the seventeenth century on, every Englishman is an Imperialist, conscious or unconscious, animated by a steady patriotic flame; which, however, nearly always has an international and religious tinge; in international humanitarian efforts he sees merely the natural obverse of nationalism, and is slow to perceive that the

490

ENGLAND AND THE WORLD

nationalist and the internationalist point of view very often stand in opposition. And these qualities remain in his character to this day, though Puritanism seems to have spent its force now.

The 'Age of Reason' gave the English the mental physiognomy that remains characteristic of the majority to this day. Then, at last, fusion took place between the Puritan citizen and the knight. The product was the normal Englishman. Like the old Puritans and their peasant forebears, he gathers up money and property with a crass materialism shot by gleams of recognition of certain non-rational forces; uses hands and elbows to get on, and defends his rights and his liberties, yet, amid all this bourgeois business of his, still pays tribute to the aristocratic code of honour and, on the whole, submits gladly to the leadership of the aristocratic upper class. The springs of inner life, which used to operate merely instinctively, are now rationalized; his thought, governed by a strong empiric Utilitarianism, leaves ultimate problems alone, while keeping certain loopholes open for the non-rational. In this period the old feeling for liberty of the peasant and the nobleman is gradually developed into a great constitutional system – for the dominating class at least – and into a theoretic outlook on the whole world. It is the Englishman's philosophy of life. The system posits free, self-reliant and self-controlling citizens; it divides the world into nations free and unfree according as they do or do not resemble the English idea, and sees, in the history of the world, nothing but a gradual development of English liberty, destined to fill the whole world at last.

The nineteenth century has deepened the lines in this picture. The freedom constituting the English ideal now really became the freedom of the entire nation, as one section of the population after another wrested a share of the freedom of the privileged for itself. Economic freedom, for which the Puritans had striven, was established in unique fashion: on the basis of Capitalist Individualism, a social system was erected that satisfied all the instincts of the race; it left scope for energetic action and swift enjoyment, and provided materialism with a convenient façade of idealism: empiricism gave it a metaphysical draping, Utilitarianism an ethic of its own: a newly-invented instrument of power, the Press, served to guide the masses, while at the same time giving them the sense that they were acting on their own initiative. Old Puritanism lived on in various slightly modernized forms: new Utilitarianism is little else than old Puritanism without its strong religious groundwork, and Puritan conceptions of Eng-

491

CONCLUSION

land's destiny to fulfil the bidding of God, were occasionally revivified in order to lend a religious sanction to a policy of force abroad. But the nineteenth century at the same time also brought radical transformations. The state of the privileged gentry was broken down: access to rights previously confined to the higher orders was achieved not only by the middle classes but also by the lower. This meant the complete abolition of privilege and, what is even more far reaching, a gradual restriction of the traditional idea of liberty. To win for themselves a bare minimum standard of life, the lower classes had to demand such far-reaching changes in the structure of the State that little remained of unrestricted individual liberty, in the older sense. The new State, as developed after 1832, interferes drastically in industry, it even fixes wages: it deprives the great landowner of his *latifundia* to create small-holdings: it limits freedom of building by inspection and restrictions: by the levy of immense inheritance taxation, it deprives citizens of large part of their wealth: it imposes compulsory education – in a word, it is on the way to become a State in the Continental sense, and the army of its civil servants affords outward and visible sign of the transformation. At the same time, continuity with the past is everywhere preserved; individual liberty is respected, so far as possible – but it is no longer the sole criterion. For the first time in his history, the Englishman recognizes the State as an entity, possessing over-riding rights because it represents the nation as a whole. Since the average man sees, lurking behind this ideal, the bogey of Socialism, there is a powerful Individualist reaction against it, but hardly such as can arrest its evolution in the long run.

For the national outlook has undergone a notable change in the course of the nineteenth century; Puritanism, in the old sense, is to-day in its death-throes. Not Puritanism as such. On the contrary: one side of Puritanism, its missionary aspect, did not fully develop until the nineteenth century. Once again, religious forces served to enrich the Anglo-Saxon drive to action. Nineteenth-century Imperialism, as preached, for example, by Carlyle, was thoroughly impregnated with Puritanism. It seeks not merely to conquer but to impose its ideals on the world: its vague mixture of the conquering and the missionary idea bears the authentic Cromwellian stamp. So strong is this side of Puritanism that it has survived the destruction of its original individualistic economic and political ideals.

But – and this is the most important point – it is only in the region

492

of foreign policy that the Englishman is still the pure Puritan, seeking
to set up the Kingdom of the God of the Anglo-Saxons. Even here,
the religious colouring is fading; although religious zeal may inspire
the Englishman's sense of his mission to the future, the emotion
behind it has suffered a secular transformation, and its high lights
are liberty and peace. The point of view is still Puritan, but the
religious stimuli are dead. Where religious life does exist, it is not
chiefly of the Puritan but of the High Church Anglican type. This
new conception of piety, centred in the Church rather than in the
religious edification of the individual, which has gained ground ever
since the days of the Oxford Movement, is a phenomenon precisely
parallel to the new idea of the State, which puts the welfare of the
whole above the absolute freedom of the individual. It is also the exact
analogue of contemporary pacifist Imperialism, which puts the diffusion of English culture above the economic advantage of single traders.
In their combination, these phenomena would seem to indicate a
far-reaching transformation of outlook, of far greater significance
than any transitory reactions to individualistic modes of thought.

§ 2

Egotism and Materialism are some of the ground tones in English
life though they by no means fill the whole picture. Many traits
illustrate this, which in the midst of a refined twentieth-century
civilization strike the Continental observer as fossilized relics from
earlier stages. It will serve the purpose of clearness to study these
traits in their entirety and refer for the obvious qualifications to other
parts of the text (pages 157 seq., 169 seq., 396). In the law, there is the
damages awarded to an injured husband at the expense of the co-
respondent in a divorce suit: in education, abundant money prizes
must serve to stimulate the ambition of the schoolboy; offices in the
State, commissions in the Army, presentations to livings have long
been considered as material rights which to a large extent were even
saleable; the same spirit is expressed in the high salary expected as
a matter of course by anyone of consideration in the community,
whether minister of the Crown, high ecclesiastic, or judge. Further,
we have seen English society powerless to interfere effectively to
prevent the exploitation of entire classes in the population by the
rapacity of a few. Centuries pass, and nothing is done either to
relieve the poverty of the agricultural labourer or the penury of the
lesser curate; in the cities, slums, though diminished in extent, still

exist: to this day, the interests of barristers are strong enough to resist any radical simplification or cheapening of legal procedure. The influence of big finance is carefully veiled, but extraordinarily tight. It works strongest through the press, but it can also count on the mighty influences both in the House of Lords and in city government. Capitalism successfully protected the City of London against the democratization of the rest of local government.

Throughout English history, the powerful will to action of the people has been in conflict with a contrary impulse, hardly less strong, to enjoy without too much effort. As early as 1500, foreigners were struck by the high level of material well-being[2]; and from that time on, England and its American offshoot have been distinguished for the comfort of their dwellings, the luxury of their meals, their well-cut and convenient masculine apparel, and the handsome appointments and padded arm-chairs of their clubs. The taste for active sport has always been to a large extent neutralized by a taste for looking on in comfort at the athletic contests of others; there is nothing new in the plaint that sport is becoming less and less a means of national discipline, more and more an opportunity for a crowd to look on at the performance of professional footballers or boxers. Adventurous daring has always been confined to comparatively small sections, the desire of the masses being set to enjoyment. The complaint about the competition of others is a recurrent feature of English history; in one century it was the Spaniard, in the next, the Frenchman, the Dutchman, or the German. And instead of beating the antagonist by doing better themselves, the method is, every now and then, to gird up their loins for a single gigantic exertion, and crush him by force. The great seafaring nation in early mediæval times was not the English but the Scandinavians; it was not till the fourteenth century, after they had possessed the best harbours in the world for nearly a thousand years, that anything like a fleet was created; in the Age of Discovery men like Drake and Hawkins and Raleigh only appear when a tolerably safe material reward awaits any notable exertion. Typical, again, is the dislike for the profession of the soldier which distinguished the Englishman from other nations. In the eighteenth century, cant had an explanation ready for this – the soldier's lack of personal freedom, and the fact that he was the tool of absolutism, was repugnant to the free-born Englishman. As early as the sixteenth century, however, foreigners[3] would note that the true reason of this strange dislike was love of comfort; further that the efficiency of the

English soldier was lessened by the necessity of feeding him too well. No nation felt an equal resentment of necessary war-time restrictions. A temporary sugar shortage assumed the proportions of a national calamity. Special fodder for race-horses had to be produced, at a time when victory might turn on the last bag of oats. The first war-loan was a fiasco – the interest was too low. Many individuals accepted as self-evident the obligation to make the personal sacrifice of military service; but such was not the view of the mass.

§ 3

At every turn, throughout this book, we have come into contact with the Englishman as the man of action, of will. Here again we enumerate traits in general and refer the reader for the obvious qualifications to other parts of the text. We have seen that English institutions are in constant modification, always with the result of giving fuller scope to leadership. Wherever the Englishman scents a leader, he bows before him, clears a way for him – even if he is a Socialist workman. We have discovered the well-nigh omnipotent monarch in the Prime Minister (p. 219), the Speaker of the House of Commons (p. 225), the Headmaster of the public school (p. 466), the Trade Union Secretary and Labour leader, and have seen a new monarch gradually developing, behind the scenes of municipal organization, in the Town Clerk (p. 263). We have seen the Englishman's religion voicing itself in the most potent moral appeal ever made to the human will – Thou art to build the Kingdom of God upon earth! To that art thou called, thou and thy people! We have found democratic forms prevailing wherever the English dwell: in the State, in the city, in the jury system, even in the school, with its tendency to self-government, and in the Congregation of the Universities. But we found also, that these democratic forms are mainly so much stage scenery, behind which the few, or, it may be, a single individual, exercise almost unlimited command because they invariably leave to the commanded the sense that they co-operate in ruling, nay, are really ruling themselves. We have seen the Anglo-Saxon founding and developing colonies, without the admixture of missionary spirit, which characterizes similar French and Spanish enterprises, simply and solely in order to rule and make money. We found that in him, the sense of law and love of truth are forces that, though real enough, are grounded, in the last analysis, purely on will, and not infrequently limited by it; while hardly recognizing the almost automatic compul-

495

sive force of truth and justice as abstract virtues, he is always ready to extend them, in action, to those who exact his respect by resistance: they are prizes he has ready for strength of will, when he encounters it in others (pages 284, 402). Finding pleasure only in the discipline of sport, conceiving of education as the conscious steeling of the will at the expense of feeling and intelligence, his constitution is the most perfect system imaginable for combining various and opposing wills. His legal system is based not on the assumption that men are calm, moderate and objectively-minded, but on the assumption that they are passionate and strong-willed; it is a machine of protection, designed to safeguard most admirably an accused person from being violently man-handled by his fellow-men of a similar constitution (p. 309 seq.).

This will is harsh and egotistic. It is, in the process of history, again and again qualified by the gentleman's instincts, but only where it meets resistance. Bentham's view of civilization as the development of the diagonal forces of the endless egotism of man was thoroughly English: so was Darwin's vision of a struggle for food as the basis of all existence. Forceful personalities, like the early Norman Kings, Henry VIII, or Cromwell, Cecil Rhodes or Joseph Chamberlain, occur at the opening of each of the great periods in English history. From the time of Milton down to that of the World War, English ascendancy has been accompanied by forceful repression of the antagonist at home as well as abroad. Where nobody was there to defend himself, the distinguishing marks of the aristocratic regime of the eighteenth century are its egotistic oppression of the defenceless, artfully concealed, and, in the individual case, controlled by the gentleman's code: and the ruthless exploitation of the community in the interest of the ruling class – the felling of forests, destruction of the peasantry; present-day city slums bear living witness to the rapacious egotism of that time, as did the Irish countryside and the Scottish Highlands for more than a century. The form, not the fact, of exploitation was changed by the Industrial Revolution; the fact remained for long in the hours of the working day of tiny children. Right down to the nineteenth century, Army and Navy, the foundation stones of England's power, were dependent on forceful impressment for their recruits. England was the one country in Europe where every one was said to be free, but, in fact, a minority only enjoyed a full share of the blessings of the State.

But England's power always recognizes its own limits. That is why its effect, instead of being destructive merely, has always created fresh centres of power. The man of power who breaks down in the attempt to make possible the impossible does not occur in English history. The record of their Kings includes monarchs of the Hapsburg type, but no Hohenstaufen, no Charles the Bold, no Charles XII of Sweden, no Gustavus Adolphus. Politics, in most of the great periods of English political history, are of a surprising coolness and dryness. The part of protagonist of Protestantism was left to Gustavus Adolphus: first Elizabeth and then Cromwell toyed with the notion, but dropped it as too audacious. Always the minimum expenditure of strength is preferred – witness Elizabeth's attitude to the Dutch Protestants, or the policy employed against Richelieu, Mazarin or Napoleon, or by Palmerston on behalf of Liberalism in Europe. Rational limitations always control the sense of power: Is not this the root of the measured calm of the gentleman? and high diplomacy is brought in to increase the effect of a moderate dose of force. Instead of fighting, they levy foreign mercenaries or foreign allies. Such was Sir Thomas More's recipe.[4] Ever since the Reformation, the vein of artful diplomacy has struck the Continental observer as specifically English.[5] All the time-honoured arts of diplomacy have been developed by British cabinets to the full: raising hope and then fulfilling only a tithe thereof, making allies out of opponents and setting them to work, or putting the opponent suddenly in the wrong, where he least expected it. Nor has any other State ever touched the English in the invention of slogans which at once inspire the native masses and create enemies for their opponents within the opponents' camp. The strength of English colonial policy has always been the skilful way in which the Mother-Country, without any visible expenditure of force, retained so firm a grip – economic, political and spiritual – on its Colonies that, their sense of independence notwithstanding, they have to stay in the English fold. It is the same at home; the legislators are not commanded but led with supreme art by some statesman or other. The democratization of the constitution means, in effect, that forty millions of people, told every day that they rule the land they live in, are in fact kept roped to pulleys which are worked by incessant appeals at once to all the noble and to all the egotistic strains in the human mind. Lord Northcliffe was the Machiavelli of the turn of the century.

Love of power, in alliance with love of comfort, will always recognize its own limitations. The Englishman has never been a Don Quixote. When France was lost, in the fifteenth century, he let it

497

CONCLUSION

be: when North America slipped out of his hands in the eighteenth, he reconciled himself to the inevitable: after winning the World War, he capitulated to three million Irish rebels. So, individual love of comfort trains a nation of strong-willed people to a high point of effective statecraft. And the constant democratization of the English constitution, from the eighteenth century Whig oligarchy to the admission to a share of the power of the bourgeoisie in 1832, and the Labour Cabinet of 1924, is the most notable proof of a political compromise, which readily adapts itself to new circumstances and prefers the safe keeping of part of the power to the doubtful issue of a fight for dwindling monopolies.

§ 4

English civilization is predominantly – of course not exclusively – based on the most powerful factors of the mass-mind, the will, and the egotistic and materialistic instincts. Its political institutions are democratic. This is possible because in England the population is less diversified in character than in most other countries (page 154), because even the great man is not really different from the mass, but incarnates the common traits with special strength and purity. The constitution is built on the basic assumption of the equality of all Anglo-Saxons, all setting their wills to mastery; we have seen how it has failed wherever the attempt has been made to introduce it in the absence of this previous Anglo-Saxon condition. It depends on the assumption, peculiar to the Anglo-Saxon, that an entire nation will react, uniformly, to certain great mass-slogans, represented by a great man whom it trusts and reveres, and can be ruled through the machinery of suggestion, represented in the Press. Advertisement technique – an Anglo-Saxon invention – corresponds, in the economic sphere, to this political slogan technique. English literature, to its great detriment, subsists largely on the exploitation of those same simple mass-instincts. In no other literature does one find an equal skill in playing on the suggestibility of the mass and using its reactions to catchwords. There is no essential difference between the way in which Dickens, with inexhaustible virtuosity, plays on the tune of Captain Cuttle's hook,[6] rousing storms of delight in English (and non-English) readers, and the way in which Lord Northcliffe or Lord Rothermere deploys endless fresh women and children, in danger from some enemy or other, at home or abroad; they produce precisely analogous mass-reactions.

498

There is an undifferentiated quality about every mass. The motives, that move a human mass to action, are seldom or never quite clear to it: they are generally a crowd of various impulses. The crowd-man thinks first of himself, but, all the time, some vague altruistic ideal floats before him, undefined. He thinks first of his pleasure, and his own advantage, but at the same time he believes, with a naïve optimism, that in so doing he is somehow serving others also. The peasant in all countries is the primitive egotist, who while tilling his field for his own use, nevertheless feels himself a pillar of the community, which ought therefore to be grateful to him. And all the other pillars in society think just as he does. A higher stage of evolution has to be reached before religious and ethical influences teach a man to distinguish between egotistic and altruistic impulses in his action. In England, the number which has reached this stage seems to be much smaller than in other countries. Action, in the Englishman, derives from a primitive conception of the undifferentiated will; which is at the bottom of the cant which the foreigner has always noted as his special characteristic. Wherever he (rightly or wrongly) uses force, he will do so with an ethical tinge; when he studies æsthetics and economics, the ethical tinge will reappear; a great man like Ruskin who, in all æsthetic and economic questions is hunting for the ethical, is characteristically English. The specialist, who follows a given question or aspect to its last conclusion, is always suspect to the Englishman. He will, therefore, never be in danger of losing touch with realities. But it is difficult for him to clear religious and scientific conceptions from the surrounding ideas with which they are generally connected. It is difficult for the Englishman, for instance, in the religious sphere to detach what is religious and proper to God from the tangle of innocent, but decidedly worldly adhesions. To him not only the intercourse of man with God is sacred, but all the institutions designed to that end – the Church and Sunday, the hierarchy and the State, and, ultimately, the existing organization of society, the political constitution, and by easy stages even property, capital and the cheque-book (page 404). And wherever a scientific chain of ideas is to be pursued to its utmost limits his famous common sense may come in, the crowning virtue of the mass mind, confusing issues, darkening problems, the soft pillow for the un-thinking. A thinking Scotsman, Reid, developed it into the basic faculty of what he called human nature (page 150).

For the Englishman, at any rate, it has become one of the pillars

CONCLUSION

of his civilization. It is the great force which is at the bottom of his State. It makes slow evolution without revolution the great achievement of his history. It is at the root of the truly English love of compromise. It is the force that has made possible the English party system, in which every so-called party is a coalition of groups of the most diverse tendencies, and has enabled the original incumbents of privilege, time after time, to take their antagonists, after protracted struggles, into their own ruling group. Common sense interpenetrates the ideal of the gentleman, and secures his rigid observance of all the main points of the code, leaving alone the more arduous ethical precepts, Christian or chivalric (page 165). Common sense prevents the development in England of the professional man with definite class idiosyncrasies, and substitutes the ideal of the man who is at home everywhere, and everywhere pursues the golden mean; so making the well-meaning universal amateur a statesman who may be in charge of the shipbuilding or the telephones of a nation. Common sense makes a Departmental minister of the mere M.P., a J.P. of the landowner – and very often an excellent one – and concentrates the most specialized governmental functions in the hands of committees of gentlemen. It abolishes no old law and alters as few as possible; it dispenses so far as may be with fixed rules of procedure and settled codes, in the serene assurance that the presence of the gentleman ensures due regard for right – whether he be Speaker in the House of Commons, Minister of the Crown, Judge, or Civil Servant.

Common sense, again, is the central thread in the evolution of English literature. It is often destructive of the sense of form, of the appreciation of the highest genius. It explains the habitual denigration of everything romantic, practised, a century ago, by the *Quarterly*, or why a mystic like William Blake had to wait for a century after his death for recognition. Common sense, further, is responsible for the limited success of the classic model in the drama or the Italian sonnet in poetry: for the narrow appeal of the problem novel and the problem play; above all, for the universal avoidance of the high tragic note, and the reduction of three-fourths of English literature to the mental level of the schoolgirl. But on the other hand it has developed as its finest flower the gift of humour in English literature from Chaucer to Dickens and H. G. Wells. Common sense extends to wide spheres outside the confines of this study. Let a man deviate, for good or evil, from the norm, and the laugh of the English humourist – a glorious laugh it is, too – is swiftly at work, building a bridge back to every day, with a joke as its pillars.

§ 5

But materialism and egotism, the power of will, and common sense are far from explaining everything. A force quite as potent as the others, appearing everywhere and in the most diversified forms, softening all harsher features, is the deep-rooted irrational instinct of the English mind. It appears as a profound religious sense, which may be imperfectly differentiated from worldly side-instincts, may in many individuals be tainted with self-seeking and untruthfulness, but is at the bottom sincere and a powerful force to the good. The irrational instinct will appear as deep gentlemanly feeling of chivalrousness towards the weak, an instinct so strong, that where it cannot find a legitimate object, it will force its way in the form of perverted and ludicrous sentimentalism (page 171 *seq.*). Other forms of the respect for the non-rational have also been noted – e.g. the reverence for ancient usage in the law, and the love of forms and ceremonies in public life generally. Again and again we meet an almost superstitious respect for tradition and its embodiments, notably everything that savours of aristocratic form, so the influence of the good old families persists within the contemporary framework of democracy. It operates through institutions like the House of Lords and the Conservative Party, and, behind both, the most powerful press in the world: through the Church, through the legal corporations, through the aristocratic tone of the foremost Universities and public schools, even the Stock Exchange (page 197). Daily life is deeply dyed with aristocratic memories. Any man in the lower middle classes with a claim to social consideration has himself addressed as 'Esq.' as though he were the squire of some knight; there is an aristocratic 'hall' in every little dwelling-house – used for mackintoshes and umbrellas: no literature in the world devotes anything like an equal amount of space to descriptions of upper-class life. The cheap popular novel deals not with low life but with high. Revolutionary opinions can hardly gain a lasting hold in a country where the workman has a feeling for aristocracy and all the ideals of the gentleman, gladly pays his tribute to a Lord, and cheerfully submits to an aristocracy of his own in the form of Trade Union officialdom.

In other countries, the Universities are apt to be hotbeds of Radicalism; in England they have been and probably will remain pillars of aristocratic tradition. Easy enough to assign 'hypocrisy' as a convenient formula to cover all the conflicting elements of the national character in a cheap formula; we have tried to show that the combination of the struggle for power with the pursuit of ethical aims which underlies all these discrepancies is, in the last analysis, a healthy symptom of internal national equilibrium – far from pleasing as some of its by-products may be (page 106).

§ 6

What has Anglo-Saxon culture done for the world? It is the great last question to which any investigation of fundamental issues naturally leads up, but a question which any author, whether English or foreign, will try to answer only with an almost overwhelming feeling of risk. It does not only tax to the limits all his powers of critical detachment, it also 'implies a fixed scale of values, historical and philosophical, individual and national, which in a century of doubt and criticism he cannot expect all his readers to share. It further is not even a question which every reader will understand. It cannot be answered by a catalogue of great Englishmen, however weighty, however long. For there are other nations from which equal lists could be gathered strong enough to balance any superior merit of the former. The question is not, whether there have been many Englishmen who have made contributions of the first order to modern civilization – any schoolboy can answer this question in the affirmative. The question rather is which of our modern ideals find a more complete embodiment in England than in any other country, and by which historical movements of the very first order English civilization has put a distinctively English stamp on the whole world?

First of all, the English nation is one of the sanest of nations. It gives the picture of a nation sound in body and soul. The constant exercise of the will, trained in the youthful Englishman, by games, and the teaching dinned into his ears by others to expect nothing from them, but everything from his own exertions, have bred in the nation a virile strain such as even the tendency to idle enjoyment continually arising in England is powerless to efface. Spiritually, too, the English are a healthy people. Sheer strength of will inhibits intellectual over-subtleties; common sense, while it may militate against supreme individual achievement, outside the political sphere guarantees at once a high minimum in the performance of day-to-day tasks and an ethical minimum in action generally – wherever, that is to say, a supreme gust of passion in man or nation does not come in to make the course uncertain. Perversion, either hyper-intellectual, hyper-æsthetic or moral, is the rarest of all phenomena. (Present-day London Bohemianism is hardly important enough, in the history of the world, to be expressly called an exception.) Throughout the British Isles there prevails a robust, masculine and sound sexual morality, which amounts to more than the pious phrases of most Continental nations. No British colony records any notable miscegenation of British origin. Not sophistication, but an excess of the primitive and the barbarous is the real danger – and it is serious enough.

Further, the English are politically sound. For all its lip-service to fashionable democratic catchwords, the people, at heart, is sound and thoroughly aristocratic, submitting readily to leadership from above, so long as it is not dragooned, but inspired, led (or maybe bamboozled). In great things as in small, it contentedly takes its standards, political, social, religious and personal from its betters, and these standards are sensible and serviceable. The knightly ideal before which it bows may not be the loftiest, but it is a lofty ideal. It is no mean achievement to have made self-control the instinct of a whole nation, which only rarely yields to volcanic outbursts of primitive strength. The steady hardening process to which it has submitted under the aristocratic rubric, *noblesse oblige*, is what has saved the tremendous force of will of the Anglo-Saxon from degenerating into a merely destructive passion.

The English State rests on two specifically English assumptions, common sense and the transformation of the antagonist into a privileged colleague. It is characterized by freedom; no one need obey the laws if his conscience rejects them. Freedom carried to this point is rendered possible by the essential similarity of all citizens, their immunity from large religious or other conflicts such as might split the State, and the fact that, on all vital matters, most Englishmen prefer to be just like their neighbours, and obediently follow the lead given by the upper classes, whether in religion or the cut of a tie. Such freedom, often tantamount to a tyranny of public opinion, would be intolerable to nations more sensitive to liberty in the personal sphere. Yet it is good for the world, and good for nations with other ideals, that the world contains a state such as has made the State well-nigh superfluous, where most of the functions of the State are administered by society. England's contribution to civilization is this free state. It is a structure in which free play is given to the natural forces that go to the building of society. It rests on the *instinctive* forces of humanity; on naïve egotism, naïve imitativeness, and on the instinctive need of man to lead and be led. The Englishman has shown that great things can be achieved along these lines. His achievement is, in the last analysis, not the individual achievement of single statesmen, single legislators, single generals or single thinkers, but the collective achievement of the Anglo-Saxon race. England can live without great men comparatively longer than any other country. Whether or no, at a given period in history, England stood in the forefront of human development, may have depended on whether or no it happened then to possess dominating minds. But at no time did it stand still altogether; always there were – if not in England itself, then in the Colonies – men, simple, of average endowment, and little or no intellectual or artistic claims, who quite naturally, good-naturedly and egotistically pushed with their elbows and kept on making the world more and more English: men who, at any crisis would be slow to sacrifice themselves, but when there was nothing else for it, came forward and did what was necessary. On such men rests England's greatness: because of them it has survived, without notable loss, periods when its statesmen were definitely mediocre, periods when the world was looking forward to England's downfall. Over against the best organized state in the world, pre-war Prussia: over against the model organization of spiritual things, the Catholic Church, England sets its society state, with its minimum of organization. It is, in truth, not the ideal state: its faults are plain to see, nor could it work at all with other than Anglo-Saxons: but it is an advantage for humanity that the English model is there, to enable the one-sidedness of other systems to be improved and offset by comparison with it.

All England's other achievements pale by the side of this. It developed the idea of the gentleman more thoroughly and consistently than other nations have done, and by this gave an ethical ideal of great – though certainly not unique – value to the world. It often led in the mission field: it freed the slave throughout the world. The first great truly modern tendencies through which Scholasticism passed beyond itself, came out of England with Roger Bacon, Duns Scotus and William of Occam, while Wycliffe started the Reformation itself. England gave birth to the modern idea of toleration, England led in the rationalistic world of the eighteenth century, the first wave of Romanticism came from England. In the nineteenth century, English engineers and scientists conquered space and bent matter to their will. With William Morris it gave the world a new domestic culture. These are mighty achievements; but the English free state is even more original. Here, too, the entire contribution is England's, whereas its scholastics and reformers only won importance for the world as the result of the further developments to which their thoughts were carried on the Continent, in Italy, France and Germany. Shakespearian drama is the only other English contribution that can compare in importance with the free state. Without these two, civilization as we know it would be unthinkable.

These seem to be the points where England raises itself to the heights of human achievement. But the demonstration has also its negative force, for there are ultimate and supreme impulses in the last centuries which did not come from England, and England essentially only took over and carried on – the German Reformation, the Italian Renaissance (without which even Shakespeare is hardly conceivable), the French Revolution. Time will show whether German Idealism of the time of Fichte and Hegel should be added to the list. The authentic contribution made by the modern nations of Europe to the spiritual treasures of mankind is as important, perhaps in the last analysis more important, than England's. Even England does not possess an independent civilization, even the English are not the chosen people

And against all the great achievements which the world owes to England one fact must be set: the Englishman's one domineering quality, his lust for power which all the outside world feels as a danger, readily as it admits his lasting contributions to civilization. It is a basic fact of his character, it appears not only in wars and forceful colonization, but quite as well in English home politics so long as there is no adversary willing to accept the challenge. Few Englishmen will admit it and it is a hopeless task to try and make them see consciously what exists in their subconscious minds only. It is not a mere force of destruction: wherever the Englishman appears as a conqueror, he will bring with him not only material benefits in abundance, but also his religious and high ethical sense in all questions which do not touch his sense of supremacy. The Englishman is apt to point to this pleasant accompaniment, he is generally deaf to the tune. But it is the tune that grates upon the ears of others. Ready as they are to admit the great achievements of the English race, these achievements are not sufficiently unique to give the moral warrant for absolute world power. All world conquerors have degenerated into maniac Cæsars and all would-be world monarchies have failed before their task. England would hardly be an exception. Nations, like individuals, and the English nation even more than others, require the moral control supplied by the resistance of something like an equal opponent. It would be a loss to the world if there were no powerful England, but it would be a lasting detriment to the world, inclusive of England if ever England, were to become all-powerful.

NOTES

BOOK I

CHAPTER I

1 (p. 15). At the 1921 Congress of the Gaelic League, occupied since 1893 with the revival of the Irish tongue, it was reported that more than 80 per cent of all school children were receiving instruction in Irish. At the present moment it seems probable that the next generations of Ireland will have a certain reading knowledge and a certain speaking phraseology of Irish – but it is a long way still from this point to the re-establishment of Irish as the national language.

CHAPTER II

1 (p. 41). This oath of allegiance is the perfect example of a political egg-dance. It had to be acceptable both to (1) the English at home, who naturally desired Ireland's complete submission to the British Crown, and (2) the radical Irish who swear faith only to Ireland and regard any tie with England as a merely formal arrangement: i.e., really reject any oath of allegiance whatsoever. The result is the following diplomatic formula: '(1) *I do solemnly swear true faith and allegiance to the Constitution of the Irish Free State as by law established; (2) and that I will be faithful to H.M. King George V, his heirs and successors by law; (3) in virtue of (a) the common citizenship of Ireland with Great Britain and (b) her adherence to and membership of the group of nations forming the British Commonwealth of Nations.*' To the English Imperialist these words are to imply that Ireland swears true faith to the King and to the realm (2), and that Ireland and England are intimately united together (3*a*). To the Irish radical, on the other hand, they are to imply that (I) true faith *and allegiance* is sworn to the Irish Free State, while every member of the British, the Canadian, the South African, the Australian Parliament swears *allegiance* to the English King (1); to the latter, on the other hand, the Irishman swears only *true faith*, in the sense in which, e.g., equals may swear true faith to a mutual contract. (II) Ireland is an independent member of the British Empire (3*b*), and between it and England there merely exists a common citizenship (3*a*). What further does the introductory formula of 3 imply? The Imperialist will read '*in virtue of*' as an *affirmation* of the existing bond between the two countries, the radical enemy of England as implying the exact opposite – as a *condition* on which what is said

in (1) and (2) depend, but which can lapse, in which case the oath would automatically cease to operate. The oath is thus completely ambiguous and therefore worthless.

2 (p. 42). The name *Sinn Fein* means 'ourselves' in contradistinction to the Nationalism of Redmond, which, so it was suggested, aimed at achieving everything 'through England.'

CHAPTER III

1 (p. 66). These duties, nominally in force from 1894, were rendered practically inoperative by an internal excise on Indian cotton production of equal amount. It was not till 1917 that a real tariff wall was erected, by raising the level of duty.

2 (p. 74). The testament of Cecil Rhodes, a document highly characteristic of the best type of British Imperialism, is reproduced in the *Life of the Right Hon. Cecil J. Rhodes* by Sir Lewis Mitchell, Vol. I, pp. 68, 69.

3 (p. 76). Populations (1921): The Cape, 651,554; Transvaal, 543,481; Orange Free State, 189,142; Natal, 137,458.

CHAPTER V

1 (p. 113). Cf. The Government Return of Landowners, 1873 (reproduced in C. Brodrick, *English Land and English Landlords*, 1881, p. 173).

2 (p. 114). Taking the peers as given in Whitaker for 1928 and discounting all double titles, Princes of the Blood Royal and spiritual Lords, the total number is 836. Of these only 43 or 5 per cent date from a time earlier than 1500; 369 from between 1501 and 1831; and no less than 424 or 52 per cent from a year later than 1832.

3 (p. 115). Compare for this Hatschek, *Staatsrecht*, Vol. II, p. 401.

4 (p. 118). Cf. Levy, on page 535 [31, 32].

5 (p. 120). The English social 'season' is entirely determined by the habits of the upper classes. August 12 sees the opening of the grouse-shooting period; on November 1 fox-hunting begins. The hunting season does not close till April 1; therefore it is not till the beginning of May that social functions open in London, and last till the end of July. Even the Metropolis continues to be so dependent on the habits of the aristocracy that the social season, instead of being the winter, is in the full heat of summer.

6 (p. 126). Max Weber and Troeltsch, *op. cit.*, page 535 [21, 22].

NOTES

7 (p. 127). Cf. W. Dibelius, *Dickens*, p. 42 *seq.* and Chapters I, V.

8 (p. 129). Schulze Gaevernitz, in his *British Imperialism and English Free Trade*, points out that the whole of English life has been gradually influenced by the *rentier* ideal, or what, in contradistinction to the French *petit rentier*, I should prefer to call the *respectable rentier* ideal.

BOOK II

CHAPTER II

1 (p. 210). Hatschek, *Constitutional History*, p. 628.

2 (p. 210). Lowell, II, p. 58.

3 (p. 211). A vote at a by-election can be cast in any constituency in which the elector is on the Register in virtue of a residential qualification, as well as for his University; but at the General Election, no one may exercise more than two votes. It has been stated in the House that out of 17 million electors, 159,000 were plural voters in virtue of the residential paragraph.

4 (p. 214). The extent to which the Commons have lost control over finance has been abundantly demonstrated in recent years. Since 1919 reduction of public expenditure has been urgently demanded by all parties and by public opinion. But in Parliament, which has to sanction all expenditures, nothing to the purpose was done for years. Where the Treasury and the spending departments are in agreement, the Commons really can do little – for the majority is under compulsion to support the administration. In the beginning of 1921, however, pressure from the House induced the Cabinet to impose a 20 per cent cut in the estimates of all Government departments. A cut was actually effected – but of 12, not 20 per cent. Since nothing substantial was done either by the House or by the Ministry (in fact bureaucracy has already become a power in England!), a committee of business men (mostly not Members of Parliament!) was appointed under Sir Eric Geddes, which systematically reviewed all administrative departments with a view to effecting economies. The outsiders at last effected what Parliament had proved unable to do.

5 (p. 215). Lowell, I, pp. 260, 267.

6 (p. 217). Hatschek, *Staatsrecht*, II, p. 125.

7 (p. 225). Originally, he was the nominee of the King and appointed by him; gradually, however, the House of Commons acquired the right of appointment of the Speaker. When Speaker

Lowther retired in 1921, Mr. Lloyd George (as representing the King!) endeavoured to transfer the right of appointing the Speaker to the Ministry. The attempt failed, almost before it could be seriously undertaken, in view of the universal opposition both in the House and from public opinion.

8 (p. 227). In March, 1922, Lady Rhondda, as a Peeress in her own right (an independent Viscountess, not the wife of a Viscount) endeavoured to establish her right to a seat in the House of Lords – an attempt designed in the interest of some twenty other Peeresses in the same position. Despite the Sex Disqualification Removal Act of 1919, the House of Lords rejected her claim, on the ground that admission to the Upper House was in virtue of a specific Royal summons, which was not included in Lady Rhondda's patent.

CHAPTER III

1 (p. 248). On the clerical characters of the English bureaucracy, see Hatschek, *Staatsrecht*, II, p. 568.

2 (p. 251). In the. Metropolitan Police alone administrative posts are nearly always filled by ex-constables.

3 (p. 251). On the form of protection extended to officials, see Hatschek, *Staatsrecht*, II, p. 543 *seq.*

4 (p. 258). Only for certain special administrative purposes is there national machinery. Thus the Post Office has local offices everywhere, the Customs at all the ports, the Board of Trade has Receivers in Bankruptcy in all commercial centres, the Home Office has Factory Inspectors located in the industrial areas, local offices have been set up by the Ministry of Labour to administer the Unemployment Insurance Acts, and 'Regional Directors' under the Ministry of Pensions. These newer organizations show how rapidly the country is being bureaucratized.

5 (p. 265). Universal complaint of the vast burden of local rates has been growing louder throughout the last two decades. The system has not been radically altered by the Local Government Act of 1928, though a certain part of the local rates has been replaced by block grants from the Exchequer.

6 (p. 269). London, as well as being divided into 28 administrative boroughs, is divided into parliamentary boroughs – 61 in number – returning 62 M.P.s, since the City, included for this purpose, returns two.

7 (p. 275). Under the municipal franchise each elector has one

NOTES

vote only. Under the county franchise, he has the right to vote in every district in which he can establish his claim to be on the Register; with the result that, in practice, the rich landowner may be a pluralist on an extensive scale. Redlich, p. 424; Lowell, I, p. 269.

CHAPTER IV

In the description of the organization of justice, I have largely followed Gerland (see p. 540, line 32), and, in many respects, my opinions also, while independently arrived at, coincide with his.

1 (p. 282). The owner hands the land over to a trustee (who naturally cannot sell it) under an ingenious system of clauses which import that the owner and his eldest son retain the use of the land and that the latter undertakes to waive his right to free disposition of its inheritance. Cf. Hatschek, *Staatsrecht*, II, p. 400.

2 (p. 285). Not till 1827 was the owner forbidden to protect his land against poachers and trespassers by setting automatic guns and man-traps designed to crush the foot if caught in them. Dicey, p. 87 *et seq.*

3 (p. 287). The oldest Anglo-Saxon law takes a brutally material view of the breach of marriage vows: 'If a free man lie with the wife of a free man, let him pay him his were geld and procure another wife with his own money and take her to that other.' (Law of Æthelberht, translated by Liebermann, *Gesetze der Angelsachsen*, 1, 5, No. 31.) One would not infer, on the basis of this single text, that the Anglo-Saxon regarded his wife merely as a thing: we are dealing here with legal prescriptions which regulate the material side of marriage, and do not thereby express any view of its ethical imponderabilia. But the persistence of this primitive material point of view beyond Anglo-Saxon times, notably for instance in the 'damages' still paid to the 'injured' husband in divorce actions, shows that, side by side with the chivalrous and spiritual reverence for the lady, a coarsely materialist view of the woman still persists. Only as late as 1923 did the Matrimonial Causes Act put the two sexes on an equality so far as divorce is concerned.

4 (p. 287). Sale of offices – cf. Hatschek, *Staatsrecht*, II, p. 576.

5 (p. 288). On Habeas Corpus – cf. Hatschek, *Staatsrecht*, II, p. 61 *seq.*

6 (p. 295). This complaint goes right back to the sixteenth century. Cf. Harrison, *Description of England*. New Shakespeare Society, VI, Part I, page 102.

NOTES

CHAPTER V

1 (p. 331) Lowell, II, p. 48, estimates the costs of a contested election at between £500 and £1,000; and the costs of getting voters' names on to the Register (taken over by the State since 1918) and of all the expenses incidental to 'nursing' a constituency, at another £400 to £600 per annum. The Labour Party nowadays puts the costs of an election at £200 to £400.

BOOK III

CHAPTER 1

1 (p. 343). Out of certain secularized Church revenues, Queen Anne established a fund for the assistance of ill-paid clerics, known since as Queen Anne's Bounty. Between 1809–1820 substantial additions were made to this fund by Parliament. In 1818 and in 1825 Parliament voted considerable special grants for church buildings.

2 (p. 345). The members of the House of Laymen are elected on a system of indirect (proportional) election, in which all parishioners who are members of the Church take part.

It represents a compromise between the High Church tendency, representing the power of the Bishops as against the layman and the State, and the Low Church, representing the opposite aim. The existing rights of the State and of the Bishops remain essentially intact. Any definition of doctrine is outside the competence of the Assembly. Contact between Parliament and the Assembly of the Church is provided for through the establishment of an Ecclesiastical Commission, consisting of 15 Peers and 15 M.P.s, who must all be Anglicans. All more important resolutions passed by the Church Assembly must be forwarded by the Committee, with its endorsement, to Parliament. It was hoped that this endorsement by the Parliamentary Church Committee would suffice to secure a parliamentary majority for the proposal thus sponsored (which, however, it did not do, on the first occasion when it was tried). In this fashion, it was sought to devise a means by which – without questioning the authority of Parliament – what were in fact Church decisions could be withdrawn from the interference of non-Anglican Members of the House. The Enabling Act of 1919 gave the Church Assembly the right to present Bills on Church matters to Parliament – a right otherwise reserved to M.P.s. Any changes relevant to the creed, rites

NOTES

and sacraments of the Church are subject, not to Parliament, but only to the Church Assembly. The procedure then adopted (1) separate discussion and voting in either House; (2) final formulation of proposals in the House of Bishops; and (3) acceptance or rejection by the Church Assembly as a whole – leaves the preponderating power in the hands of the Bishops. So, in 1926, and in 1927, the Revision of the Prayer Book was actually undertaken by the Bishops, and then carried through with a large measure of lay co-operation (only to be rejected by the House of Commons).

CHAPTER III

1 (p. 362). Definite statistics are not available. The official Census has only once (1851) contained a question on religious profession; then, the returns showed, in England and Wales, 3,773,474 Church members (i.e. not including children) and 3,487,558 Catholics and Nonconformists, divided as follows: Methodists, 1,565,705; Independents, 793,142; Baptists, 587,978; Presbyterians, 60,131; Unitarians, 37,156; Quakers, 18,172; Catholics, 305,393.

2 (p. 366). In the winter of 1702–03, when a special law was passed designed to make Occasional Conformity impossible, Daniel Defoe threw himself into the controversy with his famous *The Shortest Way with the Dissenters*.

3 (p. 373). The reunion of the two Churches, in fact, took place already in October, 1929.

4 (p. 379). The Quakers are now organized on Presbyterian-Congregationalist lines, in Preparative Meetings (single communities), which are then gathered together in monthly, yearly and quarterly meetings – the Yearly Meeting being their general synod for Great Britain. Resolutions passed at meetings have considerable moral but no legally binding force. There is a Meeting for Sufferings (whose name records the old days of persecution) which acts as a sort of supreme executive. Each body of Friends has its own elders and overseers.

5 (p. 383). Sixteen lines taken almost verbatim from B. Guttman, *England im Zeitalter der bürgerlichen Reform*, 1923, p. 182.

CHAPTER V

1 (p. 397). Introduction to the Tract on Divorce. For this and other references cf. Brie, *Imperialismus*, p. 30 *seq.*

2 (p. 397). Ibid.

NOTES

3 (p. 398). No really well-educated Englishman takes these ideas seriously, of course. But they have still a strange attraction for the masses of the half-educated, with a considerable following even in higher circles. A pamphlet of the British Israel World Federation which sets forth these 'ideas' in their crudest form, mentions as patrons of the society five members of the nobility, including one princess, one (colonial) bishop, and, among deceased patrons, no less than eight High Church dignitaries.

4 (p. 398). Cf. Max Weber, *Archiv für Sozialwissenschaft*, XX.

BOOK IV

CHAPTER I

1 (p. 412). (1) The first examination (taken as a rule before coming to the University, at school before one of the examination boards, or at the University by one of the colleges) is called, in Oxford, Responsions or 'Smalls'; in Cambridge, the Previous Examination or 'Little-Go.' (2) The intermediate examination, in Oxford, First Public Examination or Moderations; in Cambridge, General Examination. (3) Final examination, in Oxford, Second Public Examination or 'Greats'; in Cambridge, Special Examination. Undergraduates reading for an Honours degree pass the intermediate examination in a stiffer form and end with a Final Honours examination in one of the Honours schools (at Oxford); or take a Tripos (at Cambridge).

2 (p. 414). The degree of democratization can be tested arithmetically. According to the Report of the Royal Commission of 1922 (p. 132) the number of undergraduates to Oxford and Cambridge, coming from ordinary day schools (i.e. schools for the middle-class), where the fees were no higher than £10 p.a.) was, in 1912, 157, and, in 1913, 237) = 394 undergraduates at the two Universities, or an annual average of 197. In 1913 there were 7,538 undergraduates at Oxford and Cambridge together; allowing for an average period of three years and a half per student, the annual entry is 2,154. In other words, the students without means amount to something like 9 per cent of the whole. This is quite a satisfactory figure: high enough to guarantee that the aristocratic majority will have a sensible influence on the democratic minority, and far too low to justify any apprehension of the University's being democratized.

3 (p. 416). The (Cambridge) Tripos was originally a renowned

mathematical examination. As firstfruits of the new reforming spirit, a Classical Tripos was introduced in 1824, gradually followed by analogous examinations in other subjects.

4 (p. 416). The nominal Head of the University is the Chancellor. He is, as a rule, an eminent political personage who is expected to be able to attract wealthy benefactors and donors. The election of Chancellor is a big political event, though so far candidates have been confined to the two older political parties. All M.A.s are entitled to vote, and they crowd up to the University for the purpose. The Chancellor takes no part in current University business, but is expected to be interested in reform and able to remove political difficulties in its way. Current business is wholly in the hands of the Vice-Chancellor, nominated in Oxford by the Chancellor from among the Heads of Colleges, generally in order of seniority, nominally for one but practically for four years: in Cambridge by the whole body of Magistri (known here as the Senate) on the basis of a list put forward by the Senatus Academicus for (in practice) two years.

5 (p. 419). In Cambridge, the Electoral Roll corresponds to Congregation; i.e. to the resident members of Convocation who are therefore entitled to vote. Its rights are limited to electing the Council of the Senate; all other business is transacted by the Senate as a whole, which thus corresponds to Convocation.

6 (p. 419). Oxford has (since the reorganization of 1917) ten faculties – theology, law, medicine, litterae humaniores (classics), modern history, English language and literatures, mediæval and modern languages, Oriental languages, physical sciences (including mathematics), biological sciences). Cambridge has twelve Boards of Studies corresponding to these faculties. On these faculties and special boards all University teachers in the faculties sit, without any distinction of rank; a smaller sub-committee (partly of *ex-officio* members, partly of members elected by the faculty) deals with ordinary business. In addition to the Special Boards there are, in Cambridge, Boards of Studies, without the full faculty status, for subjects that are not yet fully developed or less important. Subjects of importance will go (1) to the Faculty Board or Boards; (2) the General Board of Faculties, i.e. a Committee composed of the Vice-Chancellor and representatives of the various Faculties; (3) the Hebdomadal Council; (4) the Congregation. Many lectures are free: for some, fees are charged. As a rule the proceeds are carried to the

body financially responsible (College, University, special endowment, etc.). No settled principle governs the payment of fees for lectures. In so far as fees are paid, the professors do not, as a rule, receive any share of them, though the lecturers sometimes do when their stipend would be inadequate.

7 (p. 426). The following remarks will give an idea of the present organization of University Extension: All Universities now have a Board of Extramural Studies. This Board provides (a) University Extension courses of the old type (6 to 12 lectures) and (b) new types of lectures in conjunction with the Workers' Educational Association. The latter are organized by a Central Joint Advisory Committee on Tutorial Classes, composed of University men and workers. The lectures given correspond more or less to one of four prevailing types: (a) Study Circles, loosely organized, with private work of the students expected but not exacted; (b) Terminal Courses, i.e. courses for which some voluntary body, not the University, is responsible; (c) Tutorial Classes under University supervision. These are the main feature of the work, two hours weekly, during three winters, with much written work by the students. They are supported by the Board of Education. About 60 per cent of the students will, according to present experience, persist to the end; (d) Summer· Schools in Universities or other centres. From the Tutorial Classes there lies an entrance to the University by a special examination. During the years 1925–28, however, only thirteen students entered Oxford this way. The newest attempt to further University Extension is the establishment of centres in rural areas near Oxford.

CHAPTER III

1 (p. 435). In Wales, there further is St. David's College, Lampeter, founded in 1827 (affiliated to Oxford and Cambridge). Lampeter is a small theological and philosophical college for the training of Anglican clerics.

2 (p. 435). Founded by a famous pill manufacturer, Thomas Holloway, who left £700,000 for the college, in the hope (which has not been realized) that it would develop into an independent Women's University.

CHAPTER IV

1 (p. 445). In the Principality of Wales a flourishing system of private schools was established as far back as the eighteenth century

by the clergyman Griffith Jones (1683–1761). The staunch Non-conformist Protestantism of the population always guaranteed a strong interest in education there. By 1889 the Welsh Intermediate Education Act had established an organized educational system in the country; in 1907 a special Welsh Education Department of the Board of Education was set up.

2 (p. 447). Strictly speaking, religious teaching is to be 'unde-nominational' – defined by Campbell-Bannerman when Prime Minister as meaning 'the common elements of Christianity with, no doubt, a flavour of Protestantism in them.' Cf. Lowell, *Government of England*, II, 138.

3 (p. 452). The housing conditions of the very poor are so wretched that it is impossible to occupy the children at home – hence this provision. The extension of the school-leaving age to at least fourteen implies a great progress; for before the war by all sorts of exemptions no less than two-fifths of the children were wont to leave school earlier. (Cf. Report on Education of the Adolescent, p. 141.)

4 (p. 454). Elementary school statistics. (1) *Denominational and undenominational.* According to the Report of the Board of Education for 1926–7, there were, in that year, 20,723 Public Elementary Schools. (In addition to these the Board notes 563 Special Schools for blind, deaf, etc., children, and 22 Certified efficient schools, i.e. a small and diminishing total of schools not supported by the Board.) Of these 20,723 schools, there were (a) Council schools – i.e. unde-nominational schools – 9,170, with 4,444,809 places; and (b) Volun-tary schools (i.e. denominational) 11,553, with 2,611,411 places. (2) *Training of Teachers* (see Report, 1926–7, p. 124). Of teachers in England and Wales, 73·7 per cent were certificated, 20·9 uncertificated, and 5·4 supplementary. (In rural districts the number of uncertificated teachers rises to 32, in London it is only 7·9 per cent.) By no means all the certificated teachers, however, had attended training colleges: only 85·4 per cent, according to the Report for 1925–6. If the total of all teachers in England and Wales – 162,205 in 1925–6 – be compared with the total of college-trained teachers – 88,496 – it appears that only 54·6 per cent of the teachers in English schools then had received a college training. In Scotland, the teacher without college training has to all intents and purposes disappeared. In 1917–26, 1,915 new male teachers were appointed, of whom only 60 were untrained; and 9,645 female teachers, of whom only 112 were un-

trained. (Scottish Education Department: Report on Training of Teachers, 1924–6, p. 40.)

5 (p. 455). Eleven University representatives co-operate in the formation of the Register. In 1920 it included 39,340 names. All sorts of State examinations, University diplomas, credentials for games instructors, handicraft teachers and music teachers are accepted as qualifying.

6 (p. 455). An association representing the Heads of public schools and other similar institutions is the Head Masters' Conference (1870). The Heads of other schools of slightly inferior status are associated in the Headmasters' Association. Elementary school teachers are organized in the National Union of Teachers (1870), while a body, comprising the teachers of rather higher social status is the Teachers' Guild of Great Britain and Ireland (1885); there is also the Association of Assistant Masters, founded in 1892; as well as an Association of University Teachers.

7 (p. 456). In *Scotland* the organization of education is entirely different from anything existing in England. In this intensely Protestant country, ability to read the Bible was a condition of the soul's salvation, and from 1696 on, the establishment of schools was therefore regarded as the primary duty of every parish; while almost every town had its High schools. In the country the school was a Church institution, and the Church exercised a certain supervision over schools in the towns. Since the manifold divisions and splits in the Church never reached the point of creating distinct social groups, composed of the members belonging to this Church or that, as in England, there was never a conflict between the State Church and the sects for the ownership of the schools; nor have there been schools reserved for the upper classes; therefore the course of development has been rather on the tranquil lines found in Germany. After 1872 the Elementary schools were administered by School Boards, based on direct election, which gradually took over the older Church schools. In 1918 the many small school boards disappeared, and the schools are now administered by 37 Education Authorities. The religious instruction given in schools is broadly Presbyterian, dispensation being provided for under a conscience clause. Real Church schools are rare and generally Catholic. The State makes grants and supervises their expenditure. The standard of the schools is almost uniformly high. The completely untrained Elementary school-teacher is almost extinct, the educational aims are almost universally higher

NOTES

than the English average, and the average Elementary school is of the Intermediate type. Secondary education has, since 1885, been under a separate Scottish Education Department, under the Secretary for Scotland. There are a certain number of high-class boarding-schools (Fettes, Merchiston, Loretto, Glenalmond), and also a large number of admirable day schools (formerly called Academies) in nearly all the larger cities. The connexion with the system of public supervision is much closer than in England: thus, the State Leaving examination is a feature of nearly all the Secondary schools.

8 (p. 457). In addition to those mentioned, the college counted among its teachers the lawyer Thomas Hughes, author of *Tom Brown's School Days*, as well as Ruskin, Burne-Jones, Ford Madox Brown, and Dr. Furnivall, the philologist.

9 (p. 459). There are 60,000 members of the Boys' Brigade, founded by the Scottish Colonel Sir William A. Smith. The Church Lads were founded by another Colonel, W. W. Gee. There are also the Nonconformist Boys' Life Brigades, founded in 1899 by J. B. Paton, and boy-and-girl group organizations of the Salvation Army. But all these organizations have to-day been eclipsed by the Boy Scouts.

CHAPTER V

1 (p. 470). This Department of Science and Art is an instructive example of the perfectly unsystematic way in which anything new comes into being in England. The Great Exhibition of 1851 produced in many minds a vague feeling that something ought to be done for scientific and technical education. No one at that time grasped the idea that the only way to assure an adequate influence to any group of subjects is by influencing the general curriculum. What was actually done was to use the Privy Council, that grand general reservoir for meeting vague aspirations in the way of State activity, to create a department to support instruction of the desired type; this department was soon loosely attached to the Board of Trade. All schools giving any sort of technical instruction were then unsystematically subventioned; in the sixties, a series of special Science Schools sprang up, something between the Elementary and the Secondary School, with a plan of studies based on the ideas of Huxley, but, as a rule, carried out in a very amateurish fashion. Not till the Board of Education was formed were these schools thoroughly reorganized.

2 (p. 471). The education of girls was for long the most pathetic

521

scene in the whole tragi-comedy of English education. It was wholly abandoned to private effort, without any kind of supervision by the State. Not till about 1850 was there any new life stirring in this field. Then, in 1847, Frederick Denison Maurice founded an institution in London for the higher education of women, which still exists as Queen's College. In 1869 Emily Davies set up a college for women at Hitchin, out of which Girton College, Cambridge, developed (see p. 414). In 1858 Dorothea Beale was made Head of the Ladies' College at Cheltenham, and developed this institution into a model school for the education of young maidens of good family, while contriving, at the same time, to do something for the minds of her charges as well as for their manners. The Schools Enquiry Commission of 1867-8 considered the education of girls as well as boys, and was indirectly responsible for the foundation, in 1871, of the National Union for the Education of Women by Maria Grey, out of which arose, a year later, the Girls' Public Day School Company – an organization which founded a large number of excellent girls' schools (many of them High Schools) throughout the country. Gradually, State grants were extended to girls' schools, and inspection by the Joint Board likewise.

3. (pp. 471, 472). *Higher Education Statistics*. (1) Expenditure. In 1923-4 there was expended on Secondary Education (a) from Rates (i.e. from the resources of municipalities and counties), £3,321,555; and (b) from taxes (i.e. from the resources of the State), £4,376,829. (2) *Teachers*. Of the teachers in Secondary schools, the proportion of University graduates (inclusive of the Elementary school teachers who held the University B.A.) was, in 1926-7: 7,575 out of 9,572 men, 5,956 out of 9,682 women. Training-college education had been received (1921-2) by men, 39·6 per cent; women, 52 per cent. (3) In 1926-7 there were in England and Wales: (a) 1,319 Secondary schools on the grant list, with 371,493 pupils. Of these, 668 were county and municipal schools; 473 Foundation schools (i.e. older schools of the public school type, which have accepted State supervision); 77 schools belonging to Catholic orders and associations; 101 Welsh Intermediate Schools. (b) 326 schools with 59,141 pupils which, though not on the grant list, were recognized as efficient. Earlier statistics (1923-4) show that this number included a few (17) Catholic schools, and for the rest consisted in equal parts of purely private schools and old endowed schools which have maintained their independence. (c) 108 Preparatory schools, which are not counted as Secondary.

NOTES

(4) At the first examination of the Secondary Schools Examination Council (average age 16), in 1926–7, Latin was taken by 41·6 per cent of the pupils, Greek by 3·7 per cent, French by 98·5 per cent, and German by 6·5 per cent. (Every examinee must submit at least one foreign language.) At the second examination (average age 18, wide list of optional subjects) the figures were: Latin 22·8 per cent, Greek 10·7 per cent, French 38·7 per cent, and German 2·8 per cent.

(5) In 1924–5, among the pupils at Secondary schools 36·2 per cent had free places.

4 (p. 473). For a time, the College of Preceptors (founded in 1846) inspected schools, organized examinations and maintained both a training college and a teachers' training fund.

5 (p. 474). Written examination is the normal type in both systems. The set tasks are uniform for all schools (except in cases where very wide deviations present themselves), including those of the Colonies. Thus almost all the pupils in the upper forms in higher schools throughout the British Empire are studying the same narrow range of school authors in the various subjects. This makes the system dreadfully rigid. Examiners correct papers at home and draw up their results very often even without knowing so much as the names of their examinees. It is open to them to use a wide latitude in the grant of extra marks for clear thinking, originality, etc. Broadly speaking, the system does ensure a maximum degree of impartiality, but at the same time there is about it a soulless dead level of equality that is really thoroughly un-English. It must be explained as a first reaction of democracy against the nepotism that cared greatly for the antecedents of candidates and little or nothing for their intellectual achievements. Recently, oral examinations have been introduced in modern languages, and a breach thus made in the cast-iron rigidity of the older examination system.

CONCLUDING REMARKS

1 (p. 487). Cf. the instructive essay by Fr. Kern, *Recht und Verfassung im Mittelalter*. *Histor. Zeitschrift*, Vol. 120–1.

2 (p. 494). Cf. Dr. Levinus Lemnius, in Harrison, *Description of England* (New Shakespeare Society, VI, 1, p. lxiv; also L. de Rosmital, about 1465–67 (*Literarischer Verein*, Stuttgart, 1844, p. 47).

3 (p. 494). Cf. Pietro Ubaldini, in Lewis Einstein, *Italian Renaissance in England* (1902), p. 218.

NOTES

4 (p. 497). Cf. *Utopia*, II, chap. 6, ed. H. B. Cotterill (Macmillan, 1908), p. 88: 'They keep at home all the treasure which they have . . . especially and chiefly to hire therewith . . . strange soldiers. For they had rather put strangers in jeopardy than their own countrymen knowing that for money enough their enemies themselves many times may be bought or sold, or else through treason be set together by the ears among themselves. For this purpose they keep an inestimable treasure.' Thus it was a maxim of English statecraft by 1500 to wage war as far as possible with foreign mercenaries, and aim at the destruction of the enemy not by honourable battle but by the fostering of treachery within his own camp. In the eighth chapter it is (p. 119) fully set out how the Utopians seek always to win war, without bloodshed, by craft, e.g. by putting a price on the head of the enemy's leader. In foreign policy, they aim at the utmost freedom of commerce, without alliances (p. 115 *seq.*). The reasons for war are the defence of one's own soil, the defence of foreign friends against invasion, and the freeing of an oppressed people (p. 117 *seq.*) – exactly as in the twentieth century. Moreover, contemporary cant is there too: the method of winning war by bribing a traitor in the enemy's camp is praiseworthy: 'They count it a deed of pity and mercy (!) because by the death of a few offenders (!) the lives of a great number of innocents, as well of their own men as also of their enemies be ransomed and saved.' They feel deep compassion for the unhappy subjects of the foreign Prince, 'knowing that they be driven and enforced to war against their wills by the furious madness of their princes and heads!' If none of this avails, the Utopians seek to foment a rebellion within the country of their adversary or to set some neighbour upon him – 'under the colour of some old right such as kings do never lack.' These neighbours then become the Utopians' allies, they receive rich subsidies but no troops – 'but of their own citizens, they (i.e. the Utopians) send to them few or none' (p. 122). The art of British statecraft is very old indeed.

5 (p. 497). Cf. Leo de Rosmital (Czech) about 1465–67 (quoted *Literarischer Verein*, Stuttgart, 1844, p. 47): 'Angli (sunt) homines, ut mihi videtur, infidi et astuti, vitae hominum peregrinorum exitium molientes, qui licet submisse genu inflectant, non tamen illis fidem habeas.' – Scaliger. *Poetices*, III, chap. 17: 'Angli perfidi, inflati, feri, contemptores, stolidi, amentes, inertes, inhospitales, immanes.'

6 (p. 498). For typical English humour, cf. Dibelius, *Dickens* (Teubner), 1916, p. 245 *seq.*

BIBLIOGRAPHY

BOOK I: GREAT BRITAIN AND THE EMPIRE

CHAPTER I: HISTORICAL FOUNDATIONS

I. ENGLISH CULTURE IN GENERAL.

H. T. Buckle, History of Civilization in England, 2 vols., 1857–1861. – T. H. S. Escott, England, its People and Pursuits (Cassell), 1879, 2 vols. – C. F. G. Masterman, The Condition of England (Methuen), 1909. – Matthew Arnold, Culture and Anarchy, 1869 seq. – Social England, ed. H. D. Traill (Cassell), 6 vols, 1901 seq. – H. G. Wells, Mankind in the Making, 1903. – H. G. Wells, An Englishman looks at the World, 1914. – L. Cazamian; Modern England (Dent), 1916. – Emile Boutmy, Essai d'une Psychologie politique du Peuple anglais au 19e siècle (Colin), 1903. – Jacques Bardoux, Essai d'une Psychologie de l'Angleterre contemporaine I, Paris, 1906. – Price Collier (American), England and the English (Duckworth), 1909.

II. ENGLISH HISTORY.

The Political History of England, 12 vols., by different authors (Longmans), 1905–1910. – A History of England, ed. Chas. Oman (Methuen), 7 vols., 1904–1913. – Cambridge Modern History, 14 vols. – J. R. Green, History of the English People (Macmillan), 1905. – S. R. Gardiner, A Student's History of England, 3 vols. (Longmans), 1899.

III. SINGLE PERIODS.

(a) Chas. Elton, Origins of English History, 1890 – T. R. Holmes, Ancient Britain, 1907. – J. Rhys, Celtic Britain, 1904. – F. J. Haverfield, The Romanization of Britain (Proceedings of British Academy II), 1906. – H. M. Chadwick, The Origin of the English Nation (Cambridge University Press), 1907.

(b) E. A. Freeman, History of the Norman Conquest of England, 6 vols., 1867–1879.

(c) J. A. Froude, History of England from the Death of Wolsey to the Death of Elizabeth, 12 vols. (Longmans), 1856–1878.

(d) S. R. Gardiner, History of England, 17 vols. (1603–1660), (Longmans) 1863–1903. – L. von Ranke, History of England, principally in the 17th. century (Macmillan), 1875. – Thos. Macaulay, History of England, 5 vols., 1848 seq.

(e) Wm. Lecky, History of England in the Eighteenth Century, 8 vols. (Longmans), 1878–1890. – Wolfg. Michael, Engl. Geschichte im 18. Jahrhundert, 2 vols. (Hamburg, Voss), 1896 seq.

(f) Justin McCarthy, History of our own Time, 5 vols., 1899 (popular). – E. Halévy, Histoire du Peuple anglais au 19e siècle (Hachette), 1926, History of English Foreign Policy, 1783–1919, ed. A. W. Ward and G. P. Gooch, 1922 seq. – T. H. S. Escott, Social Transformations of the Victorian Age (Seeley), 1897. – The same, King Edward and his Court (Unwin), 1903. – B. Guttmann, England im Zeitalter der bürgerlichen Reform (Deutsche

BIBLIOGRAPHY

Verlagsanstalt), 1923. – Leslie Stephen, The English Utilitarians, 3 vols. (Duckworth), 1900.

(g) G. P. Gooch, History of our Time, 1885–1911 (Home Univers. Libr.) – R. H. Gretton, Modern History of the English People, 1880–1910, 2 vols., 1912. – J. R. Raynes, The Pageant of England, 1900–1920 (Swarthmore Press), 1920.

CHAPTER II: ENGLAND AND THE BRITISH ISLES

I. GENERAL.

Montagu Burrows, History of the Foreign Policy of Great Britain (Blackwood), 1895. – M. Macdonald and Lord Charnwood, The Federal Solution (Unwin), 1914. – J. A. Murray Macdonald, The Case for Federal Devolution (King), 1920.

II. SCOTLAND.

J. H. Burton, History of Scotland (Blackwood), 1873. – Same title, A. Lang (Blackwood), 1908 seq.; P. Hume Brown, 3 vols. (Cambridge Univ. Press), 1911; H. Macpherson, The Intellectual Development of Scotland (Hodder), 1911. – Jas. MacKinnon, The Social and Industrial History of Scotland (Blackie), 1920.

III. IRELAND.

(a) M. J. Bonn, die englische Kolonisation in Irland, 2 vols. (Cotta), 1906. – J. Pokorny, Irland (Perthes), 1916. – W. Dibelius, Englands irisches Problem, Zeitschrift für Politik VIII, 1915.

(b) Single Periods: Alice S. Green, The Making of Ireland and its Undoing, 1200–1600 (Macmillan), 1908. – R. Dunlop, Ireland under the Commonwealth, 2 vols. (Manchester Univ.) 1913. – John Prendergast, The Cromwellian Settlement of Ireland (Longmans), 1865. – W. H. Lecky, History of England in the 18th Century (Longmans), 1878–1890. – The same, Leaders of Public Opinion in Ireland (Longmans), 1872 – O'Connor Morris, Ireland from 1798–1898 (Innes), 1898. – Frank H. O'Donnell, History of the Irish Parliamentary Party (Longmans), 1910.

(c) Nationalism, Sinn Fein, Gaelic League, Easter Rising: Gavan Duffy, Young Ireland (Simpkin), 1896. – W. Dibelius, Neue irische Probleme, Preussische Jahrbücher 126 (1906). – The same, Die Sinn Feiner in Irland, Internationale Monatsschrift XII, 1411 (1918). – The same, Der irische Aufstand. Same publication, X, 1338. – Friedrich Brie, Der irische Aufstand (Schwetschke), 1917. – S. Brooks, The New Ireland (Maunsel), 1907. – L. Paul-Dubois, L'Irlande contemporaine, 1907. – F. P. Jones, History of the Sinn Fein Movement, New York, 1919.

(d) Irish Culture: Michael MacCarthy, Priests and People in Ireland (Simpkin), 1906. – W. P. Ryan, The Pope's Green Island (Nisbet), 1912.

(e) Economic Problems: Jas. Connolly, Labour in Irish History (Maunsel), 1914. – W. P. Ryan, The Irish Labour Movement (Dublin, Talbot Press), 1919. – D. A. Chart, An Economic History of Ireland (Talbot Press), 1920. – M. Bonn, Die irische Agrarfrage, Archiv für Sozialwissenschaft XIX. XX. – Horace Plunkett, Ireland in the New Century (J. Murray), 1905. – Hein-

526

BIBLIOGRAPHY

rich Martens, Agrarreformen in Irland (Staats und Sozialwissenschaftliche Eorschungen 177), 1915. – G. O'Brien, Economic History of Ireland from the Union to the Famine (Longmans), 1921.

(f) *Home Rule, Ulster, etc.:* St. John G. Ervine, E. Carson and the Ulster Movement (*Maunsel*), 1915. – Erskine Childers, The Framework of Home Rule (Arnold), 1911. – Home Rule Problems, ed. Basil Williams (King and Son), 1912. – Against Home Rule (F. Warne), 1912. – J. H. Morgan, The New Irish Constitution (Hodder and Stoughton), 1912. – Jas. W. Good, Ulster and Ireland (Maunsel), 1919. – Michael Macdonagh, The Home Rule Movement (Talbot Press), 1921.

(g) *Catholic Church:* Alfons Bellesheim, Geschichte der katholischen Kirche in Irland, 3 vols. (Mainz, Kirchheim), 1890.

CHAPTER III: THE RISE OF IMPERIALISM. THE COLONIAL EMPIRE

I. IMPERIALISM.

J. R. Seeley, The Expansion of England, 1883. – The same, Growth of British Policy, 1896. – Chas. Dilke, Greater Britain, 1868. – The same, Problems of Greater Britain, 2 vols., 1890. – J. A. Froude, Oceana, 1887. – von Schultze-Gävernitz, Britischer Imperialismus und englischer Freihandel (Duncker & Humblot)[2] 1915. – Fr. Brie, Imperialistische Strömungen in der englischen Literatur (Halle, Niemeyer),[2] 1928. – J. A. Hobson, Imperialism[2] 1905 (Constable). – J. A. Cramb, The Origins and Destiny of Imperial Britain, 1915 (Murray).

II. COLONIAL POLICY.

General: H. E. Egerton, Short History of British Colonial Policy (Methuen),[3] 1910. – C. P. Lucas, Historical Geography of the British Colonies, 15 vols., by various authors (Clarendon Press), 1905–25. – A. W. Tilby, The English People Overseas, 6 vols. (Constable), 1911–1914. – The Oxford Survey of the British Empire, ed. A. J. Herbertson and O. J. R. Howarth, 6 vols. – W. Dibelius, Die Selbständigkeitsbewegung in den englischen Kolonien (Anglia, Festschrift für A. Brandl, Palaestra No. 147–148). – A. B. Keith, Responsible Government in the Dominions, 3 vols. (Clarendon Press), 1912. – The same, Imperial Unity and the Dominions, 1916.

III. INDIA.

(a) *General:* Buckland, Dictionary of Indian Biography (Sonnenschein), 1906; The British Gazetteer of India, 26 vols. (Extensive Cyclopedia, Statistics, Maps, etc.), Clarendon Press. – Ch. Joppen, Historical Atlas of India (Longmans), 1910. – The Indian Yearbook, ed. Stanley Read, from 1913; yearly; Rulers of India, 27 vols. (Clarendon Press).

(b) *History:* M. Elphinstone, The Rise of British Power in the East (Murray), 1887. – The same: History of India (Trench, Trubner), 1908. – Alfr. Lyall, The Rise and Expansion of the British Dominion in India (Murray), 1911. – Cambridge History of India.

BIBLIOGRAPHY

(c) *Shorter Summaries:* T. W. Holderness, Peoples and Problems of India (Home Univ. Libr.). – W. W. Hunter, Brief History of the Indian Peoples (Clarendon Press), 1892. – John Strachey, India (Macmillan), 1911. – Vincent A. Smith, The Oxford Student's History of India (Clarendon Press), 1917.

(d) *Single Periods and Problems:* Jos. Chailley, Administrative Problems of Br. India (Macmillan), 1910. – Lord Curzon in India, Selection from his Speeches (Macmillan), 1906. – Lovat Fraser, India under Curzon and after 1911. – W. Lee Warner, The Native States of India (Macmillan), 1906. – W. R. James, Education and Statesmanship in India, 1911. – Daniel J. Fleming, Schools with a Message in India (Milford), 1921. – F. W. Younghusband, India and Tibet, 1911 (Murray). – Val. Chirol, The Middle Eastern Question, 1903 (Murray). – Lord Curzon, The Place of India in the Empire (Murray), 1909.

(e) *Indian Nationalism:* Val. Chirol, Indian Unrest (Macmillan), 1910. – J. Ramsay MacDonald, The Awakening of India (Hodder), 1910. – Henry Cotton, New India or India in Transition (Paul), 1907. – Verney Lovett, History of the Indian Nationalist Movement (Murray), 1920. – Lord Meston, India at the Crossways (Cambridge Univ. Press), 1921. – G. M. Chesney, India under Experiment (London), 1918. – Al. Carthill, Lost Dominion, 1923. – Katherine Mayo, Mother India (Cape), 1927. – Lajpat Rai, Unhappy India (Banna Publishing Co., Calcutta), 1928. – The same, Young India.

(f) *Law and Constitution:* Courtenay Ilbert, The Government of India (Clarendon Press), 1907. – Papers relating to the Application of the Principle of Dyarchy to the Government of India, ed. L. Curtis (Clarendon Press), Report on Indian Constitutional Reform (C. 9109), 1918.

(g) *Economic:* Theod. Morison, The Economic Transition in India (Murray), 1911.

IV. EGYPT.

(a) *General:* Alfred Viscount Milner, England in Egypt (Arnold),[4] 1909. – Lord Cromer, Modern Egypt, 2 vols. (Macmillan), 1908. – Auckland Colvin, The Making of Modern Egypt (Seeley), 1906. – Basil Worsfold, The Redemption of Egypt (Allen), 1899. – S. Low, Egypt in Transition (Macmillan), 1914. – A. Hasenclever, Gesceichte Ägyptens im 19. Jahrh. (Nihcmeyer), 1917. – M. v. Hagen, E. u. Ägypten (Bonn, Marcus u. Weber), 1915. – Val. Chirol, The Egyptian Problem (Macmillan), 1920.

(b) *Economic:* Franz Magnus, Ägypten (Siebeck), 1913.

(c) *Single Periods and Problems*: Wilfrid Scawen Blunt, Secret History of the English Occupation of Egypt (anti-English), Fisher Unwin, 1907. – E. Dicey, The Story of the Khedivate (Rivington), 1902 and The Egypt of the Future (Heinemann), 1907. – O. v. Dungern, das Staatsrecht Ägyptens (Graz, Leykam), 1911. – C. de Freycinet, La Question d'Egypte (Lévy), 1905. – W. Willcocks, Egyptian Irrigation (Spon), 1913.

V. SOUTH AFRICA.

(a) *Detailed History:* George Theal, History and Ethnography of (South)

BIBLIOGRAPHY

Africa, 1505–1795, 3 vols. (Allen), 1910. – The same, History of South Africa since 1795, 5 vols. (Sonnenschein), 1908–1911, and History of South Africa 1873–1884, 4 vols. (Allen, Unwin), 1920.

(b) *Shorter Histories:* H. A. Bryden, The Victorian Era in South Africa, 1897, and History of South Africa (Sands), 1907. – F. R. Cana, South Africa from the Great Trek to the Union, 1910 (Chapman).

(c) *Boer War:* A. Conan Doyle, The Great Boer War (Smith, Elder), 1901. – Edward Garrett, The Story of an African Crisis (Jameson Raid), (W. Constable), 1897. – F. W. Reitz (Boer), A Century of Wrong (Review of Reviews Office), 1900. – History of the War in South Africa (official), 2 vols. (Hurst), 1907. – W. Basil Worsfold, Lord Milner's Work in South Africa, 1897-1902 (Murray), 1906.

(d) 1902–1914: E. B. Iwan-Müller, Lord Milner and South Africa (Heinemann), 1902. – R. Violet Markham, The New Era in South Africa (Smith) 1904. – H. E. S. Freemantle, The New Nation (Ouseley), 1909.

(e) *Single Periods and Problems:* John Martineau, Life of Sir Bartle Frere, 2 vols. (Murray), 1895. – W. L. Rees, Life of Sir George Grey, 2 vols. (Hutchinson), 1893. – Paul Krüger, Memoirs, 2 vols. (Unwin), 1902. – Lewis Mitchell, Life of Cecil Rhodes, 2 vols. (Arnold), 1910. – Vindex, Cecil Rhodes (Chapman & Hall), 1900. – Schowalter, Deutsche, Engänder und Buren (Hirzel), 1915. – Ch. S. Goldman, South Africa, Finance and Mining, 2 vols. (Essington), 1915–16. – P. Lederer, Die Entwickelung der Südafrikanischen Union auf verkehrspolitischer Grundlage (Schmollers staats – und sozialwissenschaftliche Forschungen. Bd. 149, 1910).

(f) *Constitution:* The Government of South Africa, 2 vols. (semi-official), (W. H. Smith), 1918.

VI. CANADA.

(a) F. X. Garneau, Histoire du Canada, 2 vols., Paris (Alcan)[5], 1920. – W. Kingsford, History of Canada, 10 vols. (Toronto), 1887–1898. – The Makers of Canada, ed. G. N. Morang and W. L. Grant, 12 vols. (Oxford Univ. Press).

(b) *Shorter Histories and General Works:* A. G. Bradley, Canada in the twentieth Century (Constable), 1905. – W. L. Griffith, The Dominion of Canada (Pitman), 1911. – J. G. Bourinot, Canada (Story of the Nations), 1909.

(c) *Single Questions:* Lord Durham's Report, 3 vols. (Clarendon Press), 1912. – O. D. Skelton, Life and Letters of Sir Wilfrid Laurier, 2 vols. (Milford), 1921. – J. G. Bourinot, Intellectual Development of The Canadian People (Toronto), 1881.

(d) *Constitutional:* J. G. Bourinot, Manual of the Constitutional History of Canada (Montreal), 1888. – The same, How Canada is governed, 1895, and: Canada and the United States (Philadelphia), 1898. – F. Bradshaw, Self-Government in Canada (King), 1903. – H. E. Egerton and W. L. Grant, Canadian Constitutional Development (Murray), 1907.

(e) *French Element in Canada:* W. B. Munro, The Seignorial System in Canada (Harvard Historical Studies XIII (New York), 1907. – A. Siegfried, The Race Question in Canada (Nash), 1907. – J. Ch. Bracq, L'évolution du Canada français (Plon), 1927.

529

BIBLIOGRAPHY

VII. AUSTRALASIA AND NEW ZEALAND.

(a) *Extensive History:* G. W. Rusden, History of Australia, 3 vols. (Melville), 1898.

(b) *Shorter Histories:* R. Schachner, Australien in Politik, Wirtschaft, Kultur (Jena, Fischer) 1909. – G. Tregarthen, The Australian Commonwealth (Fisher, Unwin) 1893. – E. Jenks, History of the Australian Colonies (Cambridge Univ. Press), 1912. – Ernest Scott, Short History of Australia (Oxford Univ. Press), 1918.

(c) *Economic and Social:* R. Schachner, Die soziale Frage in Australien und Neuseeland (Fisher), 1911. – V. S. Clark, The Labour Movement in Australia (Constable), 1906. – A. St. Ledger, Australian Socialism (Macmillan), 1909. – A. Métin, Le Socialisme sans Doctrine (Paris), 1901. – T. A. Coghlan, Labour and Industry in Australia, 4 vols. (Oxford Univ. Press), 1918.

(d) *Single Periods and Problems:* R. Garnett, E. G. Wakefield (Colonizer of South Australia and New Zealand), (Fisher, Unwin), 1898. – Henry Parkes, Fifty Years in the Making of Australian History, 1892. – Australia: Economic and Political Studies, ed. M. Atkinson (Macmillan), 1921. – D. Sladen, Hughes of Australia (Hutchinson), 1916.

(e) *New Zealand:* G. W. Rusden, History of New Zealand, 3 vols. (Melville), 1896. – André Siegfried, La démocratie en Nouvelle Zélande (Colin), 1904. – W. Pluegge, Innere Kolonisation in Neuseeland (Jena, Fischer), 1916. – Guy H. Scholefield, New Zealand (Fisher, Unwin), 1909. – J. Hight and H. D. Bamford, The Constitutional History of New Zealand, 1914 (Whitcombe).

(f) *Constitution:* Harrison Moore, The Constitution of Australia (Melbourne, Maxwell), 1910. – B. R. Wise, The Making of the Australian Commonwealth (Longmans), 1913.

(g) *Geography:* J. G. Bartholomew, Austr. School Atlas (Clarendon Press), 1915.

CHAPTER IV: IMPERIALISM. ENGLAND, GERMANY, AND AMERICA

(a) England as seen by Foreigners in the Days of Elizabeth and James I, ed. W. B. Rye (London, J. R. Smith), 1865.

(b) *England and Germany:* A. Zimmermann, Der englisch-deutsche Gegensatz, Ztschr. für Politik II (1901). – W. Dibelius, Englische Berichte über Hamburg und Norddeutschland aus dem 16–18. Jahrhundert: Zeitschrift des Vereins für Hamburgische Geschichte, XIX, 1914. – J. A. Cramb, Germany and England (Murray), 1914. – E. Marcks, Männer und Zeiten, Quelle and Meyer II, 199. – Ch. Saroléa, The Anglo-German Problem (Nelson), 1912. – Ad. W. Ward, Germany, 1815–1900 (Cambridge Univ. Press, 1919). – Wm. H. Dawson, The German Empire, 1867–1914 (Allen & Unwin), 1919. – G. P. Gooch, Germany (E. Benn), 1926. – E. Koeppel, Deutsche Strömungen in der englischen Literatur (Strassburg), 1910. – S. Pfeiffer, George Eliots Verhältnis zu Deutschland (Anglistische Forschungen, ed. Hoops LX, 1925). – Fr. Meinecke, Geschichte des deutschenglischen Bündnisproblems, 1890–1901 (Oldenbourg), 1928.

BIBLIOGRAPHY

(c) *England and America:* W. A. Dunning, the British Empire and the United States (1814-1914), (Allen & Unwin), 1914. – Concerning English Public Opinion about America, *see* W. Dibelius, Dickens (Teubner 1916), 147 *seq.* – Chas. Dilke, Greater Britain, 1886. – W. T. Stead, the Americanisation of the World (Review of Reviews), 1902.

(d) Oil Question: Karl Hoffmann, Ölpolitik und angelsächsischer Imperialismus (Ring Verlag), 1927. – L. Denny, We fight for Oil (Knopf), 1928.

CHAPTER V: ECONOMICS

I. ECONOMIC HISTORY AND GENERAL ECONOMIC PROBLEMS.

W. Cunningham, Growth of English Industry and Commerce during the Early and Middle Ages (Cambridge Univ. Press), N.E. 1910. – The same, Growth of English Industry and Commerce in Modern Times, 2 vols. (C. J. Clay), N.E. 1907. – J. E. Th. Rogers, The Industrial and Commercial History of England (Fisher Unwin), N.E. 1920. – Social England, a Record of the Progress of the People, by various writers, ed. H. D. Traill and J. S. Mann, 6 vols. (Cassell), 1901-1904. – W. J. Ashley, Economic History and Theory, 2 vols. (Longmans), 1888-1893. – Georg Brodnitz, Englische Wirtschaftsgeschichte, vol. I, (Jena, Fischer), 1918. – J. F. Rees, A Social and Industrial History of England, 1815-1918 (Methuen), 1920. – Lujo Brentano, Geschichte der wirtschaftlichen Entwickelung Englands, 3 vols. (G. Fischer), 1927. – H. Levy, Die englische Wirtschaft (Teubner), 1921. – E. Tröltsch, Soziallehren der christlichen Kirche (Siebeck), 1912. – Max Weber, Archiv f. Sozialwissenschaft XX. – E. Obst, England, Europa und die Welt (Vowinckel), 1927.

II. AGRICULTURE.

J. E. Th. Rogers, History of Agriculture and Prices in England, 1259 1793, 7 vols. (Frowde), 1866-1902. – H. Rider Haggard, Rural England, Account of Agricultural and Social Researches carried out in 1901 and 1902, 2 vols. (Longmans), 1902. – R. E. Prothero, Pioneers and Progress in English Farming 1888 (Longmans). – The same, English Farming Past and Present (Longmans), London, 1912. – Hermann Levy, Soziologische Studien über das englische Volk (Fischer) Jena, 1920. – The same, Die englische Agrarreform (Archiv f. Sozialwissenschaft), 1914. – W. Hasbach, A History of the English Agricultural Labourer (King), 1920. – G. C. Brodrick, English Land and English Landlords (Cassell), London, 1880. – J. L. and Barbara Hammond, The Village Labourer, 1760-1832 (Longmans), London, 1911 (1913, 1920). – F. E. Green, History of the English Agricultural Labourer, 1870-1920 (King), 1921. – Joseph Arch, Story of his Life, told by him and ed. by Countess of Warwick (Hutchinson), 1898. – F. E. Green, A New Agricultural Policy (Parsons), 1921. – The Land Report of the Land Enquiry Committee, 2 vols., London, 1913. – F. W. Green, The Awakening of England (Nelson), 1912. – B. Skalweit, Die Englische Landwirtschaft (Berichte über Landwirtschaft, her. im Reichsamt des Inneren 37), Berlin, 1915. – Forestry Sub-Committee Final Report (Cd. 8881), 1918. – Agricultural Tribunal of Investigation, Final Report (Cd. 2145), 1924. – The Land and

BIBLIOGRAPHY

the Nation, Rural Report of the Liberal Land Committee (Hodder and Stoughton), 1926 (with bibliography).

III. INDUSTRIALISM: SOCIAL QUESTION, LABOUR PROBLEM.

(a) see: Cunningham and Rogers. – A. Toynbee, Lectures on the Industrial Revolution of the Eighteenth Century (Longmans), 1908. – Alfred (= Sam. Kidd), History of the Factory Movement, 1857. – G. v. Schultze-Gävernitz, Zum sozialen Frieden 2 vols. (Duncker), 1890. – W. Dibelius, Charles Dickens (Teubner), 1916, Chaps. I and VI. – G. v. Schultze-Gävernitz, Britischer Imperialismus und englischer Freihandel (Duncker), Leipzig, 1906. – Hermann Levy, Monopole, Kartelle und Trusts (G. Fischer),[2] 1927. – The same, Wirtschaftsliberalismus in England (G. Fischer), 1928.

(b) L. Brentano, Die Arbeitergilden der Gegenwart, 2 vols. (Duncker & Humblot), 1871–72. – Sidney and Beatrice Webb, The History of Trade Unionism. (Longmans), 1920. – The same, Industrial Democracy, 2 vols. (Longmans), 1897. – The same, Problems of Modern Industry, (Longmans), 1898. – G. Güttler, Die englische Arbeiterpartei (G. Fischer), 1914. – M. Beer, A History of British Socialism (Bell), 1919. – The same, Der britische Sozialismus der Gegenwart (Dietz), 1920. – Whitley Report on Works Committees (Cd. 9001), 1917. – Chas. Booth, Life and Labour of the People of London, 4 vols. (Macmillan), 1892 seq. – G. F. Steffen, Studien zur Geschichte der englischen Lohnarbeiter, 3 vols. (Hobbing & Büchle), 1900–1905.

(c) Actual Problems: M. B. Hammond, British Labour Conditions and the Legislation during the War (Milford), 1920. – Charlotte Leubuscher, Sozialismus und Sozialisierung in England (G. Fischer), 1921.

S. G. Hobson and A. K. Orage, National Guilds (Bell), 1914. – G. D. H. Cole, The World of Labour (Bell), 1913. – G. R. Stirling Taylor, The Guild State (Allen and Unwin), 1919. – The same, Guild Politics (Cecil Palmer), 1921. – A. J. Penty, The Restoration of the Guild System (Sonnenschein), 1906. – Guild Socialism (Fabian Tracts 192), 1920. – Bertrand Russell, Roads to Freedom: Socialism, Anarchism and Syndicalism (G. Allen), 1918. – S. G. Hobson, Guild Principles in War and Peace (Bell), 1918. – G. D. H. Cole, Self-Government in Industry (Bell), 1917.

Committee on Industry and Commerce (Stationery Office): (I) Survey of Overseas Markets, 1925–6, (II) Survey of Industrial Relations, 1926; (III) Factors in Industrial and Commercial Efficiency, 1927. – Report of the Royal Commission on the Coal Industry (Cmd. 2600), 1926. – Ministry of Labour: Report on the Establishment and Progress of Joint Industrial Councils, 1923. – England's Industrial Future (Liberal Industrial Inquiry), 1928. – Ch. Leubuscher, Liberalismus und Protektionismus in der englischen Wirtschaftspolitik nach dem Kriege (G. Fischer), 1927.

(d) Proletariate and Poor Law: G. Nichols, a History of the English Poor Law, New ed., 2 vols., 1898; as supplement to above: Thos. Mackay, History of the Poor Law, vol. III: From 1834 to Present Time (King), 1899. – J. Marburg, Die sozialökonomischen Grundlagen der englischen Armenpolitik im ersten Drittel des 19. Jahrhunderts. Volkswirtschaftliche Abhandl.

der badischen Hochschulen. Neue Folge, Heft 11 (Karlsruhe, Braun), 1912. – P. F. Aschrott, Das englische Armenwesen in seiner historischen Entwickelung und heutigen Gestalt (Staats- und sozialw. Forschungen, vol. V, 4) (Duncker).

CHAPTER VI: NATIONAL CHARACTERISTICS

(a) K. Wildhagen, der englische Volkscharakter. Leipzig, Akademische Verlagsgesellschaft 1925. – L. L. Schücking, der englische Volkscharakter (Deutsche Verlagsanstalt), 1915. – R. N. Bradley, Racial Origins of English Character (Allen & Unwin), 1926. – Rye (see Chapter IV, line 32).

(b) H. Spies, England im Urteil des Auslandes, 1911.

(c) The Gentleman: W. Göricke, Das Bildungsideal bei Addison und Steele (Bonner Studien zur engl. Philol. XIV), 1921. – W. H. Schofield, Chivalry in Elizabethan Literature (Harvard Studies in Comparative Literature II), 1912.

English Philosophy: W. R. Sorley, A History of English Philosophy (Cambridge Univ. Press), 1920. – Leslie Stephen, History of English Thought in the Eighteenth Century, 2 vols., 1876–1880. – The same, The English Utilitarians, 3 vols. (Duckworth), 1900.

BOOK II: THE CONSTITUTION

Historical: W. Stubbs, Constitutional History of England, 3 vols. (Macmillan), 1874–1878. – Thos. Erskine May, Constitutional History of England since the Accession of George III, 1760–1860 (Longmans), 1861, continued by F. Holland, 1912. – F. W. Maitland, The Constitutional History of England (Cambridge Univ. Press) 1908. – George B. Adams, A Constitutional History of England (New York, Holt), 1921. – R. v. Gneist, Engl. Verfassungsgeschichte (Springer), 1882. – J. Hatschek, Englische Verfassungsgeschichte (Oldenbourg), 1913.

Present-day Conditions: Wm. R. Anson, Law and Custom of the Constitution I [5] 1922, II [3] 1907–8 (Frowde). – W. Bagehot, The English Constitution (Chapman), 1891. – A. Lawrence Lowell, The Government of England (Macmillan), 2 vols.,[2] 1920. – Sidney Low, The Governance of England (Fisher Unwin),[7] 1915. – C. F. G. Masterman, How England is Governed (Selwyn & Blount), 1921. – John A. R. Marriott, English Political Institutions,[2] 1913. – The same, The English Constitution in Transition, 1910–24. – The same, The Mechanism of the Modern State, 2 vols. (all three published by Clarendon Press), 1926. – J. Hatschek, Engl. Staatsrecht, 2 vols., 1905 (Handbuch des öffentlichen Rechts, ed. Piloty IV 2, Abt. IV 1, 2, Siebeck), 1914. – The same: Das Staatsrecht des vereinigten Königreichs Grossbritann und Irland (Das öffentliche Recht der Gegenwart XXV, Siebeck), 1914. – O. Koellreuter, Verwaltungsrecht und Verwaltungsrechtsprechung im modernen England (Siebeck) 1912. – A. V. Dicey, Lectures on the Relation between Law and Public Opinion in England during the Nineteenth Century (Macmillan), 1915.

BIBLIOGRAPHY
CHAPTER I: PARTIES

I. GENERAL.

G. W. Cooke, History of Party, 3 vols. (Cunningham), 1840. – H. P. Belloc and Cecil Chesterton, The Party System (Swift), 1911. – M. Ostrogorski, Democracy and the organization of the Political Parties (Macmillan), 1902.

II. CONSERVATIVE.

J. E. Kebbel, Toryism, from Pitt to Beaconsfield (Allen), 1885. – C. B. Roylance Kent, The Early History of the Tories, 1660–1702 (Smith), 1908. – Lord Bentinck, Tory Democracy (Methuen), 1919. – J. A. Hobson, Imperialism (Nisbet), 1902. – The same, The Psychology of Jingoism (Richards), 1901. – F. E. Smith, Unionist Policy and other Essays (Williams), 1913. – W. F. Monypenny and G. E. Buckle, Life of B. Disraeli, 6 vols. (Murray), 1910–20.

III. LIBERAL.

B. L. T. Hobhouse, Liberalism (Home Univ. Library), 1911. – J. A. Hobson, The Crisis of Liberalism; New Issues of Democracy (King), 1909. – G. P. Gooch, History of English Democratic Ideas in the Seventeenth Century (Clay), 1897. – John Morley, Life of Cobden, 2 vols. (Chapman), 1881. – The same, Life of Gladstone, 3 vols. (Macmillan), 1903. *Radicalism:* Roylance Kent, The English Radicals (Longmans), 1899. – J. Holland Rose, The Rise of Democracy (Blackie), 1897. – Leslie Stephen, The English Utilitarians (Duckworth), 3 vols., 1900. – Graham Wallas, The Life of Francis Place, 1771–1854 (Longmans), 1898.

IV. LABOUR PARTY.

(See also works quoted on page 532). – B. L. T. Hobhouse, The Labour Movement (Unwin), 1893. – J. Ramsay MacDonald, The Socialist Movement (Home Univ. Library), 1911. – The same, Social Unrest (Foulis), 1913; The same, Socialism and Government, 2 vols., (Independ. Labour Party), 1909. – J. H. Thomas, When Labour Rules (Collins), 1921.

CHAPTER II: PARLIAMENTARY GOVERNMENT

I. PARLIAMENT.

(a) see page 533, *Historical* and *Present-day Conditions.*

(b) R. Gneist, Das englische Parlament in seinen tausend-jährigen Wandlungen,[2] 1886. – Alpheus Todd, On Parliamentary Government in England, 2 vols. (Longmans), 1867–1869. – E. Porritt, The Unreformed House of Commons, 2 vols. (May), 1903. – Th. E. May, Parliamentary Practice (Butterworth), 1917. – Courtenay Ilbert, Parliament (Home University Library), 1911. – The same, Legislative Methods and Forms (Clarendon Press), 1901. – The same, The Mechanics of Law-making (Milford), 1914. – Michael MacDonagh, The Pageant of Parliament, 2 vols. (Fisher Unwin), 1921. – J. Redlich, The Procedure of the House of Commons (Constable), 1908.

Manual of Procedure in the Public Business of the House of Commons, prepared by the Clerk of the House, 1919.

(c) *National Finance:* H. Higgs, The Financial System of the United Kingdom (Macmillan), 1914. – E. Hilton Young, The System of National Finance (Murray), 1924. – W. F. Willoughby, W. W. Willoughby, and S. M. Lindsay, The Financial Administration of Great Britain (United States Institute of Government Research, Appleton, 1917).

Parliament issues the following series of Parliamentary Papers:

(1) Bills Public, (2) Reports from Committees, (3) Reports from Commissioners, Inspectors and others, (4) Accounts and Papers (chiefly Statistics) The Papers of 3 and 4 are Cmd. Papers, i.e. printed by command of the House of Commons – they are quoted as Cmd. (or Cd.), etc. According to the colour of their binding they are called Blue Books or White Papers.

The enormous contents of these publications is made accessible by the following indices: (1) For the years 1801–1852: General Index to Accounts and Papers, Reports of Commissioners, Estimates, etc., 1853, Index to Bills and Reports, 1854, General Index to the Reports of Select Committees, 1854, General Index to Bills 1854. (2) For the years 1852–1899: General Alphabetical Index to the Bills, Reports, Estimates, Accounts and Papers printed by order of the House of Commons and to the Papers presented by Command 1852–1899, published in 1910. (3) For the years 1852–1909: Title as under 2, published in 1912. – There are further two private Indices: H. Vernon Jones (1) Catalogue of Parliamentary Papers, 1801–1900, and (2) same title, 1901–1910 (King).

II. CABINET.

Besides the works quoted under I (a) and (b): W. Michael, Entstehung der Kabinettsregierung in England: Zeitschrift für Politik 1903 VI 549 and W. Hasbach, Die parlamentarische Kabinettsregierung (Deutsche Verlagsanstalt), 1919.

CHAPTER III: THE ADMINISTRATION

I. LOCAL GOVERNMENT.

Joseph Redlich, Local Government in England (Macmillan), 1903. (This work has been largely used for this chapter.) – John T. Clarke, The Local Government of the United Kingdom (Pitman), 1922. – Edw. Jenks, Outline of English Local Government (Methuen),[2] 1907. – P. Ashley, Local Government (Jack), 1905. – The same, Local and Central Government (Murray), 1906. – Fred. Hackwood, The Story of the Shire (Heath Cranton), 1921.

II. SCOTLAND.

N. Atkinson, Local Government in Scotland (Blackwood), 1904.

III. CIVIL SERVICE.

R. Eaton, The Civil Service in Great Britain: A History of Abuses and Reform (New York), 1880.

BIBLIOGRAPHY

IV. BOROUGHS.

H. A. Merewether and A. J. Stephens, History of Boroughs, 3 vols. (Stevens), 1853. – F. Pollock and F. W. Maitland, History of English Law before Edward I, 2 vols. (Clay),[2] 1898. – Chas. Gross, Bibliography of British Municipal History (New York), 1897.

V. LONDON.

Ludwig Sinzheimer, Der Londoner Grafschaftsrat I (Gotha), 1900. – G. L. Gomme, The London County Council (Nutt), 1888.

VI. POOR LAW ADMINISTRATION.

see p. 532, *Proletariate and Poor Law.*

CHAPTER IV: THE LAW

I. HISTORY.

(a) W. S. Holdsworth, History of English Law, 3 vols. (Methuen), 1903–09. – F. Pollock and F. W. Maitland, History of English Law, 2 vols. (Cambridge University Press), 1898. – H. Brunner, Geschichte der englischen Rechtsquellen (Duncker & Humblot), 1909. – J. F. Stephen, History of the Criminal Law of England, 3 vols. (Macmillan), 1883. – F. Liebermann, Die Gesetze der Angelsachsen, 3 vols. (Niemeyer), 1903–1916. – A. V. Dicey, Law and Public Opinion in England during the Nineteenth Century (Macmillan), 1915.

II. THE LAW SYSTEM.

(a) William Blackstone, Commentaries on the Laws of England, 4 vols. (Oxford), 1765–1768, ed. Stewart, 1854 (considered as classical). – J. H. Stephen, New Commentaries on the Laws of England, 4 vols. (Butterworth), [10] 1883–1886. – Earl of Halsbury, etc., The Laws of England (Butterworth), 1907 *seq.* – N. B. Odgers, The Common Law of England, 2 vols. (Sweet & Maxwell), 1911. – The Times Law Reports (yearly).
Encyclopædia of the Laws of England with Forms and Precedents by the most eminent legal authorities, 15 vols., 1906–1909, and Annual Supplements, 1910 *seq.*

III. ORGANIZATION.

H. B. Gerland, Englische Gerichtsverfassung (Göschen), 2 vols., 1910 (extensively used on the following pages).

CHAPTER V: THE PRESS

Directories (yearly): Willings' Press Guide. – Mitchells' Newspaper Directory.
Histories: F. K. Hunt, The Fourth Estate, 2 vols. (Bogue), 1850. – Jas. Grant, The Newspaper Press, 2 vols. (Tinsley), 1871. – H. Simonis, The Street of Ink (Cassell), 1917. – Quarterly Review, June, 1823, gives a short History of *The Times.*

BIBLIOGRAPHY
BOOK III: RELIGION AND CHURCHES

I. GENERAL.

J. Hastings' Encyclopædia of Religion and Ethics. – W. R. W. Stephens, Church Dictionary (Murray), 1896. – Fred. G. Lee, Glossary of Liturgical and Ecclesiastical Terms (Quaritch), 1876. – J. S. Bumpus, Dictionary of Ecclesiastical Terms (Laurie), 1910.

II. CHURCH HISTORY.

(a) *General:* Wm. Hunt and W. R. W. Stephens, A History of the English Church, 9 vols. (Macmillan), 1899–1910, by various authors. – Jas. Stoughton, History of Religion in England, 6 vols. (Hodder), 1881. – Epochs of Church History, ed. Mandell Creighton, 15 vols., by various authors (Longmans), 1886–1889. – Handbooks of English Church History, ed. John H. Burn, 6 vols. (Methuen), 1909 *seq.* – R. W. Dixon, History of the Church of England from the Abolition of the Roman Jurisdiction, 6 vols. (Smith, Elder), 1878–1902. – A. Plummer, English Church History, 3 vols. (Clark), 1900–1907. – S. L. Ollard and G. Crosse, A Dictionary of English Church History (Mowbray), 1912.

(b) *Single Periods:* Heinrich Böhmer, Kirche und Staat in England und in der Normandie im 11 und 12. Jahrhundert, Leipzig, 1899 (Dieterich). – G. Lechler, John Wiclif and his English Precursors (Kegan Paul), 1878. – Gairdner, Lollardy and Reformation in England, 4 vols. (Macmillan), 1908–1913. – H. E. Jacobs, The Lutheran Movement in England during the Reigns of Henry VIII and Edward VI and its Literary Documents, Philadelphia, 1894. – W. A. Shaw, The English Church, 1640–1660, 2 vols. (Longmans), 1900. – A. H. Hore, The Church in England from William III to Victoria, 2 vols. (Parker), 1886.

Oxford Movement: R. W. Church, History of the Oxford Movement, 1833–1845 (Macmillan), 1891. – H. P. Liddon, Life of E. B. Pusey, 4 vols., 1893–1894. – J. H. Newman, Apologia pro Vita sua 1864. – Report of the Royal Commission on Ecclesiastical Courts, 1833. – Report of Royal Commission on Ecclesiastical Discipline, 1906. – The Faiths, ed. L. P. Jacks (Methuen): (1) T. A. Lacey, Anglo-Catholic Faith, (2) P. Gardner, Modernism in the English Church.

(c) *Scotland:* A. F. Mitchell, The Scottish Reformation (Blackwood) 1900. – John Cunningham, Church History of Scotland, 2 vols. (Simpkin) 1883. – The Church of Scotland, Past and Present (by different authors), ed. Rob. H. Story, 5 vols. (Mackenzie), 1890. – Alex MacEwen, History of the Church in Scotland (down to 1560), 2 vols. (Hodder), 1913–1918. See also V and VII.

(d) *Ireland:* T. Olden, The Church of Ireland (London, W. Gardner) 1892. – J. T. Ball, The Reformed Church of Ireland, 1537–1886 (Longmans), 1887. See also page 542, lines 9, 31–33.

III. THEOLOGY.

J. Hunt, Religious Thought in England (down to 1800), 3 vols. (Isbister), 1884, and Religious Thought in England in the Nineteenth Century (Gib-

BIBLIOGRAPHY

bings), 1896. – Leslie Stephen, English Thought in the Eighteenth Century, N.E., 2 vols. (Murray), 1927. – William James, The Varieties of Religious Experience, A Study in Human Nature (Longmans), 1903.

IV. CATHOLICISM.

A. O. Meyer, England und die katholische Kirche unter Elisabeth (Bibl. des preuss. histor. Instituts in Rom VI), 1911. – P. Thureau-Dangin, La Renaissance du Catholicisme en Angleterre au 19. siècle, 3 vols. (Plon), 1899–1906. – A. Bellesheim, Geschichte der katholischen Kirche (a) in Schottland, 2 vols., 1883; (b) in Irland, 3 vols. (Mainz: Kirchheim), 1890.

V. PURITANS, NONCONFORMISTS, DISSENTERS, FREE CHURCHES.

General: D. Neal, History of the Puritans, ed. J. Toulmin, 3 vols., 1837, and H. S. Skeats and C. S. Miall, History of the Free Churches of England, 1688–1851, 1891. – Henry Clark, History of English Nonconformity from Wiclif to the Close of the Nineteenth Century, 2 vols. (Chapman & Hall), 1911–1913. – Ch. Burrage, The Early English Dissenters, 2 vols., 1550–1641 (Cambridge University Press), 1912. – Rob. Barclay, The Inner Life of the Religious Societies of the Commonwealth (Hodder), 1877. – D. Masson, Life of John Milton, 6 vols., 1859–1880,[2] 1881, Vols. II, III, V.

Short Survey of Present Times: Arthur Reynolds, English Sects, 1921 (Mowbray). – Max Weber, Die protestantische Ethik und der Geist des Kapitalismus: Archiv für Sozialwissenschaft, Bd. 20, 21, 25, 26, 30, 31. – Ernst Tröltsch, Die Soziallehren des christlichen Kirchen unf Gruppen Tübingen (Mohr), 1912. – E. Dowden, Puritan and Anglican (Kegan Paul), 1900.

VI. PRESBYTERIANISM, SCOTLAND.

The Church of Scotland (v.s. IIc). Otto Dibelius, Das kirchliche Leben Schottlands: Stud. zur prakt. Theologie V, 2 (Töpelmann), 1911. – J. Vant Stephens, Presbyterian Churches, Unions and Divisions (Philadelphia), 1910. – A. H. Drysdale, History of the Presbyterians in England, 1889. – Walter Lloyd, The Story of the Protestant Dissent and English Presbyterians (Green), 1899. – P. Adair, Rise and Progress of the Presbyterian Church in Ireland (Belfast, Hamilton), 1866. – W. J. Latimer, A History of the Irish Presbyterians (Belfast), 1902.

VII. CONGREGATIONALISM.

H. M. Dexter, The Congregationalism of the last 300 years (Hodder), 1880. – R. W. Dale, History of English Congregationalism (Hodder), 1907. – W. B. Selbie, Congregationalism in: The Faiths, ed. L. P. Jacks (Methuen).

VIII. BAPTISTS.

Th. Crosby, History of the English Baptists from the Reformation to the Beginning of the Reign of George I, 4 vols., 1738–1740. – H. C. Vedder, A Short History of the Baptists (Baptist Tract Society, 1897.) – John Clifford, The Place of the Baptists in the Evolution of British Christianity, 1908.

538

BIBLIOGRAPHY

IX. UNITARIANS.

Walter Lloyd (v. VI). – Alex Gordon, Heads of English Unitarian History (Green), 1895. – I. E. Manning, The Religion and Theology of Unitarians, 1906.

X. QUAKERS.

George Fox, Journal (ed. Penney, 1911, Cambridge University Press). – W. C. Braithwaite, Beginnings of Quakerism (Macmillan), 1912, and: The Second Period of Quakerism (Macmillan), 1919. – E. Grubb, Quakerism in England (Headley), 1901. – J. S. Rowntree, The Society of Friends (Headley) 1901. – Rufus M. Jones, The Later Periods of Quakerism, 2 vols. (Macmillan) 1921, and: The Faith and Practice of the Quakers (The Faiths, ed. L. P. Jacks, 1927). – Book of Discipline: (1) Christian Life, Faith and Thought in the Society of Friends, 1927; (2) Christian Practice, 1925; (3) Church Government, 1927.

XI. METHODISM.

John Wesley, Journal, ed. N. Curnock (Kelly), 1906. – J. Whitehead, The Life of John Wesley, 2 vols., 1793–1796. – L. Tyerman, The Life and Times of John Wesley, 3 vols., 1877. – W. J. Townsend, A New History of Methodism (Hodder & Stoughton), 2 vols., 1909. – J. F. Hurst, The History of Methodism, 7 vols. (New York), 1902–1904. – W. Redfern, Modern Developments in Methodism (Law), 1906. – H. W. Williams, The Constitution and Policy of the Wesleyan Methodist Church, N.E. by D. J. Waller (Kelly), 1899.

XII. SALVATION ARMY.

Harold Begbie, Life of Wm. Booth, 2 vols. (Macmillan), 1920. – Th. Kolde, Die Heilsarmee (A. Deichert),[2] 1899. – P. A. Clasen, Der Salutismus (Schriften zur Sozialogie, ed. Alfred Weber II), Diederichs, 1913.

XIII. ACTUAL QUESTIONS.

J. F. Laun, Soziales Christentum in England (Furcheverlag), 1926. – C.O.P.E.C. Commission Report: (I) Nature of God; (II) Education, (III) The Home, (IV) Relation of the Sexes, (V) Leisure, (VI) Crime, (VII) International Relations, (VIII) Christianity and War, (IX) Industry and Property, (X) Politics and Citizenship, (XI) Social Function of the Church, (XII) Social Effects of Christianity (Longmans), 1924.

BOOK IV: EDUCATION

I. EDUCATION IN GENERAL.

1. Chief Sources are: Reports of Royal Commissions (abbreviated R.C.) on Education and the Annual Reports of the Board of Education since 1899, especially; R. C. on popular Education in England (Newcastle Commission), 6 vols., 1861. – R. C. appointed to enquire into the Revenues and Management of certain Colleges and Schools (=Lord Clarendon's Commission on Secondary Schools), 4 vols., 1864. – Lord Pakington, Report on Education, 2 vols., 1865. – Schools Enquiry C. 21 vols., 1868. – Elementary Education

BIBLIOGRAPHY

Acts, Lord Cross C., 10 vols., 1888. – R.C. on Secondary Education., 9 vols., 1895 (=Lord Bryce Commission). – R. C. on Technical Instruction, 5 vols., 1882–1884. – Interim Report of the Commission on National Expenditure (=Geddes Report) 1922. – Statistics of Public Education for 1926–7, England and Wales, Board of Education, 1928.

Special Reports of the Board of Education on Educational Subjects, 1896, etc., 28 vols. – The Teaching of English in England, 1921. – Modern Studies, 1918. – The Classics in Education, 1923. – The Education of the Adolescent, 1926.

History and Criticism: Graham Balfour, Educational Systems of Great Britain and Ireland (Clarendon Press), 1903. – Sir Hugh Owen, The Education Acts, 1870–1902 (Ch. Knight), 1903. – J. E. G. de Montmorency, State Intervention in English Education from earliest times to 1833 (Clay), 1902. – Henry Craik, The State in its Relation to Education (Macmillan), 1896. – Robert Gregory, Elementary Education: its Rise and Progress in England, 1895. – The Nation's Need, ed. H. Sp. Wilkinson (Constable), 1903. – L. F. Anderson, History of Common School Education (Bell), 1909. – Geraldine Hodgson, Rationalist English Educators, 1912. – Norman Lockyer, Education and National Progress (Macmillan), 1906–1907. – F. J. Gould, British Education after the War, 1917. – B. Dressler, Geschichte der englischen Erziehung (Teubner), 1928.

A. S. Barnes, The Catholic Schools of England (Williams & Norgate), 1926.

II. SCOTLAND.

Report of the Commission to inquire into the Schools of Scotland, 10 vols. 1865–67. – John Kerr, Scottish Education, School and University, from early times to 1908 (Cambridge Univ. Press), 1910. – W. J. Gibson, Education in Scotland: a Sketch of the Past and the Present (Longmans), 1912.

III. IRELAND.

M. E. Sadler, the National System of Education in Ireland (=Board of Education, Special Reports on Educational Subjects, I, 2), 1896.

IV. ELEMENTARY SCHOOLS.

(1) *Sources* v. I. – (2) *History and Criticism:* M. E. Sadler and J. W. Edwards, Public Elementary Education in England and Wales, 1870–1895 (=Board of Education, Special Report I, 1), 1896. – J. L. Kandel, Elementary Education in England with special reference to London, Liverpool, Manchester (United States Bureau of Education Bulletin, 568), 1914. – Jos. Lancaster, The British System of Education, 1810. – J. M. D. Meiklejohn, An old Educational Reformer, Dr. A. Bell (Blackwood), 1881. – Dean Gregory, Elementary Education, National Society, 1895 (History of Nat. Soc.). – H. B. Philpott, London at School, The Story of the School Board, 1870–1904 (T. Fisher Unwin), 1904.

V. CONTINUATION SCHOOLS AND ADULT EDUCATION.

(a) *General:* Two books by Ernst Schultze (both published by Oldenbourg at Munich, 1912, in Die Kultur des modernen Englands, ed. Sieper I, II).

BIBLIOGRAPHY

(1) Die geistige Hebung der Volksmassen in England (2) Volksbildung und volkswohlfahrt in England.

(b) *Adult Education, Sources:* Final Report of the Committee on Adult Education. Ministry of Reconstruction (Cd. 321), 1919. – Reports of the Adult Education Committee, Board of Education from 1922. – Oxford and Working Class Education (Clarendon Press), 1909. – Handbook and Directory of Adult Education. *History and Criticism:* G. Currie Martin, The Adult School Movement, 1924. – J. Llewellyn Davies, The Working Men's College (1854–1904), 1904. – T. W. Price, The Story of the Worker's Educational Association, 1913–24 (1924). – A. Mansbridge, An Adventure in Working-class Education (=W. E. A. 1903–16), 1920. – W. H. Draper, University Extension; Survey of Fifty Years (Cambridge Univ. Press), 1923.

(c) *Continuation Schools:* M. E. Sadler, Continuation Schools in England and elsewhere (Manchester Univ. Press), 1908. – Report on the Education of the Adolescent (Stationery Office), 1926.

(d) *Youth Movement:* Rob. Baden-Powell, Scouting for Boys (Pearson) N.E. 1920. – R. E. Young, Boy Scout Tests and how to pass them (Brown), 1922.

VI. TEACHERS.

Chas. H. Judd, The Training of Teachers in England, Scotland and Germany (United States Bureau of Education, Bulletin 609), 1914. – Lance G. E. Jones, The Training of Teachers in England and Wales, 1924. – The Modern Teacher, Essays on Educational Aims and Methods (Methuen), 1921. – The Department of Education in the Univ. of Manchester, 1891–1911 (Publ. of the Univ. of Manch., Educ. Series IV).

VII. OXFORD AND CAMBRIDGE.

J. B. Mullinger, History of Cambridge (Longmans), 1888. – H. C. Maxwell Lyte, Hist. of the Univ. of Oxford to 1530 (Macmillan), 1886 – J. B. Mullinger, Hist. of the Univ. of Cambridge 3 vols. (Cambridge Warehouse) 1873–76. – H. Rashdall, The Universities of Europe in the Middle Ages II (Clarendon Press), 1895. – A. J. Tillyard, A History of University Reform, Cambridge (Heffer) 1913. – Oxford University Commission. Report of the Commissioners concerning the State, Discipline, Studies and Revenues of the Univ. and Colleges of Oxford, 1852. – Same title, for Cambridge, 1852. – Report of proposed Measures of Improvement in the University of Oxford and Cambridge, 1854. – Oxford and Cambridge Univ. Comm. 1874. Report of Commission, 3 vols., 1874. – Principles and Methods of Univ. Reform. Report of the Hebdomadal Council (Oxford Univ. Press), 1910. – Lord Curzon, Principles and Methods of Univ. Reform (Oxf. Univ. Press), 1909. – Report of the Royal Comm. (Asquith Comm.) on Oxford and Cambridge Universities, 1922.

VIII. OTHER UNIVERSITIES.

Reports from Univ. Colleges participating in the Grant of £15,000; yearly from 1896 (Stationery Office).

BIBLIOGRAPHY

Wales: W. C. Davies and W. L. Jones, The Univ. of Wales and its Constituent Colleges (F. E. Robinson), 1905. – Report of the Royal Commission on University Education in Wales, 1918.

Scotland: Report of the University Commission of Scotland (Lord Inglis), 4 vols., 1858. – J. M. Bulloch, Hist. of the Univ. of Aberdeen, 1495–1895 (Hodder), 1895. – P. J. Anderson, Studies in the History and Development of the Univ. of Aberdeen (Aberdeen Univ. Studies XIX), 1906. – Alex. Grant, The Story of the Univ. of Edinburgh, 2 vols. (Longmans), 1883. – Jas. Coutts, Hist. of the Univ. of Glasgow, 1451–1909 (Glasgow), 1909.

Macneile Dixon, Trinity Coll., Dublin (Robinson), 1902. – J. T. Fowler, Durham Univ., Earlier Foundations and present Colleges (Robinson), 1904. – The Univ. of London. A Sketch of its Work and History from its Foundation to the Present Time (Stationery Office), 1900.

IX. UNIVERSITY EXTENSION (see also V).

H. J. Mackinder and M. E. Sadler, Univ. Exten. Past, Present and Future (Cassell), 1891. – R. D. Roberts, 18 years of Univ. Exten. (Cambridge Univ. Press), 1891.

Settlements: J. M. Knapp, Univ. and the Social Problem (Rivington), 1896. – W. Picht, Toynbee Hall (Siebeck: Ergänzungs-Hefte zum Archiv für Sozialwissenschaften und Sozialpolitik No. 9), 1913. – Univ. and Social Settlements, ed. by W. Reason (Methuen), 1898.

X. SECONDARY EDUCATION.

Sources see under I. – Foster Watson, The English Grammar Schools to 1660 (Cambridge Univ. Press), 1908. – C. Norwood and A. H. Hope, The Higher Education of Boys in England (Murray), 1909. – R. A. Archer, Secondary Education in the Nineteenth Century (Cambridge Univ. Press), 1921. – H. B. Gray, The Public Schools and the Empire (Williams and Norgate), 1913. – H. C. Maxwell Lyte, History of Eton College (Macmillan), 1877. – W. H. D. Rouse, History of Rugby School (Duckworth), 1909. – A. P. Stanley, Life and Correspondence of Thomas Arnold, 1844. – H. G. Wells, The Story of a Great Schoolmaster (Sanderson of Oundle), (Chatto), 1923. – Cecil Reddie, Abbotsholme, 1889–1899 (Allen), 1900. – Friedrich Grunder, Le Mouvement des Ecoles Nouvelles en Angleterre et en France (Paris, Thèse), 1910. – J. H. Badley, Bedales School (Cambridge Univ. Press), 1912.

Scotland: John Strong, History of Secondary Education in Scotland, (Clarendon Press), 1909.

XI. WOMEN'S EDUCATION.

Alice Zimmern, The Renaissance of Girls' Education (Innes), 1898. – Annie E. Ridley, Frances Mary Buss (Longmans), 1895. – Elizabeth Raikes, Dorothea Beale of Cheltenham (Constable), 1908.

CONCLUSION

Two books by J. M. Keynes (both Macmillan), The Economic Consequences of the Peace, 1919. – The same, A Revision of the Treaty, 1922. – Erich Obst, England, Europa und die Welt, Vowinckel, 1926. – Dean Inge,

BIBLIOGRAPHY

England (Benn), 1926. – C. E. Montague, Disenchantment (Chatto and Windus), 1922. – André Siegfried, L'Angleterre d'aujourd'hui (Paris) (Crès), 1927. – Samuel Dumas, and K. O. Vedel-Petersen, Losses of Life caused by War (Carnegie Endowment for International Peace), (Clarendon Press), 1923. – C. F. G. Masterman, England after the War (Hodder and Stoughton), 1922.

INDEX

545

INDEX

INDEX

547

INDEX

Habeas Corpus, 287 f., 307
Hague Conference, 84, 105, 393
Haldane, Lord, 34, 93, 160
Halibut Treaty, 86
Ham, 102
Hamburger Fremdenblatt, 328
Hampden, 28
Hampshire, 14
Hanover, House of, 21, 189, 195, 228, 241
Hanseatic League, 46, 51, 121, 124
Hapsburg, 497
Harbours, 247, 257
Hardie, Keir, 200
Hargreave, John, 460
Hardy, Thomas, 167
Harland and Wolff, 123
Harmsworth, Alfred (see Northcliffe)
Harold, King, 16
Harrington, James, 397
Harrison, 164
Harrow, 463
Harvey, Gabriel, 161
Hastings, Warren, 59, 153, 304
Havana, 81
Hawkins, 50, 494
Hay-Pauncefote Treaty, 100
Health, Board of, 247, 261
Health Insurance, 234
Health, Ministry of, 218, 242, 258, 260 f., 276 f.
Hebdomadal Council, 416, 419
Hebrides, 358
Hedjaz, 71
Hegel, 505
Heine, 149
Henley, 120
Henry II, 17, 31, 34
Henry III, 46, 342
Henry IV, 208
Henry V, 16
Henry VI, 235, 463
Henry VII, 50
Henry VIII, 18 f., 31, 50, 242, 342 f., 362, 490, 496
Herbert, Edward (of Cherbury), 161

Herbert, William, 355, 396
Hereford, 242
Heriot Watt College, 433
Herrenhaus, 227
Herschel, 415
Hertzog, General, 76 f.
Hewley, Lady Sarah, 378
Hibbert, Robert, 378
Hibbert Journal, 378
Highbury (St. John's Hall), 436
High Church, 353, 428
High Commissioner (in General Assembly), 372
High Court of Justice, 291, 299 f., 302
Hinduism, 63, 177
Hogarth, 230
Hogg, Quintin, 456
Holbein, 46
Holland, 51, 108, 124, 374, 376
Holstein, 397
'Holy Places,' 105
Home Office, 218, 244
Home Reading Union, 457
Home Rule, 32, 37
Home Secretary, 246
Hong-Kong, 102, 194
Hooker, Richard, 349
Hops, 110
Horace, 161 (and see p. 47, 'Horatian mode')
Horses (and racing), 111, 168
Hospitals, 271, 276, 436
Houses of Parliament, 23
Housing, 257, 262, 265, 269, 488
Howard, John, 446
Hughes, W. M., 80
Hull, 110
Hulton, Sir Edward, 317
Humanism (and Humanists), 47, 152, 156, 160 f.
Humber, 14
Hume, David, 150
Hume, Joseph, 432
Hutcheson, Francis, 150
Huxley, Thomas, 413, 422, 450
Hyde, Douglas, 42
Hyndman, H. M., 201

554

557

INDEX

Metropolitan Water Board, 270
Mexico, 99
Middle class, 24
Middle Temple, 292
Middlesex, 267
Military preparations, 221
Mill, James, 192, 256, 432, 444
Mill, John Stuart, 150, 160, 192, 212, 250, 412 f., 422, 444, 451
Milner, Alfred, 75
Milton, John, 21, 61, 160, 168 f., 173, 178, 235, 330, 375, 397, 409, 496
Mines (and mining), 122, 125, 247, 257, 484
Mines inspection, 246
Mining Minimum Wage Act, 193
Minimum wage, 29, 119, 145, 200, 202, 237, 278, 390, 484
Ministers, 203
Ministry, candidates for the, 482
Ministry of Labour, 202
Minnesaenger, 17
Minorca, 67, 81, 102
Minors, 290
Mission-field, 101, 104, 105, 106, 504
'Moderates,' 370
Moderator, 370
Modern languages, 420, 438
Mogul dynasty, 196
Mohammedans, 58
Monaghan, 44
Monasteries, dissolution of, 463
Mond, Sir Alfred, 141
Money bills, 226
Monmouth, 14 (county), 424
Monroe doctrine, 72
Montagu, Edwin, 64
Montesquieu, 97
Montrose, Duke of, 117
Morals, 165
Moravians, 381
More, Sir Thomas, 101, 497
Morel, E. D., 106 f.
Morning Post, 197, 318, 328, 332
Morocco, 93
Morris, William, 170, 201 (and Soc. Dem. Fed.), 462, 487, 507

Mortgages, 290
Moscow, 142, 202, 203, 482, 484 ff.
Moslems, 58, 63
Motor-car, 100
Mudirs, 70
Müller, von, 169
Municipalities, 259, 261
Municipal administration, 255
Municipal bodies, 260
Municipal Corporations Act, 255, 262
Municipal government, 24 f., 192, 241, 271
Municipal socialism, 453
Municipal undertakings, 257
Munitions Act, 202
Munster, 35
Murder, 308
Museums, 256
Music, 21
Music-halls, 314
Mutiny (Indian), 60

Nacion, 324
Name, change of, 276
Napier, Lord John, 160
Napoleon, 27, 34, 51, 148, 195, 330, 497
Natal, 72, 75
Nation, 335
National Assembly, 345
National Church League, 355
National Conference of Unitarian, Liberal Christian and kindred Organizations, 378
National Covenant, 32
National Debt, 213, 245 f., 481
National Education Association, 449
National Free Church Council, 369
National Health Insurance, 245
National Review, 335
National Society for the Education of the Poor, 444
National Union of Teachers, 455
National University of Ireland, 435
Nationalism, 15, 42, 46 f., 62 f., 71, 359, 391
Nationalization, 132, 319

559

INDEX

INDEX

INDEX

567

INDEX

INDEX

Wycliffe, 17, 19, 340, 360, 362, 382, 397, 407, 409, 428, 504
Wye, 436
Wykeham, William of, 463
Wyndham, George, 39, 195

Yorkshire, 122 f.
Yorkshire Post, 328, 332
Young, 22, 348
Younger, Sir George, 206

Y.M.C.A. and Y.W.C.A., 459
Youth Movement, the, 106

Zaghlul, Saad, 71
Zanzibar, 67
Zeppelins, 84
Zinc monopoly, 80
Zionism, 71, 102, 105
Zollverein, 92
Zulu, 72

A LIST OF TITLES

ACADEMY
BOOKS

Demy 8vo.   7s. 6d. net each
Usually the volumes are illustrated

JONATHAN CAPE   30 BEDFORD SQUARE   LONDON

BAINVILLE, Jacques   Napoleon

No.
13

'What many British readers are likely to find most admirable in the work of M. Bainville is the breadth and soundness of his views. He comprehends fully the part played by Britain in the long struggle . . . Over and over again one comes upon paragraphs or phrases which throw a ray of light upon the most vital problems. It is these vital problems which always engage the writer; and it is in his treatment of them that he appears at his best . . . One can hardly imagine a better introduction to Napoleonic study than this well-balanced, deeply pondered, and very readable book.'

THE TIMES LITERARY SUPPLEMENT

BEDOYERE, Count Michael de la   Lafayette

'M. de la Bedoyere has written a very good biography of Lafayette. The book is compact with information. It is also easy to read. One finishes it with regret, having extracted from it much pleasure, much information, and that satisfaction which is conveyed by a difficult task competently executed.'   HAROLD NICOLSON in the DAILY TELEGRAPH

No.
22

'This new life of Lafayette is undoubtedly the best account that we have in English of the position of Lafayette in the world of his time.'   CATHOLIC HERALD

'Count Michael de la Bedoyere has given a convincing sympathetic picture of Lafayette. In doing so he has written interestingly on sixty years of history, three revolutions, and a group of the world's most dramatic characters.'

NEW STATESMAN AND NATION

COOPER, Duff   Talleyrand

No.
14

'Its main quality, to my mind, is that it is written throughout from the intellectual rather than from the ethical or sensational standpoint. We have had so many biographies of late which are brilliant and amusing; it is a relief to find one which is sensible as well. In the second place Mr. Duff Cooper treats the English Language with respect. In the balance of his periods one catches an echo of the greater periods of English prose, whereas his deft, sharp phrases have all the nimbleness of modernity. And in the third place Mr. Duff Cooper has a perfect gift of selection. He has woven his tangled material into a tissue of silken smoothness. If biography is to be defined as "the history of an individual conceived as a work of art", then Mr. Duff Cooper's book should serve as an exhibit. It is historical in that it conveys the proportions of events; it describes an individual, since it concentrates on character; and it is, without question, a deliberate work of art.'

HAROLD NICOLSON in the NEW STATESMAN AND NATION

DIBELIUS, Wilhelm England

'He gives us a very thorough, very detailed, very learned picture of every department of English life. Regarded from this point of view alone the book is one which will be of the greatest service to all serious students. It can be read with advantage and profit, even by well-informed English readers ... His accuracy and insight are remarkable. We have noted few errors and few omissions ... But this account is not merely a text-book compilation: it is accompanied by constant criticism and comment, which are none the less valuable because they often take the form of a contrast between the English and German institutions and attitude of mind.' THE TIMES LITERARY SUPPLEMENT

No. 8

ELWIN, Malcolm Charles Reade

'Mr. Elwin is extremely just to Reade; he unravels for us with patience and sympathy the contradictions and perplexities of his character and actions. And the result is to give us the portrait of a man we should all like to see again, in our age which is so deficient in the qualities Reade most showed – enthusiasm, impetuosity, and magnanimity.' THE LISTENER

No. 6

ELWIN, Malcolm Thackeray: a Personality

'The vivid and exciting portrait of a man, naturally sociable and pleasure-loving, a devoted son, scrupulously honourable, erratic in his habits, enjoying the sunshine of fame though it

No. 21

was often darkened for him by pain and illness. It would have been easy to make the story of such a life as Thackeray's seem comparatively lacking in great events; but Mr. Elwin has made it seem extraordinarily eventful . . . this excellent biography — the best life of Thackeray that has yet appeared.'

NEWS-CHRONICLE

GREIG, J. Y. T. — David Hume

No.
10
'Mr. Greig has written a first-rate biography of a very interesting man. He describes Hume's adventures in Paris, his relations with the Encyclopaedists, and his unhappy experiences with Rousseau with a delightful humour. He gives his readers not only an excellent picture of Hume, but also of Edinburgh society in the eighteenth century and of the brilliant circle in Paris in which Hume moved and shone.'

MANCHESTER GUARDIAN

GWYNN, Denis — The Life and Death of Roger Casement

No.
11
'It is balanced, accurate, and admirably written. Mr. Gwynn has not only served his own and Casement's country by the difficult labour of tracing a fine and varied career, he has served all who detest cruelty as the one crime that has no forgiveness . . . Worn out and distracted by the horrors of his brave service against cruelty, blinded to realities by a passion for his country and a quixotic ideal of patriotism, Casement remains none the less one of the noblest characters I have ever known, and I have known many noble.'

H. W. NEVINSON in the NEW STATESMAN

HACKETT, Francis — Henry VIII

No.
1
'He draws vivid pictures and vivid characters; indeed, it is a remarkable feat that not only Henry himself and the chief actors like Wolsey, Cromwell, and Cranmer, but even the minor figures and supers, and all the six wives stand out in the book as real and distinct characters. His use of dialogue is very good; it is never invented, for as he says, "Thanks to the

astonishingly full diplomatic correspondence, I could stick to the record and yet quote direct speech". I found it a fascinating book.'
LEONARD WOOLF

HART, Liddell 'T. E. Lawrence' In Arabia and after
NEW AND ENLARGED EDITION

'A fascinating book with not a dull page – but with many brilliant ones . . . Lawrence is an Elizabethan; a born adventurer of the highest kind; a natural soldier as well as an artist with a spark of the divine afflatus. The results of these endowments, first his inspiring leadership of guerrilla bands in the Syrian Desert, and, second, his brilliant record of those events in his two books, *The Seven Pillars of Wisdom* – a classic, and the *Revolt in the Desert*, have carried him to a peak of achievement that is unassailable. His prose is the finest that Arabia has inspired in this generation . . . The author describes vividly, and at the right sharp tempo, the series of adventurous stages of the revolt – the Battle of Wijh, the brilliant Aqaba coup, the dashing assaults on the railway behind the enemy lines, the amazing camel rides, and the masterful operations on the flanks of the victorious forces of Allenby, leading first to the capture of Jerusalem, and then of Damascus.'
BERTRAM THOMAS in the OBSERVER

No. 20

LEVINE, Isaac Don Stalin

'Mr. Levine is much to be congratulated upon this book. It is a bountifully documented study into which his personal views scarcely intrude at all, and which yet provides an exceedingly complete and obviously adequate picture of this Eurasian despot of Communist Russia.' NEWS-CHRONICLE

No. 2

MEIER-GRAEFE, Julius Pyramid and Temple

'It proves to be full of art criticism of the most penetrating kind. It would not be too much to say that it is one of the most valuable books which have yet been written about Egyptian art and architecture. On every period and on every feature of Egyptian art he has something wise to say, so much

No. 15

so that his book is to be recommended not merely to the traveller but to the professional Egyptologist. Roger Hinks, his translator, has carried out a most difficult task with courage and insight; the rendering could not be improved.'

MANCHESTER GUARDIAN

MUMBY, Frank A.   Publishing and Bookselling

No.
12

' "Ten ordinary histories of kings and courtiers", wrote Carlyle, "were well exchanged against the tenth part of one good History of Booksellers"; and, having set that quotation in the forefront of his ingenious and exhaustive volume, Mr. Mumby proceeds to justify it by as deft, comprehensive and entertaining a piece of workmanship as ever invited the gratitude of all sorts and conditions of bookmen. The more the reader knows of the history of bookselling, the better he will appreciate the industry, judgment, and constructive skill which have gone to the making of this closely packed but never congested record.'

ARTHUR WAUGH in the WEEK END REVIEW

PARES, Bernard   My Russian Memoirs

No.
17

In this book Sir Bernard Pares, Professor of Russian in the University of London, surveys the twentieth century historical and political development of Russia. The writer is in a unique position. He chose this subject for his life work and has been in close personal relations with the most prominent characters in the story independently of all party views and, having the confidence of the most various persons, was able at each event, of many of which he was an eye-witness, to have the frankest explanation of their actions, views and objects. The end of the book follows the fate of the principal actors since the revolution, deals with the Bolshevist propaganda in England and gives a sketch of the main trend of events in Russia up to date.

POURTALÈS, Guy de   Richard Wagner

No.
18

'For the future, the features of Wagner, of Cosima, of Liszt, of Ludwig of Bavaria, as of their teeming world, will be seen in M. de Pourtalès' drawings of them, for the simple reason that his drawings are instinct with the authentic breath of life. With them, learning has passed beyond the point where it has any need to display itself; the process of revivification, like the fundamental brain-work of organization and argument, has become organic, and emerges, for the reader, as an incontestable but never asserted authority. One believes in M. de Pourtalès; one accepts from him Liszt, Ludwig, and Richard Wagner, because, in his pages, they live, not in outline, but solid and warm.'   MARY AGNES HAMILTON

PRINGLE, Henry F.   Theodore Roosevelt

' "An interesting combination of St. Vitus and St. Paul," was Lord Morley's description of Theodore Roosevelt. The task of writing a well-balanced and judicial biography of such a personality must have been extraordinarily difficult, but Mr. Pringle has achieved it with conspicuous success. As a record of the career of its subject this volume is in no respect lacking. *No.* It brings together all the significant facts not only with regard 16 to Roosevelt's political activities but also concerning his excursions into the diverse unrelated spheres in which from time to time he found an opportunity of working off the surplus of his superabundant energy. Its outstanding merit, however, lies in its admirable delineation of the character with which it deals.'   THE TIMES

TAYLOR, G. R. Stirling   Robert Walpole and His Age

'It is a book with a great deal of reading behind it; it is not flashy or flimsy, though it is entertaining. It is well documented, and is the most complete life of Walpole written up to date.'   DESMOND MacCARTHY in the SUNDAY TIMES *No.*
'This new study is humane and sympathetic in its treatment   7
of the hero ... A living biography, and one which in its appreciation of Walpole's foreign Policy corrects certain easy and common misconceptions.'   MANCHESTER GUARDIAN

THOMPSON, Grace E.   The First Gentlemen

'Miss Thompson has retold the familiar tale with gaiety and sympathy. She deals with an age when life was gross and muddy, but wits ran gaily as the sparkling Thames. Every phase and incident in the outrageous procession is equipped with its contemporary epigram. The diaries and memoirs of the time have been ransacked for the right word. Such are the ingredients for a feast of good reading and good writing.'

No.
19

THE OBSERVER

TOUR DU PIN, La Marquise de la
Recollections of the Revolution
and the Empire

'The book is fascinating . . . Whether as political history, or as a portrait of social life in two brilliant eras, or as a "thriller" of the first water, this book is to be read and to be treasured!'

No.
9

THE TIMES LITERARY SUPPLEMENT

'Makes life under the *ancien régime* unveil before the mind's eye in all its natural carriage and motion.'   THE OBSERVER